(shep)

D0303701

Good Faith and Fault
in Contract Law

BPP University

089938

Good Faith and Fault in Contract Law

Edited by

JACK BEATSON
AND
DANIEL FRIEDMANN

CLARENDON PRESS · OXFORD

*This book has been printed digitally and produced in a standard specification
in order to ensure its continuing availability*

OXFORD
UNIVERSITY PRESS

Great Clarendon Street, Oxford OX2 6DP

Oxford University Press is a department of the University of Oxford.
It furthers the University's objective of excellence in research, scholarship,
and education by publishing worldwide in

Oxford New York

Auckland Bangkok Buenos Aires Cape Town Chennai
Dar es Salaam Delhi Hong Kong Istanbul Karachi Kolkata
Kuala Lumpur Madrid Melbourne Mexico City Mumbai Nairobi
São Paulo Shanghai Singapore Taipei Tokyo Toronto

Oxford is a registered trade mark of Oxford University Press
in the UK and in certain other countries

Published in the United States
by Oxford University Press Inc., New York

© The contributors severally
© in this collection OUP 1995

The moral rights of the author have been asserted
Database right Oxford University Press (maker)

Reprinted 2002

All rights reserved. No part of this publication may be reproduced,
stored in a retrieval system, or transmitted, in any form or by any means,
without the prior permission in writing of Oxford University Press,
or as expressly permitted by law, or under terms agreed with the appropriate
reprographics rights organization. Enquiries concerning reproduction
outside the scope of the above should be sent to the Rights Department,
Oxford University Press, at the address above

You must not circulate this book in any other binding or cover
and you must impose this same condition on any acquirer

ISBN 0-19-826578-6

Contents

Part 1 Introduction

Part 2 Formation of Contract

(a) Pre-contractual duties and good faith

(b) Consideration

**Part 3 The Contractual Obligation:
Good Faith, Control and Adaptation**

(a) *The effect of good faith and implied terms on
contractual obligations*

(b) *Legislation and public law influences*

(c) *Relational and long-term contracts*

(d) *Extent of contractual obligation*

Acknowledgments

This collection originated at a colloquium held at Merton College, Oxford in September 1993. Earlier versions of all but two of the contributions were presented as papers at that meeting. Our aims in organizing the colloquium and putting together the book are stated in our introductory chapter. We are grateful to the contributors and to those who attended and commented on the papers, in particular to Sir Thomas Bingham MR, Lord Justice Steyn and Lord Justice Peter Gibson who chaired sessions. We are also grateful for generous support for the colloquium from the Hamlyn Trust, the Hulme University Fund, Merton College's Higher Studies Fund, Travers Smith Braithwaite, and the Faculty of Law of the University of Oxford. Richard Hart of Oxford University Press has been a steadfast friend of the project, and Stephen Brett provided invaluable assistance at the colloquium, as did Imogen Maclean in preparing the papers for publication.

Jack Beatson   Daniel Friedmann
Cambridge   Tel Aviv

19 September 1994

Essayists

H. G. Beale:	Professor of Law, University of Warwick
J. Beatson:	Rouse Ball Professor of Law, University of Cambridge
P. B. H Birks FBA:	Regius Professor of Civil Law, University of Oxford
M. G. Bridge:	Hind Professor of Law, University of Nottingham
J. W. Carter:	Associate Professor of Law, University of Sydney
Chin Nyuk Yin:	Associate Professor of Law, University of Western Australia
M. Chen-Wishart:	Fellow and Tutor in Law, Merton College, Oxford
N. Cohen:	Professor of Law and Vice-Rector, Tel Aviv University
W. K. Ebke:	Professor of Law, Business and Tax Law Chair, University of Konstanz
M. Eisenberg:	Koret Professor of Law, University of California, School of Law, Berkeley
M. Fabre Magnan:	Professor of Law, University of Nantes
E. A. Farnsworth:	Alfred McCormack Professor of Law, Columbia University
D. Friedmann:	Dean, School of Law; The College of Management; Professor of Law, Tel Aviv University
W. Lorenz:	Professor of Law, University of Munich
E. G. McKendrick:	Fellow and Tutor in Law, St Anne's College, Oxford; Linnells Lecturer in Law, University of Oxford
B. Nicholas FBA:	Formerly Professor of Comparative Law, University of Oxford
B. Steinhauer:	Assistant, University of Konstanz School of Law

T. D. Rakoff:	Professor of Law, Harvard Law School
G. H. Treitel QC FBA:	Vinerian Professor of English Law, University of Oxford
S. M. Waddams:	Albert Abel Professor of Law, University of Toronto

Colloquium Participants

Sir Thomas Bingham: Master of the Rolls

S. Bright: Fellow and Tutor in Law, St. Hilda's College, Oxford

A. S. Burrows: Professor of Law, University College London; Law Commissioner for England and Wales

J. Cartwright: Tutor in Law, Christ Church, Oxford

P. L. Davies: Reader in the Law of the Enterprise, University of Oxford

A. de Moor: Fellow and Tutor in Law, Somerville College, Oxford

Rt. Hon. Lord Justice Peter Gibson

R. Goode Q.C. F.B.A.: Norton Rose Professor of English Law University of Oxford

C. G. Hale: Travers Smith Braithwaite, Solicitors

H. McGregor Q.C.: Warden of New College, Oxford

F. H. Oditah: Fellow and Tutor in Law, Merton College, Travers Smith Braithwaite Lecturer in Corporate Finance Law, University of Oxford

D. D. Prentice: Allen and Overy Professor of Corporate Law, University of Oxford

S. Smith Fellow and Tutor in Law, St. Anne's College, Oxford

C. Starnes: Professor of Law, Detroit College of Law

Rt. Hon. Lord Justice Steyn

S. J. Whittaker: Fellow and Tutor in Law, St. John's College Oxford

Abbreviations

ABGB	Austrian General Civil Code
AcP	Archiv für die civilistische Praxis
ALR	Allgemeines Landes Recht 1794 (Prussian General Land Law)
BGB	Bürgerliches Gesetzbuch (German Civil Code)
BGE	Entscheidungen des schweizerischen Bundesgerichtes
BGH	Bundesgerichtshof (West Germany's Federal (Supreme) Court)
BGHZ	Entscheidungen des Bundesgerichtshofes in Zivilsachen (Decisions of the West German Supreme Court in civil matters)
Cass	Cour de cassation
CISG	The United Nations (Vienna) Convention on Contracts for the International Sale of Goods (1980)
JW	Juristische Wochenschrift
JZ	Juristenzeitung
NJW	Neue Juristische Wochenschrift
OLG	Oberlandesgericht (Decision of a German Court of Appeal)
OR	Swiss Code of Obligations
Restatement 2d Contracts	American Law Institute's Restatement of the Law (Second): Contracts (1979)
RG	Reichsgericht
RGZ	Entscheidungen des Reichgerichts in Zivilsachen (Decisions of the German Imperial Court in civil matters)
UCC	Uniform Commercial Code (USA)
UCTA	Unfair Contract Terms Act 1977 (UK)

Table of Cases

Canada

United States

Table of Legislation

Part 1
Introduction

1

Introduction: From 'Classical' to Modern Contract Law*

JACK BEATSON AND DANIEL FRIEDMANN

I

The English law of contract is the origin of modern contract law to be found in the United States and in the nations of the British Commonwealth which adopted the common law system. It has also been particularly influential in a number of jurisdictions with civilian roots, eg Scotland, where it is sometimes regarded as a cuckoo in the nest, South Africa and other 'mixed jurisdictions'.[1] Not surprisingly the different systems have developed in different ways. This is most marked in the case of the United States, although it has been argued that the perception of US jurisdictions gradually diverging from their old world common law roots may not be accurate, and that the colonists took much less of the common law with them to the new world than was commonly supposed.[2] In the last 20 years, the gradual divergence of contract doctrine within the Commonwealth has been more apparent, with particularly significant developments in Australia.[3] In the same period English trade, and with it the English law of contract, has been exposed to the influence of the European Community and the predominantly civilian systems of its members. 1993 saw the most significant European Community initiative affecting contract law, the Directive on Unfair Terms in Consumer Contracts.[4] This seems an opportune time to take stock. This collection of essays presents some of the main topics and issues facing the modern law of contract. In this introduction we seek to give an overview of the current state of play and of the matters covered in the individual essays.

One of the motivating factors in organizing the conference on which

---

* Copyright © 1994, Jack Beatson and Daniel Friedmann.

[1] See generally K Zweigert and H Kötz, *An Introduction to Comparative Law* (2nd ed 1992) pp 226–45.

[2] LM Friedman, *A History of American Law* (1973) pp 9–32, 69–77.

[3] See the development of a general doctrine of unconscionability (*Commercial Bank of Australia Ltd v Amadio* (1983) 151 CLR 447), a reliance model of liability (*Waltons Stores (Interstate) Ltd v Maher* (1987/88) 164 CLR 387) and third party rights under contracts (*Trident General Insurance Co Ltd v McNeice Bros Pty Ltd* (1988) 165 CLR 107). On Canadian contract law, see e.g. *Hunter Engineering Co Inc v Syncrude Canada Ltd* (1989) 57 DLR (4th) 321.

[4] Council Directive 93/13/EEC (OJL 95, 21.4.1993, p 29); UK SI 1994 No. 3159.

this collection is based was the perception that in the last decade English contract law has been less innovative and perhaps less open to the influence of other systems. One of the features of nineteenth-century law was a willingness to look to other systems, whether the French Civil Code, as in *Hadley* v *Baxendale*[5] in respect of damages or Roman law, as in *Kennedy* v *Panama, New Zealand and Australian Royal Mail Co.*[6] That occurred at the height of Empire and in an age when the United Kingdom's influence on world trade was significant, if not paramount.[7] It was not surprising that the English law of contract had an undisputed international influence. Even today the Commercial Court in London is much resorted to by the nationals of a wide range of states for the resolution of disputes.[8] The willingness to look elsewhere was, however, coupled with confidence, perhaps excessive confidence, in the merits of English law. For instance, in 1919 Greer J, discussing the conference which settled the form of the Baltic and White Sea Conference Charter in 1908, stated:

That Conference, I think, took place in some foreign town, but the people represented there were some of them British shipowners, some British coal exporters, and some importers of coal into importing countries, but there can be little doubt that the dominating minds at that Conference were the minds of the British representatives, who were dealing with matters generally regarded throughout the commercial world as matters of British trade. One of the objects of the Conference was to adopt a contract that would produce uniformity of rates, duties, and obligations on the part of those who entered into the contract. I have very little doubt that the British representatives imposed their views—and rightly imposed those views—on the foreign representatives in a matter which was very properly describable as mainly concerned with British trade.[9]

English contract lawyers have shown a greater willingness to export ideas than to import them. For instance, the process of imperial fertilization led to reproduction of the Marine Insurance Act 1906 in far corners of the globe, with the result that in many countries the standard form of English marine policy is in regular use.[10] By contrast, the success of the Indian Contract Code 1872 did not serve as a catalyst at home.[11]

---

[5] (1854) 9 Exch 341; 156 ER 145. See also the citation of Pothier on mistake of identity; *Anson's Law of Contract* (26th ed 1984) p 277 gathers the authorities.

[6] (1867) LR 2 QB 580 per Blackburn J. But cf FH Lawson, 'Error in Substantia' (1936) 52 LQR 79.

[7] Between 1880 and 1980 the UK's share of world trade in manufactures fell from c 40% to c 7%: Craft & Woodward eds, *The British Economy since 1945* (1991), p 148.

[8] *Amin Rasheed Corpn* v *Kuwait Insurance Co* [1984] AC 50, at 67, per Lord Diplock. See also Lord Goff, Hansard (HL) 4 February 1992, vol 535, cols 230–31, Second Reading debate on what became the Carriage of Goods by Sea Act 1992.

[9] *Aktieselskab August Freuchen* v *Steen Hansen* (1919) 1 Ll L Rep 393, at 396.

[10] *Amin Rasheed Corpn* v *Kuwait Insurance Co* [1982] 1 WLR 961, at 968 per Bingham J.

[11] Attempts by the Law Commission and the Scottish Law Commission to produce a contract code were abandoned but an early draft of the proposed code has recently been

Although today the tone is likely to be far less chauvinist than that of Greer J, English law has recently turned its back on the UNCITRAL Model Law of Arbitration[12] and appears to be doing so on the Vienna Convention on Contracts for the International Sale of Goods.[13] One of the reasons given in each of these cases was the greater sophistication of English law and the uncertainty that would result from the broadly formulated provisions of the Model Law and the Convention. One distinguished commercial judge has stated that: '[i]nternational Commerce is best served not by imposing a deficient legal schemes upon it but by encouraging the development of the best schemes in a climate of free competition and choice.'[14]

Other jurisdictions have proved less suspicious of cross fertilization. The adoption of the duty of good faith by the United States's Uniform Commercial Code reflects the influence of German law.[15] Israel, which came within the common law orbit during the British Mandate, has adopted statutes based on continental laws (notably the German BGB) and on international conventions for the unification of private law.[16]

In England a consensus developed among judges during the 1960s that major developments, even in areas hitherto the preserve of the common law, should be achieved by legislation. This meant that a broad principle of unconscionability and inequality of bargaining power[17] or the recognition that non-parties may claim under contracts intended to give them enforceable rights[18] were less likely to be imported judicially. This judicial consensus was formed at a time the legislature was relatively active in the matter of private law. Thus, between 1967 and 1987 a number of statutes

---

published: H McGregor, *The Contract Code*, 5 *Studi Sulla Fenomenologia Negoziale Nell'Area Europea* (ed Gandolfi) 1993.

[12] The Rt Hon Lord Justice Mustill, 'A New Arbitration Act for the United Kingdom? The Response of the Departmental Advisory Committee to the UNCITRAL Model Law' (1990) 6 *Arbitration International* 3. For more recent proposals for reform, see (1994) 10 *Arbitration International* 189 (proposed Arbitration Bill) and commentary, *ibid*; 163 (B Davensport), 179 (J Uff & D Keating) and 185 (AH Hermann).

[13] See B Nicholas, 'The United Kingdom and the Vienna Sales Convention: Another Case of Splendid Isolation' (1993) 9 *Saggi, Conferenze e Seminar*: 1.

[14] Sir John Hobhouse, 'International Conventions and Commercial Law: The Pursuit of Uniformity' (1990) 106 LQR 530, 535. Cf. Sir Johan Steyn, 'A Kind of Esperanto?' in P Birks (ed), *The Frontiers of Liability* (1994) Vol 2, p 11.

[15] J Whitman, 'Commercial Law and the American *Volk*: A Note on Llewellyn's German Sources for the Uniform Commercial Code' (1987) 97 Yale LJ 156. See generally W Twining, *Karl Llewellyn and the Realist Movement* (1973).

[16] D Friedmann, *The Effect of Foreign Law on the Law of Israel* (1975) pp 99–101.

[17] *National Westminster Bank plc v Morgan* [1985] AC 686, at 708; *Barclays Bank plc v O'Brien* [1994] 1 AC 180.

[18] *Beswick v Beswick* [1968] AC 58, at 72; *Woodar Investment Development Ltd v Wimpey Construction UK Ltd* [1980] 1 WLR 277 at 297–8, 300; *Swain v The Law Society* [1983] 1 AC 598, at 611.

dealing with contracts in general were enacted.[19] However, more recently the pressure for space in a crowded legislative timetable has meant that reform of private law and, in particular, of contract and tort law has lost out to legislative initiatives with a higher political profile. In the fight for legislative space, the major impetus for changes appears to be the fear of losing trade to other centres.[20]

However, the continued vitality of common law lies in its capacity to change in the way Lord Goff graphically described in his Maccabean lecture. He described the common law as a kaleidescopic mosaic 'in the sense that it is in a constant state of change in minute particulars'.[21] Its vitality also lies in the willingness, in appropriate situations, to import as well as to export. If a system is not capable of changing it is liable to wither on the wine. In an atmosphere in which the prospects of legislation appear less likely it is possible that the consensus favouring judicial restraint will break down and there will be greater judicial activism. The Court of Appeal has recently shown willingness to develop the law of contracts for the benefit of a third party[22] and the House of Lords has also taken a more activist stance, albeit not yet in the context of contract.[23] In any event, change may be imposed on English law by European Community Law which, as we have noted, is beginning to make its presence felt on contract law.[24]

---

[19] The Misrepresentation Act 1967, the Unfair Contract Terms Act 1977, the Civil Liability (Contribution) Act 1978 and the Minors Contract Act 1987. Additionally, the Supply of Goods and Services Act 1982, the Law of Property (Miscellaneous Provisions) Act 1989 and the Carriage of Goods by Sea Act 1992 dealt with particular types of contract. There were also particular statutory provisions addressing particular defects. For example the Financial Services Act 1986. Ss 132 gives the insured the option of enforcing a contract of insurance made by an unauthorized insurer and reverses the decision in *Phoenix General Insurance Co of Greece SA* v *Halvanon Insurance Co Ltd* [1988] QB 216 (CA). See also the Property Misdescriptions Act 1991.

[20] This was so in the case of rights of suit by consignees of goods carried by sea (Carriage of Goods by Sea Act 1992) and is an important factor in calls for reform of s 16 of the Sale of Goods Act to make it possible, as under the Uniform Sales Act and the Uniform Commercial Code, for the parties to a sale of an undivided share in a bulk to agree that title to a proportionate share shall pass before appropriation of specific goods by separation from the bulk: Sale of Goods Forming Part of a Bulk (1993) Law Com No. 215; Scot Law Com No. 145.

[21] 'The Search for Principle' (1983) 59 Proc Brit Acad 169, 186.

[22] *Darlington BC* v *Wiltshier Northern Ltd* [1995] 1WLR 68.

[23] *Woolwich Building Society* v *IRC* [1993] 1 AC 70, at 176 F–G (Lord Goff, deciding to recognize a new right to restitution of ultra vires tax payments, said 'this opportunity will never come again. If we do not take it now it will be gone forever . . . [H]owever compelling the principle of justice may be, it would never be sufficient to persuade a government to propose its legislative recognition . . .') In other contexts see *R* v *R* (*Rape: Marital Exemption*) [1992] 1 AC 599; *R* v *Kearley* [1992] 2 AC 228 (reform of the hearsay rule in criminal proceedings).

[24] See also J Beatson, below pp 285–6 (EC procurement regime); H Beale, ch 9 below (EC Directive on Unfair Terms in Consumer Contracts).

II

It has become usual to describe the law of contract as developed during the nineteenth century and the first part of the present century as 'classical' contract law.[25] This body of law has been said to have been shaped by the conditions created in the wake of the industrial revolution and the prevalent social and economic outlook. These were seen as fostering freedom of contract founded upon the centrality of the individual, the creed in the creative power of his will and a restricted role of intervention for either the court or the state.[26] Although this interpretation has been said to be inaccurate historically,[27] it has been influential. Moreover, it has in recent years been advanced in a new form using the tools of micro-economic analysis and re-presented by new adherents in a modern and sophisticated way.[28]

An important feature of classical contract theory is the endeavour to develop a general body of contract law applicable to all types of contracts and overshadowing the various branches of specific contracts.[29] In the past, a number of commercial contexts, such as shipping, construction and insurance, have been particularly influential in the development of contract law. Some have suggested that they have been disproportionately influential. Whatever the influence of particular contexts, however, and despite much discussion, apart from statutory intervention the ideology of the common law of contract remains that of a single body of principles worked out with some differences in particular contexts.

At its zenith, the concept of freedom of contract had a twofold meaning. One related to its positive aspect, namely the creative power of the participants in the contractual process to act as private legislators and to

[25] eg LM Friedman, *Contract Law in America* (1965) pp 20–4; G Gilmore, *The Death of Contract* (1974) p 6; PS Atiyah, *The Rise and Fall of Freedom of Contract* (1979) ch 21. H Collins, *The Law of Contract* (2nd ed 1993), xi states, somewhat extravagantly, that the result of fidelity to tradition in exposition of the law of contract is that 'students learn in their early years a misleading and almost irrelevant set of rules' and that the subject can claim 'sublime irrelevance'. But see the reviews of the first edition by JA Weir [1986] CLJ 503, 504 ('perverse, inaccurate and obscure') and FMB Reynolds (1986) 102 LQR 628, esp 629–30.

[26] M Cohen, 'The Basis of Contract' (1933) 46 Harv L Rev 553, 558; PS Atiyah, *The Rise and Fall of Freedom of Contract* (1979) p 25; G Gilmore, *The Ages of American Law* (1977) p 65. See also S Williston, 'Freedom of Contract' (1921) 6 Cornell LQ 365.

[27] JL Barton, 'The Enforcement of Hard Bargains' (1987) 103 LQR 118; AWB Simpson, 'The Horwitz Thesis and the History of Contracts' (1979) 46 U Chi LRev 533; J Gordley, *The Philosophical Origins of Modern Contract Doctrine* (1991) ch 8.

[28] RA Posner, *Law and Economics* (4th ed 1992) ch 4; R Cooter & T Ulen, *Law and Economics* (1988) ch 6. For discussion, see PS Atiyah, 'Freedom of Contract and the New Right' Cassel Lecture of 1988, University of Stockholm; H Collins, *The Law of Contract* (2nd ed 1993) pp 24–6.

[29] Cheshire, Fifoot and Furmston's *Law of Contract* (12th ed 1991) p 24.

legislate rights and duties binding upon themselves. The other meaning
was concerned with what may be termed its negative aspect, namely, the
freedom from obligation unless consented to and embodied in a valid
contract.[30] This concept was no less important than that of contractual
freedom in the positive sense. The idea of freedom from liability without
consent was often extended to mean no liability without contract. It was
highly instrumental in narrowing the scope of those parts of the law
which deal with liability ex lege, namely, torts and restitution. In the field
of torts, duties which originated in contract were confined to the parties
to the particular agreement by what became known as 'the privity of contract fallacy'.[31] In the field of restitution (then known as quasi-contracts)
the famous dictum by Bowen LJ that '[l]iabilities are not to be forced upon
people behind their backs[32] left a deep imprint. Indeed, Lord Mansfield's
conception of a broad principle of unjust enrichment was replaced by narrow rules of liability based on 'implied contract'.

The law of torts was mainly concerned with the protection of proprietary interests and with providing remedies against physical injury. The
protection offered against pure economic loss was meagre, although a
number of economic torts were developed, notably deceit,[33] injurious
falsehood,[34] inducement of breach of contract[35] and conspiracy.[36] It is,
however, typical that they are all based on wilful misconduct. The rising
wrong of negligence, which was to engulf much of the tort area, was carefully confined to physical injuries. No liability was imposed for negligent
misrepresentation that caused mere economic loss.[37] This area remained
within the domain of contracts although equitable relief, which recent
scholarship has shown could include compensation, was available.[38]

The freedom of contract approach was said to have led to the reduction
of supervision over contractual terms to a bare minimum.[39] A contract
could not be invalidated on the ground of unreasonableness or unfairness. These matters were for the parties to decide. Contractual justice

[30] N Cohen, ch 2 below.
[31] *Winterbottom* v *Wright* (1842) 10 M & W 109; 152 ER 402. See BS Markesinis and SF
Deakin, *Tort Law* (3rd ed 1994) pp 66, 254.
[32] *Falcke* v *Scottish Imperial Insurance Co* (1886) 34 Ch 234, at 248.
[33] *Pasley* v *Freeman* (1789) 3 TR 51; 100 ER 450.
[34] *Ratcliffe* v *Evans* [1892] 2 QB 524. On the history of this tort see Prosser & Keeton on *The
Law of Torts* (5th ed, 1984) pp 962 *et seq.*
[35] *Lumley* v *Gye* (1853) 2 El & Bl 216; 118 ER 749.
[36] Salmond & Heuston on *The Law of Torts* (20th ed, 1992) 366 *et seq.*
[37] *Le Lievre* v *Gould* [1983] 1 QB 491. The decision was followed by the majority in *Candler*
v *Crane, Christmas & Co* [1951] 2 KB 164. See also note 80 below and accompanying text.
[38] IE Davidson, 'The Equitable Remedy of Compensation' (1982) 13 Melb UL Rev 349; PM
McDermott, 'Jurisdiction of the Court of Chancery to award damages' (1992) 108 LQR 652;
The Hon Mr Justice WMC Gummow, 'Unjust Enrichment, Restitution and Proprietary
Remedies' in PD Finn (ed), *Essays on Restitution* (1990) ch 3.
[39] PS Atiyah, *The Rise and Fall of Freedom of Contract* (1979).

meant honouring the parties' agreement with little regard to its contents. The tools available for control over the agreement were deprived of much of their effectiveness. The doctrine of public policy was given a narrow interpretation. A contract was not regarded against public policy merely because its terms were harsh or grossly unfair.[40] The doctrine of consideration acquired a formal meaning and, although it was on occasion utilized to invalidate unfair agreements,[41] it could not provide effective means for ensuring contractual justice. It should, however, be pointed out that the argument that the judges of the nineteenth century were less willing to interfere with contracts than their predecessors has been challenged on the grounds that

the various factors, whether of confidence between the parties, or of affluence on the one side and distress on the other, which at an earlier period would have been treated at most as circumstances of evidence, from which the court might infer that a grossly unequal bargain had been fraudulently obtained, were [by the nineteenth century] held to oblige the other party to prove the justice of the bargain.[42]

The general emphasis on the severely restricted role of the court in supervising the contract or particular terms may have been due in part to the concentration by the textbooks on common law doctrine and the relative neglect of equitable principles, the consequences of which still affect contract scholarship.[43]

On the theoretical level, the reluctance to impose upon the parties obligations to which they had not consented led to the attribution of a substantial part of contract law to the parties' agreement. Thus, a term was not to be implied into the contract merely because it was just or reasonable. It had to be based upon the parties' consent.[44] In the case of implied terms based on trade custom this was said to be presumed consent[45] and, perhaps because of the artificiality of this, the custom had to be strictly proved.[46] It had to be consistent and had to be more than a course of

[40] See note 73 below and accompanying text.

[41] *Stilk v Myrick* (1809) 2 Camp 317; 170 ER 1168. Cf the report in 6 Esp 129, 170 ER 851, which bases the decision on public policy. See generally, GH Treitel, *The Law of Contract* (8th ed 1991) pp 88–9.

[42] JL Barton, 'The Enforcement of Hard Bargains' (1987) 103 LQR 118, 143–4 comparing, in particular, *Prees v Coke* [1871] LR 6 Ch App 645 and *Proof v Hines* (1735) Cas T Talbot 111, 25 ER 690 (Lord Talbot). See also AWB Simpson, 'The Horwitz Thesis and the History of Contracts' (1979) 46 U Chi L Rev 533, 561–73.

[43] Cf. the approach of English courts since *United Scientific Holdings Ltd v Burnley BC* [1978] AC 904; eg *Associated Japanese Bank (International) Ltd v Crédit du Nord* [1989] 1 WLR 255, at 267–8; *Westdeutsche Landesbank Girozentrale v Islington LBR* (1993) 91 LGR 323, at 349 aff'd [1994] 1 WLR 938. For a sketch of how an integrated system might work, see J Beatson, *The Use and Abuse of Unjust Enrichment* (1991) pp 253–4.

[44] *Shirlaw v Southern Foundries (1926) Ltd* [1939] 2 KB 206, at 227, aff'd [1940] AC 801. GH Treitel, *The Law of Contract* (8th ed 1991) p 187. See further T Rakoff, ch 8 below.

[45] eg *Product Brokers Co Ltd v Olympia Oil & Cake Co Ltd* [1916] 1 AC 314, at 324 per Lord Atkinson.　　　　[46] *Nelson v Dahl* (1879) 12 ChD 568, at 575 per Jessel MR.

conduct which was habitually followed; it had to be shown that it was recognized as binding and intended to affect the legal rights and duties of the parties involved. Thus, although not necessary, proof of past enforcement is valuable and might be conclusive in establishing the custom.[47] Even the doctrines of mistake and frustration were said to be based upon the parties' intent.[48]

Another dominant tendency of classical contract theory was reflected in the endeavour to attain the highest degree of stability and predictability so as to ensure the parties' ability to rely upon the binding effect of the contract. To achieve this purpose, judicial discretion was seen as having little place in contract law and in many areas, notably those relating to contract formation and consideration, the rules assumed an almost mathematical guise. Again equity, with its discretionary remedies, and its ability to subvert common law rules such as the parol evidence rule,[49] appears to have been marginalized.

Some of the greatest paradoxes of classical contract law lay in the fundamental incongruity between the ethos of the will of the parties and the quest for certainty in contract law. Thus, the supremacy of the parties' intention means that if consent was not 'real', for instance if it was vitiated by such elements as mistake, misapprehension or duress, the contract should be avoided. On the other hand, the requirements of certainty and reliability lead to the circumscription of the grounds upon which it is possible to avoid contractual obligations. This tendency, which culminated in *Bell* v *Lever Bros Ltd*,[50] has resulted in the upholding of contracts which did not reflect genuine intention and in narrowing the scope of the doctrines of mistake and duress.

Another, perhaps more important aspect of the quest for certainty is reflected in the adoption of the 'objective theory' in English contract law. This provides, in essence, that no matter what a person's real intention is, if he so conducts himself that the other party reasonably believes that he assents to the terms of the contract, he would be bound as if he actually agreed to them.[51] This obviously leads to the imposition of nonconsensual obligations. A person may be under an obligation to which he never consented, simply because he acted as if he did consent. Indeed, the

---

[47] *Cunliffe-Owen* v *Teather & Greenwood* [1967] 1 WLR 1421, at 1438; *General Reinsurance Corpn* v *Forsakringaktiebolaget Fennia Patria* [1983] QB 856, at 874.

[48] *Anson's Law of Contract* (26th ed 1984) p 252 (mistake); GH Treitel, *The Law of Contract* (8th ed 1991) pp 818–19 (frustration).

[49] Compare *Godd* v *Lord Nugent* (1833) 5 B & Ad 58, at 64–5, 110 ER 713, at 715–16 (Lord Denman CJ on the common law position) with *Redgrave* v *Hurd* (1881) 20 Ch D 1 (evidence of oral warranty could be given in equity because the words amounted to a misrepresentation). See DW Greig and JLR Davis, *The Law of Contract* (1987) pp 440–1, 465.

[50] [1932] AC 161.

[51] *Smith* v *Hughes* (1871) LR 6 QB 597, at 607; GH Treitel, *The Law of Contract* (8th ed 1991) p 1; W Howarth, 'The Meaning of Objectivity in Contract' (1984) 100 LQR 265.

objective test is in direct conflict with the very idea that bases liability upon agreement. This test is typical of non-consensual liability, notably in the field of torts where it is routinely applied. The paradoxical result is that while English law strongly resisted the imposition of liability for pure economic loss in the field of torts, which is primarily concerned with non-consensual liability, it lavishly allowed such liability to be imposed in the field ostensibly dedicated to consented obligations.

Classical contract law embodied a number of features which offered considerable advantages to the powerful and the knowledgable, while posing substantial risks to the ignorant and the unwary. Pre-contractual duties were minimal. The imposition of contractual liability was often dependent upon formal requirements which the unscrupulous could at the last minute refrain from fulfilling and thus avoid liability. In *Pitt* v *P.H.H. Asset Management Ltd*[52] Sir Thomas Bingham MR graphically described the process of buying or selling a house as a profoundly depressing and frustrating experience, because after a deal is struck and hands are shaken either party can decide not to proceed without any explanation or apology. The vendor who may have made plans for his own move and taken the house off the market 'has to embark on the whole dreary process of putting his house on the market all over again.' The purchaser may have instructed solicitors to act, commissioned an architect to plan alterations, made arrangements to borrow money and put his own house on the market or even to move but is unprotected. The Master of the Rolls stated that the reasons why purchaser and vendor are able to indulge their self interest, even their whims, without exposing themselves to any legal penalty and to act in an apparently unprincipled manner are to be found in two legal rules of long standing: first, the rule that contracts for the sale and purchase of land must be evidenced (or now made) in writing: secondly, the rule that terms agreed subject to contract do not give rise to a binding contract.

Freedom of contract in the sense that the content of the contract was almost completely exempt from external supervision, coupled with the objective test, often enabled business corporations to draft their contracts as they pleased, and once the contract was formed escape routes were very narrow. By contrast, as the cases on breach of condition illustrate, if what occurred *happened* to fall within an escape route, in the case of a 'condition' an escape route designed by the parties, it could be used for opportunistic reasons.[53]

The presentation of broad general trends in classical contract law must necessarily admit the existence of exceptions, variations and even inexactitudes. Equitable rules, although as we have seen accorded a secondary

---

[52] [1994] 1 WLR 327, at 333–4.   [53] See *Arcos Ltd* v *Ronaasen & Son* [1933] AC 470.

role and sometimes marginalized, did lead to some deviation from the strict classical model. It was thus held that a contract can be avoided for misrepresentation even if it was innocent,[54] and the doctrine of undue influence, which greatly expands the possibility of avoiding unfair contracts, was maintained throughout the period.[55]

In the modern period there is evidence of the reshaping of contract law accompanied by an expansion of the non-contractual fields of liability.[56] Harbingers of the new era appeared in England by the 1940s. The decision in the *High Trees*[57] case was perhaps the most prominent among them, but there were others, including a realistic and fairly relaxed approach to requirements of contractual certainty[58] and an approach to discharge of contract, whether by breach or frustration, that gave greater emphasis to the ex post consequences of an event and less emphasis on the (often fictional) intentions of the parties.[59] The evolution of new doctrines and approaches has been gradual and slow, and there have also been exceptions and inconsistencies. For instance, when economic duress was first recognized as a vitiating factor, its theoretical basis was said to be 'coercion of the will',[60] ie absence of intention. But the overall impression of contract law today as the end of the century approaches shows the transformation clearly. The contrast between duress and frustration is instructive in this context. Whereas it took frustration almost a hundred years to reject the implied contract theory,[61] the process was achieved in a decade in the case of duress.[62]

Modern contract law is characterized by an increased control over the contractual regime. This control is reflected both by general supervision over the process of contract formation and by intervention in the very con-

---

[54] *Redgrave* v *Hurd* (1881) 20 ChD 1.

[55] See eg *Wright* v *Carter* [1903] 1 Ch 27; *Ellis* v *Barker* (1871) LR 7 Ch App 104. See also JL Barton, 'The Enforcement of Hard Bargains' (1987) 103 LQR 118, note 42 above and accompanying text.

[56] See generally PS Atiyah, *The Rise and Fall of Freedom of Contract* (1979). An extreme approach is taken in G Gilmore, *The Death of Contract* (1974).

[57] *Central London Property Trust Ltd* v *High Trees House Ltd* [1947] KB 130.

[58] *Hillas & Co* v *Arcos Ltd* (1932) 147 LT 503 per Lord Wright. Cf. N. Cohen, pp 36–7 below for a more restrictive approach today.

[59] *Hongkong Fir Shipping Co Ltd* v *Kawasaki Kisen Kaisha Ltd* [1962] 2 QB 26; *Davis Contractors Ltd* v *Fareham UDC* [1956] AC 696.

[60] *The Siboen* [1976] 1 Lloyd's Rep 293, at 336; *The Atlantic Baron* [1979] 1 QB 705, at 717, 719; *Pao On* v *Lau Yiu Long* [1980] AC 614, at 635. See further, J Beatson, *The Use and Abuse of Unjust Enrichment* (1991) pp 109–17.

[61] The modern doctrine was first recognized in *Taylor Caldwell* (1863) 3 B & S 826, 122 ER 309; an alternative to the implied term theory was only found in *Davis Contractors Ltd* v *Fareham UDC* [1956] AC 696, at 729.

[62] *The Universe Sentinel* [1983] 1 AC 366, at 383, 400; *B & S Contracts and Design Ltd* v *Victor Green Publications Ltd* [1984] ICR 419; *The Evia Luck* [1992] 2 AC 152.

tents of the contract. The first category deals with the topic that in US law has been described as 'procedural unconscionability'.[63] It is mainly concerned with confining the caveat emptor idea and with ensuring that the contract when formed is free from elements which vitiate consent. The developments in this area are due in the main to innovations introduced by case law. The courts apparently felt free to reshape the law because the result does not conflict with the 'freedom of contract' paradigm. A conspicuous example of the modern approach can be found in the rules regarding the inclusion of exemption and unfair terms in the contract. Such terms may be included by reference or notice. Modern law, however, requires the notice to be manifested in a way that is proportionate to the onerousness or unusualness of the term. In extreme cases the well known statement by Lord Denning may apply. Under it '[s]ome clauses ... would need to be printed in red ink on the face of the document with a red hand pointing to it before the notice could be held to be sufficient.'[64]

The grounds for rescinding a contract because there has been no genuine consent have been greatly expanded. We have noted that modern contract law recognizes economic duress as a vitiating factor.[65] Doubts as to the extent of the right to rescind a contract on the ground of innocent misrepresentation have been removed.[66] In the field of mistake, the restrictive approach of *Bell* v *Lever Bros Ltd*[67] has been circumvented by resorting to the equitable jurisdiction.[68] The law of undue influence has also evidenced remarkable development, and in the context of guarantees it may be incumbent upon a lender, who knows or ought to know that the debtor has a dominating influence over the guarantor, to ensure that the guarantor is not induced by undue influence exerted by the debtor.[69] Furthermore, the requirement that the transaction be manifestly disadvantageous to the party subjected to the influence has been greatly diluted

[63] AA Leff, 'Unconscionability and the Code—The Emperor's New Clause' (1967) 115 U of Pa L Rev 485; RA Epstein, 'Unconscionability: A Critical Reappraisal' (1975) 18 JL & Econ 293. Cf. MA Eisenberg, 'The Bargain Principle and its Limits' (1982) 95 Harv L Rev 741.

[64] *J Spurling Ltd* v *Bradshaw* [1956] 1 WLR 461, at 466, recently applied in *Interfoto Picture Library Ltd* v *Stiletto Visual Programmes Ltd* [1989] QB 433. Contrast this approach with *Thompson* v *LM & S Ry Co* [1930] 1 KB 41 which was decided in the classical period. See also GH Treitel, *The Law of Contract* (8th ed 1991) p 199 who concludes that the result in the *Thompson* fact situation would probably be now otherwise.

[65] R Goff and G Jones, *The Law of Restitution* (4th ed, 1993) p 250 *et seq*.

[66] *Leaf* v *International Galleries* [1950] 2 KB 86; GH Treitel, *The Law of Contract* (8th ed 1991) p 335.

[67] [1932] AC 161.

[68] *Solle* v *Butcher* [1950] 1 KB 671; *Grist* v *Bailey* [1967] Ch 532; *Magee* v *Pennine Insurance Co Ltd* [1969] 2 QB 507; *Associated Japanese Bank (International) Ltd* v *Crédit du Nord SA* [1989] 1 WLR 255, at 267–8.

[69] See eg *Avon Finance Co* v *Bridger* [1985] 2 All ER 281; *Barclays Bank plc* v *O'Brien* [1994] 1 AC 180; *CIBC Mortgages* v *Pitt* [1994] 1 AC 200.

[70] *Barclays Bank plc* v *O'Brien* [1994] 1 AC 180; *CIBC Mortgages plc* v *Pitt* [1994] 1 AC 200; *Cheese* v *Thomas* [1994] 1 WLR 129. See further Birks and Chin, Ch 3 below.

and, in some instances, completely eliminated.[70] In addition, legislation has introduced what may be termed 'statutory undue influence', which enables consumers to rescind a contract in certain cases on the ground of pressure that is beyond the reach of traditional undue influence.[71]

However, once the contract passes the test of initial validity, the control of its terms on the ground of unfairness becomes problematical since it is in direct conflict with the notion of freedom of contract. Nevertheless, the law has for centuries possessed tools that could be utilized in order to exercise such control, notably the doctrine of public policy and the equitable rules against penalty and forfeiture. The doctrine of public policy was applied to various types of agreements such as agreements detrimental to the institution of marriage and agreements involving sexual immorality.[72] In the purely economic area it applied mainly to agreements restraining competition. However, other 'economically immoral' contracts, ie contracts which were grossly unfair, were beyond the reach of the public policy doctrine. Indeed, the rise of the classical contract theory bred attempts to circumscribe the doctrine of public policy, which was naturally viewed as a potential threat to freedom of contract. It thus earned pejorative descriptions such as an 'unruly horse',[73] and it was even suggested that courts may not 'invent a new head of public policy'.[74] Another way of diminishing the effectiveness of public policy was by presenting the doctrine as requiring the enforcement of contracts rather than their invalidation.[75]

The doctrine of good faith provides another important tool for the control of contractual terms and their application. The doctrine has long been recognized by continental law. Recently it has been gradually absorbed by a number of common law jurisdictions.[76] English law has hitherto declined to adopt a general principle of good faith but was able to offer specific solutions to a wide range of issues which involve the question of

---

[71] See eg Consumer Credit Act 1974, ss 67–8; GH Treitel, *The Law of Contract* (8th ed 1991) p 376.

[72] *Ibid.* p 387 *et seq.*

[73] *Richardson v Mellish* (1824) 2 Big 229, at 252; 130 ER 294, at 303.

[74] *Janson v Driefontein Consolidated Mines Ltd* [1902] AC 484, at 491 per Lord Halsbury LC.

[75] *Printing & Numerical Registering Co v Sampson* (1875) LR 19 Eq 462, at 465 per Jessel MR. On the two aspects of public policy, the one supporting freedom of contract while the other requiring its limitation, see GL Williams, 'Language and the Law' (1946) 62 LQR 387, 399.

[76] See eg Restatement of Contracts 2d §205. Moreover, under the prevailing view in US jurisdictions, courts may interfere in cases of grossly excessive price and presumably also where the terms of the terms of the contract are extremely unfair ('Substantive Unconscionability'). See JD Calamari and JM Perillo, *The Law of Contracts* (3rd ed 1987) p 406; MA Eisenberg, 'The Bargain Principle and its Limits' (1982) 95 Harv L Rev 741. See also the Australian developments, cited in note 3 above; P Finn, 'Commerce, The Common Law and Morality' (1989) 17 Melb UL Rev 87.

[77] *Interfoto Picture Library Ltd v Stiletto Visual Programmes Ltd* [1989] QB 433, at 439, at 445 per Bingham LJ.

unfairness.[77] Even before the European Community Directive on Unfair Terms in Consumer Contracts, which imposes obligations of good faith, there were signs that the influence of other legal systems and the European environment were leading to a gradual recognition of the doctrine or at least to parallel solutions by other means.[78]

The reluctance of the courts to develop principles that will allow direct control over substantive unfairness has led to legislative intervention. Legislation exercising or permitting direct control over various types of contracts and contractual terms has been adopted in many countries. Indeed, such legislation constitutes an important part of modern contract law. England has enacted the Unfair Contract Terms Act 1977, which is of broad application, as well as statutes dealing with specific contracts such as the Consumer Credit Act 1974 and the Financial Services Act 1986.

Another tendency of modern contract law is to dilute formal requirements and to attach greater weight to substantive fairness. A conspicuous example is the erosion of the doctrine of consideration in the context of contract renegotiation, and its replacement by the rules of equitable estoppel and economic duress.[79]

These developments coincide with the rise of non-contractual fields of obligations, namely, torts and restitution. Liability in torts may now be imposed for negligent misrepresentation that causes a mere financial loss,[80] and a party who fails to perform a contract is sometimes liable in tort to a third party who is an intended beneficiary.[81] The greater sophistication of tort law and the transformation of the defence of contributory negligence coupled with the emphasis upon substantive justice, have somewhat undermined the 'all or nothing' approach of contract law. There are now clear indications that contributory negligence will have a role, albeit a modest one, in the field of contracts. It is clear that contributory negligence applies where the defendant has breached a contractual duty of care (as is generally owed by professionals and others rendering services) and his conduct also amounts to a tort.[82]

Under classical law the exact point of contract formation assumed crucial importance. It marked the boundary between the pre-contractual regime of no liability and the regime in which the parties are subject to contractual liability. The modern expansion of torts and restitution, cou-

---

[77] *Ibid.* See also *Chitty on Contracts* (27th ed 1994) ss 1–010–1–011.

[79] J Beatson, 'Innovations in Contract: An English Perspective' in P Birks (ed) *The Frontiers of Liability* (1994) vol. 2. Cf. M Chen-Wishart, ch 5, below.

[80] *Hedley Byrne & Co Ltd v Heller & Partners Ltd* [1964] AC 465.

[81] *Ross v Caunters* [1980] Ch 297; *White v Jones* [1993] 3 WLR 730.

[82] *Forsikringsaktieselkapet Vesta v Butcher* [1989] AC 852 (aff'd without discussion of this point *ibid.*, 880). For a review of the present law and proposals for extending the role of contributory negligence to breaches of contractual duties to take care which do not amount to torts, see Contributory Negligence as a Defence in Contract (1993) Law Com No. 219.

pled with the erosion of the formal requirements for contract formation, have somewhat blurred the line between these two regimes, though it still maintains much of its significance.

On the theoretical level, the approach which attributes the main body of contract law to the parties' intention has been largely abandoned. It is now openly recognized that a substantial part of contract law derives from ex lege rules[83] although the parties are, in many instances, free to deviate from them. The greater emphasis on substantive justice and the growing role of ex lege rules has also led to greater differentiation between diverse types of contracts. Consumer contracts are often treated differently from other contracts. Standard contracts have been the subject of specific rules in some countries. Various other contracts, such as employment contracts, hire-purchase contracts and credit contracts are subject to specific legislation. The process of control over the contractual regime is thus accompanied by considerable fragmentation of contract law.[84]

Another question of ex lege intervention in the contractual regime relates to the possible adaptation of the contract to change of circumstances. Classical contract law developed the doctrine of frustration. It is a rather rigid doctrine. Under it, if the change which occurred is sufficiently drastic, the contract is discharged. If the change does not amount to frustration the contract as originally formed remains in force. However, sometimes an intermediate solution may be more appropriate. The issue is of particular significance in long term contracts, although it may arise in other contracts as well.

Developments in contractual remedies are of considerable interest, notably because of the particular importance which this field occupies in the common law tradition. It may however be pointed out that contract remedies were subject to judicial control even in the classical period. Here, therefore, changes are less drastic than in other parts of the law of contract. Still, in modern times legal control over contractual remedies, notably those agreed upon by the parties, has been extended by legislation.[85] Another important change in contract remedies relates to the

---

[83] Thus, the doctrine of frustration was once attributed to an implied term (see note 48 above and accompanying text). Under the modern approach it is founded on an ex lege rule applied by the court. See *Davis Contractors Ltd v Fareham UDC* [1956] AC 696, at 728, per Lord Radcliffe; PS Atiyah, *Introduction to the Law of Contract* (4th ed 1989) pp 255–6.

[84] Cheshire, Fifoot and Furmston's *Law of Contract* (12th ed 1991) pp 24–5.

[85] See PS Atiyah, *The Rise and Fall of Freedom of Contract* (1979) p 439 with regard to statutory limitations upon self-help remedies in the context of certain type of contracts.

[86] The initial position of Anglo-American law was that the promisee is not entitled to specific performance if damages are adequate. However, it seems that the modern test is not the 'adequacy' of damages but which remedy is the most appropriate: GH Treitel, *The Law of Contract* (8th ed 1991) p 902. Cf also EA Farnsworth, *Contracts* (2nd ed 1990) p 858.

greater availability of specific performance[86] and the mitigation of the formal rules that limited its application.[87] This development which strengthens the contractual right can be probably be attributed to the greater emphasis upon substantive justice and to the decline of formal requirements that fetter judicial discretion. The field of remedies provided a most fertile ground for theoretical developments. Topics such as the relation between rights and remedies and the nature of the interests protected by contract remedies, became the subject of intense discussion.[88] For the adherents of economic analysis contract remedies became a most attractive testing ground for their theories.

III

This book is divided into four parts. This first part is introductory. The second part deals with the formation of contract; pre-contractual duties and fairness in the process of contract formation and consideration. Nili Cohen considers a broad spectrum of duties and liabilities at the pre-contractual stage. She addresses the interrelations of freedom in the bargaining process, the duty of good faith and a contract to negotiate. Two categories of potential defects in the process of contract formation are analysed, the one relating to a defect in the will and the other to a breach of promise or frustration of expectation. It is pointed out that English law grants adequate protection in the first category, but is more reserved in the second. Peter Birks and Chin Nyuk Yin consider undue influence and Muriel Fabre-Magnan duties of disclosure. Neither paper is concerned with duties in the strict sense (i.e. requirements the breach of which gives rise to liability), but with conditions for the creation of contractual obligations.[89]

Birks and Chin analyse undue influence, not as a matter of 'victimisation', which implies wicked exploitation by the defendant, but as a matter of 'excessive dependence' on the part of the plaintiff. Resisting current tendencies to assimilate undue influence to unconscionable behaviour, they argue that all cases of improper pressure which have been litigated

---

[87] Thus, the award of specific performance was not considered conditional upon mutuality. As to the present state of the law see GH Treitel, *The Law of Contract* (8th ed 1991) pp 916–18; SM Waddams, Ch. 18 below.

[88] No attempt will be made to list the publications which appeared in the wake of LL Fuller and WR Perdue, 'The Reliance Interest in Contract Damages' (1936) 46 Yale LJ 52, 373.

[89] Cf *Banque Keyser Ullman SA v Skandia (UK) Insurance Co Ltd* [1990] 1 QB 665, aff'd [1991] 2 AC 249 (in the context of the duty of disclosure). Compare also the principle of mitigation, which does not impose a duty in the strict sense. Failure to mitigate damages may affect the plaintiff's right of recovery against the other party, but does not impose on him liability to pay damages.

as undue influence can and should now be classified as duress. In the cases which then remain, which Birks and Chin see as 'true' undue influence, the ground of rescission is, in their analysis, solely the marked impairment of the plaintiff's capacity to make an independent judgment, that impairment arising from loss of autonomy brought about by the nature of the relationship between the two parties.

Fabre-Magnan uses economic analysis to examine the duty of disclosure against the background of French law in which this duty is particularly extensive. She distinguishes between duties of disclosure relating to the party's own performance or consideration (*prestation*) and that of the other party. She concludes that the imposition of such a duty is justified in the former category (eg a requirement that the seller will disclose information pertaining to the property he sells), while in the second category there is ordinarily no room for such a duty (eg the buyer should usually not be required to disclose information relating to the property he intends to purchase).

Mindy Chen-Wishart deals with the doctrine of consideration which is sometimes conceived as reflecting a mere formal requirement, but may also represent notions of fairness. This chapter critically examines the decision in *Williams v Roffey Bros and Nicholls (Contractors) Ltd*[90] and the concept of 'practical benefit' which it adopted. The author argues that the introduction of this concept undermines the functions of the doctrine of consideration, notably that of defining the category of promises, the breach of which entitles the promisee to expectation damage. Rather than broadening the definition of consideration, she argues that it is preferable to recognize exceptions to its application, within which the normal remedy would be based upon the reliance interest.

The third part of the book is concerned with the contents of the contract, its control and adaptation. It is divided into four sections. The first section considers the concept of good faith in general and implied terms which, in the common law system, fulfil some functions analogical to that of good faith. Allan Farnsworth points out the great variety of situations in which the issue of good faith in contract performance arises in United States law. The chapter traces the historical origins of the good faith doctrine and discusses a number of its important applications. It also examines the theoretical debate over the meaning of the concept of good faith and the major issues that currently arise in US law regarding its ambit.

Werner Ebke and Bettina Steinhauer describe the cardinal role of good faith in German law. The concept has been utilized to fill gaps (lacunae) in the rules on breach of a contract, to develop secondary (or ancillary) contractual obligations, including the obligation to furnish information

[90] [1991] 1 QB 1.

and to cooperate in the performance of the contract. In addition, the requirement of good faith had a role in the developments of the law relenting to frustration and contract modification where circumstances have drastically changed.

Todd Rakoff addresses the question of how courts should deal with the process of gap filling by what are variously called 'background terms', 'default rules' or 'implied terms'. The issue may arise in standard situations such as landlord and tenant, seller and buyer or employer and employee, or in more individual or 'one-off' contracts in which there is a gap in the terms. He is concerned with the first of these and discusses the difficulties and abstractness of a number of approaches including 'fairness', 'a common sense notion of implied consent', a 'hypothetical bargain' test and an efficient risk allocation test. He proposes a 'situation sense' approach which depends on a considerably more explicit, tight, and structured model of the transactional situation at issue in its societal context.

The second section examines legislation and public law influences, which furnish additional tools for the control of the contractual obligation. Hugh Beale deals with the topic that has assumed major importance in modern contract law, namely legislative control of unfairness. The chapter discusses the difficulties raised by standard contracts and argues that usually the issue is not unconscionable behaviour but unfair surprise and lack of choice. The chapter also analyses the provisions of the United Kingdom's Unfair Contract Terms Act 1977 as well as the European Commission's Directive on Unfair Terms in Consumer Contracts and its possible impact on English law. In this context the author discusses the conceptual problem raised by the Directive's test of unfairness which is based, inter alia, on the concept of good faith. He also points to the need to face up to the phenomenon of mass contracting and welcomes the fact that the Directive enables and welcomes collective action by consumer organizations while expressing disappointment with its substantive requirements.

Jack Beatson explores the limited situations in which public law values have influenced developments in contract law. He argues that, although there are more such instances than is generally recognized, the fact that they are regarded as isolated atypical cases has meant that the common law has not been able to solve a number of problems, particularly pre-contractual disputes and difficulties arising from the existence and exercise of contractual discretions. He suggests that the concepts first developed in public law to limit the unbridled exercise of discretions and to protect legitimate expectations should not be marginalized in contractual contexts.

The third section deals with relational and long term contracts and the related issue of change of circumstances (an issue which at least theoretically may also arise in other contracts). Relational and long-term contracts are discussed in two chapters, one by Melvin Eisenberg and the other by Ewan McKendrick. Both authors conclude that there is no room for a separate category of long term (or relational) contracts to which specific rules will apply. McKendrick points out that there may be a great need for adjustment in long term contracts but the parties often insert force majeure, hardship and other clauses intended to deal with change of circumstances. What is required is a liberal approach by the courts that will recognize the need for flexibility, and will permit the enforcement of such clauses even though they may be drafted in vague flexible terms. Melvin Eisenberg points out that the relational contract literature cannot offer a definition of relational contracts, to which special rules are to apply. He then advances the theory that most contracts are in fact relational, and that the weakness of both classical law and modern relational theory derives from their shared implicit assumption that most contracts are discrete. Because most contracts are relational, a special body of law for relational contracts cannot be created. Instead, the general principles of contract law should be sufficiently expansive to deal appropriately with both relational and discrete contracts.

The final section of this part of the book is devoted to three issues relating to the extent of the contractual obligation. Barry Nicholas presents the French model of contractual liability which includes three categories. The first requires the use of reasonable care. The second imposes strict liability to achieve a result subject to possible exemption if the failure was due to a cause for which the party not responsible and could not surmount. The third category includes cases of absolute liability. The common law contractual liability is analysed against this model, and it is pointed out that there are analogues to the three categories of liabilities in French law. The author discusses the common law technique of implied terms which was employed to base liability on fault as well as the doctrine of frustration.

German law has particular experience with contract adjustment as a result of change of circumstances. The topic is addressed by Werner Lorenz, who presents a broad picture of continental legislation. French and German court decisions and a variety of legal theories advanced to cope with this universal problem. The discussion analyses the great complexities involved in an attempt to modify the contract and reach a fair solution.

Guenter Treitel's chapter on alternative obligations considers contracts which give one of the parties the right to choose between two or more ways of rendering performance. He discusses the general rule that a party is not excused when one alternative becomes impossible or illegal after the contract is made and the exceptions to it. One exception is where the contract creates a liberty to substitute rather than a true alternative. Treitel analyses how courts have distinguished between the two situations. He also considers alternative methods of discharge and alternative and contingent obligations.

The fourth part of the book deals with remedies. Daniel Friedmann discusses the theory that gaps created in English law by the lack of good faith doctrine are filled in part by the law of remedies. The discretionary remedies of specific performance and injunction are likely to be denied to a party who acted unfairly or in breach of the requirement of good faith. These remedies are thus utilized to control contractual behaviour. Even the non-discretionary remedy of damages embodies rules, such as those on mitigation, which discourage unfair conduct. He also discusses the self-help remedy of termination and the various limitations upon its application which are based upon ideas akin to that of good faith.

Michael Bridge addresses the issue of assessment of expectation damages. The assessment of such damages is based upon supposition as to the position the plaintiff would have been in had the contract been performed. Bridge deals with the many difficulties that this supposition entails. The discussion relates inter alia to cases of the loss of a chance, situations in which the other party has a discretion as to his performance, and those in which recovery is measured by reliance loss.

Stephen Waddams deals with the choice of remedy for breach of contract. He points out that remedy should be fashioned so as to do justice to both parties. An unrestricted right to specific performance might expose the defendant to extortionate demands and does not accord with the principle of mitigation. The absence of specific performance often reduces the cost of the breach to both parties. Hence, while the availability of specific performance is being expanded, it is important for the courts to retain flexibility and to use discretion so that this remedy is granted only where appropriate.

In his chapter on suspending performance John Carter advocates the adoption of the possibility of suspending performance as a remedy for breach. Rather than forcing the injured party to choose between terminating the contract and keeping it alive, it is argued that he should, in an appropriate case, be entitled to suspend his performance or to require an assurance that the other party will fulfil his obligation. Carter analyses the various functions and advantages of suspension. Also discussed are the pertaining legal rules in English and Australian law, which do not openly recognize suspension, as well as the provisions in the Convention on International Sale of Goods (the Vienna Convention) and the United States's Uniform Commercial Code and Restatement 2d Contracts.

Part 2
Formation of Contract

(a) Pre-contractual duties and good faith

2

Pre-Contractual Duties: Two Freedoms and the Contract to Negotiate*

Nili Cohen

Freedom to contract

In *Four Essays on Liberty* Isaiah Berlin distinguishes between the negative and the positive sense of liberty. Negative liberty means the freedom *from* (intervention) whereas positive liberty means the freedom *to* (self accomplishment).[1] The distinction is rooted in the law of contract, which is predicated upon these two notions of freedom: the positive freedom of contract, which means that the parties are free to create a binding contract reflecting their free will, and the negative freedom of contract, which means that the parties are free from obligations so long as a binding contract has not been concluded.

As to the positive freedom of contract, this principle means that the formation of a contract and the selection of its terms are the result of the free will of the parties. The crucial question relates then to the necessary preconditions guaranteeing the existence of the freedom upon which a valid contract may be founded. In other words: when is a contract considered as a product of the free will of the parties?[2]

Freedom of contract admits contest between the contracting parties themselves as to the terms of the contract, but the value of reinforcing self-reliance and initiative, underlying any contest, is not absolute. No legal system would legitimize use of violence, fraud or other unlawful means in the negotiating process; such methods subvert the very idea of positive freedom of contract. A contract concluded by violence or fraud is not a product of the free will of the contracting parties. Such a contract can be

---

* Copyright © 1994, Nili Cohen.

[1] In the essay 'Liberty' in *Four Essays on Liberty* (1969) p 118.

[2] This problem indicates that the distinction between the two freedoms is far from being clear-cut (for a critical comment on the distinction see SJ Heyman, 'Positive and Negative Liberty' (1992) 68 Chicago-Kent L Rev 81). The issue of defects in the will of the contracting parties can be conceived as pertaining both to positive and negative freedoms. As to the positive freedom, this reflects the free will of the parties to be bound under contract. As to the negative freedom from contract, subjecting the parties to an agreement which is not a product of their free will amounts to imposing upon them coercive contract, which is contradictory to the very concept of contract. For reasons of methodology the issue of defects in the formation of contract will be discussed within the ambit of positive freedom to contract.

avoided and, in extreme cases, is not binding at all. Furthermore, violence or fraud are likely to constitute civil wrongs and may impose liability in tort on the contracting party. This has nothing to do with the question whether the legal system contains a general principle of good faith in the bargaining process. The freedom to act in the bargaining process is limited in the following way: the contracting party is not allowed to act so as to frustrate the pre-conditions for the existence of freedom of contract. If he does so, the contract may not be binding, or it may be invalidated, and sometimes the party at fault might be subject to liability in tort.

It should be stressed, however, that not every difference between the parties calls for the intervention of the law. The freedom of action on which freedom of contract is founded is a relative one. There can be no doubt that violence is incompatible with freedom of contract, but what about economic or emotional compulsion? There is also no doubt that fraud is incompatible with freedom of contract, but what about non-disclosure of a material fact of which the other party is unaware?

The determination of the pre-requisites guaranteeing the positive freedom of contract 'already implies a judiciary enforced redistribution of advantages from the strong to the weak'[3] and raises doubts and controversies as to its scope. Such doubts are prevalent in every legal system, but a system which recognizes a principle of good faith in the bargaining process is likely to broaden the minimal pre-conditions guaranteeing freedom of contract. This means that the grounds of rescission of contract may be expanded[4] and, at the same time, this might also lead to the expansion of the causes for imposing compensatory liability on the party to blame.[5]

The desire to accomplish a positive freedom of contract stimulates every system to create rules imposing liability on those violating the minimal pre-conditions guaranteeing this freedom. In this respect the absence of a duty to act in good faith in the bargaining process is not decisive.

---

[3] A Brudner, 'Reconstructing Contracts' (1993) 43 UTLJ 1, 5. On the relative character of consent see L Brilmayer, 'Consent, Contract and Territory' (1989) 74 Minn L Rev 1; R Craswell, 'Property Rules and Liability Rules in Unconscionability and Related Doctrines' (1993) 60 U Chic L Rev 1.

[4] Thus it is argued that there is a general duty of disclosure in French law: J Ghestin, 'The Pre-contractual Obligation to Disclose Information—French Report' in D Harris and D Tallon (eds), *Contract Law Today—Anglo-French Comparisons* (1989) pp 151–66, whereas in English law a duty to disclose is imposed only in some specific categories.

[5] However, the grounds for rescission of contract are generally wider than those for imposing compensatory liability. Thus, misrepresentation and sometimes non-disclosure might invalidate a contract; misrepresentation may provide a ground for tort liability: *Esso Petroleum Co Ltd v Mardon* [1976] QB 801; but non-disclosure will scarcely entail liability in damages: *Banque Keyser Ullman SA v Skandia (UK) Insurance Co Ltd* [1991] 2 AC 249 (HL). The same applies to undue influence: EA Farnsworth, 'Precontractual Liability and Preliminary Agreements: Fair Dealing and Failed Negotiations' (1987) 87 Colum L Rev 217, 221, n 11.

Freedom from contract

Matters are different with respect to the second notion of freedom in the bargaining process, namely the negative freedom of contract or the freedom from contract. So long as a contract has not been concluded, the contracting parties are free to withdraw. According to this reasoning, if they are not contractually bound (and have not committed any tort), why should they be bound at all? 'By permitting liabilities to arise before agreement has been reached, the courts sense a danger that this would amount to the imposition of liability without consent.'[6]

Even if the parties strongly wish to be bound by a contract, the law will not always give effect to their mutual assent. Each system may impose additional conditions for the validity of a contract, eg the requirement of consideration or that of a formal document. These rules impose a limitation on the positive notion of freedom of contract. If such requirements are not complied with, the contract does not exist or is unenforceable. Imposing liability on the parties before the formal requirements are met would be contradictory to the very existence of those requirements.

The rules governing the formation of a contract leave the parties an ample negative freedom from contract. Before the conclusion of a final contract, each party is free to withdraw from the negotiations, each party bears his own expenses, each party acts at his own risk.[7] These are the rules of the game.

But strict adherence to freedom from contract might transform it into a freedom to manipulate the rules of the game. Freedom of action which is the underlying idea of freedom of contract may be abused. If a party makes a non-contractual promise, namely a promise that is not binding according to the formal rules, should he always be entitled to renege even if he induced the other party to rely on that promise? How is the tension between the need to keep the formal requirements and the protection of misplaced reliance to be handled?

English law tends to enable the contracting party to act according to the rules of the game and to benefit from the freedom granted by these rules. Hence, the merger of freedom in the negotiation process and formal requirements has led English law to rule that an offer promised to be irrevocable, is still revocable, as it is not supported by consideration, and is thus good to create only a *nudum pactum*.[8]

---

[6] H Collins, *The Law of Contract* (2nd ed 1993) p 169.

[7] EA Farnsworth, 'Precontractual Liability and Preliminary Arrangements: Fair Dealing and Failed Negotiations' (1987) 87 Colum L Rev 217, 221–2.

[8] *Dickinson v Dodds* (1876) 2 ChD 463. But see the arrangement in American law under UCC, § 2–205 and Restatement 2d Contracts, § 87(2) which provide for a limited scope of irrevocability. For prospects of a change in this rule see text following note 114, below.

By contrast to English law, Continental systems empower the offeror to bind himself by an irrevocable offer, if he so wishes.[9] Negative freedom in the negotiations is not sacred:[10] even a non-contractual promise or a mere expectancy may have a certain binding force under the doctrine of good faith in negotiations.

The duty of good faith is likely to limit the negative freedom from contract and the possibility of abusing the contractual rules of the game. In fact, this duty has also become part and parcel of the rules of the games themselves.

The imposition of duty of good faith in the bargaining process means a rejection of the adversarial approach which characterizes the position of the negotiating parties in English law.[11] The contracting parties in a good faith regime are no strangers. They have to be considerate towards each other. They rely on each other. This reliance is translated into a legal duty of fairness, the breach of which usually entails liability in damages.

ENGLISH AND CONTINENTAL LAWS

I have presented the English and the Continental systems as diametrically opposed with regard to the notion of negative freedom in the bargaining process. Nevertheless, the difference between the systems is not as wide as might initially appear.

In the case of *Interfoto Picture Library Ltd* v *Stiletto Visual Programmes Ltd*[12] which dealt with the rules of offer and acceptance as a regulating mechanism of unfair conditions in a contract, Bingham LJ opened his judgment by stating:

In many civil law systems, and perhaps in most legal systems outside the common law world, the law of obligations recognises and enforces an overriding principle that in making and carrying out contracts parties should act in good faith. This does not simply mean that they should not deceive each other, a principle which any legal system must recognise; its effect is perhaps most aptly conveyed by such metaphorical colloquialisms as 'playing fair', 'coming clean' or 'putting one's

---

[9] In German law: § 145 BGB and RB Schlesinger (ed), *Formation of Contracts: A Study of the Common Core of Legal Systems* (1968) vol I, pp 780–3. In French law there are some doubts as to the theoretical basis of the irrevocability of an offer. Some regard it as a unilateral obligation; others base it on the doctrine of good faith in negotiations grounded in torts; still others regard it as a preliminary contract (*avant-contrat*) regulating the negotiations: J Ghestin, *Traité de Droit Civil: Les Obligations, Le Contrat: Formation* (2nd ed 1988) s 213 *et seq*.

Section 3(b) of the Israeli Contracts (General Part) Law 1973 states that an offer is irrevocable if that was the declared intention of the offeror or if a specific time was provided for its acceptance (27 LSI 1972/3 117).

[10] For the polar approaches of English and Continental systems: HK Lücke, 'Good Faith and Contractual Performance', in PD Finn (ed), *Essays on Contract* (1987) 155, 170–1.

[11] As termed by Lord Ackner in *Walford* v *Miles* [1992] 2 AC 128, at 138 (HL).

[12] [1989] QB 433.

cards face upwards on the table.' It is in essence a principle of fair and open dealing . . .

English law has, characteristically, committed itself to no such overriding principle but has developed piecemeal solutions in response to demonstrated problems of unfairness.[13]

I shall briefly refer to the piecemeal solutions offered by English law imposing some limitations on freedom of action in the bargaining process. One of them is the rule of promissory estoppel, which is a hybrid creature, comprising elements of contract (promise) and tort (reliance). But this institution, which has been highly developed in the United States[14] and Australia,[15] is of somewhat limited application in English law.[16]

Another tool is offered by the law of restitution. This is available where some benefits have been transferred from one party to the other in the belief that a contract will eventually be concluded.[17] If no benefit has been transferred to the other party, a restitutionary remedy could not be used

---

[13] *Ibid.*, at 439. For examples: HK Lücke, 'Good Faith and Contractual Performance', in PD Finn (ed), *Essays on Contract* (1987) pp 155, 157–8.

[14] The seminal case is *Hoffman v Red Owl Stores Inc* 133 NW2d 267 (Wis 1965), regarded by Professor Farnsworth as a 'decision which might fit better into that field of liability for blameworthy conduct that we know as tort': EA Farnsworth *Contracts* (2nd ed, 1990) p 208. See also *Skycom Corpn v Telstar Corpn* 813 F2d at 810, 817–18 (7th Cir 1987) (liability imposed mainly under a theory of representation to compensate the plaintiff for negotiations expenditures). Cf. note 117, below.

For relatively recent discussions of promissory estoppel in US law: RE Barnett and ME Becker, 'Beyond Reliance: Promissory Estoppel, Contract Formalities, and Misrepresentations' (1987) 15 Hofstra L Rev 443; ME Becker, 'Promissory Estoppel Damages' (1987) 16 Hofstra L Rev 131; MB Metzger and MJ Phillips, 'Promissory Estoppel and Reliance on Illusory Promises' (1990) 44 SW L J 841.

[15] CNH Bagot, 'Equitable Estoppel and Contractual Obligations in the Light of *Waltons v Maher*' (1988) 62 A LJ 926; K Lindgren, 'Estoppel in Contract' (1989) 12 U NSW LJ 153; J Carter, 'Contract, Restitution and Promissory Estoppel' (1989) 12 U NSW LJ 30. See also: *The Commonwealth v Verwayen* (1990) 170 CLR 394.

[16] But see *AG of Hong Kong v Humphreys Estate (Queen's Gardens) Ltd* [1987] AC 114, at 127–8, where the Privy Council indicated that negotiations 'subject to contract' may give rise to some form of estoppel. See note 123, below.

Proprietary estoppel may be used as a cause of action (*Crabb v Arun District Council* [1976] Ch 179; *Taylor Fashions Ltd v Liverpool Victoria Trustees Co Ltd* [1982] QB 133. On a proposition that the former decision should be based on contract: PS Atiyah, 'When is an Enforceable Agreement not a Contract? Answer: When it is an Equity' (1976) 92 LQR 174; and its refute: PJ Millett, '*Crabb v Arun District Council*: A Reposte' (1976) 92 LQR 342; IW Duncanson, 'Equity and Obligations' (1976) 39 MLR 268). For the contrasts between proprietary and promissory estoppel: GH Treitel, *The Law of Contract* (8th ed 1991) pp 134–6. See also: C Davis, 'Estoppel: An Adequate Substitute for Part Performance?' (1993) 13 Ox JLS 99, 103.

For the argument that in English law a non-contractual promise might be used as a cause of action: MP Thompson, 'From Representation to Expectation: Estoppel as a Cause of Action' [1983] CLJ 257.

[17] *British Steel Corpn v Cleveland Bridge and Engineering Co Ltd* [1984] 1 All ER 504; SN Ball, 'Work Carried Out in Pursuance of Letters of Intent—Contract or Restitution' (1983) 99 LQR 572.

to redress expenses incurred during negotiations.[18] Such expenses may be recovered under the collateral contract theory,[19] which might treat a pre-contractual promise as a contractual one, antecedent to the principal contract and sometimes operating along it. Other contractual means change the contractual rules themselves[20] by predating the point at which the contract is concluded,[21] thus altogether preventing a party from exercising his freedom from contract. This device is reflected in the rules about postal acceptance.[22] The law of torts might be applied as well to impose pre-contractual duties, although in the past it was not frequently employed.[23] As will be indicated later, the collateral contract and the tort of negligence currently serve as the main tools for imposing pre-contractual liability.

The principle of good faith, which was adopted by Continental law,[24]

---

[18] For a generous definition of 'benefits' in US law which also covers expenses not conferred on the defendant but incurred under his request see *Earhart* v *Low William Co* 600 P2d 1344, at 1345 (Cal 1979) (note 27 below); EA Farnsworth, 'Precontractual Liability and Preliminary Agreements: Fair Dealing and Failed Negotiations' (1987) 87 Colum L Rev 217, 223–4; GR Shell, 'Opportunism and Trust in the Negotiation of Commercial Contracts: Toward a New Cause of Action' (1991) 44 Vanderbilt L Rev 221, 242–3.

[19] *Blackpool and Fylde Aero Club Ltd* v *Blackpool Borough Council* [1990] 1 WLR 1195 (plaintiff's bid not considered, as the tender box was not cleared in time due to the negligence of the Council. The Council was under no obligation to enter a contract, but the Court of Appeal held that the plaintiff was entitled to damages since there was a collateral contract to observe the rules of the tender which were broken. The measure of damages was not considered).

Cf. *Record* v *Bell* [1991] 1 WLR 853 in which the collateral contract device was used to evade the formalities of s 2 of the Law of Property (Miscellaneous Provisions) Act 1989.

[20] For an interesting exposition: H Collins, *The Law of Contract* (2nd ed 1993) pp 163–86.

[21] Predating the point of time in which the contract is concluded may also serve as a technique to exclude unfair provisions from the contract. See eg, *Thornton* v *Shoe Lane Parking Ltd* [1971] 2 QB 163.

However, the rules of offer and acceptance might be applied so as to postpone the stage of an offer in order to exempt altogether a party from contractual liability. See *Gibson* v *Manchester City Council* [1979] 1 WLR 294 (for a critical approach according to which the plaintiff in *Gibson* should have been compensated for his reliance: H Collins, *The Law of Contract* (2nd ed 1993) pp 168–9). For a different result where a collateral contract is identified see note 19, above.

[22] For various explanations to the postal acceptance rule, including the argument that it serves as a corrective mechanism for the rule of the revocability of an irrevocable offer: S Gardner, 'Trashing with Trollope: A Deconstruction of the Postal Rules in Contract' (1992) 12 Ox JLS 170, 177 *et seq*.

[23] EA Farnsworth, 'Precontractual Liability and Preliminary Agreements: Fair Dealing and Failed Negotiations' (1987) 87 Colum L Rev 217, 233–5: '. . . courts have rarely applied the law of misrepresentation to failed negotiations.' See MP Gergen, 'Liability for Mistake in Contract Formation' (1990) 64 S Cal L Rev 1; S Levmore, 'Strategic Delays and Fiduciary Duties' (1988) 74 Va L Rev 863, 905, note 123.

The collateral contact and the tort liability for misrepresentation often form twin channels of liability. See eg *Esso Petroleum Co Ltd* v *Mardon* [1976] QB 801, where liability was finally founded in tort.

[24] In Germany within the doctrine of culpa in contrahendo (fault in negotiations): F Kessler and E Fine, 'Culpa in Contrahendo', Bargaining in Good Faith, and Freedom of Contract: A Comparative Study' (1964) 77 Har L Rev 401.

postulates an a priori limitation of freedom of action in the bargaining process,[25] subject to excuses or justifications exempting from liability. On the other hand, the position of English law is just the opposite: it is an a priori assumption of freedom in the bargaining process, subject to special rules imposing liability.

These special rules regulate the bargaining process and some of them impose liabilities on contracting parties, even though the ultimate contract has not been concluded. It is clear that the imposition of liabilities grounded in tort, restitution and (collateral) contract, deviates from the aleatory concept of negotiations and derogates to some extent from the negative freedom granted to negotiating parties.[26] If we take liability in restitution for services rendered in the stage of negotiations as an example, that liability is based in our context on benefits inured to the defendant by the plaintiff at the defendant's request. A rule which gives supremacy to the freedom from contract in the course of negotiations would reject a restitutionary remedy as imposing a liability which was not contractually assumed. Indeed, some courts seek to evade this difficulty by labelling the liability as grounded in an implied collateral contract,[27] but terminology cannot hide the fact that the area of negotiations which was supposed to be liability-free is, as a result of such a rule, subject to liability which limits the freedom in negotiations.[28]

Although under the specific categories mentioned above pre-contractual liability puts limits on freedom of action during negotiations, it might be well justified. Commercial contracts require complicated and lengthy negotiations. The aleatory nature of the negotiations is not self-evident. The parties should not always bear their own expenses. When, in the course of negotiations, trust is being built and consequently expenses are incurred, the rule of freedom should be substituted by another rule of risk allocation.[29] In the absence of a general principle of good faith in the

[25] HK Lücke, 'Good Faith and Contractual Performance' in PD Finn (ed), *Essays on Contract* (1987) 155, 170, observes that '[t]he courageous protection of the liberty of the individual is not a dominant theme in the civilian tradition.'

[26] Cf. G Kuehne, 'Reliance, Promissory Estoppel and Culpa in Contrahendo: A Comparative Analysis' (1990) 10 Tel-Aviv U Stud in Law 279, 288, note 35, referring to the argumentation by German scholars that limiting withdrawal from negotiations impairs the freedom of contract.

[27] See *Earhart v William Low Co* 600 P2d 1344, at 1345 (Cal 1979); *Hill v Waxberg* 237 F 2d 936, at 938–9 (9th Cir 1956). Cf. EA Farnsworth, 'Precontractual Liability and Preliminary Agreements: Fair Dealing and Failed Negotiations' (1987) 87 Colum L Rev 217, 224, nn 19 and 232, n 47. But the construction of an implied contract was rejected in *British Steel Corpn v Cleveland Bridge and Engineering Co Ltd* [1984] 1 All ER 504, at 510–11.

[28] J Beatson, 'Benefit, Reliance and the Structure of Unjust Enrichment' in *The Use and Abuse of Unjust Enrichment* (1991) p 21.

[29] GR Shell, 'Opportunism and Trust in the Negotiation of Commercial Contracts: Toward a New Cause of Action' (1991) 44 Vanderbilt L Rev 221 and text to notes 63–9, below. I Brown, 'The Contract to Negotiate: A Thing Writ in Water?' [1992] JBL 353, 356.

negotiations, the development of piecemeal solutions to cure problems of unfairness in the bargaining process is a reasonable substitute. Although inevitably imposing some burdens on the judiciary, which must be responsive to the special needs of the case and adjust the application of the rules accordingly,[30] it purports to strike a balance between freedom (non-liability rule) and fairness (a limited rule of liability).

ISRAELI LAW

Israeli law, as a mixed system, contains both sets of norms governing the bargaining process: the duty of good faith and the variety of devices which have been employed by English law to mitigate the absence of the duty of good faith.

Section 12(a) of Contracts (General Part) Law 1973[31] states that: 'in negotiating a contract, a person shall act in customary manner and in good faith.' The sanction for the breach of this duty is imposed by s 12(b) which reads: 'A party who does not act in customary manner and in good faith shall be liable to pay compensation to the other party for the damage caused to him in consequence of the negotiations or the making of the contract . . .'

Section 12 has received more attention in the legal literature than any other section of the Contracts Law.[32] Judicial decisions are also saturated with its application and evaluation. No wonder it has been regarded as the most revolutionary provision in the Israeli Contract Law. Yet the other devices which were borrowed from English law can still be invoked, and they all form an umbrella of liability governing the bargaining process.[33]

The development of Israeli law, insofar as it exposes the attitude of a common-law-oriented system with a certain continental inclination, may offer us a unique opportunity to study this process in the short term. I will address this topic later.[34]

Two types of defects in negotiations

I have introduced the problem of liability in the bargaining process from the point of view of freedom of action. From the point of view of the

---

[30] I Brown, *ibid.*, 360 argues that the techniques English courts used to circumvent the formal rules, especially the rules of offer and acceptance, engender uncertainty, while the recognition of an implied term of good faith would offer greater clarity. But see text to notes 112–15, below.

[31] 27 LSI 1972/3 117.

[32] For a general survey: N Cohen, 'Good Faith in Bargaining and Principles of Contract Law' (1990) 9 Tel-Aviv U Stud in Law 249.

[33] *Ibid.*, 256–63.   [34] Text around nn 114–15, below.

injured party, we can say that the two notions of freedom correspond to two types of defects in the bargaining process: the first concerns a defect in the will of the contracting party and occurs when one party makes a contract as a result of a mistake, misrepresentation, duress or undue influence; the second concerns breach of a promise given or expectation created in the course of negotiations.

In both instances the party's expectations are frustrated, but for different reasons. In the first case, the frustration arises out of the difference between the true will and the one expressed in the contract: the contracting party either does not want the transaction as formed or wants a different one. In the second case, that of a breach of promise during negotiations, the expectation is frustrated because the negotiations did not materialize into a contract. In the first case, an unwanted contract is formed; in the second, the desired contract has not been created.

Indeed, the two kinds of defects operate in different fact situations. A defect in the will of the contracting party assumes, generally speaking, that a contract has been concluded but a defect in its formation occurred. On the other hand, a breach of a promise given in the course of negotiations generally assumes that a contract has not been created.

As stated above, the duty of good faith does not play a major role with regard to a defect in the will of the contracting party. A contract defective in its formation deviates from the basic requirements of contract law. It does not accomplish the 'freedom to', as it is not a product of a 'freedom from'. Every legal system will seek to allow the injured party to free himself from such a contract, and will sometimes impose sanctions on the party at fault. From that point of view, the duty of good faith is of little moment. Its significance is reflected, however, with regard to the other defect in the negotiating process, namely that of a breach of a promise or frustration of expectation created during negotiations.

It should be emphasized that, although the division between the two defects is methodologically useful, it is not always clear. Take for example the case in which a contract has been concluded, but either it does not contain an undertaking which was promised during the negotiation, or it contains a condition which was not mentioned during the negotiations and was 'smuggled' into the contract. In such cases both defects are involved: breach of a promise given during negotiations and defect in the will of the contracting party consisting of a mistake as to the contents of the contract. Should the law of mistake and misrepresentation govern the case or the parol evidence rule?[35] Or take the case of a promise given during the

---

[35] EA Farnsworth, *Contracts* (2nd ed 1990) pp 477–8, who points out the rules of collateral contract and promissory estoppel as means of mitigating the effects of the parol evidence rule. But the most prevalent mitigating device is liability for misrepresentation, which 'has produced the most litigation': *ibid.*, 483.

negotiations, which was not intended to be performed. In this case no contract has been executed and therefore no defect in the will of the contracting party has occurred. But there was a defect in the negotiating process which motivated in vain the entire negotiations or their continuation.[36] Should it be remedied? That kind of defect has arisen in the case of *Walford* v *Miles*,[37] to which I shall shortly refer.

Breach of promise made during negotiations

I shall now focus on the negative freedom of contract, involving the situation in which negotiations are broken off or terminated. In the case under consideration, a negotiating party breaks a promise or frustrates an expectation created in the course of negotiations. The promise is broken (or expectation frustrated) at an advanced stage of the negotiations, but prior to the formation of the contract. Does that promise (or expectation) have any binding force?

As has been observed earlier, the freedom to enter into a contract also implies the freedom not to do so. If a party decides not to go through with the agreement, he is exercising his freedom of contract in its negative sense. The rule of the game in this example derives directly from the principle of freedom of contract. A rule which subjects the withdrawing party to liability limits his contractual freedom and in a way compels him to an earlier contractual liability. The English rule would, in principle, exempt a negotiating party from liability for breaking off negotiations. A system which contains a duty to act in good faith in the bargaining process would react otherwise.[38]

But what would be the approach of English law with regard to a contract which attempts to regulate the process of negotiations? Does English law allow for a positive contractual limitation on the negative freedom from contract? What would be the position of such a contract in a system rejecting a general duty of good faith in the negotiation process?

These questions have been raised in the case of *Walford* v *Miles*,[37] where the facts were as follows. Owners of a photographic processing company wished to sell their company and the premises on which it conducted its business. They received an offer of £1.9 million from the auditor of the company (the third party), which they rejected. Shortly afterwards they received an offer of £2 million from the plaintiffs. They agreed in principle to sell the business to them and warranted a certain sum as net profit for the first year after the completion of the sale. In a phone conversation

---

[36] Cf. note 23, above. [37] [1992] 2 AC 128.

[38] G Kuehne, 'Reliance, Promissory Estoppel and Culpa in Contrahendo: A Comparative Analysis' (1990) 10 Tel-Aviv U Stud in Law 279; and text to notes 49–55, below.

it was also agreed that, if on a certain date the plaintiffs provided a comfort letter from a bank, the vendors 'would terminate any negotiations with a third party'. The plaintiffs duly provided the comfort letter within the time specified, and the defendants confirmed in letters that, subject to a contract, they agreed on the sale. But several days later the defendants withdrew from the negotiations and decided to sell the business to the third party for the same price. They said that they did it because they were concerned that the plaintiffs would not get along with the staff and would put the warranted profit in jeopardy. They were also worried that they would be burdened with assisting the plaintiffs, who had no experience in the business.

It was held by the trial court as a fact that the negotiations with the third party were never terminated, notwithstanding the oral agreement.

The plaintiffs claimed damages for misrepresentation in continuing to deal with the third party. They were awarded £700 which reflected their expenses incurred in the negotiations and in the preparation of the contract documents.[39] This point was not challenged. The controversy related, however, to the contractual cause of action. The plaintiff claimed that the vendors broke a collateral contract, which imposed on them a positive duty to negotiate with them in good faith, and a negative duty not to negotiate with third parties. The consideration for that undertaking was the supplying of the comfort letter by the plaintiffs. They determined their loss as a result of the breach to be £1 million, ie the difference between the contract price and the present value of the company.

The trial judge ruled that the vendors broke the collateral contract and ordered that the damages for the loss of opportunity be assessed. The Court of Appeal, by a majority (Dillon and Stocker LJJ), allowed the appeal, holding that the action relied only on an agreement to negotiate which was unenforceable under English law. Bingham LJ, who dissented, held, however, that the vendors broke the negative agreement not to deal with third parties.

The House of Lords affirmed the Court of Appeal's position. Lord Ackner, who rendered the judgment, held that the cause of action failed on both grounds: the positive ground failed, because an agreement to negotiate was not binding under English law for lack of certainty; the negative cause, not to deal with others, failed because it did not specify any time limit.

The twofold agreement failed for uncertainty: its first limb, the contract to negotiate, failed because of an inherent incertainty, which leads to a total rejection of this type of contract in English law; the second limb, the lock-out agreement, failed because of a concrete uncertainty. That

---

[39] The sum was agreed upon by the parties: *ibid.*, 135.

uncertainty could not be cured *ex post* by a normative supplementation. Only an *ex ante* agreed time specification could cure it, and this element was absent.[40]

Walford v *Miles* has stirred critical reaction among legal scholars, both with regard to its argument and its result.[41] The case presents a legal culture protecting vigorously the negative freedom from contract. Other legal systems would most likely have treated such a case differently. The Israeli system, for example, might have recognized the following bases of liability: the preliminary contract subject to contract;[42] the collateral contract to negotiate including the lock-out agreement; and also the non-contractual liability of fair dealing in negotiations. English law has rejected the contractual claim, but imposed on the plaintiffs liability in tort. Its approach will now be examined in more detail.

A contract to negotiate—problem of completion

The fate of the contract to negotiate was doomed in English law about 20 years ago in the Court of Appeal's decision in *Courtney & Fairbairn Ltd* v *Tolaini Brothers (Hotels) Ltd*,[43] where Lord Denning MR held that it is unenforceable because:

If the law does not recognise a contract to enter into a contract (when there is a fundamental term yet to be agreed) it seems to me it cannot recognise a contract to negotiate. The reason is because it is too uncertain to have any binding force. No court could estimate the damages because no one can tell whether the negotiations would be successful or would fall through: or if successful, what the result would be.[44]

That decision rejected the approach enunciated by Lord Wright some 40 years earlier, in an obiter dictum in *Hillas & Co Ltd* v *Arcos Ltd*, which

---

[40] The problem of filling-in contractual gaps will be discussed below, text to notes 81–7.

[41] BJ Davenport, 'Lock-Out Agreements' (1991) 107 LQR 366 (a comment on the decision of the Court of Appeal); P Neill, 'A Key to Lock-Out Agreements?' (1992) 108 LQR 405; J Cumberbatch, 'In Freedom's Cause: The Contract to Negotiate' (1992) 12 Ox JLS 586; I Brown, 'The Contract to Negotiate: A Thing Writ in Water?' [1992] JBL 353; E Peel, 'Locking-Out' and 'Locking-In': The Enforceability of Agreements to Negotiate' [1992] CLJ 211; RP Buckley, '*Walford* v *Miles*: False Certainty About Uncertainty—An Australian Perspective' (1993) 6 JCL 58; B Jamieson, 'Lock-Out Agreement is Unenforceable' [1992] LMCLQ 16; 'When Lock-Out Agreement Enforceable' [1992] LMCLQ 186.

[42] There is no compelling reason to reject the validity of a contract to enter a contract (see eg, *Morton* v *Morton* [1942] 1 All ER 273), and such an approach was adopted by Israeli law even with regard to land transactions.

On the legal regime of a binding contract subject to a contract and similar transactions: EA Farnsworth, 'Precontractual Liability and Preliminary Agreements: Fair Dealing and Failed Negotiations' (1987) 87 Colum L Rev 217, 244–9. See also WH Holmes, 'The Freedom Not to Contract' (1986) 60 Tul L Rev 751.

[43] [1975] 1 WLR 297.　　　　　　　　　　　　　　　　　　[44] *Ibid.,* 301.

gave effect to the intention of the parties to be bound by an agreement to negotiate.[45]

Indeed, on the face of it, it seems logical that if a contract to agree on one term fails, a contract to negotiate a whole contract, should a fortiori fail. It is submitted, though, that the analogy is flawed. The reason is that a contract to negotiate is not dependent upon reaching an agreement. Its target is the process of the negotiations, not the end result of the contract.[46] Therefore, the quantitative difference—one term in a contract to enter a contract, or the whole contract in the contract to negotiate—is irrelevant. The two contracts are targeted at different purposes: one is result-oriented, the other is process-oriented.

The difficulty then relates to the substance of the contract to negotiate: what is the content of that contract? Such contract imposes a positive duty to negotiate where such a duty has not previously existed. However, it still enables the party to withdraw for a proper cause. As suggested by the plaintiffs, a proper cause should be tested according to the standard of good faith. But how is this standard to be applied, or, in the words of Lord Ackner in *Walford* v *Miles*: 'How is the court to police such an "agreement"?'[47] Implied in his question is the apprehension that a vague standard such as good faith cannot serve as a solid guideline either to negotiating parties, or to the court. Lord Ackner goes on to say: 'A duty to negotiate in good faith is as unworkable in practice as it is inherently inconsistent with the position of a negotiating party . . . [W]hile negotiations are in existence either party is entitled to withdraw from those negotiations, at any time and for any reason.'[48]

This language reflects the inherent tension between the position of the law and the intention of the parties. It is clear, however, that by imposing upon themselves a contract to negotiate, the parties did intend to limit their freedom to withdraw 'at any time and for any reason'.

The real question then is whether their intention could have been accomplished in light of the vague language they used and the position of English law with regard to the duty of good faith in negotiations. In other words: are English courts equipped to supplement such an agreement?

Indeed, the apprehension regarding a contract to negotiate may be justified. It seems quite difficult to assess the propriety of the causes of the breakdown of the negotiations.[49] Some may be legitimate. An objective

---

[45] [1932] All ER Rep 494, at 505.

[46] J Cumberbatch, 'In Freedom's Cause: The Contract to Negotiate' (1992) 12 Ox JLS 586, 587. However, a contract to enter a contract where there is only one term to agree, may be construed as impliedly imposing a duty to negotiate.

[47] [1992] 2 AC 128, 138H.   [48] *Ibid.*, 138.

[49] P Neill, 'A Key to Lock-Out Agreements?' (1992) 108 LQR 405, 410, who nevertheless argues that the court should have completed the contract, as it always does with other contracts containing open terms. See notes 82–3, below.

criterion for evaluating the causes of withdrawal is not always available, and the court is required at times to examine the motives of the parties. A system which has never built the common law notion of good faith into negotiations, and which is actually hostile to this concept, might feel unable to fill gaps in a contract predicated on the notion of good faith.

Other legal systems, like the German law, have developed rules regarding good faith in negotiations. Since the late 1960s, the courts have consistently held that a late withdrawal from negotiations and frustration of reliance investment will entail liability if the withdrawal is not supported by a proper cause.[50] The following cases may serve as examples: calling for part performance of a contract which has not yet materialized and breaking off relations with no proper excuse; breaking off negotiations where there has been an almost complete agreement on all terms; breaking off negotiations where expenses have been incurred as a result of the encouragement by the other party who promised that a contract would eventually be concluded.[51]

These decisions may serve as a guideline to the contents of a contract to negotiate in German law. But it seems unlikely that English courts will transplant foreign legal categories of bad faith[52] as a means of supplementing gaps in a similar English contract.

On the basis of the elaboration of an already existing duty of good faith in negotiations, it is easy to give an effect to an express contract to negotiate in good faith, and possibly also to such an implied contract. This has been the development of French law: by virtue of *tort* law, the parties are subject to a duty to negotiate in good faith,[53] but once the negotiations have attained a mature stage, the parties are subject to a 'contractual obligation ... to continue to negotiate in good faith. This obligation is sometimes express, but most often implicit in the structure of the preliminary dealings. A sort of *affectio contrahendi* grows between the parties. . . . this obligation strengthens as negotiation proceeds. Its extent grows: it makes one party furnish information to the other, it prevents his putting up unacceptable proposals with the aim of . . . causing a break-off of negotiations, or of merely pretending to negotiate seriously, while in fact he

---

[50] G Kuehne, 'Reliance, Promissory Estoppel and Culpa in Contrahendo: A Comparative Analysis' (1990) 10 Tel-Aviv U Stud in Law 279.

[51] *Ibid.*, 279, 287.

[52] On the difficulties regarding the transplant of rules from a foreign system: H Collins, 'Methods and Aims of Comparative Contract Law' (1991) 11 Ox JLS 396, 397–8.

[53] A party who negotiates without a serious intention to enter a contract or who breaks off negotiations abruptly with no proper reason may be liable to the other party (in tort): Cass Com, 20 March 1972, JCP 1973 2 17543 note J Schmidt; G Durry, 'La nature contractuelle ou délictuelle de la responsabilité', Rev trim dr civ 1972, 779 para 1 and generally, J Schmidt, 'La sanction de la faute précontractuelle' Rev trim dr civ 1974 p 46; J Ghestin, *Traité de Droit Civil, Les Obligations* (2nd ed 1988) no 228, p 252.

has decided to deal with a competitor, it compels him to work towards the reaching of a definite decision within a reasonable period.'[54]

It might also be useful to refer briefly to Israeli law and to see what has been done in the 20 years since the introduction of the concept of good faith in negotiations into our law.

The scope of the duty of good faith in Israeli case law has not been clearly defined and there are controversies which have yet to be resolved. But for the sake of depicting a general outline, we can categorize the following conducts under the bad faith umbrella: initiating negotiations without serious intent (whether intentionally or negligently) to reach agreement; continuing negotiations without serious intent to reach agreement; calling for performance of a contract which has not yet materialized and breaking off the relations without proper excuse; retracting the negotiations at a late stage for illegal reason.[55]

With regard to the position of a contract to negotiate, the direct doctrine imposing a pre-contractual duty to negotiate in good faith, which has been generously and frequently applied in Israel, saves in most cases the urgent need to create a collateral contract to negotiate. But on the theoretical level such a contract was recognized in Israel long ago.[56] Currently, the categories of bad faith in negotiations could be utilised to fill in gaps in the Israeli contract to negotiate.

The last comparative observation will describe the developments in US law with regard to the contract to negotiate. US law is familiar with the notion of good faith in the performance of contract, but has not yet expressly recognized a general duty of good faith in negotiations.[57] Hence

[54] C Jauffret-Spinosi, 'The Domain of Contract—French Report' in D Harris and D Tallon (eds), *Contract Law Today: Anglo-French Comparisons* (1989) pp 113, 131 (eg letters of intent if not expressly excluding contractual liability, impose a contractual duty to negotiate in good faith); for a comparative analysis: RB Lake and U Draetta, *Letters of Intent and Other Precontractual Documents* (1989) esp pp 153 *et seq*. On preliminary contracts in French law: J Ghestin, *Traité de Droit Civil, Les Obligations* (2nd ed 1988) no 229 *et seq*. Some preliminary contracts are fully binding (no 230–9). Other preliminary contracts which are not binding and are only preparatory, nevertheless impose a contractual duty to negotiate in good faith (no 241 pp 269–70). See also J Cedras, 'L'obligation de négocier' Rev trim dr com 1985, p 265.

[55] N Cohen, 'Good Faith in Bargaining and Principles of Contract Law' (1990) 9 Tel-Aviv U Stud in Law 249, 272 *et seq*.

[56] In CA 615/72 *Gelner v Haifa Theatre*, 28 PD(1) 81, where the validity of such a contract was recognized even before the introduction of the duty of good faith, on the basis of the dictum in *Hillas & Co Ltd v Arcos Ltd* [1932] All ER Rep 494, at 505. *Gelner* dealt with a contract between a theatre and a director. The theatre argued that the parties had formed a mere contract to negotiate which was not effective. But the court held that such a contract was valid, and that as the parties had previously worked together several times, they formed a usage, which could be used as a means of completing the contract.

[57] Restatement 2d Contracts, § 205; UCC § 1–203. Both sources disclaim any good faith duty in the negotiations: Restatement 2d Contracts, § 205, comment c. See *Feldman v Allegheny International Inc* 850 F2d 1217, at 1223 (7th Cir 1988), where the court states: 'No particular demand in negotiations could be termed dishonest, even if it seemed outrageous to the other party. The proper recourse is to walk away from the bargaining table, not to sue

it is not surprising that US courts have conflicting views as to the effect of a contract to negotiate. Some courts follow the English approach, which does not give any effect to this contract; others tend to give it a binding force, and that seems to be the prevailing view.[58]

In his seminal article on 'Precontractual Liability', published in 1987, Professor Farnsworth advocates the recognition of this contract.[59] Being aware of the problem of the substance of such a contract in a system which lacks a general duty of good faith in negotiations,[60] and assisted by analogies from labour law, where such a duty exists with regard to collective agreements,[61] he enumerated causes of unfair dealing that can serve as a gap filler of the contract to negotiate.[62] The causes include, inter alia: refusal to negotiate, imposing improper conditions, non-disclosure of parallel negotiations where a promise to exclusively negotiate has been undertaken, breaking off negotiations without any excused reason.

Some courts, encouraged by the willingness to recognise express contract to negotiate, approved of an implied contract to negotiate.[63] Professor Farnsworth remarked critically that the tendency to give effect to contract to negotiate, even 'in the absence of a clear indication of assent . . . if carried to an extreme . . . would enable courts to impose a general

---

for "bad faith" in negotiations' (cited by and followed in: *A/S Apothekernes Laboratorium* v *IMC Chemical Group Inc* 873 F2d 155, at 159 (1989)).

[58] EA Farnsworth, 'Precontractual Liability and Preliminary Agreements: Fair Dealing and Failed Negotiations' (1987) 87 Colum L Rev 217, 265–7. See *Itek Corpn* v *Chicago Aerial Industries* 248 A2d 625, at 629 (Del 1969) (provisions in a letter of intent obligated each side to attempt in good faith to reach final and formal agreement).

Doubts as to the validity of the contract to negotiate have emerged also in Australian law, but recently it was stated, although not unanimously, that 'in some circumstances a promise to negotiate in good faith will be enforceable, depending upon its precise terms': *Coal Cliff Collieries Pty Ltd* v *Sijehama Pty Ltd* (1991) 24 NSWLR 1, at 26E per Kirby P with whose reasons Waddell A-JA generally agreed, but Handley JA dissented on this point, preferring to follow *Courtney & Fairbairn Ltd* v *Tolaini Bros (Hotels) Ltd* [1975] 1 WLR 297. Finally, on the facts of this case the contract was held to be unenforceable. See RP Buckley, '*Walford* v *Miles*: False Certainty About Uncertainty—An Australian Perspective' (1993) 6 JCL 58; P Neill, 'A Key to Lock-Out Agreements?' (1992) 108 LQR 405, 411–12.

[59] EA Farnsworth, *ibid*., 267–9; CL Knapp, 'Enforcing the Contract to Bargain' (1969) 44 NYU L Rev 673, 679.

[60] The fact that American law imposes contractual duty of good faith may theoretically support the contract to negotiate, but actually the requirements of good faith applying to such a contract are those which have been developed under the duty of good faith in negotiations.

[61] National Labor Relations Act, 29 USC, s 158(d).

[62] EA Farnsworth, 'Precontractual Liability and Preliminary Agreements: Fair Dealing and Failed Negotiations' (1987) 87 Colum L Rev 217, 269–84.

For a cautious proposal to adopt the American categories of good faith in negotiations: I Brown, 'The Contract to Negotiate: A Thing Writ in Water?' [1992] JBL 353, 361–2.

[63] EA Farnsworth, 'Precontractual Liability and Preliminary Agreements: Fair Dealing and Failed Negotiations' (1987) 87 Colum L Rev 217, 266 and note 207.

obligation of fair dealing'.[64] This prophecy was almost accomplished shortly afterwards in a relatively recent case where, although a preliminary contract to negotiate had not been recognized, the court held that promissory estoppel could be used to redress expenses incurred as a result of the defendant's promise to co-operate fully in consummating the contract.[65] This case, which has been followed in later decisions,[66] opened an avenue for recognition of a non-contractual promise to negotiate in good faith and reinforces earlier decisions which paved the way to an implied duty of good faith in negotiations.[67] According to this line, an express or implied contract to negotiate is no longer needed as a vehicle to impose a duty of good faith: a promise to consummate the final contract which induces substantive reliance will suffice. Such promises change the aleatory nature of the negotiations, and impose the risk of the incurred expenses on the promisor.

Following these developments, one author has suggested that the law should recognize, even in the absence of a contract, a new cause of action which he labels 'opportunistic breach of the bargaining relationship'. This cause of action consists of an assurance (express or implied) of trustworthiness (eg an assurance that the conclusion of a contract is a mere formality) and a substantive reliance on that asssurance consisting of investing assets in the trust-building process.[68] Another author has suggested the adoption of a new default rule, according to which each party to the negotiations would be subject to a duty to disclose any changes in the intention to reach an agreement.[69]

In the light of these significant developments it seems that US law is on the verge of recognizing an explicit duty to act in good faith in the

---

[64] *Ibid.*, 266. Professor Gergen regards the implication of a contract to negotiate a natural consequence of a preliminary non-binding agreement: MP Gergen, 'Liability for Mistake in Contract Formation' (1990) 64 S Cal L Rev 1, 31–2 and note 149.

[65] *Arcadian Phosphates Inc v Arcadian Corpn* 884 F2d 69, at 73–4 (2nd Cir 1989); GR Shell, 'Opportunism and Trust in the Negotiation of Commercial Contracts: Toward a New Cause of Action' (1991) 44 Vanderbilt L Rev 221, 244–5; EA Farnsworth, 'Developments in Contract Law During the 80's: The Top Ten' (1990) 41 Case Western L Rev 203, 212.

[66] See *Marilyn Miglin Inc v Gottex Industries Inc* 790 F Supp 1245, at 1252 (SDNY 1992) (plaintiff was induced to part performance and other expenditures by the defendant who gave assurance that it would execute a draft agreement); *Budget Marketing Inc v Centronics Corpn* 927 F2d 421 (8th Cir 1991) (assurance of acquiring company that it would close the merger deal induced substantial reliance by the target company). See also *West Financial Services Inc v Tollman* 786 F Supp 333, at 334 (SDNY 1992) (where the rule was followed in principle but not applied due to the vagueness of the promise).

[67] *Hoffman v Red Owl Stores Inc* 133 NW2d 267 (Wis 1965) (note 14 above) about which Farnsworth remarks that 'its influence has been more marked in the law reviews than in the law reports': EA Farnsworth, 'Precontractual Liability and Preliminary Agreements: Fair Dealing and Failed Negotiations' (1987) 87 Colum L Rev 217, 237.

[68] GR Shell, 'Opportunism and Trust in the Negotiation of Commercial Contracts: Toward a New Cause of Action' (1991) 44 Vanderbilt L Rev 221, 276–7.

[69] JP Kostritsky, 'Bargaining with Uncertainty, Moral Hazard and Sunk Costs: A Default Rule for Precontractual Negotiations' (1993) 44 Hast L J 621.

negotiations. This duty has borrowed its normative force from three sources: the general duty of good faith in the performance of a contract; the doctrine of promissory estoppel; and the norm grounded in labour law, imposing a duty of good faith in negotiations. It is interesting to note that these developments in US law are similar to those undergone in German and French law, where the general duty of good faith, which literally applied to parties to an already existing contract, served as a vehicle to impose a duty of good faith on negotiating parties.[70]

Let us return now to the *Walford* case, assuming that the contract to negotiate was effective. How is this case to be analysed by a system adhering to the duty of good faith in negotiations? Was the contract to negotiate broken by Miles? Did they have a proper cause to withdraw? The facts of the case pose the difficulties we have addressed earlier. On the face of it the fear that the plaintiffs would not get along with the staff and thus put in jeopardy the condition regarding the net profit, seems a proper cause for withdrawal. However, this reason existed from the outset. It could presumably be argued by the vendors that they were not aware of its implications. Yet, if the contract to negotiate would have been valid, it is doubtful whether a party would have been permitted to withdraw at a late stage because of a point that was agreed upon and raised no difficulty at an earlier stage.

Furthermore, a heavy shadow is cast on the defendants' reliability by virtue of the fact that, notwithstanding their promise not to negotiate with a third party, they maintained their negotiations with that third party at all relevant times. Such a breach may indicate that the vendors used the plaintiffs instrumentally as a trap to improve the bargain which they really wished to conclude with the third party. Needless to say, such conduct is not in line with the doctrine of good faith where such doctrine is recognized. This brings us to the question whether a promise not to negotiate with third parties is effective in English law.

---

[70] The duty of good faith is embodied in § 242 of the BGB. Y Sussman, 'Problems in the Law of Contract' (1976) 2 Tel-Aviv U Stud in Law 17, 28. The duty of good faith in French law is embodied in art 1134(3) of the Code Civil and it applies to the performance of contracts, but has been expanded to its formation and interpretation as well: J Ghestin, *Traité de Droit Civil, Les Obligations* (2nd ed 1988) nos 184, 227.

A parallel development in German and American law is also apparent with regard to the gradual process of imposing pre-contractual liabilities: in both systems the liability was first imposed to redress reliance on a contract which has not been materialized due to lack of formal requirements (written documents in German law and consideration in American law). Subsequently, liability has been expanded to encompass cases of breaking off negotiations: G Kuehne, 'Reliance, Promissory Estoppel and Culpa in Contrahendo: A Comparative Analysis' (1990) 10 Tel-Aviv U Stud in Law 279, 282 *et seq*.

A lock-out agreement

The position of the House of Lords with regard to a lock-out agreement can be summarized as follows: a lock-out agreement may be valid, but it is ineffective if it does not specify any time limit for its duration.

On the theoretical level, the House of Lords treated this agreement more leniently (capable of being effective) than the agreement to negotiate (inherently ineffective).

Indeed, in his dissenting judgment in the Court of Appeal, Bingham LJ, in order to cure the time deficiency, stated that the agreement not to deal with others should be construed as binding the vendors for such time as was reasonable. Bingham LJ, whose favourable attitude to the concept of good faith, has already been pointed out,[71] continued by saying:

the defendants could not . . . bring the reasonable time to an end by procuring a bogus impasse, since that would involve a breach of the duty of reasonable good faith . . .[72]

Lord Ackner indicated that the construction which Bingham LJ had suggested would again impose indirectly on the vendors a duty to negotiate in good faith, a duty not recognized in English law.[73]

I would like first to refer to the association between the lock-out agreement and the duty of good faith, and then to address the question of the effectiveness of the lock-out agreement.

In contrast to the contract to negotiate, the parties gave to the lock-out agreement specific contents: a specified negative conduct which purported to impose a negative duty on the vendors. The content of the duty in the lock-out agreement was clear and so was its breach. Since no bogus impasse was contended in this case, there was no need for assistance from the standard of good faith in order to specify the time limit. As there was no need to associate the lock-out agreement with the notion of good faith, the objection raised by Lord Ackner against its enforceability is not convincing.

Admittedly the reluctance of the House of Lords to enforce a lock-out agreement is not peculiar to English law. The same controversy concerning the effect of a contract to negotiate has also divided US courts with regard to lock-out agreements.[74] Nevertheless, there is support for the view that, despite the absence of a time specification, such a contract is effective.

[71] Text to note 13, above.   [72] [1992] 2 AC 128, at 140.
[73] Some American courts read into a lock-out agreement a positive duty to deal in good faith: EA Farnsworth, 'Precontractual liability and Preliminary Agreements: Fair Dealing and Failed Negotiations' (1987) 87 Colum L Rev 217, 279, n 266.
[74] Ibid., 279–80.

Indeed, in *Walford*[75] the House referred to the US case of *Channel Home Centers Division of Grace Retail Corpn v Grossman*[76] which was described by the plaintiffs as 'the clearest example' in their favour. Similarly to *Walford* the case of *Channel Home Centers* was first analysed in terms of the doctrine of consideration: the lock-out obligation given by the defendants was supported by the withdrawal of the store from the rental market by the plaintiff. The US court was prepared to give effect to a contract to negotiate including a lock-out agreement seemingly with no time limit.[77] The court held that the standard of 'a reasonable time would be applicable'[78] to cure the time deficiency.

The House of Lords interpreted the case as giving validity to a contract to use best endeavours, and regarded equating this contract with a contract to negotiate as 'an unsustainable proposition'.[79]

The House of Lords' indication that, in contrast to a contract to negotiate, a contract to use best endeavours does not suffer from uncertainty, is problematic. First, the contract in *Channel Home Centers* is described as a contract to negotiate in good faith, and the duty to use best endeavours is only mentioned in one of the references[80] to be equated with the duty to negotiate in good faith. Secondly, in both cases the duty is evaluated according to a vague standard, and the 'best endeavours' formula is no more certain than that of good faith.

The reluctance of the court in *Walford* could be explained by reference to the classical will theory: if a contract is supplemented by the court, the contract no longer derives from the parties' agreement, but from the position adopted by the court.

However, the concept of freedom of contract is prejudiced in either solution: whereas a system which rejects the validity of the contract to negotiate or a lock-out agreement violates the very freedom to create a contract, a system which gives effect to such contracts, but supplements them with normative provisions, violates the freedom of the parties to give the contract the contents they wish. Yet it seems that the total rejection of a contract is more harmful to the free will of the parties than the introduction of supplementing elements to a contract whose main features had already been agreed upon.

---

[75] [1992] 2 AC 128, at 138.
[76] 795 F2d 291 (3rd Cir 1986). *Channel* was distinguished (on the facts) in *STV Engineers Inc v Greiner Engineering Inc* 861 F2d 784, at 787 (3rd Cir 1988) (by a majority opinion holding the lock-out agreement was not breached) and in *Phoenix v Shady Grove Plaza Ltd* 734 F Supp 1181 (DMd 1990) (where no promise was deduced from the letter of intent and where promissory liability was denied on the facts as well).
[77] This point was controversial: 795 F 2d 291, at 301 (3rd Cir 1986).   [78] *Ibid.*
[79] *Walford v Miles* [1992] 2 AC 128, at 138.
[80] 795 F 2d 291, at 299 (3rd Cir 1986).

Indeed modern contract law tends to minimize the doctrine of certainty and to fill in incomplete contracts by implied norms.[81]

This approach leads the transfer of a greater part of the problem of certainty from the formation into the interpretation level and thus enables validity to be conferred to a broader spectrum of contracts.[82] Hence, where no time limit is specified, the tendency is to complete the contract by reference to the standard of reasonableness in light of the surrounding circumstances.[83] The contract is not regarded as non-existent, but rather as curable.[84]

The reluctance of the court in *Walford* to fill in the incomplete contracts in this case can be explained more easily by reference to an internal

---

[81] Much of the discussion devoted to the problem of certainty focusses on devices mitigating its harshness: Cheshire, Fifoot and Furmston's *Law of Contract* (12th ed 1991) pp 67–9; GH Treitel, *The Law of Contract* (8th ed 1991) pp 50–8; EA Farnsworth, *Contracts* (2nd ed 1990) pp 208 *et seq*.

Cf. the parallel relaxation of the requirement of certainty with regard to the award of damages: Farnsworth *ibid*. 922.

[82] Cf. D Tallon (ed), *La détermination du prix dans les contrats, etude de droit comparée* (1989) where he points out the vast possibilities for filling in the missing vital element of price. For a liberalized approach by the House of Lords with regard to an open contract containing a future machinery for establishing a price: *Sudbrook v Eggleton* [1983] 1 AC 444 (the price was to be a reasonable price).

Similarly, in *Hillas & Co Ltd v Arcos Ltd* [1932] All ER Rep 494, the House of Lords upheld an agreement for the sale of timber 'of fair specification', made between merchants of the same trade.

See also *Paula Lee Ltd v Robert Zehil & Co Ltd* [1983] 2 All ER 390 (where sole distributors for the sale of the plaintiff's manufactured garments claimed that they had the right to choose the cheapest garments. The court dismissed this contention, holding that the freedom of choosing garments was limited to a reasonable choice); *Queensland Electricity Generating Board v New Hope Collieries Pty Ltd* [1989] 1 Lloyd's Rep 205 (an open price term imposed a duty on parties to use reasonable endeavours to agree on price, and if that did not occur, to procure the appointment of an arbitrator); GH Treitel, *The Law of Contract* (8th ed 1991) pp 55, 57.

See generally MP Gergen, 'The Use of Open Terms in Contract' (1992) 92 Colum L Rev 997.

[83] *Hick v Raymond & Reid* [1893] AC 22, at 32, per Lord Watson: 'When the language of a contract does not expressly, or by necessary implication, fix any time for the performance of a contractual obligation, the law implies that it shall be performed within a reasonable time.'

See generally Restatement 2d Contracts, § 33, comment d (addressing the problem of uncertainty from the formation of contract level); § 204, comment d (addressing the problem from the interpretation-construction level). Both sources employ the standard of reasonableness to fill in the absent element of time.

Cf. s 41 of Israeli Contracts Law (27 LSI 1972/3 117): 'An obligation the date for the fulfilment of which has not been agreed upon shall be fulfilled within a reasonable time after the making of the contract at a date of which the creditor has given the debtor reasonable notice in advance'.

[84] But non-specification of time may preclude the granting of an injunction: EA Farnsworth, 'Precontractual Liability and Preliminary Agreements: Fair Dealing and Failed Negotiations' (1987) 87 Colum L Rev 217, 279–80, especially note 267. However, in *Channel Home Centers Division of Grace Retail Corpn v Grossman* 795 F2d 291, at 301 (3rd Cir 1986), specific performance was available.

'contractual' public policy,[85] which is motivated by a wish to keep clear-cut the contractual boundaries and not to destabilize commercial standards.

One commentator has pointed out that some of the facts in *Walford v Miles*, 'strained and sieved through successive levels of appeal, were overlooked.'[86] He goes on to clarify that the trial judge held that there was an intent to conclude the deal as soon as possible after 6 April. The significance of that date was that it took the transaction into the next financial year. The court thus could have held that the Miles' were bound not to deal with third parties until a reasonable time had elapsed after 6 April. Furthermore: even if the Miles' were to determine for themselves the reasonable time limit,[87] they could not have exempted themselves from liability, as the breach occurred from the very beginning of the contract and it was certainly within the reasonableness limitation.

Though a bit latent, the court laid down a positive rule under which a time-specified lock-out agreement is valid. This rule was shortly afterwards applied by the Court of Appeal in *Pitt v PHH Asset Management Ltd*[88] in the following circumstances. Pitt was competing with a third party for the purchase of a residential property. His final bid of £200,000 was accepted by the vendor, acting through an agent, subject to contract. The third party increased her offer to £210,000. The vendor was informed that the acceptance of his offer was withdrawn. Pitt told the vendor's agent that he would seek an injunction to prevent the sale to the third party; alternatively, that he would tell that third party that he was withdrawing and that she could lower the price and also that he could exchange as quickly as the agent wished. Consequently an oral agreement was reached between Pitt and the vendors, which was confirmed by letters, whereby the vendor would stay with Pitt's offer and that he would not consider any other offer provided Pitt exchanged contracts within two weeks of its receipt. Eight days after he received a draft contract, Pitt was ready to exchange contracts. However, the vendor decided to sell it to the third party at her offer price of £210,000. Pitt sued for damages for breach of the oral agreement.

The preliminary question whether an enforceable contract had been made between Pitt and the vendor, was answered positively by the court.

---

[85] J Cumberbatch, 'In Freedom's Cause: The Contract to Negotiate' (1992) 12 Ox JLS 586, 588–9.

[86] RP Buckley, '*Walford v Miles*: False Certainty About Uncertainty—An Australian Perspective' (1993) 6 JCL 58, 60.

[87] This technique is labelled by Farnsworth as 'cure by concession' (EA Farnsworth, *Contracts* (2nd ed 1990) p 204). The party who seeks the enforcement of the agreement may give the other party the power to fix the contents of the missing term or may provide the best term which the other party could reasonably expect (eg offering the price in cash where the terms on which the price is payable have not been agreed upon).

[88] [1994] 1 WLR 327.

The parties had reached a lock-out agreement, whereby the vendor would not negotiate with anyone for the period of two weeks following Pitt's receipt of the draft contract. The consideration for the lock-out agreement consisted of three elements: Pitt did not sue for an injunction; would not cause trouble with the third party; and agreed to exchange contracts within two weeks.

Apparently the elements of the consideration raise problems: if Pitt did not have any substantive cause of action, how could his promise not to sue be regarded as valid consideration? Was there a sufficient doubt as to the reasonableness of the claim to include it in the category of 'a settlement of a doubtful claim'?[89] Is a nuisance value good consideration? And if a promise to contract is not binding on each party, how could the agreement to exchange contracts be regarded as consideration being based on an invalid promise?[90] It seems that the court applied a rather loose concept of consideration, presumably following the modern trend depicted earlier in *Williams* v *Roffey Brothers and Nicholls (Contractors) Ltd* (concerning renegotiations) in order to give binding force to the lock-out agreement.[91]

By relaxing the element of consideration, the court has broadened the ambit of contractual liability, and opened the gate for the recognition of binding promises given during the negotiation. Parties to negotiations now have to be more cautious. A promise supported by consideration in its broader sense might give rise to a contractual liability. Consequently, the borderline between negotiations and contract has been blurred to some extent. The legal rules are now less certain but, on the other hand, the decision gives some certainty to negotiating parties who in the sphere of land contracts are struck twice: by the invalidity of a contract subject to contract; and by the unenforceability in the past and invalidity in the present of an oral agreement.[92] The decision mitigates the harshness of these

---

[89] For consideration based on invalid claim see GH Treitel, *The Law of Contract* (8th ed 1991) pp 82–3.

[90] But see C MacMillan, 'How to Lock Out a Gazumper' [1993] CLJ 392, who is aware of the problematic nature of consideration of the first two elements, but is satisfied with the third one.

The court of Appeal also held that the requirement of a written document under s 2 of the Law of Property (Miscellaneous Provisions) Act 1989 does not apply, because the agreement is not a positive agreement by the vendor to sell an interest in land but rather 'a negative undertaking that he will not for the given period deal with anyone else': [1994] 1 WLR 327, at 334, per Sir Thomas Bingham MR.

[91] [1991] 1 QB1, thoroughly analysed by M Chen-Wishart, ch 5 below.

Cf. J N Adams and R Brownsword, 'More in Expectation than Hope: The Blackpool Airport Case' (1991) 54 MLR 281, remarking that the relaxation of consideration in *Roffey* has indirectly contributed to the decision in *Blackpool and Fylde Aero Club Ltd* v *Blackpool Borough Council* [1990] 1 WLR 1195, where a collateral contract was created by implication.

[92] As analysed by Sir Thomas Bingham MR in *Pitt* v *PHH Asset Management Ltd* [1994] 1 WLR 327, at 333.

rules. It clarifies that the process of negotiations is not norm-empty. Oral promises which regulate the negotiation process could at times be held valid even though supported by dubious consideration.

Remedies for breach of a contract to negotiate

The two recent English cases which dealt with contractual liability for promises given during negotiations both redressed the injured parties. The vendor in *Pitt* v *PHH Asset Management Ltd* had already sold the property to the third party and Pitt's claim was for damages. The court dealt only with the question of the validity of the lock-out agreement, and the assessment of damages had yet to be made by the lower court. In *Walford* v *Miles*, although the court rejected the contractual cause of action, it imposed tort liability on the vendors who had to compensate the plaintiffs for the misrepresentation they had made in continuing to deal with the third party. Might the application of the contract to negotiate as well as of the lock-out agreement have offered the plaintiffs a more generous measure of damages?

What remedies are available for the breach of a contract to negotiate and a lock-out agreement?

Even if a contract to negotiate is effective, it seems unlikely that it would be specifically enforced, because of its personal character. There is no reason, however, not to issue an injunction to prevent the breach of a lock-out agreement.[93]

As to damages; the remedy available for the breach of duty to act in good faith in the negotiations is usually aimed at putting the injured party in the position he would have been in, had the contract not been created or the negotiations not begun. In contrast, contractual compensation aims at putting the injured party in the position he would have been, had the contract been performed. In sum, the damages granted for the breach of duty of good faith in negotiations are reliance not expectation damages. Thus, in a system that imposes a duty to bargain in good faith, if a party improperly withdraws from the negotiations, he would ordinarily pay damages reflecting the expenses of negotiations (and possibly also the value of forgone opportunities, if these could be proved with reasonable certainty).[94] That is precisely the sum the plaintiff was awarded in *Walford*.

---

[93] I Brown, 'The Contract to Negotiate: A Thing Writ in Water?' [1992] JBL 353, 363. Cf. n 84 above; C MacMillan, 'How to Lock Out a Gazumper' [1993] CLJ 392, 394: 'the analogy to be made is with that of restrictive covenants in contracts for personal services.'

[94] Promissory estoppel liability to negotiate in good faith entails under US law reliance damages as well: see cases cited at notes 65, 66 above. But see note 123, below.

Would a contract to negotiate or a contract not to deal with a third person make any difference? None of these guarantee the creation of the ultimate contract; they are merely designed to ensure the negotiation process. Therefore, it is submitted, the proper measure of damages is still reliance damages, as awarded in *Walford*.

But is there really no difference between a mere breach of the duty of good faith in bargaining and a breach of a contract regulating the bargaining? Such a contract, it may be argued, fortifies the plaintiff's prospects of getting the contract, and the measure of damages should reflect it.

A possible suggested measure of damages, following the rule in *Chaplin v Hicks*,[95] would reflect the chances of the plaintiffs in obtaining the contract. Indeed that was the direction of the trial judge in *Walford*.[96] Such measure of recovery entails an assessment of probabilities, and it may lead to a higher amount of damages. Thus, if the alleged damages of a contractual right were £1 million (as was argued in *Walford*), and the plaintiffs had a fifty per cent chance of obtaining the contract, their loss would be £0.5 million (although if negotiations had been properly conducted, the plaintiff would have received either nothing or one million).[97]

Admittedly, there is a distinction between the situation in *Chaplin v Hicks* and that in *Walford*. In *Chaplin* the fifty contestants had a vested right to participate in the contest, and it was guaranteed that twelve of them would win. In *Walford* the vendors did not bind themselves to enter a contract. Their obligation related only to the negotiation procedure. No candidate had any vested right to the contract. Should that make any difference?

An analogy, which could even lead to the expectation measure of recovery,[98] may be drawn from US cases which dealt with a competition between two bidders: following a bid, the contract was awarded to a non-eligible bidder who performed the work. In *Iconco v Jensen Construction Co* the

---

[95] [1911] 2 KB 786. See also *Brewer Street Investments Ltd v Barclays Woollen Co Ltd* [1954] 1 QB 428. For a thorough analysis: MG Bridge, ch 17 below.

[96] As reported in *Walford v Miles* [1992] 2 AC 128, at 135. See Lord Wright's dictum in *Hillas & Co Ltd v Arcos Ltd* [1932] All ER Rep 494, at 505: '. . . the damages may be nominal, unless a jury think that the opportunity to negotiate was of some appreciable value to the injured party.'

[97] In such a case they would not be compensated for expenses incurred during negotiations, because such expenses were necessary for the production of the contractual gain. The trial judge awarded £700 as special damages for misrepresentation and also ordered that damages for the lost opportunities be assessed: *Walford v Miles* [1992] 2 AC 128, at 135. Presumably, this sum reflected wasted expenses. Cf. note 99, below.

[98] Some US courts awarded expectation damages for the breach of a contract to negotiate: *Teachers Ins v Tribune Co* 670 F Supp 491 SDNY (1987); *Teachers Ins v Butler* 626 F Supp 1229 (SDNY 1986). This measure of recovery seems excessive: GR Shell, 'Opportunism and Trust in the Negotiation of Commercial Contracts: Toward a New Cause of Action' (1991) 44 Vanderbilt L Rev 221, 279–80 and note 253.

second low bidder brought an action against the winner and claimed the latter's profits. The court awarded the lost profits to the second low bidder, though the other party, similarly to the Miles', was under no duty to enter a contract with any of the bidders. The court stated that, if the unsuccessful bidder 'proves by a preponderance of the evidence that it would have received the contract award absent the successful bidder's wrongdoing, we find no persuasive reasons why recovery should be denied.'[99] The court awarded a restitutionary remedy to the plaintiff, and actually placed him in the position he would have been had the contract been awarded to him.[100]

In *Iconco's* case the defendant was a party who profited from a contract by breaking a Federal law whose purpose was to protect the class to which the plaintiff belonged.[101] The appropriate analogy could have been drawn had the action in *Walford v Miles* been directed against the third party, on the ground that he had unlawfully acquired the profits, eg by comitting the tort of interference with contractual relations (knowing about the lock-out agreement, and nevertheless negotiating with the vendors).[102] But imposing expectation measure of damages only on the third party raises a difficulty: why should the position of a third party be worse than the position of the party to the contract who broke the contract?

Recent developments in tort law reflect a reluctance to ascribe liability based on chance. In *Hotson v East Berkshire Area Health Authority*[103] the plaintiff was injured in an accident. Had the injury been diagnosed in

---

[99] *Iconco v Jensen Construction Co* 622 F2d 1291, at 1300 (1980). On the restitutionary protection of expectancies: D Friedmann, 'Restitution of Benefits Obtained through the Appropriation of Property or the Commission of a Wrong' (1980) 80 Colum L Rev 504, 512–13, 548–9.

Cf. French law, which awards damages for loss of opportunity (*perte de chance*) in these cases: J Ghestin, *Traité de Droit Civil, Les Obligations* (2nd ed, 1988) no 241, p 270. The award of damages is a matter of fact and is dependent on proof of probabilities. Thus, where a company had been wrongfully excluded from participating in a gas pipeline project, after it had incurred preliminary expenses, it recovered losses of profits as well as actual expenses wasted: 'The Binding Nature of Contractual Obligations—Summary of Discussion' in D Harris and D Tallon (eds), *Contract Law Today: Anglo-French Comparisons* (1989) p 75.

[100] This line of reasoning was followed in *Service Engineering Co v Southwest Marine Inc* 719 F Supp 1500 ND Cal (1989) to support recovery of damages for lost profits for fraud, but not for restitution, as the plaintiffs could not establish that 'they had a "right" to [the] contract' (*ibid.*, 1510).

[101] Small Business Act s 2(2) 15 USCA, the purpose of which is to assist small businesses at the federal level. There is a conflict as to the question whether the causes of action stated in the above law pre-empt state law's causes of action. *Iconco* and its followers answer in the negative (see also *Tectonics Inc of Florida v Castle Construction Co* 753 F2d 957 (1985) (majority opinion)). For an approach denying state law causes of action: *Integrity Management International Inc v Tomb & Sons Inc* 614 F Supp 243 (DC Kan 1985).

[102] For a doubtful answer with regard to the possible liability of the third party in torts: EA Farnsworth, 'Precontractual Liability and Preliminary Agreements: Fair Dealing and Failed Negotiations' (1987) 87 Colum L Rev 217, 280, n 268, relying on the Canadian case of *Cineplex Corpn v Viking Rideau Corpn* (1985) 28 BLR 212, at 218 (Ont HC).

[103] [1987] AC 750 reversing the Court of Appeal decision.

time, there would have been a 25 per cent chance of recovery. The negligence precluded any possibility of recovery. The Court of Appeal held that the plaintiff was entitled to 25 per cent of the full loss, but the House of Lords reversed the decision and adopted the all-or-nothing approach. It held that on the balance of probabilities the sole cause of the damage was the original accident, and exempted the defendants altogether. But the court emphasized that its holding did not cast any doubts upon the contractual rule of *Chaplin* v *Hicks*.[104] Other cases, dealing mainly with solicitor's liability,[105] reflect a more generous approach to the possibility of recovering damages in torts for loss of chances.

To conclude, although there is a room for the argument that damages for loss of chances may be awarded, apparently reliance damages are mostly apt to redress the injured party in the context of a contract to negotiate. This measure strikes an appropriate balance between the protection of the misplaced reliance of the promisee and the respect for the freedom of the promisor still allowed by such a contract.[106]

In the two last sections of this chapter I wish to refer to two dichotomies which stand at the centre of our discussion and, probably, at the centre of current contract debate: rules and standards on the one hand and tort and contract on the other hand. I shall address these topics briefly.

Rules and standards

The creation of a contract is governed by fixed rules dictated by the law. If these rules are not complied with, the parties are not contractually bound. One of these rules relates to the requirement of certainty. This was the focus of the discussion in *Walford*. Another rule relates to the

---

[104] Lord Ackner rendered one of the judgments (see especially, *ibid.*, 793). The explanation given by the court for the difference between *Chaplin* and *Hotson* was that in *Chaplin* the chance was dependent upon an hypothetical fact in the future, whereas in *Hotson* the chance depended on a past fact. G Cooper, 'Damages for the Loss of a Chance in Contract and Tort' (1988) 6 Auckland U L Rev 39.

In the case of CA 231/84 *Koopat-Holim* v *Fatah* 42 (3) PD 312, the Israeli Supreme Court (Levin J) preferred the approach of the Court of Appeal to the nothing-or-all approach of the House of Lords.

[105] For a general survey: McGregor, *Damages* (15th ed 1988) paras 360–7.

In an Israeli tender case, where the tender procedure was broken but the defendants were under no duty to enter a contract, the court awarded reliance damages, and was not willing to compute chances: CA 207/79 *Moshe Raviv* v *Beit Yules* PD 37(1) 533 (reversed on other grounds in 43(1) PD 441). Cf. *Blackpool and Fylde Aero Club Ltd* v *Blackpool Borough Council* [1990] 1 WLR 1195 where the measure of damages was not discussed.

[106] This approach is supported by EA Farnsworth, 'Precontractual Liability and Preliminary Agreements: Fair Dealing and Failed Negotiations' (1987) 87 Colum L Rev 217, 267 and GR Shell, 'Opportunism and Trust in the Negotiation of Commercial Contracts: Toward a New Cause of Action' (1991) 44 Vanderbilt L Rev 221, 279–80.

requirement of consideration. This point was briefly referred to both in *Walford* and in *Pitt*, but the problem is much broader.

The crucial question regarding rules concerns their mandatory nature. To what extent are the parties free to deviate from rules? To what extent will the court co-operate in mitigating the formal requirements of contract law? Are there any standards which might override the formal rules, particularly when insisting on the rules is contrary to basic principles of fairness?[107]

A system based on the duty of good faith in negotiations will impose pre-contractual duties which will mitigate the harshness of the formal rules. Good faith is a standard which might override the formal rules. In English law, equity has been used similarly 'to mitigate the rigours of strict law'.[108]

Obviously, if the rule is protective, ie imposed for the benefit of the public, a protected class or a protected party, it is unlikely to be waived.[109] Were the rules intended to protect one of the parties in the cases under consideration?

Walford v *Miles* made use of classical contract law by adhering to rules (certainty and definiteness) and the rejection of standards (good faith, reasonableness). The purpose of the formal rule (certainty) in *Walford* was to guarantee the true intention of the parties, but its application destroyed that very purpose. The case gave primacy to the formal rule, which was initially intended to protect the intention of the parties, but which ultimately ignored that clear intention. As one commentator pointed out: 'If business persons choose to bind themselves to negotiate in good faith, why should the law not enforce that promise as best as it can . . . ?'[110]

Lacking the tradition of a good faith system, English law has shown a reluctance to be assisted by this standard as a means to subdue the formal rule. By preserving the governance of rules, English law has thus reinforced the values of certainty and security[111] and undermined those of cooperation and solidarity, regarded as the underlying values of modern

[107] For some recent articles on the much discussed distinction between rules and standards: KM Sullivan, 'The Justices of Rules and Standards' (1992) 106 Har L Rev 22; L Kaplow, 'Rules versus Standards: An Economic Analysis' (1992) 42 Duke LJ 557.

[108] Cf. the similar tensions between estoppel and statutory formalities: C Davis, 'Estoppel: An Adequate Substitute for Part Performance?' (1993) 13 Ox JLS 99, 120–3.

[109] *Crabb* v *Arun District Council* [1976] Ch 179, at 189 per Lord Denning MR.

[110] RP Buckley, '*Walford* v *Miles*: False Certainty About Uncertainty—An Australian Perspective' (1993) 6 JCL 58, 61.

[111] On the uncertainty and instability of the good faith doctrine: MG Bridge, 'Does Anglo-Canadian Contract Law Need a Doctrine of Good Faith?' (1984) 9 CBLJ 385 and M Tancelin, 'Does Anglo-Canadian Contract Law Need a Doctrine of Good Faith? A Comment' (1984) 9 CBLJ 430). In the same vein: GR Shell, 'Opportunism and Trust in the Negotiation of Commercial Contracts: Toward a New Cause of Action' (1991) 44 Vanderbilt L Rev 221, 275–6. But see note 30, above.

contract law.[112] Indeed, Professor Atiyah is of the opinion that since 1980 there is a post-modern return to the classical principles,[113] and no doubt the case of *Walford* exemplifies such a trend.[114]

But the decision in *Pitt v PHH Asset Management Ltd* goes in another direction. It relaxed the element of consideration so as to give binding force to promises inducing reliance given during negotiations. Such construction might pave the way for the validity of irrevocable offer and other agreements made during negotiations, hitherto considered *nudum pactum*, provided they are supported by the required meager consideration.

The clash between fixed requirements embodied in rules, and the principle of fairness embodied in the duty of good faith, reveals the advantages and disadvantages of rules when counterposed to standards. Rules save the courts from the need to employ discretion and, further, accelerate the judicial process. Yet their application might be over- or under-inclusive. Standards which serve as corrective to the over- or under-inclusiveness of formal rules, may frequently increase uncertainty on the part both of the courts and of contracting parties. Discretion creates potential for abuse—an unevenness in application of standards because of the difficulty in ascertaining precedents from the application of fluid norms to concrete facts. It enlarges the 'grey area' and may encourage non-compliance with the rule: just as the rule creates expectations as to its application, so does deviation from it.

The experience of Israeli law indeed demonstrates that a price must be paid for the desire to enhance the standard of moral behaviour in the contractual arena, at least in the formative years while the duty of good faith is being shaped.

Although its introduction into Israeli law has been occasionally praised, the scope of this duty and its application under Israeli law are not altogether clear, either to litigants or to the judiciary and legal scholars.[115] To

---

[112] H Collins, *The Law of Contract* (2nd ed 1993) pp 16–39 points at avoidance of unjustifiable domination, equivalence of exchange and cooperation as the underlying values of modern contract law. See also IR Macneil, 'Values in Contract: Internal and External' (1983) 78 NW U L Rev 340, 348–9. For the argument that communitarian and individualistic values complement each other: A Brudner, 'Reconstructing Contracts' (1993) 43 UTLJ 1.

[113] PS Atiyah, *An Introduction to the Law of Contract* (4th ed 1989) pp 30–9.

[114] Cf. A Phang, 'Positivism in the English Law of Contract' (1992) 55 MLR 102, who traces this approach in other recent decisions, notably *Kleinwort Benson Ltd v Malaysia Mining Corpn Berhad* [1989] 1 WLR 379: a comfort letter given by a company to a lender in respect of a loan to one of its subsidiaries, declared that 'it was the policy of the company that the subsidiary is at all time to meet its liabilities'. The House of Lords held that this language entailed no contractual liability in respect of the loan. The letter did not contain a promise, but rather a declaration of the company's policy at the time it was given. Since the company had a right to change its policy, no liability ensued.

[115] See eg CA 579/83 *Sonnenstein v Gabaso Brothers*, PD 42(2) 278 discussed in N Cohen, 'Good Faith in Bargaining and Principles of Contract Law' (1990) 9 Tel-Aviv U Stud in Law 249, 281–2.

the uncertainty about whether a contract has been concluded, another uncertainty has been added, namely whether, even in the absence of a contract, the negotiations involved a breach of the duty to act in good faith. Hence, almost any negotiation is susceptible to future litigation, the results of which are unpredictable. It is difficult to evaluate at present whether the market has changed its moral code, but it is absolutely clear that certainty is not one of the characteristics of Israeli contract law.

Tort and contract

The decision of *Walford* v *Miles* which strengthened the non-binding character of the negotiations can be regarded as the ultimate incarnation of the notion of negative freedom from contract.

The extremely restrained approach of the court, reflected particularly in its reluctance to fill in the gap in the lock-out agreement, indicates that with regard to the stage of negotiations the value of freedom from contract has been considered much heavier than that of the freedom to contract. The House of Lords maintained a precise demarcation between the stage of negotiations and that of a contract by adhering to the all-or-nothing characteristic approach of the common law.[116] But in the light of the facts and the end result, the significance of the case is not as decisive. The plaintiffs received reliance damages for misrepresentation concerning the negotiation process.[117] The law of misrepresentation has been

---

[116] The problematic implication of this approach is demonstrated in the *Pennzoil Co* v *Texaco Inc* (729 SW2d 768 (Tex 1987)) saga. In the proceedings between Pennzoil and Getty, it was held that no binding agreement had been entered into by the parties; consequently, Pennzoil did not recover anything. In the tort case, however, it was held that Texaco unlawfully interfered with Pennzoil's contract with Getty, and Pennzoil was awarded expectation damages (including punitive damages). The possibility of reliance damages was not considered: EA Farnsworth, 'Developments in Contract Law During the 80's: The Top Ten' (1990) 41 Case Western L Rev 203, 210–11.

See also VV Palmer, 'A Comparative Study (From a Common Law Perspective) of the French Action for Wrongful Interference with Contract' (1992) 40 Am J Comp L 297, 336 who remarks that imposing tort liability for interference with contract expectancies is a substitute for the lack of a general principle of pre-contractual liability.

[117] For a similar case in American law: *Markov* v *ABC Transfer & Storage Co* 457 P2d 535 (Walsh 1969) where a lessee was awarded damages resulting from the lessor's deceptive representation of his intention to renew the lease. See also *Heyer Products Co Inc* v *US* 140 F Supp 409 (1956) which imposed liability for not seriously considering the plaintiff's bid. The rule can be framed as liability for false inducement of bids, and it might be limited to government contract: EA Farnsworth, *Contracts* (2nd ed 1990) p 204.

See also GR Shell, 'Opportunism and Trust in the Negotiation of Commercial Contracts: Towards a New Cause of Action' (1991) 44 Vanderbilt L Rev 221, 145–6. For an approach which conceives most cases of pre-contractual liability as predicated upon misrepresentation: MP Gergen, 'Liability for Mistake in Contract Formation' (1990) 64 S Cal L Rev 1 and cf. notes 14 and 23, above.

expanded to cover a case where no contract has been concluded at all.[118] By awarding reliance damages for improper tactics in the negotiation, English tort law was response to the modern needs of contract law.

The phenomenon of tort law supplementing shortcomings of contract law is no novelty.[119] Furthermore, liability for misrepresenting promises during the negotiations, even though a final contract has not been concluded, has been already imposed by lower courts. Thus, in *Box v Midland Bank Ltd*,[120] the plaintiff sought to borrow money from his bankers for a business venture. The manager of the bank gave the impression that the authorisation of the loan by the management would be a mere formality, and in the meantime he approved only that part of the loan which was within his authority. The loan was not confirmed by the manager's superiors, and the plaintiff lost the part loan, as the venture was impossible to accomplish without the entire loan.

The manager's negligent misrepresentation that a contract would eventually be concluded and the money lent, imposed on him liability in torts for a non-contractual promise and he was liable for the loss the plaintiff incurred.[121] A system predicated on the duty of good faith would similarly have protected the misplaced reliance. Such protection could be grounded on misrepresentation in the negotiations, on a breach of a non-contractual promise given in the negotiations, and on a breach of a contract to negotiate. The expansion of the law of negligent misrepresentation to promises may justify the argument that English law imposes on contracting parties a general duty of care during negotiations,[122] but such a general duty is still more limited than the duty to act in good faith.

[118] For support for such an expansion see Cheshire, Fifoot and Furmston's *Law of Contract* (12th ed 1991) p 282.

The Misrepresentation Act 1967 provides remedies for misrepresentation only where a contract has been concluded. Hence, Professor Treitel remarks that, where a contract has not been concluded, the remedy will lie in negligence or fraud at common law: GH Treitel, *The Law of Contract* (8th ed 1991) p 313.

[119] See eg *Ross v Caunters* [1980] Ch 297. BS Markesinis, 'An Expanding Tort Law—The Price of a Rigid Contract Law' (1987) 103 LQ R 354; J Swanton, 'The Convergence of Tort and Contract' (1989) 12 Syd L Rev 40, 45.

But the decline of liability for economic loss can be explained by reference to the desire to keep clear the traditional borderlines between contract and torts: KM Stanton, 'The Decline of Tort Liability for Professional Negligence' [1991] CLP 83.

[120] [1979] 2 Lloyd's Rep 391.

[121] PS Atiyah, 'The Binding Nature of Contractual Obligations: The Move from Agreement to Reliance in English Law and the Exclusion of Liability Relating to Defective Goods', D Harris & D Tallon (eds), *Contract Law Today: Anglo-French Comparison* (1989) pp 21, 29. Another decision in this vein is *Crossan v Ward Bracewell* (1986) 1236 NLJ 849, where liability was imposed on a solicitor who failed to notify a prospective client (who never actually became a client) that the fees are covered by the insurance. See PS Atiyah, *An Introduction to the Law of Contract* (4th ed 1989) p 109.

[122] Cf. H Collins, *The Law of Contract* (2nd ed 1993) p 171 *et seq*, who tries to embrace the categories imposing pre-contractual liability under the heading of 'the duty to negotiate with care'.

Conclusion

Thus we may conclude that the position of English law is as follows: if, in the course of negotiations, a party gave a promise by which he did not intend to be bound, that promise would bind him to the extent of the reliance the other party placed on it and any resulting loss. Breach of a promise which amounts to misrepresentation will not be tolerated. The case of *Walford* v *Miles* shows that English law, like systems adhering to the doctrine of good faith in negotiations, puts barriers to the freedom to manipulate with the rules.

Where no misrepresentation is involved, the negative freedom from contract in English law would allow a breach of a mere promise or frustration of expectation created in the course of negotiations. Hence, a promise to negotiate in good faith is wholly ineffective in English law; the same applies to a non-specified lock-out agreement and to a mere promise unsupported by consideration.

Under English law breaking a mere promise given during negotiations is permitted, even though that promise induced reliance by the other party. The promise can be a ground of liability only when it is coated with a contractual garment, that is when it complies with the formal requirements set out by contract law.

Although the formal application of consideration is less rigorous than that of certainty in the sphere of negotiations, reliance has not yet become an explicit substitute for consideration, and liability based on promissory estoppel has not yet substituted conventional contractual liability.[123] Thus, where no misrepresentation is involved in the negotiations, the barriers to the freedom to manipulate with the rules are lower than those obtaining in a good faith regime.

---

[123] In such a case under conventional rules of English law, the remedy might be specific (*AG of Hong Kong* v *Humphreys Estate (Queen's Gardens) Ltd* [1987] AC 114, at 127–8), but preferably it should be limited to reliance damages: note 94, above.

3

On the Nature of Undue Influence*

PETER BIRKS AND CHIN NYUK YIN

An awesome 60 years separated the first and tenth editions of *Pollock on Contracts*. Its introduction to the subject of undue influence remained substantially unchanged. This is what Pollock said in 1876:

In equity there is no rule defining inflexibly what kind of compulsion shall be sufficient for avoiding a transaction, whether by way of agreement or gift. The question to be decided in each case is whether the party was a free and voluntary agent.

Any influence brought to bear upon a person entering into an agreement, or consenting to a disposal of property, which, having regard to the age and capacity of the party, the nature of the transaction, and all the circumstances of the case, appears to have been such as to preclude the exercise of free and deliberate judgment, is considered by the courts of equity to be undue influence, and is a ground for setting aside the act procured by its employment . . .

[I]t may perhaps be said that undue influence, as the term is used in the courts of equity, means an influence in the nature of compulsion or fraud, the exercise of which in the particular instance to determine the will of the one party is not specifically proved but is inferred from an existing relation of dominion on the one hand and submission on the other.[1]

The elusiveness of the doctrine is apparent, not least from Pollock's tentative tone. A decade later in *Allcard* v *Skinner*[2] Lindley LJ affirmed: 'As no Court has ever attempted to define fraud, so no Court has ever attempted to define undue influence, which includes one of its many varieties.' In the intervening century, the doctrine has enjoyed remarkable success in resisting attempts to pin it down. The word 'undue' which fades into the background in Pollock's discussion, as in that of many others, is fundamentally

---

* Copyright © 1994, Peter Birks and Chin Nyuk Yin.

[1] F Pollock, *Principles of Contract at Law and Equity* (1876) pp 503–4; cf. 10th ed (1936) pp 599–600. Pollock died in 1937, aged 92. Very interesting are also the provisions of the Indian Contracts Act, 1872—essentially a codification of English law—esp s 14 (free consent) and 16 (undue influence). It is to be noted that, like the text quoted above, although in different language, the latter is careful not to treat undue influence simply as a species of pressure. 'Fraud' in the text means equitable fraud, and the enormous difficulty of extracting a well-defined doctrine from that miscellany can be seen in Story, *Commentaries on Equity Jurisprudence* (12th ed, revised by Jairus Perry 1877) p 252 *et seq*. Cf. the commentary on *Huguenin* v *Baseley* (1807) 14 Ves 273 in *White and Tudor's Leading Cases in Equity*. (8th ed 1910) vol 1, p 259.

[2] (1887) 36 ChD 145, at 183. The surprising but persistent note of pride in this uncertainty, as though unpredictable empiricism were to be encouraged notwithstanding its expense, is justly attacked by D Tiplady, 'The Limits of Undue Influence' (1985) 48 MLR 579, 580.

unstable. Which way does the doctrine turn? Is it a doctrine about excessively impaired consent? Or is it a doctrine about the improper exploitation of people whose capacity to consent is excessively impaired? Those are the questions which this chapter seeks to tackle. It takes the view that the doctrine of undue influence is about impaired consent, not about wicked exploitation. It is not a view that has many supporters.

Introduction, aims and methods

'As its name suggests, undue influence, which is a creation of equity, involves a wrongful exercise of influence by one contracting party over another. This raises the major question: what sort of influence is wrongful or "undue"?' This quotation is from the introductory section of John Cartwright's treatment of undue influence.[3] His chapter ends on a similar note: '[T]he basis of the law of undue influence is the prevention of *active* abuse of a position of influence.'[4] It will be evident therefore that the author supports an analysis which puts the emphasis on wrongful abuse or exploitation by the stronger party. In this chapter we call that a defendant-sided analysis. It is convenient to refer to the party against whom relief for undue influence is sought as the defendant, even though in some configurations it is in fact the plaintiff in the action who is obliged to resist a defence based on undue influence: a defendant-sided analysis is one which explains the relief in terms of the bad conduct of the party against whom the relief is sought.

By and large, albeit not without equivocation and even on occasion contradiction, the writers of textbooks support the defendant-sided analysis typified in Cartwright's chapter.[5] There are in addition innumerable instances of judicial language which show that the judges intuitively adopt the same approach. It is striking, for example, that in the recent case of *Barclays Bank plc* v *O'Brien* the House of Lords repeatedly referred to undue influence as wrongful or improper conduct.[6] And in *CIBC*

---

[3] J Cartwright, *Unequal Bargaining* (Oxford, 1991) p 170.

[4] *Ibid.* p 196. Cf. WHD Winder, 'Undue Influence and Coercion,' (1939–40) 3 MLR 97, 103 who rightly pointed out that pressure and undue influence were different but wrongly propounded a view of the latter which would make it indistinguishable from unconscionable behaviour. See also MH Ogilvie (1986) 11 Can Business LJ 503, 511: '. . . undue influence consists of the "victimisation of one party by the other".' Cf. D Tiplady, *op cit* note 2 above, 580, who rejects victimization for a policy in support of the sanctity of some relationships, which, however, both focuses too closely on certain prominent relationships and fails fully to spell out the policy in question.

[5] A selection of textbook positions is given in the Appendix to this chapter.

[6] *Barclays Bank plc* v *O'Brien* [1994] AC 180, noted [1994] 110 LQR 167 (JRF Lehane); [1994] LMCLQ 34 (AJ Berg); more extended discussion: SM Cretney, 'Mere Puppets, Folly and Imprudence: The Limits of Undue Influence' [1994] Restitution LR 3. At [1994] AC 180, 189 one who uses undue influence is referred to as a 'wrongdoer' six times, while at 190–2 the

Mortgages plc v *Pitt*, decided at the same time, Lord Browne-Wilkinson, who gave the leading speech in both cases, expressly described actual undue influence as 'a species of fraud.'[7] In *National Westminster Bank plc* v *Morgan* Lord Scarman also used the word 'wrongful' of transactions voidable for undue influence, and he said that the principle justifying rescission was 'not a vague "public policy" but specifically the victimization of one party by the other.'[8]

The judgments of the High Court of Australia in *Commercial Bank of Australia Ltd* v *Amadio*[9] include statements which put the matter rather differently. They seek to distinguish between relief given for undue influence and relief given for unconscionable conduct. Unconscionable conduct is portrayed as defendant-sided: the relief is given because of the bad behaviour of the defendant in exploiting the plaintiff's vulnerable position. By contrast, undue influence is projected as plaintiff-sided: the relief is given because of the impairment of the capacity of the plaintiff to make the decision which is impugned. The passages which follow both make the same kind of distinction, although they leave room for divergences in the fine tuning.

Mason, J, as he then was, said:

Although unconscionable conduct . . . bears some resemblance to the doctrine of undue influence, there is a difference between the two. In the latter the will of the innocent party is not independent and voluntary because it is overborne. In the former the will of the innocent party, even if independent and voluntary, is the result of the disadvantageous position in which he is placed and of the other party unconscientiously taking advantage of that position.[10]

Deane, J said:

The equitable principles relating to relief against unconscionable dealing and the principles relating to undue influence are closely related. The two doctrines are, however, distinct. Undue influence, like common law duress, looks to the quality of the consent or assent of the weaker party . . . Unconscionable dealing looks to the conduct of the stronger party in attempting to enforce, or retain the benefit of, a dealing with a person under a special disability in circumstances where it is not consistent with equity or good conscience that he should do so.[11]

---

proper understanding of *Turnbull & Co* v *Duval* [1902] AC 429 is said to turn on the absence of any allegation of undue influence by and hence of 'wrongdoing' in Mr Duval. Subject to one matter which is addressed in the text to note 9 below, *O'Brien* and two associated cases (see following note), although of great general importance, have only oblique bearing on the present theme.

[7] *CIBC Mortgages plc* v *Pitt* [1994] AC 200, at 209. *Pitt* provided an ideal counter-example to *O'Brien*. See also *Midland Bank plc* v *Massey The Times* 23 March 1994.

[8] [1985] AC 686, at 70–705. Cf. *Geffen* v *Goodman Estate* (1991) 81 DLR (4th) 211, at 227–8, 237, per Wilson J.

[9] (1983) 151 CLR 447.   [10] *Ibid.* 461.   [11] *Ibid.* 474.

These quotations are unequivocal as to there being a distinction between the two bases for relief. They clearly make undue influence plaintiff-sided: the relief follows from the impairment of the plaintiff's capacity to make decisions. However, an element of ambiguity can be detected in relation to unconscionable conduct. The words of Deane, J, in particular, appear to leave room for something less than intentionally exploitative behaviour on the part of the defendant at the time of the transaction. They can embrace cases in which the unconscientiousness consists only in attempting to enforce or to retain the benefit of a transaction which was not unconscientiously entered. We might call this 'unconscientiousness *ex post*' or 'unconscientiousness in retention.' It is important at the outset to demonstrate that this is not really a species of unconscientiousness at all.

UNCONSCIENTIOUSNESS *EX POST*

When unconscientiousness is extended in this way, the distinction between plaintiff-sided and defendant-sided relief becomes blurred because, while the language suggests bad behaviour on the part of the defendant, the only substantial reason why his behaviour is described as bad is that there is some other and antecedent reason why he should forego the benefit in question. A comparison can be made with relief given for mistake.

In *Kelly* v *Solari*,[12] for example, an insurer claimed to be entitled to recover a mistaken payment. The ground of recovery was the mistake. One strand of counsel's argument was that the defendant, a widow who had honestly believed that her husband's life had been insured, had made her demand in good faith, so that her conscience could not be affected. As to that, the court's view was that, despite her innocence in acquisition, she would be unconscientious in seeking to retain such a payment. Rolfe, B said:

With respect to the argument, that money cannot be recovered back except where it is unconscientious to retain it, it seems to me, that wherever it is paid under a mistake of fact, and the party would not have paid it if the fact had been known to him, it cannot be otherwise than unconscientious to retain it.[13]

This is a clear assertion that unconscientiousness solely in retention is no more than an inference from the plaintiff's right to recover, that right itself being grounded on the purely plaintiff-sided factor of mistake. If the law allowed relief to be ascribed to such unconscientiousness *ex post*, it would be inviting confusion. The line between unconscientious behaviour in acquisition and inferential unconscientiousness in retention would be too unstable in practice. In no time at all courts would find themselves suc-

---

[12] (1841) 9 M & W 54.   [13] *Ibid.* 59.

cumbing to the argument that there had to be bad behaviour on the part of the defendant in all cases.[14]

There is another diluted use of the word 'unconscionable' which is similarly misleading, because it too does not in fact indicate any kind of shabby behaviour on the part of the defendant but only the objective fact that the transaction sought to be impugned by the plaintiff was disadvantageous to him. Thus, in discussing the requirement of manifest disadvantage in *National Westminster Bank plc v Morgan*, Lord Scarman listed a number of expressions used by judges to express this requirement. The transaction might be 'hard and inequitable' or 'immoderate and irrational' or—here Lord Scarman drew on Lord Shaw in *Poosathurai v Kannappa Chettiar*[15]—it might be 'unconscionable' in being 'a sale at an undervalue.'[16] Used in this way the word perhaps means 'prima facie unconscionable', a usage best avoided. It is certainly impossible to draw a final inference of unconscionable conduct from the mere fact that a transfer has been obtained on terms which are highly favourable to one party and correspondingly disastrous to the other.

PRINCIPAL AIMS

The first aim of this chapter is to defend the plaintiff-sided nature of undue influence: the relief is given because of the impairment of the integrity of the plaintiff's decision to transfer the benefit in question. It is not necessary for the party claiming relief to point to fraud or unconscionable behaviour on the part of the other. We are conscious of the weight of the academic and judicial usage we have cited, especially of that in *Barclays Bank plc v O'Brien* and *CIBC Mortgages plc v Pitt*.[17] On the other hand, we do not think that the truth of this matter as we perceive it runs counter to any structural reasoning in the cases, except for that of *National Westminster Bank plc v Morgan*[18] the deliberate tendency of which was to restrict undue influence by grafting on to it the conditions of relief for unconscionable conduct. In *Pitt* Lord Browne-Wilkinson reinforced the elimination of a substantive requirement of manifest disadvantage as a condition of relief for undue influence by likening undue influence to

---

[14] The dangerous attractions of a universally fault-based law of restitution are considered in Birks, *Restitution: The Future* 26–60. See M Chen-Wishart, *Unconscionable Bargains* (1989) esp p 117 for exposure of the mismatch between what is said and what is done and the conclusion that what is done offers covert relief against bad bargains (substantive unfairness). We would say the relief given is plaintiff-sided and given for substandard judgmental capacity but is then sometimes pragmatically restricted, sometimes to bad or ill-advised bargains.

[15] (1919) LR 47 Ind App 1, 3.

[16] [1985] AC 686, at 704.

[17] Notes 5–7 above and text thereto.

[18] [1985] AC 686.

fraud,[19] but he might equally have drawn the analogy with mistake, an unequivocally plaintiff-sided basis for relief where it is equally evident that the plaintiff is not required to establish that he has suffered a manifest disadvantage. With equal, albeit less obvious, truth he might have drawn the analogy with duress. Relief for duress is also plaintiff-sided. The defendant does not have to be shown to have behaved badly and has indeed often acted in absolutely good faith.[20]

A consequential aim must be to resist the tendency to blur the line between plaintiff-sided relief and defendant-sided relief, in particular between undue influence and unconscientious behaviour. The contrary habit goes back to a time when many problems were solved by an undifferentiated appeal to 'equitable fraud'. Nowadays the principal engines of confusion are unconscientiousness *ex post*,[21] the ambiguity of 'undue' in the phrase 'undue influence,'[22] and failure to distinguish scrupulously between, on the one hand, relief which is founded on bad behaviour by the defendant and, on the other, plaintiff-sided relief which is nevertheless pragmatically restricted by reference to a requirement, such as the defendant's knowledge of the plaintiff's disability, which might, but need not, belong to a picture of unconscionable behaviour on the part of the defendant.[23]

The distinction between relief given on the ground of the impaired integrity of the plaintiff's decision and fault-based relief given on the ground of the defendant's unconscientious behaviour is clear and robust in principle. On many, but not all, facts it can nevertheless appear opaque and fragile because many fact-situations lend themselves to alternative analyses: relief could be given by either the plaintiff-sided or the defendant-sided route.[24] That does not justify blurring the distinction or attempting to merge the two doctrines.

It is no part of this chapter to review the whole law relating to unconscionable dealing, and no more will be said of that than is necessary to establishing the nature of undue influence. Similarly, no more will be said than is strictly necessary of other examples of impaired autonomy, such as minority, mental illness and socio-economic disability. These personal disadvantages are the closest congeners of undue influence, and in

---

[19] Text to note 7 above.

[20] It is well established that bad faith is not a requirement: see GE Palmer, *The Law of Restitution*, vol 2 s 9.6, p 270. Cf. *Morgan v Palmer* (1824) 2 B&C 729; *Chase v Dwinal*, 7 Me 134, 20 Am Dec 352 (1830); *Maskell v Horner* [1915] 3 KB 106; *Mason v NSW* (1959) 102 CLR 108.

[21] Text to note 12 above.   [22] Note 110 below and text thereto.

[23] A requirement of 'manifest disadvantage', for example, can have at least three roles: see text to note 94 below.

[24] Alternative analyses would certainly have been possible in *Tufton v Sperni* [1952] 2 TLR 516 and *O'Sullivan v Music and Management Agency Ltd* [1985] QB 428, in both of which the defendant behaved unconscientiously, see notes 45 and 64 below.

relation to all of them there is the same tension between plaintiff-sided relief, based on the impaired autonomy, and defendant-sided relief, based on unconscientious exploitation of that impairment.

The argument in defence of the plaintiff-sided explanation of undue influence requires a careful identification of the precise nature of the impairment of the plaintiff's judgmental capacity upon which it is based. If undue influence is a plaintiff-sided ground for relief, what is it precisely that must have been wrong with the party seeking relief? It is central to our argument that this question cannot be answered so long as the picture is dominated by pressure. Our method therefore requires the separation of those cases in which the impairment arises from illegitimate pressure. We will then concentrate on the instances of undue influence in which the impairment does not arise from pressure applied by the other party.

This inquiry will not in itself be objectionable even to anyone who may favour transforming undue influence into a defendant-sided species of unconscientious behaviour. For them the underlying issue will seem to be what precise weakness it is that the defendant is said unconscientiously to exploit when he is guilty of undue influence. However, our argument is that the relief is given simply on the ground of the impairment itself, not on the ground of its unconscientious exploitation. That is not to deny that it has a remoter justification as a prophylactic instrument against wicked exploitation. It is, however, a mistake to read the remoter justification as directly dictating the conditions upon which the relief is granted, and dicta which refer to the danger of exploitation must therefore be handled with great care.[25]

Separating the pressure cases

Some years ago Professor Malcolm Cope suggested that all cases of duress should be treated as undue influence.[26] We believe the decanting should go the other way: all cases of pressure should be treated as duress. It is unfortunate if this must still be expressed as transferring them from equity to common law. It is time that in this field we overcame the old jurisdictional duality. It would be better to say simply that pressure should be litigated as pressure, or as 'duress' if that synonym is preferred. The reasons are, first, that pressure or duress is a relatively easily understood and distinct notion; secondly, that pressure has been allowed to dominate the picture and has concealed the nature of relational undue influence; and, thirdly, whatever the precise future of the requirement of

[25] Text from note 86 below.
[26] M Cope, *Duress, Undue Influence and Unconscientious Bargains* (1985) para 125.

manifest disadvantage in the context of undue influence, nobody has ever suggested that it has any role whatever in duress.[27]

A consolidation of the law relating to pressure would not have been possible in earlier times because of the narrowness of the concept of operative duress. Duress to goods and other economic duress was thought not to give relief from a contract. Thanks in large measure to an influential article by Professor Beatson,[28] that picture has been transformed. Nowadays it is clear that duress includes all illegitimate pressure and that all forms of duress can ground relief from a contract. The defendant must have done or threatened to do something 'illegitimate', a word which is chosen precisely because it has softer edges than, say, 'unlawful',[29] with a view to inducing action by the plaintiff. In addition, action or threat must have induced the plaintiff to act or, more accurately, must have been one of his reasons for so acting.

It is now difficult to conceive of any pressure which will not be relieved satisfactorily, if it should be relieved at all, within the category of duress. To suggest otherwise would be to claim relief for a species of pressure which could not be characterized as illegitimate. That point will be revisited below, where it will be suggested that a legitimate pressure can never ground a claim whether framed as duress or as undue influence.[30]

There are a number of cases where relief for pressure has in the past been given under the head of undue influence. In *Williams v Bayley*,[31] for example, the aged plaintiff-respondent had yielded to pressure to give security over his colliery for the repayment of losses inflicted on the appellant bankers by his son's habitually forging his signature on promissory notes accepted by the appellants. Lord Chelmsford summed up the basis on which the father would be relieved in this way:

[T]his negotiation proceeded upon an understanding between the parties that the agreement of James Bayley, to give security for the notes, would relieve William Bayley [the son] from the consequences of his criminal acts; and the fears of the father were stimulated and operated on to an extent to deprive him of free agency,

---

[27] *Goff & Jones, Law of Restitution* (4th ed 1993) p 280. Between *Bank of Credit and Commerce v Aboody* [1990] 1 QB 923 and *CIBC Mortgages plc v Pitt* [1994] AC 200 this created an immediate practical reason for reclassification of pressure as duress, albeit one which showed up the probable error of *Aboody*.

[28] J Beatson, 'Duress as a Vitiating Factor in Contract,' (1974) 33 CLJ 97, see now ch 5 of his *Use and Abuse of Unjust Enrichment* (1991).

[29] *Universe Tankships v ITWF* [1983] AC 366. The conditions for duress were elegantly summarized by McHugh J in *Crescendo Management Pty Ltd v Westpac* (1988) 19 NSWLR 40, at 45 *et seq* further considered, in terms which raise in the context of duress, the relationship between plaintiff-sided and defendant-sided analyses, in *Equiticorp Financial Services Ltd v (NSW) v Equiticorp Financial Services Ltd (NZ)* (1992) 29 NSWLR 260, at 296–301. (The appeal from this case was dismissed on the ground that there had been no illegitimate pressure, *sub nom. Equitcorp Financial Ltd (in Liq) v Bank of New Zealand* (1993) 11 ACLC 952 (NSW Court of Appeal).)

[30] Text from note 115 below.   [31] (1866) LR 1 LH 200.

and to extort an agreement from him for the benefit of the bankers. It appears to me, therefore, that the case comes within the principles on which a court of equity proceeds in setting aside an agreement where there is an inequality between the parties, and one of them takes an unfair advantage of the situation of the other, and uses undue influence to force an agreement from him.[32]

We need not analyse the precise angle of Lord Chelmsford's approach to the relief. It is sufficient to say that a case such as this can and should be litigated as illegitimate pressure.

Mutual Finance Ltd v *John Wetton & Sons Ltd*[33] is similar. In connection with the hire-purchase of a lorry by a friend, one of the Wetton brothers, Joseph, had forged a guarantee so that it appeared to have been given by the Wetton company. When the friend defaulted, the finance company agreed that another purchaser could take the contract over but, now knowing of the forgery, felt in a position to insist upon a new guarantee from the company. No explicit threats were made that Joseph would be prosecuted if no guarantee were forthcoming, but the other brother gave the company's guarantee feeling that the threat of prosecution or exposure existed and that his elderly father's fragile health would be endangered if he discovered the facts. The narrowness of the common law's prevailing concept of duress obliged Porter J expressly to negative duress.[34] He rested the relief on undue influence. Nowadays we should not hesitate to reclassify the case as one of pressure and hence of duress. In *Kaufman* v *Gerson*[35] where the pressure was not dissimilar, there is indeed already some instability in the language used to describe it. Collins MR speaks chiefly of undue influence but he also uses the word 'duress.'[36]

A PRESUMPTION OF DURESS?

If we say that pressure cases should be litigated as duress, we have nevertheless to enter one possible caveat. An obvious advantage of litigating under the head of undue influence is that the plaintiff may be able to take the advantage of a presumption that the decision or transfer in question was attributable to undue influence. The next section will argue that the facts which support the presumption hardly ever have anything to do with pressure. However, there is a rare exception where a particular relationship is characterized by a history of violence.

---

[32] *Ibid.* 215–16. [33] [1937] 2 All ER 657.
[34] *Ibid.* 661. Cf. *Mustafa* v *Hudaverdi* (1972) 223 Estates Gazette 1751 (Goff J), in which a deed renouncing interests in two houses was set aside when it was shown that the plaintiff executed it because of veiled threats made by the patriarchal and dictatorial defendant that he would not see much of his son, the defendant's grandson, if he did not.
[35] [1904] 1 KB 591. Cf. *Silsbee* v *Webber* 171 Mass 378, 50 NE 555 (1898).
[36] *Ibid.* 596–7.

A grisly example is provided by *Farmers' Co-operative Executors &
Trustees Ltd v Perks*.[37] There a wife had transferred her interest in land to
her husband who was later convicted of murdering her. Her personal representatives sought, successfully, to have the transfer set aside. The relationship between husband and wife is not on the list of nominate
relationships which automatically support the presumption.[38] The evidence of the wife's personal representatives as to the character of this particular relationship was that the husband had routinely kicked, beaten
and otherwise maltreated her throughout their marriage, and that she had
lived in constant fear of such attacks. The question was whether the particular transfer had been induced by these beatings and her resulting fear.
The judge was prepared to hold that the plaintiffs had affirmatively
proved that it had been. However, he also held that the plaintiffs were
entitled to the benefit of the presumption of undue influence, on the
strength of the evidence of the nature of this particular relationship. Had
he proceeded solely on that basis, it would still have been reasonable to
infer that the fact which was presumed, under the head of undue influence, was (as it rarely is) the use of duress to obtain the transfer.

A less extreme example is provided by *Re Craig*,[39] where a bullying
housekeeper extracted numerous gifts from an old man. There Ungoed
Thomas J was prepared to go beyond the presumption and to find actual
undue influence affirmatively proved. However, he made that finding
only in support of a conclusion already reached through the presumption
of undue influence. Again it is reasonable to say that what was proved or
presumed was illegitimate pressure.

It is an intriguing question whether, in order to gain the benefit of the
presumption, plaintiffs such as these who face some difficulty in proving
a causal nexus between a transfer and a particular episode of violence or
other illegitimate pressure, must invoke undue influence, rather than
duress, there being no tradition of a presumption of duress from a history
of violence within a relationship. The rational step would be to hold that,
if the presumption is justified under one label, it must be no less justified
under the other. There is in any case a fine line between the presumption
and a simple shifting of the onus of proof.[40] Nevertheless, it must be
admitted that, in a less than perfectly rational world, the familiar availability of the presumption in association with undue influence may still
constitute, in some cases, a practical reason for describing a case of
pressure as a case of undue influence. Even if that is right, it provides no

[37] (1989) 52 SASR 399.
[38] Settled in *Howes v Bishop* [1909] 2 KB 390 and *Bank of Montreal v Stuart* [1911] AC 120,
reconfirmed in *Barclays Bank plc v O'Brien* [1994] AC 180, at 190.
[39] [1971] 1 Ch 95.
[40] 'Some common lawyers refer to this as the shifting of the evidential burden of proof' *Re
Brocklehurst* [1978] Ch 14, at 33, per Lawton LJ.

argument against the distinctness of the concept of illegitimate pressure, nor against the desirability on the grounds of intellectual order of drawing a line between all cases of pressure and all other cases of undue influence.

Relational undue influence

It may be thought that there is nothing left. Undue influence is not infrequently envisaged as being only about pressure. Professor Treitel, for example, introduces it in these words: 'Equity gives relief for undue influence where an agreement has been obtained by certain kinds of improper pressure which were not thought to amount to duress at common law because no element of violence to the person was involved.'[41] In probate cases, the words are indeed confined to coercive force.[42] In this section we argue that relational undue influence rarely involves pressure, and try to show that in all these cases, actual or presumed, the relevant weakness of the plaintiff is that, within the relationship, by reason of excessive dependence on the other person, he or she lacks the capacity for self-management which the law attributes to the generality of adults. This is a difficult exercise, merely from the standpoint of language.

Duress has many synonyms. One problem with undue influence is that it does not. 'Excessive dependence' is an important phrase, but there is no doubt a series of subtly different relational conditions which impair autonomy. Religious enthusiasm, for example, or sexual fixation might be thought to be distinct from dependence. The word 'excessive' creates its own difficulties. It is intended to indicate that the abdication of the one judgment to the other need not be absolute but must be out of the ordinary. The judgmental capacity of the party seeking relief must have been markedly sub-standard.

THE CASES: PRESUMED RELATIONAL UNDUE INFLUENCE

In cases in which the presumption is relied upon, it is clear time and again that facts upon which it arises suggest excessive dependence. The relationships do not suggest pressure, and the fact presumed is neither pressure nor misconduct by the defendant. In *Allcard* v *Skinner*[43] the plaintiff had left an Anglican convent to become a Roman Catholic. She sought to

---

[41] GH Treitel, *The Law of Contract* (8th ed 1991) p 366.
[42] *Boyse* v *Rossborough* (1857) 6 HLC 1; *Parfitt* v *Lawless* (1872) LR 2 PD 462, esp 469 (Lord Penzance); *Wingrove* v *Wingrove* (1885) LR 11 PD 81. Cf. recently, *Winter* v *Crichton* (1991) 23 NSWLR 116, noted P Hannen (1992) 66 ALJ 538.
[43] (1887) 36 ChD 145.

recover some of the wealth which she had surrendered to the Mother Superior of the convent at and after the time when she became a full member. She failed, but only because she had let the claim lie too long after she left the order. In presuming the undue influence the Court of Appeal was not presuming recourse to threats, express or implied, either by the Mother Superior or by the clergyman who had been the co-founder of the convent. The plaintiff had been under a spell compounded of her enthusiasm for the sisterhood and devotion to its rules, which included an obligation to seek advice only within the order. Her weakness consisted in her impaired capacity *vis-à-vis* the head of the order to judge her own best interests. She was excessively dependent or, if 'dependent' is a shade wrong, she was excessively spell-bound. Either way, her autonomy was impaired to an exceptional degree.

This type of analysis must also apply to other nominate relationships which are nowadays said to support the presumption of undue influence without further evidence.[44] The relations between doctor and patient, solicitor and client, and parent and child typically contain strong elements of dependence, trust and gratitude, together in each case with a similar tendency to exclude others from the relationship and from the matters passing between the parties to it. It would be unreasonable to analyse the presumption in such cases as resting on a common experience of illegitimate threats. The relief based on the presumption is founded on the contrary upon the common experience of impaired autonomy within such relationships. They are relationships in which the patient, client or child is excessively dependent.

Turning to cases in which the plaintiff reaches the presumption by evidence of the quality of the particular relationship, we see the same picture. What has to be shown is not a relationship raising the probability of illegitimate threats, but one in which the integrity of the plaintiff's judgment is likely to have been impaired by excessive dependence. In *Tufton* v *Sperni*[45] a convert to the Muslim faith determined, so far as his means could achieve it, to set up a centre of Muslim culture in London. He had no experience of business. A committee was formed to bring that project to fruition. The defendant, who was experienced in local government and business and was also a Muslim, albeit no zealot, was brought on to the

---

[44] Goff & Jones, *The Law of Restitution* (4th ed 1993) pp 278–9 lists in the class which supports the presumption without further inquiry into the particular characteristics of the relationship: parent/minor child; parent/very ill adult child; solicitor/client; doctor/patient; spiritual advisers/followers; trustee/beneficiary; guardian/ward; step-parent/step-child; manager/young entertainer. GH Treitel, *The Law of Contract* (8th ed 1991) pp 367–8 has a similar list but, no doubt rightly, draws a soft line between the nominate relationships in which the presumption arises without more and those in which only the proven particular character of the relationship supports the presumption.

[45] [1952] 2 TLR 516.

committee to provide business know-how. The defendant sold a house of his own to the plaintiff for the project. He not only charged more than twice its market value, but also reserved numerous privileges for himself, including a right, with no corresponding obligation as to quality or state of repair, to substitute other premises if he so chose.

The trial judge refused to set the transaction aside. He thought that there was insufficient evidence that the plaintiff had been dominated by the defendant. An appeal succeeded. It was held that it was not necessary to show that the relationship was one in which the plaintiff had 'abdicated all his authority' to the defendant or given himself over to 'blind, unquestioning trust.'[46] This confirms that, while there must be excessive dependence, there need not be an absolute surrender of one will to another. If Mason J's 'overborne will' were to suggest the need for a mind absolutely paralysed by the relationship of dependence, it would be setting too extreme a condition.[47]

The word 'dominated' which was rejected by the Court of Appeal in *Tufton* v *Sperni* is unreliable, above all because its meaning is unstable. Different people use it to denote different degrees of submissiveness or subservience. It is sometimes used to suggest a relationship in which one person is the other's puppet, and it therefore contains the danger, repulsed in *Tufton*, of requiring too absolute a loss of autonomy. Favoured again by Lord Scarman in *National Westminster Bank plc* v *Morgan*,[48] it was again rejected in *Goldsworthy* v *Brickell*,[49] only to be taken up by the Supreme Court of Canada in *Geffen* v *Goodman Estate*.[50] What matters is not the word itself, but the degree of dependence or abdication which it is taken to suggest. The relationship must be such as to impair the autonomy of the weaker party to a serious and exceptional degree. He need not have been reduced to an automaton.

In *Lloyds Bank* v *Bundy*[51] an old farmer had remortgaged the family farm in support of his son's business and had given a personal guarantee as well. The question for the Court of Appeal was whether the mortgage and guarantee should be set aside. It held that they should be. Sir Eric Sachs, with whom Cairns LJ agreed, came to that conclusion by an orthodox application of the presumption of undue influence. The bank manager had gone to the house to get the documents signed and in the discussion he had crossed the line which divides the banker dealing at arm's length and the banker as a trusted counsellor. The relation between counsellor and client had about it the elusive character of 'confidentiality' which 'imports some quality beyond that inherent in the confidence that

[46] *Ibid.* 524, per Lord Evershed MR.
[47] *Commercial Bank of Australia Ltd* v *Amadio* (1983) 151 GLR 447, 461, text to note 10 above.
[48] [1985] AC 686.   [49] [1987] 1 Ch 378.
[50] (1991) 81 DLR (4th) 211, at 227.   [51] [1975] 1 QB 326.

can well exist between trustworthy persons who in business affairs deal with each other at arm's length'.[52]

Sir Eric Sachs emphasized the difficulty of capturing in language the quality of the relationship which he finally elected to call 'confidentiality'.[53] He based the relief on the quality of the relationship so described, expressly rejecting the notion of 'domination'. The difference between trust or reliance, on the one hand, and this 'confidentiality' on the other is, in other language, nothing other than the notion of excessive dependence: 'confidentiality' supposes an element of exclusiveness, an abdication of judgment to the confidant and a dropping of the client's guard. The law merely presumes, not that the act was then done under pressure, but that it was attributable to that loss of autonomy. The presumption compels the other to show that, on the contrary, the judgment of the client was emancipated from its excessive dependence by independent advice and information.

The word 'confidentiality' is not in the end a completely satisfactory solution to the search for the right vocabulary. It was criticized in *National Westminster Bank v Morgan*.[54] It has to be read and understood in the light of the descriptive difficulty which it was trying to solve. Some relationships which connote dependence or subservience are certainly of a different kind. Even 'dependence' is not always quite right.

Re Brocklehurst[55] is on the other side of the line. An aristocratic owner of a large estate in Cheshire had in his last years made many very substantial gifts in money and in kind to friends and helpers. One such gift had been made to the owner of a small local garage who, across a social gulf, had become both a friend and a helper. The gift, a 99-year lease of the shooting rights over the entire estate, heavily reduced the value of the estate. The lease had been drawn up by the recipient's solicitor. The donor had kept the matter from his own lawyer and had taken no independent advice. However, the majority of the Court of Appeal found that there was no room for a presumption of undue influence.

The court did not find it easy to indicate the missing ingredient. Bridge LJ attached importance to the fact that no evidence suggested that the donee was either in the habit of advising the donor or under any duty to give advice. But there can be dependence on and subservience to persons other than advisers. More illuminating is his observation that there was plenty of evidence that, far from taking advice, let alone depending on it or deferring to it, the donor was even in old age a strong-minded and independent person. In short, although between donor and donee there was certainly friendship and to a degree both reliance and trust, there was nothing to suggest a surrender or impairment of the donor's autonomy.

[52] [1975] 1 QB 341.　　　[53] *Ibid.*　　　[54] [1985] AC 686, at 706.
[55] [1978] 1 Ch 14.

Eccentric as he may have been, the donor was in the habit of making his own decisions.[56] Neither his age nor his relationship with the defendant impaired his capacity to make his own choices or to manage his own affairs. The element of 'confidentiality' in the sense of that word intended by Sir Eric Sachs in *Lloyds Bank v Bundy* was absent. There was no cession of autonomy, no excessive dependence.

Goldsworthy v Brickell[57] falls back on the other side of the line from *Re Brocklehurst*. An Oxfordshire farmer in his eighties found it difficult to keep up his farm. He came to rely on his neighbours, the Brickells. As he became more frail, they became more indispensable. They were in effect running the farm and looking after him. He granted them a tenancy and an option to purchase the freehold. He shut out other advice. He was not on speaking terms with his son and he kept the matter from his usual solicitor. The deal was extremely favourable to the defendants. Later, after a reconciliation with his son, the old farmer successfully sought to have the transaction set aside. He had not become a puppet in the defendants' hands. He was not 'dominated' by them in that sense. As we have noticed, the Court of Appeal took the view that that kind of domination was not necessary.[58] He was certainly not subjected to threats, nor should the presumption be construed as imputing pressure of that kind. There was merely a cession of trust and confidence to the defendants, a loss of autonomy.

In *Simpson v Simpson*[59] a famous professor of forensic medicine, now emeritus, had made large transfers of property to his third wife in the last months of his life. He was under treatment for a malignant brain tumour. Morritt J was prepared to find that he had lost the capacity to understand what he was doing and that the transfers were therefore void. They were in any case voidable for undue influence. There was no presumption of undue influence from the relationship of husband and wife.[60] However, in the particular case, the presumption arose from the professor's diminishing mental capacity due to the progress of the tumour, his intense anxiety to be cared for at home and not in hospital, and his absolute dependence on his wide for all his needs.[61]

A clearer picture of extreme dependence—emotional, intellectual and physical—could hardly be drawn. However, it is a picture drawn for the purpose of generating the presumption of undue influence, and the crucial question is: what is the fact presumed? Is it causation or, in other words, was it the judgmental dependence that brought about the transfers? Or is the abuse of the vulnerably dependent party by the other? Even Morritt J's careful judgment gives no clear answer, although it might be

---

56 [1978] Ch 14, at 44, per Bridge LJ.
58 Text to notes 47–50 above.
60 *Howe v Bishop* [1909] 2 KB 11.
57 [1987] 1 Ch 378.
59 [1992] 1 FLR 601.
61 *Ibid.* 621–2.

said to incline towards the latter, if only by emphasizing the defendant-sided aspect of the phrase 'undue influence': 'By that date, [the wife] had acquired actual or potential dominance over the Professor, or, if that is too high, a capacity to influence the Professor, giving rise to a duty on her to care for him in any transaction between them.'[62]

If the crucial question is faced without forgetting that the defendant will often have been a person of unchallenged integrity—nothing was said against Professor Simpson's wife—the notion that the fact presumed is some kind of improper or unconscionable behaviour becomes not merely superfluous but embarrassing. What is presumed from the morbid dependence which is shown by evidence to characterize the relationship in general is that that judgmental disability did indeed cause the transfer. In *Simpson* v *Simpson* the professor's illness and his consequent dependence on his wife cost him his autonomy, and not just marginally but to an excessive degree. The restraint of the judge's own language shows that it would have been wrong to suggest that what was being presumed was something which had never been alleged, namely that the wife had abused her husband's weakness for her own advantage.

The crucial role of loss of autonomy, and again the irrelevance of pressure or 'wrongdoing' on the defendant's part, are underlined by the unusual recent case of *Stivactas* v *Michaletos* (*No 2*).[63] An aged woman, still very feeble after a cerebral haemorrhage, transferred her land to her great-nephew for a nominal consideration of Aus $1. Later, somewhat recovered, she repented. Despite her weakness, it was she who had taken the initiative. The great-nephew had put up some resistance to the plan and had both been to his own lawyer and had another lawyer visit his aunt before falling in with it. In the opinion of Kirby P and Shaller JA the relationship was one from whose particular facts a presumption of undue influence arose. That meant that the integrity of the aunt's consent to the transfer was taken to have been impaired unless he could affirmatively prove that she had acted of her own free and independent will. He could not do so, partly because of the extremity of her condition and partly because the lawyer whom he had had sent to her had given inadequate information.

To Kirby P and Shaller JA undue influence was a distinct doctrine focussed on the defective capacity of the transferor and not safely to be merged in a broader principle. Mahoney JA by contrast preferred to set

---

[62] *Howe* v *Bishop* [1909] 2 KB 11 622. The very similar New Zealand case *Roberts* v *Brown and Beattie* [1924] NZLR 851, cited in *Simpson* at 628, inclines the other way, chiefly because Reed J picks out Pollock's words 'all the circumstances of the case appear to have been such as to preclude the exercise of a full and free judgment' *Pollock on Contract* (9th ed) p 648, cf. text to note 1 above.

[63] Court of Appeal of NSW, 31 August 1993, as yet unreported.

aside the transfer for unconscionable behaviour. He thought undue influence was just one species of that wider doctrine, and to him it was crucial that the nephew's knowledge of her condition and the surrounding circumstances including the interests of the wider family was such that he was morally bound not to allow the transfer to happen.

The approach of the majority is much to be preferred. It ought not to be inferred from the fact that a finding of unconscionable conduct will often be possible that the two doctrines are capable of being merged. Developed law must respect analytical distinctions. There are, of course, many cases in which the defendant has in fact behaved badly and in which it is possible to rest the conclusion on wicked exploitation. *Tufton* v *Sperni* is an obvious example; *O'Sullivan* v *Management and Music Agency Ltd* is another. By alternative analysis, but not by fusion of analyses, such cases can be turned into examples of defendant-sided, fault-based relief.

The Court of Appeal in *O'Sullivan* v *Management and Music Agency Ltd* [64] was concerned less with the nature than the consequences of undue influence. The singer Gilbert O'Sullivan successfully sought to escape the burdensome contract he entered into when he was an unknown beginner. He put his future entirely in the hands of an experience;d manager, Mills. 'It is I think clear,' said Fox LJ 'that Mr O'Sullivan, who was at all material times a young man with no business experience, reposed complete trust in Mr Mills and executed those agreement . . . because of his trust in Mr Mills'. [65] The detailed account of the facts makes clear that the emphasis in this statement should be on the word 'complete'. In the fierce world of commercial music, the beginner did not merely trust and rely on his manager, but committed his future to him.

Pressure was not in question. But the trial judge did also find that the defendants had been guilty of knowingly exploiting the young singer. They knew that they could not have secured his services at a bargain basement price if he had been able to exercise a mature judgment or had been independently advised. This finding caused the court some difficulty in awarding, as part of the plaintiff's counter-restitution, a full allowance for the defendant's labour, including a fair element of profit. [66] If our approach is correct, the inconvenient finding of some moral blame on the part of the defendants was superfluous to the grant of relief on the basis of undue influence and showed only that, on the facts as they were, it would have been possible to make an alternative analysis according to which the relief would have been based on unconscientious exploitation of the plaintiff's weakness.

Cheese v *Thomas* [67] is also a case in which the focus was on the consequences of undue influence. Mr Cheese was an octogenarian. He did a

---

[64] [1985] QB 428.   [65] *Ibid.* 463.   [66] [1985] QB 428, esp 448, 458, per Dunn LJ.
[67] [1994] 1 All ER 35.

deal with his great-nephew, Mr Thomas, that the latter would buy a
house, and Mr Cheese would contribute to the purchase and in return
have a licence to live in the house until his death. The house was bought
for £83,000, of which Mr Cheese contributed £43,000. Mr Thomas contributed £40,000, which he raised on a mortgage. Mr Cheese moved in but
found out almost at once that Mr Thomas had stopped making the mortgage payments. Mr Cheese left and demanded his money back.

The trial judge found that Mr Cheese was entitled to relief on the
ground of presumed undue influence arising from the particular character of the relationship. The court also held that Mr Thomas had not been
guilty of any improper conduct,[68] and that finding has some weight since
it bears on the resolution of the principal issue. That issue arose out of the
fact that the house had fallen in value. When it was sold it fetched only
£55,400. Did the undue influence entitle Mr Cheese to recover the full sum
that he had paid? Or did he have to bear his share of the loss? The novel
answer both in the court below and in the Court of Appeal was that he
must share the loss: he could recover only forty-three eighty-thirds of the
sum realized by the sale.

It is extraordinarily difficult to explain Mr Cheese's reduced measure of
recovery. A person who has entered into a transaction under undue influence is usually able to recover his input on making counter-restitution.
One possible explanation is that the case involves an intuitive application
of the defence of change of position.[69] Mr Thomas had gained by the
money paid to him by Mr Cheese, but he had suffered a causally related
loss by the depreciation of the asset in which, with money of his own, that
payment had been invested. Although the details of the defence of change
of position still have to be worked out, it can be predicted with confidence
that it will not be made available to defendants who have obtained the
benefit in question by wrongful or improper conduct. Hence, on this interpretation, *Cheese v Thomas* brings to the surface a further practical reason
for insisting on the difference between plaintiff-sided relief for undue
influence and defendant-sided relief for unconscionable behaviour. Relief
which is plaintiff-sided and in no way dependent on the proof of fault in
the defendant must be subject to the defence of change of position.

---

[68] [1994] 1 All ER 43.

[69] Cf. M Chen-Wishart, 'Loss Sharing, Undue Influence and Manifest Disadvantage,'
(1994) 110 LQR 173, 176–8. The author astutely draws a parallel with *Allcard* v *Skinner* (1887)
36 ChD 145, at 171, 180, 186, where it was accepted that the defendant would not have been
liable for money spent on charitable purposes which when it was spent both parties had
been anxious to promote (at 177). Cf. *Quek* v *Beggs* (1990) 5 Butterworths Property Cases
11761, at 11779, an undue influence case in which, before change of position had been fully
recognized, McLelland J citing *Australia and New Zealand Banking Group Ltd* v *Westpac
Banking Corporation* (1988) 164 CLR 662, at 673–4, was prepared to treat money spent on the
purposes for which it was given as bringing the defendant within the agent's defence of min-
isterial receipt.

REBUTTING THE PRESUMPTION

The plaintiff-sided interpretation of undue influence also explains the nature of the task which faces a defendant who seeks to rebut the presumption. He rebuts it by evidence that the plaintiff was able to think for himself. Typically this means showing that he had been emancipated from his dependence by independent information and advice. The defendant cannot rebut the presumption by showing that he had no unconscientious intention to take advantage of the other's weakness, much less by showing that he made no illegitimate threats. A case such as *Allcard* v *Skinner*[70] would otherwise pose serious problems, since the Court of Appeal needed no convincing in that case that the Mother Superior was a person of the utmost rectitude who had certainly not been guilty of unconcientious behaviour. The bank manager in *Lloyds Bank* v *Bundy*[71] was no doubt in a similar position. We have seen that in *Stivactas* v *Michaletos (No 2)*[72] the great nephew had to give up the land because he could not affirmatively prove that his aunt's transfer had been her own free and independent choice.

The law was authoritatively laid down by Lord Hailsham LC in *Inche Noriah* v *Shaik Allie Bin Omar*[73] in words which have been cited repeatedly ever since. That was a case, not dissimilar from *Stivactas*, in which the Privy Council set aside a deed by which an aged aunt gave to her nephew, who lived with her and looked after her, virtually all her property. The nephew failed to rebut the presumption. Lord Hailsham LC said:

It is necessary for the donee to prove that the gift was the result of the free exercise of independent will. The most obvious way to prove this is by establishing that the gift was made after the nature and effect of the transaction had been fully explained to the donor by some independent and qualified person so completely as to satisfy the Court that the donor was acting independently of any influence from the donee and with full appreciation of what he was doing . . .[74]

---

[70] (1887) 36 ChD 145, text to note 43 above. See also *Quek* v *Beggs* (1990) 5 Butterworths Property Cases 11761, where it was the dependence which had to be negatived. It follows that, though there may be a background fear of impropriety (cf. text from note 88 below), it is the dependence which attracts the relief. Nor is it only cases of religious dependence in which the relief would be markedly narrowed by an insistence upon improper abuse as the gist of the relief, which would logically invite direct rebuttal by proof of ethical intent and conduct. In *West* v *Public Trustee* [1942] SAR 109, Mayo J set aside a gift of money from an adult daughter to her mother; the autonomy of the former, although she was capable and experienced in money matters, was heavily impaired by her habit of obedience to her ailing mother, compounded by affection and concern not to upset her.

[71] [1975] 1 QB 326, text to note 51 above.

[72] Above, note 63 and text thereto.

[73] [1929] AC 127. Cf. *Parfitt* v *Lawless* (1872) LR 2 PD 462, at 469 (Lord Penzance).

[74] *Inche Noriah* v *Shaik Allie Bin Omar* [1929] AC 127, at 135.

His Lordship quoted Cotton LJ's statement in *Allcard* v *Skinner* that:

In such a case the Court sets aside the voluntary gift, unless it is proved that in fact the gift was the spontaneous act of the donor acting under circumstances which enabled him to exercise an independent will and which justify the Court in holding that the gift was the result of a free exercise of the donor's will.[75]

ACTUAL RELATIONAL UNDUE INFLUENCE

Cases litigated as actual undue influence have nearly always been examples of pressure. *Bank of Montreal* v *Stuart*[76] is a rare example of extreme submissiveness. A rich wife has given mortgages in support of her husband's hopeless business ventures. The evidence was that she was a confirmed invalid, acted in passive obedience to her husband and had no will of her own.[77] Even though she herself protested that she had known what she was doing and done it of her own free will, the Privy Council decided that she was entitled to relief. However, the court left open the very question which we want to answer, whether the excessive submissiveness is sufficient in itself without evidence of abuse: 'It may well be argued that when there is evidence of an overpowering influence and the transaction brought about is immoderate and irrational, as it was in the present case, proof of undue influence is complete'. The court, however, went on to hold that the husband and his solicitor had taken unfair advantage of the wife and decided the case on the ground of defendant-sided unconscionable behaviour. The question whether the morbid passivity of the wife would have sufficed was left open.

It has only very recently been realized that every case of presumed undue influence can be turned into a case of actual undue influence by claimant who is able and willing to renounce the help of the presumption. This seems obvious, but it was always left out of account because there was no apparent reason why anyone should renounce the presumption in a case in which it was available. However, the novel insistence upon the requirement of manifest disadvantage is now held to apply where the claimant relies on the presumption but not where he proves the undue influence by evidence.[78] It follows that a plaintiff may indeed derive advantage from trying to prove actual undue influence by evidence, rather than relying on the presumption. This makes it all the more important to know precisely what fact is presumed when the presumption is relied upon. If the argument which we have advanced is right, it should be enough to prove the excessive dependence and, in addition, to prove that that dependence caused the transfer.

---

[75] *Allcard* v *Skinner* (1887) 36 ChD 145, at 171.   [76] [1911] AC 120.

[77] *Ibid*. 136.   [78] *CIBC Mortgages plc* v *Pitt* [1994] AC 200, at 207–9.

In *Bank of Credit and Commerce International* v *Aboody*[79] this tactic was used experimentally. In fact, though the House of Lords has since held otherwise,[80] it was decided that it would not work: manifest disadvantage was a requirement, the court thought, even where the claim to relief was based on actual undue influence. Mrs Aboody sought in vain to escape a series of transactions by which she had given security for the debts of the family business of which she and her husband were directors. She was a competent and educated person. However, she was wholly ignorant of business matters. In effect she looked after the domestic front, and her husband ran the business. Whenever her signature was needed in business matters, she signed where he told her to do so. He could take her compliance for granted. When the company finally collapsed, it owed the plaintiff bank nearly £1 million. Mrs Aboody had executed personal guarantees and mortgaged the family home, of which she was the sole beneficial owner, to support the company's borrowing. She now sought to avoid both species of security on the basis of undue influence exercised by her husband.

It is important to notice that this was not a case of pressure. In relation to the guarantees which Mrs Aboody had given there was no evidence of threats or any kind of positive conduct of an unpleasant kind. There was only evidence that Mrs Aboody did whatever she was told in business matters without thinking for herself at all, and that Mr Aboody never troubled to explain the meaning of the steps he caused her to take or the risks involved in them. *Vis-à-vis* the world outside Mr Aboody was certainly a rogue, but that was not relevant to the dealings between him and his wife. There was also some suggestion that he had misstated the risks to her, but the Court of Appeal proceeded on the basis that he had merely failed to give a full explanation. In relation to the mortgage of the house, there was also some slight evidence of bullying. During her interview with the solicitor whom the bank had insisted on sending to advise her, Mr Aboody had lost his patience and had burst into the room. A shouting match had followed between the two men. In relation to that episode the solicitor's subsequent note did record that she was being pressurized and would sign to get peace. It is doubtful whether even this loss of temper could have been considered as providing evidence of duress. The truth of the relationship between Mrs Aboody and her husband was that within that relationship she exercised no independent judgment in relation to business matters. Her judgment was excessively dependent on his.

There will be some similar cases in which it will not be unrealistic to find that there was duress. *CIBC Mortgages plc* v *Pitt*[81] may be one example. The wife in that case was very reluctant to go ahead with the

---

[79] [1990] 1 QB 923.   [80] Text to note 78 above.   [81] [1994] AC 200.

husband's project. She had to be bullied into doing so. In many more there will only be routine dependence or submissiveness, often with no hint of unpleasantness. The more old-fashioned the relationship, the more absolute this excessive dependence is likely to be. Moreover, the plural nature of modern society means that it contains groups whose religious traditions as yet make very little allowance for female emancipation.

Just as there will be similar cases which shade off into pressure, so there will also be cases in which there is no more than a *modus vivendi* in which the wife defers absolutely to her husband in business matters. In *Aboody* itself the Court of Appeal took the view that in business matters Mrs Aboody's dependence was more or less absolute: 'On the particular facts of this case we think it could fairly be said that Mrs Aboody's mind was in effect "a mere channel through which the will of [Mr Aboody] operated." '[82]

Behind the dominant issue of manifest disadvantage, there are, however, elements of this case which, according to the view which this paper seeks to defend, will require to be reconsidered. The court held that, even if Mrs Aboody had been able to establish that she had suffered a manifest disadvantage, she could not have qualified for relief because she would have signed the documents even if her husband had given her a full account of the risks that she was taking. And if he had given her a full account it could not be said of him that he had unconscientiously abused his power: he would not have exercised 'undue' influence.[83] In other words the court took the view that undue influence required influence improperly and unconscientiously exercised, and decided that, since she would have signed anyway, her signature was not attributable to the only element of unconscientiousness to which on the facts she was able to point.

In our submission, this reasoning leads to undesirable consequences and derives from a misunderstanding of the word 'undue'. Where the presumption of undue influence operates, the word 'undue' cannot mean 'improper' or 'unconscionable' but only 'excessive', and it is dangerous to exploit its natural ambiguity by giving it a different meaning when the presumption is renounced.[84] In some relationships and, in particular, within those religious traditions mentioned above, it would be impossible to characterize the husband's failure to give the wife a full account of business risks as in any way unconscientious, and it would always be true that the wife would agree whether or not such an explanation was given. That merely reflects the *modus vivendi* in conditions of unchallenged inequality.

---

[82] [1989] 1 QB 923, at 969, referring to Jenkins and Morris, LJJ, in *Tufton v Sperni* [1952] 2 TLR 516, at 530–2, where this extreme degree of inertia is said not to be essential, cf. text to note 46.
[83] [1990] 1 QB 923, at 968–71.   [84] Cf. text from note 70 above.

To insist that the transaction be attributable to an element of unconscientious abuse is therefore to obstruct the finding of undue influence in the most extreme case, where it is systematic and unchallenged. Furthermore, there is a logical difficulty in insisting upon proof of a fact which is not a one which the presumption, when it is allowed to operate, supposes to be true. We have shown that the presumption does not suppose pressure or unconscionable exploitation, but only that the transfer was attributable to one shade or another of loss of autonomy. Renunciation of the presumption cannot entail the assumption of a burden of proving any facts other than those which would, if the presumption were not renounced, fall to the defendant to deny.

In addition to these objections, the one substantial and the other logical, it is also of course true that to focus on Mr Aboody's concealment of the risks as importing a necessary element of unconscionable behaviour is to merge the doctrines of undue influence and unconscionability, at least so far as concerns cases of actual undue influence. Quite apart from the question whether that is analytically objectionable in itself, such a merger would then raise very awkward questions in relation to duress and the classification of most actual undue influence cases as duress. Just as it has never been said that manifest disadvantage is a requirement of relief for duress, so also it has not been said that the application of pressure must be unconscionable. In some cases it is not, the pressure being applied in absolutely good faith under a claim of right.[85] If words are to mean anything, a defendant who applies pressure because he believes on reasonable grounds that he may lawfully do so cannot be described as behaving unconscionably.

PROPHYLAXIS

There are some passages in *Allcard v Skinner*, especially in the judgment of Lindley LJ, which do suggest the contrary analysis, namely that undue influence is a matter of improper behaviour on the part of the defendant. Lindley LJ went out of his way to say that the law does not relieve a person from the consequences of folly, imprudence or lack of foresight.[86] These passages can be read as supporting the view that relief must be based on the wrongful, exploitative conduct on the part of the defendant, not on the weak or crippled judgment of the plaintiff. However, that is an incorrect construction of their meaning. Lindley LJ was in no doubt that the Mother Superior was the model of rectitude. Closer examination shows that these passages bear on the ultimate justification for the intervention.

---

[85] eg *Maskell v Horner* [1915] 3 KB 106; *Mason v New South Wales* (1959) 102 CLR 108.
[86] (1887) 36 ChD 145, at 182–3.

The ultimate justification of the relief is here presented as the need to meet the danger of wicked exploitation to which foolish or fixated people are exposed. Lindley LJ's meaning was not that the party seeking relief must prove wicked exploitation by the other, but only that it was to obviate the danger of wicked exploitation that relief was given, without proof of wicked exploitation, to those whose capacity to make judgments was impaired by relational influence. In other words, in his view, the justification for relieving the weak has to found in prophylaxis against abuse by the strong. The case itself shows that the relief thus justified remains entirely plaintiff-sided.

The same prophylactic justification for the relief was expressed by Dixon J in *Johnson v Buttress*,[87] when he said:

The basis of the equitable jurisdiction to set aside an alienation of property on the ground of undue influence is the *prevention* [emphasis added] of an unconscientious use of any special capacity or opportunity that may exist or arise of affecting the alienor's will or freedom of judgment in reference to such a matter.[88]

Dixon J was a master of the English language. When he used the word 'prevention' he intended it to bear its proper meaning: the jurisdiction was designed to anticipate the danger of exploitation.[89] It was not based on proof of exploitation in the particular case but on what Dixon J referred to as the impairment of the alienor's 'free act'. In the second quotation, at the beginning of this chapter, Cartwright also uses the word 'prevention,' but both the context and the emphasis given to the word 'active' show that he is using 'prevent' to mean 'undo'.[90] The prophylactic element has been eliminated.

THIRD PARTIES

It is clear from *Barclays Bank plc v O'Brien*[91] that, genuine agency apart, a partly outside the relationship in which one person is morbidly dependent on another or, in the case of misrepresentation, outside the relationship between misrepresentor and misrepresentee will not be subject to relief unless that party has notice of the vitiating factor. Constructive notice suffices. This is true even where the transfer which is impugned is made directly by the impaired party to the outsider. This raises a prima facie difficulty for the plaintiff-sided analysis. If what matters is the vitia-

---

[87] (1936) 56 CLR 113. Cf. Story, *Equity Jurisprudence*, note 1 above, pp 252, 258.

[88] *Johnson v Buttress* (1980) 56 CLR 113, at 134.

[89] In *Louth v Diprose* (1992) 175 CLR 621, at 628 Brennan J cites the passage with emphasis on the references to unconscientiousness, as part of his assimilation of the plaintiff-sided and the defendant-sided doctrines, but, with respect, that seems to be an abuse of Dixon J's intentions.

[90] Text to note 4 above.   [91] [1994] AC 180.

tion of the judgment of the impaired party, why is it relevant to ask whether the outsider had constructive notice of the impairment? Does not the fact that this question must be asked show that what matters is wicked exploitation by the transferee?

It is perfectly true that the impairment could be given effect as against anyone, without more. However, that possibility encounters a routine anxiety: the fear of too much restitution. Where the impairment is inherently associated with one particular person other than the plaintiff (as misrepresentation and undue influence are, but spontaneous mistake is not) the law has a choice, in contemplating that anxiety, whether to treat the vitiated decision bad as against that one person, or as against some people, or as against everyone. The third possibility is easily excluded, to reduce the range of the relief which is on offer. Hence the reason why an innocent bank, outside the relationship, is allowed an immunity from this relief, despite the impairment of the person granting security, is simply that this relief is given grudgingly, and no more is given than need be. The law looks for defensible cut-off points.[92]

In summary, therefore, the reason for restitution in cases of relational inequality is that the morbidly dependent party is, or is presumed to be, unable to think freely for himself. His dependence on the judgment of the other means that he lacks the standard capacity for managing his own affairs and defending his own interests. This, like mistake, is a factor impairing the integrity of the plaintiff's decision-making process. However, like induced mistake (misrepresentation), it is an impairment which is tied to a particular defendant and which the law chooses not to relieve as against third parties unless they have notice of the impairment. That is an inhibition of the natural scope of the relief. Both the nature of the fact presumed and the means of rebutting the presumption show that the law of relational undue influence is no more concerned with wicked behaviour than is the law of mistake or innocent misrepresentation.

Victimization, manifest disadvantage, and knowledge

It is evident that the House of Lords in *National Westminster Bank plc* v *Morgan*[93] was motivated by a desire to limit the incidence of relief for undue influence. Moreover, it seems that this desire was expressed

---

[92] See *Barclays Bank plc* v *O'Brien* [1994] AC 180 (per Lord Browne-Wilkinson). We are grateful to Mr Andrew Dickenson (St Edmund Hall, Oxford) for insisting on the importance of this point. The position which is taken in the text, which differs slightly from that which Mr Dickinson himself proposed, might equally be rendered as a grant to the innocent outsider of a total defence based on change of position.

[93] [1985] AC 686.

through a programme which amounted, in effect, to an assimilation of undue influence and unconscientious conduct. It is difficult to employ the word 'victimization' in connection with relief for undue influence without meaning to add an additional requirement that, in addition to the impaired autonomy of the plaintiff, there must also be wicked exploitation of that weakness by the defendant. To victimize someone is to cheat them, to make them suffer by exceptional treatment.[94]

The language of victimization appeared to be further supported by the introduction of a requirement that the victim prove the transaction in question was manifestly disadvantageous. Later, in *Bank for Credit and Commerce International* v *Aboody*[95] that requirement was doubly reinforced since it was held that manifest disadvantage was a condition of relief for both presumed and actual undue influence. Mrs Aboody's renunciation of the presumption did not therefore enable her to escape it. Secondly, the court decided that full weight must be given to the word 'manifest.' If the transaction was not obviously disadvantageous, there could be no relief. Mrs Aboody's case fell because the overall disadvantageous nature of the transaction only emerged after a fine and close evaluation of its various beneficial and detrimental features.[96] The picture of undue influence as wicked exploitation seemed to be complete.

In fact, however, it was not complete. The reason is that a requirement of manifest disadvantage does not necessarily indicate a commitment to an interpretation of undue influence as unconscientious exploitation. There are at least two other roles which such a requirement can play. In the first it pragmatically restricts relief for impaired autonomy, meeting the fear that otherwise too many transactions might be unsettled,[97] and in the second it is evidence in support of the presumption of undue influence, completing the facts upon which the presumption arises. This second role was rejected in *Aboody* when the Court of Appeal held that the requirement was not confined to cases in which the party seeking relief invoked the presumption. Mrs Aboody's counsel argued strongly to the contrary. Indeed the tactical renunciation of the presumption had been based on the assumption that manifest disadvantage could be assigned to its evidential role, in support of the presumption. Nevertheless, only one of the remaining two possible explanations of manifest disadvantage

---

[94] *The New Oxford Shorter English Dictionary* (1993): '*victimize* 1. Make a victim of; cause to suffer inconvenience, discomfort, harm, etc. Also, single out for punitive or unfair treatment; *spec.* impose penalties on (an employee taking industrial action). *b* Cheat, defraud. . . .'

[95] [1990] 1 QB 923.   [96] *Ibid.* 964.

[97] For an extreme reaction to this fear, see *Tommey* v *Tommey* [1983] Fam 15, where Balcombe J following *Thwaite* v *Thwaite* [1982] Fam 1 (CA) and distinguishing *Apsden* v *Hildesley* [1982] 1 WLR 264, decided that to allow undue influence to be invoked would be too unsettling to consent orders made on divorce and therefore refuses altogether to recognize it as a ground of challenge.

pointed towards an assimilation of undue influence and unconscionable conduct.

This is still important in relation to other examples of impaired autonomy,[98] but not in relation to undue influence. In *CIBC Mortgages* v *Pitt*[99] the House of Lords repudiated the notion that a plaintiff seeking relief for actual undue influence must establish that the transaction entered was manifestly disadvantageous. Their Lordships held that manifest disadvantage had no role except in relation to presumed undue influence, as part of the factual pattern which generates the presumption. They thus in effect adopted the argument which was rejected in *Aboody*. Lord Browne-Wilkinson, who gave the leading speech said:

Whatever the merits of requiring a complainant to show manifest disadvantage in order to raise a class 2 presumption of undue influence, in my judgment there is no logic in imposing such a requirement where actual undue influence has been exercised and proved . . . I therefore hold that a claimant who proves actual undue influence is not under the further burden of proving that the transaction induced by undue influence was manifestly disadvantageous: he is entitled as of right to have it set aside'.[100]

His Lordship then gave a broad hint that the requirement of manifest disadvantage may be insecure even where the presumption is invoked.[101] The effect in Australia of this shift in the position of the House of Lords will no doubt be to stiffen resistance to a requirement which has never been welcomed even in cases of presumed undue influence.[102]

Manifest disadvantage thus retains a much reduced role in relation to undue influence. Where it does have a part to play, there will still be questions about its proper construction. In *Aboody* itself, the court adopted a surprisingly extreme version, very unfavourable to the plaintiff, which emphasized the meaning of the word 'manifest.' If the basis of relief is the impairment of autonomy, the best approach will be to ask whether the transaction is one which an unimpaired adult would have entered in the circumstances. This approach would apply equally, as the words 'manifest disadvantage' do not, to transactions of different kinds, not only to sales but also to gifts and to grants of real and personal security. Gifts explicable by ordinary motives would then be upheld without having to ask the awkward question whether a gift can ever be, or ever not be, manifestly disadvantageous. This approach also allows factors other than the adequacy of consideration, such as the common desire to keep land in the family, to be considered more naturally. A sale of land at full value may

---

[98] Text from note 115 below.   [99] [1994] AC 200.   [100] *Ibid*. 209.
[101] *Ibid*.
[102] *Johnson* v *Buttress* (1936) 56 CLR 113, *Baburin* v *Baburin* [1990] 2 Qd R 101 per Kelly, SPJ, aff'd [1991] QLR 143. Cf. *James* v *Australian and New Zealand Banking Group* (1986) 64 ALR 347, at 390; *Farmers' Co-operative Executors and Trustees Ltd* v *Perks* (1989) 52 SASR 399.

nonetheless be a transaction which an unimpaired person would not have entered, since family roots and related sentiments normally play a strong role in the debate whether to sell.

Such a development would find a sufficient element of manifest disadvantage in the existence of a sensible doubt whether it would have been natural for an unimpaired person to have acted in the way in which the plaintiff did. This would tie in with the prophylactic purpose of the relief and is essentially the approach of Dixon J in *Yerkey v Jones*[103] which, like *Aboody*, was a case of security given by a wife. In that case he said:

[I]n the relations comprised within the category to which the presumption of undue influence applies there is another element besides the opportunity of obtaining ascendancy or confidence and of abusing it. It will be found that in none of those relations is it natural to expect the one party to give property to the other. That is to say, the character of the relation is never enough to explain the transaction and to account for it without the suspicion of confidence abused.[104]

The question should therefore be whether the transaction was one which an adult *sui iuris* would naturally have made in the given circumstances. The word 'manifest' will probably turn out to be too strong. The word 'ill-advised', which is broader than 'disadvantageous', will be better suited to the kind of inquiry which Dixon J had in mind. It will often be easier and more straightforward to handle the ideas expressed by 'ill-advised' than the ideas expressed by 'disadvantageous'.[105]

KNOWLEDGE

A minor avoids a contract because of his or her minority, without showing that the adult knew.[106] It seems, however, that a person suffering from a mental handicap has to show that the other knew of the disability.[107] So far as concerns actual undue influence, in *Mutual Finance Co Ltd v Wetton and Sons Ltd*[108] where no explicit threats were made but veiled threats were in the air, Porter J certainly thought that the fears of the party seeking to avoid the transaction must be shown to have been known to the

---

[103] (1940) 63 CLR 649. See also *Johnson v Buttress* (1936) 56 CLR 113 (note 87 and text thereto above).

[104] At 675. This test obviates the difficulties in integrating the law relating to contracts and the law relating to gifts: *Geffen v Goodman Estate* (1991) 81 DLR (4th) 211, at 227–8 (Supreme Court of Canada). Cf. *Quek v Beggs* (1990) 5 Butterworths Property Cases 11761, at 11777–9.

[105] Even, for example, in a case such as *Zamet v Hyman* [1961] 1 WLR 1442, where a widow of 71 anxious to marry a fiancé 8 years older than herself released claims against him for less than a tenth of their value, a transaction variously described as 'ridiculous' and 'remarkable'.

[106] *R Leslie Ltd v Sheill* [1914] 2 KB 607 (adult lender fraudulently deceived).

[107] *Hart v O'Connor* [1985] AC 1000, text to note 124 below.

[108] [1937] 2 KB 389, text to note 33 above.

other, and he held that they were known. But that was not a relational case, but rather a one-off application of pressure.

Since in cases of relational dependence plaintiffs hardly ever renounce the assistance of the presumptions, the question whether the defendant's knowledge of the loss of autonomy is required cannot be firmly answered. In the automatic class, it is the species of relationship which matters, not knowledge (although knowledge is always present). In the other case, it is the particular character of the relationship in question, a matter necessarily within the knowledge of the parties to it. This does not me that knowledge is formally a requirement, only that it is necessarily implicit.

Where the presumption is renounced, the better view would appear to be similar. The nature of the disability in question supposes a relationship, and a relationship cannot subsist without its general characteristics being known to both parties. If that is right, knowledge of the relationship and its general characteristics is simply implicit in the nature of this type of disability is not a separate and distinct requirement. If X were secretly obsessed, sexually and emotionally with Y,[109] the obsession might at a certain point begin to count as a mental handicap but it could not create a relationship with Y. A question remains whether, given the parties' necessary knowledge of the general nature of their relationship, the law might not insist on specific knowledge of the precise depth and degree of the dependence. The answer is that it probably could not do so. There are two reasons. One is that plaintiffs would simply run back to the presumptions. The other, if we try to contemplate the matter in a landscape from which the presumptions have been removed, is that such a burden would cut too deeply into the relief.

The meaning of 'undue influence'

In our discussion of relational undue influence, we sought to show that relief for undue influence is given, putting the matter somewhat broadly, on the ground of impaired judgmental capacity usually arising from morbid dependence on another. We have also argued that a requirement of 'manifest disadvantage' need not and should not exercise a gravitational pull towards a defendant-sided analysis in terms of unconscientious exploitation. That point retains some general importance, notwithstanding the fact that within undue influence itself the role of manifest disadvantage has been much reduced. In this section it is necessary to address the meaning of the words 'undue influence' and the relation of undue influence to a number of related figures.

---

[109] A unilateral variation of *Louth* v *Diprose* (1992) 175 CLR 621, as to which see text note 127 below.

The ideas involved in this area of law are elusive. It is always difficult to find the right language, and always dangerous to make too much of any single word or phrase. 'Undue influence' itself is difficult. Judges have fought shy of definition, even of exposition. A tendency to circularity can be detected: the requirements of relief for undue influence are that there must be influence and that it must be undue. In struggling towards a more stable understanding, it must be acknowledged that the phrase's natural orientation is to the defendant's side, ie it tends to draw the mind towards the person who has influence. At the same time, despite having that tendency, it is not wholly inappropriate to describe, neutrally or bi-polarly, the relationship in which one is dependent or otherwise easily led, while the other has the power to influence. Dependence and influence are two sides of the same coin. The phrase 'undue influence' is not unsuitable to describe the entirety of such a relationship. Its tendency to draw the mind to active abuse of influence is distracting, but it is not so powerful as to necessitate a change of terminology. We should therefore say, first, that the phase 'undue influence' supposes the existence of two parties and, secondly, that the word 'influence' indicates, in relation to some decision to be taken or some class of such decisions, a degree of reduced autonomy on the part of the one and a corresponding degree of control or ascendancy on in the other.

Next, the ambiguity of the word 'undue' is awesome. It is naturally capable of meaning both 'excessive' and 'unfitting' or 'improper'.[110] Worse, there is a point where, in general usage, that which is excessive also becomes improper or unacceptable. A person who is unduly talkative talks too much and, in doing so, offends the canons of social behaviour. The excess is also out of place. This ambiguity must be resolved in favour of 'excessive.' If the question is whether the plaintiff's autonomy was impaired by the relationship to a degree which deprived him of the capacity for self-management which the law attributes to the generality of adults, and if no inquiry has to be made about the wickedness of the defendant, there is, logically, no warrant for saying that the influence must be 'undue' in any sense other than 'excessive.'

The same conclusion follows from another proposition, namely that a moderate loss of autonomy cannot found relief even if attributable to an influence exercisable or exercised by the other which can be qualified as improper. Appetites, even far short of addiction, create a degree of dependence, and some appetites, as for illicit commodities, invite improper influence. But a rich man who wants ivory or rhinoceros horn does not, in

---

[110] *The New Shorter Oxford English Dictionary* (1993) gives: '1. Not owing or payable. Now rare. 2. That ought not to be done; inappropriate, unsuitable, improper, unrightful, unjustifiable. 3. Going beyond what is warranted or natural, excessive, disproportionate.'

equity's sense, thereby come under the undue influence of the poachers. Whatever the precise quality of the contract by which he pays a vast price, it is not voidable for undue influence. It is not the impropriety of the influence upon which the relief is based, but the excessive and exceptional degree of lost autonomy.

'Undue influence' is therefore too much influence, too much to be compatible with the general presumption that adults all have the standard common law capacity to manage their own affairs. Where there is too much influence on one side there is insufficient autonomy on the other, and it is that insufficient autonomy on which the relief is founded. 'Too much' and 'insufficient' are matters of degree, but the degree in question is exceptional. Although adults are in reality of widely differing intelligence and personality, by and large they must be presumed equally able to cope with their own affairs. Similarly, adults come under all sorts of different influences, and again they have to be assumed able to cope. The law relieves only an extreme loss of autonomy.

Finally, there is the word 'exercise.' Is it correct to speak of exercising undue influence or to ask of a defendant whether it can be said of him that he 'exercised undue influence' so as to obtain an advantage? In pressure cases the application of pressure can of course be described as an exercise of undue influence.[111] However, the usage which derives from those cases should not be allowed to spread into all other examples of undue influence. We have shown that, where undue influence is presumed, the presumption concedes causation, so that it falls to the defendant to show that the plaintiff's want of autonomy did not cause the transfer, usually done by showing that independent advice emancipated the plaintiff from his or her excessive dependence.

In a pressure case 'causation' and 'exercise' are the same thing, but in other cases the causation which the presumption concedes does not imply activity on the party of the defendant. Similarly, where a plaintiff renounces the presumption to avoid affirmative proof that the bargain was disadvantageous or ill-advised, the usage based on the pressure cases should not carry over a requirement of active causation to actual relational influence. The plaintiff renounces the concession of causation and must therefore prove that the excessive dependence (or other shade of lost autonomy) did cause the transfer. We have argued that the Court of Appeal in *Aboody* ought not to have added additional facts to the plaintiff's voluntarily assumed evidential onus.[112] Renouncing the presumption, Miss Allcard a century ago, and Professor Simpson or Mrs Stivactas in our own day would have had to prove only that their want of

---

[111] The subtle relation between undue influence and duress is briefly considered immediately below, text note 113.
[112] Text note 83 above.

autonomy caused the transfer, not that their defendant 'exercised undue influence' to obtain it.[113]

DURESS, PERSONAL DISADVANTAGE AND BREACH OF FIDUCIARY DUTY

It is necessary at this point to make three brief digressions, because the meaning of 'undue influence' must be secured by differentiation from and comparison with other nearby grounds for relief, namely pressure (duress), non-relational personal disadvantage and breach of fiduciary duty.

Duress

'Undue' as used in 'undue influence' should not be regarded as analogous to 'illegitimate' as used in relation to pressure.[114] Pressures are commonplace in society. Freedom of the will or, synonymously, of judgmental capacity is intelligible only within the context of pressures inherent in ordinary social life.[115] Freedom is precisely and definitively the freedom to cope with those pressures, and it is impaired only when a pressure alien to that context is introduced.

The ubiquity of pressure and the sensitivity of context compels the law of duress to discriminate between pressures which are legitimate and those which are illegitimate. In relational undue influence, only the quantum of disablement is in issue. There is nothing in undue influence comparable to legitimate pressure, no case in which someone excessively dependent nevertheless lacks a prima facie right to relief. Cartwright is nevertheless exactly to the contrary: 'In undue influence, as much as in the law of duress, there is a problem in distinguishing between pressures which are legitimate and so must be endured . . . and pressures which are illegitimate.'[116] This is only true when the vice in question is indeed pressure. It is not true of dependence and other forms of fixation.

A case of severe illegitimate pressure, ie a case in which the pressure in question does impair judgmental capacity to an extreme degree, can be presented as a case of undue influence. The excessive dependence or deference is produced in such a case, not by trust and confidence, but by the pressure. Our decanting such cases back into duress merely creates better intellectual order.

It is also important to underline the point that, although pressure must be illegitimate if it is to ground relief, this does not imply that pressure is

---

[113] Text to notes 43, 59, and 63 above.   [114] Cf. note 29 above.
[115] PW Young, *Law of Consent* (Sydney, 1986) p 9. Cf. Birks, *Introduction to the Law of Restitution* (1989) p 175.
[116] *Op cit* note 3 above, 173.

not also a plaintiff-sided phenomenon, so that the relief flows from the impairment of the plaintiff's decision-making capacity, not from unconscientiousness on the part of the other. The person applying the pressure may know that he is acting wrongly and in that case the relief may be referred to his unconscientious behaviour, but as we have seen the proof of bad behaviour is additional to and not part of the proof of duress, which can be exerted conscientiously and in good faith.[117]

Non-Relational Personal Disadvantage

In undue influence the plaintiff gets his relief because he has, to a sufficiently extreme degree, a sub-standard judgmental capacity, and the source of the impairment is the character of the relationship in which he finds himself. If we use 'unequal' instead of 'substandard' to denote his failure to match up to the common standard of judgmental capacity, we can say that he suffers from 'relational inequality'. It is important to notice that the nearest congeners of 'relational inequality' are other non-relational examples of sub-standard capacity—minors, persons of impaired intellect, intoxicated persons, persons under socio-economic disadvantage, and so on. If we call the one category 'relational inequality', the other must be 'personal inequality'.[118]

The orderliness of the law, and ultimately its regular application, requires that relational and personal inequality be kept close together in lawyers' minds. This is not because the law must necessarily be exactly the same across all examples of inequality, but because the underlying unity of the whole category is strong enough to require differences in the law within it to be carefully explained and because all cases of inequality involve the same difficulties in relation to the line between plaintiff-sided relief based on the impairment of judgmental capacity and defendant-sided relief based on wicked exploitation by the unimpaired party.

These latter difficulties are exacerbated, first by the overlap on many facts between the two, and, secondly and more distractingly, by the possibility that the plaintiff-sided liability may in a given case be inhibited or restricted by a requirement which seems at first sight to belong in a defendant-sided picture. The case of overlap is straightforward: if the unimpaired party does exploit the impaired party, there will in principle be a choice between impairment-based and fault-based relief. The case of inhibited plaintiff-sided relief entails a delicate but lucid distinction between, on the one hand, the requirements which indicate

---

[117] Note 20 above.
[118] The inequality is measured by reference to an abstract standard, not the strength of the other party to the transaction which is impugned. Two minors dealing together are both 'unequal'—not up to the common standard of self-management.

unconscientious exploitation and are invoked precisely because they do justify that conclusion and, on the other hand, the use of one such requirement—as it might be, manifest disadvantage or knowledge of the plaintiff's disability—merely to subject plaintiff-sided relief for impaired autonomy to a pragmatic restriction. The restrictor, where there is one, can all too easily be read as part of a picture of defendant-sided unconscientiousness.

For example, between *Morgan* and *Pitt*, and therefore before *Pitt* confined manifest disadvantage to an evidential role in support of the presumption,[119] undue influence exemplified 'inhibited plaintiff-sided relief'. That is, relief for undue influence rested on the plaintiff's loss of autonomy, but it was restricted or inhibited by a further requirement that the plaintiff must have suffered a manifest disadvantage. Accordingly, as will always be the case where plaintiff-sided relief is inhibited by a factor capable of belonging in a picture of unconscionable exploitation, there was an ever-present danger, deliberately encouraged in *Morgan*, of its being misconstrued with the effect of collapsing the plaintiff-sided relief into an over-extended form of unconscionable behaviour. However, since *Pitt*, relief for undue influence is once more an instance of pure plaintiff-sided liability.

It is possible to work this through only for a single example of non-relational disability, mental handicap, and then only in outline. Schematically, our model suggests four possible categories of liability, of which the fourth is only added out of extreme caution:

(1) plaintiff-sided relief on the basis of impaired autonomy;
(2) the same, subject however to an inhibiting factor, typically
    (a) manifest disadvantage, but possibly
    (b) some other restrictor, such as knowledge of the defendant's disability;
(3) defendant-sided relief for unconscionable exploitation;
(4) other shades or refinements of the foregoing.

As we have said, there is no imperative for the law to be identical for every species of impaired autonomy, but good law will be able to explain any differences there may be and will not seem to pick at random from the available menu. For the mentally inadequate, *Archer* v *Cutler*[120] appeared to represent a choice in New Zealand of (2)(a), relief for impaired autonomy restricted by a requirement of manifest disadvantage. *Hart* v *O'Connor*[121] rejects that choice, preferring, it would seem, (2)(b), relief for

---

[119] Text to note 99 above.   [120] [1980] 1 NZLR 386.
[121] [1985] AC 1000. Invaluable discussion: AH Hudson, 'Mental Incapacity in Property and Contract Law' [1984] Conv 32; AH Hudson, 'Mental Incapacity Revisited' [1986] Conv 178.

impaired autonomy restricted by a requirement of knowledge on the part of the unimpaired party. Both options leave open on suitable facts the alternative of (3), defendant-sided relief for unconscientious exploitation.

The obvious criticism of the handling of mental handicap, and the obstacle to relating it to the pattern of relief for relational inequality, is the absence from the judgments of explicit reasons for rejecting the pure plaintiff-sided relief, option (1)[122] which now applies to undue influence. Given that both mental handicap and relational undue influence are species of loss of autonomy, why do the requirements differ?

The suspicion must be that the differences are accidental, but that conclusion is a last recourse. We might prefer to guess that the underlying anxiety in relation to mental handicap is the danger of destroying the credit of a wide class of adults, especially aged adults, who might find it impossible to deal with their property without demeaning medical reports on their mental health or, perhaps worse, without the cooperation of those junior members of their family from whom allegations of impaired competence might later be expected. Besides the fear of infantilizing adults, there is probably a second anxiety, namely about the danger of fabrication after the event, whether by the repining alienor or, after his death, by his disappointed relatives. These good reasons for restricting plaintiff-sided relief should be brought out into the open, to allow a rational choice between the various options. The extreme would be to bar plaintiff-sided relief altogether and to give relief only against wicked exploiters of the mentally infirm.[123]

Breach of fiduciary duty

The true congeners of undue influence are the cases of personal disadvantage. It is less useful, even dangerous, to create a close relationship between undue influence and breach of fiduciary duty. Professor Finn writes that reasons of history rather than sound principle have kept relational undue influence and the law of fiduciary duties apart and, citing *O'Sullivan* v *Management Agency and Music Ltd*,[124] applauds their modern assimilation.[125] Yet for many purposes, and in particular for setting aside transactions between the parties, it is superfluous to characterize the relationship in which one is unduly dependent on another as fiduciary. The undue dependence being sufficient in itself to explain the relief, the intrusion of a complex term such as 'fiduciary' can only confuse. These

---

[122] Contrast, in Scots law, *John Loudon & Co* v *Elder's CB* 1923 SLT 226.
[123] Cf. *Tommey* v *Tommey* [1953] Fam 15, at 25–6; see also note 96 above.
[124] [1985] QB 428.
[125] P Finn, 'The Fiduciary Principle,' in TG Youdan (ed), *Equity, Fiduciaries and Trusts* (1989) 1, 43–4.

difficulties can be seen rising to the surface in both *Aboody* and *Pitt*.[126] When they come to be considered directly and in detail, the most important thing to remember will be that undue influence and breach of fiduciary duty are different grounds for relief, with different consequences. It is again a matter of alternative analyses. Just as undue influence and unconscionable behaviour must be kept analytically distinct, so breach of fiduciary obligation must be distinguished from both. On some facts all three analyses will be available.

Conclusion

This conclusion takes the form, not of a summary or overview, but of an application of what has been said to be an important recent case. In *Louth* v *Diprose*[127] in the High Court of Australia, the substantive question was whether the respondent, who was a lawyer but not wealthy, was able to recover a gift of Aus $58,000 which he had made to a woman for whom he had suffered the pains of obsessive and unrequited love for some 7 years. The respondent had been so infatuated with the appellant that, when she moved from Tasmania to the mainland, he gave up his legal practice on the island to follow her. She needed somewhere to live. He paid for the house and it was conveyed into her name. There was a crucial finding that the appellant had exploited his emotional dependence on her and played upon it. The gift of the house had been his response to her acute need and her despair at the prospect of homelessness. But, on the facts as found below, with which the majority of the High Court would not interfere, she had manufactured the atmosphere of crisis, even threatening suicide.

The respondent won this case. Claims based on resulting trust and undue influence dropped away in the lower courts, and with them some intriguing legal questions about their operation and interrelation. The respondent therefore won by the defendant-sided route. His infatuation had made him emotionally dependent on the appellant: she played on that dependence to obtain a home. It was not difficult for the court to characterize that behaviour as unconscientious. The trial judge declared that

---

[126] [1990] 1 QB 923, at 962–4; [1994] AC 200. It is difficult to read between the lines of Lord Browne-Wilkinson's reference in *Pitt* to fiduciaries and to the policy underlying their discipline, but it is possible that he is alerting a future court to the need to remain alive to different analyses, to avoid overlooking an analysis which, even within the field prima facie covered by the presumption, would not encounter the requirement of manifest disadvantage: [1994] AC 200, at 209. In *Midland Bank plc* v *Massey* (1994) *The Times* 23 March (note 7 above) the Court of Appeal did contemplate two bases for rescission, one being the impaired judgmental capacity of the female partner, the other a wrong committed by the male (Transcript, 7–8).

[127] (1992) 175 CLR 621; (1993) 67 ALR 95; noted: S Hepburn, 'Equity and Infatuation' (1993) 18 Altern LJ 208.

the appellant held the land on trust for the respondent and must convey it to him. That relief was upheld, because no variation was asked for, but both the High Court and the Court of Appeal of South Australia indicated that restitution in money would have been more appropriate.[128]

Toohey J dissenting, would have reviewed the facts and then have allowed the appeal. He noted that the plaintiff-respondent had accepted that if he could not win on the basis of unconscionable behaviour, he could not make out a case in undue influence and that he had not argued undue influence in the High Court.[129] Lest it be later suggested that Toohey J's remarks acquiesce in that position, as though in a general proposition that one who cannot win in unconscionable behaviour cannot win in undue influence, it is as well to emphasize that, on his view of the facts, the respondent had retained his autonomy and was not 'emotionally dependent' on the appellant.[130]

Brennan J assimilated the two bases of relief. Although he said that the doctrines were 'distinct,' he immediately followed that observation with a sentence in which he seemed to be saying that they were very similar: 'Gifts obtained by unconscionable conduct and gifts obtained by undue influence are set aside by equity on substantially the same basis.'[131] And again: 'The similarity between the two jurisdictions gives to cases arising in the exercise of one jurisdiction an analogous character in cases involving the same points in the other jurisdiction.'[132]

Brennan J then proceeded with an analysis which in effect merges or at least interlaces unconscionable, exploitative behaviour and either all cases of undue influence or, more certainly, all cases of actual undue influence.[133] This may be one programme for the future, but there is no denying that it is incompatible with everything written in this paper.

The leading judgment was given by Deane J with whom, so far as concerned the law applicable to the facts as found below, Mason CJ and

---

[128] (1992) 175 CLR 621, at 638, 643.　　[129] *Ibid*. 655.　　[130] *Ibid*.　　[131] *Ibid*. 627.

[132] *Ibid*. 628. Brennan J supported his approach by reference to the association of the two ideas in *White and Tudor's Leading Cases in Equity*. It was, however, a curse of that species of literature that it associated ideas in the manner of a fugue. There was little attempt at analysis. Dicey condemned that kind of anti-rational flow of consciousness in his famous inaugural lecture. AV Dicey, 'Can English Law be Taught at the Universities?' (London, 1883) 12–13.

[133] (1992) 175 CLR 621, at 628–9. Hepburn, 'Equity and Infatuation' (1993) 18 Altern LJ 208, 210, appears to overemphasize the degree to which Brennan J, was willing to treat the doctrines as alternatives. His is a strategy of merger, cf. JRF Lehane, 'Undue Influence, Misrepresentation and Third Parties,' [1994] 110 LQR 167, 173, and Mahoney JA in *Stivactas v Michaletos*, note 63 above and text thereafter. As for the uncertainty indicated in the text as to the scope of the contemplated merger, any notion of dividing undue influence along a line which rigidly separates actual from presumed is misconceived, as is revealed by the possibility of renouncing the help of the presumption and proving that which the presumption would have presumed. There is, however, a sound line between relational (actual and presumptive) and non-relational (always actual) undue influence: see text from note 80 below.

Dawson, Gaudron and McHugh JJ agreed. That judgment says nothing about undue influence, and in it the immediate ground of the decision is clearly that the appellant deliberately played on the respondent's vulnerability.[134] In other words, it is based squarely on the defendant's unconscionable behaviour. The appellant had been unconscientious in the mode of and at the time of the acquisition.

Deane J's more general statement of the law for unconscionable dealing is similar to his analysis in *Commercial Bank of Australia Ltd* v *Amadio*[135] but is differently modulated: given the one party's 'special disability', the jurisdiction to relieve unconscionable dealing arises where:

that special disability was sufficiently evident to the other party to make it prima facie unfair or 'unconscionable' that the other party procure, accept or retain the benefit of the disadvantaged party's assent to the impugned transaction in the circumstances in which he or she procured or accepted it. Where such circumstances are shown to have existed, an onus is cast upon the stronger party to show that the transaction was fair, just and reasonable . . .[136]

Although the words 'or retain' might suggest the contrary, this statement does not in fact extend into the dangerous terrain of unconscientiousness *ex post*,[137] for it insists on unconscionable knowledge at the time of acquisition. A cruder paraphrase would make the relief of unconscionable dealing turn on

(1) the plaintiff's special disability;
(2) knowledge on the defendant's part of that weakness sufficient to render the acquisition prima facie unconscientious; and
(3) failure by the defendant to show that the transaction was fair.

These conditions are analytically distinct from those which govern relief for undue influence. On the other hand, it is undeniable that many plaintiffs who might rest their claim on undue influence will also be able to satisfy them and, further, that, of those, any who still have to face the proof of manifest disadvantage will be attracted by the reversed burden of proof in condition (3).

When will it be advantageous to stay with undue influence? Proof of actual undue influence puts an end to the matter. The plaintiff need not show that the facts add up to unconscientious knowledge on the defendant's part, and no issue whatever can arise as to substantive unfairness (manifest disadvantage). If we, so to say, cleaned up the facts of *Bank of Credit and Commerce* v *Aboody*[138] we would produce a situation in which, with no background of fraud or bullying, a husband simply took his

---

[134] (1992) 175 CLR 621, at 638.   [135] (1983) 151 CLR 447, at 474, note 11 above.
[136] (1992) 175 CLR 421, at 637.   [137] Text to note 14 above.
[138] [1990] 1 QB 923, text from note 83 above.

wife's opinion for granted in business matters and she was happy to accept that regime. From one perspective that kind of relationship is deplorable, from another it is merely old-fashioned. Either way it would be impossible to characterize that husband's behaviour as unconscionable, and that wife would be better advised to rest her claim to relief on the actuality of her excessive dependence.[139]

In the case of presumed undue influence, recourse to the presumption will save the plaintiff from having to enter into questions of causation and from having to build up a picture of unconscientious knowledge on the part of the defendant, but it seems these advantages will be brought at the cost of accepting the onus of proving manifest disadvantage. In Australia that price may not have to be paid, since the requirement of manifest disadvantage has not taken root even within the field of the presumption.[140]

Some jurists will still be attracted by the simplicity of the defendant-sided analysis, and they will point out, correctly, that the number of cases in which there is no unconscionable behaviour will be very small. However, the rationality of the law cannot tolerate abbreviations or approximations. If there are two doctrines, there are two doctrines; and the fact that one might do perhaps ninety-five per cent of the work is no reason for pretending that the other does not exist. The correct approach will be to treat both undue influence and duress as plaintiff-sided factors which ground relief on a degree of impairment of the plaintiff's capacity to make decisions. In every case we should accept not a dogma of priority and subsidiarity, but a voluntary intellectual discipline of exhausting the plaintiff-sided analysis before proceeding to the question whether relief might be rested on unconscientious behaviour on the part of the defendant. That discipline will serve to protect all plaintiff-sided grounds for relief—spontaneous and innocently induced mistake no less than undue influence and duress, not to mention others—and will avert the unnecessary injustice which happens when plaintiffs lose cases because lawyers fail to see their winning argument.

Lawyers will disagree whether relief for undue influence could have been claimed on the facts of *Louth* v *Diprose*. Some go so far as to doubt whether it should have been conceded on any ground.[141] It would not perhaps be surprising if some relational conditions capable of counting as

---

[139] Cretney has recently warned against enlarging soft grounds for reopening family transactions and thus tempting the weak into the dangers of litigation: SM Cretney, 'Mere Puppets, Folly and Imprudence: The Limits of Undue Influence,' [1994] Restitution LR 3. The proper response to that danger is to emphasize the point made in this paper to the effect that the loss of autonomy must be extreme and to recall the availability of inhibitors to reduce the incidence of relief without denying its availability. In this regard, the doctrine of undue influence may yet be glad of what survives of 'manifest disadvantage.' Cf. text from notes 97 and 110 above.

[140] Cf. note 102 above.

[141] Hepburn, 'Equity and Infatuation' (1993) 2 Altern LR 208.

exceptional disabilities for relief based on unconscionable behaviour[142] did not suffice as exceptional impairments of autonomy for the purposes of the doctrine of undue influence. That probably constitutes another important difference between the two doctrines. However, we know that Miss Allcard's zeal for religion and charitable works did suffice. Mr Diprose's obsession was of a lower order but for these purposes of the same genus. His case was exceptional, 'different in kind from the ordinary relationship of a man courting a woman'.[143] Common or garden lovesickness is a source of misery, but does not disable its victims' capacity to judge their own interests, manage their own affairs and make their own decisions.

[142] There has undoubtedly been a tendency to dilute the requirement of 'special disadvantage' which provides the foundation for relief in respect of unconscionable exploitation. See the authorities collected by J Phillips and J O'Donovan, *The Modern Contract of Guarantee* (2nd ed 1992) pp 152–4. At p 155 the learned authors correctly attempt to draw a line across this development before the point is reached at which the onerous nature of the contract itself becomes the special disadvantage. Cf. L Peterson, 'Unconscionable Conduct after *Amadio—Baburin v Baburin*' [1992] JCL 167, 169–70.

[143] (1992) 175 CLR 621, at 629 per Brennan J.

Appendix: Textbook positions on undue influence

What follows is no more than a selection of opinions as to the nature of undue influence. It properly belongs at footnote 5 but would have overloaded the apparatus at that point. The key question is whether the writer sees undue influence as consisting in wrongful conduct by the defendant. It is not uncommon for a writer to sit on or on both sides of the fence.

AS Burrows, *The Law of Restitution* (1993) pp 193–9 handles undue influence under the heading of 'exploitation' but at the same time resiles from the suggestion that that word necessarily connotes wickedness on the part of the defendant.

JW Carter and DJ Harland, *Contract Law in Australia* (3rd ed 1991) deals with the matter briefly but might be said to incline against the defendant-sided analysis, see esp p 1404.

Cheshire and Fifoot and Furmston's Law of Contract (12th ed 1991) pp 309–11, 316–21 is clearly defendant-sided, being committed to the notion of 'unfair and improper conduct' and apparently content for the reader to understand undue influence as a species of duress, similarly defendant-sided.

Lord Goff of Chieveley and GH Jones, *The Law of Restitution* (4th ed 1993) p 276 *et seq* emphasizes the breadth and subtlety of the doctrine of undue influence, but abstains from any attempt to choose between the different analyses under consideration.

DW Greig and JLR Davies, *The Law of Contract* (1987, with 1992 supplement) p 961 is unequivocally defendant-sided.

AG Guest (ed), *Chitty on Contracts* (26th ed 1989) p 523 speaks of undue influence as directed against the retention of benefits from fraud or wrongful acts.

JE Martin, *Hanbury and Martin's Modern Equity* (14th ed 1993) inclines in favour of a plaintiff-sided analysis on p 815, but explicitly prefers the defendant-sided analysis on p 818.

RP Meagher, WMC Gummow and JRF Lehane, *Equity Doctrines and Remedies* (3rd ed 1992) favours the defendant-sided analysis and describes undue influence as 'the malign production of intent,' at s.1503, although the word 'malign' might be thought to be underplayed in the subsequent discussion, esp at s.1506 and s.1524 (see also JRF Lehane, 'Undue Influence, Misrepresentation and Third Parties,' (1994) 110 LQR 167, 173, arguing for assimilation to unconscionable behaviour).

JG Starke, NC Seddon and MP Ellinghaus, *Cheshire and Fifoot's Law of Contract* (6th Australian ed 1992) vacillates between the two analyses, at s.810 and s.818.

4

Duties of Disclosure and French Contract Law: Contribution to an Economic Analysis*

Muriel Fabre-Magnan

The main aim of this chapter is to investigate the economic analysis which is usually made of pre-contractual duties of disclosure and the widely accepted conclusion that such duties are economically inefficient.[1] Some of the distinctions made under French contract law will be used to show that, in some circumstances, imposing such a duty may be more efficient than relying on each party to safeguard his own interests. This is not to say that French law is beyond criticism in this area, and this chapter will also use economic analysis to show that in some respects French law goes too far.

The development of duties of disclosure in French contract law

One of the most striking recent evolutions of French contract law has been the multiplication of pre-contractual duties of disclosure. Such duties now exist not only in the traditional areas of the law of sale and insurance, but also in many others, eg money lending and franchising. Not only sellers but also doctors, garage owners, architects, distributors, bankers and lawyers have to disclose information before entering into contracts with their clients.

Duties of disclosure arise either pursuant to legislation or through the evolution of case law. Numerous direct duties of disclosure have been

---

* Copyright © 1994, Muriel Fabre-Magnan.
[1] The purpose of this chapter is deliberately narrow. It only deals with pre-contractual duties of disclosure which impose on a party to a prospective agreement an obligation to inform the other party of factors likely to influence his decision. It does not deal with contractual duties of disclosure which concern the performance of the contract, nor does it purport to discuss the exact scope of duties of disclosure in each individual case, should such duties be imposed, although some criteria for the determination of circumstances in which duties of disclosure should be imposed are described briefly. Moral issues have also been deliberately left aside, even though it is obvious that duties of disclosure are a powerful means of enforcing the moral duty of honesty, which should be taken into account when choosing a proper legal rule.

imposed by legislation which tend to be aimed at particular circumstances. In addition to the traditional example of insurance law,[2] numerous specific duties of disclosure have been imposed in recent years, for instance on banks (which must inform clients as to the full cost of credit[3] and guarantors as to the extent of their obligations[4]), distributors who enter into exclusive agreements with retailers,[5] and issuers of publicly traded securities.[6]

[2] The law of 13 July 1930, which forms part of the Insurance Code, has been extensively amended, in particular in matters of duties of disclosure, by the Law no 89–1014 dated 31 December 1989 on the adaptation of the Insurance Code in view of the opening of the European market (OJ 3 January 1990, p 63; D 1990, Leg p 66). The duty of disclosure is, like under English law, a reciprocal duty which falls both on the insurer and the insured. On these duties of disclosure in French law, see articles L 112–2, L 112–3, L 113–2, L 113–4 of the Insurance Code.

[3] Law no 66–1010 dated 28 December 1966 (as amended) on Usury, Moneylending and Certain Acts relating to Canvassing and Advertising. Article 4 of this law provides that: 'the effective global interest rate computed in accordance with the above provisions must be stated in all written acknowledgments of a loan agreement governed by this law' (le taux effectif global déterminé comme il est dit ci-dessus doit être mentionné dans tout écrit constatant un contrat de prêt régi par la présente loi).

[4] Law no 84–148 dated 1 March 1984 on the Prevention and the Amicable Settlement of Difficulties of Enterprises. Article 48 of this law provides that: 'credit institutions which have extended financial support to an enterprise, on the basis of the grant of a guarantee by a natural or legal person must, at the latest on 31 March in each year, notify the guarantor of the amount o fprincipal and interest, commissions, costs and incidental expenses outstanding as at 31 December in the previous year pursuant to the obligation covered by the guarantee, as well as the term of such commitment. If the commitment is for an unlimited duration, they must mention the power to revoke it at any time and the conditions in which it will be invoked' (les établissements de crédit ayant accordé un concours financier à une entreprise, sous la condition du cautionnement par une personne physique ou une personne morale, sont tenues au plus tard avant le 31 mars de chaque année de faire connaître à la caution le montant du principal et des intérêts, commissions, frais et accessoires restant à courir au 31 décembre de l'année précédente au titre de l'obligation bénéficiant de la caution ainsi que le terme de cet engagement. Si l'engagement est à durée indéterminée, ils appellent la faculté de révocation à tout moment et les conditions dans lesquelles celle-ci est exercée).

[5] Law no 89–1008 dated 31 December 1989 on the Development of Commercial and Personal Enterprises and on the Improvement of their Economic, Legal and Social Environment. Article 1 of this law provides that: 'any person who makes available to another person a tradename, a trademark or a service mark requiring him to enter into an exclusive or quasi-exclusive agreement in order to conduct his activity must, prior to the execution of any contract entered into for the mutual benefit of the parties, provide the other with a document containing truthful information enabling him to enter into such a commitment with full knowledge of the circumstances' (toute personne qui met à la disposition d'une autre personne un nom commercial, une marque ou une enseigne, en exigeant d'elle un engagement d'exclusivité ou de quasi-exclusivité pour l'exercice de son activité, est tenue préalablement à la signature de tout contrat conclu dans l'intérêt commun des deux parties de fournir à l'autre partie un document donnant des informations sincères, qui lui permette de s'engager en connaissance de cause).

[6] Under the regulations of the *Commission des Opérations de Bourse* (the COB), in particular Regulation 88–04 relating to information to be published on publicly traded companies, as amended, all companies whose securities are publicly traded must prepare and submit for approval to the COB and information memorandum prior to an issue of new securities. Regulation 90–02 relates to information provided to the public and specifies that 'information provided to the public must be exact, precise and truthful'.

Legislation even seems to be moving towards the imposition of a general duty of disclosure in the context of contractual relationships between consumers and professionals. Thus, a law dated 18 January 1992 reinforced the level of protection for consumers[7] by providing that:

before the conclusion of a contract, every professional selling goods or providing services must put the consumer in a situation where he is able to know the essential characteristics of the goods or the service. In addition, the professional seller of goods must tell the consumer the period during which it is likely that spare parts needed for using the goods will be available on the market. This period must be brought to the knowledge of the professional by the manufacturer or by the importer.

This provision has been reproduced in the first two articles of the *Code de la consommation* created by a statute dated of 26 July 1993, under the title 'chapter I: general duty to inform'.

Parallel to legislation, case law has developed duties of disclosure on the basis of the provisions of the Civil Code relating to lack of consent (*vices du consentement*).[8] Thus, in the absence of a statutory duty to disclose information in a given situation, a failure to disclose information can give rise to a remedy indirectly, for instance on the grounds of mistake (*erreur*)[9] or fraud (*dol*).[10] Invoking *dol* in the context of a failure to disclose is made considerably easier by the fact that *dol* can result not only from acts

---

[7] Law no 92–60, art 2: 'Tout professionnel vendeur de biens ou prestataire de services doit, avant la conclusion du contrat, mettre le consommateur en mesure de connaître les caractéristiques essentielles du bien ou du service. Le professionnel vendeur de biens meubles doit, en outre, indiquer au consommateur la période pendant laquelle il est prévisible que les pièces indispensables à l'utilisation du bien seront disponibles sur le marché. Cette période est obligatoirement portée à la connaissance du professionnel par le fabricant ou l'importateur).

[8] The Civil Code defines four requirements for a contract to be valid: the parties must have consented freely to enter into the agreement; they must have had proper capacity to contract; the contract must have an *objet* (ie a subject matter); and it must have a *cause* which is both real (in the sense approximately, that there is a proper equivalent, or return, for each obligation) and not illegal (as regards the purpose of the contract). For a more complete description of French contract law concepts and principles, see B Nicholas, *The French Law of Contract* (2nd ed 1992).

[9] *Erreur* is defined under art 1110 of the Civil Code as a mistake relating to the essential characteristics (*qualités substantielles*) of the *objet* of the agreement. These are not confined to the physical components of the subject matter of the contract; they also encompass all the main attributes of the subject matter of the contract which induced the relevant party to enter into it. As a consequence of this extensive definition, *erreur* is used very widely under French law as a basis for challenging the validity of contracts.

[10] *Dol* vitiates consent when the fraud causes a mistake in the other party. However, an important difference between *dol* and *erreur* is that, while *erreur* must concern the essential characteristics of the subject matter of the agreement, *dol* may be invoked when the resulting mistake did not relate to the subject matter of the agreement (eg *erreur* as to the value or to the other party's motives). In an action based on *erreur*, only the state of mind of the mistaken party will be analysed, while in an action for *dol*, the deceiving party's intention to defraud will have to be established.

designed to deceive the other party, or from lies, but also from, remaining silent and failing to dispel a known misunderstanding of the other party. As the Cour de cassation[11] has regularly held since a case dated 1 April 1954 '*dol* may consist of the silence of one party concealing from the other a fact which, if it had been known by him, would have prevented him from entering into the contract; but such silence must relate to a circumstance or a fact which the other party could reasonably be expected not to know'.[12] These *vices du consentement* are a ground for annulling the contract. But damages can also be awarded on the basis of art 1382 of the Civil Code, which states a general principle of tortious liability[13] and which can apply in case of breach of a duty of disclosure. These damages can be awarded together with annulment of the contract.

Although the provisions on which judges rely in order to penalize a failure to disclose information concern different questions relating to the formation of contracts, it can be argued that French judges have extended the scope of these provisions so widely that they have transformed them into a coherent doctrine of obligatory pre-contractual disclosure of information. It is beyond the scope of this paper to describe in detail all criteria developed by French case law for invoking duties of disclosure. What follows therefore is only a brief outline of the main criteria, which concern the content of the information to be disclosed and the knowledge of both parties.

INFORMATION TO BE DISCLOSED

First, a party has only to disclose such information as is relevant having regard to the subject matter of the contract and to the obligations undertaken by the parties. For instance, it is the seller's duty to inform the buyer of the conditions of use of a machine; however, the same obligation does not arise for the person who repairs it. Relevant information can either be

---

[11] The Cour de cassation, which supervises all civil, commercial, social and criminal courts, usually hears appeals made only on points of law against decisions rendered by one of thirty-three Cours d'appel located throughout France. In those cases, the Cour de cassation will either quash the decision which is challenged or dismiss the appeal. If a decision is quashed, it will be remitted for further consideration not to the original court, but to another court of equal jurisdiction. Although there is no doctrine of binding precedent in France, decisions of the Cour de cassation clearly enjoy very strong persuasive authority.

[12] Chambre sociale of the Cour de cassation, 1 April 1954, Bull civ, Section Sociale, no 223, p 171 (Le dol peut être constitué par le silence d'une partie dissimulant à son cocontractant un fait qui, s'il avait été connu de lui, l'aurait empêché de contracter; mais le silence ainsi gardé doit être relatif à une circonstance ou à un fait que le cocontractant était excusable de ne pas connaître).

[13] According to this text, any human act which causes prejudice to another obliges the person by whose fault the prejudice has occurred to make it good (tout fait quelconque de l'homme qui cause à autrui un dommage, oblige celui par la faute duquel il est arrivé à le réparer).

essential, in which case the conclusion of the contract depends upon it, or simply material, in which case it will only influence the conditions under which the contract is concluded. Failure to disclose essential information will entail the nullity of the contract, since had the information been disclosed, the contract would not have been entered into. In case of non-disclosure of other relevant information, the only remedy available is damages.

Relevant information only includes information likely to be useful when deciding to contract. Information which would be of no help when taking a decision or which could even be damaging does not have to be disclosed. For instance, when a patient has a terminal disease for which no treatment is available, his doctor can choose whether or not he must disclose this to him. For the same reason, a surgeon has no duty to disclose the exceedingly rare risks arising out of an operation, because such knowledge could cause a patient to refuse to undergo a very beneficial operation. Nevertheless, there is a very wide duty of disclosure to warn patients of potential complications arising out of their diseases in order to enable them to avoid them. The 'usefulness' test should be objective. Information which it would be illegal to use in order to reach a decision, such as the pregnancy of the applicant in an employment situation, does not have to be disclosed.

These principles are, in fact, quite close to those developed under the English law of insurance. Thus, it is stated 'the proposer is obliged to disclose to the insurer at the time of making (or remaking) the contract of insurance all material information affecting the risk';[14] material information or material facts 'must be distinguished from opinion' (in the same sense as in the law relating to misrepresentation)[15] and '[t]he materiality of information is a question of fact, determined by reference to the judgment of the prudent insurer at the time that the proposer is obliged to disclose',[16] the test being objective.[17] In a recent case, *Pan Atlantic Insurance Company* v *Pine Top Insurance Co*[18] the House of Lords held that, in order to avoid an insurance contract on the basis of non-disclosure, it must be established that, in addition to the objective test of materiality of information (ie whether it would have been material for a prudent insurer), the misrepresentation or non-disclosure induced the actual insurer to enter into the contract. The introduction of such a subjective test restricts the duty of disclosure imposed on the insured under previous cases.[19] The five Law Lords nevertheless disagreed on the criteria of materiality in the

---

[14] MA Clarke, *The Law of Insurance Contracts* (2nd ed 1994) p 549, para 23–1A.
[15] *Ibid*. p 561, para 23–5.
[16] *Ibid*. p 562, para 23–6.
[17] *Ibid*. p 563, para 23–6.
[18] [1994] 3 All ER 581.
[19] Following the Court of Appeal decision in *CTI* v *Oceanus* [1984] 1 Lloyd's Rep 476, it had been argued that the imposition of too onerous a duty of disclosure on the insured

objective test. For two of them, information is material for a prudent insurer only if, knowing of the undisclosed fact, he would have either refused the risk, or accepted it but at an other premium (the 'decisive influence test').[20] For the other three,[21] the decisive influence test should be rejected. According to them, for a circumstance to be material, it would be enough that it had an impact on the mind of a prudent insurer in weighing up the risk, even though it had no decisive effect on his eventual decision whether to accept the risk and, if so, at what premium.

KNOWLEDGE OF BOTH PARTIES

Duties of disclosure arise due to the parties' unequal information.[22] Thus it is necessary to ascertain the knowledge of the party who may have a duty to disclose and the knowledge of the party who complains that he has not been informed in order to assess whether such unequal information existed.

Knowledge of the party who may have a duty of disclosure

The conditions for the existence of a duty of disclosure are the actual knowledge of both the relevant information and the fact that such information is useful to the other party. In other words, a party can generally be under a duty to disclose only information which he knows. The words 'duty of disclosure', more than those of 'duty to inform', imply this knowledge.

However, in certain exceptional circumstances, an absence of knowledge does not constitute a valid defence and a party is not allowed to escape from a duty of disclosure if his ignorance was illegitimate. Thus, a party must sometimes seek information to inform others.[23] For instance, a professional car salesman could not claim to be ignorant about the state of the cars he sells. But such a duty must remain exceptional. Once again, strikingly similar principles have been developed under English insurance law. Thus, although in principle, '[t]he proposer is required to disclose only material information actually known to him ... he may be deemed to know things, which he does not actually know, if they are

---

enabled insurers to avoid their contractual obligations too easily. The detailed judgments rendered by their Lordships in the *Pan Atlantic* case illustrate the degree of sophistication of English law in that field.

[20] Lord Templeman and Lord Lloyd of Berwick. Their criteria would restrict yet further the scope of the duty of disclosure of the insured.

[21] Lord Goff of Chieveley, Lord Mustill and Lord Slynn of Hadley.

[22] J Ghestin, 'The Pre-contractual Obligation to Disclose Information: French Report', in D Harris and D Tallon (eds), *Contract Law Today: Anglo-French Comparisons* (1989) pp 151, 157.

[23] French jurists speak of an *obligation de s'informer pour informer*.

known to his agents or if he should have known them ... [or] he should have inferred them from things he actually did know'.[24] In England, unlike the United States, the proposer may breach the duty of disclosure, not only when he does not appreciate the significance of facts he knows, but also when he does not know facts which he should now.

To be under a duty of disclosure a party must be aware not only of the information, but also of its influence on the consent of the other party. He ought to have disclosed the information because he knew that the other party would not have entered into the contract if he had also known it.[25]

Knowledge of the party who complains that he has not been informed

There is obviously no duty of disclosure when the party who needs the information already knows it. Only a party who is unaware of information needs to be informed. Furthermore, his lack of knowledge also has to be legitimate. The Cour de cassation states that the contracting party who made a mistake by being too gullible or careless in checking some information has only himself to blame. For instance, the party cannot have the contract annulled if the mistake is the result of his own negligence. French law calls this *erreur inexcusable*. Duties of disclosure must be limited to cases where there is a legitimate ignorance of one party. In particular, a party is allowed to be unaware of information if it was impossible for him to know it or if he could legitimately rely on the information given by the other party.[26] This argument explains why, in English law, there are duties of disclosure in contracts *uberrimae fidei*, ie of the utmost good faith, because in these kinds of contracts, a party cannot do otherwise than rely on the other party.[27] For instance, in a contract of insurance, it would be too costly and difficult for the insurance companies to have to check all material information given by the policy-holders, so that they have no option but to rely on them.

These criteria may sometimes seem quite wide, but in practice the rules relating to the burden of proof restrain them considerably, because it is for the party who complains not to have been informed to prove that all conditions for a duty of disclosure existed. The onus of proof is upon the

[24] MA Clarke, *The Law of Insurance Contracts* (2nd ed 1994) p 576, para 23–8.

[25] If the plaintiff only claims damages and not to have the contract annulled, it is sufficient to prove that if he had known the information, he would have asked for more favourable conditions in the contract. It is not necessary to prove that he would not have entered into the contract in view of the fact that he does not want the contract to be set aside.

[26] For more details, see J Ghestin, 'The Pre-contractual Obligation to Disclose Information: French Report' in D Harris and D Tallon (eds), *Contract Law Today, Anglo-French Comparisons* (1989) pp 151, 160 *et seq.*

[27] See G Spencer Bower, *The Law Relating to Actionable Non-Disclosure and other Breaches of Duty in relations of Confidence, Influence and Advantage* (2nd ed 1990 by Sir Alexander Kingcome Turner and R Sutton) pp 83 *et seq.*

person who alleges that there has been non-disclosure. Furthermore, as will be seen below, even if these conditions are satisfied, there ought to be no duty to disclose information about what a party receives from the other, because such a duty would not be economically efficient.

The traditional hostility of English law towards duties of disclosure

In contrast, English law has been traditionally hostile to the imposition of duties of disclosure.[28] The caveat emptor rule has remained as one of the fundamental principles of contract law and there are exceptions to it only in certain circumstances, such as contracts *uberrimae fidei* or in situations expressly defined by statute.[29] It should be noted that, in the latter case, many of the statutory duties of disclosure existing in English law derive from the implementation of EEC Directives, relating in particular to the information to be provided to consumers as to the contents and the use of products.

The main reason for such hostility of common law jurists is explained by Marshall CJ in the US case *Laidlaw* v *Organ*.[30] To deny the existence of any duty of disclosure in this case, he stated that '[it] would be difficult to circumscribe the contrary doctrine within proper limits, where the means of intelligence are equally accessible to both parties. But at the same time, each party must take care not to say or do anything tending to impose upon the other.' This argument against the imposition of any duty of disclosure is not beyond discussion: is it satisfactory to acknowledge that imposing duties of disclosure would be fair in many circumstances, but yet to rule this out and give up because of the difficulty of circumscribing such duties within proper limits?

It is obvious that multiplying duties of disclosure creates a risk of opening the floodgates of litigation. But this risk can be considerably reduced by finding appropriate criteria. As has been seen above, the English law of insurance illustrates the fact that it is both possible to assert a very wide duty of disclosure and yet to succeed in defining proper criteria which could easily be transposed to other fields.

If the scope of duties to inform under French law is wider than under English law, it does not mean that the two systems cannot be compared. Often, many cases which are analysed by French lawyers in terms of a

[28] See P Legrand, 'Pre-Contractual Disclosure and Information: English and French law Compared' (1986) 6 Ox JLS 322.
[29] See B Nicholas, 'The Pre-contractual Obligation to Disclose Information: English Report' in D Harris and D Tallon (eds), *Contract Law Today: Anglo-French Comparisons* (1989) p 166 *et seq*.
[30] 15 US (2 Wheat) 178 (1817).

duty of disclosure will lead to the same solutions in English law, even if not qualified as such. For instance, French law does not make a distinction as to whether information has been given or not so that, whether or not information has been given to the other party, there is still a breach of the duty of disclosure. In this case, English law would also find a remedy on the grounds of misrepresentation or undue influence. The recent judgment of the House of Lords in *Barclays Bank plc v O'Brien*[31] is, in this respect, quite revealing: the bank was unable to enforce a wife's obligation to secure her husband's debt, on the ground that it had not checked that the wife was sufficiently aware of her liability as a surety and, if she was not aware, had not informed her of the risks incurred.[32] Under French law, the reasoning would have been almost exactly the same, except that the remedy would have clearly been the breach of a duty to inform.

The classical economic analysis of duties of disclosure

The traditional hostility of English law towards a general duty of disclosure has been supported by the development of the economic analysis of law. Under the economic analysis of law, rules are appraised according to their economic efficiency. From this perspective, when solutions are being selected, the most cost-effective rule in any given situation will be the one which should, in the absence of overriding reasons to the contrary, be favoured.

In recent years, duties of disclosure have been analysed from this economic perspective by eminent authors (see for instance, Anthony Kronman,[33] Richard Posner,[34] Patrick Atiyah,[35] Bernard Rudden[36]) most of them English or American.[37] The unanimous conclusion of these studies was that, if a person who has invested in the search for information is forced to give it away to the co-contracting party, 'he will have an incen-

---

[31] [1994] 1 AC 180.

[32] According to Lord Browne-Wilkinson, *ibid.*, 196, 'for the future in my judgment a creditor will have satisfied these requirements if it insists that the wife attend a private meeting (in the absence of the husband) with a representative of the creditor at which she is told of the extent of her liability as surety, warned of the risk she is running and urged to take independent legal advice'.

[33] In a key article published in 1978, he proposed a detailed economic analysis of the duty of disclosure in the context of the law of contracts: AT Kronman, 'Mistake, Disclosure, Information, and the Law of Contracts' (1978) 7 JLS 1.

[34] *Economic Analysis of Law* (3rd ed 1986) p 96 *et seq.*

[35] *An Introduction to the Law of Contract* (4th ed 1989) p 265 *et seq.*

[36] 'Le juste et l'inefficace pour un non-devoir de renseignements' Rev trim dr civ, 1985, p 91.

[37] See B Nicholas, 'The Pre-contractual Obligation to Disclose Information: English Report', in D Harris and D Tallon (eds), *Contract Law Today: Anglo-French Comparisons* (1989), pp 166, 184 *et seq.*

tive to reduce (or curtail entirely) his production of such information in the future.'[38] If he is allowed to make use of his knowledge and skill in negotiating contracts without having to disclose material information, he will be encouraged to invest in the acquisition of information which will ultimately benefit society as a whole. To use the terminology of Kronman, the law should maximise the production of 'socially useful information'[39] by allowing those who discover it to benefit from their knowledge of it. Thus, to take the classic example of the purchase of land on which, due to an extensive (and expensive) search for information, the purchaser suspects oil might be found, it would be unreasonable to force him to disclose his knowledge to the seller. If the law imposed such a duty of disclosure, the result would seem to be that the search for new oil resources would be abandoned, due to the lack of reward for this type of investment.

However, this reasoning, according to the authors, only applies where information has been deliberately acquired with a view to a potential reward. In contrast, in the case where information has been casually acquired (ie without any special investment), imposing a duty of disclosure will not affect the behaviour of the person subject to such duty. In the case of the seller of a house, the information he possesses about the defects in the house (eg that the roof is infested with termites) will, according to the authors, have been casually acquired, as the seller has this information simply by reason of his living in the house. There would in this case be no reason for not imposing a duty of disclosure of such information.

Therefore, if one is to follow the traditional findings of economic analysis, the evolution of French contract law runs counter to a greater economic efficiency of the rule of law. It has been argued that his evolution is due to the French obsession with the morality of the rule of law, rather than its efficiency. More prosaically, however, the question of the economic efficiency or inefficiency of duties of disclosure has never been methodically addressed in France. The scientific study of the respective costs entailed by different legal solutions to a given problem, which is the basis of the economic analysis of law, remains to a large extent something which French academics and practitioners alike have so far not been used to taking into account.[40]

---

[38] AT Kronman, 'Mistake, Disclosure, Information, and the Law of Contracts' (1978) 7 JLS 1, 13–14.   [39] *Ibid.*, p 33.

[40] This situation may however be changing and, perhaps belatedly, major authors are being discovered, seminars organized and articles published. The article by Bernard Rudden, 'Le juste et l'inefficace pour un non-devoir de renseignements' Rev trim dr civ, 1985, p 91, published in one of the leading journals of French jurisprudence, is one of the first to have succeeded in convincing a large number of French authors of the usefulness and the interest of an economic approach to duties of disclosure. Recent court decisions have also shown that judges are increasingly aware of the economic impact of their decisions, and that they are willing to use certain legal techniques in order to mitigate the negative effects of some of their decisions.

However, even from an economic perspective, the evolution of French law in relation to duties of disclosure is not necessarily towards lesser efficiency.[41] Thus the economic analysis which is usually made of duties of disclosure and the widely accepted conclusion that such duties are economically inefficient is not beyond criticism. For reasons which will be explained below, it seems that the cost of acquisition of information is not always the most appropriate criterion for testing the efficiency of duties of disclosure. More precisely, a criterion—which has been developed under French law in the context of *erreur*—based upon the nature of information to be disclosed, seems to offer a better basis for determining in which situations duties of disclose are economically efficient. It will then be possible to conclude that in some circumstances imposing such a duty may be more efficient than relying on each party to safeguard his own interests.

To assert that duties of disclosure cannot be efficient in circumstances where information has been acquired deliberately, in other words at a certain cost, is not always satisfactory. There are several reasons why this 'cost of acquisition' criterion seems not to be very practical.

First, if we are to follow the indications of Kronman, there are very few cases where information is truly casually acquired (ie at no cost). One of the few examples of casual acquisition he gives is when a businessman 'acquires a valuable piece of information when he accidentally overhears a conversation on a bus'.[42] For him, the term 'costs' covers a wide range of expenses and 'may include not only direct search costs but the costs of developing an initial expertise as well (for example, the cost of attending business school)'. If strictly applied, this criterion would exclude a duty of disclosure in most circumstances.

Secondly, it is often difficult to determine exactly when information has been deliberately acquired. According to this author, as soon as information is obtained through prior study or expertise, such information is deemed to have been deliberately acquired. In many cases the seller of a

---

[41] It should be mentioned in this context that the general denial of duties of disclosure seems to contradict the usual findings of the most classical economic analysis, since it is widely acknowledged that one of the pre-conditions of perfect competition is equal access to information for both buyers and sellers. Equal access means that all buyers and sellers have complete information about the price of the product and of what is used to produce it and that buyers know all they need to know about product characteristics, while producters have equal knowledge of production techniques. The imposition of duties of disclosure is certainly a way of achieving this equality of knowledge. Many other economists who have studied the concept of information have underlined the danger of 'information asymmetry' (information asymmetry is a situation in which some parties to a transaction possess relevant information that other parties do not possess). See, for the most notable, FA Von Hayek, 'The Use of Knowledge in Society' (1945) American Economic Review p 519 *et seq*; GA Akerlof, 'The Market for "Lemons", Qualitative Uncertainty and the Market Mechanism' (1970) Quarterly Journal of Economics, p 488 *et seq*.

[42] AT Kronman, 'Mistake, Disclosure, Information, and the Law of Contracts' (1978) 7 JLS 1, 13.

house may discover that the roof is infested by termites simply by living in it. In these circumstances it is argued that the information has been casually acquired and that nothing should prevent the existence of a duty of disclosure. But take the case of the seller of a house who discovered a defect when he had a survey done prior to putting it on the market. Why should he be allowed to hide this information from prospective buyers? What should be the solution when, for example, the seller is an architect and is able to detect a structural defect which would not have been apparent to someone not so qualified? This criterion will, therefore, always be a matter for discussion and subjective appreciation.

Thirdly, in a given situation, information could be acquired casually or deliberately by different persons, and it would seem absurd to rule out the possibility of imposing a duty of disclosure in one case while allowing it in the other. To take the example of the auction at which a painting which may be a masterpiece is to be sold; two people know this—an expert who invested a lot of time and effort to discover this fact and a person who casually overheard the expert talking to his wife. Why should no duty of disclosure be imposed on the expert while a duty should be imposed on the other person?

In reality, in most cases (if not in all of them), the application of the criterion proposed by Kronman will lead to there being no duty of disclosure, even where (eg in the case of the house) it is clearly in the public interest that information should be required to be disclosed.

Although the distinction drawn by Kronman between 'efficient' and 'inefficient' duties of disclosure is usually considered to be the most sophisticated economic approach to this area of the law, other authors have put a different emphasis on what distinguishes useful from damaging duties to inform. Thus, Cooter and Ulen[43] have proposed a different analysis based upon a distinction between productive facts and redistributive facts.[44] For these authors, productive facts include 'information that can be used to increase wealth'[45] and redistributive facts 'information creating a bargaining advantage that can be used to redistribute wealth in favour of the knowledgable party but that does not lead to the creation of new wealth'.[46] Therefore, 'incentives for discovery of productive facts are efficient when the discoverer is compensated at a rate commensurate with the increase in wealth yielded by his discovery' but in contrast, 'efficiency does not require compensating the discoverers of merely redistributive facts'. Their conclusions are thus that: '1. trades on private knowledge of

---

[43] R Cooter and T Ulen, *Law and Economics* (1988). [44] *Ibid.*, p 259.

[45] They illustrate this kind of information by 'the discovery of a vaccine for polio and the discovery of a water-route from Europe to China'.

[46] An example of such information would be the knowledge 'a week in advance of the public where a new highway will be located' which 'provides a powerful advantage in the real estate market'.

mixed facts (productive and redistributive) are enforceable; 2. trades on private knowledge of purely redistributive facts may be set aside'.[47] Finally, Cooter and Ulen identify a third category of facts, destructive facts, by which they mean 'information that, if not disclosed, will cause harm to someone's property or person'.[48] In order to prevent those losses, 'there may be a duty to divulge facts whose non-disclosure is destructive'.[49]

As the authors themselves acknowledge, the main weakness of this analysis lies in the difficulty in distinguishing between productive, redistributive and destructive facts. For example, Eli Whitney's invention of cotton gin in 1792 was enormously productive but also provided a basis to speculate on increases in the value of land suitable for growing cotton.[50] If we take the example of a painting whose buyer discovers that it is worth much more than the price paid: is this information about the authenticity of the painting merely redistributive, because the painting has always been genuine so that no wealth has been discovered, or is it productive because if nobody had known about this authenticity, it is as if the wealth did not exist? The authors solve this difficulty by applying the same rule for mixed facts as for productive facts, ie that they should not be subject to a duty of disclosure. However, it is arguable that in most cases information contains an element of productive facts. Thus this analysis, like Kronman's, almost always results in denying the efficiency of duties of disclosure.

Nevertheless, there is one idea in their analysis which is convincing: that the efficiency of duties of disclosure mainly depends not on the cost of acquisition of information, as in Kronman's analysis, but on the nature or content, of the information to be disclosed.

A different economic analysis of duties of disclosure

The distinction to be drawn according to the nature of the information to be disclosed may be illustrated by one of the most famous recent cases of French contract law, the case of the Poussin painting. In the course of this case, a legal distinction was proposed to limit the circumstances in which a contract could be rescinded on the grounds of mistake.[51] The facts of this case were as follows.

---

[47] *Ibid.*, p 261.

[48] For instance 'failing to disclose the side effects of drugs can harm their users'.

[49] *Ibid.*, p 265.

[50] The conclusion would be the same with their previous example of the discovery of a vaccine.

[51] Among the many decisions rendered in the course of this litigation, the judgment of the Versailles Cour d'appel, of 7 January 1987, which put an end to the case, is certainly the one

M and Mme Saint-Arroman wanted to sell an antique painting which the family had long believed had been painted by Nicholas Poussin. They consulted M Rheims, a well-known auctioneer and art expert, who had the painting examined by M Lebel, an expert specializing in works from the neo-Classical period. The painting was auctioned in 1968. It was described in the catalogue as a work from the school of the Caracci (which was the opinion of the experts), and sold for the modest sum of 2,200 francs. The Réunion des Musées Nationaux, which represents all state museums, exercised its legal right of pre-emption and acquired the painting. Some time later, articles appeared in the press in which it was explained how an important work by Nicholas Poussin had been discovered by a team of young specialists from the Louvre. The painting was then exhibited at the Louvre as *Olympos et Marsyas* by Poussin.

M and Mme Saint-Arroman started an action against the Réunion des Musées Nationaux to have the contract declared void on the grounds of *erreur*. Their argument was that they had been mistaken at the time of the sale as to the essential characteristic of the painting; they had thought it to be a work of the school of the Caracci while it was probably by Poussin; therefore, their consent to the sale was not valid. After legal proceedings which lasted more than 15 years (with two judgments from the Cour de Cassation which quashed the first two decisions from the Cours d'appel they finally succeeded before the third Cour d'appel and recovered their painting. The painting was then auctioned again and fetched a price of 7,400,000 francs.

One of the numerous arguments raised in the course of the litigation was that mistake could only be invoked by a party to avoid a contract when the mistake related to what the other party offered or provided, and not when it related to what he himself offered. In this case, the Saint-Arromans were mistaken not as to the obligations of the Musées Nationaux but as to the characteristics of the painting which they themselves were selling. To use French terminology, they were mistaken as to their own *prestation*.[52] This is not a common situation: usually when a party makes a mistake it relates to what the other party promised,

in which the facts and arguments raised at all stages are best explained. This judgment was extensively reported and commented upon in legal publications and in the general press (D 1987, p 485, commentary by J-L Aubert; Rev trim dr civ, 1987, p 741, commentary by J Mestre: JCP, 1988, II, 21121, commentary by J Ghestin; A Piedelièvre, 'Le dernier état de la jurisprudence du Poussin, Gaz Pal, 1987, 1er sem, doct, p 196; J-P Couturier, 'La résistible ascension du doute (quelques réflexions sur l'affaire Poussin), D 1989, chron p 23; R Lindon 'Post-face au roman judiciaire du Poussin', D 1989, chron p 121).

[52] Under French law, the *prestation* is approximately what a party has an obligation to provide under the contract and which can consist in transferring, doing or abstaining from doing (*dare, facere, non facere*). For a fuller definition, see B Nicholas, *The French Law of Contract* (2nd ed 1992) p 114. The French word *prestation* is used in this chapter since there is no single English term which truly corresponds to this concept.

eg where the buyer of a painting believes it is genuine when it is in fact a fake. Cases where a party is mistaken as to his own *prestation* are much less frequent.

Many arguments have been formulated against allowing the concept of mistake to be invoked when the mistake relates to a party's own *prestation*.[53] One of the most convincing is that a mistake about one's own *prestation* can never be reasonable,[54] which is a prerequisite to having a contract avoided for mistake. If we revert to the example of the seller of an antique painting, the mistaken party, the seller, was in possession of the painting and could examine it as much as necessary. Therefore, he should not be able to complain if he was mistaken. However, these arguments were dismissed by the courts in the Poussin case. It is now an accepted principle of French law that mistake is a ground for having a contract annulled whether the mistake relates to a party's own *prestation* or to that of the other party,[55] although numerous authors disagree with this result.[56]

This distinction, used in the context of the French law of mistake, provides an interesting criterion for distinguishing different types of duties of disclosure. It will be seen that an economic analysis of the duty of disclosure leads to different conclusions depending upon whether the duty to disclose relates to information about a party's own *prestation* or that of the other party.

ECONOMIC ANALYSIS OF DUTIES OF DISCLOSURE RELATED TO THE OTHER PARTY'S *PRESTATION*

Most of the examples used to illustrate the economic analysis of the duty of disclosure, both those devised by academics and those derived from case law, share a common characteristic: they concern information about the obligation—or more precisely about the *prestation*—of the other party. Whether the example chosen concerns the sale of a Stradivarius by an unsuspecting violin dealer,[57] of an art masterpiece by a seller who is

---

[53] It is argued, for example, that such a mistake is only a mistake as to value which, under French law, cannot be invoked to challenge the validity of a contract. A mistaken valuation is a ground for nullity only if it is a consequence of a mistake as to the essential qualities of the *objet* of the contract.

[54] And therefore constitutes, according to French legal terminology, an *erreur inexcusable*.

[55] See B Nicholas, *The French Law of Contract* (2nd ed 1992) p 95.

[56] See, for instance, Ph Malaurie et L Aynes, *Droit civil, Les obligations*, Cujas, 4th ed 1993, no 409, p 223; J Carbonnier, *Droit civil*, t 4, *Les obligations*, PUF, 14th ed 1993, no 48, p 106; H Capitant, *Les grands arrêts de la jurisprudence civile*, 9th ed by F Terre and Y Lequette, Dalloz, 1991, cases no 83–4, p 365 *et seq*; J Chatelain, 'L'objet d'art, objet de droit', in *Etudes offertes à Jacques Flour, Répertoire du Notariat Defrénois*, 1979, p 77 *et seq*, esp p 80.

[57] Quoted by AT Kronman, 'Mistake, Disclosure, Information, and the Law of Contracts' (1978) 7 JLS 1, 29.

unaware of its true value[58] or of a plot of land under which oil may be found,[59] the basic scenario remains the same: because of his superior knowledge, a purchaser manages to acquire an asset at a price far below its true value. The question which is then examined is whether the purchaser should have been subject to a duty to inform the seller about his suspicions.

As regards case law, the decision most often analysed from an economic perspective, *Laidlaw* v *Organ*[60] concerns a similar type of situation. Organ, a New Orleans tobacco merchant, learned on the morning of 19 February 1815 that a peace treaty had been signed between Britain and the United States which put an end to the war of 1812. Before this information became public knowledge, he contracted to buy 111 hogsheads of tobacco from Laidlaw. The peace treaty brought an end to the sea blockade and the price of tobacco quickly rose by between 30 and 50 per cent. Laidlaw considered that the failure to disclose the information was sharp practice and refused to deliver the tobacco. But the United States Supreme Court ruled in favour of the buyer, who was under no duty to disclose his information.[61]

In such cases, it is true that if the buyer is obliged to disclose to the seller the information which leads him to believe that the violin, the painting or the land sold is worth in excess of the proposed price, there is no incentive for the buyer to acquire that information as his efforts in doing so will only benefit the seller.[62] This is ultimately detrimental to society. The logical consequence of imposing a duty of disclosure in these circumstances would be that buyers would be reluctant to buy a painting which they suspected of being a masterpiece. In the real world, the consequence is more likely to be that buyers would try to keep their discovery secret until claims about the validity of the sale contract were barred by limitation. The negative effect of such a duty of disclosure would thus be that masterpieces would stay unknown, and therefore most probably in the wrong hands. Thus, in order to maximize the economic usefulness of a genuine painting, the law should encourage its authenticity to be discovered.

[58] The example used in particular by B Rudden, 'Le juste et l'inefficace pour un non-devoir de renseignements', Rev trim dr civ, p 99 *et seq*, and PS Atiyah, *An Introduction to the Law of Contract* (4th ed 1989) p 269.

[59] The example used by AT Kronman, 'Mistake, Disclosure, Information, and the Law of Contracts' (1978) 7 JLS 1, 20 and by PS Atiyah, *An Introduction to the Law of Contract* (4th ed 1989) p 265.

[60] 15 US (2 Wheat) 178 (1817). This case has been much analysed from an economic perspective. See, for instance, AT Kronman, 'Mistake, Disclosure, Information, and the Law of Contracts' (1978) 7 JLS 1, 9 *et seq*.

[61] Cf. above for the statement of Marshall CJ in this case.

[62] B Rudden, 'Le juste et l'inefficace pour un non-devoir de renseignements', Rev trim dr civ, 1985, no 20, p 101.

Furthermore, to quote Posner, 'resources tend to gravitate toward their most valuable uses if voluntary exchange—a market—is permitted' and '[w]hen resources are being used where their value is highest, we may say that they are being employed efficiently'.[63] It is therefore most efficient, economically speaking, that masterpieces and undervalued Stradivarius violins become the property of persons who can give them proper value.

Another argument against the imposition of a duty of disclosure is that sellers, who would benefit without cost from the discovery made by the buyers, would have no incentive to invest in the search for information. This argument seems less convincing since, in such a case, the seller would depend entirely upon the ability of the buyer to discover the true value of what he bought and upon his honesty in disclosing it.

French judges seem to have acknowledged that their current approach is not beyond criticism. In particular, one of the most unjust consequences of annulling the contract is that the buyer may have spent substantial sums of money in ascertaining the authenticity of the painting—in experts' fees, in scientific tests and in restoration costs. Yet when a contract is annulled, the seller normally recovers the object of the sale, while the buyer only recovers the purchase price. The seller thus benefits at no cost from the efforts of the purchaser.

In order to mitigate this unjust effect, the courts have tried in a recent case[64] (not very efficiently) to correct some of the more blatant inequities associated with an absolute right of rescission. In the case,[65] although the seller was allowed to rescind the contract, damages were awarded to the buyer on the grounds that the seller was unjustly enriched (*enrichissement sans cause*).[66] It is nevertheless obvious that such compensation will never be quite adequate since, under French law, damages granted on the grounds of unjust enrichment amount to the lesser of either the expenses incurred or the gain realized. In the case of the discovery of a masterpiece, damages awarded to the buyer after the contract has been avoided will always amount only to the expenses incurred, and the huge increase in

---

[63] RA Posner, *Economic Analysis of Law* (3rd ed 1986) p 9.

[64] Civ lère 25 mai 1992, Contrats, Concurrence, Consommation, October 1992, no 174, commentary by L Leveneur; Rép Defrénois, 1993, art 35484, p 311, no 13, commentary by J-L Aubert.

[65] This is another case concerning the discovery of a masterpiece. In this instance, the purchaser of a painting which was believed to be a copy of a lost Fragonard established, following a meticulous enquiry, that it was in fact the original.

[66] Unjust enrichment was created by case-law and occurs when a person derives a benefit without consideration from a third party. This remedy was first granted in a decision of the Chambre des Requêtes of the Cour de cassation dated 15 June 1892 (*Boudier v Patureau-Mirand*). Due to his insolvency, the tenant of a farm was unable to pay for the fertilizers he had already used in his fields. The lease was terminated and the owner was made to pay for the fertilizers, since he had derived a benefit from their use without any consideration.

value resulting from the discovery of the authenticity of the painting will still benefit the seller entirely.

There are therefore a number of economic reasons, which are convincing, against imposing a duty of disclosure with respect to the other party's *prestation*. Recent developments of French case law fail not only to provide proper economic incentives, but also to offer a just reward for knowledge and effort. This opinion is limited to cases where duties of disclosure concern the *prestation* to be provided by the other party. Where duties of disclosure concern a party's own *prestation*—in other words the *prestation* of the person subject to that duty—it appears that such duties should often be encouraged because they can be economically efficient.

ECONOMIC ANALYSIS OF DUTIES OF DISCLOSURE RELATED TO PARTY'S OWN PRESTATION

Informing a potential co-contracting party about one's own *prestation* is in fact much more frequent than informing such a party about what he is expected to deliver or perform. For example, it is much more likely that the seller of a painting or of land will inform a potential buyer about its characteristics than *vice versa*. In other words, it is much more frequent for purchasers to be disappointed and to complain that they were not sufficiently informed about what they bought, than for sellers to plead their own mistake and to argue that they were unaware of the value of what they sold.

Yet most of the examples used in order to analyse the economic usefulness of duties of disclosure involve information about the other party's *prestation*. One of the few examples involving a duty of disclosure relating to a party's own *prestation* which has been extensively discussed from an economic perspective[67] comes from a US case, *Obde* v *Schlemeyer*.[68] In that case, the seller, knowing that his house was infested by termites, failed to reveal this fact to the buyer. The question which was raised before the courts was whether the seller was subject to a duty to disclose this information.[69] This example shows that imposing upon the seller a duty to disclose the main characteristics and defects of a house to the buyer will not entail the negative economic consequences described above. In other words, imposing a duty of disclosure in those circumstances will not discourage either the seller or the buyer from searching for information and thereby from giving a proper value for the house.

---

[67] See, for instance, RA Posner, *Economic Analysis of Law* (3rd ed 1986) p 97.

[68] 56 Wash 2d 449, 353 P 2d 672 (1960). This case has been analysed, for instance, by R Cooter and T Ulen, *Law and Economics* (1988) p 264.

[69] The court awarded damages to the buyer because of the seller's failure to disclose the termite infestation.

First, the seller will not be discouraged from looking for information about what he is selling. On the contrary, if he is subject to a duty of disclosure, he will have an incentive to do so, knowing that if he fails to disclose information his breach of duty may be penalized. There is no real risk either that the imposition of a duty of disclosure would discourage the seller from entering into the contract (eg from selling his house) since such a refusal could make the remedy worse than the disease. In the case of the painting, the only advantage of acquiring it was to be able to do so without having to disclose any information, so that any imposition of a duty of disclosure would make the buyer renounce the purchase. But of course the situation is very different here and a seller does not only sell his house because he does not have a duty to disclose any information. In any event, if the seller declines to sell his house because he is prevented from cheating, this was have the socially beneficial consequence that no buyer will be deceived. This reasoning applies in all instances when duties of disclosure are related to a party's own *prestation*. To take another example, imposing upon a prospective policy-holder a duty to disclose all relevant facts concerning the subject matter of the insurance (such as for instance the state of his health, or the state of the car insured) will not discourage him from finding out such information in the future. On the contrary, he has an incentive to find out this information, because he knows that if he fails to disclose it he could lose the benefit of the insurance. This argument assumes that the duty is not mainly to disclose facts actually known, but also to seek information in order to pass it on to the other party. Nevertheless, duties of disclosed related to a party's own *prestation* do not entail the negative economic consequences described by Kronman, and the seller or the insured have no reason to want to reduce their production of such information in the future.

Secondly, the buyer will not be discouraged from looking for information concerning what he is buying. The fact that a seller is subject to a duty of disclosure is not in practice a sufficient reason for the buyer to avoid being careful. The expenses and the time involved in the enforcement of legal rights—not to mention the inherent risks involved in litigation—are such that any reasonable buyer would rather look for information himself as far as practicable. The existence of a duty of disclosure will nevertheless provide some comfort in cases where the buyer could not inform himself.

Thirdly, imposing a duty of disclosure in such circumstances may be economically efficient, since it will reduce the global cost of the search for information. If all buyers have to inform themselves about the defects of houses they want to buy, the practical impact of this obligation will be that each potential buyer will have to invest in the search for information. Thus, each potential buyer will have to carry out a survey of the house to know its state of repair. If, on the contrary, sellers are obliged to disclose key elements concerning the state of their houses to all potential buyers, the cost of surveying the houses will be incurred only once.

Similarly, duties of disclosure ought to be imposed on the party best able to obtain information at the least cost. In the context of a house sale, it will be the seller who, by living in the house, will usually have acquired the relevant information at no extra cost. More generally, in the context of a sale or of a contract of insurance, it will normally be the party who is in possession of the thing to be sold or of the object of the insurance policy who will be in the best position to acquire such information and pass it on to the other party. Thus, duties of disclosure appear to be an economically efficient way of allocating the task of collecting information. It should be noted that this is implicitly taken into account by English law, which includes insurance contracts in the category of contracts entered into *uberrimae fidei*.

It would appear then that, particularly in the context of duties of disclosure relating to a party's own *prestation*, the cost of acquisition criterion becomes to a large extent irrelevant in testing the economic efficiency of these duties. As has been stated above, the efficiency of duties of disclosure is usually appraised by reference to their impact on the generation of 'socially useful information'. However, allowing a party to enter into contracts without having to disclose material facts does not necessarily provide an incentive for socially useful information to be generated. Whether an incentive will exist depends in reality upon the nature of the information.

When a party knows a valuable piece of information concerning the other party's *prestation*, eg he is aware that the painting offered for a modest price is a masterpiece, the most effective way of promoting investments in this kind of socially useful information is to allow the party in possession of it to buy the painting without having to disclose it to the seller. But this reasoning no longer applies when the duty of disclosure relates to one's own *prestation*. To revert to the example of a house sale, it is clear that information about the state of a house for sale is socially useful. It is socially useful to know if houses are infested with termites or if roofs need to be repaired. However, allowing a seller to enter into a contract without disclosing to a buyer that his house is infested with termites will not incite him to invest in the search for such information; the contrary is much more likely. Likewise, imposing upon sellers a duty to disclose this information to buyers will not discourage the latter from seeking to discover such information in the future.

In addition, whether or not information has been deliberately acquired (ie at a certain cost) does not have an impact on this reasoning. Even if expenses have been incurred to produce the information, eg if the seller has had his house surveyed to check the state of the roof, imposing on the seller a duty to disclose all material facts relating to what he is selling will not discourage him from searching for information, because if he wants to sell his house he has to disclose material information. Imposing a duty of disclosure on the seller thus remains the most efficient way of promoting the production of socially useful information. In the circumstances, duties of disclosure relating to a party's own *prestation* clearly appear beneficial from an economic perspective, not to mention the moral issues.

Thus, a distinction must be drawn depending on the kind of information concerned. Information can either increase or diminish the *prestation*, ie approximately the value of the obligation undertaken. For instance, in the case of a sale the law does not need to impose on the seller a duty to disclose information which will increase the value of the thing sold, nor to impose on the buyer a duty to disclose information which will diminish this value: if they are aware of such information, they will be keen to disclose it spontaneously. The only areas where the law may have to interfere is to make the seller disclose information which diminishes the value of what he sells or to make the buyer disclose information which increases this value. The economic analysis proposed leads to the conclusion that only duties of disclosure imposed on the buyer or, more generally, on the person in possession of information which increases the value of what he gets from the contract are inefficient. Therefore nothing, certainly not an economic analysis, prevents imposing a duty of disclosure on a seller and, more generally, on a person in possession of information which diminishes the value of what he provides in the contract. Not only are these duties of disclosure morally very satisfactory in that they prevent people from trying to obtain fraudulently more than they deserve from the contract, but they are economically efficient in that people pay only for what they receive and no more.

This criterion is not too difficult to implement. It is quite easy to determine whether or not information increases the value of what a party offers or receives from a contract. In the example of the cotton gin provided by Cooter and Ulen,[70] a party aware of the discovery could buy land suitable for growing cotton without having to disclose the information because it increased the value of what he got from the contract. Imposing a duty of disclosure in this case would not be efficient because it would discourage people from seeking information. One of the main differences with the analysis proposed by Cooter and Ulen is that information is not in itself 'to be or not to be' disclosed. It depends rather on the kind of advantages it gives to the parties to a contract. It is more important to check the fairness of the bargain and, thus, to analyse the information in the context of the exchange.

[70] R Cooter and T Ulen, *Law and Economics* (1988).

Conclusion

Economic analysis can serve as a helpful tool in making a critical assessment of a legal system's rules relating to duties of disclosure. However, it
is only one tool among many, and it should be noted that one of the main
weaknesses of the economic analysis of law is that the findings will
always depend on the underlying assumptions which have been made.
Thus, duties of disclosure may have negative effects when they are a dis-
incentive to invest in the search for information while, on the other hand,
they sometimes permit a better allocation of resources and a diminution
of the total cost of research for information.

Therefore, the efficient legal solution is certainly not to resist systematically the imposition of duties of disclosure; nor to multiply them 'at any
cost' as if they were a panacea, which French lawyers sometimes seem to
think. European law is helping these two legal traditions to move closer;
and much European legislation is now imposing duties of disclosure
throughout the Community in everyday situations, from the labelling of
products to contracts of employment.[71]

It may be argued that it would not be satisfactory to base the law
entirely upon an economic analysis which is so subjective and diverse. In
matters of duties of disclosure in particular, moral issues should have
much more influence on the legal solutions.

[71] Directive 91/533 EEC of 14 October 1991, defining minimum information to be provided by employers to employees prior to entering into an employment contract.

(b) Consideration

5

Consideration: Practical Benefit and the Emperor's New Clothes*

MINDY CHEN-WISHART

The doctrine of consideration provides the principal criterion of contractual liability in the common law. Redefining the contents of consideration will effect a consequential shift in the boundaries of contractual liability. *Williams v Roffey Brothers and Nicholls (Contractors) Ltd*[1] heralds such a redefinition in the most far reaching manner: This chapter explores the nature and desirability of this redefinition, the reasons motivating it and how these reasons might have been alternatively accommodated in the law.

On its face, the approach in *Roffey* is consistent with the orthodox view that the consideration which grounds contractual liability represents the exchange or bargain element in a contract. Something which counts in law must be given in exchange for a promise to make that promise enforceable as a contract.[2] While there have always been exceptional examples of non bargain enforcement, bargain provides the overwhelming, and commercially, most important explanation of contractual liability. The strength of this orthodoxy is such that bargain consideration has had to be 'invented'[3] where it is lacking to justify enforcement. Moreover, preserving a distinct category for bargain transactions serves two important functions. First, it gives the party seeking to enforce the promise a compelling justification because he or she has given some enforceable agreed exchange for that promise. Secondly, at the remedial end, it provides the basis for determining the extent of liability on the promise. The expectation measure, 'the distinctive feature of a contractual action',[4] gives the promisee the value of the promised performance because 'she has paid the agreed equivalent of that performance.'[5]

These two functions of bargain consideration are seriously undermined

* Copyright © 1994, Mindy Chen-Wishart.
[1] [1991] 1 QB 1 (hereafter *Roffey*).
[2] GH Treitel, *The Law of Contract* (8th ed 1991) p 63.
[3] eg *Hamer* v *Sidway*, 27 NE 256 (1891); *Shadwell* v *Shadwell* (1860) 9 CB (NS) 159, 142 ER 62; *Ward* v *Byham* [1956] 1 WLR 496; and see generally GH Treitel, *The Law of Contract* (8th ed 1991) p 67.
[4] GH Treitel, *The Law of Contract* (8th ed 1991) p 831.
[5] SM Waddams, *The Law of Contracts* (3rd ed 1993) p 17, para 24.

by the incorporation of practical benefit into the definition of consideration effected by *Roffey*. Promises of more for the same are traditionally
regarded as unenforceable, because the promisee logically gives no more
for the reciprocal promise to pay more. A confirmatory promise, therefore, has not 'counted' as valid currency for the purchase of contract
rights. To say now that it *can* count because it confers a 'practical benefit'
on the promisor is a trick no less than that played by the tailor of the
emperor's new clothes. It cannot disguise the fact that practical benefit
neither confers any enforceable benefit additional to that contained in the
original contract, nor buys any enforceable expectation to the reciprocal
promise to pay more. Like the emperor's new clothes, the benefit
described as 'practical' turns out to be a lot less than presented. The words
'illusory' and 'naked' would not be inapt.

Acceptance of practical benefit as consideration, indeed, 'practically
alter[s] the sense of the word'[6] with consequential distortion, dilution and
muddying of what we mean by contractual liability. The reach of this
adjusted view of contract is undoubtedly extended, but its desirability is
highly suspect. However, to deny full contractual effect to practical benefits is not to deny that some enforcement of promises of more for the same
may be desirable for reasons other than bargain. The question is, whether
such reasons for enforcement are best addressed indirectly via a redefined
notion of bargain consideration, or directly via a widened meaning of
'consideration' or some other doctrine which acknowledges such enforcement to be exceptional to the doctrine of consideration.

Practical benefit as consideration

WILLIAMS V ROFFEY

Roffey Brothers contracted to refurbish a block of twenty-seven flats. They
subcontracted the carpentry work to Williams for the sum of £20,000.
Williams finished nine flats but was at risk of non-completion of the rest
due to financial difficulties arising partly from the underprice of the sub-
contract and partly from deficiencies in Williams' supervision of his
workers. Realising this, Roffey Brothers called a meeting at which they
agreed to pay Williams the additional sum of £575 on the timely completion of each of the remaining eighteen flats. Eight further flats were substantially completed, but because Roffey failed to pay the additional sums
promised, Williams discontinued work and brought an action claiming
£10,847. Meanwhile, Roffey engaged other carpenters to complete and
incurred a week's time penalty under the main contract. Roffey denied

---

[6] *Foakes v Beer* (1884) 9 App Cas 605, at 613, per the Earl of Selborne LC.

that the amount claimed by Williams was enforceable since he had given no consideration for it. Roffey counterclaimed for damages of £18,121.46 arising from Williams' non completion. The judge at first instance held in favour of Williams and awarded damages of £3,500. Roffey appealed.

In dismissing the appeal, the Court of Appeal reaffirmed that consideration, in the orthodox bargain sense, is still required but that, in the context of promises of more for the same, consideration includes practical benefits.[7] Glidewell LJ said:[8]

(i) if A has entered into a contract with B to do work for, or to supply goods or services to, B in return for payment by B; and (ii) at some stage before A has completely performed his obligations under the contract B has reason to doubt whether A will, or will be able to, complete his side of the bargain; and (iii) B thereupon promises A an additional payment in return for A's promise to perform his contractual obligations on time; and (iv) as a result of giving his promise, B obtains in practice a benefit, or obviates a disbenefit; and (v) B's promise is not given as a result of economic duress or fraud on the part of A; then (vi) the benefit to B is capable of being consideration for B's promise, so that the promise will be legally binding.

The court found practical benefits to Roffey in:[9]

(1) Williams' continued performance;
(2) avoiding the trouble and expense of obtaining a substitute;
(3) avoiding the penalty payment for untimely performance under the main contract; and
(4) the institution of a systematized scheme for payment of the additional amount which occasioned a more orderly performance by Williams, allowing Roffey to direct their other subcontractors more efficiently towards timely completion of the main contract.

Hitherto, none of these would have counted as valuable consideration for the additional promise. The first two benefits are the very ones due to Roffey in the existing contract and the third is directly consequential on them. As for the fourth, in the absence of an undertaking to perform sequentially, it is hard to see how Williams' mere acceptance of the mode of payment of the additional sum can constitute consideration for that sum.

Despite strenuous insistence to the contrary,[10] *Roffey* clearly overturns the pre-existing duty rule for which *Stilk* v *Myrick*[11] is authority. Consideration there still must be, but it need not comprise something additional to the obligations owed under the existing contract. Nor is

---

[7] [1991] 1 QB1, at 16, 19, 22, described as benefits (or the avoidance of disbenefits) 'resulting' or 'accruing' from the promised performance assessed 'practically' or 'pragmatically'.
[8] *Ibid.*, at 15–16.   [9] *Ibid.*, at 11, 19, 20, 21.   [10] *Ibid.*, at 16, 18–19, 20.
[11] (1809) 2 Camp 317, 6 Esp 129; 170 ER 851 and 1168.

additional detriment to the promisee necessary.[12] Practical benefit moving from the promisee is enough. Thus, Roffey's promise to pay the additional sums was enforceable in contract. Roffey's failure to make due payment on the finished flats constituted a breach[13] which entitled Williams to terminate performance before completion and claim damages.[14]

THE MEANING OF PRACTICAL BENEFIT

To assess the nature of the enlargement of contractual liability effected by practical benefit, we need to define the limits of this term. What precise advantages conferred are regarded as practical benefit? Two meanings are consistent with *Roffey*. First, it is the advantage of obtaining actual (or an increased chance of) contractual performance already due to the promisor over the right to seek legal redress for non-performance. Secondly, it is the chance of obtaining additional benefits (or of avoiding disbenefits[15]) from the promisee's already due performance other than that expressly stipulated in the original contract.

Increased chance of performance already due

The first two practical benefits accepted by the Court of Appeal fall in this category. Williams' continued performance and Roffey's not having to find a substitute are irreducibly the benefits to which Roffey is entitled under the existing contract. A number of formulations have been suggested for this category. Professor Treitel equates it with 'factual benefit'.[16] Thus, so long as an original promise (consideration) conferred factual benefit on the promisor, so will the repromise.[17] Logically, practical or factual detriment to the promisee must follow. This formulation necessitates a distinction between *factual* benefit (invoking the idea of something conferring objective benefit and actually sought by the

---

[12] *Roffey* [1991] 1 QB 1, at 16.

[13] It does not appear that Roffey breached the original contract.

[14] *Roffey* [1991] 1 QB 1, at 7.   [15] *Ibid.*, at 16.

[16] GH Treitel, *The Law of Contract* (8th ed 1991) pp 65, 88 and 90. *Roffey* is seen as sanctioning, in the context of a confirmatory promise, the sufficiency of 'factual benefit to the promisor ... even in the absence of a legal benefit to him or of a legal detriment to the promisee', bringing the two party cases into line with the three party cases.

[17] B Coote, 'Consideration and Benefit in Fact and in Law' (1990–91) 3 JCL 23, 25. Practical benefit will exist so long as 'actual performance would provide more benefits to the promisor than would non-performance (or, for that matter, fewer harms than would breach). It would be absent only where the promisor had stood to obtain no advantage under the existing contract when first made, or where the change of circumstances meant that all chances of the promisor's obtaining an advantage from performance had been lost. In the latter cases no rational party is likely to offer further payment for the completion.'

promisor as the bargain equivalent of his or her own reciprocal promise)[18] and *legal* benefit (something not previously owed but which may confer only nominal or trivial benefit to the promisor or may be 'invented'). This distinction involves an open inquiry into factors hitherto said to be non-justiciable or non-dispositive (the adequacy of consideration and a party's motives) in determining prima facie contractual liability.[19] The formulation entails the further corollary that contracts involving factual value can be modified at will while those involving only legal value cannot be modified unless supported by further legal value. Further explanation is required.

It has been suggested that the benefit conferred by Williams' repromise is the comfort Roffey could derive 'from their own perception of a greater chance of completion of the project on time'.[20] But this is no more than sentimental value and, despite some questionable decisions,[21] rightly repudiated as valid consideration.[22] To regard them now as practical benefit collapses the doctrine of consideration from within. All promises, whether to perform an existing duty, to be loving, good or not complain, confer reassurance on the promisee (unless known not to be intended seriously). Indeed one can even be said to derive reassurance and satisfaction from one's own altruistic promises without receiving any reciprocal promise. Benefit is confused with motive, and consideration becomes meaningless as a criterion of enforceability. There is always a motive unless the promisor acts entirely irrationally.

A promisor of additional payment is not intending to buy the same promise of reciprocal performance twice. He or she agrees does so to in the hope of obtaining either actual performance, or a better chance of actual performance. This is what each member of the Court in *Roffey* fastened upon.[23] While the first formulation has the support of Professor Treitel[24] and the New Zealand High Court,[25] Professor Coote points out that consideration 'is required for the formation of a contract. Performance, ex hypothesi, comes too late to qualify'.[26] The second

---

[18] C Dalton, 'An Essay in the Deconstruction of Contract Doctrine' (1985) 94 Yale LJ 997, 1066–73.

[19] GH Treitel, *The Law of Contract* (9th ed 1991) pp 68, 70–2, 79–81.

[20] R Hooley, 'Consideration and the Existing Duty' [1991] JBL 19, 28.

[21] For examples see note 3, above.

[22] *White v Bluett* (1853) 23 LJ Ex 36; *Thomas v Thomas* (1842) 2 QB 851.

[23] B Coote, 'Consideration and Benefit in Fact and in Law' (1990–91) 3 JCL 23, 26.

[24] GH Treitel, *The Law of Contract* (8th ed 1991) p 90, a party's 'actual performance of his earlier contract . . . will normally suffice to constitute consideration'.

[25] *Newman Tours Ltd v Ranier Investments Ltd* [1992] 2 NZLR 68, at 80. In applying *Roffey*, Fisher J said that 'the agreement to perform [its] existing contractual obligations, followed by actual performance in reliance upon that subsequent agreement, can constitute fresh consideration.'

[26] B Coote, 'Consideration and Benefit in Fact and in Law' (1990–91) 3 JCL 23, 26. This objection may be overcome by a unilateral contract analysis, but more of this later.

formulation (an objectively better chance of performance of the existing contract) is more apt. Consistently, Glidewell LJ's test of consideration requires the promisor to have 'reason to doubt whether A [the promisee] will, or will be able to, complete his side of the bargain'.[27] If so, it is a benefit to the promisor to secure an objectively better chance of completion by promising an additional payment, than to resort to what may be unsatisfactory or incomplete remedies. The practical benefit of performance over the right to sue is assumed. There appears to be no need to show that damages would in fact be inadequate to compensate the promisor.

The court abandons the language of existing rights and obligations. Consideration to support the promise to pay more need not be additional to that baseline of benefits already owed under the existing contract. It need only be additional to the baseline of losses consequential on a real likelihood of breach of that existing contract. As Purchas LJ recognized, it amounts to saying 'that a contracting party can rely upon his own breach to establish consideration'.[28]

Practical benefit as the 'objectively better chance of performance' is the least problematical formulation. It is determinable at contract formation, is more than motive or sentiment and does not require a distinction between factual and legal benefit. However, in common with other formulations, it is morally neutral about the reasons for the promisee's likely non-performance and shifts the burden of assessing the merits of these reasons under some other legal rubric such as duress or hidden behind a functional definition of consideration. More problematically, however formulated, we are still essentially talking about the *same* performance to which the promisor is already entitled under the original contract. The practical benefit consists only of the promisor's hope that he or she will be put in as good a position as if the *original contract had been performed*. In the words of Professor Coote, this

provides nothing that is not already the promisor's right. It could constitute fresh consideration only if the law were to recognise some break in that link between a contract and its performance which is inherent in the concept of enforceable legal obligation.[29]

Such a break makes a contract no more than a point for further negotiation.[30] This is no small problem of academic logic. Acceptance that an increased chance of performance of a contract is consideration for its variation reflects a disrespect for the very idea of contract as creating binding obligations.

It could be argued, of course, that contract law itself does not have an

---

[27] *Roffey* [1991] 1 QB 1, at 15.   [28] *Ibid.*, 23B.

[29] B Coote, 'Consideration and Benefit in Fact and in Law' (1990–91) 3 JCL 23, 28.

[30] P Birks, 'The Travails of Duress' [1990] LMCLQ 342, 346.

adequately high view of contractual obligations.[31] A number of doctrines and rules are said to weaken the commitment of the law to the protection of the expectation interest.[32] Damages given on breach are often inadequate to compensate even the ordinary losses of breach, while the nonpecuniary costs of seeking legal redress, typically delay, hassle, time and effort are not normally susceptible to compensation at all. This inadequacy of remedies provides the occasion for the parties to seek and agree to modifications of the more-for-the-same or the same-for-less variety. It lies at the heart of arguments that such modifications are commercially necessary, realistic and in the parties' own best interests. It is also central to concerns about opportunistic renegotiations discussed under the rubric of economic duress.[33]

Holmes[34] supports the separation of the promise to perform from performance itself since, in his view, a contract party has an option to perform or to pay damages for not performing. Thus it was said in *Roffey* that it was 'open to the plaintiff to be in deliberate breach of the contract in order to "cut his losses" commercially.'[35] Nevertheless, inadequacy of remedy is not peculiar to contract law and the rights and liabilities created in its exploitation should not be accorded the same recognition as that created by an exchange.[36] The chance to avoid the inadequacies of contract redress ought not be recognized as valid currency for the purchase of additional contract rights.

Practical benefit as chance of consequential benefit

Practical benefit is used in *Roffey* in a second sense, to designate the chance of obtaining benefits additional to that expressly stipulated in the existing contract. Purchas LJ emphasized the need for 'some *other* consideration

---

[31] See, eg, PS Atiyah, *Essays on Contract* (1986) pp 29–30, 124–5.

[32] The exceptional nature of the remedy of specific performance, the limits relating to causation, remoteness, mitigation and the disregard for subjective losses, sentimental uniqueness or the consumer surplus.

[33] *Roffey* [1991] 1 QB 1, at 13 the promisee may be guilty of securing the promise 'by taking unfair advantage of the difficulties he will cause if he does not complete the work'.

[34] *The Common Law* (1881) p 298. See PS Atiyah, 'Holmes and the Theory of Contract' in his *Essays on Contract* (1986) pp 59 *et seq*, describing it as a 'brilliant but wholly unsound paradox'. It is inconsistent with established rules of law such as anticipatory breach and the tort of inducing breach of contract and with the remedy of specific performance; it obscures the distinction between damages as part of the remedial response to non-performance and as part of a promise in the alternative; it is unrealistic and artificial to say that a contract party is merely betting on performance rather than buying the performance itself.

[35] [1991] 1 QB 1, at 23.

[36] See further S Williston, 'Successive Promises of the Same Performance' (1894–95) 8 Harvard LRev 27, 30–1.

... to support the agreement to pay the extra sum'.[37] The third and fourth practical benefits accepted in *Roffey* (avoiding the time penalty under the main contract and obtaining the chance of a more orderly mode of performance) fall into this category. *Anangel Atlas Compania Naviera SA* v *Ishikawajima-Harima Heavy Industries Co Ltd (No 2)*[38] provides a further illustration of this type of practical benefit. There, the defendant ship builder was faced with a serious slump in the shipping industry. Many buyers were threatening cancellation, seeking delays in delivery and price reductions. In response, the defendant promised various concessions, inter alia, to the plaintiffs if they would accept the timely delivery of a hull as they were already contractually bound to do. Applying *Roffey*, Hirst J held that the concessions were supported by practical benefit as it was 'conclusively demonstrated' that the defendants' main objective 'was to make sure that the plaintiffs, who they described as their "core" customers, did indeed take delivery ... in order to encourage their other reluctant customers to follow suit.'[39] That is, practical benefit consisted of the *chance that other buyers would follow the promisee's example of due acceptance and be deterred from breach*. These are presented as benefits (or avoidance of disbenefits) 'resulting' or 'accruing' from the promised performance assessed on a 'practical' or 'pragmatic' approach.[40] They are spin-off advantages, not guaranteed or assured by the promisee but, desired and hoped for by the promisor. Their potentially all-encompassing nature threatens to destroy the traditional boundaries of contractual liability. How far can it go?

Practical benefit obviously includes avoiding liability to a third party for breach of contract, the fulfilment of which relies on the promisee's performance of *its* contract with the promisor, as in *Roffey*. It would also logically include the avoidance of other consequences of such a breach, such as damage to the promisor's reputation, loss of a valuable commercial relationship with that third party, and consequential threat to the financial viability of the promisor's business. A case like *Atlas Express Ltd* v *Kafco (Importers and Distributors) Ltd*[41] may now be reversed on the issue of consideration. Additionally, 'practical benefit' includes the hope of obtaining a performance which will set an example for others to follow. Would it also include the good will of or favourable future dealings with the promisee, or the enhancement of the promisor's reputation in the industry which will translate into some commercial gain in the future? Would *Gilbert Steel Ltd* v

---

[37] *Roffey* [1991] 1 QB 1, at 21 (emphasis added). Glidewell LJ, at 12–13 purported to follow the majority in *Ward* v *Byham* [1956] 1 WLR 496, who found additional consideration albeit on rather questionable facts.
[38] [1990] 2 Lloyd's Rep 526 (hereafter [1956] 1 WLR 496, *Anangel*).
[39] *Ibid.*, at 544.   [40] *Roffey* [1991] 1 QB 1, at 16, 19, 22.   [41] [1989] QB 833.

University Construction Ltd[42] also now be decided differently on consideration?

But if practical benefit includes the chance, as opposed to the assurance, of obtaining a specified benefit, how small must the chance be before it ceases to count as consideration? If any hope of benefit by the promisor, however speculative, vague or tangential, is to count, consideration amounts to little more than a requirement of motive for a promise. Moreover, the requirement that consideration 'move from the promisee'[43] is stretched to breaking point where the hoped for practical benefit, if it eventuates at all, must come from parties other than the promisee, as in *Anangel*.

Three limits may be implied to the definition of practical benefit. First, the courts can require very clear evidence of the promisor's *intention* to bargain for the practical benefit. Secondly, courts may take into account the objective likelihood of benefit eventuating. Where there is no actual or reasonable belief in the risk of non-completion by the promisee, or the objectively assessed chance of obtaining actual performance or other 'additional' benefits is too remote, the court may question the existence of the relevant promisor intention. Consistently *Roffey* emphasizes the importance of giving effect to the intention of the parties in finding consideration.[44] In both *Roffey* and *Anangel*[45] the promisors clearly spelt out the practical benefits which they subjectively hoped to obtain. There was also much evidence of the chance of objective benefit which the promisors stood to gain in the particular circumstances of the cases.[46] Such evidence is treated as corroborative of the promisor's intention. The use of objective value as evidence of intention to bargain is evident elsewhere,[47] but to discount clear

---

[42] (1973) 36 DLR (3d) 496, affirmed (1976) 67 DLR (3d) 606, in which the promisee agreed to give the promisor 'a good price' on the steel for the second building. The judge remarked at 504 that factually this 'might have been more than adequate compensation for an increase in the cost of the first building'.

[43] *Roffey* [1991] 1 QB 1, at 16, Glidewell LJ interprets this to mean that it must be 'provided by the promisee, or arise out of his contractual relationship with the promisor'.

[44] *Ibid.*, at 18.

[45] *Ibid.* at 11; *Anangel* [1990] 2 Lloyd's Rep 526, at 544.

[46] *Roffey* [1991] 1 QB 1, at 19 per Russell LJ; 20, 23 per Purchas LJ ('there were clearly incentives to both parties to make a further arrangement'; and 'As a result of the agreement the defendants secured their position commercially'); *Anangel* [1990] 2 Lloyd's Rep 526, at 528, 544–5.

[47] The consideration-conditional gift distinction is said to depend on whether 'a reasonable man would or would not understand that the performance of the condition was requested as the price or exchange for the promise'; Williston on Contracts (3rd ed 1961) s 112. C Dalton, 'An Essay in the Deconstruction of Contract Doctrine' (1985) 94 Yale LJ 997, 1068, notes that the commitment of contract law to objective intentions and subjective values means that reliance on subjective intention in the realm of consideration is 'frequently "objectivised" by derivation from notions of objective value.' Objective value appears 'often by reference to the intention of the parties.' This raises the same problems as the attempt to distinguish between factual and legal value.

evidence of subjective intention because of an absence or inadequacy of objective value would require independent justification.

Thirdly, a substantive limit can be imposed by excluding benefits of a purely sentimental nature or requiring that the benefit be of a commercial nature or conferred in a commercial context. Both *Roffey* and *Anangel* involved commercial transactions and certainly the judges in the former emphasized the need for a more flexible notion of consideration in this context.[48] Such a pragmatic limit would meet calls for reform of the pre-existing duty rule based on reasonable commercial expectations or necessity. But precisely what is it about the commercial context that is being responded to? Is it the promotion of economic efficiency, the protection of a promisee's reasonable reliance, or the recognition of the promisor's serious intention to be bound, which are commonly considered desirable in a commercial context? If so should they not be responded to directly, rather than mediated through the doctrine of consideration and the notion of commercial context? Anyway, how is a 'commercial context' to be identified away from the core? How and why should non-commercial modifications be dealt with differently ?

Uncertainty in defining practical benefit and so consideration has serious implications in the uncertain enlargement of contractual liability. Rules of contract 'should not make contracting so easy that it hooks the unwary signer or the casual promisor.'[49] It should protect parties' freedom to contract as well as freedom from contract. The impact of a consistently applied notion of practical benefit to other questions of contract enforcement are discussed in below. Before that, the precise legal consequences triggered by a transfer of practical benefits are examined.

THE LEGAL EFFECT OF PRACTICAL BENEFIT

Rights conferred by practical benefit

The exchange of consideration in a contract traditionally provides the basis for the assessment of each party's expectation at the remedial stage.[50] If consideration is to be found not in what was promised but in a party's hopes of benefits, then it is unclear what the appropriate

---

[48] *Roffey* [1991] 1 QB 1, at 21. Russell LJ, at 18, emphasizes the intention of the parties where the bargaining powers are not unequal and commercial transactions are commonly assumed to be such cases; and Glidewell LJ, at 15, relies on *Pao On v Lau Yiu Long* [1980] AC 614, at 634–5 in which Lord Scarman noted the undesirability of interference in the absence of duress 'where businessmen are negotiating at arm's length'. However, he also relies on cases within a family context.

[49] EW Patterson, 'An Apology for Consideration' (1958) 58 Colum LR 929, 948.

[50] GH Treitel, *The Law of Contract* (8th ed 1991) p 831.

measure is. These benefits have by definition not been promised. To what extent can their expectation be protected?

If the promisee (of the additional payment) performs the existing contract there can be no remedy if the promisor's hopes of consequential benefits fail to eventuate. The promisor has got the chance bargained for. Thus, practical benefit in the second sense cannot be independently enforced. If the promisee ultimately fails to perform, the promisor's expectation of practical benefits, whether in the first or second sense (performance and the chance of consequential benefits), are either already protected by the original contract[51] or, if not, derive no more protection from having been purchased twice.

Consequential losses on breach (eg loss of profits or time penalties[52]) are compensable within the rules of remoteness and causation.[53] Where the loss is too remote and so uncompensable the promisor's position is not improved by paying more for it.[54] Where the promisor has lost the chance of some consequential gain, damages may be awarded in proportion to the chance of loss,[55] unless the chance was purely speculative. It is doubtful whether loss of benefits such as the hope of favourable future contracts or, as in *Anangel*, the hope that other buyers would follow suite and perform their contracts with the promisor are within the remoteness rules. The compensability or quantifiability of such practical benefits is not increased by the payment of an additional sum. Halson's suggestion,[56] that the scope of practical benefit should be confined to avoiding uncompensable losses on the promisee's breach, thus takes us no further in remedial terms. Practical benefits, comprising of chance rather than assurance, confer benefits of an illusory and unenforceable kind.

Rights bought by practical benefits

Going the other way, what enforceable right does practical benefit buy? Not, it appears from *Roffey*, an expectation to the reciprocal promise of the additional sum. It is often overlooked that it was Roffey Brothers who were in breach by failing to make due payment and that

---

[51] *Ibid.*, 831: 'A contract may give rise to two quite separate expectations: that of receiving the promised performance and that of being able to put it to some particular use.'

[52] Roffey could have claimed these if Williams had breached.

[53] *Hadley* v *Baxendale* (1854) 9 Ex 341, at 354; 156 ER 145, at 151.

[54] Unless the promisee expressly accepts that additional risk of loss which would constitute legal consideration.

[55] *Chaplin* v *Hicks* [1911] 2 KB 786. See generally M. Bridge, ch 17 below; AS Burrows, *Remedies for Torts and Breach of Contract* (2nd ed 1994) pp 33–4; GH Treitel, *The Law of Contract* (8th ed 1991) p 845. The quantification 'depends on the value of the expected benefit and the likelihood of the plaintiff's actually getting it.'

[56] See R Halson, 'Sailors, Sub-Contractors and Consideration' (1990) 106 LQR 183, 184.

this entitled Williams to terminate his performance before completion. On a contract action, Williams should prima facie be entitled to the full expectation on the additional promise.[57] This was not what the court awarded.[58] Williams' total expectation can be calculated as:[59] £20,000 (original promise) + £10,300 (additional promise) − £17,700 (benefit received) − £x (cost avoided by not having to complete) − £y (deductions for defective performance on the flats substantially completed) = £12,600 − £x − y (as the potential claimable sum). Williams claimed £10,847.

The court awarded only £3,500. The figure is based on the extent of Williams' performance at the point of Roffey's breach calculated as:[60] £4,600 (actual performance on eight flats at £575 each) + £z (a reasonable proportion of the unpaid original sum of £2,300) − £y (deductions for defective performance) − £1,500 (the sum already paid). While it may be possible to maintain an expectation calculation by virtue of a bad bargain for Williams resulting in a high £x, such a scenario was never suggested by the court. Indeed this is unlikely given the contract was originally underpriced by £3,783, but topped up by an enforceable promise of £10,847.

The award to Williams appears to be reliance- and not expectation-based. On an orthodox contractual analysis, the real question on the facts of *Roffey* is not 'why was the plaintiff's claim treated so generously?'[61] posed by Adams and Brownsword, but 'why so mean?' The suggestion must be that practical benefits impose a less than expectation liability on the promisor, and confer a less than expectation right on the promisee. To describe such rights and liabilities as contractual seriously compromises contract as an action which enforces expectations.

That is not to suggest that expectation is the appropriate measure. Indeed, it is particularly inappropriate where the promisees, through breach, eventually fail to perform their existing obligations, despite being promised greater payment. A contractual analysis would treat that greater sum as cost avoided or saved by the promisors and deduced from their damages. Thus, promisors faced with breach would find that while they have obtained no more enforceable rights

---

[57] To put the plaintiff 'so far as money can do it . . . in the same situation . . . as if the contract had been performed' *Robinson* v *Harman* (1848) 1 Ex 850, at 855, 154 ER 363, at 365; and see generally GH Treitel, *The Law of Contract* (8th ed 1991) pp 830–1.

[58] *Roffey* [1991] 1 QB 1, at 7.

[59] See AS Burrows, *Remedies for Torts and Breach of Contract* (2nd ed 1994) p 141 for the general formulae in assessing pecuniary loss.

[60] *Roffey* [1991] 1 QB 1, at 7.

[61] J Adams and R Brownsword, 'Contracts, Consideration and the Critical Path' (1990) 53 MLR 536, 538. The assumption here seems to be that the non-completion was due to the promisee's default. They refer, at note 11, to the 'promise of additional payment having failed to keep the plaintiff working.'

than were already due, their own promises to pay more *are* enforceable to reduce the quantum of their damages and make them worse off than if no additional promise had been made. The intuitive unfairness and inappropriateness of contract analysis to this situation is recognized by the Ontario Law Reform Commission. In such an instance, the appropriate deduction is the original sum promised, and not the greater sum of the variation, because 'it would be an implicit understanding between the parties that failure to comply with the terms of the new agreement would revive the old one.'[62] The promisor's liability on the additional promise is therefore conditional on the other's performance thus implicitly revocable without performance. This is inconsistent with a view of the additional promise as a contractual obligation supported by consideration.

The rights and liabilities created by the exchange of a promise to pay more for a practical benefit do not, and should not, have full effect as a contractual exchange. To treat practical benefit as consideration is no minor adjustment in the definition of consideration. The suggestion that valid consideration may now be unenforceable, may be previously owed, and may not support an expectation to the reciprocal promise represents a serious challenge to contract fundamentals and has far reaching implications for other questions of contractual enforceability.

PRACTICAL BENEFIT AND OTHER QUESTIONS OF ENFORCEMENT

Promises to relieve: part performance and promissory estoppel

The Court of Appeal has already had to contend with the argument that practical benefits, which support the enforcement of promises of more for the same, must also logically support the enforcement of promises of the same for less.[63] Practical benefit in the latter case consists of obtaining part of the benefit already contractually owed by the other party, rather than insisting on the whole and getting even less or none at all while incurring delay, effort, and expense.[64] Practical ben-

---

[62] Ontario Law Reform Commission, Report on Amendment of the Law of Contract (1987) p 13, discussing the promise to accept part performance.

[63] *Re Selectmove Ltd, The Times* 13 January 1994. See, in support of this extension, GH Treitel, *The Law of Contract* (8th ed 1991) p 116 and J Adams and R Brownsword, 'Contracts, Consideration and the Critical Path' (1990) 53 MLR 536, 540.

[64] *Foakes v Beer* (1884) 9 App Cas 605, at 622, Lord Blackburn ('all men of business . . . do every day recognize and act on the ground that prompt payment of a part of their demand may be more beneficial to them than it would be to insist on their rights and enforce payment of the whole'); *Robichaud v Caisse Populaire de Pokemouche Ltée* (1990) 69 DLR (4th) 589, at 595, Angers JA ('The consideration . . . was the immediate receipt of payment and the saving of time, effort and expense').

efit may also consist of avoiding losses consequential on breach (such as inability to trade or survive economically[65]) or obtaining the chance of other benefits (such as enhanced reputation for fair dealing and good will which may translate into future dealings with the promisee or others).

In *Re Selectmove Ltd*,[66] the plaintiff company challenged an order for its compulsory winding up on the petition of the Revenue to which the company owed arrears in taxes. The company argued that the debt had not become due, because the Revenue had agreed to an enforceable deferral in payment. The company had given practical benefit in the increased likelihood of the Revenue 'recover[ing] more from not enforcing its debt against the company which was known to be in financial difficulties, than from putting the company into liquidation'. Peter Gibson LJ saw the force of the analogy with *Roffey*. He recognized that any creditor who accommodates a debtor at arm's length 'will no doubt always see a practical benefit to himself in doing so.' However, since this was expressly rejected as consideration in *Foakes v Beer*[67] and *Foakes v Beer* was not even referred to in *Roffey*,[68] he declined to make the extension since it would leave that well established principle without any application. Any extension, he felt, should be made by the House of Lords, 'or more appropriately, by Parliament after consideration by the Law Commission.'

Quite apart from precedent, which did not deter the court in *Roffey*, other reasons caution against the extension. The present rule of unenforceability is mitigated by a functional (if inconsistent) approach to its exceptions[69] and by resort to the rules relating to waivers and promissory estoppel. These exceptions and doctrines allow the courts some flexibility in assessing a broad range of circumstances in determining appropriate enforcement. This flexibility would be lost if practical benefit could support the blanket enforcement of relieving promises. Unlike promissory estoppel, promises supported by consideration are enforceable without reliance, are unrevocable and unaffected by equitable considerations (such as the conduct of the parties and changes of circumstances) short of duress or other established defences.

Like the promise to pay more, the promise to accept less should be

---

[65] eg *D & C Builders Ltd v Rees* [1966] 2 QB 617.

[66] *The Times* 13 January 1994. The quotations in the text are taken from the transcript.

[67] (1884) 9 App Cas 605.

[68] [1991] 1 QB 1. The ratios are directed at promises of more for the same. See Glidewell LJ at 15–16, Russell LJ at 19, and Purchas LJ at 21.

[69] For example, rescission followed by a new contract, accord and satisfaction, compromise, new (legal or invented) consideration. See BJ Reiter, 'Courts, Consideration and Common Sense' (1977) 27 UTLJ 439 and R Halson, 'The Modification of Contractual Obligations' [1991] CLP 111.

regarded as conditional on the promisee's actual part performance and revocable without it. For, if the promisee does not render even the less performance it is surely unfair to allow damages to the promisor to be reduced to this lesser performance. The Ontario Law Reform Commission recommends that promises to accept part performance in satisfaction of the whole be binding 'subject to actual performance'.[70] It is implicit in the promise to relieve that if the promisee fails to honour the new arrangement the promisor should be able to enforce the rights under the original contract. A consideration analysis cannot directly address this concern but a different approach can, as *Re Selectmove* shows. There, Peter Gibson LJ held that even if the Revenue had agreed to the part performance raising promissory estoppel, 'it was not inequitable or unfair' to go back on that agreement 'because the company failed to honour its [lesser] promise'.

Illusory consideration, bad faith forbearance and firm offers

Practical benefit can be extended to contract formation. Currently where B gives A a real promise in exchange for A's promise of no value (which B is duped into believing has real value),[71] A's promise imports illusory consideration and B's promise is unenforceable. If A's promise is now accepted as importing practical benefit of a broad, subjective kind then B's promise is enforceable subject only to the defence of unconscionability.

Promises conferring factual but not legal value may now also be enforceable by virtue of practical benefit. Forbearance to enforce a bad faith claim can no longer be assumed to import no consideration. In *Pitt v PHH Asset Management Ltd*[72] the plaintiff successfully made out an enforceable obligation by the defendant to sell property at a set price. The consideration for this included the plaintiff withdrawing the threat of an injunction which had no chance of succeeding and refraining from making trouble for the defendant by telling a third party that he was withdrawing from the contest for the property so that the third party would reduce her offer. To accept the avoidance of such bad faith nuisance as importing consideration encourages opportunistic behaviour and circumvents the policy against abuse of the judicial process.

---

[70] Report on Amendment of the Law of Contract (1987) p 10. At pp 12–13 the Commission explains that the promisor 'has agreed to accept less on the ground that "a bird in the hand is worth two in the bush". It would be unfair, in such a case, to limit the rights absolutely to the single bird of the subsequent agreement'.

[71] See MA Eisenberg, 'The Principles of Consideration' (1982) 67 Cornell LR 640, 651.

[72] [1994] 1 WLR 327, see p 11 above.

Where B promises A a firm offer (to keep an offer open for a period of time) or some other performance in exchange for A's promise to perform at A's discretion, the traditional position has been that A's promise is illusory, and B's promise is unenforceable. This is now open to challenge. In English law[73] A's actual performance of the terms of the agreement may import consideration, even though A was not legally bound to do it. On this unilateral contract analysis, B can revoke before acceptance by A of the firm offer or so long as the agreement is executory, ie not performed by A. It is now arguable that 'performance' is rendered by the conferral of practical benefit, and practical benefit can connote giving B a chance of a benefit, including the benefit of a contract with A.[74] In that case, B is bound immediately on making the promise.

The line between practical benefit to the promisor and the promisor's commercial motive would be indistinguishable. This result is in line with calls for some enforcement of firm offers[75] based on the reasonable expectations and needs of the business community, the promisor's commercial motive,[76] and the induced reliance of the promisee in deliberating on the offer, not seeking alternatives, or in submitting its own tender.[77] However, full enforcement of B's promise may be neither fair[78] nor necessary. Enforcement as justice requires to protect A's induced reliance is generally thought to be enough.[79] This result is incompatible with enforcement based on the presence of consideration. A different approach is warranted.

[73] *Cambridge Nutrition Ltd* v *BBC* [1990] 3 All ER 523, at 538, noted by GH Treitel, *The Law of Contract* (8th ed 1991) p 81.

[74] MA Eisenberg, 'The Principles of Consideration' (1982) 67 Cornell LRev 640, 649, 653, proposes an analysis in terms of 'a promise for an act-the act of giving the promisor a chance.' But he favours enforcement here not on the basis of consideration but because 'the law should enforce promises that facilitate or augment the likelihood of exchange.'

[75] See eg, Ontario Law Reform Commission, Report on Amendment of the Law of Contract (1987) pp 20–5; JP Dawson, *Gifts and Promises: Continental and American Law Compared* (1980) pp 211–21; The Law Revision Committee, *Sixth Interim Report* (Statute of Frauds and the Doctrine of Consideration) (1937), Cmd 5449, Para 50(6); Firm Offers (1975) Law Com Working Paper No 60.

[76] JP Dawson, *Gifts and Promises: Continental and American Law Compared* (1980) p 215 'no one surely would suggest that such transactions should fail because they are conceived on either side as promises of gift. The purpose clearly is to effect an exchange that both parties desire.' And see MA Eisenberg, 'The Principles of Consideration' (1982) 67 Cornell LRev 640, 649–50, the promise by restricting the promisor's freedom, conveys information about the attractiveness of the promisor's offer and alters the promisee's incentives.

[77] *Ibid.*, p 653: 'In deciding whether to accept an offer, an offeree must make an investment of time, trouble, and even money. The offeree is more likely to make such an investment if he is sure the offer will be open while the investment is being made than if the offer may be revoked during that period.'

[78] It would bind the offeror while the offeree remains free to continue bid shopping.

[79] MA Eisenberg, 'The Principles of Consideration' (1982) 67 Cornell LRev 640, 652.

Gratuitous promises

Despite strenuous insistence in *Roffey* that gratuitous promises not under seal are unenforceable,[80] the reality of this position will depend on how rigorously the courts are prepared to limit the notion of practical benefit. If it is accepted that practical benefit includes avoiding the expense, time, delay and hassle of suing or finding a substitute (in the context of contract modifications); and the chance of a contract or some other unpromised benefit or the chance of avoiding some nuisance threatened by the promisee (in the context of contract formation) it will be impossible to hold the line against enforcing all promises. *Any* motive or desire of the promisor is capable of being turned into practical benefit.

Past consideration

Consideration may be past and so be insufficient consideration to support a counter promise in two senses. First, the promise may have been executed before the counter promise is given. *Roffey* does not change its legal effect. Secondly, the promise may be executory but, being already enforceable, have been regarded as incapable of supporting the enforcement of any additional counter promise.[81] In such cases it is now arguable that actual performance or even an increased chance of performance of that past promise confers practical benefits and imports valid consideration. *Roffey* was so applied in a recent New Zealand case.[82]

Frustration

Roffey deprives the frustration principle of its sting where the increased difficulty or cost of performance (short of that necessary to satisfy the frustration principle) can be passed onto the other party, by obtaining from that party, a promise to pay more or to accept less. Such promises are now enforceable if supported by practical benefit to the promisor.

---

[80] [1991] 1 QB 1, at 16, 19, 21.

[81] eg *Roscorla v Thomas* (1842) 3 QB 234, where the plaintiff had purchased a horse from the defendant who subsequently assured the plaintiff that the horse was sound and free from vice. The horse failed to match that description but the assurance was held to be unenforceable because what consideration *was* given for it, the price, was past.

[82] *Newman Tours Ltd v Ranier Investments Ltd* [1992] 2 NZLR 68, at 80.

Promissory estoppel and economic duress

Roffey's dilution of the consideration requirement will alter the significance of related doctrines. While *Re Selectmove* preserves the utility of promissory estoppel in respect of relieving promises, practical benefit will circumvent any incentive to develop the doctrine in respect of promises to create or extend existing rights. The effect of practical benefit in conferring prima facie enforceability to promises of more for the same, shifts the burden of evaluating the merits of such enforceability on the doctrine of economic duress. The relative merits of mediating decisions as to enforceability through economic duress and promissory estoppel is discussed later.

LEGAL CONSIDERATION AND *ROFFEY*

The question posed is, whether the vexing effects of practical benefit could have been avoided in *Roffey* by finding consideration within its existing definition. Indeed there are a number of ways by which legal consideration could have been found, but none provides a satisfactory way forward in determining the enforceability of promises to pay more for the same. For instance, consideration could take the form of the repromise which the promisee is under no obligation to give, or consist in the fact that the new promise will 'survive after the old claim is barred by statute of limitations.'[83] However, these 'invented' considerations[84] are not what Roffey bargained for and to regard the muscular effort in reuttering the promise or the extension of the limitation period as consideration is both artificial and a clear distortion of the notion of consideration as a test of bargain enforcement. Additionally, they fail to explain the limited enforcement given in *Roffey*.

An alternative analysis is that the modification is a bilateral entire contract, consisting of a number of divisible obligations (a promise to pay the additional sums on the completion of each flat). However, this interpretation would explain *Roffey*'s limited enforcement only if partial completion is accompanied by Williams' breach. It is inconsistent with the actual finding that Williams' partial completion is justified by Roffey's breach. A better 'fit' is to treat the additional promise as a *unilateral offer*.[85] Williams accepts and earns each divisible unilateral offer to pay £575 as he completes each flat. He is, therefore, only entitled to

[83] JB Ames, 'Two Theories of Consideration' (1899) 13 Harv LRev 29, 41.

[84] See GH Treitel, *The Law of Contract* (8th ed 1991) p 67.

[85] Denning LJ in *Ward v Byham* [1956] 1 WLR 496, at 498, regarded the father's promise to pay for the mother's performance, of her existing statutory duty, as a unilateral contract, '[s]o long as she looked after the child, she would be entitled to' the promise. See also B Coote, 'Consideration and Benefit in Fact and in Law' (1990–91) 3 JCL 23, 27–8.

his expectation on the completed flats and not in respect of the uncompleted flats since Roffey had impliedly revoked these offers by conduct (not paying) before Williams' acceptance. This functional (or manipulative) finding of consideration,[86] as the others, invokes the same Holmesian heresy. There is no bargain (although there is reliance). And even the unilateral device cannot handle other adjustments in enforcement which may be necessitated by a legitimate evaluation of the conduct of the parties, any changes in the economic environment surrounding the contract, the assumptions on which the promise to pay more was given, or the circumstances of the parties.

NON-BARGAIN ENFORCEMENT OF PROMISES OF MORE FOR THE SAME

While the variation in *Roffey* is enforced as if it imported a contractually enforceable exchange, it has been argued that there was neither exchange nor *contractual* enforcement. If it was not a bargain, why indeed was the modification in *Roffey* enforced, albeit limitedly? Four motivations can be identified consistent with the dicta in *Roffey*: respect for the serious intention of the promisor;[87] the absence of exploitation or duress by the promisee in obtaining the variation;[88] the unfairness of the original contract to the promisee,[89] and the promisee's reliance on the promise.[90] These concerns are reflected in rival non-bargain theories of contractual liability but, it is submitted, none provides an adequate sole test of enforceability for promises of more for the same. They are all relevant to the particular determination.

On the intention theory of contractual liability,[91] bargain merely provides the best informal test of intention to be bound. It is unnecessary if the relevant consent can otherwise be proved. But clearly, unless under seal, contract law has never enforced all promises even if

---

[86] BJ Reiter, 'Courts, Consideration and Common Sense' (1977) 27 UTLJ 439, 445–7 citing the objections of lack of reckonability, inconsistent reasoning and results, and an absence of open balancing of the relevant considerations.

[87] [1991] 1 QB 1, at 18, per Russell LJ; and 21, per Purchas LJ.

[88] *Ibid.*, at 13–14, 16, 17, 21, 23.

[89] All the judges noted that the original contract price was too low to allow Williams to operate satisfactorily and at a profit: [1991] 1 QB 1, at 10, 19, 23. In fact, the judge at first instance accepted the argument that 'a main contractor who agrees too low a price with a subcontractor is acting contrary to his interests. He will never get the job finished without paying more money.' He held that a promise of additional payment will not fail for want of consideration 'where the original sub-contract price is too low: *ibid.* at 10.

[90] Russell LJ said it would be unconscionable to allow Roffey to go back on a promise upon which Williams had acted in reliance: [1991] 1 QB 1, at 17. Cf. Glidewell LJ at 13.

[91] There is a number of versions of consent based theories. See for example, C Fried, *Contract As Promise* (1981); RE Barnett 'A Consent Theory of Contract' (1986) 86 Colum LRev; Lord Wright, 'Ought the Doctrine of Consideration to be Abolished From the Common Law?' (1936) 49 Harvard LR 1225; LL Fuller 'Consideration and Form' (1941) 41 Colum LRev 799.

seriously intended, and it cannot be sufficient to say that the promisor intended to be bound. The question is: bound to what legal effect? What rights and liabilities were intended to be transferred, created, waived or suspended by the promisor? Was this to be absolute or conditional? There is no reason to suppose that the promise to pay more is made with the intent to extinguish the promisor's own original rights absolutely, irrespective of changes of circumstances, changes of mind, or failure by the promisee to perform under the new arrangement. Indeed, it has been argued that the reverse is probably true. In *Roffey*, the additional payment was described by the promisor as something 'over and above the contract sum',[92] and by the judge at first instance as a 'bonus'.[93] These are more consistent with a concession than with a fully enforceable contractual promise. *Roffey*, of course, did not enforce the contractual measure of the promise to pay more. To say that the issue is determinable by employing the criteria of 'consent to liability'[94] simply begs the same question.

A duress sensitive view of contractual liability may follow from the intention view since duress can be said to vitiate intent. Duress may also be consistent with an economic theory of contract. The latter would support the enforcement of contract modifications to 'minimise the waste and inconvenience between parties already embarked on a project, and to bring projects safely to a conclusion without interruptions and unnecessary ill-will'.[95] But controls are needed to ensure that the efficiency end of certainty in risk allocation is not undermined for unlimited renegotiation would:

increase the over-all costs of contracting by creating incentives for opportunistic behaviour in cases where 'hold-up' possibilities arise during contract performance . . . even where a genuine change has occurred in the economic environment of the contract . . . allowing recontracting may facilitate the reallocation of initially efficiently assigned risks. This leads to moral hazard problems that may attenuate incentives for efficient risk minimisation . . . by the party who subsequently seeks the modification.[96]

Opportunism and reallocation of risks are to be constrained by limiting the legitimate circumstances for modifications and this is to be

[92] [1991] 1 QB 1, at 7, 17.
[93] *Ibid.*, at 10.
[94] RE Barnett, 'A Consent Theory of Contract' (1986) 86 Colum LRev, 316.
[95] P Birks, 'The Travails of Duress' [1990] LMCLQ 342, 346. See VA Aivazian, MJ Trebilcock and M Penny, 'The Law of Contract Modifications: The Uncertain Quest for a Benchmark of Enforceability' (1984) 22 Osgoode Hall LJ 173. For empirical support, see H Beale and T Dugdale, 'Contracts Between Businessmen: Planning and the Use of Contractual Remedies' (1975) 2 Brit J Law & Soc 45.
[96] VA Aviazan, MJ Trebilcock and M Penny, 'The Law of Contract Modifications: The Uncertain Quest for a Benchmark of Enforceability' (1984) 22 Osgoode Hall LJ 175.

worked out under the rubric of economic duress.[97] The difficulty lies with the as yet unstable nature of the duress doctrine as discussed below.[98]

An important theory of contractual liability is based on the protection of the reasonable, foreseeable or justifiable reliance of the promisee.[99] The problem is that the standard of reasonableness or foreseeability can only be generated from outside the fact of reliance itself. Invariably it begs the very question sought to be answered: whether the promise is enforceable in the first place such that reliance can reasonably be placed by the promisee or foreseen by the promisor.

Nevertheless, the decision in *Roffey* is fairly consistent with a reliance-based view. Williams' reliance in completing the eight further flats could be said to be reasonable because it was induced by Roffey's promise and because Roffey stood by knowing of Williams' reliance. The remedy given protected this reliance by awarding Williams a figure based on the promise as the best surrogate of an uncertain measure of reliance.[100] It can also be said to recognize the promisor's ability to revoke before, or to limit, reliance. Williams is thus protected to the extent of his reliance up to the point it became clear that Roffey is repudiating its promise. The requirement of reasonable reliance may be able to accommodate a wide ranging evaluation of the circumstances of the case. But the question remains as to how this is best expressed in the law.

The attractive suggestion that the substantive unfairness[101] of a contract should be a factor for the enforcement of its variation[102] raises the obvious difficulty of the standard to be applied.[103] For example, how

[97] See TE Robison, 'Enforcing Extorted Contract Modifications' (1983) 68 Iowa LRev 699; R Halson, 'Sailors, Sub-Contractors and Consideration' (1990) 106 LQR 183; VA Aviazan, MJ Trebilcock and M Penny, 'The Law of Contract Modifications: The Uncertain Quest for a Benchmark of Enforceability' (1984) 22 Osgoode Hall LJ 173. Glidewell LJ's test of enforceability includes the requirement that the additional promise should not have been obtained by economic duress (*Roffey* [1991] 1 QB 1, at 16).

[98] See text accompanying notes 106–14, below.

[99] RE Barnett, 'A Consent Theory of Contract' (1986) 86 Col LRev 269, 274 n 17, observes that while 'a comprehensive reliance theory of contract has never been systematically presented', the literature is replete with suggestions of 'the reliance principle'. See eg G Gilmore, *The Death of Contract* (1974) pp 71–2, 88; PS Atiyah, *The Rise and Fall of Freedom of Contract* (1979) p 779; LL Fuller, 'Consideration and Form' (1941) 41 Col LRev 799, 810–12.

[100] LL Fuller and WR Perdue, 'The Reliance Interest in Contract Damages' (1936–37) 46 Yale LJ 52, 66–7.

[101] See generally on the importance of substantive unfairness as a test of contractual liability, PS Atiyah, 'Contract and Fair Exchange' in his *Essays on Contract* (1986) p 329 and J Gordley, 'Equality in Exchange' (1981) 69 Cal LRev 1587.

[102] GH Treitel and FMB Reynolds, 'Consideration For the Modification of Contracts' (1965) 7 Mal LR 1, 20, a promise to pay more should be enforceable, inter alia, where the promisor has 'secured some harsh or unfair advantage over the promisee—if, for example, he employed the promisee at rates of pay well below the current ones.'

[103] See RE Barnett, 'A Consent Theory of Contract' (1986) 86 Col LRev 269, 283–6.

would it accommodate notions of bad bargain, responsibility in contract formation, bad faith under bidding with a view to later renegotiation[104] and attempts to reallocate a foreseeable risk? Such uncertainties would, no doubt, increase the incidence of renegotiation for substantive unfairness, and give rise to claims that any modification obtained, in the absence of substantive unfairness, is nevertheless the valid compromise of a bone fide belief in such a valid ground for renegotiation. It has been argued that correcting an inadequacy of consideration is desirable only 'where the parties themselves have reopened it on this ground'.[105] But why should respect for the intention of the parties be limited to specifically approved grounds? Moreover, should the fairness of the modification be relevant to its enforcement? In *Roffey*, while the original contract was said to be under-priced by £3,783, the additional promise was to pay an extra £10,847. Substantive fairness was clearly an important factor in the court's decision to enforce the modification and, interestingly, the figure awarded on the promisor's breach was £3,500.

Assuming that the concern raised by each approach is relevant to the enforceability of contract modifications, the question becomes how best to accommodate them in the law. The first avenue is that adopted in *Roffey*—the redefinition of bargain consideration. Non-bargains are transformed into bargains and there is, prima facie, unlimited enforcement of modifications. Limits on enforcement, based on an evaluation of the intention, reliance, pressure and fairness factors, can then be mediated through a number of channels. The most obvious is through the doctrine of economic duress. The question is whether that doctrine is up to the task. Economic duress is said to rest on the finding of an 'unlawful threat' (usually to breach) which gives the other party 'no practicable alternative' but to agree to a variation[106] and so vitiates the latter's consent to that variation. As such, the doctrine is too coarsely calibrated to adequately distinguish between meritorious and unmeritorious variations. It cannot easily accommodate the sort of wide ranging inquiry which may be thought necessary to the assessment: the circumstances prompting the parties' renegotiation,[107] the quality of the promisee's conduct in obtaining a variation,[108] the quality of the

---

[104] P Birks, 'The Travails of Duress' [1990] LMCLQ 342.

[105] GH Treitel and FMB Reynolds, 'Consideration For the Modification of Contracts' (1965) 7 Mal LR 1, 20.

[106] *The Universe Sentinel* [1983] 1 AC 366; *Atlas Express Ltd v Kafco (Importers and Distributors) Ltd* [1989] QB 833.

[107] Was the risk of the change of circumstances reasonably foreseeable and was it allocated? What are the consequences of performance on the original terms for the promisee?

[108] What was the promisee's knowledge of the promisor's position? What was threatened? Was this commensurate with the need to preserve the promisee's economic position? Did reasonable discussion or negotiation take place?

promisor's decision to consent to the modification,[109] the reasonable-ness of the modification;[110] and any subsequent change in the circum-stances of the parties.

One suggestion is to allow the modification if it is reasonably related to the impact of 'unanticipated circumstances' upon the performing party where the promisor had an adequate alternative to the modifi-cation. Otherwise, the modification is tainted by duress.[111] *Roffey* is a very questionable application of such an approach. The court's finding of no duress[112] was based on there being no threat to breach by Williams and on Roffey's having taken the initiative in increasing the contract price. Nevertheless, the circumstances necessitating the mod-ification, the bad bargain made by Williams and his defective supervi-sion of his workers, can hardly be described as 'unanticipated'. And, despite the absence of a threat to breach, it was nevertheless clear to Roffey that Williams would not complete on time without additional payment.[113]

More problematically, the inadequacy of contract remedies, which provides the incentive for the promisee's opportunism and creates 'no practicable alternative' for the promisor, factors against enforcement, is paradoxically also the substance of the 'practical benefits' favouring enforcement. Consistently, Robison argues that duress should not be dispositive, so long as remedies do not fully protect the promisor's expectation interests in the original contract: 'when an antiextortion rule will not deter extortion, the law should value the recipient's suc-cessful attempt and future ability to save himself more highly than the understandable but misplaced reluctance to enforce any extorted promises.'[114]

There is no clear boundary between the presence of consideration which indicates enforceability and the presence of economic duress which denies it. A threat which leaves the promisor with no practica-ble alternative but to agree to a modification (and so compulsion) is par excellence the situation in which the promisor can be said to obtain a practical benefit from the modification. Moreover, if the threat of

---

[109] What did the promisor obtain from the modification? Was the fear of breach actual and reasonable? What were the likely consequences for the promisor? Was substituted perfor-mance or a resort to legal remedies realistic alternatives? Was any reluctance to give consent made clear to the promisee? Did the promisor act with knowledge of the legal position?

[110] Was the original contract manifestly unfair? If so, what was the cause of this? Does the modification better reflect the values exchanged in the light of any changes of circumstance, or does it result in unjust enrichment to the promisee?

[111] R Halson, 'Sailors, Sub-Contractors and Consideration' (1990) 106 LQR 183.

[112] [1991] 1 QB 1, at 17, 21, 23.

[113] See *B&S Contracts and Design Ltd v Victor Green Publications Ltd* [1984] ICR 419, in which an *implied* threat to breach was found.

[114] TE Robison, 'Enforcing Extorted Contract Modifications' (1983) Iowa LRev 699, 751.

unlawful breach is too readily implied or no practical alternative is too
lightly found, then what practical benefit gives with one hand, duress
takes away with the other. Even if these difficulties are sensitively
resolved, we are still left with a potentially all or nothing result. The
additional promise is either fully enforceable as a contract in the
absence of duress or unenforceable in its presence. Limited enforcement in the absence of duress, such as in *Roffey*, would need further
justification.

The liability opened up by *Roffey* can also be controlled by manipu-
lating the finding of practical benefit to reflect a court's covert assessment of the merits of the modification. The drawbacks of such an
approach, lack of reckonability, inconsistent reasoning and results,
and an absence of open balancing of the relevant considerations, are
well known.[115] Enforcement can also be limited by simply refusing to
extend practical benefit beyond promises of more for the same. But,
such a refusal in *Re Selectmove*,[116] without substantive explanation,
contributes little to the orderly development of the law.

An alternative to *Roffey's* redefinition of bargain, is to redefine consideration as bargain *plus*. It has been suggested that *Roffey* signals a
new approach in determining the enforceability of a promise. Courts
may now 'be guided less by technical questions of consideration [as
bargain] than by questions of fairness, reasonableness and commercial
utility',[117] consistent with a view of contractual liability based on an
assessment of all the reasons (or considerations) for enforcement. The
chief exponents of this pluralistic interpretation of contractual liability[118] argue that the courts have always, though inconsistently,
adopted a functional approach to the question of enforceability and
the ostensible finding of bargain consideration. The manipulation of
rules and the resort to avoidance devices go to achieve just results and
a finding of consideration is conclusory, rather than explanatory of
enforcement.[119]

While an open articulation and development of these covert considerations would be a welcome evolution in the law, it is not the way the
court proceeded in *Roffey*, nor is it a likely development of the com-

[115] BJ Reiter, 'Courts, Consideration and Common Sense' (1977) 27 UTLJ 439, 445–7.

[116] *The Times* 13 January 1994.

[117] J Adams and R Brownsword, 'Contracts, Consideration and the Critical Path' (1990) 53
MLR 536, 537.

[118] *Corbin on Contracts* (rev'd ed 1963) vol 1, ss 109 *et seq*; PS Atiyah, 'Consideration: A
Restatement' in his *Essays on Contract* (1986) p 179; MA Eisenberg, 'The Principles of
Consideration' (1982) 67 Cornell LRev 640; BJ Reiter, 'Courts, Consideration and Common
Sense' (1977) 27 UTLJ 439.

[119] Consistently the Law Revision Committee recommended that promises ought to be
enforceable subject to considerations of public policy: Sixth Interim Report (Statute of
Frauds and the Doctrine of Consideration) (1937), Cmd 5449.

mon law. The old problem of uncertainty will remain, because courts have never systematically articulated the relevant considerations, nor how they might balance any conflicts between them. More problematically, such an expansion into non-bargain criteria for enforcement necessitates enormous compromises in contract orthodoxy.

Contract orthodoxy sets a relatively high threshold of enforceability based on a finding of bargain consideration, is restrictive of operative defences and normally enforces to the full extent of the promisee's expectations.[120] Increasing the number of grounds for enforcement must entail appropriate adjustments of the conditions of liability, the relevant defences,[121] and the extent of enforcement[122] that justice requires, which will vary with the particular *type* of circumstance involved (whether commercial, consumer, charitable, family and so on).[123] In any particular case it would have to be asked whether a promise should be:

(1) fully enforceable if there has been performance or substantial performance or substantial reliance by the promise; or
(2) enforceable *to the extent* of performance or reliance; or
(3) enforceable to the extent of performance or reliance not *revoked*; or
(4) enforceable to the extent of performance or reliance not *revoked* and not *'inequitable'*[124] to go back on the promise; or
(5) some other basis and extent?

If enforcement is to be divorced from exchange, it is not obvious what the proper measure is.

The notion of consideration as bargained for 'benefits' and 'detriments' is firmly entrenched. Counsel and judges will continue to speak its language. Acceptance of a wider meaning of consideration is

---

[120] MA Eisenberg, 'The Principles of Consideration' (1982) 67 Cornell LRev 640, 665.

[121] PS Atiyah, 'Consideration: A Restatement' in his *Essays on Contract* (1986) p 242, favours the enforcement of 'gratuitous promises . . . but not to the same extent as ordinary commercial promises . . . It may be wise to provide for a much wider defence of frustration . . . [and] mistake. Perhaps we need to consider the possibility of the conduct of the promisee depriving him of the right to enforce a gratuitous promise. Perhaps we need to consider a shorter limitation period. And perhaps after all some . . . may be better treated as merely giving rise to a defence . . .'

[122] *Ibid.*, p 243, 'we must look to the reasons (or considerations) which make it just or desirable to enforce promises, and also to the extent to which it is just to enforce them.' See also MA Eisenberg, 'The Principles of Consideration' (1982) 67 Cornell LRev 640, 665, we need to 'tailor the extent of enforcement to the substantive interest that enforcement is designed to protect.'

[123] PS Atiyah, 'Consideration: A Restatement' in his *Essays on Contract* (1986) pp 242–3.

[124] Like that employed by the doctrine of promissory estoppel, see GH Treitel, *The Law of Contract* (8th ed 1991) p 106.

neither imminent nor particularly useful.[125] As Professor Waddams observes:

There seems little point in arguing strenuously for the use of a single word for all enforceable promises if an immediate division is to be required between fully enforceable promises and promises that are only partially enforceable.[126]

Moreover, to expand consideration in this way dilutes the distinctiveness of a contract as an action which gives the promisee the value of the promised performance because he or she has paid the agreed equivalent for that performance. But, to advocate the retention of bargain enforcement, is not to deny some legitimate enforcement for non bargain promises such as that in *Roffey*. '[C]ontract does not exhaust the category of statements which are actionable or otherwise capable of producing legal effects.'[127] But such enforcement should be regarded as an exception to the doctrine of consideration, rather than an application of a redefined notion of consideration. In Professor Waddams' views:

It is surely simpler to follow the American Restatement in continuing the present usage of reserving 'consideration' for bargains leading to fully enforceable contracts and to recognise that though some promises may be enforceable without consideration the full 'normal' panoply of contract remedies, in particular damages measured by the value of the promised performance, may not always be appropriate.[128]

Promissory estoppel,[129] based on the protection of induced assumptions, provides a ready framework for assessing the fairness, pressure and change of circumstance factors presented by promises of more for the same. The major conceptual obstacle is the orthodoxy that promissory estoppel merely 'prevents the enforcement of existing rights, but it does not create entirely new rights or extend the scope of existing ones'.[130] It rests on the artificial distinction between relieving promises (of the same for less), and promises which create or extend existing rights (of more for the same). Professor Treitel insists on the distinction to limit the application of promissory estoppel,[131] but eschews the distinction when he advocates the extension of practical benefit to both types of promises as 'more consistent, as well as more satisfactory in its practical operation'.[132] *Anangel*,[133] a case analysed as a promise

---

[125] These and following criticisms apply also to the non-bargain theories of consideration discussed above.

[126] SM Waddams, *The Law of Contracts* (3rd ed 1993) p 17, para 24.

[127] GH Treitel, 'Consideration: A Critical Analysis of Professor Atiyah's Fundamental Restatement' (1976) 50 ALJ 439, 441.

[128] SM Waddams, *The Law of Contracts* (3rd ed 1993) p 17, para 24.

[129] GH Treitel, *The Law of Contract* (8th ed 1991) pp 101 *et seq*.   [130] *Ibid.*, p 107.

[131] *Ibid.*   [132] *Ibid.*, p 116.   [133] [1990] 2 Lloyd's Rep 526.

to create additional rights (to be relieved from some existing obligations) in exchange for practical benefit shows how illusory the distinction is. In the High Court of Australia, Brennon J said:

If a promise by A not to enforce an existing right against B is to confer an equitable
right on B to compel fulfilment of the promise, why should B be denied the same
protection in similar circumstances if the promise is intended to create in B a new
legal right against A? There is no logical distinction to be drawn . . .[134]

The distinction was not insisted on in *Roffey*. It was suggested that
promissory estoppel *may* have operated to prevent the promisor 'from
claiming that there was no consideration for his promise.'[135] Russell LJ
thought it would be unconscionable to allow Roffey to go back on a
promise upon which Williams had acted in reliance and would have
'welcomed the development of argument . . . on the basis that there
was here an estoppel' to prevent it.[136] Estoppel so used would have
created rights contrary to the orthodoxy that it is a 'shield and not a
sword'. In the light of this and the lack of proper arguments put before
it, the court channelled its impulse for enforcement toward an inappropriate expression—the invention of practical benefit to justify
enforcement within the bargain model. Promissory estoppel would
have provided greater flexibility and accuracy in targeting the relevant concerns in contract modifications. And, as a distinct doctrine it
would not have compromised the important functions currently performed by consideration. Moves are afoot in its development as a
cause of action. While it is not established in English law,[137]
Australasian cases[138] and the American Restatement 2nd[139] already
recognize its ability to create new rights. Such a position has been recommended by the Law Revision Committee[140] and the Ontario Law
Reform Commission.[141] However, if the law is to recognize a new type
of enforceable promise, it will need rigorously to clarify the parame-
tres and the effect on consideration of such a recognition.

---

[134] *Walton Stores (Interstate) Ltd v Maher* (1987–88) 164 CLR 387, at 425.
[135] [1991] 1 QB 1, at 13.
[136] *Ibid.* at 17.
[137] Although see the rare operation of estoppel by convention, *Amalgamated Investment &
Property Co Ltd v Texas Commerce International Bank Ltd* [1982] QB 84.
[138] *Walton Stores (Interstate) Ltd v Maher* (1987–88) 164 CLR 387; *Commonwealth v
Verwayen* (1990) 95 ALR 321; *Burbery Mortgage, Finance & Savings Ltd v Hindsbank Holdings
Ltd* [1989] 1 NZLR 356; *Gold Star Insurance Co Ltd v Graunt* (1991) 3 NZBLC 102 294.
[139] § 90(1): 'A promise which the promisor should reasonably expect to . . . and which
does induce such action or forbearance is binding . . . as justice requires'.
[140] Sixth Interim Report (Statute of Frauds and the Doctrine of Consideration) (1937),
Cmd 5449.
[141] Report on Amendment of the Law of Contract (1987) pp 25–32.

Conclusion

As *Re Selectmove*[142] demonstrates, the effect of *Roffey* will not be systematic. The common law does not automatically expand outwards in
conformity with a central core but develops on a case-by-case basis,
pragmatically, incrementally, even fragmentally. The object of this
essay has not been to refute this 'life of the law'. Rather, it has been to
caution against any rush to embrace the deceptively simple and seduc-
tive notion of practical benefit as valid currency in a bargain exchange.
In the context of contract modifications, practical benefit neither confers any enforceable benefits additional to that contained in the existing contract, nor supports the enforcement of the expectation on the
reciprocal promise. The boundary of a contract action, redrawn to
accommodate practical benefit, will be uncertain in its much expanded
outer limits, but certain in its loss of distinctiveness as an action which
enforces the promisee's expectation on a promise, because he or she
has given some enforceable agreed exchange for it. Some enforcement
of promises of more for the same performance is to be welcomed. But
this result is better worked out, with clearer articulation of the basis
and extent of appropriate enforcement, and without distortion to contract fundamentals, elsewhere in the jurisprudence. Using a tool for a
job for which it is not designed has the tendency not only to warp the
tool so that it can no longer perform its original task, it does nothing to
encourage the acquisition of more appropriate tools. To achieve
Roffey's result by *Roffey*'s solution, of allowing the illusory notion of
practical benefit to support an action in contract, is to sacrifice too
much in the orderly development and understanding of the law of
enforceable promises.

---

[142] *The Times* 13 January 1994.

Part 3
The Contractual Obligation: Good Faith, Control and Adaptation

(a) The effect of good faith and implied terms on contractual obligations

6

Good Faith in Contract Performance*

E ALLAN FARNSWORTH

Brian Dalton, a junior at Holy Cross High School in New York, took the Scholastic Aptitude Test (SAT), widely used by American colleges to evaluate candidates for admission. The test is administered by the Educational Testing Service (ETS), a not-for-profit corporation. It requires its 2,400,000 applicants each year to agree to the terms of a bulletin that states:

ETS reserves the right to cancel any test score if . . . ETS believes there is reason to question the score's validity.

Brian's score was a disappointing 620, so, after a coaching course, he took the SAT a second time and scored 1030, a spectacular increase of 410 points. A test security officer and a handwriting examiner, however, concluded that the two exams were not written by the same person.

After review, ETS notified Brian of its preliminary decision to cancel his second score and explained his options, which included submitting additional information and taking the test again to confirm the validity of his scores. Brian claimed that he had mononucleosis on the first occasion and submitted a variety of evidence, including a statement from the proctor, who said that she remembered Brian as present on the second occasion, and the report of a document examiner, retained by Brian's family, who disagreed with the conclusion of the ETS examiner. The final decision of ETS, however, was to cancel the score of his second exam; the only way that Brian could successfully controvert the opinion of the ETS handwriting analysts was to take a retest.

Rather than return to the examination room, however, Brian went to court, and the judge ordered ETS to release the score of his second exam:

The requirement of the good faith performance of a contract is not merely abstract legal theory . . . In face of two mutually exclusive factual premises, that an impostor took the SAT or that Brian took the SAT, ETS arbitrarily chose to rely solely on handwriting analysis . . . [B]y failing to make even rudimentary efforts to evaluate or investigate the information furnished by Brian, information that was clearly relevant to a rational decision-making process, ETS reduced its contractual undertaking to an exercise in form over substance. ETS, therefore, breached its adhesion contract with Brian by failing to act in good faith in the

* Copyright © 1994, E Allan Farnsworth.

course of determining whether there was reason to question the validity of Brian's SAT score.[1]

I will not presume to guess how Brian would have fared in a British court, but his case is suggestive of the variety of situations in which the doctrine of good faith performance is called into play in my country.

A lot has happened to the doctrine of good faith performance in the three decades since I first wrote on the subject,[2] and I must be selective. I will deal with the subject under seven heads: the doctrine's historical origins; the sources of the doctrine in United States law; the reaction to the doctrine in other common-law countries; some important applications of the doctrine in the United States; the debate over the meaning of the doctrine in the United States; current issues as to the doctrine in the United States; and the future of the doctrine.

I shall discuss only good faith in the *performance* of contracts and not good faith *purchase* or good faith in either the *negotiation* or *enforcement* of contracts. Furthermore, I shall say nothing of the good faith that is required of an agent or other fiduciary. Certainly the standard of good faith performance of contracts is not as exacting as the standard of good faith applied to fiduciaries, who are required to act consistently with the self-interest of another person. As the Supreme Court of Utah put it, the duty of good faith performance of contracts 'does not mean that a party vested with a clear right is obligated to exercise that right to its own detriment for the purpose of benefiting another party to the contract'.[3]

Historical origins

I shall resist the temptation to trace the historical origins of the doctrine of good faith performance back to Roman times. Coming closer to today, in 1766, in a leading insurance case, Lord Mansfield referred to good faith as the 'governing principle . . . applicable to all contracts and dealings'.[4] But, to the best of my understanding, in this country the course of the doctrine of good faith performance has been downhill since the time of Lord Mansfield. Credit—if that is the correct word—for the contemporary

---

[1] *Dalton v Educational Testing Service* 588 NYS 2d 741, at 747–8 (Supreme Court, Queens County, 1992), aff'd, 614 N.Y.S. 742 (Supreme Court Appellate Divison 1994). Affirmance came after the Oxford conference. In its opinion, the Appellate Division explained that 'ignoring Dalton's evidence without even initiating a preliminary investigation clearly demonstrates a lack of good faith.' *Ibid.* at 744.

[2] EA Farnsworth, 'Good Faith Performance and Commercial Reasonableness Under the Uniform Commercial Code' (1963) 30 U Chi L R 666. See also *Farnsworth on Contracts* (2nd ed 1990) s 7.17.

[3] *Rio Algom Corpn v Jimco Ltd* 618 P 2d 497, at 505 (Utah 1980).

[4] *Carter v Boehm* (1766) 3 Burr 1905, at 1910; 97 ER 1162, at 1164.

recognition of the doctrine of good faith performance goes not to the Scotsman Lord Mansfield but to the Welshman Professor Karl Llewellyn, Chief Reporter for the Uniform Commercial Code, who was inspired not by Mansfield but by the *Treu und Glauben* provision of the German Civil Code, with which Llewellyn was familiar.[5] Even before the Code, a common law doctrine of good faith performance had been recognized by a few states, notably New York and California. As a federal Court of Appeals judge put it:

The contractual duty of good faith is . . . not some newfangled bit of welfare-state paternalism or . . . the sediment of an altruistic strain in contract law, and we are therefore not surprised to find the essentials of the modern doctrine well established in nineteenth-century cases. . . .[6]

Nevertheless, today's general acceptance of the doctrine in the United States is due, at least in good part, to the doctrine's inclusion in the Code.

Sources in United States law

In the United States, the doctrine of good faith performance now has three textual underpinnings: the Uniform Commercial Code, the American Law Institute's Restatement (2d) of Contracts, and the United Nations Convention on Contracts for the International Sale of Goods.

The first of these, the Uniform Commercial Code, in § 1–203, provides:

Every contract or duty within this Act imposes an obligation of good faith in its performance or enforcement.

In addition, over fifty of some 400 Code sections mention good faith specifically. Section 1–201(19) contains the Code's general definition of good faith as 'honesty in fact in the conduct or transaction concerned.' Some of the Code's substantive articles contain variant definitions of good faith. The best known of these is § 2–103(1)(b), which provides with respect to the sale of goods, that in the case of a merchant, good faith means not only honesty in fact but also 'the observance of reasonable standards of fair dealing in the trade'.[7]

This merchant's definition of good faith was the inspiration for § 205 of the Restatement (2d) of Contracts, which states:

[5] W Twining, *Karl Llewellyn and the Realist Movement* (1985) p 313 (mentioning the Uniform Commercial Code's 'emphasis on "good faith" ' as one of the 'general indications of Llewellyn's familiarity with civil law').

[6] *Market Street Associates Ltd Partnership v Frey* 941 F 2d 588, at 595 (7th Cir 1991), *per* Posner J.

[7] The definition of 'good faith' in Art 3, Negotiable Instruments, which applies mainly to good faith purchase, has recently been revised. UCC § 3–103(a)(4) defines 'good faith' as 'honesty in fact and the observance of reasonable commercial standards of fair dealing'.

Every contract imposes upon each party a duty of good faith and fair dealing in its performance and its enforcement.

This section, which does not of course have the force of legislation, is of particular importance for contracts not covered by the Code, notably contracts for services including Brian's contract with ETS.

Finally, because the United States has ratified the Convention on Contracts for the International Sale of Goods (the Vienna sales convention) contracts for the international sale of goods are subject to its Art 7(1), which reads:

In the interpretation of this Convention, regard is to be had to its international character and to the need to promote uniformity in its application and the observance of good faith in international trade.

A proposal to require the observance of good faith in the performance of contracts was rejected in favour of this awkward compromise, which plainly falls short of imposing such a duty. But, as Professor Barry Nicholas noted recently, one finds 'an increasing number of suggestions [from civil law scholars] that good faith is nevertheless to be applied to the performance . . . of the contract', which he supposed would 'be disturbing for the English lawyer'.[8] Given the expansive reading likely to be given to 'good faith' by civil law scholars in an international context, I suspect that we American lawyers would find these suggestions just as disquieting, even though we are comfortable with the concept of good faith performance in the domestic context. But it would be premature to hazard a guess as to what a US judge would make of this provision. As of now, the Vienna sales convention has played no role in the development of the US doctrine of good faith performance.

Reaction in other common-law countries

Reaction in other common law countries to these US developments has sometimes been critical. In 1984, Professor Michael Bridge, then of McGill University, took aim in a major article at the doctrine of good faith performance as it had been developed south of the Canadian border. He speculated that, 'Far from involving the community ethic in the day-to-day task of law-making and decision-making . . . good faith is more likely to produce idiosyncratic judgments'.[9] It was Bridge's conclusion that

---

[8] B Nicholas, 'The United Kingdom and the Vienna Sales Convention: Another Case of Splendid Isolation?' 9 Saggi, Conferenze e Seminari 9 (Centro di studi e ricerce di diritto comparato e straniero, Roma 1993).

[9] MG Bridge, 'Does Anglo-Canadian Contract Law Need a Doctrine of Good Faith?' (1984) 9 Can Bus LJ 385, 413.

'Anglo-Canadian law does not need to legislate a standard of good faith because it has evolved sufficiently towards the protection of justified expectations'[10] and that while 'a preoccupation with [good faith] is useful in articulating contract theory and in defining the goals that our contract law is harnessed to serve,'[11] 'good faith could well work practical mischief if ruthlessly implanted in our system of law'.[12] Professor Roy Goode told an Italian audience that 'we in England find it difficult to adopt a general concept of good faith'. He seemed not at all overcome by regret and added that 'we do not know quite what [good faith] means'.[13]

Other English jurists, however, have been more positive about a doctrine of good faith performance. As far back as 1956, Professor Raphael Powell observed that 'there are a number of individual cases in which the [English law of contracts] contains an element of ... good faith'[14] and opined that '[f]or want of a rule of good faith the courts have upon occasions had to resort to contortions or subterfuges'[15] or 'to fictitious implied promises.'[16] In 1991 Steyn J, in a lecture on good faith at Oxford University, explained that, lacking a doctrine of good faith, 'English law has to resort to the implication of terms'.[17] He urged rather that 'in using the high technique of common law the closest attention is paid to the purpose of the law of contract, ie, to promote good faith and fair dealing'.[18] Even more support for a doctrine of good faith has come in other parts of the common-law world.

Australia is a leading example. In 1987, Professor HK Lücke admitting that 'the United States legal system has some special characteristics which make it necessary for lawyers to embrace broad principles and policies', nonetheless thought it not unreasonable to hope that good faith would ultimately make a significant and beneficial impact upon [Australian] private law'.[19] He was supported by Professor Paul Finn, who noted in the same year that equity 'has no exclusive proprietorship of "good faith" '[20] and, in 1989, that the 'doctrine of "good faith" in contract performance is now squarely upon contract's agenda'.[21] It was also in 1989 that Priestley JA published an article in which he turned his attention to the

---

[10] *Ibid.*, 425–6. [11] *Ibid.*, 426. [12] *Ibid.*

[13] R Goode, 'The Concept of "Good Faith" in English Law', 2 Saggi, Conferenze e Seminari 3, 3 (Centro di studie ricerche di diritto comparato e straniero, Roma 1992).

[14] R Powell, 'Good Faith in Contracts' (1956) 9 CLP 16, 23.

[15] *Ibid.*, 26. [16] *Ibid.*

[17] The Hon Mr Justice Steyn, The Role of Good Faith and Fair Dealing in Contract Law: A Hair-Shirt Philosophy? [1991] Denning LJ 131, 133.

[18] *Ibid.*, 141.

[19] HK Lücke, 'Good Faith and Contractual Performance' in PD Finn (ed), *Essays on Contract* (1987) 155, 156, 182.

[20] PD Finn, 'Equity and Contract' in PD Finn (ed), *Essays on Contract* (1987) 104, 106.

[21] P Finn, 'Commerce, the Common Law and Morality' (1989) 17 MULR 87, 89.

[22] The Rt Hon Mr Justice LJ Priestley, 'A Guide to a Comparison of Australian and United States Contract Law' (1989) 12 UNSWLJ 4, 17.

doctrine of good faith as a 'feature ... of much United States contract law'[22] and wondered whether 'Australian law has reached the point where terms may readily be implied into contracts, having substantially the same effect as the good faith formulation in the United States.'[23] In 1992 he elaborated this view in a case involving the power of a government agency to terminate a construction contract on default by the contractor if the contractor did not 'show cause to the satisfaction' of the agency why the contract should not be terminated. After reviewing US and other common law authorities on good faith, Priestley JA concluded 'that people generally, including judges and other lawyers, from all strands of the community, have grown used to the courts applying standards of fairness to contract which are wholly consistent with the existence in all contracts of a duty upon the parties of good faith and fair dealing in its performance.'[24]

The doctrine of good faith has also stirred interest in Canada. In 1983, BJ Reiter, a Toronto lawyer, called good faith 'a vital norm in contract law'[25] and argued that 'the pervasiveness of good faith in contracts has important implications for theories of contract law, for the relationship between law and society, and for the law in its practical, day-to-day operation'.[26] Significantly, two Ontario studies have advocated rules on good faith. In 1979, the Ontario Law Reform Commission's Report on Sale of Goods recommended the adoption of a good faith standard for performance of contracts of sale. The recommendation defined 'good faith' as 'honesty in fact and the observance of reasonable standards of fair dealing'.[27] In 1987, in its Report on Amendment of the Law of Contract, the Commission recommended that legislation recognize the doctrine of good faith in the performance of contracts generally, that this statutory obligation of good faith should not be disclaimable, and that the provision should take the form of Restatement (2d) § 205.[28]

One can only speculate as to how these various authorities would have resolved Brian's case. Was the decision of the New York judge one of Professor Bridge's 'idiosyncratic judgments', or was it a proper application of one of Priestley JA's 'standards of fairness'?

---

[23] The Rt Hon Mr Justice LJ Priestley, 'A Guide to a Comparison of Australian and United States Contract Law' (1989) 12 UNSWLJ 4, 23.
[24] *Renard Constructions (ME) Pty v Minster for Public Works* (1992) 26 NSW LR 234, at 268F.
[25] BJ Reiter, 'Good Faith in Contracts' (1983) 17 Val UL Rev 705, 707.
[26] *Ibid.*, 706.
[27] Ontario Law Reform Commission, Report on Sale of Goods (1979), vol I, pp 163–71.
[28] Ontario Law Reform Commission, Report on Amendment of the Law of Contract (1987), ch 9.

Important applications in the United States

As Brian Dalton's case suggests, the doctrine of good faith performance has been applied in a wide variety of situations. In many of these, as in Brian's case, the doctrine restrains a party in its exercise of discretion conferred on it by the contract.

For example, an output contract confers discretion on the seller, and a requirements contract confers discretion on the buyer in determining the quantity of goods to be sold. Under the Uniform Commercial Code, an output on requirements term 'means such actual output or requirements as may occur in good faith'.[29] Any reduction in output or requirements, including the extreme case of complete cessation on going out of business must be in good faith. Any increase must also be in good faith, so that, for example, a buyer under a requirements contract has no right to goods for the purpose of stockpiling or speculation.[30]

Courts have constrained the exercise of discretion by imposing a common law requirement of good faith even where the Code does not apply. Thus, where a contract prohibits assignment by a party without consent of the other party, there is a growing tendency to require that, if consent is withheld, this must be done in good faith.[31] And, where a contract between an author and a publisher provides for 'approval' of the manuscript by the publisher, courts have regularly required that if approval is to be withheld, this must be done in good faith.[32] Other interesting, and more controversial, decisions have involved attempts by borrowers to impose liability on a lender that has exercised its discretion to call in loans or to refuse further advances without giving what, in the borrower's view, is fair warning.[33]

A great deal of litigation has arisen from termination of agreements that are ostensibly terminable 'at will'. Courts have traditionally regarded franchise and distributorship agreements as terminable at will, in the absence of provision to the contrary. In recent years, however, a growing number of courts have recognized the substantial investment that is often required of the franchisee or distributor. Some of these courts have

---

[29] UCC § 2–306(1).

[30] *Homestake Mining Co* v *Washington Public Power Supply System*, 476F Supp 1162, at 1168 (ND Cal 1979) (buyer under requirements contract 'is not acting in good faith if it insists on delivery of unneeded goods, even if at the time delivery was first requested it had actual requirements'), aff'd per curiam, 652 F 2d 28 (9th Cir 1981).

[31] eg *Cheney* v *Jemmett*, 693 P 2d 1031, at 1034 (Idaho 1984) (vendor must 'act reasonably and in good faith').

[32] *Doubleday & Co Inc* v *Curtis*, 763 F 2d 495 (2nd Cir 1985); cert dismissed, 474 US 912, 88 L Ed 2d 247 (1985).

[33] See text at n 62 below.

invoked the doctrine of good faith performance to protect the franchisee or distributor.[34]

Courts have been less willing to invoke the doctrine of good faith performance in employment contracts. Tenaciously clinging to a rule rooted in nineteenth-century liberalism, US courts treat employment contracts that are silent as to duration as terminable at will by either party. Courts have generally rejected claims by employees that the duty of good faith performance means that they can be fired only for 'good cause'. As the Supreme Court of Utah explained in 1991:

The covenant of good faith ... cannot be construed to change an indefinite-term, at-will employment contract into a contract that requires an employer to have good cause to justify a discharge.[35]

Or, as New York's highest court put it some years earlier:

No obligation can be implied ... which would be inconsistent with other terms of the contractual relationship.[36]

In some instances, the duty of good faith performance may not only proscribe conduct but may mandate affirmative action as well. A party may thus be under a duty to take steps to co-operate with the other party in achieving the objectives of their contract. In a case arising under the 'approval' provision of a contract between an author and a publisher, the court said that the publisher's 'wilful failure to respond to a request for editorial comments on a preliminary draft' might be a breach of the duty of good faith performance.[37]

A 1991 decision of the US Court of Appeals for the Seventh Circuit is graphic. A lessee of a shopping centre had the right to ask its lessor for financing of improvements and, if turned down, to exercise an option to purchase the property. It requested financing, making no reference to the option provision in the lease, and, when the lessor refused the request, the lessee exercised the option. When the lessor refused to convey, the lessee sought specific performance. On appeal, the Court of Appeals, through Judge Richard Posner held that there had been a breach of the lessee's duty of good faith performance, because:

it is one thing to say that you can exploit your superior knowledge of the market ... [but] another thing to say that you can take deliberate advantage of an oversight by your contract partner concerning his rights under the contract.[38]

[34] *Bak-A-Lum Corpn of America* v *Alcoa Building Products* 351 A 2d 349 (NJ 1976).
[35] *Brehany* v *Nordstrom Inc* 812 P 2d 49, at 55 (Utah 1991). See also Eisenberg, p 302 below.
[36] *Murphy* v *American Home Products Corpn* 448 NE 2d 86, at 91 (NY 1983).
[37] *Doubleday & Co Inc* v *Curtis* 763 F 2d 495, at 500 (2nd Cir 1985).
[38] *Market Street Associates Ltd Partnership* v *Frey* 941 F 2d 588, at 592, 594 (7th cir 19910).

Debate over meaning in the United States

If, as Professor Goode suggests, the English have difficulty in attaching any meaning to good faith, the difficulty in my country is quite the opposite: the Americans have, or so it might seem, too many meanings of good faith. What do Americans mean by 'good faith' in the context of performance of contracts?

The most restrictive answer is that the duty of good faith is 'simply a rechristening of fundamental principles of contract law',[39] as Justice Antonin Scalia put it in the days when he was a federal Court of Appeals judge. Three decades ago, in my article on good faith, I took much the same position, to which Scalia alluded in observing, 'correct . . . is the perception of Professor Farnsworth that the significance of the doctrine is "in implying terms in the agreement" '.[40] I suspect that when English lawyers think of good faith—if they do so at all—they tend to think of it in these terms. The earlier quotations from Priestley JA and Steyn J confirm this. This restrictive answer has not satisfied US academics, however, and their search for the meaning of good faith has sparked a spirited debate.

In 1968, Professor Robert Summers published an influential article on good faith in which he sketched the contours of this mandate in terms of an 'excluder' analysis. He suggested 'that in cases of doubt, a lawyer will determine more accurately what the judge means by using the phrase "good faith" if he does not ask what good faith itself means, but rather asks: What . . . does the judge intend to rule out by his use of this phrase?'[41] Summers argued that 'good faith . . . is best understood as an "excluder"—it is a phrase which has no general meaning or meanings of its own, but which serves to exclude many heterogeneous forms of bad faith.'[42] This excluder analysis, despite what Lücke characterized as its 'agnostic' flavour,[43] found its way into the commentary to the good faith provision in the Restatement 2d, which notes:

A complete catalogue of types of bad faith is impossible, but the following types are among those which have been recognized in judicial decisions: evasion of the spirit of the bargain, lack of diligence and slacking off, willful rendering of imperfect performance, abuse of a power to specify terms, and interference with or failure to cooperate in the other party's performance.[44]

---

[39] *Tymshare Inc v Covell* 727 F 2d 1145, at 1152 (DC Cir 1984). [40] *Ibid.*

[41] RS Summers, ' "Good Faith" in General Contract Law and the Sales Provisions of the Uniform Commercial Code' (1968) 54 Va L Rev 195, 200.

[42] *Ibid.*, 196.

[43] HK Lücke, 'Good Faith and Contractual Performance' in PD Finn (ed), *Essays on Contract* (1987) p 155, 160.

[44] Restatement 2d Contracts § 205, Comment d.

This list is taken almost literally from Summers. Bridge thought that the drawback of Summers' approach 'is that it seems tantamount to saying that the good faith duty is breached whenever a judge decides that it has been breached ... [which] hardly advances the cause of intellectual inquiry and ... provides absolutely no guide to the disposition of future cases, except to the extent that they may be on all fours with a decided case.'[45] But Priestley JA's opinion described Summers' approach as having 'the great merit of being workable, without involving the use of fictions often resorted to by courts where the good faith obligation is not available, and reflects what actually happens in decision making.'[46]

In 1980, Professor Steven Burton, of the University of Iowa, in a major article on good faith, introduced a 'forgone opportunity analysis'. Taking a swipe at Summers by lamenting that 'neither courts nor commentators have articulated an operational standard that distinguishes good faith performance from bad faith performance',[47] he attempted to fashion a standard based on the expectations of the parties. 'Good faith,' he argued, 'limits the exercise of discretion in performance conferred on one party by the contract', so it is bad faith to use discretion 'to recapture opportunities forgone upon contracting' as determined by the other party's expectations—in other words, to refuse 'to pay the expected cost of performance'.[48] Bridge also found Burton's theory wanting. Burton's 'elegant' model 'amounts to little more than the proposition that bad faith is a breach of contract and a breach of contract is bad faith',[49] and 'the notion of recapturing forgone opportunities is hardly an accurate characterization of the entire range of breaches of contract',[50] yielding a theory that is 'very modest in its application'.[51] But Lücke, though also noting that Burton's formula is 'rather narrow in its scope', thought it 'a legitimate and important application of the good faith concept'.[52]

Burton and Summers fought it out in the law reviews. Summers struck back at Burton by faulting his formulation as not 'necessarily any more focused' than the Restatement 2d's 'in a novel good-faith performance case'.[53] Burton responded by faulting the excluder analysis as implying

[45] MG Bridge, 'Does Anglo-Canadian Contract Law Need a Doctrine of Good Faith?' (1984) 9 Can Bus LJ 385, 398.

[46] *Renard Constructions (ME) Pty Ltd v Minister for Public Works* (1992) 26 NSWLR 234, at 266G.

[47] SJ Burton, 'Breach of Contract and the Common Law Duty to Perform in Good Faith' (1980) 94 Harv L Rev 369, 369.

[48] *Ibid.*, 372–3.

[49] MG Bridge, 'Does Anglo-Canadian Contract Law Need a Doctrine of Good Faith?' (1984) 9 Can Bus LJ 385, 402.

[50] *Ibid.*   [51] *Ibid.*, 403.

[52] HK Lücke, 'Good Faith and Contractual Performance' in PD Finn (ed), *Essays on Contract* (1987) 155, 161.

[53] RS Summers, 'The General Duty of Good Faith—Its Recognition and Conceptualization' (1982) 67 Cornell L Rev 810, 831.

that courts 'typically use the doctrine to render agreed terms unenforce-able or to impose obligations that are incompatible with the agreement reached at formation . . . [rather than] 'to effectuate the intentions of the parties'.[54]

Courts have looked to all three of these views—Burton's, Summers', and mine—for support, often without recognizing a conflict among them, which is scarcely surprising, because in the context of performance the meaning of good faith may turn on which of its several functions is in issue. Sometimes good faith is the basis of a limitation on the exercise of discretion conferred on a party, as under Burton's view. Sometimes good faith is the basis for proscribing behaviour which violates basic standards of decency, as under Summers' view. Sometimes it is merely the basis of an implied term to fill a gap or deal with an omitted case, as under the view in my Chicago article—the most restrictive of the three views. Which view would be preferable in Brian's case? Good faith in the sense of lim-iting ETS's exercise of its discretion 'to recapture opportunities forgone on contracting'? Good faith in the sense of proscribing 'evasion of the spirit of the bargain' by ETS? Or good faith in the sense of 'implying terms' requiring ETS to cooperate in resolving the dispute?

Current issues in the United States

Although US judges have often cited these academic views, courts have not often been called upon to take sides in the disputes that these views have engendered. Litigation has centred on rather different questions. From the tangle of case law generated by arguments over good faith—and there are a great many cases—three major questions of great practical importance can be teased. The first is whether the test of good faith performance is purely subjective or whether it has an objective compo-nent as well. The second is whether the duty of good faith performance creates 'an independent cause of action'. The third is whether the duty of good faith performance prevails over the explicit provisions of the con-tract.

As for the first question, it is undisputed that good faith has a subjective component that requires a party at least to make an honest judgment. An honest judgment in one's own self-interest is sufficient to meet this sub-jective component. As a federal Court of Appeals judge wrote, contract law 'does not require parties to behave altruistically . . . [or to] proceed on the philosophy that I am my brother's keeper . . ., [a philosophy that] may

---

[54] SJ Burton, 'More on Good Faith Performance of a Contract: A Reply to Professor Summers' (1984) 69 Iowa L R 497, 499.

animate the law of fiduciary obligations . . .'[55] Thus when a seller under an output contract decided that operations were no longer profitable, 'there was no question for the jury of . . . good faith . . .'[56] Nevertheless, a party must not, in the words of the Supreme Court of New Jersey, 'do anything which will have the effect of destroying or injuring the right of the other party to receive the fruits of the contract.'[57] The emphasis on this subjective component is a legacy of the early development of the concept of good faith in the context of good faith purchase rather than good faith performance. Three decades ago, I questioned whether 'a subjective standard [is] sufficient to test good faith'[58] in the context of contract performance, and I would ask the same question today.

Some courts have also asked whether making an honest judgment in accord with self-interest is always enough. In a distributorship-termination case, the Supreme Court of New Jersey concluded that a manufacturer's:

selfish withholding from [a distributor] of its intention seriously to impair its distributorship although knowing [that the distributor] was embarking on an investment substantially predicated upon its continuation constituted a breach of the implied covenant of dealing in good faith.[59]

Although the manufacturer may have made an honest judgment, it fell short of an objective component of good faith, which might appropriately be called fairness. In some situations, a court's own sense of fairness may suffice to guide it, as in Brian's case. In other situations, such as an author's claim that a publisher had failed to give necessary editorial assistance, a court might be aided by evidence of what is considered to be fair in the trade or other activity concerned.

Unfortunately, the Code's general definition of good faith, in contrast to that of the Restatement (2d), says nothing about fairness. For a time during 1993 it appeared that it might be possible to amend § 1–201(1) to read:

'Good faith' means honesty in fact and the observance of reasonable commercial standards of fair dealing in the conduct or transaction concerned.

This would have made it clear that good faith performance has an objective component under the Code, just as it does under the Restatement

---

[55] *Original Great American Chocolate Chip Cookie Co Inc v River Valley Cookies Ltd* 970 F 2d 273, at 280 (7th Cir 1992), *per* Posner J.

[56] *Neofotistos v Harvard Brewing Co* 171 NE 2d 865, at 868 (Mass 1961). But see Comment 2 to UCC § 2–306 ('A shut-down by a requirements buyer for lack of orders might be permissible when a shut-down merely to curtail losses would not').

[57] *Association Group Life Inc v Catholic War Veterans* 293 A 2d 382, at 384 (1972) (quoting *Williston on Contracts* (3rd ed 1961) s 670, 159–60).

[58] EA Farnsworth, 'Good Faith Performance and Commercial Reasonableness Under the Uniform Commercial Code' (1963) 30 U Chi LR 666, 671–2.

[59] *Bak-A-Lum Corp of America v Alcoa Building Products* 351 A 2d 349, at 352 (NJ 1976).

(Second), which couples 'good faith' with 'fair dealing.' But it was decided to leave this matter to each separate article of the Code, in the way it was done in Art 2 with the merchant's definition, a decision that strikes me as unfortunate. But then if one could start afresh, I would abandon the term 'good faith' entirely in connection with performance and use it only in connection with purchase. For me, 'fairness' says all that needs to be said in connection with performance. But, also, it is too late in the day to start afresh.

The second question, going to a possible independent cause of action, aroused such concern that the Code's Permanent Editorial Board went to the extreme of issuing a PEB Commentary to support the conclusion that 'UCC § 1–203 does not create an independent cause of action'. Some of this Commentary shows remarkable timidity: witness such statements as 'good faith merely directly attention to the parties' reasonable expectations' and 'Section 1–203 does not support a cause of action where no other basis for a cause of action exists'.[60] If these statements were taken seriously, the duty of good faith performance would be mere surplusage. Indeed, the conclusion quoted above cannot be correct, since there are well-accepted instances in which it would be difficult to find a basis for the cause of action aside from the duty of good faith performance. What of the duty of cooperation frequently imposed on a party whose cooperation is essential and not unreasonably burdensome? What of the duty to give notice within a reasonable time of some important fact of which the other party would otherwise be unaware? In explaining the basis for UCC § 2–309(3), which imposes such a duty of 'reasonable notification' for termination of a contract, the Official Comment states that 'the application of principles of *good faith* and sound commercial practice normally call for such notification of the termination of a going contract relationship as will give the other party reasonable time to seek a substitute arrangement' (emphasis added).[61] And what, for that matter, of the duty imposed on ETS in Brian's case? Would it have withstood scrutiny under the language of the PEB Commentary?

Although the Commentary may be guilty of overkill, it does respond to a serious concern that will certainly be understood by English lawyers, a concern about those 'idiosyncratic judgments' against which Bridge inveighed. We Americans—from high-school students like Brian on up— are a litigious lot, and a doctrine couched in the vague language of good

---

[60] PEB Commentary on the Uniform Commercial Code, Commentary on § 1–203, pp 4–5.

[61] A revised footnote, designed to meet this criticism, notes that a 'breach of such duties gives rise to a cause of action for breach of the contract of which the implied term becomes a part,' but says that although 'such a cause of action arguably has the same practical content as a cause of action based on a purported breach of § 1–203, there is an important methodological difference in that this commentary requires . . . that the focus be upon the agreement of the parties and their reasonable expectations'.

faith invites abuse. Take, for example, the claim of bondholders outraged by a multimillion dollar loss in the value of their bonds following the fabled RJR Nabisco leveraged buy out, which the bondholders saw as 'misappropriating the value of those bonds to help finance the LBO and to distribute an enormous windfall to the company's shareholders'. Lacking any explicit covenant in their bond indenture on which they could rely, the bondholders sought relief for breach of an implied covenant of good faith and fair dealing. A federal district court judge granted that if:

while the express terms may not have been technically breached, one party has nonetheless effectively deprived the other of those express explicitly bargained-for benefits . . ., a court will read an implied covenant of good faith and fair dealing into a contract to ensure that neither party deprives the other of 'the fruits of the agreement'.[62]

Nevertheless, the court held that:

the 'fruits' of these indentures do not include an implied restrictive covenant that would prevent the incurrence of new debt to facilitate the recent LBO . . . These plaintiffs do not invoke an implied covenant of good faith to protect a legitimate, mutually contemplated benefit of the indentures; rather, they seek to have this Court create an additional benefit for which they did not bargain . . . [The silence of the indentures] does *not* mean that the Court should imply into those very same indentures a covenant of good faith so broad that it imposes a new, substantive term of enormous scope . . . While the Court stands ready to employ an implied covenant of good faith to ensure that such bargained-for rights are performed and upheld, it will not, however, permit an implied covenant to shoehorn into an indenture additional terms plaintiffs now wish had been included.[63]

The likelihood that either PEB Commentary or stern judicial language will head off future claims of this kind is slim. But if this is all the Commentary is taken to stand for, it is at least unobjectionable.

The third question, going to whether the duty of good faith performance prevails over explicit contract provisions, is a particularly troublesome one. Section 1–103 of the Code provides:

The effect of provisions of this Act may be varied by agreement, . . . except that the obligations of good faith, diligence, reasonableness and care prescribed by this Act may not be disclaimed by agreement but the parties may by agreement determine the standards by which the performance of such obligations is to be measured if such standards are not manifestly unreasonable.

Plainly this means that ETS could not have protected itself by revising its brochure to read:

---

[62] *Metropolitan Life Ins Co* v *RJR Nabisco Inc* 716 F Supp 1504, at 1517 (SDNY 1989).
[63] *Ibid.*

ETS reserves the right to cancel any test score . . . if ETS believes, *whether or not in good faith*, there is reason to question the score's validity.

On the other hand it would be startling if the parties were powerless to agree to terms that might vary implied terms that are based on the duty of good faith performance. According to UCC § 2–309(3), as we have seen, reasonable notification is required for termination of a contract, and although this notification is said by the Official Comment to be based on principles of good faith and is normally such 'as will give the other party reasonable time to seek a substitute arrangement,' the Comment goes on to say that an agreement 'dispensing with notification or limiting the time for the seeking of a substitute arrangement is, of course, valid' unless unconscionable. Thus, although the duty of good faith performance cannot be disclaimed, an explicit provision varying an implied term based on that duty will prevail over the implied term. Can sense be made of this? A goodly number of courts have tried to do so, but with conflicting results.

In a leading case in the US Court of Appeals for the Sixth Circuit in 1985, a bank gave a borrower a $3.5 million line of credit to finance its wholesale and retail grocery business. Loans were secured by the borrower's inventory and accounts receivable, with all the borrower's receipts to go into a 'blocked account' to which the bank had sole access. When the bank without notice refused a requested advance of $800,000, which would have brought the balance nearly to the limit, the borrower sued, claiming that the sudden discontinuance of financing resulted in the collapse of its business. The court pointed out that the 'blocked account' mechanism left the borrower 'without operating capital until it had paid down its loan,'[64] putting its 'continued existence entirely at the whim or mercy'[65] of the bank. Looking by analogy to the Code's notice rule in § 2–308(3), mentioned earlier, for contracts for the sale of goods, the court concluded that the 'obligation to act in good faith would require a period of notice to [the borrower] to allow it a reasonable opportunity to seek alternative financing, absent valid business reasons precluding [the bank] from doing so'.[66]

For contrast, take the decision of the US Court of Appeals for the Seventh Circuit in a 1990 case involving a secured line of credit granted by a bank to a bankrupt Chicago shoe retailer that was in reorganization. The

[64] *Ibid.*

[65] *KMC Co Inc* v *Irving Trust Co* 757 F 2d 752, at 759 (6th Cir 1985).

[66] *Ibid.* While Canadian courts have not gone to this extreme, they have held—without a doctrine of good faith performance—that where payment is to be on demand the debtor is entitled to reasonable notice, which means more than just sufficient time to enable the debtor to withdraw the money from a financial institution. See JS Ziegel, 'The Enforcement of Demand Debentures—Continuing Uncertainties' (1990) 69 Can B R 718. English law is not as generous, see *Bank of Baroda* v *Panessar* [1987] Ch 335.

contract granting the $300,000 line of credit provided for cancellation on five days' notice and added that 'nothing provided herein shall constitute a waiver of the right of the Bank to terminate financing at any time'. The bank terminated in accordance with these provisions, without giving any reasons, when a $65,000 debt was outstanding. A federal district court judge held that the bank had acted inequitably and, having no valid business reason, without just cause in refusing to grant further advances. Because of the bank's breach of its duty of good faith and fair dealing, the judge equitably subordinated the bank's secured claim in the reorganization, reducing it to an unsecured claim.

The Court of Appeals reversed the decision. An opinion by Judge Frank Easterbrook, explained:

When the contract is silent, principles of good faith ... fill the gap. They do not block use of terms that actually appear in the contract ... Any attempt to add an overlay of 'just cause' ... to the exercise of contractual privileges would reduce commercial certainty and breed costly litigation ... The Bank was entitled to advance its own interests, and it did not need to put the interests of Debtor and Debtor's other creditors first.[67]

What, one might ask, would Easterbrook have done in Brian's case if the language in the brochure had been the following:

ETS reserves the right to cancel any test score ... if ETS believes *in its sole discretion* there is reason to question the score's validity.

Would this language allow ETS to 'advance its own interests' by asking Brian to take a third test? Might it even be defended as a permissible attempt to 'determine the standards' for measuring the *performance* of the duty of good faith, something that § 1–102(3) explicitly permits?

Easterbrook's reverence for contract language was the subject of a scathing attack in an article by Professor Dennis Patterson. Patterson faulted Easterbrook for failing 'to render a thorough analysis of the meaning of "good faith under the Code" ' and for revisiting 'the formalist era of plain meaning and literal reading of contractual terms,' concluding that the opinion 'does not live up to the author's claim to legitimacy—working within the common-law tradition' and, by both invoking and ignoring that tradition, 'does violence to the law'.[68] Patterson does not, however, suggest what, if anything, the bank could have added to its contract to give it a right to terminate without just cause. One may wonder how he

[67] *Kham & Nate's Shoes No 2 v First Bank* 908 F 2d 1351, at 1357–8 (7th Cir 1990). The court noted, *ibid.*, 1358, 'The principle is identical to that governing a contract for employment at will: the employer may sack its employee for any reason except one forbidden by law, and it need not show "good cause".'
[68] DM Patterson, 'A Fable from the Seventh Circuit: Frank Easterbrook and Good Faith' (1991) 76 Iowa L Rev 503, 505, 506, 533.

would resolve Brian's case if the ETS brochure contained the language just quoted.

The Supreme Court of California expressed a similar sentiment in another context in holding that a lessor's termination under a recapture clause:

in order to claim for itself appreciated rental value of the premises was expressly permitted by the lease and . . . such conduct can never violate an implied covenant of good faith and fair dealing.[69]

Similarly, a federal Court of Appeals has held that, although 'the obligation good faith and fair dealing pervades all contracts,'[70] nevertheless, to give 'full effect to express, definite, umambiguous contract provisions',[71] retailer was not required to act in good faith in terminating an agreement with a catalog merchant where the agreement gave either party the power to terminate on sixty days' notice.[72]

Future of the doctrine

What conclusions can we draw from all this? First, the doctrine of good faith performance is alive and well in the United States, where it provided employment to many US lawyers, who have produced the tangled case law that has marked the doctrine's somewhat uncertain course. Secondly, it has given pleasure to at least some American academics, who have found the subject a congenial one for spirited disagreement. Thirdly, it has occasioned some difficulties for the courts, which have had to wrestle with such current issues as the three I singled out for discussion. Fourthly, lest we forget, it furnished the basis for a teenager named Brian to overturn a decision of one of the United States' most entrenched institutions, ETS.

It also seems that the doctrine is about to burst out beyond its geographical borders to other common law countries such as Australia and Canada. While speaking to a civil law audience of comparative law students in 1994, I remarked that, although the study of how one civil law system has influenced another, through the spread of ideas and the borrowing of principles, is grist to the mills of many comparative law centres on the Continent, there are no comparable centres for the study of how

---

[69] *Carma Developers v Marathon Development California* 826 P 2d 710, at 729 (Cal 1992).
[70] *Davis v Sears, Roebuck & Co* 873 F 2d 888, at 894 (6th Cir 1989). [71] *Ibid.*, at 895.
[72] *Ibid.* See *Pennington's Inc v Brown-Forman Corpn* 785 F Supp 1412 (D Mont 1991) (provision in distributorship agreement for termination on 30 days' notice negated the implied covenant of good faith and fair dealing).

one common-law system has influenced another.[73] It seems unlikely that such a centre will be created, but were it to be, study of the doctrine of good faith performance should be high on its agenda.

[73] EA Farnsworth, The Concept of Good Faith in American Law, 10 Saggi, Conferenze e Seminari 12–13 (Centro di studi e di ricerche di diritto comparato e straniero, Roma 1993).

7

The Doctrine of Good Faith in German Contract Law*

Werner F Ebke and Bettina M Steinhauer

Introduction

The doctrine of good faith (*Treu und Glauben*) is now a favorite subject in German contract law. Growing from little more than a legislative acorn,[1] the doctrine of good faith has ripened into a judicial oak that overshadows the contractual relationship of private parties. In the past 90 years, numerous contract liability theories have emerged on the basis of the doctrine of good faith, which is set forth in § 242 of the German Civil Code (*Bürgerliches Gesetzbuch*). The body of law that has developed on a case-by-case basis is by now a substantial one. Taken literally, § 242 of the BGB refers only to how the debtor is to perform. The question whether the debtor has an obligation to perform or whether non-performance is excused is not dealt with in the good faith provision of § 242 of the BGB.[2] German courts, however, have had little theoretical difficulty in recognizing, as a fundamental principle of contract law, that good faith regulates the debtor's obligation to perform as well as the creditor's right of performance. In reaching this conclusion, the courts not only have relied upon § 242 of the BGB Code, but also have invoked § 157.[3]

In German contract law, the doctrine of good faith fulfils three basic functions: it serves as the legal basis of interstitial law-making by the judiciary, it forms the basis of legal defences in private law suits, and it provides a statutory basis for reallocating risks in private contracts. The doctrine of good faith has been used by the courts to create new causes of action where no cause of action existed in statutory law. According to the

---

* Copyright © 1994, Werner F Ebke and Bettina M Steinhauer.
[1] See § 242 of the German Civil Code (*Bürgerliches Gesetzbuch*) (hereinafter referred to as BGB) which reads as follows:

'The debtor is bound to perform according to the requirements of good faith, ordinary usage being taken into consideration.'

See AT von Mehren and JR Gordley, *The Civil Law System* (2nd ed 1977) p 1190.
[2] See *Palandt's Bürgerliches Gesetzbuch* (51st ed 1992) s 242 annot 1 a aa.
[3] According to § 157 of the BGB, 'Contracts shall be interpreted according to the requirements of good faith, ordinary usage being taken into consideration.' See AT von Mehren and JR Gordley, *The Civil Law System* (2nd ed 1977) p 1190.

courts, the doctrine may also be relied upon as a defence in cases where, unforeseen by the parties, the basic assumptions underlying their contractual relationship have changed fundamentally between the time the contract was entered into and the agreed upon time of performance. In a third group of cases, the doctrine of good faith has been employed by the courts to reallocate risks between parties to a contract where stringent adherence to traditional principles and rules of law would have led to undesirable results.

Although the three functions of the doctrine of good faith are generally well settled today, it is often difficult in modern contract cases to determine the exact scope of the causes of action, the defences, and risk allocation devices based upon §§ 242 and 157 of the BGB. This essay discusses selected German court decisions in which the doctrine of good faith has played a seminal role. The essay will confine itself to a discussion of German contract law as set forth in the BGB. The legal significance of the doctrine of good faith under the Vienna Sales Convention will not be dealt with in this chapter.[4] Similarly, the legal impact of the doctrine of good faith upon standard term contracts is beyond the scope of the chapter.

The first part of this essay focusses upon the judicially created cause of action of breach of contract (*positive Vertragsverletzung*). The development of secondary contractual obligations will be discussed in the second part of this chapter. In the third part, cases involving the doctrines of impracticability (*Äquivalenzstörung*) and of frustration of purpose (*Zweckstörung*), change of economic circumstances (*Wegfall der Geschäftsgrundlage*) and mutual error (*Doppelirrtum*) will be analysed. Throughout, this chapter emphasizes the historical and theoretical aspects, as well as the practical implications of the doctrine of good faith in German contract law.

Breach of contract

In German contract law, the doctrine of good faith plays an important role in the course of the formation of a contract. In the final analysis, the theory of *culpa in contrahendo*, or pre-contractual liability, finds its statutory foundation in § 242 of the BGB.[5] The breach of a precontractual duty entitles the injured party to claim damages.[6]

---

[4] For a detailed exposition of the meaning of good faith within the ambit of the Vienna Sales Convention, see eg P Winship, 'Private International Law and the UN Sales Convention' (1988) 21 Cornell Int LJ 487.

[5] See judgment of 2 January 1920, RGZ 97, 326; judgment of 1 March 1928, RGZ 120, 351.

[6] See WF Ebke, 'Federal Republic of Germany', in International Chamber of Commerce (ed), *Formation of Contracts and Precontractual Liability* (1990) pp 35–50.

SPECIFIC PERFORMANCE: RULE AND EXCEPTIONS

When the contract has entered into force, § 242 of the BGB requires the parties to perform in good faith. Under German law, the creditor, as a general rule, is entitled to specific performance. Actions for damages based upon non-performance of contractual obligations[7] are the exception rather than the rule.[8] While in common law systems such actions are grouped together under the heading of 'breach of contract', the BGB has no such comprehensive notion of breach of contract.[9] Rather, the BGB provides that the creditor can claim damages if performance has become impossible for the debtor (*Unmöglichkeit*).[10] Similarly, a cause of action for damages exists where performance has been delayed due to the debtor's fault (*Schuldnerverzug*).[11] If defective goods have been delivered, the buyer can claim damages in cases in which the seller fraudulently concealed the defect or warranted the promised performance (*Gewährleistung*).[12]

THE RISE OF A NEW CAUSE OF ACTION

As early as 1902, Dr Staub[13] pointed out, however, that there are cases of non-performance that cannot be dealt with under the legal concepts of impossibility (*Unmöglichkeit*), delay (*Schuldnerverzug*) or warranty (*Gewährleistung*) as codified in the BGB. Thus, a new cause of action was required to remedy a wrong for which there was no statutory relief. The new cause of action has become known as *positive Vertragsverletzung* or 'positive breach of contract', a term coined by Staub.[14] In 1907, the Reichsgericht, Germany's highest court in civil matters from 1879–1944, adopted Staub's view by recognizing a cause of action for breach of contract.[15]

In the case before the court, the plaintiff had bought fodder for his horses. Upon delivery, the fodder was contaminated. Two of the buyer's horses died after eating it. The plaintiff sought compensation for the damage suffered. The plaintiff could not bring an action for damages on

---

[7] Throughout this article, the term 'obligation' will refer to express or implied contractual obligations. The term 'duty' will be used to refer to non-contractual obligations which are imposed by law irrespective of the existence of a contractual relationship. See also WF Ebke and JR Griffin, 'Good Faith and Fair Dealing in Commercial Lending Transactions: From Convenant to Duty and Beyond' (1989) 49 Ohio St LJ 1237, 1238.

[8] See K Zweigert and H Kötz, *An Introduction to Comparative law* (2nd ed 1992) pp 505–6.

[9] *Ibid.*, pp 524–53.   [10] See BGB, §§ 275, 280, 323–5.

[11] See BGB, §§ 284–92.   [12] See BGB, §§ 459–80, 537–40.

[13] See H Staub, *Die positive Vertragsverletzung* (2nd ed 1913).

[14] The term 'positive' seems to have been used to indicate that the injured party is entitled to expectation damages rather than reliance damages.

[15] See judgment of 9 July 1907, RGZ 66, 289.

grounds of impossibility, because the delivery of proper fodder was still possible.[16] An action for damages for delayed performance could not be brought either, because the plaintiff's damage was not due to the defendant's delay in performance. Neither did a contractual cause of action for damages for selling defective goods exist, because the defendant had not expressly warranted to the plaintiff that the fodder would not be poisonous, nor had he fraudulently concealed the defect.[17] Thus, there seemed to be no statutory relief available to the plaintiff. In order to remedy the situation, the court resorted to the new doctrine of *positive Vertragsverletzung* developed by Staub. Under this doctrine, plaintiffs who are damaged by the defendant's breach of a secondary obligation (*Sekundärpflicht*) are entitled to damages. Recognizing a cause of action for breach of contract, the court based its holding upon an analogy to the rules on delay[18] and impossibility[19] a well as on § 242 of the BGB.[20] By resorting to the methodological instrument of analogizing the doctrine of *positive Vertragsverletzung* to statutorily recognized causes of action, the court implied that, in the final analysis, there is a statutory foundation for the newly created cause of action for breach of contract.

The judicially recognized cause of action for breach of contract reflects the fact that, in German law, delivery of defective goods does not constitute a case of non-performance (*Nichterfüllung*). Rather, it constitutes a case of poor performance (*Schlechtleistung*). While the seller can still fulfil his primary contractual obligation (ie the obligation to deliver the promised goods) by delivering defective goods, the buyer is not left without a remedy in such a case. Under the BGB, the buyer in such a case may cancel the sale, return the goods delivered and claim a refund of his money (*Wandelung*). In the alternative, the buyer is entitled to a reduction of the contract price paid or to be paid (*Minderung*).[21] In cases of fraud, the buyer may also claim damages.[22] The same rule applies when the seller has expressly or impliedly warranted that the promised goods are of a certain nature or quality.[23] There are, however, commentators who are of the opinion that the theory of liability for impossibility should be applied in a much broader sense. According to these authors, performance also includes the quality of performance. Thus, defective performance means

---

[16] See D Medicus, *Schuldrecht I: Allgemeiner Teil* (4th ed 1988) p 185.

[17] See BGB, §§ 463, 480.   [18] See BGB, §§ 286, 326.

[19] See BGB, §§ 280, 325.

[20] See judgment of 11 November 1953, BGHZ 11, 80, 84.

[21] Under § 366 of the German Commercial Code, the buyer can only bring an action for damages for defective goods, if he has inspected the goods delivered and reported the defect to the seller within a reasonable time.

[22] See BGB, §§ 463, 480. As to the damages the plaintiff may recover see, eg NG Foster, *German Law and Legal System* (1993) pp 220–1, 228–9.

[23] See BGB, §§ 459–80.

partial non-performance and thus partial impossibility of performance.[24] Consequently, these commentators would have applied the law of impossibility of performance to the poisonous fodder case discussed above.

ELEMENTS OF THE NEW CAUSE OF ACTION

While the cause of action for breach of contract has never been codified in German contract law, the elements of a cause of action based upon the doctrine of breach of contract become clear when one looks at the numerous cases that have been decided by German courts since the poisonous fodder case in 1907. The elements of a cause of action for breach of contract may be summarized as follows:[25]

(1) The party's failure to perform must not fall within the categories of impossibility, delay or delivery of defective goods, because the cause of action for breach of contract is a residual one.[26]
(2) The contract in question has become effective.
(3) A breach of primary or secondary contractual obligations has occurred, either by means of act or omission.
(4) The debtor is at fault.
(5) The plaintiff's damage would not have occurred but for the defendant's breach of his contractual obligations.

The defendant's breach of contract entitles the plaintiff to claim damages or, in the case of a reciprocal contract (*gegenseitiger Vertrag*), to rescind the contract.[27] The right to rescind is, however, limited to cases of a material breach where enforcing the contract would be unreasonable in light of the doctrine of good faith.[28] In case of a long term contract, the injured party may terminate the contractual relationship *ex nunc*.[29]

CONTRACTS FOR THE BENEFIT OF THIRD PARTIES

An action for damages resulting from the debtor's breach of contract may be brought by a third party who is not party to the contract. Thus, for example, if the contract is one for the benefit of a third party (*Vertrag zugunsten Dritter*), the third party is as much entitled to damages as if it were in privity of contract.[30] If the third party suffers personal injury or

---

[24] See D Medicus, *Schuldrecht I: Allgemeiner Teil* (4th ed 1988) pp 185–6.
[25] *Ibid.*, pp 184–91.   [26] The action may also be based upon the law of torts.
[27] See note 20 above. See also judgment of 5 February 1929, RGZ 123, 241.
[28] See D Medicus, *Schuldrecht I: Allgemeiner Teil* (4th ed 1988) p 185.
[29] See, eg judgment of 27 September 1938, RGZ 158, 326. See also judgment of 10 July 1968, BGHZ 50, 312.
[30] See BGB, § 328.

property damage due to the debtor's breach of a secondary obligation, the third party may bring an action for damages under the doctrine of breach of contract. The plaintiff's rights under the doctrine of breach of contract, however, are limited to the right to claim damages. The right to rescind the contract may be exercised only by the contracting parties themselves.[31]

VERTRAG MIT SCHUTZWIRKUNG FÜR DRITTE

German courts have further broadened the class of potential third party plaintiffs by extending the right to sue to individuals who are not formally in privity of contract and not a third party beneficiary but who do have a close personal relationship with one of the parties to the contract (eg spouses or children). In some cases, courts have gone even further and have given a right to sue to persons who, expressly or impliedly, were intended by the contracting parties to fall within the ambit of the contractual relationship (*Vertrag mit Schutzwirkung für Dritte*).[32] The sole purpose of these court rulings has been to provide injured third parties a contractual remedy where the law of torts, because of the possibility of exculpatory proof (*Entlastungsbeweis*), provides no satisfactory remedy.[33] A case decided by the Reichsgericht[34] illustrates this point.

In the case before the court, a tenant contracted with a repair firm for the repair of a gas-operated water heater which was in the dwelling. Owing to fault on the part of the gas fitter, the heater exploded and caused injuries to a cleaning lady employed by the tenant. The cleaning lady could, of course, bring a tort action against the gas fitter.[35] She could also bring a tort action against the repair firm under the principle of *respondeat superior*, or vicarious liability.[36] Under German tort law, however, employers are not liable for acts or omissions of their employees, if the employer can prove that he was not personally at fault. To satisfy the requirement of exculpatory proof, the defendant must establish only that he took all requisite precautions in selecting, training, instructing and supervising the employee.[37]

Under German contract law, by contrast, a similar defence is not available to persons employing others to perform their obligations under a

---

[31] See *Palandt's Bürgerliches Gesetzbuch* (51st ed 1992) s 328, annot 1 c aa.
[32] See judgment of 22 January 1968, BGHZ 49, 350, 353.
[33] See WF Ebke, 'Federal Republic of Germany' in International Chamber of Commerce (ed), *Formation of Contracts and Precontractual Liability* (1990), p 42.
[34] See judgment of 10 February 1930, RGZ 127, 218.
[35] See BGB, §§ 823(1), (2).   [36] See BGB, § 831.
[37] See K Zweigert and H Kötz, *An Introduction to Comparative Law* (2nd ed 1992) pp 670–6.

contract.[38] Thus, a party to a contract is personally liable to the other party to the contract for any damage caused by his employees, irrespective of the party's own care and without the possibility of exculpation. In the above-mentioned case, however, the cleaning lady was not party to the contract between her employer (ie the tenant) and the repair firm. Accordingly, there seemed to be no basis for a contract action for damages by the cleaning lady against the repair firm. Nevertheless, the court held that, under the doctrine of good faith, a secondary obligation of care arose from the contract between the repair firm and the tenant, which was owed not only to the tenant but also to the tenant's cleaning lady.[39] In view of her employment relationship with the tenant, the cleaning lady was held to be in so close a relationship to the tenant as to be entitled to bring a contract action for damages against the repair firm, based upon the doctrine of breach of contract.

The development of secondary obligations

Today, the doctrine of good faith plays its most important role in the emerging field of secondary contract obligations, the breach of which may make the party in breach liable to the other party under the doctrine of breach of contract. Under German law, the primary obligation of the parties to a contract is to perform. In addition, both parties may be subject to additional 'secondary' or 'auxiliary' obligations. The purpose of those secondary obligations is to specify how the parties have to perform under the contract. Secondary obligations include, but are not limited to, obligations expressly provided for by statute, contract or agreement.[40] In addition, the courts have implied obligations where the parties were found to have contemplated such obligations as part of their contract or agreement.

CATEGORIES OF CASES

The cases involving implied secondary obligations can be divided into five categories. The first category of secondary obligations includes cases in which the law imposes upon each contracting party an obligation

---

[38] See § 278 of the BGB which reads as follows:

A debtor is responsible for the fault of his statutory agent and of persons whom he employs in fulfilling his obligation to the same extent as for his own fault.

See AT von Mehren and JR Gordley, *The Civil Law System* (2nd ed 1977) p 1193.

[39] See K Zweigert & H Kötz, *An Introduction to Comparative Law* (2nd ed 1992) pp 492–3, 674–5.

[40] See, eg BGB, §§ 368, 402, 444, 618, 666.

of care (*Obhutspflicht*) with respect to the other party's life, limb or property.[41] Cases falling into the second category can best be described as those in which courts have recognized an obligation to bargain in good faith and to deal fairly with each other (*Aufklärungspflicht*).[42] The third category involves a broad variety of cases in which the parties can be expected to refrain from everything which might impair the purpose of the contact. Thus, the debtor is under an obligation to do what he can to secure the promised performance (*Leistungstreuepflicht*).[43] The fourth category of cases concerns the parties' obligation to assist each other so that the contract can be carried out (*Mitwirkungspflicht*).[44] The fifth category includes the obligation of one party to disclose material facts to the other party (*Auskunftspflicht*).[45]

CONTRACTUAL NATURE

The secondary obligations mentioned arise from the contract. In the final analysis, such obligations are based on § 242 of the BGB. If a party negligently or intentionally breaches an express or implied secondary contract obligation, and if such breach proximately causes damages on the part of the other party to a contract, the injured party may, under the doctrine of breach of contract, claim damages or rescind the contract. Whether the creditor also has a right to claim performance of a secondary obligation is a matter of dispute between courts and commentators. A claim for performance of a secondary obligation would seem to be justified where the parties have reached an agreement on this question.[46] If there is no such agreement, it is widely held that the debtor cannot demand specific performance of a secondary obligation.[47] Some authors suggest, however, that secondary obligations are specifically enforceable if the exact scope of the obligation is clear, and if the remedies provided under the doctrine of breach of contract are not adequate.

---

[41] See judgment of 10 March 1983, BGH, NJW 1983, 2813, 2814.
[42] See judgment of 12 November 1969, BGH, NJW 1970, 653, 655.
[43] See judgment of 24 January 1910, RGZ 54, 394.
[44] See judgment of 4 June 1954, BGHZ 14, 1, 2. See also judgment of 25 June 1976, BGHZ 67, 34.
[45] See judgment of 4 May 1923, RGZ 108, 7. See also judgment of 28 October 1953, BGHZ 10, 385, 387.
[46] See eg R Stürner, 'Der Anspruch auf Erfüllung von Treue- und Sorgfaltspflichten' (1976) 31 Juristenzeitung 384, 385.
[47] See judgment of 26 June 1984, OLG Frankfurt, JZ 1985, 337; see also J Esser and E Schmidt, *Schuldrecht I: Allgemeiner Teil* (7th ed 1992) pp 110–11; J Gernhuber, *Das Schuldverhältnis* (1989) pp 24–5.

The following two examples concerning the obligation of care and the obligation to refrain from impairing the purpose of the contract will illustrate this point.

OBLIGATION OF CARE

Under § 536 of the BGB, a lessor is obliged to keep the let room in a condition that enables the lessee to use it as agreed in the lease. Suppose rain leaks through the roof causing damage to the lessee's furniture. The question arises whether the lessee may sue for the roof to be repaired or whether he is only entitled to terminate the lease and claim damages for the damage to the furniture. While under German contract law, the lessee may terminate the lease[48] and claim damages for the damage he suffered,[49] contract law does not deal expressly with the right to specific performance. Specifically, in the case in question, German law is silent on the issue of whether or not the lessee may demand that the lessor repair the roof. As the specific performance required can be put into precise terms, the answer depends upon whether the lessee could find relief by revoking the contract. Under these circumstances, however, revoking the contract will in most cases not be an appropriate remedy. Thus, the plaintiff may claim performance of the lease and sue for the roof to be repaired.[50]

Obligation to refrain from impairing the purpose of the contract

A claim for performance of the obligation to refrain from impairing the purpose of the contract can be brought when the date of performance lies sometime in future. If, for example, the seller has to transfer the title to a horse to the buyer 12 months following the date of making the contract of sale for the horse, the seller owes the buyer a secondary obligation to feed the horse. In the absence of an express contractual provision to that effect, courts will have little theoretical or practical difficulty in implying such an obligation and rendering a declaratory judgment to that effect. The plaintiff can then enforce the declaratory judgment. If, by contrast, the seller had to transfer the title to a horse to the buyer 2 days following the contract of sale of the horse, the buyer could only seek a preliminary injunction to secure performance of the main obligation.[51]

---

[48] See BGB, § 542. [49] See BGB, § 538.
[50] See R Stürner, 'Der Anspruch auf Erfüllung von Treue- und Sorgfaltspflichten' (1976) 31 Juristenzeitung 384, 388.
[51] *Ibid.*, 390, 391.

Impracticability and frustration of purpose[52]

The doctrine of breach of contract and the emerging secondary obligations have been used to remedy situations where no statutory relief
existed. The doctrines of impracticability and frustration of purpose,
change in economic circumstances and mutual error, by contrast, have
been utilized by the courts to correct undesirable results reached under
traditional concepts and rules of law. Like the doctrine of breach of contract and secondary obligations, the doctrines of impracticability and frustration of purpose, in the final analysis, find their statutory foundation in
the good faith provision of the BGB.

IMPRACTICABILITY

The doctrine of impracticability[53] applies where events have occurred
which have rendered performance, or performance in the contemplated
fashion, impracticable. Such events may be the result of fire, increased
costs, inflation etc. To insist upon performance in accordance with the
terms and conditions of the contract, to the detriment of the party
adversely affected by such events, might amount to bad faith. This part of
the chapter traces the development by the German courts of comprehensive relief in cases of changed or unforeseen circumstances.

The doctrine of impossibility

The seminal case was decided by the Reichsgericht in 1904.[54] In this case,
the defendant had promised to deliver specified goods, a type of flour
which was produced in one mill only. The mill was destroyed by a fire.
The plaintiff brought an action for damages based upon the defendant's
failure to deliver. The seller defended the action on the ground that performance had become economically impossible and that, consequently,
non-performance was excused under § 275 of the BGB.[55] The court did not

---

[52] See W Lorenz, Ch 14 below.
[53] For a detailed comparative study on the theory of impracticability, see GH Treitel,
Unmöglichkeit, Impracticability und Frustration im Anglo-Amerikanischen Recht (1991).
[54] See judgment of 23 February 1904, RGZ 57, 116. See also AT von Mehren and JR
Gordley, *The Civil Law System* (2nd ed 1977) pp 1067–8.
[55] Section 275 of the BGB reads as follows:

The debtor is relieved from his obligation to perform if the performance becomes impossible because of
a circumstance for which he is not responsible and which occurred after the creation of the obligation.
    If the debtor, after the creation of the obligation, becomes unable to perform, it is equivalent to a cir-
cumstance rendering the performance impossible.

See AT von Mehren and JR Gordley, *ibid.*, p 1193.

treat this case as a case of economic impossibility, however. Rather, it ruled that performance had, as a practical matter, become impossible because the goods in question could not be produced by the mill within the foreseeable future, and because the seller could not be expected to locate flour that had left the mill by ship the night before the fire broke out.

The doctrine of economic impossibility

The doctrine of impossibility of performance has also been referred to in cases in which, due to war or scarcity of goods, the costs of manufacturing had become prohibitive. Thus, if the costs by far exceeded the contract price stipulated by the parties,[56] performance was ruled to be impossible; provided, however, that performance would result in the debtor's financial ruin. It was not necessary, however, that the performance of the obligation in question would have ruinous effects. It sufficed if performing all the obligations affected by the rise in price would result in the debtor's ruin.[57] This argument in effect granted preference to those debtors whose businesses were built on shaky ground.[58] Therefore, other judgments stressed the requirement of identity of performance: where the economic essence of what could still be done was different from the act that was agreed to be done, performance had become essentially different and therefore impossible.[59] The debtor could then terminate the contract. But terminating the contract did not provide an appropriate remedy in cases in which both parties wanted the contract to be carried out.

The clausula rebus sic stantibus

In 1920, the *Reichsgericht* had to decide a case[60] in which both parties wanted the contract to be performed. In 1912, the plaintiff had let a business space to the defendant. Under clause 20 of the contract, the defendant was entitled to receive steam to be furnished by the plaintiff. The plaintiff in turn was to be compensated for the steam in accordance with the lease. In 1917, due to a considerable increase in steam prices, the plaintiff refused to furnish further steam unless the defendant was willing to pay an additional sum of money. Relying upon the principle of *pacta sunt*

---

[56] See judgment of 7 December 1917, RGZ 91, 312; judgment of 25 March 1918, OLG Stuttgart, (1918) 22 Recht 240.

[57] See judgment of 22 October 1920, RGZ 100, 334.

[58] See EJ Cohn, 'Frustration of Contract in German Law' (1946) 28 J Comp Leg & Int L 15.

[59] See judgment of 2 February 1921, (1921) 50 JW 833; judgment of 29 November 1921, RGZ 103, 177. See also AT von Mehren and JR Gordley, *The Civil Law System* (2nd ed 1977) p 1074.

[60] See judgment of 9 September 1920, RGZ 100, 129. See also AT von Mehren and JR Gordley, *ibid.*, pp 1075–8.

servanda, the defendant refused to pay more. The Reichsgericht, however, held for plaintiff.

The court based its decision upon the *clausula rebus sic stantibus*. This principle had been expressly recognized in the Code Maximilaneus Bavaricus[61] and in the Prussian Allgemeines Landrecht,[62] which were legal predecessors of the German Civil Code. The drafters of the BGB, however, generally rejected the *clausula rebus sic stantibus* and made it applicable only to a few exceptional circumstances.[63] The *clausula rebus sic stantibus* nevertheless found its way into the BGB by means of §§ 242, 157 and 325. Under §§ 242 and 157 of the BGB, the debtor's obligation to perform may be limited where, as a result of complete change in economic circumstances, performance has become economically different from the performance originally contemplated by the parties. Similarly, under § 325, impossibility may be understood as including economic impossibility.[64]

The *clausula rebus sic stantibus* does not purport to provide a uniform solution for all cases. Rather, where the contracting parties do not want the contract to be carried out, each party is entitled to rescind the contract according to the rules of rescission. Where the parties prefer the contract to be carried out, courts have the power, under the *clausula rebus sic stantibus*, to adapt the parties' contractual obligations in accordance with the change in circumstances.[65]

The doctrine of contractual basis (Wegfall der Geschäftsgrundlage)

In 1921, Professor Oertmann of the University of Göttingen developed the doctrine of contractual basis (*Geschäftsgrundlage*) by redefining the *clausula rebus sic stantibus*:[66]

'Contractual basis' is an assumption made by one party that has become obvious to the other by the process of the formation of the contract and has received its acquiescence, provided that the assumption refers to the existence, or coming into existence, of circumstances forming the basis of the contractual intention. Alternatively, 'contractual basis' is the common assumption on the part of the respective parties of such circumstances.

Thus, the doctrine of *Wegfall der Geschäftsgrundlage* was born. Translated literally, the doctrine applies to cases in which the contractual

---

[61] See Code Maximilianeus Bavaricus, Civilis (1756), Part 4, ch 15, p 2.

[62] See Prussian Allgemeines Landrecht I, 5, pp 377–9.

[63] The *clausula rebus sic stantibus* has been incorporated only in a few provisions of the BGB. See, eg BGB, §§ 321, 610, 519, 605, 775(1).

[64] See judgment of 21 September 1920, RGZ 100, 129.

[65] See P Oertmann, *Die Geschäftsgrundlage: Ein neuer Rechtsbegriff* (1921) p 165.

[66] *Ibid.*, p 37 (translation by EJ Cohn, 'Frustration of Contract in German Law' (1946) 28 J Comp Leg & Int L 15, 20).

basis has 'collapsed'. The courts first referred to the doctrine of contractual basis in cases in which, due to inflation, the relationship between the value of the goods to be sold and the price to be paid had changed fundamentally.

The aftermath of World War I

In the aftermath of World War I, the impact of inflation on long-term contracts was particularly pressing. The question arose whether the seller could either rescind the contract or ask for the price to be renegotiated and adjusted. As early as in 1921, the Reichsgericht held that reciprocal contracts are based upon the notion of equivalence of the parties' promises or, at least, upon some notion of adequacy.[67] In a decision handed down in 1922, the court ruled that such an assumption constitutes the contractual basis of every contract.[68] When the conditions that form the basis of the parties' contractual relationship cease to exist, the party who would be detrimentally affected by the change in circumstances may refuse to perform on the grounds of good faith or sue for the obligations to be adjusted to the change in circumstances.[69] By thus holding, the court in effect did away with the principle of nominal value. The court was careful, however, to limit the application of the doctrine to circumstances that are not under the control of the debtor and do not fall within his 'sphere of influence' (*Risikosphäre*),[70] but that have resulted in an extreme disproportion[71] in the relationship of mutual performance and where continued persistence on the debtor's performance would be contrary to good faith.

Equitable contribution

In another case,[72] a seller had sold a house to a third party after paying off the mortgage. The seller, having paid the nominal amount of money to the mortgage creditor, sought the cancellation of the mortgage in the land register. The mortgage creditor, however, rejected the cancellation claiming that, by April 1920, when the mortgage had become due, the cost-of-living index had risen by about 10 per cent. Thus, he could not be compelled to accept worthless paper money in exchange for the mortgage debt. The Reichsgericht held for the mortgage creditor. Consequently, the mortgage creditor was entitled to a fair share of the revalued amount of the mortgage debt (*Aufwertungsanspruch*). The court based its judgment

---

[67] See judgment of 29 November 1921, RGZ 103, 177.
[68] See judgment of 3 February 1922, RGZ 103, 328. [69] *Ibid.*
[70] See judgment of 25 February 1993, BGH, NJW 1993, 1856, 1859.
[71] An extreme disproportion may exist where the manufacturing costs have risen by 60%. For further examples, see, eg *Palandt's Bürgerliches Gesetzbuch* (51st ed 1992) § 242 annot. 6 c a aa.
[72] See judgment of 28 November 1923, RGZ 107, 78. See also AT von Mehren and JR Gordley, *The Civil Law System* (2nd ed 1977) pp 1084–7.

upon § 242 of the BGB generally, rather than upon the theory of contractual basis.[73]

Revaluation

In subsequent cases, the Reichsgericht extended the theory even further. In a comparable case, the seller of a house was granted a right to claim for adjustment of the price to be paid from the buyer for further payments he had to make to the mortgagee because of the revaluation of the mortgage debt (*Ausgleichsanspruch*). The *Reichsgericht* was of the opinion that the basis of the contract between the seller and the buyer, ie the assumption that the mortgage had been paid off, had changed completely.[74] The idea underlying the decision of the *Reichsgericht* was that creditors cannot expect that only the debtors should carry the crushing burden of the economic turmoil following World War I.

Subjective versus objective basis

The doctrine of contractual basis has been developed further by legal writers who draw a distinction between the objective basis of contract and the subjective basis of contract. The term 'subjective basis of contract' refers to circumstances which have become obvious in the negotiation process and that induced the parties to conclude the contract. The term 'objective basis of contract', by contrast, refers to circumstances which logically had to exist in order to achieve the objectives of the contract. Thus, the term 'objective basis of contract' refers to circumstances that the parties did not have in mind when they concluded the contract.[75] As a result, the doctrine of *Wegfall der Geschäftsgrundlage* applied to all changes in circumstances, whether or not the parties had had these circumstances in mind when they concluded their contract.

FRUSTRATION OF PURPOSE

While under the doctrine of impracticability the debtor of an obligation can find relief, the doctrine of frustration of purpose (*Zweckstörung*) applies to cases in which performance is still possible, but in which the creditor has lost interest in the performance.[76] Thus, the rules of impossibility normally do not apply, nor does the doctrine of *Wegfall der Geschäftsgrundlage*. For example, non-performance is not excused under the doctrine of *Wegfall der Geschäftsgrundlage* when the buyer has lost

---

[73] See text accompanying note 62, above.
[74] See judgment of 10 February 1926, RGZ 112, 329.
[75] See K Larenz, *Geschäftsgrundlage und Vertragserfüllung* (3rd ed 1963) p 17.
[76] For a detailed comparative study on frustration of purpose, see GH Treitel, *Unmöglichkeit, Impracticability und Frustration im Anglo-Amerikanischen Recht* (1991) pp 91–121.

interest, because an event has occurred which frustrated his assumption that he would gain profit from further selling the goods he contracted for. In such a case, the purpose of the contract is not frustrated; rather, the frustration relates to the profits to be made from further transactions. One could also argue that the buyer has assumed the risk of mistake with respect to the use of the goods.[77]

The coronation cases

There might, however, be cases in which the specific use of the purchased goods has become the basis of the contract between the parties. This is the case when both parties understand the purpose for which the contract has been made, and the failure of this purpose makes the contract perfor- mance completely or almost totally worthless to the party seeking relief.[78] The doctrine of contractual basis can best be applied where one party can make its profits only because of the intended use of the other party. The case most often discussed in this context by German writers is *Krell* v *Henry*, one of the 'coronation cases'.[79]

In this case, the plaintiff had contracted to permit the defendant to occupy his flat on Pall Mall for two days during which the coronation parades would be passing by. The illness of King Edward VII led to the cancellation of the pagentry. The contract made no express reference to the coronation. The question was whether the defendant had to pay rent for the flat. According to some German commentators, the case was one of impossibility because the plaintiff had contracted to perform in such a way that the defendant could watch the parade and this performance had become impossible.[80] Other authors, by contrast, argue that the issue is whether or not the objective basis of the contract has collapsed.[81] More recently, commentators suggested solving cases of this sort by applying § 537 of the BGB: the plaintiff was not in a position to permit the use by the defendant which was agreed upon in the contract. Thus, the flat had a 'defect' and the rent to be paid would be reduced.[82]

Some other cases

Frustration of purpose should be distinguished clearly from cases in which the purpose of the contract has been achieved without any efforts

---

[77] See judgment of 1 June 1979, BGHZ 74, 370, 374; judgment of 5 May 1955, BGHZ 17, 327; judgment of 27 February 1985, BGH, NJW 1985, 2692, 2694.

[78] See judgment of 23 March 1966, BGH, (1966) 21 JZ 409; judgment of 8 February 1984, BGH, NJW 1984, 1746.   [79] See *Krell* v *Henry* [1903] 2 KB 740.

[80] See D Medicus, *Bürgerliches Recht* (15th ed 1991) p 86.

[81] See K Larenz, *Lehrbuch des Schuldrechts I: Allgemeiner Teil* (13th ed 1982) p 203.

[82] See *Krell* v *Henry* [1903] 2 KB 740.

on the part of the debtor. If, for example, a person promises to free a grounded ship by pulling it off the ground and the ship refloats itself before the promissor arrives, performance must be treated as impossible. It is not enough that the act of pulling the ship remains possible where the agreed upon purpose can no longer be achieved. Frustration of purpose should also not be confused either with cases in which the purpose has become impossible. Where the patient dies one day before a scheduled operation, performance has become impossible. The question remains, however, on what legal grounds the deceased's estate can refuse to pay in case the hospital demands payment for the agreed upon operation. The prevailing view would seem to be to allow the deceased's estate to defend such an action on grounds of impossibility rather than the doctrine of contractual basis.[83]

CHANGE IN ECONOMIC CIRCUMSTANCES

The doctrine of contractual basis has been applied to circumstances which adversely affected the party to a contract other than the party owing money. By contrast, the question in the group of cases involving changes in economic circumstances is, whether the party owing money can defend an action for performance on the ground that his financial situation has worsened to an extent that he finds it too onerous to perform and that, therefore, his non-performance should be excused. The answer would seem to be 'no'. Section 279 of the BGB seems to support this view.[84] As a general rule, the debtor is responsible for his ability to pay.[85]

The aftermath of World War II

The courts have, however, recognized that there might be cases in which stringent adherence to the provisions and rules of law would have led to unsustainable results. Thus, for example, in the aftermath of the collapse of the Third Reich, the Decree of Judicial Assistance in Respect of Contracts (*Vertragshilfeverordnung*)[86] granted some relief to debtors who were, directly or indirectly, affected by the stoppage of payments by the government. The District Court of Tempelhof ruled that, where the Decree was not applicable, the debtor should be allowed to plead his deteriorating financial situation in defence to any claim brought against him

---

[83] See D Medicus, *Schuldrecht I: Allgemeiner Teil* (4th ed 1988) p 200.

[84] See judgment of 10 February 1982, BGHZ 83, 97, 100.

[85] An exception is made only as to alimony, child support and similar cases. See D Medicus, *Schuldrecht I: Allgemeiner Teil* (4th ed 1988) pp 161–2.

[86] See the Decree of Judicial Assistance in Respect of Contracts (*Vertragshilfeverordnung*) of 30 November 1939, RGB1 vol I, p 2329 (1939).

under a pre-war contract. Basing its unique judgment on § 242 of the BGB, the court ruled that no creditor could demand that the debtor alone was to carry the economic burden of the collapse of the Third Reich.[87] The court's holding is, however, limited to the exceptional facts of the case. The decision cannot be read to include cases of unexpected financial strain as are common in everyday life.

The reunification of Germany

More recently, the doctrine of contractual basis has been employed to deal with the challenges arising from the turmoil following the collapse of the Soviet Union. Similarly, the impact of the accession of former East Germany to the Federal Republic of Germany[88] on private contracts concluded under East German law before Germany's reunification is among the legal issues to be addressed by German courts today. In 1992, the Bundesgerichtshof, Germany's highest court in civil matters, handed down a decision[89] in which it invoked the doctrine of contractual basis to cope with these problems. In the case before the court, the East German plaintiff had contracted in January 1990 to deliver a printing machine to the East German defendant, a government enterprise. The printing machine had been imported by the plaintiff from Austria. The money for the machine was to be provided in part by the East German government and in part by an East German bank. In June 1990, the defendant was granted part of the bank loan. The defendant handed the sum over to the plaintiff. No further payments were made. On 1 July 1990, the East German currency ceased to exist as a result of the monetary union between former East Germany and the Federal Republic of Germany.

The plaintiff sued the defendant for the outstanding sum of money. The buyer defended the action arguing that he did not get any further funds from the East German government nor from the East German bank. Consequently, the contemplated means of financing the purchase, which arguably constituted the contractual basis of the contract, had failed. In view of the doctrine of contractual basis, the defendant argued, he could not be expected to pay the rest of the purchase price. The Bundesgerichtshof held that, as a general rule, the doctrine of contractual basis is applicable to contracts concluded under the laws of former East Germany. However, according to the court, the failure of the buyer to secure the contemplated means of financing the purchase generally falls within the buyer's sphere of risk. Consequently, according to the general

---

[87] For details on the Decree of Judicial Assistance, above note 86, see Editorial, (1946) 1 Süddeutsche Juristenzeitung 97.

[88] See WF Ebke, *'Legal Implications of Germany's Reunification'* (1990) 24 Int Lawyer 1130.

[89] See judgment of 14 October 1992, BGH, NJW 1993, 259.

rule, one would have expected the court to reject the defendant's argument that the doctrine of contractual basis was a valid defence in the case at hand.

The court, however, recognized the unique situation that contracting parties faced under the legal and economic system of former East Germany. Under this system, the parties to a contract did not assume any financial risk. Rather, they were obliged to carry out East Germany's Five Year Plan and could count on the necessary financing to be provided as planned. In view of this situation, the Bundesgerichtshof ruled that the contractual obligations of the defendant be adjusted on the ground of the doctrine of contractual basis. In the opinion of the court, both parties should bear, to an equal extent, the consequences of the collapse of East Germany and East Germany's accession to the Federal Republic of Germany. The court concluded that the defendant had to pay half of the difference between the purchase price originally agreed upon by the parties and the amount that the defendant had already paid to the plaintiff.

The court's reasoning was as follows: the original purchase price of the printing machine was 1.7 million East German Marks, of which the defendant had already paid 400.000 East German Marks. Thus, the difference between the purchase price and the amount paid was 1.3 million East German Marks. Based upon the exchange rate of the East German Mark to the Deutsche Mark under the Monetary Union Treaty (ie 2:1), the difference between the originally agreed upon purchase price and the amount paid was 650.000 DM. According to the court, the plaintiff was entitled to receive 50 per cent of this amount, ie 325.000 DM.

At first glance, this holding may seem remarkable. It should be noted, however, that the original purchase price of 1.7 million East German Marks was artificially inflated because it was based upon an unrealistic exchange rate of the East German Mark to the Austrian Shilling. Based upon the official exchange rate of the Deutsche Mark *vis-à-vis* the Austrian currency, the purchase price of the printing machine would have been 380.000 DM. By holding that the defendant owed the plaintiff 325.000 DM in addition to the 400.000 East German Marks (ie 200.000 DM), the plaintiff in effect received an amount equal to the realistic purchase price plus a significant profit. While it may be debatable whether courts should adjust essential contract terms where the means of financing the transaction have proved to be unavailable, the court's holding in the case at hand would seem to be acceptable or at least understandable because of the unique facts presented.

MUTUAL ERROR

The last group of cases involves cases of mutual error. Like the preceding group, this group of cases is concerned with the correction of inadequate results which would be achieved by applying the BGB's provisions on avoidance (*Anfechtung*). Where both parties are mistaken as to a basic assumption upon which the contract was based, the rules of avoidance should not be applied. If the rules were to be applied, it would depend upon mere chance which party would become liable for damages. Under § 122 of the BGB, who is the first to declare avoidance is liable to pay the expectation damages (*negatives Interesse*) to the other party.[90] This result is thought to be unreasonable. Therefore, cases of mutual error are treated as falling within the ambit of the doctrine of subjective contractual basis.[91] Consequently, the contract will be either adjusted or terminated, depending upon the will of the parties. However, no party is liable to the other party for any expectation damages that the other party may have suffered.

The mutual error can also refer to the occurrence or non-occurrence of future circumstances. In such a case, the doctrine of contractual basis can be applied when both parties wanted to base the contract upon those circumstances. The courts, however, were again careful to limit the applicability of the doctrine of contractual basis to circumstances that are not under the control of, and do not fall into the 'sphere of influence' (*Risikosphäre*) of one of the parties.[92]

Conclusion

As can be seen from the preceding discussion, § 242 of the BGB has been used by German courts as the statutory basis for deriving new general principles of law when existing rules of law proved inadequate in adjudicating actual cases. Courts have had little theoretical difficulty in over coming statutory limitations and doctrinal hurdles, if they were convinced that a just and equitable response to new social developments, and needs not anticipated by the legislature, could be achieved only by deviating from traditional rules of law. The source of such law-making by German courts has very often been § 242 of the BGB, which has been used both as a shield and a sword. The judicial 'invention' by German courts of the cause of action for breach of contract is the most important example of

[90] See § 122(1) of the BGB, which reads as follows:

If a declaration of intention given to another person is void under section 118 or voidable under sections 119 and 120, the declarant shall compensate him or any third party for any damage that the other or the third party has sustained by relying upon the validity of the declaration; the damages, nevertheless, shall not exceed the value of the interest that the other or the third party has in the validity of the declaration.

See AT von Mehren and JR Gordley, *The Civil Law System* (2nd ed 1977) p 1187.

[91] See judgment of 30 October 1928, RGZ 122, 203; judgment of 23 October 1957, BGHZ 25, 390, 392.

[92] See judgment of 10 March 1983, BGH, NJW 1983, 1489, 1490.

how judges have utilized the good faith provision as a sword. The doctrines of impracticability, frustration of purpose and change in economic circumstances, by contrast, are examples of cases in which § 242 of the BGB has been used as a shield.

The preceding discussion also shows how judges in a civil law system like Germany are more and more frequently engaged in creative interstitial law-making on the basis of, and in some cases even without the aid of, the written law. In this respect, German courts are moving in the direction of common-law jurisdictions, where judges openly admit that they are making law. Although the technique employed by the courts to achieve the desirable result may vary from one country to another, courts in both legal traditions increasingly are inclined to decide cases in a highly pragmatic and sometimes result-oriented fashion, rather than by slavishly applying traditional principles and rules of law. The doctrine of good faith is a particularly tempting instrument for interstitial law-making, because it has proved to be flexible enough to respond to novel needs of the legal system, and firm enough to serve as a foundation even for new causes of action, such as the action for breach of contract.

8

The Implied Terms of Contracts: Of 'Default Rules' and 'Situation-Sense'[1]

·Todd D Rakoff

The problem

Let us suppose that A and B have a contract. They argue about something having to do with their relationship under the contract. Unable to resolve their dispute, they come to court. Unfortunately, their agreement, even when fully interpreted in light of their actions, trade usage, and other means of getting at what they meant, does not provide a term that answers their dispute. (It might be that no term of the agreement comes close to the situation that has developed, or it might be that the court is convinced that a broad term that appears to be applicable was not in fact meant to apply to these particulars.) What is the court to do?

The court might say, courts do not make contracts for parties. Where there is no agreed term, there is no legal obligation. Or the court might say, the matter in dispute was in any case the subject of a mandatory rule. Even if the contract had provided for the eventuality, it would make no difference; what the law requires, the law requires. Courts do make such points.

Courts also, and not infrequently, say something else. They say: 'here is the term which you did not provide, which will govern your relationship, but only because you did not speak, as we would not insist on our term if the two of you had agreed to something different.' The doctrinal labels for these things are 'constructive' or 'implied' 'terms' or 'conditions' (although sometimes those labels are also used for things that are mandatory, and at other times for things that are inferred as the parties' actual intent). The process of creating them the Realists often denominated 'gap filling,' while Professor Farnsworth's treatise calls it 'deciding omitted cases'.[2] Most recently, in the US literature at least, these things have been labelled 'default rules'. US law professors, at least in their use of metaphor, share their compatriots' technological fixation; the notion is,

---

[1] Copyright © 1994, Todd D Rakoff.
[2] EA Farnsworth, *Contracts* (2nd ed 1990) pp 540 *et seq*.

that just as a computer program has settings applicable in default of user specification, so too does the legal system.[3]

What is involved in filling a gap, deciding an omitted case, or creating a default rule? Judges often describe what they are doing in terms of carrying out the intentions of the parties. Sometimes, indeed, all that is involved is an inference as to what the parties had in their minds but failed to say. To this extent, there is hardly a problem, except perhaps a question of the relationship between documents and parol evidence. For several generations, however, it has been understood by scholars that the parties' intentions, in this factual sense, often run out long before the courts stop opining.[4]

What, then, are the judges trying to say? Sometimes judicial reference to 'intent' seems to have a somewhat different descriptive content, as indicating not an inferred mental state, but rather the attention being paid by the judge to the particular circumstances in which the very parties before the court found themselves. But, very commonly, the language should be understood as answering to the needs of ideological justification rather than realistic description. The use of the word 'intent' constitutes a ceremonial bow to complete private autonomy, to the implicit limitation of obligation to intentions which can be imputed in fact to the parties. This can only be viewed as a fiction.

But if intention is often the fiction, then what is the fact? If we look at the cases, we see the judges using two very different methods to supplement the actual agreement of the parties. One is well exemplified (to rely on US decisions) by *Parev Products Co Inc v I Rokeach & Sons Inc*,[5] and the other by *Ellsworth Dobbs Inc v Johnson*.[6]

---

[3] The rise of this analogy is traced in RE Barnett, 'The Sound of Silence: Default Rules and Contractual Consent' (1992) 78 Va L Rev 821, 823–5. The terminology in fact represents something of a linguistic *renvoi*. 'Default rules' has reference to the computing usage of 'default,' ie '[a] preselected option adopted by a computer when no alternative is specified by the user or programmer', but this usage is in turn merely one variant of a general meaning of 'default' as 'failure in performance,' whose earliest usages, going back to about 1300, are legal. A modern legal use of the same meaning appears in the phrase 'judgment by default'. 'Default,' *The Oxford English Dictionary* (2nd ed 1989) vol IV, p 371.

[4] Professor Corbin's analysis of conditions, published in 1919, famously distinguished between express, implied, and constructive conditions; he lamented that 'the courts so frequently construct under the guise of mere interpretation.' See AL Corbin, 'Conditions in the Law of Contract' (1919) 28 Yale LJ 739, 741. Professor Williston's contemporaneous treatise had a whole section, placed in the middle of the discussion of implied conditions, entitled 'Fictitiously imputed intentions.' See S Williston, *Contracts* (1920) vol II p 1576. A generation later—but still a while ago—Glanville Williams wrote of the 'common form among judges to deny that they ever read into a contract . . . anything other than what, in their view, the parties actually intended'; his view was: '[t]hese statements cannot be taken seriously.' See GL Williams, 'Language and the Law—IV' (1945) 61 LQR 384, 402–3. The history of the judicial use of 'intent' to cover construction is traced in EA Farnsworth, 'Disputes Over Omission In Contracts' (1968) 68 Colum L Rev 860, 862–8.

[5] 124 F 2d 147 (2d Cir 1941).   [6] 236 A 2d 843 (NJ 1967).

Parev Products dealt with a long-term licensing arrangement for a secret formula, made between two producers of Kosher foods. Royalties were paid according to the volume of the licensed product sold. The matter in dispute—not covered by any explicit term of this custom-crafted contract—was whether the licensee could introduce a new product into the market, to meet new competition from third parties, when that product would also compete somewhat with the licensed product. The judgment was that selling the new product should not be forbidden, but that the licensee should pay royalties on the displaced sales volume of the licensed product.

In reaching its result, the court first interpreted the terms of the agreement, including the express covenants barring competition between the parties in certain circumstances, and determined that none of the terms reached the dispute at issue. Having exhausted intent, it then looked at the situation the parties had created for themselves: the dependency of the licensor on the licensee in a relationship which had gone on for 15 years, and the need of the licensee nonetheless to maintain itself in the open market. Finally, it tried to craft a judicial solution that would be, as it said, 'really equitable'[7]—that would meet the legitimate needs of both of the parties as much as possible. As the court itself described its method, what it sought, even though there was no discernible intention of the parties on point, was 'that which will most nearly preserve the status created and developed by the parties'.[8]

The primary issue in *Ellsworth Dobbs* was the claim made by a real estate broker for a commission that the sellers refused to pay because, although an agreement for sale of the property had been signed, the transaction failed to close when the buyer could not obtain financing. The opinion began much like *Parev Products*, with a careful recitation of the circumstances and terms agreed by the parties. But then it took a quite different turn. Leading off with the remark that 'there has been an immense amount of litigation over the years with respect to the commissions of land brokers',[9] the *Ellsworth Dobbs* court traced the development, in its jurisdiction, of a rule stipulating that if a seller accepts a prospective purchaser produced by a broker, and signs a purchase and sale agreement, the risk of the buyer's ability to carry through then falls on the seller, with the broker earning his or her commission in any event. 'A new and more realistic approach to the problem is necessary', said the court.[10] It then proceeded to adopt the rule that the commission is earned only when the transaction is closed, unless the failure to close is the fault of the seller: '[i]n reason and in justice it must be said that the duty to produce a

---

[7] *Parev Products Co Inc v I Rokeach & Sons Inc*, 124 F 2d 147, at 150 (2nd Cir 1941).
[8] *Ibid.*, 149.   [9] *Ellsworth Dobbs Inc v Johnson* 236 A 2d 843, at 850 (NJ 1967).
[10] *Ibid.*, 852.

purchaser able in the financial sense to complete the purchase at the time fixed is an incident of the broker's business'.[11] The court next addressed the circumstances under which a broker, 'by special contract', could change 'the general rules now declared to control the usual relationship between him and an owner'.[12] Only then did the court return to the deal these parties made: was it sufficient to change the usual rule? This particular agreement, said the court, was not.[13]

How might we describe these two different approaches to the problem of supplementation? A judge following the first approach, upon being presented with a contract and a topic of dispute, looks first to the express terms of the agreement; failing to find an answer, he or she then reasons outward from that core, first to terms inferred from context, and then to terms adapted to the particular circumstances although implied by the law. A judge following the second approach, upon being presented with a contract and a topic of dispute, might not get beyond the text if it were very clear; but otherwise he or she determines first the legally implied term that would apply to the situation as a general matter, and then looks to see if the particular undertaking of the parties should be interpreted as an agreement to adopt some other term.

Much of what has been written about implied terms and the like, seems to proceed from an unstated assumption that only one or the other of these techniques is legitimate or worth discussing. But each is consistent with the fundamental desideratum of contract law that the express agreement of the parties controls, for even under the second approach the legally constructed terms can be, and commonly are, 'yielding' rather than 'iron' (to use Karl Llewellyn's words).[14]

More broadly, each can give a plausible account of contractual freedom and exchange justice. The first approach sees contract as an expression of freedom in the, roughly speaking, libertarian sense—the ability of individuals not to be bound except as they agree to be bound—supplemented by a particular understanding of what is involved in the parties' invocation of the institution of contract: the addition of those terms needed to make the voluntary commitment to this specific undertaking a working proposition. The second approach, by contrast, views entering into deals of one sort or another as an inherent part of living in a market society; it is the power to deviate from type that represents contractual freedom, in the

[11] *Ellsworth Dobbs Inc* v *Johnson* 236 A 2d 843, 850 (NJ 1967) at 853.

[12] *Ibid.*, 856.

[13] As to what would constitute an adequate agreement to change this background rule in New Jersey, compare *Kennedy* v *Roach*, 300 A 2d 570 (NJ AD 1973) (agreement enforced) with *Kulp Real Estate* v *Favoretto*, 316 A2d 71 (NJ AD 1974) (agreement not enforced).

[14] KN Llewellyn, 'What Price Contract?—An Essay in Perspective' (1931) 40 Yale LJ 704, 729.

same way that the power to leave a job (or for that matter, a country) does: it is a juristic mobility.[15] As to exchange justice, the first approach finds it in the equivalency defined by the parties' quid pro quo, which sets the standard from which the judges work. The second approach, by contrast, finds exchange justice initially in the socially disciplined normal case, to be displaced only by the agreement of both parties.

Finally, each technique, as suggested indeed by the examples we have discussed, is fully consistent with the role of the common law judge. The first constructs terms based on the particular interaction presented; a court could avoid doing at least this much only at the cost of refusing to enforce many bargains clearly meant to be efficacious. The second uses broader grounds, with greater social content, to construct a more general norm. Common law courts reason in this way all the time under titles such as 'torts' or 'property', and in doing so often, indeed, construct background terms which the parties are free to change by agreement. There is no difference regarding judicial authority here, unless we make the artificial (and historically unwarranted) stipulation that once the rubric 'contracts' makes its appearance, the courts are not allowed to know anything about the society in which they live. In short, as Professor Eisenberg has reminded us in his book on the common law, courts are legitimately in two businesses: deciding individual disputes and enriching our body of legal norms.[16]

Thus both approaches may well be justifiable. That does not mean they are equally suited to all situations. A clear difference is that the first approach produces an individualized supplementary term (applicable to *Parev Products Co* and *I Rokeach & Sons*), while the second approach produces a standardized one (applicable to 'brokers' and 'owners'). This difference has broad implications: it affects the scope of the precedents which the court should consult before making its decision, the range of information relevant to the decision, the precedential impact of the decision this very court will make, and so forth. Perhaps different kinds of cases call for different kinds of implied terms.

US judges may well have worked on such a premise, but if they have, they have been by and large quiet about the matter. Current English doctrine, as I understand it, overtly embraces a distinction of this sort, but with uncertain consequences.[17] By far the sharpest judicial statement of

---

[15] See M Walzer, 'The Communitarian Critique of Liberalism' (1990) 18 Pol Theory 6, 11–12.

[16] MA Eisenberg, *The Nature of the Common Law* (1988) pp 4–7.

[17] According to Lord Bridge of Harwich, delivering the opinion with which the other Lords concurred in *Scally v Southern Health and Social Services Board* [1992] 1 AC 294, at 307, there is a 'clear distinction' to be drawn 'between the search for an implied term necessary to give business efficacy to a particular contract and the search, based on wider considerations, for a term which the law will imply as a necessary incident of a definable category of contractual relationship'. But this crisp statement is coupled with

the matter I have found was set out nearly twenty years ago by Lord Denning; he was speaking in *Shell UK Ltd* v *Lostock Garage Ltd* and restating the law as he understood it after a then-recent case in the House of Lords:[18]

As I read the speeches, there are two broad categories of implied terms.

(i) The first category
The first category comprehends all those relationships which are of common occurrence. Such as the relationship of seller and buyer, owner and hirer, master and servant, landlord and tenant, carrier by land or by sea, contractor for building works, and so forth. In all those relationships the courts have imposed obligations on one party or the other, saying they are 'implied terms'. These obligations are not founded on the intention of the parties, actual or presumed, but on more general considerations: [citations]. In such relationships the problem is not to be solved by asking what did the parties intend? Or would they have unhesitatingly agreed to it, if asked? It is to be solved by asking: has the law already defined the obligation or the extent of it? If so, let it be followed. If not, look to see what would be reasonable in the general run of such cases: [citation] and then say what the obligation shall be. . . . In these relationships the parties can exclude or modify the obligation by express words; but unless they do so, the obligation is a legal incident of the relationship which is attached by the law itself and not by reason of any implied term . . .

(ii) The second category
The second category comprehends those cases which are not within the first category. These are cases—not of common occurrence—in which from the particular circumstances a term is to be implied. In these cases the implication is based on an intention imputed to the parties from their actual circumstances: [citation]. Such an imputation is only to be made when it is necessary to imply a term to give efficacy to the contract and make it a workable agreement in such manner as the parties would clearly have done if they had applied their mind to the contingency which has arisen.

Lord Denning, however, claimed only to be restating the law; he did not overtly justify in any other way the distinction he drew. We must, then, speculate: why do 'relationships which are of common occurrence' present a distinct category from the point of view of determining background contract terms? It is not a necessary truth. The claims of individualism might be so strong that each person's contract should be treated as if it were the only one in the world, regardless of its type. Or it might be merely a reflection of the history of the legal system itself; for it is true that

others in the same opinion—for example, that for the second category 'the criterion to justify an implication of this kind is necessity, not reasonableness' (*ibid.*, 307)—to yield a muddy result. See A Phang, 'Implied Terms in English Law—Some Recent Developments' [1993] JBL 242. The distinction, as regards English law, is usefully developed in H Collins, *The Law of Contracts* (2nd ed 1993) pp 227–9.

[18] [1976] 1 WLR 1187, at 1196–1197.

there is a body of landlord–tenant law, a body of law governing the sale of goods; a body of law applicable to the common carrier, by land or by sea. But Lord Denning's language hints at a different analysis. His use of the word 'relationships' rather than 'contracts' to describe what are 'of common occurrence' suggests that the point is how the parties to any one contract are positioned *vis-à-vis* a broader social structure. This theme is carried through by his naming of the common 'relationships' in terms of the social roles involved: seller and buyer, landlord and tenant. The numerousness of the legal artifacts reflects a society that creates repeated patterns. One might infer, then, that it is because the law must interact in some substantial way with an existing social structure, that it makes sense to develop a method which treats 'relationships which are of common occurrence' differently from the way the other type of case is handled.

If this is right—and I think it is[19]—much more is at issue than can be captured in summary phrases. It is not a matter of allocating words like 'necessary' or 'reasonable' to various imputations, as some English cases would have it, but rather a matter of very different problems to be solved and very different materials to be used. What the best method for dealing with 'relationships which are of common occurrence' might be, I will come to in a little while. For the moment, I should just say that I am embracing Lord Denning's distinction, but that I only intend to discuss this, his 'first category' of default rules. (To my ear, a phrase like 'default rule' or 'background term' more easily captures terms implied for these standardized situations, while a phrase such as 'gap filler' or 'omitted case' more easily captures the individualized ones; but I do not claim that usage has been uniform in this regard.) This first category represents, I think, the more usual, but less understood, case. The problem to be solved, then, is this: how should courts determine the background terms—not individualized gap-fillers, but rather standardized default rules—not mandatory terms, but rather yielding terms—for contractual relationships which are of common occurrence?

Possible solutions

The most straightforward answer to the question just posed is that judges ought to, and in fact often do, simply consult their own standards as to what outcome is right. By some this is phrased as an appeal to 'basic principles of justice',[20] and this, indeed, is the language the court used in the *Ellsworth Dobbs* case. It can also be phrased more agnostically, as in

[19] See TD Rakoff, 'Social Structure, Legal Structure, and Default Rules: A Comment' (1993) 3 S Cal Interdisciplinary LJ 19.
[20] EA Farnsworth, *Contracts* (2nd ed 1990) p 547.

Holmes' famous (but off-the-bench) discussion of implied conditions: 'But why do you imply it? It is because of some belief as to the practice of the community or of a class, or because of some opinion as to policy, or, in short, because of some attitude of yours upon a matter not capable of exact quantitative measurement, and therefore not capable of founding exact logical conclusions.'[21]

The most obvious difficulty with this approach is that, while few would require 'exact quantitative measurement', most want some better ground-ing for judicial action than merely 'some opinion as to policy' or the asser-tion that 'this is just'. Many of the older articles on the problem of constructed terms and conditions are, indeed, devoted to providing the intermediate premises that could give some specificity to Holmes' dictum; some of them are outstanding examples of doctrinal scholar-ship.[22] Nevertheless, analyses which provide rules of thumb (e.g. 'the courts work to avoid credit risks'), when used as explanations of, say, implied conditions of performance, commonly run afoul of the fact that in many circumstances other rules of thumb (e.g. 'the courts work to avoid forfeitures') will generate opposite conclusions. Since it is commonly true that, not only can the parties make different claims of justice, but the court will feel that there is 'some justice' on each side, we need something more, not in terms of working rules, but in terms of an operating method to resolve normative disarray.[23]

Another possibility, recently stated with imagination and force by Professor Randy Barnett, is to extend the notion of 'consent' beyond the interpretation of what the parties said and did, to what their silence might mean in the circumstances.[24] The general result he suggests, akin to the objective theory of contract interpretation, is that default rules should reflect the conventional understanding, or 'common sense', of the parties' 'community of discourse'. Where these conventions differ between the parties, Professor Barnett thinks the law should favour the common sense of that party, if there is one, who, in the typical situation, rarely enters into the type of transaction and does not have too much at stake; his or her 'rational ignorance' of the law justifies putting the burden on the more knowledgeable party to try to negotiate a different mutual understand-ing. This approach has the merit of simplicity, as it is similar to, although

---

[21] OW Holmes, 'The Path of the Law' (1897) 10 Harv L Rev 457, 466.

[22] See, eg, AL Corbin, 'Conditions in the Law of Contract' (1919) 28 Yale LJ 739; EW Patterson, 'Constructive Conditions in Contracts' (1942) 42 Colum L Rev 903.

[23] EA Farnsworth, 'Disputes Over Omission In Contracts' (1968) 68 Colum L Rev 860, provides such a method, but is primarily addressed to the implication of individualized terms, not the present subject.

[24] RE Barnett, 'The Sound of Silence: Default Rules and Contractual Consent' (1992) 78 Va L Rev 821, 894–7. Compare SJ Burton, 'Default Principles, Legitimacy, and the Authority of a Contract' (1993) 3 S Cal Interdisciplinary LJ 115, 162–5.

at a higher level of generality than, the methods judges already use for interpreting the specific deal the particular parties have made; for the same reason, it has the merit of reducing disjunction and surprise at the boundary line between interpretation and judicial construction.

Nevertheless, this approach seems to me to ignore the legitimacy of the judicial impulse to do justice through the statement of implied terms. Looking backward, judges may see the law as implicated in the fashioning, over time, of the existing common sense of the community; looking forward, they may be unwilling to continue supporting propagation of that traditional common sense if it now seems out-of-date. Legally implied terms are commonly taken as a statement, not merely of society's conventions, but rather of the presumptive norm. Even though the parties will remain free to adopt a different rule, and to have that different rule enforced by the court, there is a real difference, both in judicial self-concept and in the meaning for society as a whole, between awarding a verdict by reason of what the parties have expressly agreed, and awarding it solely by force of law. While it is surely right to see the parties as situated, some way of seeing the situation other than merely through its conventional rules is needed.

A third approach—and the approach most commonly used as the starting point in the recent scholarly literature, although it also has a long pedigree—is to ask what rule the parties in a given type of situation would have agreed to, had they actually bargained about the matter. This hypothetical bargain method bears some resemblance to the approach Lord Denning said he would take in a case 'not of common occurrence'. Whatever its appropriate use for the unique case, when it is understood that we are talking about framing rules for general cases it is clear that we must construct the parties and their situations before we can imagine how they might bargain. The simplest way of characterizing the parties consists of deciding that by and large parties would adopt a principle of overall economic rationality and endeavor to maximize their joint output and minimize their total costs. This would mean, for example, that insofar as a term concerns a risk of loss, that risk would be allocated, say, to the party best able to take precautions, or best able to insure against the risk's eventuation.[25] However, this construction is clearly too simple, because even parties motivated solely by economic self-interest also bargain about the distribution of the joint product. The predictable strategy of that distributive negotiation can easily transform the term to which such parties would in fact bargain. It is harder than it seems to square the circle of best bargaining strategy and overall economic efficiency.

---

[25] See the discussion in RE Scott, 'A Relational Theory of Default Rules For Commercial Contracts' (1990) 19 JLS 597.

There have been several scholarly responses. Some have suggested that there are methods for determining the distributive bargain rational parties would make.[26] Others have suggested that, if one can assume not merely a hypothetical bargain, but parties who will actually bargain in the shadow of the legally-adopted background rule, then a crafty choice of rule can, by altering what are the most advantageous individual strategies, induce the parties to in fact bargain to the most productive joint solution.[27] And it has also been pointed out that if parties are actually going to bargain around the rule, then the differential transaction costs involved in bargaining around one possible rule or another must be taken into account too: implying the rule most parties would bargain for will not necessarily reduce transaction costs to the minimum.[28]

These efforts to derive default rules by modelling bargaining behaviour as if the parties were playing a game seem to me to share some fundamental weaknesses. They necessarily assume a structured context, because it is impossible to define what will constitute rational behaviour, or what will constitute a meaningful incentive, or even how parties in the future will understand that the rule which has been constructed applies as a precedent to their situation, without describing a structured context in which action takes place. At the same time, it is very hard to reach any determinate general conclusions as to what 'rational' games-players would do, if the description of the context becomes too thick. So models of this sort typically ignore elements of context, too—for example, the existence of cultural norms which relate to bargaining behaviour, even though bargaining, hypothetical though it may be, is the centre piece of the construct.[29] Offered as models for deriving rules for actual cases, the hypothetical bargaining situations seem too thin and drawn more with an eye to what will make the method work than to what is significant in reality.

That judges are deciding on the default rules applicable, not to abstract bargaining games, but to real life situations, becomes all the more important as the argument moves from the claim that parties will bargain to the most efficient rule, to the assertion that parties ought to be encouraged to

---

[26] JL Coleman, DD Heckathorn and SM Maser, 'A Bargaining Theory Approach to Default Provisions and Disclosure Rules in Contact Law' (1989) 12 Harv JL & Pub Pol'y 639, 650–70.

[27] I Ayres and R Gertner, 'Filling Gaps in Incomplete Contracts: An Economic Theory of Default Rules' (1989) 99 Yale LJ 87, 91. Later research in the same vein, even by the same authors, has raised doubt as to the general ability to locate a rule which will uniquely lead to an efficient result after bargaining takes place. See I Ayres and R Gertner, 'Strategic Contractual Inefficiency and the Optimal Choice of Legal Rules' (1992) 101 Yale LJ 729, 733; and JS Johnston, 'Strategic Bargaining and the Economic Theory of Contract Default Rules' (1990) 100 Yale LJ 615, 626–39.

[28] D Charny, 'Hypothetical Bargains: The Normative Structure of Contract Interpretation' (1991) 89 Mich L Rev 1915, 1841.

[29] See L Bernstein, 'Social Norms and Default Rules Analysis' (1993) 3 S Cal Interdisciplinary LJ 59, 67–73.

do so. The reason these life situations are structured is that society has worked them into patterns. Landlord and tenant, doctor and patient, carrier and shipper: these situations come to the courts freighted with patterns of behaviour and complexes of meaning far beyond what these models assume. Responsible judges, judges who face up to the seriousness of what they do, have to work not merely in the realm of efficiency, but also in the realms of distributive justice, cultural symbolism, procedural fairness, and so forth. Not that they want to muck up the world; but with so many things to attend to, the utmost point of efficiency is not the primary objective; rough workability is much more important.

It seems, then, that neither a simple reliance on sentiments of justice, nor constant recourse to conventional meanings, nor the possible outcomes of hypothetical bargains, are a satisfactory basis for constructing default rules. We want to attend to justice, but we need some way of resolving value conflicts; we want to treat the parties as situated in a going society, but we do not want to be bound always to follow existing conventions; we want the world to work, but efficiency is not our only goal.

The purpose of this paper is to suggest the merits, in this welter of desires, of a fourth way of determining default rules. This method is distinctly different from the other approaches which just have been sketched, distinctly different, that is, from the answers for this problem which have been suggested in the recent literature. It is the method that was expounded by the great American scholar of commercial law, Karl Llewellyn. He called it 'situation-sense'.

Situation-sense described and exemplified

What is situation-sense? According to Karl Llewellyn, situation-sense is the characteristic method of the common law at its best; he made it the centerpiece of his culminating work, *The Common Law Tradition*.[30] Some people, when they see what it is, agree that it is simply a description of what they always thought common law reasoning to be. Llewellyn, however, first worked out the idea in his early commercial law articles, and in particular in his work on the development of the law of implied warranty terms.[31] It certainly was meant to apply to the determination of the defeasible rules of contractual relationships. Moreover, Llewellyn stressed the importance of fashioning implied terms through analysis of the facts

[30] KN Llewellyn, *The Common Law Tradition: Deciding Appeals* (1960).
[31] KN Llewellyn, 'On Warranty of Quality and Society' (1936) 36 Colum L Rev 699; 'On Warranty of Quality and Society II' (1937) 37 Colum L Rev 341; for a particular example of Llewellyn's method, see 36 Colum L Rev 699, 720–2, or in even shorter scope, 711, n 39.

typical of a social pattern—what he called the 'problem-situation' or the 'type-situation'—leaving idiosyncrasies to the later stage of deciding the particular case.[32] In short, whether or not situation-sense is the archetype of common-law reasoning, it is certainly a method designed exactly for our problem, for the derivation of default rules of contract law in standardized situations.

But what is situation-sense? Llewellyn defined situation-sense as 'the type-facts in their context and at the same time in their pressure for a satisfying working result, coupled with whatever the judge or court brings and adds to the evidence, in the way of knowledge and experience and values to see with'.[33] One is tempted to respond, in the words of an early critique of Llewellyn's book, '[i]t is extremely difficult, indeed, to pin down precisely what Llewellyn means by "type-situation" and "situation-sense" '.[34] But if we look at how this definition portrays common law judges, some progress can be made. It appears that the particular virtue of judges using this method is not to be smart, as it might be if they were presented with a clear, abstract, and complex algorithm for decision and asked to stamp it onto the complicated facts of life; nor is it to be heroic, as it might be if they were presented with the claim that life is inherently contradictory and chaotic, yet told to wrest a moment of meaning from it. What judges need is 'knowledge and experience and values' and their job is to 'see' the 'pressure' of the 'type-facts'. Because this 'seeing' requires experience and values, not just prior knowledge, it does not appear that Llewellyn was stating a method for achieving demonstrable (or objective) knowledge; because what is seen arises in some strong sense from the facts, he also was not viewing it as the imposition of judges' particular (and subjective) wills. 'Situation-sense', Llewellyn added one paragraph later, is one of those 'compounds of Isness and Oughtness and what have you more'.[35] It appears that Llewellyn was in some fashion endorsing a method of practical wisdom.

Now, quite a lot of people would agree with the propositions that successful legal thought requires 'compounds of Isness and Oughtness' and that judges ought to be wise, but little is heard of Llewellyn's method these days. Partly, his writing is of the bucking-bronco sort; partly, the half-life of legal theories is getting rather short, so that a book published in 1960 has a touch of the ancient about it. But also, Llewellyn's further exposition of situation-sense has at times a mystical sound to it. He claimed, for example, that the matter was perfectly put by the German

---

[32] KN Llewellyn, *The Common Law Tradition: Deciding Appeals* (1960) p 268.
[33] *Ibid.*, p 60.
[34] CE Clark and DM Trubek, 'The Creative Role of the Judge: Restraint and Freedom in the Common Law Tradition (1961) 71 Yale LJ 255, 260.
[35] KN Llewellyn, *The Common Law Tradition: Deciding Appeals* (1960) p 61.

scholar Goldschmidt when he wrote: 'Every fact-pattern of common life, so far as the legal order can take it in, carries within itself its appropriate, natural rules, its right law.'[36] Llewellyn's actual attitude is, however, better shown by his later discussion of the same point:

Only as a judge of court knows the facts of life, only as they truly understand those facts of life, only as they have it in them to rightly evaluate those facts and to fashion rightly a sound rule and an apt remedy, can they lift the burden Goldschmidt lays upon them: to uncover and implement the immanent law. Life-circumstances ... work in appellate deciding only on and through definite human beings: the sitting judges.[37]

Finding the sense of the situation was meant to be both a practical and a creative human activity, and not mere divination.[38]

The real difficulty in coming to grips with Llewellyn's proposal, I think, is not that it is mystical, but that it is unmethodical, in the rather strict sense that we are only given many examples, and no clear description of a method. As Professor Twining pointed out, Llewellyn 'was fascinated by human institutions and transactions and he had an uncanny capacity for getting the feel for the point of view of ordinary participants and their ways of going about their work'.[39] Such a person perhaps needs no method for arriving at wisdom. The rest of us do.

So, what is situation-sense? Without being able to cite scripture in support of everything I say, I will try to give a demonstration of what I understand situation-sense to be, followed by an analysis of its methodological features.

Let us look at a very ordinary question concerning default rules: if the parties have said nothing about the matter, what must a supplier of goods or services do in order to be entitled to claim the contract price? For over two hundred years, the implied condition has been that the purchaser need not pay unless performance is tendered. But what constitutes adequate tender? In US law, at least, there are two competing rules. The first requires the supplier to make a 'perfect tender'; this gives the purchaser the right to reject, without being liable to pay, any offer of performance

---

[36] *Ibid.*, p 122.   [37] *Ibid.*, p 127 (emphasis omitted).

[38] For a useful, compressed discussion of the various positions that have been espoused regarding Llewellyn's quotation of Goldschmidt, see DM Patterson, 'Good Faith, Lender Liability, and Discretionary Acceleration: Of Llewellyn, Wittgenstein, and the Uniform Commercial Code (1989) 68 Tex L Rev 169, 195, n 176.

[39] WL Twining, *Karl Llewellyn and the Realist Movement* (1985) p 122. Twining's otherwise clear restatement of Llewellyn's conception of situation-sense, pp 203 *et seq*, seems to me to falter because it attempts to make situation-sense consistent with the fact-value distinction as ordinarily used (see pp 226–7). His overall conclusion, at p 226, that situation-sense is 'most appropriately used in respect of disputes which arise within groups or sub-groups which have an underlying consensus about relevant values' reflects this analysis, but, were it true, would make the method of very limited utility.

that fails in any respect to conform to what the contract specifies. The second allows the supplier to tender 'substantial performance'; here, the purchaser cannot reject the performance for small deviations from the contract, but rather must accept it and pay the contract price save a damage remedy for the nonconformity.

In the abstract, without addressing a particular transaction-type, one might analyse these competing doctrines in the following ways. As a general matter of obligation, perfect tender has the virtue of holding suppliers strictly to what they promised to provide, thereby taking their voluntarily assumed obligations seriously; what might be said in favour of substantial performance is that the goal of contract law should be to take promises seriously, but not too seriously. Put differently, substantial performance can be seen as a 'soft' doctrine (in a pejorative sense) or perfect tender can be seen as a 'hard' doctrine (also in a pejorative sense). What seems clear, is that perfect tender is very protective of the purchaser, who has the choice of accepting a deviant performance and deducting the value of the defect from the price, or of rejecting the performance because it is not the full measure. This, however, creates an incentive on the part of the purchaser to look for defects—especially defects that cannot be cured because there is no time, or because the law does not allow the seller two bites at the apple—whenever the market price has fallen below the contract price; for then the purchaser can do better by rescinding the contract and buying anew. However, the doctrine of substantial performance also provides an opportunity for one of the parties to take advantage of the other. If the law allows substantial performance to be tendered, it encourages the supplier deliberately to provide only substantial performance in any situation in which it is more costly to complete the distance between 'most' and 'all' than it is to pay the resultant damages. This temptation is especially great in those situations in which the law measures the damages by the loss in value, rather than by the cost of rectifying the performance. The consequence for the purchaser may well entail both being forced to accept the substandard performance and having to pay nearly the full contract price. Either of these opportunistic possibilities can be policed by a requirement that the parties act in good faith in tendering or in rejecting a tender, but if taken seriously that approach adds to the complexity and expense of the legal apparatus by requiring an inquiry into motive. Quite apart from any such doctrine, a determination of substantial performance ordinarily requires the balancing of many facts, whereas perfect tender can often be decided on a few; the competing doctrines therefore also incorporate to some extent the relative merits and demerits of flexible standards as against bright-line rules.

How has the competition between these two possible constructive conditions gone? One could imagine a clear victory for either. Perhaps the temptation to reject in a falling market, so as to avoid a looming loss, is so much greater than the temptation to render only a near performance that substantial performance should always be the rule; or perhaps the importance of protecting buyers, who often are in socially subordinate positions, is so great that perfect tender should always obtain.

One could also imagine the two rules succeeding each other as the late twentieth century has succeeded the late nineteenth. Perfect tender partakes both of the sanctity of promising that was characteristic of Victorian morality and of the crystalline purity of formalistic doctrine. If, as the United States Supreme Court ruled in 1885, the contract said 'Shipment from Glasgow', that was what was promised, and compliance therewith was all the court would inquire into; shipment from Leith, however commercially reasonable, would not do.[40] Such punctiliousness may seem hard to maintain in this age of equity and post-Freudian morality. On this view, perfect tender should have, by this time, withered away.

When we move from supposition to fact, however, we see neither a clear victory for one of the possibilities nor a succession in time. The main feature of US law in this regard is that there is no clear winner: both rules prevail now, as they have for quite a long time. The dividing line between them has been, and is, situational. The archetypical case for the implied condition of perfect tender, is a sale of goods; the archetypical case for the implied condition of substantial performance, is a building construction contract.[41]

By far the leading discussion of the distinction, is the opinion by Judge Cardozo for the majority in *Jacob & Youngs Inc v Kent*,[42] applying the substantial performance doctrine. A contract to build a residence specified that all the pipe be wrought-iron pipe 'of Reading manufacture'; in the event, some of the pipe that was installed was Reading made, and some was not; this was discovered after the plumbing had been installed but before the final payment to the builder had been made. The builder offered to prove that the brands which had been installed were fully equivalent to the one contractually specified. In a suit for the final payment which had been withheld, was this offer of proof relevant?

We think the evidence, if admitted, would have supplied some basis for the infer-

[40] *Filley v Pope*, 115 US 213 (1885). The parallel English case is *Bowes v Shand* (1877) 2 App Cas 455.

[41] For not-entirely-consistent discussions of the scope of these respective rules in American law, see EA Farnsworth *Contracts* (2nd ed 1990) p 620 *et seq* and JE Murray, *Contracts* (3rd ed 1990) p 605 *et seq*. The sale-of-goods rule of perfect tender as codified in the Uniform Commercial Code at § 2–601, is, in light of the qualifications appearing in §§ 2–508, 2–608 and 2–612, not quite as stern as its common law antecedents; it is still considerably different from the substantial performance doctrine.

[42] 129 NE 889, rehearing denied, 130 NE 933 (NY 1921). For discussion in this context, see D Patterson, 'The Pseudo-Debate Over Default Rules in Contract Law' (1993) 3 S Cal Interdisciplinary LJ 235, 280–4.

ence that the defect was insignificant in its relation to the project. The courts never say that one who makes a contract fills the measure of his duty by less than full performance. They do say, however, that an omission, both trivial and innocent, will sometimes be atoned for by allowance of the resulting damage, and will not always be the breach of a condition to be followed by a forfeiture. [Citations.] The distinction is akin to that between dependent and independent promises, or between promises and conditions. [Citations.] Some promises are so plainly independent that they can never by fair construction be conditions of one another. [Citations.] Others are so plainly dependent that they must always be conditions. Others, though dependent and thus conditions when there is departure in point of substance, will be viewed as independent and collateral when the departure is insignificant. [Citations.] Considerations partly of justice and partly of presumable intention are to tell us whether this or that promise shall be placed in one class or in another. The simple and the uniform will call for different remedies from the multifarious and the intricate. The margin of departure within the range of normal expectation upon a sale of common chattels will vary from the margin to be expected upon a contract for the construction of a mansion or a 'skyscraper'. There will be harshness sometimes and oppression in the implication of a condition when the thing upon which labor has been expended is incapable of surrender because united to land, and equity and reason in the implication of a like condition when the subject-matter, if defective, is in shape to be returned. From the conclusion that promises may not be treated as dependent to the extent of their uttermost minutiae without a sacrifice of justice, the progress is a short one to the conclusion that they may not be so treated without a perversion of intention. Intention not otherwise revealed may be presumed to hold in contemplation the reasonable and probable. If something else is in view, it must not be left to implication. There will be no assumption of a purpose to visit venial faults with oppressive retribution.

Those who think more of symmetry and logic in the development of legal rules than of practical adaptation to the attainment of a just result will be troubled by a classification where the lines of division are so wavering and blurred. Something, doubtless, may be said on the score of consistency and certainty in favor of a stricter standard. The courts have balanced such considerations against those of equity and fairness, and found the latter to be the weightier.[43]

(The court also ruled that because of the gross disproportion between the cost of ripping out concealed plumbing, and the value of doing so, the damage allowance to the owner for the shortfall of performance would be only the difference in value between the building as promised and the building as built, which, on the offered proof, 'would be either nominal or nothing'.[44])

We may start our analysis by noting that in this opinion Cardozo relies on general facts in order to frame a general implied condition. This appears to have been purposeful; commentators on the case have pointed out that

---

[43] 129 NE 889, at 890–1 (NY 1921).   [44] Ibid., 891.

Cardozo fails to use several more particular facts of the case that might have solved it.[45] He recites in his statement of facts that '[e]ven the defendant's architect, though he inspected the pipe upon arrival, failed to notice the discrepancy'; but there is no pursuit of a possible waiver or estoppel. The contract provided that specification of 'any particular brand of manufactured article' was to be 'considered as a standard', although a change of manufacturer would require the architect's signature; while this suggests that the default might have consisted of nothing more than failure to get a signature which would have been given, and while the builders stressed this provision in their brief, it does not even make it to the opinion. Perhaps more surprising, because it could have converted the losing side into the prevailing party, the opinion makes no mention of a contractual provision that defective work was to be replaced; this failure, indeed, provoked a motion for reargument, but the court merely held that its violation, too, was to be remedied by the offsetting, negligible damage award.[46]

We should also note that very little weight is placed either on the parties' intentions, or on precedent. Cardozo does at times use a language of intention, but he makes no reference to any actual state of mind of any actual party. Intention is more the consequence than the antecedent of the argument: intention is itself 'presumed' from other facts. At most this part of the argument shows not that the parties agreed to the condition of substantial performance, but that they would not be greatly surprised by it. As to precedent, much the same can be said. It is of course cited. But the argument does not begin with the language or holdings of prior cases. We get the argument, and then find out that, in Cardozo's view, the cases have agreed. This is not an argument from precedent, even if it is an argument consistent with precedent.[47]

The opinion also uses words such as 'justice' and 'fairness'. Indeed, in his well-known set of lectures, *The Nature of the Judicial Process*, Cardozo discussed the doctrine of substantial performance specifically as enunciated in this case and said: 'I have no doubt that the inspiration of the rule is a mere sentiment of justice.'[48] But if we actually look at the opinion,

[45] R Danzig, *The Capability Problem in Contract Law* (1978) pp 108–28; RA Posner, *Cardozo: A Study in Reputation* (1990) pp 106–7; Prof. A Kaufman of Harvard Law School, in his forthcoming biography of Cardozo.

[46] 130 NE 933 (NY 1921).

[47] Both the majority and the dissent agreed that there was a doctrine of substantial performance; the dissent's argument was that it only excused faults much less grievous than those presented in the instant case (129 NE 889, 892 (NY 1921)). On the precedents, the matter was surely contestible, and indeed the case was decided four to three. *Schultze* v *Goodstein*, 73 NE 21 (NY 1905), the first-relied-on case in the dissent, 129 NE at 892, had refused to allow a contractor to prove that the plumbing he had installed was just as good as what the contract called for. Cardozo's distinction of the case as based on a finding that the deviation was willful, 129 NE at 891, is probably fair, but not inevitable.

[48] BN Cardozo, *The Nature of the Judicial Process* (1921) p 44.

'justice' serves as a label only. Cardozo never states an abstract principle of justice; Cardozo presents no argument based on an analysis of its nature. Surely he thought the outcome was just; but it is not the concept of justice, in any philosophical sense, that is doing the actual work.

Not party-specific facts; not intention; not precedent; not abstract justice. What in fact drives the argument in *Jacob & Youngs Inc* v *Kent* is the depiction, partly expressed, partly implied, of two contrasting situations. To use Cardozo's own language, they comprise 'a sale of common chattels' and 'a contract for the construction of a mansion or a "skyscraper" '. It is in the movement from these two (in Lord Denning's phrase) 'relationships which are of common occurrence'—buyer and seller of goods, construction contractor and future owner of a building—to the proper allocation of the default rules of 'perfect tender' and 'substantial performance', that the force of the opinion is to be found.

Cardozo starts his comparison with the nature of the performance itself. 'The simple and the uniform', he says, 'will call for different remedies from the multifarious and the intricate.' Most buildings are, by nature, more complicated than most goods. Moreover, buildings are predominantly made by hand, even if sometimes with the aid of sophisticated tools. They are not susceptible to the precision (or uniformity) which an assembly line, if properly engineered, can impart. Perfect buildings are much more difficult to tender than perfect goods.

He then moves to the meaning to the participants, in context, of transactions in such things. 'The margin of departure within the range of normal expectation upon a sale of common chattels will vary from the margin to be expected upon a contract for the construction of a mansion or a "skyscraper".' Partly this is a statement that what has just been said about the relative complexity of buildings and chattels is not a secret, but rather is apparent to builders and owners—and sellers and buyers—themselves. But it goes beyond that, because Cardozo is now speaking about the 'margin of departure', implicitly recognizing that when we are speaking of contractual tender, we are comparing the offered performance with the contractual specification of the performance. The suggestion is that specifications in construction contracts ought to be viewed rather differently from, and taken somewhat less seriously than, specifications in a sale-of-goods contract, at least on average.

Now this is not obvious. There is a demoralization inherent in making a purchaser accept something that the law admits (through its willingness to assess damages) is not what he or she was promised. Some might say that, just because buildings are generally custom-built, the specifications for them incorporate personal decisions on the part of the owner, and that therefore deviations from the specifications should be taken very seriously. This argument was, indeed, pressed by the dissenting opinion:

Defendant contracted for pipe made by the Reading Manufacturing Company. What his reason was for requiring this kind of pipe is of no importance. He wanted that and was entitled to it. It may have been a mere whim on his part, but even so, he had a right to this kind of pipe, regardless of whether some other kind, according to the opinion of the contractor or experts, would have been 'just as good, better, or done just as well.'[49]

What could be said to support Cardozo's rejection of this way of reading the document? Because buildings are complicated, and because they are customarily designed by professionals working for the prospective owner, there is usually a great mass of detail—the architect's plans and specifications—which are, from a legal point of view, part of the 'contract' against which either 'perfect tender' or 'substantial performance' would be measured. The principal function of much of this detail, however, is not to express a purpose, or even 'whim', of the owner but, rather, to serve as communication from the architect to the builder; details are commonly changed on the authority of the architect throughout the construction process. The particular facts of *Jacob & Youngs Inc* v *Kent*—the fact that the architect did not initially notice the deviation in the brand of pipe, the fact that the contract documents described brand names as merely stipulating a standard—may have been suppressed in Cardozo's analysis, but the process of which they are examples here surfaces in its general form.

Of course, performance specifications of little importance turn up in sale-of-goods documents, too. But, especially in the sale of common chattels, much trade takes place by mere designation of the good. When that is so, the contract terms will be read to require only that the goods be merchantable within that designation—a definition of quality which has built into it, so to speak, some latitude for conformity to the 'ordinary' standards set by the market. When, as not infrequently happens, only a few specific details are added to this standardized description, they are more likely to represent purposes which are important to the particular parties.

In short, a contract simply for the construction of 'one modern house', or even 'one modern house, four bedrooms, colour yellow', is hardly imaginable, while a contract which specifies what is to be supplied as simply 'one 1994 Ford Taurus', with some additional language specifying paint colour or type of radio, is an everyday event. On the one side, then, there is an intense specificity inherent in the contracting practices; on the other side, less specificity overall, and some automatic differentiation between the general and specific performance terms. It seems Cardozo is justified in his conclusion that the meaning of a contractual term in the two contexts is different, and that the difference goes precisely to the importance of fulfilling exactly what each term requires.

---

[49] 129 NE 889, at 892 (NY 1921).

Following this consideration of complexity, Cardozo next draws our attention to a very different, very practical point: goods, when rejected, can be returned; buildings, because they are usually built on the owner's land, cannot. However, he does not simply state these factual truths about the world; instead, he finds, in their intersection with the legal system, normative conclusions. 'There will be harshness sometimes and oppression in the implication of a condition when the thing upon which labour has been expended is incapable of surrender because united to the land, and equity and reason in the implication of a like condition when the subject-matter, if defective, is in shape to be returned.' As regards goods, because they can be returned, and because they are commonly not so unique as to be suited to only one buyer, they can be resold. Insofar as the difference between the resale price and the contract price reflects the deflect in the quality of the goods, justice can be done by licensing the buyer to reject because of the defect, without the need for further judicial intervention. No such self-regulating solution is possible regarding a defect in construction. Severe forfeiture of the sort that would be involved in having a builder almost complete a structure but still get nothing indeed could be remedied—since by reason of the forfeiture the other party has retained a benefit—but only through judicial mensuration in an action in restitution. Once that far, perhaps the contract remedy is the preferable one; or, to be more precise, perhaps the doctrine of substantial performance stands for the proposition that at some point is is easier to start with the contract price, and make allowance for what has not yet been done, than to start with zero, and allow for the work which has indeed been completed.

Perhaps for practical purposes what is important is the mere presence, or not, of a legal remedy. However, if we want to press harder, and consider not merely the existence of a remedy, but its adequacy, this analysis needs some supplementation. For, in the sale-of-goods case, resale of the rejected goods will make the seller bear the cost, not only of any defect, but also of any downward shift in the market; it may also lead to a loss of volume overall. By contrast, if builders are given an action in contract, rather than in restitution, their benefit of the bargain will be protected. So, beyond the question of remedy *vel non*, there is the question why the expectation interest of the builder, but not of the seller of goods, should be protected when the tender is a bit defective. What might be said—and perhaps it relates to Cardozo's sense of what constitutes 'oppression', although he does not articulate it—is that each individual profit probably matters more to the builder of buildings than to the seller of goods. It seems likely that building contractors make fewer contracts to build houses each year than merchants or manufacturers do to sell goods—fewer by a substantial magnitude. If what is at stake in allowing the tender of substantial performance is, roughly speaking, the recovery of the profit on the deal, then it might be thought that losing that profit takes on a different colouration if the job is one of a few, or one among thousands.

Cardozo turns next to how the court's standardized term might interact with the more individualized desires of the parties. 'Intention not otherwise revealed may be presumed to hold in contemplation the reasonable and probable. If something else is in view, it must not be left to implication.' Obviously, he recognizes that what is at issue is a default rule, one that parties will be able to contract around. Even under a regime of substantial performance, if an owner wants to indicate that fulfilment of some apparently ordinary term is in fact of unusual importance, he or she can contract for its perfect performance as a condition on payment.[50] Indeed, insofar as the adoption of legal rules might affect his or her calculations, the application of the implied condition of substantial performance to construction contracts would create what could variously be described as a burden, or an incentive, to reveal information of just that sort. If the implied condition follows the meaning of the situation as the parties themselves would usually understand it—if it states what is 'the reasonable and probable' term—this incentive will operate in much the same way that the objective theory of contracts does. Cardozo's tone seems to indicate this relatively straightforward way of looking at the matter.

But, we might ask, what if the meanings in context are not so clear to the parties? How should we consider the burden of further speech if we recognize that the legal rule might come as a surprise? As an empirical proposition, one might hazard the guess that building contractors and owners are more likely to be equal in their knowledge of the law than are sellers and buyers of goods. In each case, the suppliers are likely to have some knowledge of the law governing their transactions because that is their business. On the other side of the deal, buildings are usually expensive, and thus justify a substantial investment in the costs of the transaction; moreover, owners are customarily aided, in dealing with contractors, by architects, whose business this also is, and whose trade association supports them with legal information and form documents.[51] By contrast, buyers of goods are often consumers making purchases small in comparison to buildings, and unaided by professionals. In allocating the burden of a rule which is defeasible by contract, there is much to be said for placing the burden of the rule on the party more likely to find out about it, and therefore more likely to make it a matter of express

---

[50] Cardozo's opinion ducks the question, whether one could by blanket language stipulate that 'performance of every term shall be a condition of recovery'. 129 NE 889, at 891 (NY 1921).

[51] See J Sweet, 'The American Institute of Architects: Dominant Actor in the Construction Documents Market' [1991] Wis L Rev 317, 319–22.

contract—known to both sides—if the rule is ill-suited to the particular case.[52] While there may be no class of parties systematically more knowledgeable in construction cases, in sale-of-goods cases, sellers may well be. Perfect tender is, as already discussed, the seller-burdening doctrine.

Finally, Cardozo addresses the costs and benefits of one form or another of legal doctrine itself. Some, he says, 'will be troubled by a classification where the lines of division are so wavering and blurred. Something, doubtless, may be said on the score of consistency and certainty in favor of a stricter standard.' But since Cardozo does not tell us what that 'something' is, exactly what the doctrinal problem is also remains obscure. One possibility is that the creation of a separate rule for construction contracts, from that which applies to buyers and sellers of goods, generates a more complex legal system both in itself, and in the pressure it might create for the recognition of yet further, intermediate patterns. How, for example, should the law handle custom-made goods, easily returnable but perhaps not so easily resellable, and in other ways, too, a mixed case? Another possibility is that the 'line of division' which is 'so wavering' is not that between legal categories, but rather that inherent in implementing the very test of substantial performance. Substantial performance is a judgmental standard, and lacks the hard edges of a perfect tender rule. Cardozo, a few sentences after the material already quoted, openly avows the fact that '[w]here the line is to be drawn between the important and the trivial cannot be settled by a formula'.[53] Whichever the case, Cardozo certainly concedes that there are doctrinal costs in what he is doing, but, he concludes, they are outweighed by the other considerations at play.

These points bring us back to the basic question, when should we require perfect tender, and when will tender of substantial performance suffice? We have seen that the two doctrines have the following abstract qualities: Both are default rules. Perfect tender holds suppliers strictly to the letter, while substantial performance takes promises a little less seriously. Perfect tender gives more power to the purchaser; substantial per-

---

[52] What is needed to express the parties' agreement to vary from the implied term, makes a long story. As a matter of substance, the principal question is whether the law is truly indifferent between its term and the parties' term (eg in the implied term favouring cash sales absent an agreement for credit), or whether it wants to see a justification before it yields (eg in the judicial treatment of liquidated damages clauses). For openers, see RE Scott, 'A Relational Theory of Default Rules for Commercial Contracts' (1990) 19 JLS 597, 613–15. As a matter of process, the chief doctrinal question has been the intersection between the parol evidence rule and legally constructed terms. For discussion, see H Hadjiyannakis, 'The Parol Evidence Rule and Implied Terms: The Sounds of Silence' (1985) 54 Fordham L Rev 35, 36–9. My own view is that most of the mischief lies in the use of contracts of adhesion to escape implied terms. See TD Rakoff, 'Contracts of Adhesion: An Essay in Reconstruction' (1983) 96 Harv L Rev 1173, 1180–3 and generally.

[53] 129 NE 889, at 891 (NY 1921).

formance, to the supplier. Perfect tender creates an incentive for the purchaser to look for defects when he or she wants out of a deal; substantial performance creates an incentive for the supplier to be a bit careless, or to not-quite-perform when the last bit of performance would be burdensome. Perfect tender risks depriving the supplier of a profit; substantial performance risks requiring the purchaser to accept what was not ordered. Perfect tender is a rule; substantial performance is a standard.

Now let us look at our two 'relationships which are of common occurrence', or transaction-types. First, we have transactions between building contractors and owners to build buildings. Buildings are intricate and custom-crafted, as both parties know. Architects typically draft the specifications, which are set forth in great detail in the applicable contractual documents; while some specifications set forth particular desires of prospective owners, many do not. Buildings are commonly built on the owner's land, and cannot be returned if found wanting; there will have to be some remedy to avoid substantial unjust enrichment. Building contractors typically build a small number of buildings at any one time. Owners, customarily aided by architects, are about as likely as builders to be informed about the law applicable to their negotiations.

Next, we have transactions between sellers and buyers of goods. Goods are typically mass-produced, as is known by buyers as well as sellers. The contractual performance specifications for such goods are typically straightforward: often there is a simple description, which will be supplemented by the implied requirement that they be of the usual sort, or 'merchantable'; or a simple description accompanied by a few specifics. Defective goods, if rejected, can be returned and typically can be resold, although perhaps with a loss of profit. Sellers of goods usually sell large quantities in many transactions in a given time period. If we lump together all those who are likely to be buyers, and compare them to all those who are likely to be sellers, the buyers will often be less legally knowledgeable about the law of trade than are the sellers.

The proposition is, that this analysis of the two proposed legal rules, combined with this analysis of the two situation-types, forms an argument. That upon consideration of the rules and the models, it will be apparent that it makes sense to couple the building-contractor-and-owner situation with the doctrine of substantial performance, and that it makes sense to couple the sale-of-goods situation with the doctrine of perfect tender. That, for example, a judge in a construction case, as a way of summarizing his or her thinking, will have the following soliloquy:

When people make contracts, they ought to live up to their commitments, and they are entitled to expect others to live up to theirs. But construction contracts have a great many details. Given the realities of the situation, no one can build a building that conforms to all of them. Being really strict about the matter is more than commerce can bear. And fulfilling each and every requirement is not really important to the owners, themselves, anyway. There are a lot of things owners can complain about, if they want to be 'complainy', but it's too harsh to make builders lose their profits to protect that right to complain—especially when each builder only enters into a limited number of transactions in a year. We can protect the things that are really important to most owners by requiring substantial—not just significant—performance, and let the owners tell us, and their contracting partners, if there is something unusually important. That's a bit hard on some owners, who may have to keep what they don't completely want, and perhaps not even get the money to repair it, but it is not as hard as it might seem, since they are often represented by architects, who know the ropes and can advise them how to write the necessary special specifications. And it is a bit hard on the courts, who will have to police something as vague as 'substantial performance': but there would be judicial costs on the other side too, such as deciding what the measure of unjust enrichment for an insufficient building would be. When I ask myself, if I were sometimes a builder, and sometimes an owner, what rule could I consistently favour; when I think about what is at stake for all concerned; when I recognize that each alternative entails costs for one side or the other, and ask myself which party's interests are more weighty; then I think owners should have to pay the contract price, with damage allowance, once builders tender substantial performance.

It is this whole process of thinking—a consideration of the implications of various legal rules, matched up against reasonably intricate models of social situations, and brought together in light of the force of all the claims to be made—which, I think, lies at the core of Judge Cardozo's argument, even though, admittedly, I have substantially reframed it. This process of thinking is also, I think, what Karl Llewellyn meant by 'situation-sense'.

I find this argument persuasive: not incontestable, but very forceful. Assuming that the descriptive generalizations are correct, I am convinced by it both that substantial performance is a better standard for builder-owner cases than is perfect tender, and that the case for substantial performance is much stronger in builder-owner cases than in buyer-seller cases. Cardozo's specific conclusion, that substantial performance should apply to the construction of buildings, and can legitimately do so even in a legal system that requires perfect tender for the sale of goods, is thus justified. The case was properly decided.

Some of the wider implications of the argument are perhaps more open to question. It would be possible, and consistent with what was just said, to transpose the whole scale against which to judge the determination that construction cases call for substantial performance more than sale-of-goods cases do, so that although the argument for one was stronger than for the other, both would be subject to a substantial performance test. One might, for example, think that the moral hazard of a perfect tender rule is so great, begging buyers to reject in bad faith, as to outweigh in all situations the good faith desire of buyers to get what they contracted for.[54] It would also be possible to question whether the situations are properly bounded. Should the category 'sale of goods' be bifurcated into mass-produced goods and custom-made goods, or, alternatively, bifurcated into goods sold to merchants for resale and goods sold to consumers for personal use?[55] At least some of the substantive points raised in the analysis of the models would suggest these distinctions, but jurisprudential issues, such as the best 'size' for legal categories, are also implicated. Even as to these questions, however, situation-sense usefully frames the issues so that judgment can be sensibly applied at the start, and thinking in terms of repetitive situations and their sense allows patterns to be observed over time, and default rules, if need be, corrected.

Only in an ideal world—and perhaps not even there—is the test of a legal method whether it provides answers to every question a problem might raise. In the actual world of pragmatic judicial activity, a method that allows for resolution of the precise issues tendered, and that usefully frames many of the broader concerns, accomplishes a lot, and more than most. Such, in my view, is the power of situation-sense.

But it is quite possible to have a very different reaction to it. One might view the argument which has just been exhibited, or others of its type, as too flat, or as based too much on a leap from what appears to be a descriptive sociology to a normative conclusion, or as masking a process by which judges pass off their prejudices as the common sense of the community.[56] As these objections are based largely on methodological concerns, clearly description and analysis of the method, as a method, is needed.

---

[54] The preliminary report of the American study group considering revision of the sales provisions of the Uniform Commercial Code did not, however, reach this conclusion. 'Arguably,' they wrote, 'the image of buyers engaging in strategic behavior under § 2–601 is illusory.' The report favours, although not unanimously, maintaining the basic perfect tender provision, but adding to it a requirement that the rejection of nonconforming goods be made in good faith. See American Law Institute, PEB Study Group, Uniform Commercial Code art 2, Preliminary Report (1990) 157–9.

[55] Llewellyn himself, in his role as draftsman of the Uniform Commercial Code, advocated such a division. As he saw it, 'perfect tender' was the appropriate rule for sales to consumers, but 'substantial performance' was the sensible rule for merchant-to-merchant transactions. See ZB Wiseman, 'The Limits of Vision: Karl Llewellyn and the Merchant Rules' (1987) 100 Harv L Rev 465, 509–12. His attempted bifurcation lost in the ensuing debates. The new United Nations Convention On Contracts for the International Sale of Goods, effective among signatories from the end of 1986, rejects a 'perfect tender' approach in favour of a test based on the fundamentality of the breach (Art 46); since the Convention does not apply to goods bought for personal consumption (Art 2), it might be thought to support Llewellyn's view, but might also reflect the different needs of international commerce.

[56] See, eg, J Feinman, 'Promissory Estoppel and Judicial Method' (1984) 97 Harv L Rev 678, 698ff.

Situation-sense as a general method for constructing default rules

Situation-sense, reconstructed as a method, has eight distinctive features.

First, the method depends on constructing models which describe type-situations and the relationships among type-characters. These models do not aspire to the universality present in abstract rules; they have too much social content for that. But they are also far different from a traditional statement of a case, for they try to state paradigmatic facts rather than a mass of particulars. They are neither doctrines nor cases. If models such as these are used as core elements of legal reasoning, one gets a body of thinking substantially more structured than a mere collection of decided precedents, which yet shares with the analogic method the suggestion that common law thinking is at its core based on nodal paradigms rather than linear propositions.

Second, the disparate elements of each model are joined to each other in a particular way. On the one hand, they are not tightly connected in a logical sense; it is not true, for example, that given most of the elements of either of the models we have created, the remaining elements could be deduced. The models are, in that sense, contingent. On the other hand, most or all of the elements of each model link up to large propositions about the way a given society works. The models are, in that sense, not accidental or contingent. They are put together by social processes even if not by logic. For example, the typical good (or as Cardozo would have it, a 'common chattel') is, in a modern society, mass-produced. It is no accident that the contractual specifications for mass-produced articles are relatively simple—for if the producer cannot produce to its own internal specifications (with perhaps a few add-ons), it cannot mass produce. Moreover, for goods to be mass produced there must be a mass market, and usually within such a market there will be someone who will buy goods that are somewhat defective—so a rejected but mass-produced good can usually be resold. The model of the contract for the purchase and sale of goods thus grows out of, is in some sense a sub-specification of, the modern mass market. One can imagine other markets, even other modern markets; the derivation is not from a logical analysis of the word 'market', but from an understanding of the fundamental processes of a society at a given time and place. Indeed, it is this reference to a larger structure which allows us to feel the importance, or 'weight', of the characteristics which have been combined in the model.

Third, the type-roles and their relationships are treated as constructed jointly by the law and the wider society. Existing law—other than the law in dispute—helps define the logic of the situation. For example, the claim that a building contractor needs a transactional remedy against the owner for a substantial part performance, in order to avoid forfeiture, depends in part on the prior legal determination that the contractor does not have the power to sell the nearly complete building to a third party when it sits on the owner's land. That rule is not inevitable; a law of property that can conceive of profits *à prendre* and condominiums could give the builder a salable interest in the building. If it did, it would change the situation.

To some extent; for whether any such property interest would be salable in fact is more than a legal question. Indeed, this method as a whole assumes that the legal system is merely a part, and not a conclusively determinative part, of a broader social dynamic. If the law molded society in its image, the existing social forms and the existing legal forms would already make a perfect fit, and there would be no work to do. Instead, several of the cases which are striking examples of situation-sense put into practice, have striven to bring out-of-date legal rules into congruence with a society that has passed them by.[57] Thus 'owner' and 'construction contractor', 'seller' and 'buyer', and so forth, are treated by this method as being both legal roles and social roles. Correspondingly, the judge who helps to give new content to the definitions of these roles is a participant in both the legal system and in the culture at large.

[57] For example, in *Javins* v *First National Realty Corp*, 428 F 2d 1071 (DC Cir 1970), cert denied, 400 US 925 (1970), the question was whether landlords had an obligation to maintain residential premises in a habitable condition. Judge Wright's opinion, which answered yes and held the warranty to be non-waivable, relied on many sources, including various housing codes. In the part of the opinion self-consciously described as presenting a 'common-law argument', 428 F 2d 1071, at 1077–80 (1970), the issue was whether the duty to repair the premises should, as a background norm, be allocated to the tenant or the landlord. Judge Wright admitted that the traditional rule, going back to the middle ages, put the burden on the tenant. He justified the decision to shift it to the landlord by in effect building contrasting situational models that might be schematically stated as follows:

The Medieval Agrarian Leasehold Model:
(1) The leased structure is a single, technically uncomplicated dwelling unit.
(2) The leased land is economically more important than the structure on it.
(3) The tenant is a long-term tenant, often remaining (and expecting to remain) on one piece of land for his entire life.
(4) The tenant has a broad range of skills, including those necessary to repair dwellings.
(5) The landlord does not have a highly specialized set of skills regarding the inspection and maintenance of buildings.

The Modern Urban Tenant Model:
(1) The leased unit is part of a multiple, technically interconnected dwelling structure.
(2) The economic interest of the tenant is in the structure and not the land.
(3) The tenant is potentially mobile, often does not stay for a long time, and has no long-term legal interest in the property.
(4) The tenant has a specialized occupational skill usually unrelated to inspecting or maintaining buildings.
(5) The landlord treats the rental of housing as a distinct business, and has the skills appropriate to that business.

Fourth, the legal side of the construction of situations and roles is a matter of form as well as substance. The defined classes must be usable in a workable legal system. In addition, the proposed doctrines whose 'fit' is to be tested against the models are drawn from a limited universe of possibilities: they are constrained to look like the kind of law common law judges traditionally enunciate. They must assign a 'right' or 'duty' of an 'ordinary' legal type; they must create a winner and a loser in a litigative setting, rather than splitting the difference, sending the proceeds to charity, or whatever else the parties might do in, say, a mediated settlement.[58] While 'situation-type' may not be a common element in the legal lexicon, the final result of the analysis is subject to the formal constraints of the rule of law.

Fifth, if we analyse the models using one or another of the traditional normative justifications for contract law, we find that the elements presented seem to call forth a plurality of evaluative premises. Buildings are intricate and difficult to produce to specification, while goods are simpler and commonly 'merchantable'. One of the purposes of contract law is to support ordinary commerce. One can insist on perfect tender for the sale of goods, without giving one side the power routinely to wriggle out of the usual deal; but if applied to the construction trade, perfect tender would make most contracts revocable by the purchaser, rather than binding.

Again, buildings cannot be returned if rejected, while goods can be. Another of the purposes of contract law is to maintain some balance over time between the two contracting parties. Failure to give the builder a remedy will create a pattern of gains and losses quite unlike that foreseen in the contract if it had been performed, while leaving the seller of goods to resell the goods will not.

Not only are there a multiplicity of values; they are commonly in conflict even as applied to the particular situation. Builders do promise to build according to the specifications in the contract documents. A third purpose of contract law is to make people live up to their expressed commitments. Letting builders get paid after tender only of substantial performance, especially if they do not necessarily have to pay for the cost of completing the performance, threatens to undermine this goal.

Thus, this method accepts the existence of a multiplicity of evaluative premises at a decisional node as a commonplace of life. It does not try to deny the existence of conflict among them; it does not try to evaluate each fact according to a consistent algorithm. Nowhere in the imaginary soliloquy of the deciding judge, for example, are the multiple aspects of

---

[58] For recent discussion of this presumption in the default rule context, see RE Scott, 'A Relational Theory of Default Rules For Commercial Contracts' (1990) 19 JLS 597, 613ff.

adopting a doctrine of substantial performance summed up against a singular criterion. Instead, some facts are treated in one framework, and some in another, without any announced mega-principle explaining the grounds of selection. Similarly, there is no a priori stipulation of a closed set of possible justifications.

Sixth, the relationships between doctrine and situation are tested both backwards in time and forwards. On the one hand, the proposed rule is related to the values implicated in the pattern of activities as it has been and now exists. On the other hand, the doctrine which is now embraced becomes a part of the definition of the situation for the future. Whether it will undermine or improve the situation—how role characters will respond to a chosen rule—is itself one of the factors that must be considered.

Seventh, the implicit conception of the relationship between a judge and his or her society differs from that present in many other forms of legal argument. Perhaps the anthropological near-oxymoron, 'participant observer', comes as close as any label to describing the appropriate judicial attitude. This is the judge who understands that the type-situation has to be constructed in the active sense of the term, but yet treats as being directly persuasive seeing how things work and discovering what makes them work smoothly and fairly, or could make them work more smoothly and fairly than they do.

Finally, there is the distinctive process of closure. The proposition is simply this: by consciously and methodically modelling a legal and social situation, the roles involved and how they relate, a judge can sort out the possible claims of need, the possible assertions of purpose and meaning, in order to come to grips with those which in fact have to be considered in reaching a workable and fair resolution. In the process he or she will also gain an appreciation of the weights to be accorded the various values as they appear embedded in the particular context. Looking then at the possible legal doctrines, the judge will be able, if fair minded, to see which legal resolution of this particular nodal problem, all things considered, is best. He or she will be able, in this context, for this purpose, to be wise.

Is this eight-part method sound? In evaluating it, we need to look first at its use of social models, next at its approach to value reconciliation, and finally at its vision of the common law judge.

To start, it might seem surprising to see so much use made of models of social interactions and role expectations when dealing with contract law. Contract, after all, is often viewed as pre-eminently the realm of subjective choice and the individually tailored arrangement. Is this method simply misplaced?

It is indeed true that those who have tried to define the domain of contract law have usually done so in terms of consent, promise, or agreement.[59] But such definitions are far too universal. Voluntary assent is relevant throughout much of the law, touching matters as disparate as rape, battery and the waiver of procedural rights. Nor can it be said that all contracts deal with market transactions.[60] What contract is, in fact, is a social institution compounded of elements held together by convention as much as by definition.[61] One of those elements is the truly particularistic agreement made for a commercial purpose—but only one.

There was something of a habit, in older books on contract law, of including not only the general problems such as consideration or capacity, but also discussions of particular types of contracts, taken one by one. Perhaps reflecting its lineage, the current edition of *Chitty on Contracts*—the twenty-seventh—follows in this tradition, with the fat volume called 'General Principles' being followed by an equally fat one called 'Specific Contracts'.[62] Included in the latter are 'Bills of Exchange and Banking', 'Carriage by Air', 'Carriage by Land', 'Employment', 'Sale of Goods', and so forth. These are the same types of things Lord Denning called 'relationships which are of common occurrence', and not accidentally so. What is at work here is the recognition—old and new but suppressed in the hey-day of freedom of contract—that, except for a residuum of truly bespoke arrangements, contract law consists of principles of voluntarism superimposed on underlying social patterns and statuses.[63] The result, as proclaimed in the title of an article written three-quarters of a century ago, but all the more true today, is 'The Standardizing of Contracts'.[64]

The problem we started with, is the fitting of default rules to transaction-types. As can now be seen, this definition of the task is not a stipulative trick; it is, rather, a realistic recognition of a potentiality present throughout most of contract law. The method of model building inherent to situation-sense is congruent with the subject matter to which it is

[59] Thus the first sentence of Williston's treatise: 'A contract is a promise, or set of promises, to which the law attaches legal obligation,' S Williston, *Contracts* (1920) Vol 1 p 1, and of GH Treitel's: 'A contract is an agreement giving rise to obligations which are enforced or recognized by law': *The Law of Contract* (8th ed 1991) p 1.

[60] Compare H Collins, *The Law of Contract* (2nd ed 1993) p 1. Whatever its usefulness in highlighting certain features of contract law, an emphasis on contract as the law of the market excludes many agreements in fact enforceable as contracts, for example, agreements to make a will, which are usually made between family members and deal in things not available on a market.

[61] As Wittgenstein said of the concept 'games': 'if you look at them you will not see something that is common to *all*, but similarities, relationships, and a whole series of them at that.' L Wittgenstein, *Philosophical Investigations* (3rd ed 1976) p 31 (emphasis in original).

[62] *Chitty on Contracts* (27th ed, 1994).

[63] See PS Atiyah, *The Rise and Fall of Freedom of Contract* (1979) pp 716 *et seq.*

[64] N Issacs, 'The Standardizing of Contracts', (1917) 27 Yale LJ 34. As Issacs points out, much of this standardization takes place, on the legal side, through statutes, although tending to follow the same social patterns.

addressed; the wherewithal for carrying out an analysis of type-situations exists throughout a very large part of contract law.

This congruence becomes all the clearer if we look at the matter from the standpoint of judges trying to create models of transactional situations. Certain types of information are not relevant to their task: for example, what these particular parties said to each other. (This information might, of course, be relevant to the ultimate decision in a particular case by reason of contracting-out, waiver, estoppel, and so forth.) At the same time, standardized situations give judges the raw material to do things they cannot do in more individualized situations. This is so because these recurrent transactions occur within a structured social situation; they are contracts made not between the abstract A and B, but by pairs of characters playing roles within a framework: landlord and tenant; builder and owner; merchant and consumer; carrier and shipper. A whole range of information is available about a repetitive, structured situation of this sort that cannot be had for a unique arrangement. Some of this is trade usage in the narrow sense; some of it regards practices common in the situation; some of it concerns the usual players in the situation beyond the particular pair of contracting parties; and some of it connects the particular transaction-type with other institutions, or with other already-applicable rules of law.

Moreover, the existence of structure makes it possible not merely to accumulate information, but to model the dynamics of the interaction of the type-characters. It is possible to speak of expected behaviour, or reasonable behaviour, or efficient behaviour, with some specificity because there is a structured context to give those terms some content. A social meaning can be attributed to actions, insofar as they are the typical actions of characters in role, without having to rely on the subjective understandings of any particular parties.

Yet further, because structured transactional situations are usually not merely functional units, but cultural forms as well, parties within the transaction-type will often attribute a meaning to the pattern itself which will be judicially accessible. It is realistic to assume that parties often act with reference to the cultural form—that they firstly, let us say, decide to enter a lease, as landlord and as tenant, and only secondarily haggle over the individual terms. (By contrast, in a truly unique business arrangement it may be very hard to know what the meaning of the transaction to the parties was, without explicit evidence, because they may well have viewed themselves as creating a wholly individual form.) Going further, and looking at a proposed rule as giving new definition to the form, because it may be possible to say something about how different role characters relate to that form, judges may also be able to say something about the likelihood that, and the way in which, any newly announced default rule will be accessible to, and used by, future transacting parties.

Finally, relationships of common occurrence tend to breed lawsuits of common occurrence—and with them, a richness of accumulated learning about social practices and friction points. Recurrent lawsuits also provide the opportunity for refinement of an analysis over time, and, if necessary, for reformulation of a default term.

All this makes feasible an approach to situation-sense that is dependent, not on a direct, intuitive appreciation of reality, but on a considerably more explicit, tight, and structured model of the transactional situation at issue. This is not to say that, just because social life provides the material from which a model of a transaction-type can be built, there is no work for judges to do. Clearly the contrary is the truth: these models are constructed, and judges will often have a major role in the building. The point is rather that the lumber is at hand.

Of course, since social perception helps shape the models, we would expect 'liberal' and 'conservative' judges to create somewhat different models, at least in some situations. How significant the resultant wobble would be, depends of course in part on the institutional arrangements by which judges scattered over time and space relate to each other. There are, however, at least two substantial constraints serving to prevent these acts of model building from becoming idiosyncratic. The first lies in the fact that what the models aim at, is the delineation of an actual, working situation which has some preexisting structure. To readmit Llewellyn speaking in his own words, this time cautioning judges against the false blandishments of counsel, 'the best safeguard against counsel's mispainting lies in visualizing the hands-and-feet operations in the picture, seen as a going scheme, a working setup. Such operating aspects are curiously hard to fake.'[65] The second inheres in the application of the sub-culture of the law, in the fact that judges build these models while working in their roles as judges. Many traditional jurisprudential concerns—worries about the complexity of the law, the lay intelligibility of the law, the over-inclusiveness and under-inclusiveness of the law—go also to questions such as, should the law either create or recognize a bifurcation of an existing transaction-type ('buyer and seller of goods') into two more carefully tailored types (one 'merchant buyer', the other 'consumer buyer'). And, as already mentioned, what is to be allocated in the end is a legal right of the usual sort. In short, the judicial activity needed here seems to fit comfortably within the scope accorded to the judicial craft in general, and can be subjected to the same sort of craft criticism.

If it be conceded that the necessary models can be reasonably

---

[65] KN Llewellyn, *The Common Law Tradition: Deciding Appeals* (1960) p 261.

constructed, the next issue to be addressed is the claim that situation-sense misconstrues what conclusions can be drawn from models of this sort. The description of such a model, or even of two such models back-to-back, does not, it will be said, constitute a sufficient argument for the determination of a normative result. At most, a model will furnish the basis for saying that among such-and-such proposed rules, a specific rule will best achieve a given purpose. Models assume purposes rather than provide them; the idea that models of sociological phenomena can go beyond these positive, predictive functions and serve as the basis for reconciling value conflicts is an utter confusion of 'is' and 'ought'. Or so it might be claimed.

Now, no one claims that situation-sense is a science. Llewellyn, as already pointed out, knew that situation-sense was compounded 'of Isness and Oughtness and what have you more'.[66] The issue is not, whether it is a surprise that this method is not respectful of the dogmas of the positivist theory of knowledge, but rather, whether it is a sign of rampant confusion.

I think not. In legal matters the separation of value from fact assumes importance when the law is imagined to contain a system of abstract normative propositions; one then wants a statement and justification of the law separate from the identification of particular instances to be subsumed under one rule or another. However, when the law is conceived as a set of paradigmatic decisions, of statements of the right result in a series of determinate situations, each instance will inevitably include normative and factual components. Legal reasoning based on situation-sense is, as already noticed, of this nodal, rather than linear, sort, and is thus inevitably based on compounds 'of Isness and Oughtness'. The issue is thus not a matter of confusion, but rather of the strengths and weaknesses of two different methods, each intelligible, and each, in common law systems at least, with good ground to be considered traditionally legal.

Perhaps our more common image of how we ought to think about what we ought to do, is to use more abstract concepts to give order to the plethora of more concrete ones. As the process is recapitulated, we move up a hierarchy of concepts until the grand abstractions—which in legal discourse are represented by terms such as liberty, fairness, efficiency—appear. This rationalistic approach has obvious power if, at the apex, there is only one relevant concept. However, one consequence of the Realists' destruction of the world of formal, classical legal thought—in which, in theory, all common law concepts could be traced to the macro-concept 'liberty'—is our current understanding that the legal concepts we

[66] *Ibid.*, p 61.

ordinarily use cannot be organized in a hierarchy that culminates in a single summit.[67]

One possible response is to try to recreate a monistic value system, seeking conceptual structure at the expense of whatever is excluded during the ascent to the single favoured peak. Another possibility is to conclude that since the method of ascending hierarchies results in there being many peaks, one faces an eternal conflict among incommensurable values. And yet another possibility is to recognize more than one hierarchy, but to suggest that there is some way to balance or trade-off the values which reside at the apexes.

The method of situation-sense rejects all three of these responses. It recognizes a multiplicity of values and points of view; it suggests that they can be put together coherently (not solely by rational thought but rather by a combination of reason and social understanding); and it sees this reconciliation occurring more toward the ground-level than at the peaks. Situation-sense, as said before, is a method of practical wisdom.

Does wisdom exist?

It is often said that the old are wise. If we imagine an idealized traditional society, with a simple social and economic structure, we might think of the old being wise in a rather straightforward way. Having lived long, they have been child and parent, neophyte and initiate, single and married, apprentice and master. They have partaken of most or all of the roles in their society. They have looked at the world through the viewpoints which are available in their culture. They have experienced what life, lived where they are and when they are, has to offer. Correspondingly, when a dispute arises, they are ready to consider the merits and demerits not by assuming an Olympian or abstract viewpoint, but rather by being able to call on a concrete appreciation of the multiple points of view espoused by the participants.[68] Their judgments are based, not on intuition, but rather on a practical experience that enables them to assess the probability of different versions of what transpired and the actual importance of various asserted values to the holders of different roles in the society. Assuming they have no personal stake in the outcome, they are in a position to act on the impulse to be fair-minded. They can ask the question: 'If, over a lifetime, a person will be on both sides of any rule we adopt, what rule is best?'—and give an answer based on concrete and knowing experience. Their judgments can be wise.

---

[67] Many philosophers have reached the same conclusion about ethical thinking in general. See, eg, B Williams, *Ethics and the Limits of Philosophy* (1985) p 113; S Hampshire, *Two Theories of Morality* (1977) pp 28–31.

[68] In actual traditional societies, of course, there will usually be some permanent role differentiation—for instance, by sex or by caste—that will make this unmediated process problematic in some cases.

It would be wrong to view this type of thinking as mysterious in our own place and time. The contextual consideration of multiple values, undertaken with the goal of determining a fair and workable course of action, is in fact one of our everyday patterns of thought. It is also an everyday pattern of legal argument. It corresponds, for example, to what practicing lawyers do when they, as they say, 'argue the facts', for implicit in that very phrase is the notion that facts can be made into arguments, that as a practical activity we can form the facts into patterns that will tell us what ought to be done. The practical question is not whether our minds can think this way—they can think this way quite well; the practical question is whether they can think this way on a sufficient scale to encompass situations of which we have no first-hand experience.

In other words, the problem of wisdom in any modern society, is that it is impossible to cumulate in any individual—or in any small collegial group—personal experience with more than the smallest fraction of the life-possibilities put forth by the society. Correspondingly, the danger of wisdom in our society is that its name becomes merely a sham for the assertion of a point of view derived from some very limited experience. And the challenge of wisdom in our society is to find a method—not intuition, not practical experience—but a method to use in order to gain a substantive appreciation of multiple points of view. More, it must be a method that allows not only for an identification of various interests, but for an assessment of the weight of the various claims as well.

The extent of our ability imaginatively to recreate the circumstances and understandings of persons situated differently from ourselves is of course much contested. To some degree this is a question put to one's experience of life, and all I can say is that my experience convinces me that members of a going society are usually, and to a considerable degree, more intelligible to each other that at least some theoretical constructs say they should be. But it is also a question put to one's method of thinking, and at that level it seems clear that the particular process we are considering has been created to address this very issue. For instead of dealing either with the citizen of the society as a whole (who in a modern, differentiated society does not exist) or with the unique individual litigant (who may partake of an opaque subjectivity), this method deals with social type characters. It places them in a structured context. The meanings of their actions become accessible because those actions are institutionally constrained and socially oriented.[69] A total outsider to the society still might not understand. But a judge who has an initial comprehension of his or her society and culture, of what claims of value might be valid, and of what their weight might be, can indeed learn what values are in fact

[69] This point will be a commonplace for those familiar with the sociology of Max Weber. For exposition, see T Parsons, *The Structure of Social Action* (1937) pp 640 *et seq*.

implicated, and what their weights truly are, in the type-situation which is at hand.

It is better for the common law judge to deal with normative conflict in this fashion, than to use the alternatives that situation-sense rejects: reliance on a monistic value system, the trading-off of abstract values, or acceptance of continually unresolved value conflict. When dealing with social roles and social processes, judges are constantly faced with situations that others understand as multi-valenced. It seems more responsible to recognize that than to ignore it. Even if that desideratum could be satisfied through a trade-off of macro-values, of what good would it be? What content is there in 'thirty-five per cent efficiency, twenty-five per cent fairness, forty per cent freedom'? All the problems involved in working down even a single-valued hierarchy from abstraction to practise—the looseness of entailment at each level, the need to import social vision in order to do the work of concretizing, the ability to turn an argument based on one abstraction into one based on another—are multiplied beyond question in transforming a 'grand trade-off' of several abstractions into particular decisions. At the same time, judges, given the obligation to decide and to achieve a liveable resolution of problem after problem, ought to work towards coherence, rather than chaos, if they can. Thus, the notion that a workable coherence can be achieved by relating the implicated values to a patterned social situation—the idea that claims can live together in context even if antagonistic in the abstract—is a very attractive one. Especially is this true, if the necessary delineation of the situations can legitimately be understood as, yes, a cultural activity, but, no, not a wilfully idiosyncratic business.

This brings us, then, to the matter-of-factness which characterizes the judge using situation-sense—the judge, as I previously said, who is acting as a participant-observer. This is the judge whose attitude, to quote Lon Fuller's famous article on common law reasoning called 'Reason and Fiat in Case Law', is 'more like that of a cook trying to find the secret of a flaky pie crust, or of an engineer trying to devise a means of bridging a ravine'.[70] What is involved in this approach to judging?

Fuller's explication starts from the insight that every judicial decision partakes of both reason and fiat; in a strikingly up-to-date formulation (although written in 1946) these are 'notions apparently contradictory [which] form indispensable complements for one another'.[71] Yet it is fair to say that he assumes that in modern times the idea that law is the embodiment of will needs no proof, and focusses instead on the omnipresence of the element of reason. Reason is omnipresent, because acceptance of the role of judge constitutes acceptance of a position not

---

[70] L Fuller, 'Reason and Fiat in Case Law' (1946) 59 Harv L Rev 376, 379.
[71] *Ibid.*, 381.

merely of power, but also of responsibility: the judge must seek to make the right decision. Moreover, the judge's decisions, especially insofar as they established law for the future, will have social effects; the 'rightness' he or she must seek, is a social rightness. But one cannot tell what is 'right for the group, right in the light of the group's purposes and the things that its members sought to achieve through common effort'[72] if all is flux. The judge, by force of his or her role, is 'faced with the task of mastering a segment of reality and of discovering and utilizing its regularities for the benefit of the group'.[73] In short, inherent in our conception of responsible judging is the assertion that there is a discoverable, non-chaotic order to social life.

Fuller's argument is powerful. Part of what has prevented its wider acceptance, I think, is that he assumes there will in fact be such a social order, that he grounds his discoverable order in natural processes. He uses the literary convention of a desert island, and on this island social order is a spontaneous occurrence.[74] Moreover, established institutions, once they arise, are just another circumstance, not different in kind from natural conditions. That is hard for many of his readers, including me, to accept. It seems fairer to say that the institutions that exist in modern societies have been fashioned by centuries of history and conflict; that they sufficiently dominate life in these societies that each society must be seen as more a constructed than natural reality; and that there is no supra-historical process by which even artificial creations of this sort are brought into congruence with natural social laws. But Fuller's depiction of responsible judging does not depend, logically or practically, on social processes being natural. Social order can be created order—and the corollary that there can be situations in which no responsible judging is possible without some prior political action is far from unimaginable.

It seems, then, that the judicial attitude supposed by situation-sense, the judicial attitude Fuller also supposes, is possible if we start with a going society and reason from existing social structures. But, to raise the other sticking point, if we do that, are we serving justice?

Situation-sense takes as its standard the wise result as understood by someone who comprehends all the claims of value (including their fair weight) that might be made by the different role participants in a situation, and who sees himself or herself as impartial—that is, as equally likely to be in any of the roles. The implied term that is fair, the term that we would adopt if we were ignorant of which side of the transaction we would inhabit, is adopted as the term that is just. This approach resonates with the well-known theory of justice espoused by the philosopher John Rawls, and not by accident; for Rawls' theory is ultimately contractarian in

---

[72] *Ibid.*, 378.   [73] *Ibid.*   [74] *Ibid.*, 377–80.

nature, and based on a conception of society as being a fundamentally co-operative endeavour. But the differences are instructive. Rawls asks us not only to imagine that we could be in any role—an exercise in achieving fairness—but also to abstract from actual institutional arrangements in conceiving those roles.[75] This stipulation serves the purposes of the polit-ical philosopher, interested in the normative foundations of society's basic institutions. It is a much less useful approach for a judge operating in a system already established; there, the concrete question of fairness—what ought each actual role be willing to yield to the other roles, assum-ing the participants could end up in any of them—seems much more to the point.

It is true, of course, that arguments of this type will not generate, or even necessarily incorporate, principles of what we might call 'cosmic jus-tice'. Judges are to be cultural participants; they are to use existing social relations and structures as the starting point for framing issues; they are supposed to pay attention to how a situation works and how a proposed rule will fit in with what is already there. From such a starting point, it is hard to see how one would ever appeal from the society to the heavens.

However, admitting that we are talking at most of interstitial change, it is quite a different, and I think erroneous, thing, to say that situation-sense is biased toward the conservative. That contention implicitly assumes that when law changes, it leads society, or, phrased the other way around, that any appeal to what exists will be a restraint on the law's forward motion. One need not be a Marxist to appreciate that the opposite is usually the truth, that the most dynamic elements in modern societies are not the lawmaking institutions. Legal rules are often, perhaps very often, lagging rules, and an appeal to social reality has a progressive effect. The prophetic voice, by contrast, can be reactionary, and historically often has been so.

Situation-sense will not make the poor rich. However, to be judged by the standards that fairly inhere in one's society is worth a lot; many people, especially the poor and the powerless, get much less. It is not a goal so easy to attain that its fulfilment can be assumed. Judges who enforce situation-sense do, in my view, contribute to the justice of their society.

The law as a whole may well aspire to grander things. But this em-bedded view of justice can certainly be commended to common law judges trying to determine default rules. The historical and political action which sets the basic tenor of a society not only cannot be, but should not be, left to common law judges. And, of course, it is hard to insist on radi-cal change and at the same time say that the very rules being announced legitimately admit of the parties' contrary specification.

In short, situation-sense is a very good method for determining what the default rules of contract law should be.

[75] J Rawls, *Political Liberalism* (1993) pp 15–28.

(b) Legislation and public law influences

9

Legislative Control of Fairness: The Directive on Unfair Terms in Consumer Contracts*

Hugh Beale

This chapter looks at the particular problems of trying to secure fairness when contracts are made using one party's standard form conditions, and at the EC Council Directive on Unfair Terms in Consumer Contracts.[1] In so doing we move away from the traditional grounds for relief, which for the most part[2] involve either some improper behaviour by the party against which relief is sought (eg duress) or exploitation in terms of value for money—that the weaker party has sold property for less than its true value or the transaction is manifestly disadvantageous.[3] There are certainly many cases of the 'victimization'[4] of consumers; some sad examples are given in the Report of the Director-General of Fair Trading, *Trading Malpractices*.[5] The Director-General calls for improved powers to deal with such cases.

Problems with standard form contracts

I hope it is now accepted that the problems caused by standard form contracts are rather different to those confronted in traditional cases of victimization. They are the result of the very advantages of standard form contracts—that complex transactions can be made with a minimum of negotiation and by relatively unskilled personnel, and that supplier's

---

* Copyright © 1994, Hugh Beale.
[1] Council Directive 93/13/EEC of 5 April 1993 (OJ L95, 21.4.1993, p 29).
[2] Infants' contracts are possibly an exception.
[3] See *Fry v Lane* (1888) 40 ChD 312 and on 'manifest disadvantage' in cases of undue influence, P Birks & Chin Nyuk Yin, ch 3 above. The meaning of unfairness is discussed in H Beale, 'Inequality of Bargaining Power' (1986) 6 Ox JLS 123; SN Thal, 'The Inequality of Bargaining Power Doctrine: The Problem of Defining Contractual Unfairness' (1988) 8 Ox JLS 17.
[4] The word is that used by Lord Brightman in *Hart v O'Connor* [1985] AC 1000, at 1018.
[5] (Office of Fair Trading July 1990.) See, eg p 42.

risks are reduced and standardised.[6] To restate[7] the arguments briefly, although both judges[8] and academics[9] have suggested that the frequency of harsh terms in standard form contracts is the result of 'the concentration of particular kinds of business in relatively few hands',[10] this explanation seems implausible. Standard forms and apparently harsh terms are found in industries which do not have significant market concentrations.[11] Empirical study of guarantees offered by manufacturers in the United States does not suggest a correlation between concentration and the use of exclusion clauses.[12]

Although not proven empirically, it seems more likely that harsh clauses are the result of information costs. Many customers faced with standard form contracts may not know of, or understand the meaning of, the small print and may not think it worth the time and cost to find out about it. Instead they choose products and services on the basis of things they can evaluate, such as the physical characteristics of the product and the price. In order to remain competitive in price, suppliers will tend to reduce their costs by using the small print to shift more and more risks onto the customers who, since they do not know of or understand the clauses, will not complain. So in a market which is competitive in terms of price, but where customers do not have full information about the standard terms, there will be a tendency toward harsh term—low price offerings.[13]

Even if a customer is aware of what is in the standard form and protests, it is likely to be met with a take-it-or-leave-it attitude. A supplier is unlikely to find it worth while altering its standard terms just to satisfy one customer unless that customer's business is particularly important to it—unless, in other words, the customer has bargaining power as well as bargaining sophistication.

---

[6] See F Kessler, 'Contracts of Adhesion—Some Thoughts About Freedom of Contract' (1943) 43 Colum L Rev 629, 631–2.

[7] See also the summaries in H Beale, 'Inequality of Bargaining Power' (1986) 6 Ox JLS 123, 131–2 and H Beale, 'Unfair Contracts in Britain and Europe' [1989] CLP 197, 199–201.

[8] eg Lord Diplock in *A Schroeder Music Publishing Co Ltd v Macaulay* [1974] 1 WLR 1308, at 1316.

[9] eg F Kessler, 'Contracts of Adhesion—Some Thoughts About Freedom of Contract' (1943) 43 Colum L Rev 629, 631; O Kahn-Freund, Introduction to K Renner, *The Institutions of Private Law and their Social Functions* (1949).

[10] *A Schroeder Music Publishing Co Ltd v Macaulay* [1974] 1 WLR 1308, at 1316, per Lord Diplock.

[11] See MJ Trebilock, 'An Economic Approach to the Doctrine of Unconscionability' in (BJ Reiter and J Swan (eds) 1980) *Studies in Contract Law* 379, 398.

[12] GL Priest 'A Theory of the Consumer Product Warranty' (1981) 90 Yale LJ 1297.

[13] See VP Goldberg, 'Institutional Change and the Quasi-Invisible Hand' (1974) 17 J Law & Econ 461, 483 *et seq*; MJ Trebilcock, 'An Economic Approach to the Doctrine of Unconscionability' in BJ Reiter and J Swan (eds), *Studies in Contract Law* (1980) 379. A very useful survey of the economic arguments is IDC Ramsay, *Rationales for Intervention in the Consumer Marketplace* (Office of Fair Trading, 1984). Other possible explanations for harsh terms are canvassed in H Beale, 'Unfair Contracts in Britain and Europe' [1989] CLP 197, 200.

Suppliers are not completely unconstrained in the terms other than the price that they offer, because these non-price terms may become the subject of competition. This may the result of a marketing decision to highlight the advantages of particular terms, eg the warranty offered on a new car or the cover provided by an insurance policy, or it may result from the fact that a percentage of customers are sufficiently knowledge-able to compare the small print offerings and to shop around to try to find terms with which they will be happier. If there are enough of these mar-ginal sophisticated customers, it may be worthwhile for suppliers to offer better terms in the hope of capturing their business, and since it is not often going to be worthwhile to discriminate between customers so far as the standard terms offered are concerned, the result may be that better terms are offered to all.[14]

This analysis means that often it will be impossible to say that there has been 'exploitation' in the traditional sense of over-charging or buying at undervalue. Nor will there have been procedural impropriety in any of the traditional senses; rather, just a failure to explain to the customer the content and meaning of what is being signed or perhaps a refusal to nego-tiate over the standard terms. So what are the problems of fairness associ-ated with standard form contracts? One of the best summaries is that of Lord Reid in the *Suisse Atlantique* case:

In the ordinary way the customer has no time to read [the standard terms], and if he did read them he would probably not understand them. And if he did under-stand and object to any of them, he would generally be told he could take it or leave it. And if he then went to another supplier the result would be the same. Freedom to contract must surely imply some choice or room for bargaining.[15]

In other words the problems are what the comments to Uniform Commercial Code § 2–302 calls 'unfair surprise', and lack of choice.

Legislative controls over unfair terms in consumer contracts in English law

In England attention until now has focused on clauses which exclude or limit the liability of one party to a contract. Legislative controls date back to the Railway and Canal Traffic Act 1854, but controls over such clauses in contracts in general were introduced in the Unfair Contract Terms Act

[14] See MJ Trebilcock, 'An Economic Approach to the Doctrine of Unconscionability' in BJ Reiter and J Swan (eds), *Studies in Contract Law* (1980) 379, and A Schwartz and LL Wilde, 'Intervening in Markets on the Basis of Imperfect Information: A Legal and Economic Analysis' (1979) 127 U Penn LR 630.
[15] *Suisse Atlantique Société d'Armement Maritime SA v NV Rotterdamsche Kolen Centrale* [1967] 1 AC 361, at 406.

1977 (UCTA). Despite its broad title,[16] this only affects various types of exclusion and limitation of liability clause[17] and indemnity clauses in consumer contracts.[18]

The legislation involves two types of control: some clauses are always ineffective while others may be valid but only if they satisfy the requirement of reasonableness. Thus the 1977 Act, s 2 deals with clauses which purport to exclude or restrict liability for negligence in the course of a business or arising out of the occupation of land used for the business purposes of the occupier.[19] Section 2(1) provides that any clause which purports to exclude or limit such liability for death or personal injury is of no effect. It is immaterial whether the liability arises in contract or in tort. Under s 2(2), in contrast, clauses excluding or restricting liability for other loss or damage caused by negligence in similar circumstances may be valid but only if the clause is reasonable.

Some controls are applied only to contracts for the sale or supply of goods. As against any person who deals as a consumer,[20] any attempt by the supplier to exclude or restrict liability for the goods' correspondence with description or fitness for purpose is of no effect.[21] At common law, manufacturers would normally be liable directly to a consumer in tort if negligence in the manufacture of the goods led to the consumer being injured or her property being damaged,[22] or if the manufacturer has given the consumer a contractual guarantee.[23] Section 5 of the Act prevents the manufacturer from using the terms of the guarantee to exclude or limit its liability in tort to the consumer.

Finally, any exclusion or restriction not caught by the above may fall within s 3, which applies in favour of any consumer.[24] The business may

[16] The draft Bill proposed by the Law Commission was entitled the Avoidance of Liability Bill: the new title was adopted in the Bill's passage through Parliament.

[17] See s 13, discussed by E Macdonald, 'Exclusion Clauses: the ambit of s 13(1) of the Unfair Contract Terms Act 1977' (1992) 12 LS 277.

[18] Section 4, which was also the result of an amendment in Parliament.   [19] See s 1.

[20] Section 12 defines this broadly as a sale or supply by a person acting in the course of a business to one who is not, provided that the goods are of a kind normally supplied for private use or consumption.

[21] Sections 6(2) (sales) and 7(2) (other contracts for the supply of goods). Section 6 derives from the earlier Supply of Goods (Implied Terms) Act 1973, which imposed similar but not identical controls. In non-consumer contracts (eg a sale by one business to another) such clauses may be valid if they are reasonable: ss 6(3) and 7(3).

[22] The manufacturer will then be liable under the principles established in *Donoghue* v *Stevenson* [1932] AC 562. There is no liability for a product which is defective but which has not caused any harm: *Murphy* v *Brentwood District Council* [1991] 1 AC 398.

[23] The consumer's purchase of the goods in reliance on the guarantee would normally be the consideration for the manufacturer's promise. Doubts may arise over whether the consumer relied on the guarantee and thus whether it is enforceable and the Department of Trade and Industry has canvassed making all manufacturers' guarantees of consumer goods enforceable by statute: *Consumer Guarantees: A Consultation Document* (1992).

[24] And also in favour of any party, consumer or not, who is dealing on the other party's written standard terms of business.

not exclude or restrict any liability for breach of contract[25] unless the clause is reasonable. Nor may it rely on any clause as permitting it to render a performance substantially different to that which was reasonably expected, or as justifying it in not performing, unless the clause is reasonable.[26] Thus, were a clause to purport to give a package holiday company the right to change the destination of the holiday-maker, or to cancel the holiday altogether, at its complete discretion, it would probably be invalid.

The test of whether a clause is reasonable is whether it was a fair and reasonable clause to include given the circumstances known when the contract was made.[27] The 'inclusion' test seems to mean that a clause which is very wide may be unreasonable even though the way in which the business is seeking to apply it does not seem unreasonable on the facts which have actually occurred.[28] Schedule 2 of the Act contains a non-exhaustive list of guidelines which, although they apply strictly only to decisions under ss 6(3) and 7(3),[29] the courts look at in any case:[30]

(1) the strength of the bargaining positions of the parties relative to each other, taking into account (among other things) alternative means by which the customer's requirements could have been met;

(2) whether the customer received an inducement to agree to the term, or in accepting it had an opportunity of entering into a similar contract with other persons, but without having to accept a similar term;

(3) whether the customer knew or ought reasonably to have known of the existence and extent of the term (having regard, among other things, to any custom of the trade and any previous course of dealing between the parties);

(4) where the term excludes or restricts any relevant liability if some condition is not complied with, whether it was reasonable at the time of the contract to expect that compliance with that condition would be practicable;

(5) whether the goods were manufactured, processed or adapted to the special order of the customer.

Because under the Act so many clauses in consumer contracts are automatically invalid, there has been little case law on the application of the reasonableness test to consumer contracts.[31]

---

[25] Section 3(2)(a).   [26] Section 3(2)(b).   [27] Section 11(1).

[28] In contrast the Supply of Goods (Implied Terms) Act 1973, s 4, had used the test of whether it was fair and reasonable to rely on the clause.

[29] Section 11(2).

[30] *Phillips Products Ltd* v *Hyland* (Note) [1987] 1 WLR 659.

[31] Though see *Woodman* v *Photo Trade Processing Ltd* (7 May 1981, unreported), cited in RG Lawson, 'The Unfair Contract Terms Act: A Progress Report' (1981) 131 NLJ 933, 935.

The implications of unfair surprise and lack of choice

Although it was said a long time ago that the problems with standard form contracts are usually ones of unfair surprise and lack of choice, I am still not sure that we have taken on board the full implications. We are dealing not with individual victimization, but with problems of mass contracting. First, I have argued elsewhere that this should have implications for the way in which we determine in an individual case whether or not a clause is fair and reasonable under the Unfair Contract Terms Act 1977 (UCTA).[32] Secondly, it may affect the implications of individual decisions on reasonableness for the general run of standard form contracts. Thirdly, it requires us to think carefully about mechanisms for improving the standard forms on offer, especially in the consumer field. For a traditional contract lawyer, some of the devices which are needed may 'go against the grain'.

An irreducible minimum?

There is another possible problem with standard form contracts, identified years ago by the Molony Committee: they enable well organised commerce 'to deny [the consumer] what the law means him to have.'[33] Whether English contract law is solely concerned with freedom of contract in all its many guises, or whether there is a certain irreducible minimum of obligations and correlative rights, is something on which neither the law nor policy makers seem to have made up their minds. I think that liability for fraud and other intentional harm cannot be excluded under any circumstances,[34] but do we go further than this?[35] The absolute bans on certain types of exclusion clauses under the 1977 Act seem to have been justified at least by the Law Commission primarily in terms of bargaining

---

On reasonableness in non-consumer contracts the leading cases are *George Mitchell (Chesterhall) Ltd v Finney Lock Seeds Ltd* [1983] 2 AC 803 and *Phillips Products Ltd v Hyland (Note)* [1987] 1 WLR 659. See also *Smith v Eric S Bush* [1990] 1 AC 831, a case in tort.

[32] See H Beale, 'Unfair Contracts in Britain and Europe' [1989] CLP 197, 204–11.

[33] Board of Trade, *Final Report of the Committee on Consumer Protection* (Molony Committee) (1962) Cmnd 1781 para 435. See *Exemption Clauses in Contracts, First Report: Amendments to the Sale of Goods Act 1893* (1969) Law Com No 24; Scot Law Com No 12; para 68.

[34] *Pearson & Son Ltd v Dublin Corpn* [1907] AC 351.

[35] H Collins, 'Good Faith in European Contract Law' (1994) 14 Ox JLS 229, 246–7, has argued that the decision in *Smith v Eric S Bush* [1990] 1 AC 831 represents a policy of creating a 'social market'.

power[36] or the misleading nature of the term.[37] This liberal tradition is seen as surprising by many continental colleagues.

The Directive

There are a number of questions one may address in relation to the Directive on Unfair terms in Consumer Contracts. I will discuss only three.

First, what will be its impact on the law of England and Wales? Here the means of implementation must be considered. Shortage of Parliamentary time has meant that the Directive has been implemented via regulations under the European Communities Act 1972 rather than by amendment of UCTA or other legislation; full revision of the Act before the deadline of 31 December 1994 for implementation of the Directive was impossible. The Department of Trade and Industry's initial consultation paper on implementation[38] provisionally proposed Regulations for the most part simply reciting the words of the Directive, so that there would be a dual system by which clauses might be challenged either under the Act or under the Regulations. This seems clumsy and apparently attracted a good deal of adverse comment. However, it was not clear that, given the time constraints, there was a better solution. It might have been stated in the Regulations that consumers would be excluded from the future operation of those sections of UCTA which require terms in consumer contracts to be reasonable, so as to force consumers to proceed under the Regulations and thus eliminate the overlap.[39] But it would have been arguable that consumers' protection was being reduced, as it is not wholly clear that the test of fairness under the Directive gives the same protection

---

[36] For s 2(1) (clauses excluding liability for death or personal injury) the original proposal was to limit the ban to situations such as car parks where the customer had no effective choice. For ss 6(2) and 7(2) (clauses excluding or restricting liability for failure to correspond with description, fitness for purpose etc) the First Report on Exemption Clauses stated that the burden should fall on the retailer rather than the consumer, but also rejected a reasonableness test because it would weaken the consumer's bargaining position rather than on any a priori ground (*Exemption Clauses in Contracts, First Report: Amendments to the Sale of Goods Act 1893* (1969) Law Com No 24; Scot Law Com No 12; para 73).

[37] Section 5 (clauses in manufacturers' guarantees): *Exemption Clauses, Second Report* (1975) Law Com No 69; Scot Law Com No 39; para 100.

[38] *Implementation of the EC Directive on Unfair Terms in Consumer Contracts* (93/13/EEC): A Consultation Document (1993).

[39] FMB Reynolds, 'Unfair Contract Terms' (1994) 110 Law QR 1, argued that 'all the resources of s 2(2) [of the European Communities Act 1972] should be deployed' to repeal parts of UCTA in order to avoid uncertainty.

as the test of reasonableness under the Act.[40] After a second consultation paper, regulations were laid before Parliament.[41a]

This raises the second question: what is covered by UCTA and other existing UK law but not by the Directive? This may seem to be of less importance, but one of the aims of the Directive is

... to safeguard the citizen in his role as consumer when acquiring goods and services under contracts which are governed by the laws of Member States other than his own ...[42]

If consumers do shop abroad, what minimum protection can they be sure they will have, compared to what they would have at home? Often the position will be better than the minimum, as many Member States already offer much fuller protection that the Directive requires (and Article 8 preserves their right to do so), but this will not always be the case.

Thirdly, what are the concepts and techniques employed in the Directive, and do they add anything to the debate or possible amelioration of the problems?

Scope of the Directive

The Directive is confined to the law relating to unfair terms in contracts concluded between a seller or supplier and a consumer.[43] A consumer is defined as a natural person.[44] Thus, unlike UCTA, the Regulations will not affect contracts between businesses and it will not be possible to hold that a limited company is acting as a consumer, even if it makes a transaction which is outside its normal course of business.[45]

The Directive only requires Member States to treat as potentially unfair terms which have 'not been individually negotiated'.[46] UCTA does not contain such a restriction, but many laws do; eg the German Law of Standard Contract Terms of 9 December 1976. Printed standard terms of business are obviously within this definition, unless in fact there has been some negotiated change in them. Perhaps the phrase 'standard terms' was not used to take care of the problems of definition which occur when one party has its usual terms not in a pre-printed document but on its word-

---

[40] See further below, pp 242–5.

[41] *Implementation of the EC Directive on Unfair Terms in Consumer Contracts (93/13/EEC): A Further Consultation Document* (1994).

[41a] Unfair Terms in Consumer Contracts Regulations, SI 1994 No. 3159.

[42] Council Directive 93/13/EEC of 5 April 1993 (OJ L95, 21.4.1993, p 29), preamble para 6 (my numbering).

[43] Article 1. See r 2(1).   [44] Article 2(b).

[45] Cf. *R & B Customs Brokers Co Ltd* v *United Dominions Trust Ltd* [1988] 1 WLR 321.

[46] Article 3(1).

processor, or in a precedent contract which is in effect non-negotiable. It is clear that the question is whether the consumer has been able to have some influence:

A term shall always be regarded as not individually negotiated where it has been drafted in advance and the consumer has therefore not been able to influence the substance of the term, particularly in the context of a pre-formulated standard contract.[47]

In terms of consumer contracts, the restriction of the Directive to terms which have not been individually negotiated does not seem very significant; at a guess, almost all objectionable terms[48] are pre-formulated.

In terms of the types of consumer contract covered the Directive is significantly wider than UCTA, from which several types of contract are exempted.[49] For example, insurance contracts are within it[50] and so, it seems, are contracts for the sale of land when these are part of the seller's 'trade, business or profession'.[51] This is to be welcomed. Whether a lessor of land can be regarded as a 'supplier' is unclear.

With two exceptions, which I will deal with below, the Directive requires the law of Member States to cover any unfair terms. This is, on the face of it, a sharp contrast to UCTA which, as noted earlier, covers only clauses which in one form or another restrict or exclude liability[52] and indemnity clauses.[53] It is difficult to predict what types of clause may be vulnerable under the new Regulations. The Annex contains 'an indicative and non-exhaustive list of the terms which may be regarded as unfair'.[54] This permissive wording seems to leave it to Member States whether or not to adopt the list; in any event, the terms are not ones which are automatically to be regarded as unfair; in that sense it is only a 'grey list' not a 'black list'. Yet some idea of what terms may be caught may be gained from looking at it, or at black and grey lists contained in the legislation of other Member States.[55]

Not surprisingly, a number of the clauses in the Annex would in any event be of no effect under UCTA[56] or other legislation.[57] Some would be

---

[47] Article 3(2). Regulation 3(3) omits the last phrase.

[48] Other than the price itself, which cannot be reviewed anyway. See below, p 240.

[49] See Sched 1.   [50] Though see the discussion of Article 4(2) below, p 240.

[51] Article 2(c).

[52] See UCTA, s 13: in particular, clauses which would 'exclude or restrict the relevant obligation or duty' (eg 'the seller gives no undertaking of any kind that the vehicle is of merchantable quality') are covered: s 13(1).

[53] Section 4.   [54] Article 3(3); Regulations, Schedule 3.

[55] An early draft of the Directive (June 1987: XI/124/87-EN) helpfully appended lists from the legislation of Member States and from the earlier Council of Europe resolution (76)47 of 16 November 1967. This draft is reprinted in (1988) 6 *Trading Law* 79. A very full and helpful survey is EH Hondius, *Unfair Terms in Consumer Contracts* (1987).

[56] eg Annex para 1(a), (b), (f) and (o).

[57] On para 1 (q) see Consumer Arbitration Agreements Act 1988.

caught by common law rules, eg the rules on penalty clauses.[58] Some are perhaps unlikely to arise under English law; for example, Annex para 1(c), a clause

making an agreement binding on the consumer whereas provision of services by the seller or supplier is subject to a condition whose realization depends on his will alone

may be aimed at systems which normally treat offers as irrevocable.

Other clauses in the Annex could perhaps be reached by an imaginative use of UCTA. The examples in para 1(j) and (k) giving the seller or supplier the right to alter unilaterally, and without a valid reason, the terms of the contract or the characteristics of the product or service must be within s 3(2)(b)(i) of the 1977 Act.

There will definitely be some widening of the controls. We can expect, for example, considerable activity over clauses allowing sellers and suppliers to change their prices after the contract has been made. Annex para 1(l) lists clauses 'providing for the price of goods to be determined at the time of delivery'. (It should be remembered that in some systems there cannot be a valid contract of sale if the price is 'open'.[59]) It also covers clauses allowing a price increase without a right of cancellation for the consumer if the 'final price is too high'. It would not be controversial to hold such a clause unfair but decisions under the new Regulations might go further. The German Law on Standard Contracts black-lists any clause allowing an increase of price within the first four months.[60] This may give many companies pause for thought. Luxembourg law proscribes minimum consumption clauses in contracts for the supply of gas, electricity or fuels;[61] standing charges for utilities may be at risk.

Price and definition of the main subject matter

As mentioned above, there are two exceptions to the wide coverage of types of clause. Under Article 4(2) the price may not be assessed in terms of fairness in so far as it is in plain intelligible language; nor may the definition of the main subject matter of the contract. The second exception at least seems to be another tribute to the power of the insurance lobby.[62] The nineteenth paragraph of the Preamble states that

. . . it follows, inter alia, that in insurance contracts, the terms which clearly define or circumscribe the insured risk and the insurer's liability shall not be subject

---

[58] eg Annex para 1(e).
[59] eg under French law. See generally D Tallon (ed), *Le détermination du prix dans les contrats, étude de droit comparée* (1989).
[60] Para 11.1.   [61] Consumer Protection Act of 25 August 1983, Art 2(17).
[62] Cf. the exemption of insurance from UCTA. Sched 1, s 1(a).

to . . . assessment since these restrictions are taken into account calculating the premium paid by the consumer.

The words inter alia, and the terms of Art 4.2 itself leave a considerable loophole in the Directive. In any competitive market, the terms on which the goods are sold or the service provided are taken into account in the price. Can it not be said that any exception clause defines the seller or supplier's obligations and thus cannot be reviewed?

There seem to be two possible answers. One is that the exception must be obvious. Thus a clearly understandable clause stating that travel insurance does not cover injury through winter sports would not be subject to review; but an obscure clause in the small print of a domestic insurance policy, excluding theft coverage when the theft occurred without forcible entry, would be reviewable.

The second argument may be that an insurance policy's exceptions define when the insurer is obliged to perform its primary obligation, ie to pay out; whereas many exemption or limitation of liability clauses define only secondary obligations, ie those which spring up only when there has been a failure to perform the primary obligations. But what of the kind of clause at one time so common in holiday contracts:

Steamers, sailing dates, rates and itineraries are subject to change without prior notice.[63]

As the Law Commission pointed out, such clauses also define the primary obligation and a special provision for them was made in UCTA.[64] It seems they are not covered by the Directive.

In terms of scope, therefore, the Directive does extend controls to more types of clause than are caught by UCTA. For the British consumer abroad, the picture is less happy. First, certain types of clause covered by UCTA are apparently outside the Directive. A second point is more serious. There is no guaranteed minimum. Section 2(1) of UCTA, for example, renders completely ineffective any clause excluding or restricting business liability for death or personal injury caused by negligence. Under the Directive there is no blacklist. Fortunately many countries' laws do prevent the exclusion of this type of liability[65]—but do they all?

Early drafts of the Directive seemed to contemplate black lists and grey lists but were less than clear.[66] The Economic and Social Committee said

[63] *Anglo-Continental Holidays Ltd* v *Typaldos Lines (London) Ltd* [1967] 2 Lloyd's Rep 61. See now the Package Travel, Package Holidays and Package Tours Regulations 1992, SI 1992 No 3288 (implementing the Council Directive 90/314/EEC of 13 June 1990 (OJ L158, 23.6.1990, pp 59) which might not apply to the facts of this case.

[64] Exemption Clauses, Second Report (1975) Law Com No 69; Scot Law Com No 39; para 143; UCTA s 3(2)(b), above, p 235.

[65] eg German Law on Standard Contracts, art 11(7).

[66] eg COM (90) 322 fin -SYN 285 (OJ C 243, 28.9.1990, p 2).

that this must be clarified[67] and the next draft was quite categoric: certain terms were blacklisted, some (including exclusions of liability for death and personal injury) even if they had been negotiated individually.[68] The final text is a disappointing watering down.[69]

The test of unfairness

When we turn to the test of when a term in a consumer contract is to be treated as unfair we come to one of the conceptual problems. The test laid down in the Directive is not immediately applicable to the problems which I identified earlier. It is to be regarded as unfair

... if, contrary, to the requirement of good faith, it causes a significant imbalance in the parties' rights and obligation arising under the contract, to the detriment of the consumer.[70]

The world 'imbalance' has connotations of exploitation of the old-fashioned kind. If the arguments used earlier are correct, this would open to the seller or supplier the defence that the harsh clause resulted in a cheaper deal for the consumer, with the result that there was no overall imbalance. It was on just this ground that the French legislature rejected this test when considering what was to become the *Loi Scrivener* of 1978.[71] In addition, it seems, the Directive restricts relief to cases where there has not been good faith. To English lawyers this may have connotations of conscious misleading, or at least a reckless attitude as to whether the other party has been misled by the standard form. It does not seem to apply readily to a case where the consumer has simply not read the standard form, although the form is not misleading, still less to cases where the supplier simply indicates that it is not willing to alter the form in the consumer's favour.

In this respect, earlier drafts of the Directive again seemed more satisfactory: in the 1990 version,[72] for instance, significant imbalance and incompatibility with good faith were alternatives, rather than cumulative.

---

[67] 91/C159/13 (OJ C 159, 17.6.1991, p 34).

[68] COM (92) 66 final - SYN 285 (OJ C 73, 24.3.1992, p 7), Art 3.3.

[69] It seems inconsistent with the Package Travel Directive, note 63 above, which by Art 5 blacklists any exclusion of liability for personal injury, grey-listing exclusions of liability for property damage: also with Commission Proposal for a Council Directive on liability of suppliers of services (91/C12/11, COM (90) 482 final -SYN 308 (OJ C 12, 18.1.1991, p 8). Art 7, which would have prevented exclusion of liability for either type. However the draft Services Directive has now been withdrawn, COM(94) 260 of 23 June 1994.

[70] Article 3(1); r 4. The term is to be judged by the circumstances at the time the contract was concluded, Article 4(1). section 11(1) of UCTA is the same on this point.

[71] J Ghestin, *Le contrat: formation* (2nd ed 1988), para 602.

[72] COM(90) 322 fin - SYN 285 (OJ C 243, 28.9.1990, p 2).

There were also two other grounds for unfairness: that the term caused performance of the contract to be unduly detrimental to the consumer, or that it caused the performance to be significantly different to what the consumer could legitimately expect. The Economic and Social Committee wanted to add a further criterion, the 'non-transparency of a contract term'.[73] The House of Lords Select Committee on the European Communities favoured adding the test of reasonableness, although noting that this term has a different meaning in civil law jurisdictions.[74] In contrast, in the first debate of the proposal in the European Parliament, a Spanish member protested against all the grounds except good faith as being too much the British solution; only good faith was in accord with the civil law tradition. His argument was turned down so sharply by the Commission representative that it is a little surprising to see that this voice of reaction appears to have come close to winning the day.

However, it seems probable that concerns over the tests of imbalance and absence of good faith appropriate may be premised on interpretations of those phrases which are too narrow. First, we should think of imbalance not just in a narrow 'deviation from market price' sense, but in terms of balancing overall interests. Thus there may be imbalance if, by using a term, the supplier reduces the price slightly, and thereby gains a few extra sales, but at the price of placing a very large potential loss on the small number of consumers for whom the risk will materialize.[75] It has been noted that the test adopted by the Directive is close in its wording to the German Act on Standard Contract terms of 1976.[76] The so-called 'General Clause' of that Act refers to 'undue advantage to such an extent as to be incompatible with good faith'.[77] It seems that this has been interpreted as requiring the courts to look at the overall balance of advantage in the general run of cases.[78] Witz notes that the courts have frequently rejected the argument that a harsh clause is acceptable because it leads to a lower price being charged to the consumer.[79]

Secondly, it is clear that in several civilian systems 'good faith' has been

---

[73] Opinion on the proposal for a Council Directive on unfair terms in consumer contracts (91/C159/13) (OJ C 159, 17.6.1991, p 34), para 2.5.3.

[74] House of Lords, 6th Report (1991–92) HL 28, para 74.

[75] It may be interpreted as requiring that the consumer have certain rights irrespective of the price: H Collins, 'Good Faith in European Contract Law' (1994) 14 Ox JLS 229.

[76] eg KG Weil and F Puis, 'Le droit allemand des conditions générales d'affaires revu et corrigé par la directive communautaire relative aux clauses abusives' (1994) Rev int droit comparé 125. It should be noted that the German Act contains separate provisions on surprising clauses (§2) and prohibiting certain clauses altogether (§11) but the absence of parallels from the Directive does not necessarily mean that Art 3 of the Directive must be interpreted more narrowly.

[77] Standard Contracts Law (AGB-Gesetz) of 1976, §9.1.

[78] Witz, *Droit Privé Allemand* (1992), §457.   [79] *Ibid.*, §459.

developed very much beyond what we might immediately think of. As Bingham LJ said in the *Interfoto* case.

In many civil law systems . . . [t]his does not simply mean that they should not deceive each other, a principle which any legal system must recognize; its effect is perhaps most aptly conveyed by such metaphorical colloquialisms as 'playing fair', 'coming clean' or 'putting one's cards face upwards on the table.' It is in essence a principle of fair and open dealing.[80]

French law has used the concept of good faith in performance to avoid onerous conditions.[81] Other legal systems seem to have gone beyond the kind of disclosure requirement that Bingham LJ's words suggest. The Dutch Hoge Raad, admittedly in a case of mistake, laid down as early as 1957 a very broad requirement: the parties must let their conduct be guided by the legitimate interests of the other party.[82] This kind of approach can clearly be used to hold either a failure to draw the other's attention to a harsh clause or a refusal to negotiate to be not consistent with good faith. (The new Netherlands Civil Code, Article 6.233, uses the test of whether the contract is unreasonably onerous.) Germany also uses the good faith test extensively, both under the Law of Standard Contracts and under BGB § 242. The test does not seem to be purely a procedural one. Although the 'transparency' of the clause is a very important factor,[83] commentators have noted that the German courts tend to judge the clause by whether there was any real choice open to the customer[84] and have discussed the balance of interests in general terms, rather than in relation to the particular position of the individual consumer.[85] It seems that conceptual tools have been rewrought to meet new tasks, just as the notion of unconscionability in Anglo-American law was re-worked in *Williams* v *Walker-Thomas Furniture Co*[86] to mean terms which are unreasonably

---

[80] *Interfoto Picture Library Ltd* v *Stilletto Visual Programmes Ltd* [1989] QB 433, at 439.

[81] NS Wilson, 'Freedom of Contract and Adhesion Contracts' (1965) 14 ICLQ 172; and see J Ghestin, *Le Contrat: Formation* (2nd ed 1988) para 608–2.

[82] HR 15-11-1957. See ME Storme, *La bonne foi dans la formation des contracts en droit neer-landais*, Report to the Capitant Association (1992).

[83] See Reich, 'Le Principe de la transparence des clauses limitatives relatives au contenu des prestations dans le droit allemand des conditions générales des contrats' in J Ghestin (ed), *Les clauses limitatives ou exonératoires de responsabilité en Europe* (1990), 77–93.

[84] HW Micklitz, 'La loi allemande relative au régime juridique des conditions générales des contrats du 9 decembre 1976' (1989) 41 Rev int droit comparé 101, 109: JP Dawson, 'Unconscionable Coercion: The German Version' (1976) 89 Harvard L Rev 1041, 1114. Dawson states that before the Standard Contracts Law the courts were concerned with preventing unfair surprise but also with preventing one-sided contracts and ensuring 'elementary contractual justice' (pp 1110 *et seq*). See also Schmidt-Salzer, 'Droit allemand' in J Ghestin (ed), *Les clauses limitatives ou exoneratoires de responsabilité en Europe* (1990), at p 57: 'en matière de conditions générales ce qui est inattendu est aussi déraisonable: ce qui n'est pas raisonable, est légalement inattendu'.

[85] Witz, *Droit Privé Allemand* (1992) §457.

[86] 121 US App DC 315, 350 F 2d 445 (1965).

favourable to one party and an absence of meaningful choice for the other.

Certainly the Preamble to the Directive suggests a broad interpretation of the imbalance and good faith tests.[87] The sixteenth paragraph refers specifically to the strength of the bargaining position of the parties, whether the consumer had an inducement to agree to the term and whether the goods or services were sold or supplied to the special order of the consumer—words apparently taken directly from the guidelines on reasonableness in UCTA Schedule 2—and whether the party has taken the other's legitimate interests into account. Dean notes that when the Common Position was agreed, it was made clear that reasonableness should form part of the test of unfairness.[88] The Consultation Paper suggested that the tests of unfairness and reasonableness are likely to produce similar results in most cases, but that there is no guarantee that this will always be the case.[89]

I suspect that good faith has a double operation. First, it has a procedural aspect. It will require the supplier to consider the consumer's interests.[90] However, a clause which might be unfair if it came as a surprise may be upheld if the business took steps to bring it to the consumer's attention and to explain it. Secondly, it has a substantive content: some clauses may cause such an imbalance that they should always be treated as being contrary to good faith and therefore unfair.[91] A clause excluding liability for death or personal injury caused by negligence might be an example.

Probably, as Professor Diamond said in his evidence to the House of Lords Select Committee, imprecision is inevitable.[92] In effect a great deal of discretion is left to the court or other decision maker.[93]

---

[87] On use of the preambles to interpret directives see Case C-106/89 *Marleasing SA v La Comercial Internacional de Alimentación SA* [1990] ECR 1-4135. [1992] 1 CMLR 305 and P Duffy, 'Unfair contract terms and the draft EC directive' [1993] JBL 67.

[88] M Dean, 'Unfair Contract Terms: The European Approach' (1993) 56 MLR 581, 585, referring to the Consumer Council of 29 June 1992.

[89] *A Further Consultation Document* (note 41, above), Comment on Art 3(1).

[90] Thus the requirement of good faith does more than exclude certain types of unacceptable conduct: cf. R. Brownsword, 'Two Concepts of Good Faith' (forthcoming, JCL). I have benefited greatly from extensive discussion of good faith with Professor Brownsword. The views expressed here are not necessarily his.

[91] Article 3 does not require that the significant imbalance be caused by the absence of good faith. See also H Collins, 'Good Faith in European Contract Law' (1994) 14 Ox JLS 229, 250. On this point I have to disagree with the provisional views of Brownsword, Howells and Wilhelmsson, 'Between Market and Welfare: Some Reflections on Article 3 of the EC Directive on Unfair terms in Consumer Contracts' (forthcoming), although their paper is a very interesting discussion of the various interpretations of the good faith requirement. I am very grateful to my colleague Chris Willett for useful discussions on Art 3 and for letting me see his forthcoming paper 'The Directive on Unfair Terms in Consumer Contracts'.

[92] See House of Lords, 6th Report (1991–92) HL 28, para 74.

[93] J Ghestin and Marchessaux, 'Les techniques d'élimination des clauses abusives en

Advantages of a grey list

This element of discretion gives cause for concern simply because of the uncertainty involved for business. In the United Kingdom we have black-listed clauses only after very careful consideration, but in some ways it may be easier for business to know that a particular clause is always invalid than to know that it may or may not be invalid according to the circumstances and, dare one say it, the whim of the decision maker.[94] If the clause is absolutely banned the business knows what risks it must bear or insure against, even if they are hard to quantify; whereas with a general 'fairness' or 'reasonableness' test there will always be the fear that the clause may be struck down while a competitor's clause, perhaps worded in a slightly different way or presented to the consumer in a slightly different manner, may be upheld.

Even a grey list may go some way towards reducing the uncertainty, and it is good that the Regulations incorporate one. Grey lists should be as full as possible. When any type of term is subject to review under the new unfairness test, a grey list may be much more useful as guidance to business than a set of guidelines like UCTA, Schedule 2. Section 68A of the Australian Trade Practices Act[95] is interesting: a clause limiting the liability of a supplier of goods to a non-consumer may limit the supplier's liability to replacement of the goods, repair of the goods, or payment of the cost of replacement or of repair unless reliance on the clause is shown not to be fair and reasonable. The substance of this provision, with the burden of proof on the buyer, may be thought too weak even to protect non-consumers, but the style of the section does seem to give fuller guidance than the equivalent sections of UCTA. Could a similar approach be used in grey lists?

Schedule 3 of the Regulations incorporates just the grey list in the Annex to the Directive. I would like to have seen a much fuller list. I would also be happier if the grey-listed terms were presumptively invalid, whereas the Regulations leave the burden of proving unfairness on the consumer.[96]

Europe', in J Ghestin (ed), *Les clauses abusives dans les contrats-types en France et en Europe* (1991), p 57.

[94] Kessler thought that one of the reasons for standard form contracts was to guard against judicial irrationality: F Kessler, 'Contracts of Adhesion—Some Thoughts About Freedom of Contract' (1993) 43 Colum L Rev 629, 631–2.

[95] Inserted by Trade Practices Amendment Act (No 2) 1977.

[96] *A Further Consultation Document* (note 41, above), comment to Art 3(3).

Transparency

I do think it is a shame that the Economic and Social Committee's suggestion of transparency as additional criterion was not taken up. In the present state of knowledge I can only guess, but I suspect that the vast bulk of consumer complaints about unfair terms are really questions of unfair surprise, in other words, had the consumer known and understood the implications of the clause, it would have been acceptable. Transparency has certainly been a major concern of other systems.[97] Needless to say, the problem is not just one of ensuring that the clause is understandable; the consumer must also know that it is there. In other words, clauses should be conspicuous as well as transparent.

Disclosure is already a major technique for combating problems of consumer ignorance: see eg the requirements of regulations made under Consumer Credit Act 1974.[98] The Uniform Commercial Code's requirement that disclaimers be conspicuous[99] is well-known.

The Directive goes some way in this direction. Article 5, besides stating that the contra proferentem rule shall apply,[100] states that where written terms are used (it hard to think of any other form for terms 'which have not been individually negotiated'), these must always be drafted in plain, intelligible language. This is laudable but its status is unclear. The fact that a term is not so drafted is not in itself a ground for it being held to be unfair under Article 3. Regulation 6 simply states the requirement as a preamble to the *contra proferentem* rule. Is this a proper implementation of Article 5?

There have been cases under the Directive against discrimination[101] in which the European Court has held that Member States must introduce laws to make good in full the loss suffered by persons as the result of discrimination;[102] but Art 6 of that Directive obliged Member States to provide an effective judicial remedy. There is no equivalent in the Unfair Terms Directive. It is argued that there is a general principle of Community law that effective judicial protection must be granted at least for measures which have direct effect,[103] but it is not certain that Art 5 is sufficiently clear and precise to be of direct effect.[104]

[97] See eg Reich, 'Le principe de la transparence des clauses limitatives relatives au contenu des prestations dans le droit allemand des conditions générales des contrats', in J Ghestin (ed), *Les clauses limitatives on exonératoires de responsabilité en Europe* (1990), pp 77–93.

[98] Section 60.   [99] UCC, § 2–316(2).

[100] Except in the 'collective' proceedings under Art 7. See below p 255.

[101] Council Directive 76/207/EEC of 9 February 1976 (OJ L39, 14.2.1976, p 40).

[102] Case 14/83, *von Colson* [1984] ECR 1891: Case 79/83, *Harz* [1984] ECR 1921.

[103] See van Gerven (1994) 1 Maastricht J of European and Comparative Law 6, 11.

[104] See Wyatt & Dashwood, *European Community Law* (3rd ed 1993), p 72, citing Case 126/82, *DJ Smit* [1983] ECR 73.

There is also a principle, exemplified by the *Francovich* case,[105] that an individual may bring an action against a Member State for failure to implement a Directive which is not of direct effect. However this is conditional: the Directive should entail the grant of rights to individuals, it should be possible to identify the content of those rights from the Directive and there must be a causal link between the breach of the State's obligation and the individual's loss.[106] Even if the first two conditions could be satisfied for Art 5 of the Unfair Terms Directive, it would be hard to an individual to prove that failure to provide a sanction had caused a particular loss.

Finally, if a Member State has failed to implement a Directive, the Commission has discretion to bring an action under Art 169 of the Treaty of Rome for Failure to comply with the obligations of Arts 5 and 189 of that Treaty. However, this assumes that the Directive does impose an obligation to provide a remedy, which begs the question.

If Member States are obliged to introduce a remedy where a contract is not in the plain language required by Art 5, that remedy must be no less favourable than under national law.[107] This would mean that the clarity of the language should be taken into account in assessing fairness, as it is no doubt relevant to reasonableness under Unfair Contract Terms Act 1977, s 11.[108]

Inability to assess risk

Even a clear and comprehensible clause is not necessarily fair. First, there is the problem that the individual consumer may not be able to estimate its likely impact.[109] Take a clause stating that you travel on a fairground ride entirely at your own risk, however the accident may be caused. Such a clause is almost certain to be of no effect in England,[110] but one cannot assume that it will be void elsewhere in Europe even after 31 December 1994. The clause could not be much clearer or easier to understand. But

---

[105] Case C-6/90 and C-9/90 [1991] ECR 1–5357.

[106] *Ibid.*, I-5416, para 44. See van Gerven (1994) 1 Maastrict J of European and Comparative Law 6. I am grateful to my colleague Han Somsen for allowing me to see a draft paper 'Francovich and its application to EC Environmental Law'.

[107] *Comet v Produktschap* Case 445/76 [1976] ECR 2043.

[108] See Sched 2(c) and *Stag Line Ltd v Tyne Shiprepair Group Ltd* [1984] 2 Lloyd's Rep 211. The DTI (*op cit* above n 41, p 18) has suggested that the court may take into account the way in which terms are drafted in considering whether they satisfy the requirement of good faith but proposes no stricter sanction.

[109] A point well made by Trebilcock, 'An Economic Approach to the Doctrine of Unconscionability' in BJ Reiter and J Swan (eds), *Studies in Contract Law* (1980) p 379.

[110] UCTA s 2(1) will apply unless the big dipper is not operated as part of a business. See above, p 234.

the average consumer will have little idea how much loss he will suffer if he is seriously injured, let alone how much risk there really is of the cars leaving the track. This alone seems to justify an absolute ban on such clauses.

Lack of choice

The other problem we identified earlier: lack of choice. The consumer may be only too well aware of the implications of the clause but be quite unable to get it changed—at least without offering a very high price for a 'special deal'[111]—because he lacks bargaining power.

In discussions with colleagues I have noticed that at this point many of us become slightly uneasy. Are we really going to strike down a clause as unreasonable simply because of lack of choice when the customer went into the deal with his eyes open? Lord Reid said that 'freedom of contract must imply some choice or room to bargain'.[112] But is that really so? Isn't freedom satisfied by there being a choice as to whether or not to contract, without having a choice as to the terms on which one contracts? Isn't it odd to expect bargaining over this when one wouldn't expect a seller to be prepared to drop below the market price?

In modern conditions, it seems implausible to expect explicit bargaining over much more than the item, the price and the delivery date. The effect of requiring a choice seems to be that every supplier must offer two sets of terms—the one that the run of market choices (however ill-informed) seems to suggest and another, perhaps complying fully with the general norms which would apply in the absence of any special clauses in the standard form. Isn't it moving from refusing effect to unreasonable terms to insisting that the terms offered be reasonable, even in accordance with the general norms?[113] Yet English law does it: in *Woodman* v *Photo Trade Processing Ltd*[114] a clause limiting a film developer's liability to replacement with a new film was held to be unreasonable, largely it seems because the developer did not offer a higher level of

---

[111] Cf A Schwartz, 'Seller Unequal Bargaining Power and the Judicial Process' (1974) 49 Indiana LJ 367, 370–1, who points out that customers can influence the terms offered if they devote enough resources to it. It is not unknown for suppliers on occasion to alter their standard terms to suit a customer—but it is probably rare and may be a local and unauthorized initiative.

[112] In the *Suisse Atlantique* case [1967] 1 AC 361, at 406.

[113] Also, as J Hellner, 'Consequential Loss and Exemption Clauses' (1981) 1 Ox JLS 13, 26, asked some years ago, why do we assume that the general norms are actually what is wanted by consumers? Remember that when we do have a choice, eg with extended warranties on domestic appliances, many of us prefer to take a risk and pay a lower price.

[114] Reported in RG Lawson, 'The Unfair Contract Terms Act: A Progress Report' (1981) 131 New LJ 933, 935.

service as the Code of Practice for the Photographic Industry suggested it should. If the sixteenth paragraph of the Preamble quoted earlier is to given effect, I would expect the same result to be reached under the Directive.

Transparency as a way of improving the operation of the market

Even though the Directive goes beyond requiring merely transparency, there is a second reason for disappointment that transparency was not given greater emphasis. I have argued that one cannot expect effective individual bargaining over the small print between consumers and suppliers. However, if enough consumers do raise questions about the small print, the supplier will come under pressure to offer better terms. The 'thickness of the margin', that is, the number of consumers who do ask the right questions, can be increased by the right measures.

Education is fundamental: and the value of the work of the consumer organizations and, in this country, of the Office of Fair Trading in promoting consumer awareness is tremendous. I was interested to read of a proposal in France to allow time off work for participation in consumer organizations (it was not adopted).[115] There appears to have been a steady improvement in certain types of term on offer, in particular warranties on new products, and much of this may be due to education.[116]

I am not sure how far consumer consciousness reaches to other kinds of small print, but it seems to me that if transparency is increased, so will be awareness. Elsewhere[117] I have suggested that whether a clause was conspicuous and easy to understand should be the biggest single factor in deciding whether or not it was reasonable. First, transparency will make it hard to argue that any 'surprise' on the part of the consumer was unfair. Secondly, if a clause is clear and easily understandable, and yet it is commonly used, that suggests that it may in fact represent what the active margin of consumers want—or at least that it is all they are prepared to pay for.

Here I am using a similar argument but for a different purpose. Requiring terms to be conspicuous and clear is likely to increase awareness and that, in turn, is likely to lead to the terms offered being closer to

---

[115] J Ghestin and Marchessaux, in J Ghestin (ed), *Les clauses abusives dans les contrats-types en France et en Europe* (1991), p 27.

[116] I very much regret the Government's rejection of the warranty proposals (broadly similar to Magnusson-Moss) contained in the Consumer Guarantees Bill: see C Willett, 'The Unacceptable Face of the Consumer Guarantees Bill' (1991) 54 MLR 552. The more recent DTI proposals (see *Consumer Guarantees: A Consultation Document* (1992)) are interesting, but much weaker in this respect.

[117] H Beale, 'Unfair Contracts in Britain and Europe' [1989] CLP 197.

what consumers want—in other words, to reducing the inefficiencies caused by the inadequacy of consumer information about what they are being offered.

Public and collective action

I do not believe that we can rely on individual actions, even the 'invisible hand' comprising the aggregate of individual consumers' decisions, to achieve all the results we want. Despite both consumer education and the Unfair Contract Terms Act, the level of complaints about unfair terms and conditions is still quite high. The Office of Fair Trading document 'Trading Malpractices' states that Trading Standards Authorities and Citizen's Advice Bureaux received 16,200 complains in 1989.[118] This was quite a small percentage (three per cent) of the total numbers of complaints: by comparison, forty-three per cent related to defective goods or substandard services and twenty-five per cent to selling techniques.[119] But 16,200 complaints is not a negligible number, and the real dissatisfaction is probably much higher, even if not all the grumbles are justified.

Individual challenges to unfair terms will always remain few because of the many obstacles to effective legal action by individual consumers. These are too well known to require documentation here.[120] So we must look to supplementation of individual private remedies by public action or collective action.[121]

Prevention is better than cure. Agreement on fair terms and conditions may be secured by the negotiation of Codes of Practice: some of those negotiated by the Office of Fair Trading refer to terms and conditions at least in general terms.[122] In Belgium the consumer organisation *Test-Achats* has negotiated a number of model contracts with suppliers' organizations.[123] Alternatively suppliers may be encouraged to submit terms for vetting or pre-validation, as in Israel since the Standard Contracts Act of 1964 came into force.

There are significant problems with these approaches. Neither Codes of

---

[118] (July 1990), Table 2, p 10.　　　　　　　　　[119] *Ibid.*, Table 2A, p 10.

[120] See eg AJ Duggan, 'Consumer Redress and the Legal System' in AJ Duggan and LW Darval (eds), *Consumer Protection Law and Theory* (1980) p 200; IDC Ramsay, 'Consumer redress mechanisms for poor-quality and defective products' (1981) 31 UTLJ 117.

[121] There are obvious analogies to the labour market.

[122] eg the ABTA Tour Operators Code of Conduct, s 4.4(i), provides that 'Booking conditions, if any, shall define the extent of the responsibilities as well as the limits of the liabilities of tour operators towards clients and shall be so designed that they are easily read and understood'. See now the Package Travel, Package Holidays and Package Tours Regulations 1992, SI 1992 No 3288 (implementing the Council Directive 90/314/EEC of 13 June 1990 (OJ L158, 23.6.1990, p 59).

[123] See Hondius, *Unfair Terms in Consumer Contracts* (1987) p 170, and references there.

Practice nor model contracts are compulsory and in particular they are unlikely to be used by firms which are not members of the relevant trade association. One suspects it is precisely these firms which cause a lot of the problems. Negotiating model terms and conditions is very time-consuming and difficult.[124] In this country negotiation of a model 'Fair Deal contract for Home Improvements' proved impossible.[125] I under-stand that the Israeli experiment under the 1964 Act proved disappoint-ing in that very few firms sought pre-validation.[126]

The other possibility is public or collective action against suppliers which use unfair terms. Here the United Kingdom seems to have lagged behind other countries to some extent.

Public action to prevent the use of unfair terms

The use of certain types of clause may be made a criminal offence. The Director-General has used his powers under the Fair Trading Act 1973, Part II, to outlaw terms in consumer contracts for sale or supply of goods which would exclude or restrict the seller's or supplier's liability for the description or fitness for purpose of the goods and therefore be of no effect under UCTA s 6(2) or s 7(2).[127] There is no similar provision for other terms which are equally of no effect under UCTA. Part of the expla-nation may be that procedures under this part of the Act are cumbersome and slow.[128] And criminalisation of the use of unfair terms can only be used for terms which are blacklisted.

What seems to have more potential are procedures under Fair Trading Act 1973, Part III, which gives the Director-General powers to take action against traders who persist in a course of conduct which is detrimental or unfair to consumers. He may obtain an assurance from the trader involved and, if the practice continues, obtain a court order. However, conduct which is detrimental or unfair is at present defined in terms of breaches of either the civil or the criminal law, so that it will not cover the

[124] See the personal experience of Professor Hondius reported in his *Unfair Terms in Consumer Contracts* (1987) pp 224–5.

[125] See the Annual Report of the Director-General of Fair Trading (Office of Fair Trading, 1991), p 21.

[126] See A Hecht, 'The Israel Law on Standard Contracts' (1968) 3 Israel LR 586. Possible reasons for this are discussed below, p 260.

[127] The Consumer Transactions (Restrictions on Statements) Order 1976, SI 1976 No 1813 (as amended by SI 1978 No 127).

[128] See B Harvey and D Parry, *Law of Consumer Protection and Fair Trading* (4th ed 1992), pp 314–15. The Director-General of Fair Trading has also been able to exercise some controls via his power to refuse licences for credit business and, where trade associations recommend the use of terms, under the Restrictive Trade Practices Act 1974. See GV Davies, 'Void Terms in Consumer Contracts: Should Their Use be a Criminal Offence?' (1983) 80 Law Soc Gaz 1978; H Beale, 'Unfair Contracts in Britain and Europe' [1989] CLP 197, 210–12.

use of even blacklisted terms unless an order prohibiting their use has been made under Part II. The procedures have a number of other serious defects and the Director-General has called for major improvements.[129] These would extend his powers to deal with both 'Deceptive and misleading practices'[130] and 'Unconscionable practices'. The latter would include

that the terms and conditions on, or subject to which, the consumer transaction was entered by the consumer are so harsh or adverse to the consumer as to be inequitable.[131]

Such a change seems desirable; as the Director-General points out, it would bring the law in the United Kingdom into line with that in, eg Australia[132] and many European countries.[133]

I am not wholly clear whether the Director-General envisages that any practice of using a clause which is unfair or unreasonable would count as unconscionable within this proposal. On the one hand, the Report cites as analogy the New South Wales Contracts Review Act of 1980.[134] This Act relies on the general test of whether a contract or term is 'unjust', and empowers the court to refuse to enforce the contract or the term.[135] The Supreme Court is then given power, on the application of the Minister or the Attorney General, to make orders against persons who have embarked on conduct likely to lead to the formation of unjust contacts.[136] This analogy suggests that the criterion for the Director-General to act is simply unfairness.[137] But earlier in his Report the Director-General refers to the problem that a criterion such as 'unfair' or 'improper' gives excessive discretion to the enforcement authorities. Instead:

the narrower Canadian/Australian approach is to be preferred. This refers to 'unconscionable' conduct. I broad terms it can be said that unconscionable conduct will arise in a situation where a stronger party to a transaction knowingly takes wholly unfair advantage of that position to the detriment of the less powerful party. The provision would thus be aimed at conduct which grossly contravenes ordinary principles of fair dealing.[138]

---

[129] *Trading Malpractices* (Office of Fair Trading, July 1990).
[130] *Ibid.*, s 5. 19.   [131] *Ibid.*, s 5. 27(d).
[132] eg Trade Practices Act 1974 (as amended), s 51AB, which forbids corporations from engaging in conduct 'which is unconscionable' in connection with the supply of goods.
[133] The Swedish example is very well known; the 1971 Act to Prohibit Improper Contract Terms adopts the same control mechanisms as the 1970 Marketing Practices Act. See Hondius, *Unfair Terms in Consumer Contracts* (1987), pp 143–50 and U Bernitz, 'The Swedish Marketing Practices Act' in AC Neal (ed), *Law and the Weaker Party: An Anglo-Swedish Comparative Study* (1981), vol 1 (The Swedish Experience) pp 107–25.
[134] *Trading Malpractices* (Office of Fair Trading, July 1990), s 5. 28.
[135] Section 7.   [136] Section 10.
[137] This is approach taken in the New Zealand Law Commission's provisional proposals, see Preliminary Paper No 11, *Unfair Contracts—A discussion paper* (1990): Draft Bill s 13.
[138] *Trading Malpractices* (Office of Fair Trading, July 1990), s 5. 25.

For reasons suggested earlier, this might hamper action against firms using harsh terms as a way of keeping down costs, when there have not been significant protests from consumers: it is hard to say that the firm is acting unconscionably in the sense the Director-General refers to. Perhaps continued use of such terms after their disadvantages to consumers have been pointed to the business by the Office of Fair Trading would be unconscionable in the narrow sense!

Article 7(1) of the Directive requires Member States to:

ensure that, in the interests of consumers and of competitors, adequate and effective means exist to prevent the continued use of unfair terms in contracts concluded with consumers by sellers or suppliers.

This seems to envisage either the extension of criminal sanctions against the use of unfair terms or some kind of injunctive procedure against their use. But surprisingly the Department of Industry's initial Consultation Document stated:

No specific implementing legislation is required for this Article. The legislation will automatically confer a right of civil action . . . In the UK the doctrine of precedent means that once a term has been judged to be unfair suppliers will know that if used again in the same context they will not be able to rely on it. It is not proposed that criminal sanctions be introduced.

With respect the argument that UK law already contains adequate and effective means to prevent the continued use of unfair terms, simply because such terms will be invalid, is untenable. We know from experience that businesses continue to use even terms which are automatically invalid under the Unfair Contract Terms Act; if they did not, it would not have been necessary for the Director-General to use his powers under Fair Trading Act 1973, Part II.[139] Presumably businesses continue to use invalid terms in the hope that the presence of the clause will deter consumers from seeking redress.

Powers under Fair Trading Act 1973, Part II, to make continued use of a clause a criminal offence do not seem appropriate to terms which are not automatically of no effect, as none are under the Directive. So at the least this argues for the broadening of the Director-General's powers under Part III in the way he has proposed, but to cover the use of any unfair term whether or not the use is unconscionable.[140] In the light of a 'strong consensus' among consultees that implementing action as regards Art 7(1) is required, the Regulations provide that the Director-General shall have a duty to consider complaints that a term is unfair, and the power

---

[139] See above, p 252.   [140] Article 7(1).

to seek an injunction against any person using it or recommending its use.[141]

Collective action

The Directive provides in Art 7(2) that the steps to be taken by Member States to ensure that:

... adequate and effective means exist to prevent the continued use of unfair contract terms ... shall include provisions whereby persons or organisations, having a legitimate interest under national law in protecting consumers, may take action according to the national law concerned before the courts or before competent administrative bodies for a decision as to whether contractual terms drawn up for general use are unfair, so that they can apply appropriate and effective means to prevent the continued use of such terms.[142]

This appears to contemplate proceedings by a consumer or other public interest group, or perhaps by a Government Department.

I have argued elsewhere that this provision is very important.[143] Thoroughgoing implementation of the Article would bring about the greatest single improvement in British law as the result of the Directive. Sadly, the method of implementation adopted leaves some doubt as to whether this will happen.

Before the Department of Trade and Industry's Consultation Document was published there were suggestions that the Director-General should be given power to seek a declaration from the High Court that a particular term is unfair.[144] The scheme would be parallel to the one used to implement the Directive on Misleading Advertising (1988).[145] But the initial Consultation Document's actual proposal was astonishing:

In the UK the courts decide on whether a term is unfair, there are no administrative mechanisms.

UK law at present contains no general provision for representative actions: only a party to the contract may sue under that contract. Thus according to a party may sue under the contract. Thus according to the national law concerned (ie that applying in the UK) this provision can have no effect.

---

[141] Reg 8(1). See *A Further Consultation Document* (above n 41), p 21. The DG may, instead of obtaining an injunction, accept an undertaking from the supplier or recommender.

[142] Article 7.2.

[143] H Beale, 'Unfair Contracts in Britain and Europe' [1989] CLP 197, 210.

[144] Information from Mr David Legg of the DTI, who has most helpful throughout the writing of this paper.

[145] See The Control of Misleading Advertisements Regulations 1988 (SI 1988 No 915).

This approach was rightly criticized;[146] it seemed tantamount to proposing not to implement this central element of the Directive. As a result of consultation the Department has reconsidered; but it is only the Director-General of Fair Trading who is empowered to act.[147]

Giving the Director-General power to seek an injunction against the use of an unfair term no doubt complies formally with the requirements of the Directive. I would suggest, however, that we have missed an opportunity to make a radical improvement in our law even if to do so would involve going beyond the literal requirements of the Directive. I think it is worth considering the conditions under which the type of procedure envisaged by Article 7 is likely to be really 'adequate and effective'.

(1) The mechanisms for obtaining an order prohibiting continued use of the unfair term must be speedy.

(2) There must be an effective way of publicizing decisions that particular clauses are unfair. Relying on percolation of information from the law reports is probably not enough. Under the Regulations the Director-General may arrange for dissemination of information about the operation of the Regulations to the public.[148] A public register would help, or a provision to enable clauses declared unfair to be added to the 'grey' list which I hope will form part of the Regulations to be made under the Directive.

(3) Orders made that terms are unfair should be effective not only against the individual seller or supplier but also any trade association which recommends use of the term and, preferably, other individual sellers or suppliers which use it. This is envisaged by Article 7.3.[149] Regulation 8(6) permits injunctions against 'any similar term . . . used or recommended for use by any party to the proceedings'.

(4) The order should relate not just to the use of the exact same clause in the specific circumstances of the case. The fact that the Directive is dealing with 'grey' clauses which may or may not be unfair, according to the circumstances, causes a significant difficulty in this respect. A power to enjoin the further use of an unfair term would be of little use if it could be evaded by the use of slightly different words, a different presentation or very slightly more generous terms so as to take it outside the ban without any real change in the merits. Orders would have to be made in quite general terms, with guidance as to what is and is not acceptable[149a].

---

[146] FMB Reynolds, 'Unfair Contract Terms' (1994) 110 Law QR 1: H Collins, 'Good Faith in European Contract Law' (1994) 14 Ox JLS 229, 244.
[147] Reg 8.
[148] *A Further Consultation Document* (note 41, above), p 21; Reg. 8(7).
[149] *Ibid.*, p 21.   [149a] Reg 8(6) refers to 'a term having like effect'.

(5) The decision and the order will have to take into account the circumstances in which the clause was used and might be used in the future, since a clause might not be unfair in all situations. To some extent this is a question of the degree of information given to the consumer, and guidance on that should not be hard to formulate. It gets harder when the court has to take into account other factors. In *Smith v Eric S Bush*[150] the House of Lords held that a disclaimer of responsibility by a house surveyor (who was acting for the intending mortgagee) was unreasonable *vis-à-vis* the purchaser of a modest house, but might have been reasonable for a more expensive property. The availability of insurance is also relevant.[151] So too are factors quite outside the control of the party using the term, for instance:

> ... whether the customer ... in accepting [the term] had an opportunity of entering into a similar contract with other persons, but without having to accept a similar term.[152]

It will not be easy to formulate the guidance businesses will need. The laws of other countries permit similar challenges to 'grey listed' terms, but I do not have any information on how these problems are dealt with.[153]

(6) The decision must be made by an appropriate body. In the light of the difficulties mentioned in (4) and (5), I wonder whether the questions are not much more complex and less precise than whether an advertisement is misleading, and whether it really is appropriate for the High Court or County Court to decide them. Decisions under UCTA have not produced very clear guidance as to what is or is not reasonable.[154] The range of information needed for a full consideration would be large. There seems to be a case for single, specialised tribunal which can build up experience—in Victoria there is now a Market Court consisting of a County Court judge as president and two advisers.[155] Or would it be better to give the decision to the Director-General of Fair Trading himself, perhaps with the possibility of an appeal to a court? The power to initiate action could then be

---

[150] [1990] 1 AC 831.　　　　　[151] *Phillips Products Ltd v Hyland* [1987] 1 WLR 659n.

[152] UCTA 1977, Schedule 2, (b).

[153] I am sure there is relevant on the German experience but I am limited by my inability to read German. I am also saved a great deal of work: by 1986 there had been over 2,000 decisions on the Standard Contracts Law! See H Micklitz, 'La loi allemande relative au régime juridique des conditions générales des contrats du 9 décembre 1976' (1989) Rev int droit comparé 101.

[154] H Beale, 'Unfair Contracts in Britain and Europe' [1989] CLP 197: JN Adams and R Brownsword, 'The Unfair Contract Terms Act: A Decade of Discretion' (1988) 104 Law QR 94.

[155] Market Court Act 1978 (Vic).

given to other bodies such as the National Consumer Council or perhaps Trading Standards authorities.[156]

(7) The body capable of initiating action would probably need to be pro-
active in finding out what terms are being used, and will need powers accordingly. The Swedish Consumer Ombudsman has power to
require copies of standard contracts and other information from
traders.[157]

(8) It is desirable to decentralize initiative. If the procedure is to be effective there must be a realistic prospect of action against unfair terms.
I do not mean any criticism of the Office of Fair Trading when I say
that its initiatives in this regard will necessarily be constrained by the
resources available to it—it may not, for example, be able to follow
the example of the Israeli Ministry of Justice which reportedly has a
group dedicated to reviewing contracts.[158] Under the Regulations,
the Director-General has a duty to consider any complaint that a
term is unfair, unless the complaint appears frivolous or vexatious;
but he only has a power to bring proceedings 'if he considers it
appropriate to do so'.[159] He must give reasons if he does not act, but
he might legitimately give such proceedings a low priority, eg if the
term is not widely used.

Other bodies which may have different priorities and maybe a different view should be permitted to act; in other words we should
follow the lead of several other Member States and give consumer
organisations the power to initiate action.[160] In France some 20 consumer organizations have been recognized for this purpose.[161]

(9) If organizations other than the Office of Fair Trading are to be permitted to take action, the cost of seeking a declaration must be low,
or the threat of high bills for costs if they lose will deter them.[162] The

---

[156] Trading Standards authorities might not feel that this watchdog role would be appropriate for them.

[157] Act Prohibiting Improper Contract Terms, 1971, s 3a(1).

[158] See J Ghestin and Marchessaux, *Les téchniques d'élimination des clauses abusives en
Europe*, in J Ghestin (ed), *Les clauses abusives dans les contrats-types en France et en Europe* (1991)
p 37.

[159] *A Further Consultation Document* (note 41, above); r 8(2).

[160] eg France, Law of 5 January 1988; German Law on Standard Contracts of 1976, s 13;
Luxembourg Consumer Protection Act, art 5: Portuguese Law 446/85 of 25 October 1985.
Art 25: Israeli Standard Contracts Act 1982, s 16.

[161] J Calais-Auloy, *Les clauses abusives en droit français*, in J Ghestin (ed), *Les clauses abusives
dans les contrats-types en France et en Europe* (1991), pp 113–22, 121.

[162] Though HW Micklitz, 'La loi allemande relative au régime juridique des conditions
générales des contrats du 9 décembre 1976' (1989) 41 Rev int de droit comparé 101, 118,
seems to suggest that liability for the loser's costs has not proved a deterrent to action by consumer organizations in Germany.

Victorian Market Court permits legal representation but does not award costs.[163]

Assurances and undertakings

Under the Fair Trading Act 1973, Part III, the procedure is for the Director-General first to attempt to get an assurance from the trader as to its future conduct. Under the Regulations, the Director-General may have regard to any undertakings given to him.[164] Germany has a similar procedure, but at the behest of the consumer organizations empowered to act under the Law on Standard Contracts. They can obtain a written assurance from the business and take proceedings if the assurance is broken. This has proved extremely important and effective.[165] The actions of the consumer organizations have had a significant influence at least where markets are dominated by a small number of large firms using broadly similar conditions; not surprisingly the impact on more fragmented markets has been less.[166] If, as suggested, consumer organizations were to be empowered to bring proceedings, it would be desirable to enable them to seek assurances as an alternative.

Pre-validation?

If the tribunal or administrative authority empowered to act in accordance with Art 7 is to set out the conditions under which terms are fair and unfair, as I have suggested would be very desirable, is that not tantamount to pre-validation? One doubts that any subsequent court faced with the same clause in an individual case would readily dissent from the tribunal's view. It is arguable that it should be prevented from doing so except in a case in which the circumstances were radically different from those contemplated by the tribunal. If we are coming this close to pre-validation, why not permit the seller or supplier to initiate action?

The innovative pre-validation procedure of the Israeli Standard Contacts Act 1964 did not produce many applications. One commentator

---

[163] See AJ Duggan, 'Consumer Redress and the Legal System' in AJ Duggan & LW Darvall (eds), *Consumer Protection Law and Theory* (1980) pp 200, 221.

[164] Reg 8(3).

[165] See HW Micklitz, 'La loi allemande relative au régime juridique des conditions générales des contrats du 9 décembre 1976' (1989) 41 Rev int de droit comparé 101, 118: Hondius, *Unfair Terms in Consumer Contracts* (1987), p 184.

[166] HW Micklitz, 'La loi allemande relative au régime juridique des conditions générales des contrats du 9 décembre 1976' (1989) 41 Rev int droit comparé 101, 121.

suggests that firms feared retroactive invalidation,[167] but in 1987 Hondius reported much greater success with the 1982 Standard Contacts Law—in 4 years some eighty contracts were submitted for approval.[168] Perhaps part of the reason is that the new law contains not just the carrot of pre-validation but also a stick: there are procedures for the Attorney General, the Commissioner of Consumer Protection and any approved customer's organization to seek annulment of disadvantageous conditions.[169] There was no equivalent in the 1964 law. The courts may also be taking a more severe attitude.[170]

The Law Commission considered pre-validation in its pre-UCTA report. It rejected the idea, partly because of the difficulties of pre-validating terms which may or may not be reasonable according to the circumstances.[171] I accept those difficulties but I think they will have to be faced anyway under the procedures required by the Directive. It may be necessary to validate terms under prescribed conditions of use, just as I think it will be necessary to proscribe terms under certain conditions. The House of Lords Select Committee suggested that pre-validation should be looked at again;[172] I respectfully agree.

Conclusion

I have argued that there is still need for clearer recognition that, with standard form contracts, we are not usually dealing with traditional forms of exploitation or unconscionable behaviour, but with unfair surprise, lack of choice and (perhaps) derogation from obligations which we think should be irreducible. This should be reflected in the questions we ask. The terms of general test of fairness used in the Directive must be read in this light.

We must also face up to the phenomenon of mass contracting, under which individual negotiation is unlikely but where the run of consumer preferences may influence the market for terms. We need to take this into account in assessing what is fair or reasonable. We also need to take positive steps, based on this analysis, to improve the way in which the market operates, for instance by encouraging transparency of contracts.

[167] A Hecht, 'The Israel Law on Standard Contracts' (1968) 3 Israel LR 586.

[168] Hondius, *Unfair Terms in Consumer Contracts* (1987) p 209. See also Deutch (1987) 7 Tel Aviv Univ Stud in Law 160. The Israeli Ministry of Justice has confirmed that the number of applications has increased (information from Professor Nili Cohen).

[169] Article 16(a).

[170] Eg *Israeli Football Players' Association* v *Israeli Football Association*, 825/88, 45 PD(5) 109. I am grateful to Professor Nili Cohen for this suggestion.

[171] Exemption Clauses, Second Report (1975) Law Com No 69; Scot Law Com No 39; paras 101–8.

[172] 6th Report (1991–92) HL 28, s 86.

Enabling collective by consumer organizations as envisaged by the Directive seems to have great potential.

In substantive terms the requirements of the Directive are rather disappointing. They are wider in scope than UCTA, but offer poor protection to the 'shopper abroad', particularly in the absence of a black list. Article 7, which requires Member States to ensure that there are adequate and effective means to prevent the continued use of unfair terms, does offer a significant step forward, but it would have been better if the Government had been persuaded to provide for proceedings against the use of unfair terms to be brought by consumer organizations and to be heard by a specialist tribunal.

10

Public Law Influences in Contract Law*

Jack Beatson

Introduction

This chapter seeks to explore the actual and potential influence of principles of public law and statutory regulatory regimes in the English law of
contract. It is primarily concerned with potential influence because,
although public law principles have been utilized in a few particular contexts, they have not yet influenced the general principles of English contract law. Although some commentators argue for the separation of the
analysis of the common law and statute law, it will be argued that the
issues raised by a number of the topics considered in this book, in particular good faith and fairness, pre-contractual duties, and long term or
'relational' contracts[1] can usefully be illuminated by public law principles.

It is generally recognized that modifications to the rules governing a
contract are made where the contractual capacity of one of the parties is
limited by public law principles, in particular the rule preventing the fet-
tering of discretion by contract or by pre-contractual statements.[2]
Accordingly, while the contracts of public authorities are subject to the
general rules of English contract law,[3] '[t]here is, nevertheless, a substantial body of special rules which apply only, or mainly to', such contracts.[4]
However, as we shall see, even in the case of contracting by such bodies
the influence of the general law can operate—arguably inappropriately—
to exclude public law principles.

While contracts or contractual negotiations with public authorities
must necessarily be considered, the aim here is to consider the impact, if
any, of public law concepts on private commercial and consumer contracts. The reason for this is not that the contracts of public authorities
are unimportant, either in practical or in doctrinal terms. They clearly

---

* Copyright © 1994, Jack Beatson.

[1] On these, see chs 11 and 12, below.

[2] *The Amphitrite* [1921] 3 KB 500; *Ayr Harbour Trustees* v *Oswald* (1883) 8 App Cas 623;
Western Fish Products Ltd v *Penwith DC* [1981] 2 All ER 204 (limited role of estoppel arising
from the representations of public authorities).

[3] Thus, *Chitty on Contracts* (27th ed 1994) deals with such contracts in one chapter of volume 1 (General Principles) rather than in volume 2 (Particular Contracts).

[4] S Arrowsmith, *Civil Liability and Public Authorities* (1992) p 43.

are,[5] and the difficulties in stating the modifications to contract law that obtain in such cases suggest that they merit further detailed study particularly since, in England, the fragility of the line between what is 'public' and what is 'private' has been demonstrated in recent years. But the question we now seek to address is the extent, if any, to which these special public law rules influence other areas of the law of contract, whether this influence is likely to grow, and whether such influence is to be welcomed or not.

It has been noted in the introductory chapter of this book that a limited number of contexts, such as shipping, construction and insurance, have been particularly influential in the development of English contract law. Whatever the influence of particular contexts, however, and despite much discussion, the ideology of the English law of contract remains that of a single body of principles worked out with some differences in particular contexts. Some have termed this approach 'classical' and criticized it, sometimes in rather extravagant terms. This chapter is not concerned with these criticisms, but with the question of whether in the future tendering, contracts with public or privatized bodies, and contracts made by the members of regulated professions and businesses should or will be as influential in the shaping of doctrine.

At the outset two difficulties must be identified. First, as indicated, the line that has been drawn between cases where it is clearly recognized that the contract is subject to some 'special' rules and other situations is far less definite than it was. The jurisdictional nightmare that was created by the rules that both required a person seeking public law remedies to do so by applying for judicial review and also absolutely prevented a person applying for judicial review in what were deemed to 'essentially private law matters' has produced a very technical body of law in which although issues concerning contracts are normally considered to be private law matters, they are not invariably so treated.[6] Furthermore, the onset of privatisation, market-testing and contracting-out[7] and the greatly increased

---

[5] CC Turpin, *Government Procurement and Contracts* (1989) p x estimated that in the UK central government contracts alone involved sum of c £15 billion in 1984. In 1993 terms this is £24.5 billion. In an EC context it has been estimated that the value of such contracts is, in the case of central and local government contracts, 9% of the EC's GDP and, in the case of nationalised industries, 6% of the EC's GDP: *Commission of the European Communities: Completing the Internal Market* White paper from the Commission to the European Council (1985), Cmnd (85)310.

[6] See eg S Fredman & G Morris, 'Public or Private? State Employees and Judicial Review' (1991) 107 LQR 298. The unsatisfactory position has been noted by the Law Commission: Administration Law: Judicial Review and Statutory Appeals (1993) Law Com Consultation Paper No 126, ss 3.13–3.14.

[7] The influence of these developments on tort law is discussed by B Hepple, 'Tort Law in the Contract State' in P Birks (ed), *The Frontiers of Liability* (1994) vol 2 from which I have greatly benefitted. For a powerful critique of the way public law approaches contractualisation, see M Freedland, 'Government by Contract and Public Law' [1994] PL 86.

profile accorded to contractual self-regulatory techniques are also bound
to lead to a blurring of the line. The processes of market-testing and contracting-out have sought to bring marketplace disciplines and contractual
techniques into what have hitherto been regarded as public law areas.
Thus, District Health Authorities and fund holding practices now
'contract' with Hospital Trusts,[8] and the different bits of the power industry 'contract' with each other. Mercury contracts with British Telecommunications for the use of telephone lines, and there are similar
arrangements between the rail track operator (Railtrack) and the train
operators.[9] It would be paradoxical if this process, with its blurring of the
lines between the public and the private, although designed to subject
public bodies to market forces traditionally supported by the private law
of contract, were also to lead to the infection of other areas of the law of
contract with concepts that were hitherto confined to the 'public' sphere.
The problem with contractual self-regulation is that, despite what is said,
it is neither truly contractual nor, in many cases, truly *self*-regulatory.[10]

The second difficulty with this subject concerns the treatment of the
impact of statute on contract law. For some the most interesting question
concerns the use, if any, of public law concepts in a purely common law
context. However, we shall see that, with one exception, at present these
concepts have really only been used where there has been a statutory catalyst.[11] One possible reason for this is the tension between the certainty
upon which English contract law has placed such a high premium and the
more open textured nature of public law concepts, such as procedural
fairness, propriety of purpose, *Wednesbury* reasonableness (or rationality),
legitimate expectation, and (when they finally emerge as distinct heads)
proportionality and consistency (ie the right to equality of treatment without undue discrimination). The contrast is perhaps greatest in the treatment of discretionary powers given in contracts between private parties
and those given to public authorities. The former are generally taken to
give an unfettered power of choice in the absence of bad faith, while the
latter are subject to the public law concepts listed above.[12] It is possible

---

[8] National Health Service and Community Care Act 1990, s 4(1), although s 4(3) provides
that the 'contract' does not give rise to any *contractual* rights or liabilities and that disputes
are to be resolved by the Secretary of State (in effect by arbitration).

[9] Railways Act 1993, ss 17–18, 21–2.

[10] This is especially true of the self-regulating organizations set up under the Financial
Services Act 1986 (hereafter, FSA 1986), see below. Note that the relationship between the
'Next Steps' agencies which are to operate certain public services (the benefits agency and
the Public Trust Office) and government departments is not considered since, despite the
contractual language used, they are not separate legal entities.

[11] See G Calabresi, *A Common Law for the Age of Statutes* (1982). Cf MA Eisenberg, *The
Nature of the Common Law* (1988) p vii for the view that a different set of principles governs
the interpretation of statutes and the establishment of common law rules. This suggests there
is greater value in separating the analysis of the common law from that of statute law.

[12] *Wheeler* v *Leicester City Council* [1985] AC 1054.

that the increased role of equity in contract law, a role more developed in Commonwealth jurisdictions and the United States than in England, and the increasing influence of EC Law, most recently seen in the Directive on Unfair Contract Terms,[13] will led to changes. Domestic developments may also be influential: in 1990 the Office of Fair Trading recommended that a general duty to trade fairly be introduced.[14] As far as the role of equity is concerned, it is likely that any changes will manifest themselves in cases involving joint ventures, financial advice, and the creation of security interests and guarantees in favour of banks, since those are contexts in which equitable principles have operated in a commercial context.[15]

The second aspect of the impact of statute concerns the effect, if any, of the introduction of legislation into a given area on subsequent common law development and the relationship between common law and statute. In the 1960s a consensus developed among English judges that major developments, even in areas hitherto the preserve of the common law, should be achieved by legislation. The clearest example of this has been the refusal of the courts, in the face of sustained and powerful criticism, to modify the privity of contract doctrine, which prevents third party beneficiaries from suing on contracts which were explicitly made for their benefit.[16] The other manifestation of this is that, once there has been legislative intervention in an area, courts may regard it as defining the relevant policies so as to preclude judicial activity not only within that area but also in related areas.[17] We have seen that this consensus, produced in a period in which legislative reform of contract and tort law was seen as a realistic option, may be starting to break down.[18]

Discretionary powers in contracts

One of the hallmarks of English common law is that it does not have a doctrine of abuse of rights: if one has a right to do an act then, one can, in

---

[13] Council Directive 93/13/EEC (OJ L95, 21.4.1993, p 29). Hugh Beale, ch 9 above, has discussed this.

[14] *Trading Malpractices*, A Report by the Director General of Fair Trading (Office of Fair Trading, July 1990). See generally G Borrie, 'Trading Malpractices and Legislative Policy' (1991) 107 LQR 559.

[15] See, for instance *Re Stapylton Fletcher Ltd* [1994] WLR 1182 (Judge Paul Baker QC) and see *Re Goldcorp Exchange Ltd (in Receivership)* [1994] 3 WLR 199 (PC).

[16] *Beswick v Beswick* [1968] AC 58, at 72; *Woodar Investment Development Ltd v Wimpey Construction UK Ltd* [1980] 1 WLR 277, at 291, 297–8, 300; *Swain v The Law Society* [1983] 1 AC 598, at 611. For possibilities for reform, see n 43, below.

[17] *National Westminster Bank Plc v Morgan* [1985] AC 686 (effect of the Unfair Contract Terms Act 1977 on development of undue influence and unconscionability); *Murphy v Brentwood DC* [1991] 1 AC 398 (effect of Defective Premises Act 1972 on common law liability for defective premises).

[18] p 6 above.

general, do it for whatever reason one wishes.[19] Except where the contracting parties are also in a fiduciary relationship, self-interest is permissible, and indeed is the norm in the exercise of contractual rights. It is therefore not surprising that contract law has difficulty in dealing with discretion. In a contractual context, discretion is often taken to mean that a matter is remitted to the unrestricted choice of a person. For instance, in *Weinberger v Inglis*[20] the House of Lords considered a refusal by the Committee of the London Stock Exchange to re-elect to the Exchange (ie in effect to expel) a person of German birth who had been a naturalized British subject for 30 years and whose loyalty to Britain had not been questioned. The rules of the exchange empowered the Committee to admit such persons as it 'shall think proper' and the House refused to interfere with the Committee's 'honest' exercise of a discretionary power. This case has been explained as one in which it had not been shown that the Committee had acted arbitrarily or capriciously, because the fact of Weinberger's alien birth was not an irrelevant consideration.[21]

Because discretion is often taken to mean *unrestricted* choice, the existence of discretion has been held to be inconsistent with the notion of a binding contract, either because it means that a promise is too uncertain to constitute consideration, as indicating a lack of intention to create legal relations, or as insufficiently certain.[22] Where there is a contract, discretion may prevent an alleged term from binding: thus in rejecting the argument than an employer who had agreed to pay a bonus but had not provided for a method of calculating the bonus was not obliged to do so, Lord Evershed MR said that the employer 'did not mean . . . the payment of a bonus to be purely discretionary'.[23] Alternatively, where there is a contract, the court may be reluctant to treat a right under it as limited. This is in marked contrast to public law contexts, where there is a well developed jurisprudence which controls the exercise of discretionary powers, and it is only very exceptionally that such a power would be seen as giving an unconstrained power of choice. It is also in contrast to some civil law systems where the issue is dealt with in accordance with the rules of good faith.

In fact courts are reluctant to find that a broadly phrased power in a contrast is 'discretionary' in the sense of giving an unconstrained choice particularly where this would mean there is no binding contract.[24] Thus,

---

[19] *Allen v Flood* [1898] AC 1.   [20] [1919] AC 606.

[21] *Shearson Lehman Hutton Inc* v *Maclaine Watson & Co Ltd* [1989] 2 Lloyd's Rep 570, at 627. For discussion of how this decision and others suggest public law concepts can apply to contractual powers, see p 270, below.

[22] *Halsbury's Laws of England* (4th ed 1974), vol 9, para 304.

[23] *Powell* v *Braun* [1954] 1 WLR 401, at 405.

[24] Especially where one side has performed; *British Bank for Foreign Trade Ltd* v *Novinex Ltd* [1949] 1 KB 623; *Powell* v *Braun* [1954] 1 WLR 401.

terms are implied as to the 'reasonableness' of the price, valuation, duration of the contract, and the exercise of rights under a contract.[25] For
instance, in shipping contracts, clauses permitting the ship the option of
landing a cargo at a port other than the port of discharge where that port
is unsafe or inaccessible, have been held not to give the master or
shipowner an unfettered discretion.[26] Thus, in considering whether
to exercise such a power, the master is 'bound to exercise that discretion
fairly as between both parties, and not merely to do his best for
the shipowners, his masters, disregarding the interests of the charterers'.[27]

In such cases, although the analogy of the judicial control of administrative action is said to require caution in its application, a similar
approach appears to be used. It has been stated that the essential question
always is whether the relevant power has been abused. '[N]ot only must
the discretion be exercised honestly and in good faith, but, having regard
to the provisions of the contract by which it is conferred, it must not be
exercised arbitrarily, capriciously or unreasonably.'[28] Consequently, if the
matter is not adequately considered or if no full or sufficient inquiry is
made, a purported exercise of the power will not be valid. Similarly, certification clauses in construction contracts which confer power on an
architect or engineer to certify, for instance the date on which the works
were practically complete or when defects have been made good, do not
confer an unfettered discretion. The certifier must act impartially and
within the jurisdiction conferred by the contract and may not unreasonably refuse to certify.[29]

The approach of the courts is, however, not always direct. Thus,
sometimes a widely phrased clause is construed as a power the exercise
of which is not possible until, for example, the lapse of a reasonable

[25] On reasonable time for exercise see: *United Dominions Trust (Commercial) Ltd v Eagle
Aircraft Services Ltd* [1968] 1 WLR 74; *Charnock v Liverpool Corpn* [1968] 1 WLR 1498. On
requiring the exercise of rights so as not to defeat the main purpose of the contract see *Greater
London Council v Connolly* [1970] 2 QB 100. On the principle of co-operation in contracts of
employment and on the implied provision for termination by reasonable notice in such contracts, see MR Freedland, *The Contract of Employment* (1976) pp 27–32, 151–4.

[26] *Scrutton on Charterparties* (19th ed 1984), p 134.

[27] *Tillmanns & Co v SS Knutsford Ltd* [1908] 2 KB 385, at 406 per Farwell LJ; aff'd [1908] AC
406 ('if port inaccessible on account of ice, . . . power to discharge the goods on the ice or at
some other safe port or place'). See also *Gov't of the Republic of Spain v North of England SS Co
Ltd* (1938) 61 Ll L Rep 44, at 57 (war clause empowering the master not 'to sign bills of lading for any blockaded port or for any port which the master or owners in his or their discretion consider dangerous or impossible to enter or reach').

[28] *Abu Dhabi National Tanker Co v Product Star Shipping Ltd (The Product Star)* (No 2) [1993]
1 Lloyd's Rep 397, at 404 per Leggatt LJ.

[29] See *Paramena Europea Navigacion (Compania Limitada) v Fredrick Leyland & Co Ltd (J
Russell & Co)* [1947] AC 428; *Sutcliffe v Thackrah* [1974] AC 727 and *Halsbury's Laws of England*
(4th ed 1992), vol 4(2), para 440.

time.[30] However, these cases show that it is not only where the contracting party's duty can be described as 'fiduciary' that he is precluded from acting in an entirely selfish manner. We shall, however, see that this use of the language of 'reasonableness' rather than of limited discretion means that sometimes possible solutions to questions which traditional analysis has found difficult are overlooked. If we can identify a principle to indicate when the courts will depart from the normal position in which discretion in a contract is taken to mean unrestricted choice this might be avoided. Moreover, such a principle would enable us to consider whether the fiduciary cases should be separated out in the way that they are. For instance, company directors must not exercise their powers for purposes different from which they were conferred, and must not fetter their discretion as to how they shall act, although the court leaves them a wide margin of appreciation.[31] But is it desirable for this and similar relationships based on contract to be balkanised in this way and considered as separate from 'the law of contract'?

The area in which the consideration of contractual discretionary powers is most developed in the sense that the more sophisticated public law approach to such powers has been adopted concerns mutual undertakings such as mutual insurance,[32] and bodies exercising self-regulatory powers over a business,[33] a professions,[34] or a sport.[35] In such contexts contractual discretions have been held not to be unfettered but to be subject to common law principles of procedural propriety (ie fairness or natural justice), 'Wednesbury' reasonableness (or rationality), bona fides, propriety of purpose, and relevancy. This is not a new phenomenon.[36] However, a recent example is provided by *Shearson Lehman Hutton Inc v*

---

[30] In *Tillmanns & Co v SS Knutsford Ltd*, cf. the Court of Appeal [1908] 2 KB 385 (discretion) and the House of Lords [1908] AC 406 (no power to deliver to port other than port of discharge until had waited for a reasonable time to see whether ice passed away).

[31] *Howard Smith Ltd v Ampol Petroleum Ltd* [1974] AC 821, at 832, 834. See generally *Gower's Principles of Modern Company Law* (5th ed 1992) pp 550–8.

[32] *CVG Siderurgicia del Orinoco SA v London Steamship Owners' Mutual Insurance Association Ltd (The Vainqueur José)* [1979] 1 Lloyd's Rep 557, at 574; *Shearson Lehman Hutton Inc v Maclaine Watson & Co Ltd* [1989] 2 Lloyd's Rep 570, at 624.

[33] *Shearson Lehman Hutton Inc v Maclaine Watson & Co Ltd* [1989] 2 Lloyd's Rep 570 (London Metal Exchange); *R v Life Assurance and Unit Trust Regulatory Organisation Ltd, ex p Ross* [1993] QB 17.

[34] *Swain v The Law Society* [1983] 1 AC 598; *Carmichael v General Dental Council* [1990] 1 WLR 134; *R v Visitors to the Inns of Court, ex p Calder* [1994] QB 1.

[35] *Enderby Town FC Ltd v Football Association Ltd* [1971] Ch 591; *Law v National Greyhound Racing Club Ltd* [1983] 1 WLR 1302. The *Aga Khan's* difficulties in proceeding against the Jockey Club by way of judicial review (notes 50–2, below) should not, in principle, have affected the substantive grounds upon which his action (for an alleged breach of contract) proceeded.

[36] *Wood v Wood* (1874) LR 9 Ex 190 (hearing was required in respect of every body of persons invested with authority to adjudicate on matters involving civil consequences to individuals, in that case membership of a mutual insurance association).

Maclaine Watson & Co Ltd. In that case Webster J said that the assumption
that rules of law established in public law cannot be carried over into the
field of private law was based on the premise that the rules of law established in public law and judicial review are different from those in private
law, but 'that premise, and the assumption to which it leads, is false'.[37] In
his view, the differences between private and public law rights related to
the procedures by which they are protected rather than to their substance.

Shearson Lehman Hutton Inc v *Maclaine Watson & Co Ltd* concerned the
rules of the London Metal Exchange, an administrative and regulatory
body and, although the rules constituted a contract between the members
inter se and between the members and the exchange, the powers given to
the exchange were subject to challenge on the grounds set out above. This
is similar to and consistent with the approach that has been taken in trade
union cases where, although the relationship between union and member
was contractual, the union has been obliged to adhere to the rules of natural justice[38] and (although this is not established so clearly) is subject to
control for abuse of or failure to exercise its discretion (including
Wednesbury unreasonableness).[39] It also suggests that, at the substantive
level, English law is not as distant from Scottish law as some have suggested, since it is clear that in Scottish law the court's supervisory jurisdiction extends to all 'administrative' functions, whether based on
statutory or governmental powers or on contract.[40]

The cases on regulatory bodies considered above are all ones in which
the contractual power was held by a person who was in a sense holding
the balance between different groups—one hesitates to use the much
abused phrases 'quasi-judicial' or 'administrative'—whether they be
mutual insurers, metal dealers, union members or those engaged in a particular sport. So, indeed are the cases on liberty clauses in shipping contracts and certification clauses in construction contracts considered above.
The importance of this balancing function is that, in dealing with members of the group, it does not matter whether, say self-regulating organizations under the Financial Services Act 1986 or the bodies such as the
Jockey Club, which exercise great (and monopolistic) power over certain

---

[37] [1989] 2 Lloyd's Rep 570, at 625.

[38] *Dawkins* v *Antrobus* (1881) 17 Ch D 615; *Bonsor* v *Musicians' Union* [1956] AC 104;
Edwards v *SOGAT* [1971] Ch 354. See generally HWR Wade, *Administrative Law* (6th ed 1988)
p 501.

[39] *Edwards* v *SOGAT* [1971] Ch 354; *Cheall* v *APEX* [1982] IRLR 362, at 367; [1983] 2 AC 180.
See generally P Elias & K Ewing, *Trade Union Democracy, Members' Rights and the Law* (1987)
Ch 2, esp pp 34–7, 38–44. Cf. *R* v *Disciplinary Committee of the Jockey Club, ex p Aga Khan* [1993]
1 WLR 909, at 933 (Hoffmann LJ doubted whether in the absence of legislation courts would
have imposed obligations of fairness on trade unions).

[40] *West* v *Secretary of State for Scotland* 1992 SLT 636; *The Laws of Scotland: Stair Memorial
Encyclopaedia* (1987) vol 1 para 400; WJ Wolffe, 'The Scope of Judicial Review in Scots Law'
[1992] PL 625.

sporting activities, are subject to the judicial review procedure. At the level of substance, their powers under the contract between the regulatory body and its members will be controlled in the same way and will be limited by the principles of legality, rationality and fairness. Although the public law remedies of certiorari and mandamus will not be available, injunctions and declarations cover much of the ground.

As far as the potential influence on contact law is concerned, if it is the balancing function which is crucial, the scope for the control of discretion by using the techniques that have been most fully developed in a public law context, would be limited since it would only apply to restricted types of contracts, and would not apply to, for example, contracts for the sale of goods. However, although this is an important indication that this type of control might be appropriate, it is not a necessary precondition of such control, for in the employment context similar controls have been imposed on the power of dismissal. Although no doubt influenced by the statutory regime governing unfair dismissal, these appear to be common law controls. What is important here is that the employer's discretionary power to terminate an employment or office is conditional upon him being satisfied upon a point which involves investigating some matter upon which the other party ought in fairness to be heard or to be allowed to give his explanation or put his case.[41] There are also indications that the protection goes beyond the requirement of a hearing and extends to the substantive exercise of discretion.[42]

Turning to the overlooked opportunities mentioned above, two examples will be given. The first concerns stale arbitrations and the second concerns problems concerning persons who are not parties to the contract; although the solution to the second may lie in abrogation of the much criticised doctrine of privity of contract.[43] As far as stale arbitrations are concerned, until the enactment of s 102 of the Courts and Legal Services Act 1990,[44] English law experienced great difficulties in dealing with the effect

---

[41] See *R v BBC, ex p Lavelle* [1983] 1 WLR 23 applying *Stevenson v URTU* [1977] ICR 893, at 902, per Buckley LJ. In *Roy v Kensington and Chelsea and Westminster Family Practitioner Committee* [1992] 1 AC 624, Lord Lowry said that Dr Roy had a right to a fair and legally correct consideration (by the Family Practitioner Committee) of his private law claim to payment for the work he had done.

[42] *R v BBC, ex p Lavelle* [1983] 1 WLR 23 (on which see J Beatson and MR Freedland, 'The Contract of Employment: The role of public law' (1983) 12 ILJ 43).

[43] This no longer exists in many other common law jurisdictions: eg Australia (*Trident General Insurance Co Ltd v McNiece Bros Pty Ltd* (1988) 165 CLR 107), New Zealand (Contracts (Privity) Act 1982), United States jurisdictions (*Lawrence v Fox* 20 NY 268 (1859); *Restatement 2d Contracts*, § 302). Reform is again under consideration in England either by legislation (see Privity of Contract: Contracts for the Benefit of Third Parties (1991) Law Com Consultation Paper No 121) or judicially (*Darlington BC v Wiltshier Northern Ltd*, [1995] 1 WLR 68).

[44] This inserts a new s 13A into the Arbitration Act 1950 which empowers an arbitrator to dismiss a claim where there has been 'inordinate and inexcusable delay' by the claimant in

of long delays by contractors in proceeding with arbitrations. Despite a 'scatter of judicial opinion' described as 'extraordinary',[45] it had, contrary to commercial expectations, been unable to develop a method to prevent a person who has been guilty of prolonged and inexcusable delay from thereafter continuing with his claim without at the same time imposing a duty on the other party to the arbitration to take active steps during the period of inactivity.[46] At least eight solutions had been suggested and attempted, including that the contractual right to ask the arbitration tribunal to proceed to an award should be regarded as a discretionary right to which the requirement of reasonableness could be held to apply. This argument was rejected on two grounds; first that it was inconsistent with a decision of the House of Lords in which the point had not been considered, and secondly that, insofar as it was based on the analogy of rights in public law, the contractual right to ask for directions in an arbitration or to urge the tribunal to proceed to an award was not considered to be in the nature of a discretion such as those exercised by the managers of mutual associations and self-regulatory bodies.

In his Freshfields lecture, Lord Justice Bingham said that, while the subtlety of regarding a claimant's right to ask the arbitral tribunal to proceed to an award as a contractual right in the nature of a power was incontestable, he did not see any difference between this right and other contractual rights which do not lapse on a failure to exercise them in a reasonable time.[47] But, with respect, this appears to assume that contractual rights must be absolute whereas, as we have seen, they need not be and may be subjected to requirements of reasonableness as to the time in which they are exercised.[48] Although it is often thought that the hallmark of common law rights is that they are absolute, and that the contrast between such rights and equitable and public law rights is that the latter are more qualified in character, this contrast is not entirely accurate. All these rights are qualified, but are qualified in different ways and at different stages. At common law the qualification and the flexibilty tends to

pursuing a claim which will give rise to a substantial risk that it is not possible to have a fair resolution of the issues in the claim or has caused or is likely to cause serious prejudice to the respondent.

[45] The Rt Hon Lord Justice Bingham, 'The Problem of Delay in Arbitration' (1989) 5 *Arbitration International* 333, 335.

[46] See Bingham, *ibid*. For earlier commentary, see J Beatson, 'The choice for respondents after The Leonidas D: should a turkey let a sleeping dog lie or look forward to Christmas?' (1985) 1 *Arbitration International* 192; 'Abandoning the Contract of Abandonment' (1986) 102 LQR 19; JG Wetter, 'The Importance of Having a Connection' (1987) 3 *Arbitration International* 329; FA Mann, 'Stale Arbitrations: The Antclizo (Missed Opportunities by the English House of Lords)' (1988) 4 *Arbitration International* 158.

[47] 'The Problem of Delay in Arbitration' (1989) 5 *Arbitration International* 333, 344–5.

[48] See *United Dominions Trust (Commercial) Ltd* v *Eagle Aircraft Services Ltd* [1968] 1 WLR 74 (the court implied an obligation to exercise a power to call on the other party to a recourse agreement to re-purchase aircraft, within a reasonable time).

come at the time of the ascription of the responsibility and tends to determine the extent of such responsibility, whereas in the case of equitable and public law rights the qualification and flexibility may come at the remedial stage. In the present context, it is arguable that as the arbitral process requires co-operation, having started the process, the claimant is not then entitled totally to disregard the interests of the respondent who has no control over the timetable. There are similarities both to the liberty and certification clauses considered above and, as far as the arbitrator himself is concerned, the cases on regulation considered above.[49] Statute has now intervened and the failure of the common law to furnish a solution does not matter. But it is an illustration of the way in which the marginalization of the techniques used in certain types of contract or in certain situations has not been a good thing.

Secondly, there is the problem of the non-party who is affected by the contractual arrangements. Although, the cases on regulation show that contract law can utilise techniques more familiar to public law, the fact that the language of public law is not used may be unhelpful. For instance, in considering the scope of judicial review, in *R v Disciplinary Committee of the Jockey Club, ex p Aga Khan*,[50] the court said that the Aga Khan, who was in a contractual relationship with the Club, could vindicate his rights in a contractual action and that judicial review was neither necessary nor appropriate. Hoffmann LJ did not think the position would have differed if the case had concerned a non-member who had no contractual remedy since he doubted that gaps in private law remedies against bodies such as the Jockey Club should be filled by subjecting them to public law and the judicial review procedure.[51] It was only because the Aga Khan had a contract with the Jockey Club that he was able to state that the remedies in private law in that case were adequate. Sir Thomas Bingham MR stated that where there was no contractual relationship the existence or non-existence of alternative (private law) remedies would be material to the determination of amenability to judicial review, presumably because, whatever the contractual provisions about the exercise of discretion concerning non-members and their treatment, a non-member had no private law remedy.[52] It will be argued below that the public law doctrine of legitimate expectation could have been of assistance to non-parties such as the applicant to a trade, professional or sporting association whether or not the procedure they were using was the application for judicial review.

---

[49] p 268 above.   [50] [1993] 1 WLR 909.

[51] [1993] 1 WLR 909, at 933. Cf. G Borrie, 'The Regulation of Public and Private Power' [1989] PL 552 for the suggestion that regulated utilities and bodies exercising monopoly control over for instance professions and sports should be amenable to the judicial review jurisdiction.

[52] [1993] 1 WLR 909, at 924. See also the reasoning in *R v Panel on Take-overs and Mergers, ex p Datafin Plc* [1987] QB 815.

Non-parties may also be affected by variations in the contract. Thus, in *Shearson Lehman Hutton Inc* it was held that the London Metal Exchange was entitled to change its rules so as to affect the rights of non-members (under contracts made with members) where they had agreed to be bound by its rules.[53]

The only context in which it is generally accepted that a contracting party will not be permitted to exercise his rights 'selfishly' is where his contractual duty can be characterized as fiduciary or is superimposed upon a pre-existing fiduciary relationship.[54] But when the relationship is characterized as fiduciary there are normally a number of other consequences, in particular the application of the 'no conflict', 'no profit' and 'undivided loyalty' rules.[55] The circumstances in which a relationship will be considered 'fiduciary' are notoriously difficult to define. However, the presence of certain factors such as an undertaking to act on behalf of or for the benefit of another, a discretion or power which affects the interest of that other person, and the peculiar vulnerability of that other person to the alleged fiduciary are important. Many commercial relationships involve reliance by one party on the undertaking of the other but 'high expectations do not necessarily lead to equitable remedies.'[56] The second and third of these factors exist in those situations in which contractual rights have been subjected to a common law reasonableness requirement or have been said to be limited by principles that are more familiar in a public law context (procedural fairness, propriety of purpose, relevance, and *Wednesbury* reasonableness), but without the additional rules that have normally been seen as flowing from the characterisation of a relationship as 'fiduciary'.

The impact of statute and regulation[57]

In this section we consider the impact of statute and regulation in a given area on subsequent common law development. In England there has been

---

[53] [1989] 2 Lloyd's Rep 570, at 589, 592, 594. This entitlement is, however, subject to the doctrine of restraint of trade and its requirement of reasonableness: *Eastham* v *Newcastle United FC* [1964] Ch 413; *Buckley* v *Tutty* (1971) 125 CLR 353; *Greig* v *Insole* [1978] 1 WLR 302; *Hughes* v *Western Australian Cricket Association (Inc)* (1986) 69 ALR 660, 701. See also *Falcone* v *Middlesex County Medical Society* 89 ALR 2d 952 (1961).

[54] See PD Finn, *Fiduciary Obligations* (1977). See also R Flannigan, 'The Fiduciary Obligation' (1989) 9 Ox JLS 285.

[55] This is the way the rules, which can be described in a number of ways, were summarized by the Law Commission in Fiduciary Duties and Regulatory Rules (1992) Law Com Consultation Paper No 124, ss 2.4.8–2.4.11.

[56] *Re Goldcorp Exchange Ltd (in Receivership)* [1994] 3 WLR 199, at 216.

[57] On the impact of regulation on common law and equitable doctrines, see Fiduciary Duties and Regulatory Rules (1992) Law Com Consultation Paper No 124, especially ss 1.1–1.15, 3.2, 4.1–4.6, 5.1, 5.4, 6.1–6.21.

relatively little work of a more theoretical nature on this topic.[58] There are two aspects to it. First, there is the question of whether the existence of a statute has a direct effect on the common law. In some situations, for instance, it seems clear that the existence of a statute covering part of the ground has led to the re-evaluation of a common law rule not within its scope. The two best examples of this are the effect of the Law Reform (Contributory Negligence) Act 1945 on causation (in contract where there is concurrent liability with tortious liability), and of the Unfair Contract Terms Act 1977 on the construction of exemption clauses. In the former, the possibility of apportionment of fault meant that courts were less willing to say that the chain of causation had been broken.[59] In the latter, the fact that exemption clauses in standard form and consumer contracts were subject to a statutory reasonableness test meant that courts were less inclined to construe them strictly so as to cut down their width.[60] We shall consider whether legislative duties of disclosure and the anti-discrimination legislation (both national and European Community) should similarly lead to a re-evaluation of pre-contractual duties. The second aspect concerns the more direct effect of statutes and regulations. Does the fact that a sphere of contractual activity is regulated affect the content of the contract through the medium of implied terms, or in some other way? Each will be considered in turn, although the question of implied terms or default rules is primarily considered in Tod Rakoff's contribution to this book.[61]

In the context of the issues of good faith and disclosure which are of current concern, the statutory duties of good faith and disclosure in the Consumer Credit Act 1974 and the Financial Services Act 1986 have had less influence. The statutes reflected a legislative decision that consumers buying on credit and the purchasers of the products of the financial services industry (insurance policies, investments, and advice) required protection. This was to be achieved by a licensing system and by close control of the way in which those licensed conduct their businesses. The former applies only to consumers and, in the case of financial services, private investors have a higher degree of protection than others.[62] It is required

---

[58] For important exceptions, see R Cross, *Statutory Interpretation* (2nd ed 1987) pp 41 *et seq*; Atiyah (1985) 48 MLR 1. Both rely on Roscoe Pound's important article 'Common Law and Legislation' (1908) 21 Harv L Rev 383.

[59] For a recent example of the overt recognition of this see *Schering Agrochemicals Ltd* v *Resibel NV SA* (26 November 1992 (CA)); (noted by A Burrows, 'Contributory Negligence in Contract: Ammunition for the Law Commission' (1993) 109 LQR 175) and in Contributory Negligence as a Defence in Contract (1993) Law Com No 219, ss 3.11–3.15.

[60] *Photo Productions Ltd* v *Securicor Transport Ltd* [1980] AC 827; *Ailsa Craig Fishing Co Ltd* v *Malvern Fishing Co Ltd* [1983] 1 WLR 964.

[61] Chapter 8, above.

[62] In particular they are given a right to civil damages for contravention of regulatory rules: FSA 1969, s 62A. "Private investor" is defined by SI 1991 No 489.

that financial services practitioners subordinate their own interests to those of their clients and make proper provision for disclosure of interests in and facts material to transactions entered into or advice given.[63] Unless they are transacting business on an 'execution-only' basis, practitioners are under an obligation to 'know' their customers so they can give appropriate advice, and they must explain the risks of a particular investment. Particularly detailed disclosure is required in the case of long term contracts such as those for life assurance.

Although there are many differences between the financial services and the consumer credit regimes, they have similar disclosure provisions. Also, both regimes exercise close control over the content of advertisements. The fact that the legislative schemes are so detailed means that it is not unreasonable to see them as self-contained codes. However, that part of the regimes which relates to disclosure might arguably be of wider significance. In both contexts the relationship is one of inequality: in financial services (and probably in consumer credit) there is also imbalance of information in the sense that the professional has information that the client cannot acquire from any other source—or cannot do so without incurring considerable expense. This imbalance can also be seen at the root of the equitable doctrine of undue influence, the duty of disclosure in contracts *uberrimae fidei* and employees' duties of fidelity.[64]

Accordingly, it is arguable that the fact that the legislature has imposed a duty of disclosure in one such case can be seen, alongside the cases in which a duty exists at common law, as an indication of the underlying rationale and principle of such a duty, and therefore, as a guide to a court which is considering the extension of the duty to a new fact situation.[65] If one is considering whether exceptions to a rule have become so extensive as to undermine that rule, as has happened in the case of the parol evidence rule, which has been said not to exist,[66] it would be odd to consider only the common law exceptions. Bingham LJ, in *Interfoto Picture Library Ltd* v *Stiletto Visual Programmes Ltd*,[67] considered that the cases on sufficiency of notice should be read in the context of both the statutory and the common law solutions to 'demonstrated problems of unfairness'. If this was done, he believed that the cases would be seen to be concerned not only with pure contractual analysis, but also with whether it would be fair

---

[63] FSA 1986, Sched 8, ss 3, 5–8.   [64] *Sybron Corpn* v *Rochem Ltd* [1984] Ch 112.

[65] Cf. the different approach in *Banque Financière de la Cité SA* v *Westgate Insurance Co Ltd* [1990] 3 WLR 364, at 374 where the only policy issues relevant to the imposition of a duty of disclosure addressed in the leading speech by Lord Templeman were that the information which had to be disclosed may be unreliable or doubtful or inconclusive, and that disclosure may expose the informer to criticism or litigation: 'A professional should wear a halo but need not wear a hairshirt.'

[66] See Law of Contract: The Parol Evidence Rule (1986) Law Com No 154, Cmnd 9700, and eg *Haryanto (Yani)* v *ED & F Man (Sugar) Ltd* [1986] 2 Lloyd's Rep 44, at 46.

[67] [1989] QB 433.

or reasonable to hold a party bound by a condition that was particularly unusual or stringent. However, this is exceptional. In the absence of an adequate theoretical framework for considering such statutory modifications, a court would be more likely to conclude that the necessity for statutory intervention showed the limits of any common law duty of disclosure and also precluded further common law development. The law on discrimination and refusal to contract, considered below, is perhaps the best example of this.

The contrast between these situations and public law is fundamental. In public law an appropriate partnership has been developed (albeit not without controversy) between the sovereign parliament and the courts. It is important for the future of the common law—in this context the law of contract—that an equally appropriate (albeit different) partnership be developed in private law. Without it, in view of the fact that, even granted the difficulties of legislative time, there is likely to be a steady trickle of legislation affecting contracts, the common law process of evolutionary development may not survive as the law moves in the direction of an increasing number of small, factually-based categories (or transaction types). There are, however, isolated counter-examples to the general approach of keeping common law principles and the principles underpinning statutes separate. Bingham LJ's approach in *Interfoto* has been mentioned. Another notable example is provided by the majority speeches in *Woolwich Equitable Building Society v Inland Revenue Commissioners*[68] where Lord Goff and Lord Slynn did not accept the second stage of this argument; ie that statutory intervention precludes common law development. In considering whether the presence of statutory rights to the recovery of payments precluded the development of a common law right in situations in which the statutes did not apply, Lord Goff said that 'having, where applicable, overlaid and replaced the common law principles, whatever those principles may be [the statutory provisions] become neutral in their effect when the development of those principles is considered by the courts.'[69] It is submitted that there should be a greater willingness to consider the full context of fact situations, ie statute as well as common law. In some situations, for example where it is not possible to discern a principle underlying the statute, this may not get one very far. However, modern courts have been willing to interpret statutes purposively and it may well be legitimate to do what Bingham LJ did in the *Interfoto* case.

---

[68] [1993] AC 70; on which see P Birks, ' "When Money is Paid in Pursuance of a Valid Authority . . ."—A Duty to Repay?' [1992] PL 580; E McKendrick, 'Restitution of unlawfully demanded tax' [1993] LMCLQ 88; J Beatson, 'Restitution of taxes, levies and other imposts: defining The extent of the *Woolwich* principle' (1993) 109 LQR 401.
[69] [1993] AC 70, at 170B. See also Lord Slynn at 200.

Turning to the second, more indirect, influence of statute or regulation, the fact that the contractual context is a regulated one may be influential. Where a sphere of activity is regulated by a trade or a professional association, or by the governing body of a sport, the rules of that body are likely to be adopted widely in transactions, since members of the body will be bound by its rules. It is clear that the effect of this is that the rules of bodies such as the Stock Exchange will be incorporated by implication into relevant contracts on the same principles as those applicable to trade customs.[70] It also seems that general background principles of contract law, for instance the absence of a duty of disclosure, will be affected by such rules, and that when the body changes its rules the new rules will affect existing contracts between members and non-members.[71] Where these rules provide dispute resolution machinery, or limit the manner in which contractual powers may be exercised, they are likely to be interpreted as subject to the public law principles of procedural fairness, propriety of purpose, relevance, and what is either known as *Wednesbury* reasonableness or as rationality.[72] It is also likely that the power to make changes to the rules will be subject to these principles. In this cases it is difficult to see how a non-member will be able to mount a challenge, unless the body is amenable to supervision by way of the judicial review procedure (ie on the most recent authority when it is exercising 'governmental' functions), where the rule falls foul of the restraint of trade doctrine or where it contravenes the anti-discrimination legislation.

Finally, where a sphere of contracting is subject to regulation, whether public or self-regulation, courts are likely to take account of the requirements of the regulatory regime in determining whether the contract has been broken. Thus, failure to adhere to the Take-Over Panel's Code may mean that a contractual stipulation of confidence will not be enforced,[73] and failure to warn against unsuitable investments (in breach of the Securities and Investments Boards's 'suitability' rule) may give rise to liability.[74] Conversely, compliance with regulatory rules may facilitate a finding that there was no breach of duty.[75]

---

[70] There is some authority that stock exchange rules bind regardless of their reasonableness or whether they are known to a third party who deals with a member (*Benjamin* v *Barnett* (1903) 8 Com Cas 244, at 247–8; *Union and Rhodesian Trust (Ltd)* v *Neville* (1917) 33 TLR 245; *Forget* v *Baxter* [1900] AC 467) but cf. *Fiduciary Duties and Regulatory Rules* (1992) Law Com Consultation Paper No 124 ss 3.2.8–3.2.12.

[71] See p 274 above.

[72] *Associated Provincial Picture Houses* v *Wednesbury Corpn* [1948] 1 KB 223; *CCSU* v *Minister for the Civil Service* [1985] AC 374.

[73] *Dunford & Elliot Ltd* v *Johnson & Firth Brown Ltd* [1977] 1 Lloyd's Rep 505.

[74] *Stafford* v *Conti Commodity Services Ltd* [1981] 1 All ER 691.

[75] *Lloyd Cheyham & Co Ltd* v *Littlejohn & Co* [1987] BCLC 303, at 313. Although concerned with liability in tort, the principle in this case appears equally applicable to contractual liability, particularly where there is only liability for failure to act 'reasonably'.

In the cases considered in the two paragraphs above, the statutory or regulatory contexts affect the content of the contractual duty, but formally this is done with respect to a particular contract rather than at the level of rules of contract law.

Formation: pre-contractual duties

At common law, the general rule is that there is freedom to refuse to contract. Thus, as a general rule a person may refuse to contract with another and, where the parties are negotiating but have not yet entered into a contract, courts have traditionally been reluctant to impose obligations, or 'pre-contractual duties', on them. Each will be considered.

In the context of sales, the best known manifestation of the freedom to refuse to contract is the fact that a display of goods by a shopkeeper, whether in a window or on the shelves of a self-service store,[76] constitutes an invitation to treat rather than an offer and is justified on the ground that otherwise the shopkeeper might be obligated even after he had sold all the goods, or be in convention of statutory or regulatory requirements.[77] But this freedom also permitted less defensible conduct. Thus, in *Timothy v Simpson*[78] a person who went into a shop and asked for a dress was asked to pay 7/6d although it was marked at 5/11d. One of the shopkeeper's employees said, 'don't let him have it, he's only a Jew. Turn him out'. The plaintiff had no right to have the goods marked and the shopkeeper was held to have the right to turn him out.

One or possibly two exceptions to the general rule were, however, recognized by the common law. First, there is the case of the common callings. Common innkeepers and common carriers are under a duty to serve all-comers on a reasonable basis,[79] probably because of their monopoly or near monopoly position.[80] The adequacy of their reasons for not serving is accordingly justiciable and discrimination, for example on racial grounds, has been recognised not to be an adequate reason.[81] Secondly,

---

[76] The position may be different where payment is made to a machine or where, as in many self-service petrol stations, the product purchased cannot easily be retrieved from the buyer's property: *Thornton v Shoe Lane Parking Ltd* [1971] 2 QB 163, at 169.

[77] *Pharmaceutical Society of Great Britain v Boots Cash Chemists (Southern) Ltd* [1953] 1 QB 401.

[78] (1834) 6 Car & P 499; 172 ER 1337. See also *Said v Butt* [1920] 3 KB 497 (theatre manager refused entry to critic who had someone else buy a ticket for him to a first night performance).

[79] *Chitty on Contracts* (27th ed 1994) ss 35-005–35-007, 35-009–35-011. But almost all carriers contract out of their common law liability.

[80] B Wyman, 'The Law of the Public Callings as a Solution of the Trust Problem' (1903–04) 17 Harv L Rev 156, 217.

[81] *Constantine v Imperial Hotels Ltd* [1944] KB 693.

there is the doctrine of restraint of trade. Under this, if a refusal to deal constitutes an *unreasonable* restraint on the liberty of a person to exercise his trade or a profession, ie if the 'right to work' is unreasonable affected, the excluded person may be able to obtain relief. Thus, in *Nagle v Feilden* the court refused to strike out a claim by a woman who had been refused a horse trainer's licence by the Jockey Club because of her sex and appeared favourable to injunctive as well as declaratory relief.[82] Again, what is important is that the refusal is made by a person or organization which exercises monopoly power in the area of work which it controls. These common law doctrines have not, however, been developed and the common law has left the field to the modern anti-discrimination legislation and the legislative provisions for controlling monopolies and restrictive trade practices and regulating utilities.[83]

There are now wide ranging statutory restrictions on various kinds of discrimination in the provision of services (including education)[84] and in the selection of employees and in the terms upon which they are employed.[85] The restrictions on race and sex discrimination (including discrimination against married persons) primarily give rise to compensation orders, but exceptionally can lead to specific relief.[86] In the case of discrimination against the disabled, the sanction is a criminal one and there does not appear to be any sanction for refusal to employ a rehabilitated criminal whose convictions are spent.[87] Similarly, there is legislative provision for the mandatory implication of equality clauses into contracts of

---

[82] [1966] 2 QB 633. JA Weir, 'Discrimination in Private Law' [1966] CLJ 165, criticized the willingness to give an injunction and Hoffmann LJ has stated that the possibility of an injunction has probably not survived (*The Siskina* [1979] AC 210; *R v Disciplinary Committee of the Jockey Club, ex p Aga Khan* [1993] 1 WLR 909, at 933.

[83] These are often under a duty to supply those who wish to be supplied (Gas Act 1986, s 10; Electricity Act 1989, s 16) and there tend to be prohibitions on undue preference and undue discrimination in statute (Gas Act 1986, s 14(3); Electricity Act 1989, ss 3(2) and 18(4) (for tariff customers) and see *South of Scotland Electricity Board v British Oxygen Co Ltd* (No 2) [1959] 1 WLR 587) or in the terms of the licence (Telecommunications Act 1984, ss 3, 8(1)(d); Electricity Act 1989, ss 3(2); Water Industry Act 1991, s 2(3)(a)(ii), (5) and see Part V and condition E of the licences. See further SK Bailey and RH Tudway, *Electricity Law and Practice* (1992), ch 11; J Bates, *Water and Drainage Law* (1990). Powers to disconnect, such as those in Gas Act 1986, para 7 to Sched 5, Electricity Act 1989, para 1 to Sched 6 and Water Industry Act 1991, s 61, may be exercised for commercial purposes, irrespective of the social consequences: *R v West Midlands Electricity Board, ex p Bushey, The Times* 28 October 1987.

[84] Race Relations Act 1976, s 20; Sex Discrimination Act 1975, s 29. On education, see *ibid.* ss 17 and 22 respectively and *Mandla (Sewa Singh) v Dowell-Lee* [1983] 2 AC 548, but nb the single-sex establishment exemption in Sex Discrimination Act 1975, s 26.

[85] Although, save in Northern Ireland (Fair Employment (Northern Ireland) Act 1989), these do not extend to pure religious discrimination, members of some religions such as Sikhism and Judaism, form an ethnic group which is protected: *Mandla (Sewa Singh) v Dowell-Lee* [1983] 2 AC 548.

[86] Race Relations Act 1976, s 56(1)(c); Sex Discrimination Act 1975, s 65(1)(c).

[87] Disabled Persons (Employment) Act 1944, s 9 and Rehabilitation of Offenders Act 1974, s 4(3)(c) respectively.

employment, so that an employee has contractual terms not less favourable than those accorded to a person of the opposite sex, and wide provisions make it unlawful to discriminate in other ways against employees on the ground of sex or race during employment. The prohibition on discrimination in the provision of goods, facilities and services[88] applies where the provision is made to the public or a section of the public. Thus, a shop which refuses to sell furniture on hire purchase terms to a woman without a guarantee from her husband although it would not have required a guarantee from the husband was held to have acted unlawfully, as was a wine bar which refused to serve women at the bar but required them to sit at a table.[89]

In certain contexts, exemptions seek to preserve freedom within a 'private' area. Thus, discrimination in letting accommodation is permitted where the landlord resides in the premises, and shares a significant part of the accommodation, and the premises are small.[90] So is discrimination by partnerships with less than six partners.[91] The requirements in respect of disabled persons apply only to employers of twenty or more persons. Perhaps more controversially, from a policy point of view, private clubs in which there is a genuine selection on personal grounds in electing to membership have been held not to be offering a facility to a section of the public[92] although those with twenty-five or more members are now subject to the prohibition on racial discrimination.[93]

In all these cases, as Treitel has stated, 'a relationship which results from some degree of legal compulsion is nevertheless regarded as contractual, because the parties still have considerable freedom to regulate its incidents'.[94] However, this body of law has had no impact on the common law attitude to refusal to contract, and may indeed have choked off possible developments in the context of trade and employment by deployment of the doctrine of restraint of trade in a similar way to *Nagle* v *Feilden*[95] or, in the case of those with dominant or monopoly positions, by analogy with the law on common callings.

Apart from questions of outright refusals to contract, a party in negotiations may seek to argue that the other is under obligations to negotiate in good faith or to give reasonable consideration to all offers. Such

---

[88] These terms are given a broad meaning, see Race Relations Act 1976, s 40(1); Sex Discrimination Act 1975, s 50(1) and *R* v *Entry Clearance Officer, Bombay, ex p Amin* [1983] 2 AC 818.

[89] *Quinn* v *Williams Furniture Ltd* [1981] ICR 328; *Gill* v *El Vino Co Ltd* [1983] QB 425.

[90] Race Relations Act 1976, s 22; Sex Discrimination Act 1975, s 32.

[91] Race Relations Act 1976, s 10; Sex Discrimination Act 1975, s 11.]

[92] *Charter* v *Race Relations Board* [1973] AC 868; *Dockers Labour Club and Institute Ltd* v *Race Relations Board* [1976] AC 285.

[93] Race Relations Act, s 25. They are not, however, subject to the sex discrimination legislation.

[94] *The Law of Contract* (8th ed 1991) p 5.   [95] [1966] 2 QB 633. See pp 279–80 above.

arguments have generally failed, except where the court is able to identify an implied contract.[96] Where an implied contract is found, the traditional position is formally (but perhaps not always substantively) preserved. For instance, in *Blackpool and Fylde Aero Club Ltd v Blackpool Borough Council*,[97] where the Court of Appeal considered a tendering process for the concession to operate pleasure flights from a municipally owned airport, it implied a contract to open and consider all tenders submitted before the specified deadline.

The traditional position may be challenged by the use of concepts of estoppel,[98] reliance,[99] restitution,[100] reasonable expectation (short of bargain) and unconscionability. The various 'private' law techniques which have been used to deal with this issue fall outside the scope of this chapter. Do public law concepts, in particular the concept of 'legitimate expectations' but also non-discrimination, have any role? Briefly, a person has a 'legitimate expectation' in the public law sense when the authority has, either by what it has said or by its conduct created an expectation in the citizen. The expectation may be that the authority would follow a particular procedure before granting or removing a benefit (and originally the only expectations protected were such procedural ones), or that the authority would grant or not remove a benefit if the citizen acted in a particular way (the more recent and substantive sense).[101] The principle of 'legitimate expectation' has operated to limit the exercise of public powers by holding that action inconsistent with such an expectation may be 'unfair'. It has operated in a wide variety of contexts, including ones where the authority's private rights (eg of ownership) are affected. For instance, in *Wheeler v Leicester City Council*[102] a council which had permit-

---

[96] See generally S Arrowsmith, 'Protecting the Interests of Bidders for Public Contracts; The Role of the Common Law' [1994] CLJ 104.

[97] [1990] 1 WLR 1195.

[98] In *Attorney-General of Hong Kong v Humphreys Estate (Queen's Gardens) Ltd* [1987] AC 114, at 127–8 the Judicial Committee of the Privy Council stated that '[i]t is possible but unlikely that in circumstances at present unforeseeable a party to negotiations set out in a document expressed to be "subject to contract" would be able to satisfy the court that the parties had subsequently agreed to convert the document into a contract or that some form of estoppel had arisen to prevent both parties from refusing to proceed with the transactions envisaged by the document'. On estoppel in a pre-contractual situation, see *Waltons Stores (Interstate) Pty Ltd v Maher* (1988) 164 CLR 387 (High Court of Australia). See further, N Cohen, ch 2 above.

[99] *Brewer Street Investments Ltd v Barclays Woollen Co Ltd* [1954] 1 QB 428.

[100] *British Steel Corpn v Cleveland Bridge & Engineering Co Ltd* [1984] 1 All ER 504.

[101] For examples of the protection of substantive expectations, see *R v Secretary of State for the Home Department, ex p Ruddock* [1987] 1 WLR 1482 (telephone tapping); *R v Secretary of State for the Home Department, ex p Asif Khan* [1984] 1 WLR 1337 (entry to UK for adoption). Cf. *R v Secretary of State for Transport, ex p Richmond LBC* [1994] 1 WLR 74, at 92–4.

[102] [1985] AC 1054. In the Court of Appeal, Browne-Wilkinson LJ stated that a wider ground appealed to him; that the council should not be allowed to exercise its discretionary powers so as to discriminate against those whose views differed from the views of the council.

ted a rugby football club to use one of its sports fields for matches and training for many years (for a fee) was held to have acted unfairly and unlawfully in resolving not to give permission for a period because it disapproved of the participation by three club members in a tour of South Africa. Both the *Blackpool and Fylde Aero Club* case and *R v Lord Chancellor, ex p Hibbit and Saunders*[103] suggest that such public law principles have no role whatsoever in the tendering process.

In *Blackpool and Fylde Aero Club* it was argued that the duty of the council to comply with its standing orders and its duty to ratepayers (which, in English law, is often described as 'fiduciary') meant that the council was under a pre-contractual duty to the tenderer.[104] However, even though the council was a public authority and clearly, in certain contexts, subject to the public law principles listed at the beginning of this chapter, the Court of Appeal decided the case by traditional 'private' law contractual analysis, although some would say that a little manipulation was required to achieve the result.[105] None of the statutory provisions or the European Community Directives considered below appeared to apply, and the court did not consider the applicability of the principle of 'legitimate expectation'. As it found an implied contract, it did not need to look further. But, in view of the difficulties perceived in implying a contract, should it have done so?

In *R v Lord Chancellor, ex p Hibbit and Saunders* a firm which unsuccessfully tendered for the provision of certain court reporting services claimed in judicial review proceedings that the Lord Chancellor's Department had failed to adhere to the tendering procedures that the firm had been led to believe would be followed.[106] This case is even more hostile than *Blackpool and Fylde Aero Club* to the idea that public law principles have any role to play in a tendering process. It was said that the Department had created expectations as to how the process would be conducted which it had then not observed, and had accordingly acted 'unfairly'. However, the court concluded that the public law principle protecting 'legitimate expectations' did not apply to the tendering process, and that the only remedy was an implied contract of the sort found in the *Blackpool and Fylde Aero*

---

[103] [1993] COD 326; *The Times* 12 March 1993.

[104] [1990] 1 WLR 1195, 1201D: '. . . the council as a local authority was obliged to comply with its standing orders and owed a fiduciary duty to ratepayers to act with reasonable prudence in managing its financial affairs; and that there was a clear intention on the part of both parties that all timely tenders would be considered.'

[105] See JN Adams and R Brownsword, 'More in Expectation than Hope: The Blackpool Airport Case' (1991) 54 MLR 281, 287. See also A Phang, 'Tenders and Uncertainty' (1991) 4 JCL 46. Cf. BJ Davenport, 'Obligation to Consider Tenders' (1991) 107 LQR 201.

[106] [1993] COD 326; *The Times* 12 March 1993. It claimed that, rather than contract with the lowest tenderer, the department entered into further negotiations with selected tenderers, and that it had not informed all tenderers that it had waived a requirement that the names of staff who would be employed were to be stated in the tender.

Club case. The court appeared to favour the finding of an implied contact but considered that issue could not be determined in the judicial review proceedings. Part of the problem may have related to the court's feeling that it was inappropriate for disputes of this kind to be determined in such proceedings. However, this is, as will be seen, questionable and inconsistent with a line of cases not considered. Even if judicial review was not the correct procedure, the decision also suggests that, even at the substantive level, public law principles have no role in the tendering process. It is submitted that this too is questionable.

Let us examine the possibilities which may have been overlooked. Under the general principles governing the exercise of discretionary powers and the Local Government Act 1988, refusals to contract at all or only on particular terms and failures to observe tendering procedures may be invalidated. For example, at common law, a refusal to contact may be held invalid where it is based on a policy which amounts to an improper fetter on an authority's discretion or is 'unfair' in the light of an individual's legitimate expectations. Thus, a decision not to contract with a company in part motivated by the wish to make the company cease its trade with South Africa has been held ultra vires in judicial review proceedings.[107]

The process is more obvious where contracting powers are expressly limited by statute. For example, the Local Government Act 1988 requires that local authorities exercise their functions without reference to 'non-commercial matters'. It has been held that a stipulation by a local authority that those seeking to contract with it include certain provisions prohibiting sexual discrimination in their contracts with sub-contractors is ultra vires because it infringes the requirements of the 1988 Act.[108] It follows that it would be unlawful to refuse to deal with a contractor who did not comply with the stipulation. Similarly, an authority subject to the 1988 Act may not require those contracting with it to comply with statutory requirements for the health, safety and welfare of the contractors' employees,[109] and thus may not refuse to contract with those who do not. Although the outcome may seem paradoxical because public law is used to prevent the imposition of values many consider desirable, the explanation is to be found in the fact the court considered that it was only the 1988 Act, and not the body of legislation (including the Sex Discrimination Act

---

[107] *R v Lewisham LBC, ex p Shell UK Ltd* [1988] 1 All ER 938.

[108] *R v Islington LBC, ex p Building Employers Confederation* [1989] IRLR 382. However, requiring the inclusion of terms in sub-contracts relating to race relations was not prohibited by the 1988 Act because a limited exception in s 18 of the 1988 Act allows account to be taken of the need to eliminate unlawful racial discrimination and promote equality of opportunity (see also the Race Relations Act 1976, s 71). There is no such exception in respect of sex discrimination.

[109] *Ibid.*

1975) which prescribed what values in this context were to be treated as desirable.

At present courts may be reluctant to exercise control over the pre-contractual process where they regard the authority's powers as 'man-agerial',[110] particularly where the basis of control is common law rather than statute. Nevertheless, where an authority has not complied with the requirements of procedural fairness (such as the statutory duty to give reasons under the 1988 Act), decisions will be reviewed.[111] The cases on the Local Government Act 1988 and common law ultra vires, discussed above, illustrate that public law principles can be and have been used to deal with problems that arise in contractual negotiations, and that these principles operate both procedurally (ie in judicial review proceedings) and at the level of substantive principle (for example controlling the exer-cise of discretion, ensuring fair procedures and protecting legitimate expectations[112]). We shall also see below that, even where judicial review proceedings are not possible or not appropriate, public law principles have been used in contractual contexts.

A further major change has occurred as the result of European Community Directives which seek to ensure that there is no discrimination (on national lines) in tendering procedures for major contracts for public works, supplies and services.[113] Co-ordinated and fairly elaborate proce-dures (including Community-wide advertisements and time limits to afford those in other Member States the opportunity to participate) now apply to the award of such contracts. The Directives leave the fate of a con-tract made in breach of the rules to national law,[114] and the United Kingdom's implementing regulations provide that concluded contracts are not to be set aside on the application of a third party (normally a disap-pointed tenderer).[115] Therefore, reviewing remedies such as certiorari and mandamus will not be of much assistance, unless a person complaining of

---

[110] *R v National Coal Board, ex p National Union of Mineworkers* [1986] ICR 791. Cf. *R v British Coal Corpn and Secretary of State for Trade and Industry, ex p Vardy* [1993] ICR 720 (nb neither were pre-contractual cases).

[111] *R v Enfield LBC, ex p TF Unwin (Roydon) Ltd;* [1989] COD 466, *The Times* 16 February 1989.

[112] The last two are, in a sense, 'procedural', but in a different sense: it is clear that natural justice principles apply beyond the scope of RSC, Ord 53 and it is submitted that legitimate expectation principles should too.

[113] Directives 71/305/EEC (1971 OJ L185/5); 77/62/EEC (1977 OJ L215/1); 92/50/EEC; 90/50/EEC (1990 OJ L297/1). These have respectively been implemented in the UK by SI 1991 No 2680; SI 1991 No 2679; SI 1992 No 3279. See S Arrowsmith, 'An Overview of EC Policy on Public Procurement: Current Position and Future Prospects' [1992] 1 Public Procurement Law Rev 28; F Weiss, *Public Procurement in European Community Law* (1993).

[114] Council Directive 89/665/EEC (OJ L395, 30.12.1989, p 33) Art 2(6). See HM Gilliams, 'Effectiveness of European Community Public Procurement Law after *Francovich*' [1992] Public Procurement Law Rev 292.

[115] SI 1991 No 2679, r 26(b); SI 1991 No 2680 r 31(7); SI 1992 No 3279 r 30(6).

breach can both invoke the assistance of the court before the award of the contract and persuade the court to grant interim relief. In other cases the only remedy will be monetary compensation; the Directives require there to be a damages remedy.[116] The remedies may be sui generis, and there is some debate as to whether damages for the 'loss of a chance' are available under the regulations implementing the directives as they are for breach of contract.[117] However, for a very large class of public contracts there is now a formalized pre-contractual process backed by legal remedies. Given the size of the contracts, and the fact that tenderers are likely to have incurred substantial expenses in preparing their bid and ensuring that it satisfies the rules, it is, moreover, likely that disappointed parties will seek to use these remedies.

The upshot is a mosaic of law governing tendering procedures. First, there is the purely common law position in which in the absence of an implied contract, estoppel, a restitutionary remedy or one of the other methods listed above, no obligations arise. However, it is possible that courts will be more willing to use these than they have been in the past. One reason for this is the way similar concepts have provided useful remedies in very similar situations which happen to be governed by public law. Secondly, there are tendering procedures conducted by public authorities and privatised utilities. If the 1988 Act or the EC rules apply, obligations will arise for breach. There are, however, differences; notably that there is no damages remedy for breach of the 1988 Act. If neither the 1988 Act nor the EC rules apply, there is some uncertainty. While there is authority supporting the limitation of the freedom of the person to whom tenders are submitted (the 'tenderee') by the use of the rules governing the exercise of discretionary power, in particular the doctrine of legitimate expectations, the most recent cases appear to wish to treat such 'tenderees' as subject only to the ordinary law.

As a matter of policy, it does not seem very satisfactory for public authorities to be subject to such different regimes. The expectations raised by their tendering processes may differ in degree, but they do not differ in kind. To this extent, the sentiments in *ex p Hibbit and Saunders*[118] favouring uniform treatment are to be welcomed. Is it, however, arguable that

---

[116] SI 1991 No 2679, r 26(b); SI 1991 No 2680 r 31(7); SI 1992 No 3279 r 30(6) Art 2(1)(c). For the UK provisions, see SI 1991 No 2679, r 26(2), (5)(b); SI 1991 No 2680, r 31(3), (6)(b); SI 1992 No 3279, r 30(1), (5)(b)(ii).

[117] *Chaplin v Hicks* [1911] 2 KB 786. See S Arrowsmith [1994] CLJ 104 and MG Bridge, Ch 17, below. In some systems a disappointed bidder may be able to claim to recover the profits of the successful bidder, to whom the contract was wrongly awarded: *Iconco v Jensen Construction Co* 622 F 2d 1291 (1980). In Israel, where the public law rules as to bids apply, it has been held that, where the contract should have been awarded to a disappointed bidder, he may be awarded expectation damages: *Electrical Company of Israel v Malibu Israel* 47(1) PD 667.

[118] [1993] COD 326; *The Times* 12 March 1993. See p 283 above.

the uniformity should be found elsewhere? What are the relative merits of the principles of legitimate expectation or estoppel on the one hand, and those of implied contract on the other?

The principle advantage of the implied contract is that, in principle, it will, mean that the expectations of the tenderer are protected and that damages will be awarded if the implied contract is breached. It is submitted that, broadly speaking, the tenderer's expectations are that a bid conforming to the requirements will be considered according to the specified criteria, and that the tenderer will accordingly have a chance of being awarded the contract. The arguments against the implied contract are as follows. First, as has been mentioned, it is said to be artificial to imply a contract since there is no 'bargain'. Secondly, it may be inflexible—or would be but for the fact that it is in fact fashioned *ex post* in the light of what the court thinks is reasonable. Thirdly, the measure of damages could be seen as overprotecting the tenderer insofar as it goes beyond compensating him for wasted expenditure incurred in reliance on the terms of the invitation to tender.

The advantages of estoppel and legitimate expectation lie in their flexibility. Action inconsistent with a legitimate expectation may be unfair, but is not necessarily so and the courts will not let an arrangement that has given rise to a legitimate expectation hinder the formation of policy, recognizing that administrative policies may change with changing circumstances.[119] Thus, for instance, the tenderee might chose to abandon the project which is the subject of the tendering process, or to seek fresh tenders.[120] Secondly, it has been said that it is not satisfactory to deal with pre-contractual situations by grafting another contract, a pre-contract contract, onto the negotiations and that it is preferable to deal with them with non-contractual concepts such as *culpa in contrahendo*. English law has not yet fully overcome the inhibitions on estoppel operating in this way in a pre-contractual situation. But the public law principles can and have so operated: they provide an alternative non-contractual technique.

The public law principles also provide yet another indication (if one is needed) that the inhibitions on estoppel as a sword are misplaced. If a significant part of contracting activity is conducted on the basis that the expectations created by the procedures adopted will be protected, it is arguable that, wherever such or similar procedures are used, in the absence of an express disclaimer, similar protection should be accorded. The principle of legitimate expectation is, after all, not fundamentally different from the estoppel principle (it grew out of the public law equivalent of estoppel). It is arguable that there is scope for it to be used to protect the reasonable expectations of bidders; expectations concerning,

---

[119] *Chitty on Contracts* (27th ed 1994) s 10-033.
[120] *R v Walsall MBC, ex p Yapp, The Times* 6 August 1993.

for instance, adherence to the conditions for participation and the criteria for choice. On the other hand, neither the public law principles nor estoppel as it is used in this country can provide monetary compensation, which is, as indicated by the European Community model, likely to be the most satisfactory remedy. English law has not (yet) recognized a compensatory remedy in respect of unlawful administrative action.[121]

Conclusion

Contract law, as opposed to the content of particular contracts or classes of contracts, has not been influenced either by public law principles or by the rules of statutory regulatory regimes. The unwillingness of English courts to use the statutory and regulatory material as analogues, in the way that they use common law material, can be explained by the fact that they operate in a parliamentary democracy in which Parliament is sovereign. In the case of statutory regulatory regimes, it is also explained by the feeling that the particular regime is either based on policy rather than principle, or that, if based on principle, it is not a principle that can sit comfortably with common law principle. Generally, judges and lawyers have assumed that common law and statute law are simply like oil and water, and do not mix. It is the absence of a theoretical explanation of how common law and statute law fit together that has made it difficult to challenge the traditional approach of the courts in any systematic way.

The traditional position has also been able to rely on the centrality of the notion that English private law does not recognize a concept of 'abuse of rights'. Thus, the same factors that prevent the overt recognition of duties of good faith in bargaining and in performing a contract also marginalize those contractual contexts in which ideas similar to those reflected in the public law principles have been recognized. This chapter has sought to argue that this marginalization has not been to the benefit of the law. In a number of situations, a limited concept of 'abuse of rights' has, in effect, been recognized in contractual contexts. These include situations in which formal pre-contractual tendering processes are used, or where power is given to one contracting party in circumstances in which he is to hold the balance between a number of competing interests, ie in some sense the power is administrative, or where the activity is a co-operative one, or which depends upon him being satisfied upon a point which involves investigating a matter which the other ought fairly to be heard. The question is, whether the ideas deployed in these cases will be influential in other contractual contexts.

---

[121] *R v Knowsley MBC, ex p Maguire* (1992) 90 LGR 653 (taxi licencing case).

(c) Relational and long-term contracts

11

Relational Contracts*

MELVIN A EISENBERG**

Over the last 25 years, a great deal has been written about relational contracts. Much of the literature is devoted to explaining, on economic and
sociological grounds, why parties might want to enter into contracts with
relational elements. Although many of these explanations are insightful
and illuminating, the literature has failed to show that there is a set of
legal rules that should be applied to some contracts (relational) but not
others (nonrelational). I will explain in this paper why such a showing
cannot be made.

I

I begin with the fact that it is impossible to locate, in the relational-
contract literature, a definition that adequately distinguishes relational
and nonrelational contracts in a legally operational way—that is, in a way
that carves out a set of special well-specified contracts for treatment under
special well-specified rules.

One approach to the problem of definition has been to define relational
contracts as those contracts that are not 'discrete'. This approach, of course,
requires a definition of discrete contracts. Vic Goldberg has defined a discrete contract as a contract 'in which no duties exist between the parties
prior to the contract formation and in which the duties of the parties are
determined at the formation stage'.[1] The first part of this definition fails to
distinguish relational and nonrelational contracts, because it describes all
contracts. Whether a contract is discrete or relational, no duties under the
contract can have preceded its formation. A duty may arise, prior to the formation of a contract, to negotiate the terms of a contract in good faith. That

* Copyright © 1994, Melvin A Eisenberg.
** I thank Jack Beatson, Dan Friedmann, and Ewan McKendrick for their extremely helpful comments.
[1] V Goldberg, 'Towards An Expanded Economic Theory of Contract' (1976) 10 J Econ
Issues 45, 49. I interpret this definition to mean that no *contractual* duties exist prior to contract formation. As Macneil has pointed out, in discussing this definition, if no duties of *any
kind* exist between the parties prior to a contractual exchange, 'then theft by the stronger
party is more likely to occur than is exchange'. IR Macneil, 'Economic Analysis of
Contractual Relations: Its Shortfalls and the Need for a "Rich Classificatory Apparatus" '
(1981) 75 Northwestern UL Rev 1018, 1020.

duty, however, arises as a result of a preliminary commitment, or on the basis of preliminary actions taken by one or both parties, not under the terms of the final contract.

The second part of the definition is also defective, because in the overwhelming majority of contracts all duties are determined at the formation stage. It is true that some contracts include provisions that allow or require certain duties under the contract to be determined after the contract is made. For example, a contract may provide that the exact specifications of a term are to be determined by one of the parties, or that adjustments in the contract may be ordered by a third party (like an architect), or that the parties will agree on some future term (like the rent under an option to renew). However, the presence or absence of such provisions does not serve to distinguish relational and nonrelational contracts. For example, a two-year employment contract, or a five-year partnership agreement, will be relational even though it does not contain such a provision.

Another approach to the problem of definition has been advanced by Ian Macneil. Macneil's approach is aptly summarized by Ewan McKendrick:

Macneil has identified a number of ingredients of a discrete transaction which, he argues, are not present in the case of a relational contract. These are: (1) a clearly defined beginning, duration and termination; (2) clear and precise definition of the subject-matter of the transaction, its quantity and the price; (3) the substance of the exchange is planned at the moment of formation of the contract; (4) the benefits and burdens of the contract are clearly assigned at the moment of formation; (5) there is little emphasis upon interdependence, future co-operation and solidarity between the parties; (6) the personal relationship created by the contract is extremely limited; and (7) the contract is created by a single exercise of bilateral power.[2]

Macneil's approach, however, is also unsatisfactory, because it is both overinclusive and underinclusive. On the one hand, a 25-year partnership agreement would surely be relational even though it has a defined beginning, duration, and termination, contains a clear and precise definition of the business to be engaged in and of the partners' rights, duties, and financial shares, and is created by a single exercise of bilateral power. On the other hand, a contract between strangers to buy and sell 100 bushels of wheat, with delivery on 1 February at Fargo, North Dakota at the then-market price, would surely be discrete, even though there is no precise definition of the price and the benefits and burdens of the contract remains to be determined. And what of a contract under which a consumer agrees with Macy's to buy a suit for $400, delivery in two days? Would the contract be discrete, because it has a clearly defined beginning, duration, and termination, and a precise definition of subject-matter,

---

[2] McKendrick, ch 12, below.

quantity, and price, or would it be relational, because the consumer deals with a salesman and a tailor he knows and trusts, may come back for further alterations, and may expect a rebate if the suit goes on sale within a short time?

It might be argued against such a criticism that Macneil's approach is intended as a multifactorial checklist that is suggestive, rather than definitive.[3] On this reading, a contract might have discrete aspects and yet be relational, or might have relational aspects and yet be discrete. A suggestive checklist approach is certainly acceptable if we view relational contracts only from a sociological and economic perspective. From a legal perspective, however, such an approach would be wholly inadequate, because it could not be operationalized. Since, under such an approach, many contracts would have both relational and discrete elements, there would often be no way to know whether general contract law rules or special relational contract law rules should be applied to any given contract.

What would be imperative for operational legal rules to govern relational contracts, therefore, is a definition that centred on one or more variables that meaningfully distinguished relational and discrete contracts, and did so in a way that justified the application of special legal rules to relational contracts, as so defined. One possible variable of this kind is duration. In particular, the phrase *long-term contracts* has become virtually a synonym for relational contracts. As Goetz and Scott have pointed out, 'Although a certain ambiguity has always existed, there has been a tendency to equate the term "relational contract" with long-term contractual involvement'.[4] (Indeed, when the convenors of the conference that generated the papers collected in this book listed, among possible topics, 'Long-Term Contracts', it was pretty clear that they had the problem of relational contracts in mind.) But, as Goetz and Scott have also pointed out, this variable won't do the job—'temporal extension per se is not the defining characteristic' of relational contracts.[5] For example, a long-term fixed-rent lease in which the tenant is responsible for maintenance, insurance, and taxes may involve little if any relationship between landlord and tenant. Similarly, a long-term lease of capital equipment, like aircraft, may require almost no contact between the parties, so long as periodic payments are made. In contrast, a four-week contract to remodel a room may

---

[3] Macneil himself, in answering a comparable criticism in Williamson, 'Transaction-Cost Economics: The Governance of Contractual Relations' (1981) 22 JL & Econ 233, 236, makes a somewhat different response. See IR Macneil, 'Economic Analysis of Contractual Relations: Its Shortfalls and the Need for a "Rich Classificatory Apparatus" ' 75 Northwestern UL Rev, pp 1018, 1025 note 26: 'A "rich classificatory apparatus" of *some* kind is essential if contractual relations are to be both understood and subjected to successful, realistic, and reasonably consistent analysis.'

[4] CJ Goetz and RE Scott, 'Principles of Relational Contracts' (1981) 67 Va L Rev 1089, 1091.

[5] *Ibid.*, 1091.

be highly relational, as may be a one-day contract between a photographer and a portrait sitter.

Although long duration is not a defining characteristic of relational contracts, it might be treated as an independent variable in contract law, so that there would be special rules for all long-term contracts, whether or not relational. For example, John Stuart Mill, who argued that 'laisser faire ... should be the general practice' and 'that every departure from it, unless required by some great good, is a certain evil',[6] nevertheless concluded that:

[An] exception to the doctrine that individuals are the best judges of their own interest, is when an individual attempts to decide irrevocably now what will be best for his interest at some future and distant time. The presumption in favour of individual judgment is only legitimate, where the judgment is grounded on actual, and especially on present, personal experience; not where it is formed antecedently to experience, and not suffered to be reversed even after experience has condemned it. When persons have bound themselves by a contract, not simply to do some one thing, but to continue doing something ... for a prolonged period, without any power of revoking the engagement ... [any] presumption which can be grounded on their having voluntarily entered into the contract ... is commonly next to null.[7]

Alternatively, long duration may accentuate the problems that can arise in the context of certain kinds of contracts.[8] But long duration does not of itself make a contract relational, and short duration does not of itself make a contract discrete.

Goetz and Scott, having properly rejected duration as a test for whether a contract is relational, propose yet another definition: 'A contract is relational to the extent that the parties are incapable of reducing important terms of the arrangement to well-defined obligations.'[8] This definition, however, is also inadequate. Take, for example, a very common kind of case, in which a landlord leases space to a commercial tenant for a period of years, and gives the tenant an option to renew at a rental to be agreed upon.[9] Here the parties lacked the capability of reducing a critical term to a well-defined obligation. However, if every other element in the lease is well defined, and is defined in such a manner that the interaction between landlord and tenant will be minimal (if, for example, there are no common areas, and the tenant bears all the costs of taxes, insurance, and maintenance), why should the necessity to negotiate on the rent some years down the road in and of itself mean that the contract is subject to a special set of legal rules?

---

[6] JS Mill, *Principles of Political Economy* 950 (W Ashley ed 1961).

[7] Ibid., 959–60.

[8] CJ Goetz and RE Scott, 'Principles of Relational Contracts' (1981) Va L Rev 1089, 1091.

[9] See, eg, *Joseph Martin, Jr Delicatessen, Inc v Schumacher*, 52 NY 2d 105; 436 NYS 2d 247, 417 NE 2d 541 (1981).

More generally, the fact is that parties to a contract are *never* capable of reducing all important terms of their arrangement to well-defined obligations. This point was pungently made more than 100 years ago by Lieber:

Let us take an instance of the simplest kind, to show in what degree we are continually obliged to resort to interpretation. By and by we shall find that the same rules which common sense teaches every one to use, in order to understand his neighbor in the most trivial intercourse, are necessary likewise, although not sufficient, for the interpretation of documents or texts of the highest importance, constitutions as well as treaties between the greatest nations.

Suppose a housekeeper says to a domestic: 'fetch some soupmeat', accompanying the act with giving some money to the latter; he will be unable to execute the order without interpretation, however easy and, consequently, rapid the performance of the process may be. Common sense and good faith tell the domestic, that the housekeeper's meaning was this: 1. He should go immediately, or as soon as his other occupations are finished; or, if he be directed to do so in the evening, that he should go the next day at the *usual* hour; 2. that the money handed him by the housekeeper is intended to pay for the meat thus ordered, and not as a present to him; 3. that he should buy such meat and of such parts of the animal, as, to his knowledge, has commonly been used in the house he stays at, for making soups; 4. that he buy the best meat he can obtain, for a fair price; 5. that he go to that butcher who usually provides the family, with whom the domestic resides, with meat, or to some convenient stall, and not to any unnecessarily distant place; 6. that he return the rest of the money; 7. that he bring home the meat in good faith, neither adding any thing disagreeable not injurious; 8. that he fetch the meat for the use of the family and not for himself. Suppose, on the other hand, the housekeeper, afraid of being misunderstood, had mentioned these eight specifications, she would not have obtained her object, if it were to exclude all *possibility* of misunderstanding. For, the various specifications would have required new ones. Where would be the end? We are constrained then, always, to leave a considerable part of our meaning to be found out by interpretation, which, in many cases must necessarily cause greater or less obscurity with regard to the exact meaning, which our words were intended to convey.[10]

It might be objected that Lieber's hypothetical would not fall within Goetz and Scott's definition because the unspecified terms in the hypothetical are not important. Whether an unspecified term is important, however, is basically a contextual and *ex post* question. As a practical matter, an unspecified term becomes legally important if, and only if, an issue that is not covered by the specified terms becomes salient and the parties can't agree how to deal with the issue. So, for example, if the domestic goes to a new butcher, or buys a new kind of soupmeat, and the housekeeper deems the domestic's action unacceptable, the relevant gap in the housekeeper's instructions will be very important.

---

[10] F Lieber, *Legal and Political Hermeneutics* (1880) pp 17–19 (3d ed) (emphasis in original).

What is especially striking about both the numerous efforts to define relational contracts, and the failure of all these efforts, is that the definition of relational contracts could not be more obvious. Begin with the term *contract*. Although that term is often defined to mean any legally enforceable promise, in everyday usage the term carries the more specific connotation of *bargain*. I will usage the term in that everyday sense. This usage is easily justified for present purposes, because the relational-contract literature concerns only bargain contracts and not, say, promissory estoppel or promises under seal.

Once we identify bargain as at the core of contract for this purpose, the meaning of the adjective *relational* is easy. A bargain is an exchange in which each party views his performance as the price of the other party's performance. Accordingly, every bargain contract necessarily involves an *exchange*. However, not every bargain contract necessarily involves a *relationship* between the contracting parties. Therefore, the obvious and straightforward definition of a *relational* contract is a contract that involves not merely an exchange, but also a relationship, between the contracting parties. (Correspondingly, the obvious and straightforward definition of a discrete contract is a contract that involves only an exchange, and not a relationship.) This definition can not only be operationalized, but reflects the everyday, common sense meaning of the term 'relational'. This definition also highlights a major shortcoming of competing definitions: any definition of a relational contract that fails to make critical whether the contract involves a relationship is bound to be incongruent with the ordinary meaning of the term it purports to define.

II

Because this definition of relational contracts is so obvious and straightforward, it raises the question, why has the literature on relational contracts sought other, non-straightforward definitions, none of which work, and all of which are doomed not to work, because they depart from the everyday meaning of the term they define? The answer lies at least partly in doctrinal history.

Relational theory, like much else in modern contract law, can only be fully understood against the background of classical contract law, to which it is a reaction. Classical contract law was based on certain implicit paradigm cases. The most central of these paradigms was that of a contract for a homogeneous commodity concluded between two strangers transacting on a perfect spot market. (In the parlance of relational-contract theory, this paradigm is a discrete contract—it is all exchange, and no relationship.) It is for this paradigmatic case, and often no other case, that many of the

principles of classical contract law—like the bargain theory of consideration, the objective theory of interpretation, and the rule that silence is not
acceptance—are well-suited.

That the rules of classical contract law were often suitable only for discrete contracts would have been sufficient to condemn classical contract
law even if most contracts were discrete. What made classical contract law
infinitely worse was that its tacit empirical premise was wholly incorrect.
It is discrete contracts that are unusual, not relational contracts. The great
bulk of contracts either create or reflect relationships. A contract to build
something as simple as a fence creates a relationship. A contract to sell
almost anything is likely to either create or reflect a relationship; even contracts on perfect spot markets are likely to be between traders or brokers
who have continuing relationships of some sort, not between strangers.
Many consumer contracts involve relationships, even when they are
made with huge bureaucratic organizations. Most shoppers at Macy's
have shopped there before, and expect to shop there again. Neither
Macy's nor the shopper perceives each individual exchange as an isolated, nonrelational transaction. A recent story in *The Wall Street Journal*
shows how far this relational aspect of consumer transactions has pro-
gressed:

[Merv Holtzman, a] salesman at NBO Stores, Inc., a discount menswear retailer,
asks his regular customers about their jobs, families and lifestyle. He keeps an eye
out for clothes to suit their tastes, coordinates outfits and puts aside possible selec-
tions.

'I shopped in the stores sporadically before but when I met Merv it got to be a
better marriage, so to speak,' says Michael E. Bello, a customer at Mr. Holtzman's
Paramus, N.J., store. 'Now if I go in and he's not there, I walk out.'

Once the speciality of expensive boutiques, such alternative service is being
adopted by large retailers and those for whom service was never much of an issue,
like supermarkets and bookstores. Using 'relationship marketing', these retailers
are carefully building ties to individual customers as a competitive weapon.

Dorothy Lane, a supermarket company in Dayton, Ohio, places thank-you calls
the same day to customers who spend more than $100 and pay by check. Macy's
spends time with soon-to-be college graduates helping them select an interview
suit or a wardrobe for their first job. Borders Bookstores hires avid readers as its
clerks and tests prospective employees on literature. The 44-store chain, owned by
Kmart Corp., also sends mailing on store events based on individual customers'
interests . . .

Last fall Neiman Marcus Group's flagship stores started tracking customers'
buying habits, preferences and special dates through its computer cash registers.
Sales associates can notify a client when new merchandise comes in or send a
reminder about buying a gift for a personal event, like an anniversary.[11]

---

[11] E Lisser, 'Retailers Are Trying Harder to Please Regular Customers', Wall St J, 5 May
1994, B1, col 3.

Once it is understood that most contracts are relational, it is easy to see why modern contract law has overthrown classical contract law, based, as the latter body of law was, on the mistaken premise that most contracts were discrete. The irony, however, is that relational contract theory has made the same empirical mistake as classical contract law. Classical contract law took the discrete contract as the paradigmatic case, and then made rules that failed to fit most contracts. Relational contract theory properly stresses that not all contracts fit the discrete-contract paradigm, but does not really reject the empirical premise of classical contract law, that relational contracts are unusual. Instead, relational theory tacitly accepts that premise, and then argues that these unusual contracts should be governed by special rules, rather than by the general rules of a properly formulated body of contract law.

Once relational contracts are properly defined, however, it is easy to see that they should not be governed by special rules. On the contrary, because most contracts are relational, the general principles of contract law—whatever those should be—must be catholic enough to govern relational contacts. Of course, it may be possible to identify one or more subcategories of contracts, including one or more subcategories of relational or discrete contracts, to which special rules should apply. The point is not that one rule must fit all. Rather, the general rules of contract law should fit relational contracts, because contracts that involve a relationship between the contracting parties, beyond the mere relationship of stranger-exchange, comprise the bread and butter of contracting.

What the general rules of contract law should be is too large a question to address in this chapter. I will therefore consider here only some of the rules proposed for relational contracts in the relational-contract literature. I must paint the literature here with a broad brush. For one thing, the literature does not speak with one voice. For another, it is not always easy to find operational rules in the literature. Partly this is because the literature is in large part addressed only to showing that relational contracts exist and explaining why contracting parties enter into them. A shortfall of operational rules is also a natural consequence of the lack of an operational definition.

Within these constraints, the rules that can fairly be said to be proposed in the relational-contract literature include the following: (1) Rules that would soften or reverse the bite of the rigid offer-and-acceptance format of classical contract law, and the corresponding intolerance of classical contract law for indefiniteness, agreements to agree, and agreements to negotiate in good faith, in the case of relational contracts. (2) Rules that would impose upon parties to a relational contract a broad obligation to perform good faith. (3) Rules that would broaden the kinds of changed circumstances (impossibility, impracticability, and frustration) that constitute an excuse for nonperformance of a relational contract. (4) Rules that would give content to particular kinds of contractual provisions that may be expressed or implied in relational contracts, such aᵉ a best-efforts clause or a unilateral right to terminate at will. (5) Rules that would treat relational contracts like partnerships, in the sense that such contracts involve a mutual enterprise and should be construed in that light. (6) Rules that would keep a relational deal together. (7) Rules that would impose upon parties to a relational contract a duty to bargain in good faith to make equitable price adjustments when changed circumstances occur, and would perhaps even impose upon the advantaged party a duty to accept an equitable adjustment proposed in good faith by the disadvantaged party. (8) Rules that would permit the courts to adapt or revise the terms of ongoing relational contracts, including price terms, based on changed circumstances in such a way that a loss that would otherwise fall on one party is shared, by reducing the other party's profits.[12]

The analysis in this chapter, that the general principles of contract law should be sufficiently catholic to cover (and indeed, should be based upon) relational contracts, suggests that the rules proposed in the relational-contract literature can be separated into two broad classes: those that are good for all or most contracts, and therefore should be principles of general contact law, and those that are not good for any contracts, relational or discrete. This is just the case.

For example, the relational-contract literature is correct in pointing to the deficiencies of classical contract law concerning a rigid offer-and-acceptance format and, more particularly, the intolerant treatment of such issues as indefiniteness, agreements to agree, and agreements to negotiate in good faith. If parties believe they have a deal, indefiniteness should rarely be a good defense. And if parties agree to agree, or to negotiate in good faith, that is a deal.[13] All this holds true, however, whether the contract is relational or discrete. Correspondingly, there should be a broad obligation to perform contracts in good faith, but this obligation also applies as fully to a one-day discrete contract as to a relational contract.

---

[12] See, eg, D Campbell and D Harris, 'Flexibility in Long-term Contractual Relationships; The Rule of Co-operation' 20 J Law & Soc 166 (1993); RA Hillman, 'Court Adjustment of Long-Term Contracts: An Analysis Under Modern Contract Law', 1987 Duke LJ 1; RA Hillman, 'Contract Excuse and Bankruptcy Discharge', 43 Stanf. L. Rev 99, 132–3 (1990); IR Macneil, 'Contracts: Adjustment of Long-Term Economic Relations Under Classical, Neoclassical, and Relational Contract Law', 72 Nw. L. Rev. 854 (1978); R E Speidel, 'Court-Imposed Adjustments Under Long-Term, Supply Contracts', 76 Nw. U. L. Rev. 369 (1981).

I want to underscore that I do not suggest that all of the relational-contract literature, or even more than one of the articles cited in this footnote, would support any given rule set out in the text. On the contrary, it's likely that at least some of the authors cited in this footnote would disagree with at least some of those rules. Indeed, that's one of the difficulties in locating rules in the literature. Nevertheless, I think that the rules set out in the text are fairly representative of what the literature as a whole either says or implies.

[13] See N Cohen, ch 2, above.

Similarly, whatever principles determine when changed circumstances should serve as an excuse should be equally applicable to all contracts. Indeed, some of the best-known cases in which impossibility, impracticability, or frustration were held to be excuses, like *Taylor* v *Caldwell*[14] and *Krell* v *Henry*,[15] involved contracts that were more discrete than relational. So too, rules that give content to terms like best-efforts or termination-at-will provisions should also apply to all contracts. (Of course, by their nature most provisions of this sort appear in contracts that involve a performance more extensive than a single simultaneous exchange, but the underlying principles used to determine the rules that give content to such provisions should not differ from the underlying principles used to determine the rules that give content to any other kinds of express or implied terms.) Finally, the conception that contracts are mutual enterprises, and can be analogized to partnerships, is also sound, but is also applicable to all contracts.[16]

On the other hand, the concepts that parties have an obligation to negotiate in good faith to make equitable price adjustments when circumstances change, and that the courts can revise the terms of ongoing contracts, including even price terms, seem highly questionable for any contracts. There are a variety of ways to contract for the possibility of price adjustments—for example, the use of hardship or equitable-adjustment provisions, as discussed by Ewan McKendrick.[17] In the case of long-term contracts, where such adjustments would be most plausible, normally both parties will be sophisticated and well advised, and will have the capacity to make use of such a provision if they chose to do so. The omission of such a provision therefore should normally be viewed as a deliberate decision. A corollary of this position, of course, is that the courts should liberally enforce such provisions when they are utilised.

Similarly, although the rules of contract law should impose damage remedies that prevent one party from opportunistically using an insubstantial breach by the other party, or the like, as an excuse for breaking a *deal*, the concept that legal rules can keep a *relationship* together is quixotic. Indeed, where contracts govern a thick, intensive relationship that involves personal elements, and covers a high proportion of the parties' lives, such as contracts to govern the ongoing conduct of a marriage, partnership contracts, close corporation contracts, and employment contracts in small-scale enterprises, the law should be more concerned with making rules that allow the parties to get out on fair terms than with making rules that keep the parties together. A great body of theoretical and empirical

[14] (1863) 3 Best & 5, 826.
[15] [1903] 2 KB 740.
[16] See, eg, Harrison, 'A Case for Loss Sharing' (1983) 56 So Cal L Rev 573.
[17] E McKendrick, ch 12, below.

work in cognitive psychology within the last 30 or 40 years has shown that the classical economic model, under which actors who make decisions in the face of uncertainty rationally maximize their subjective expected utility, with all future benefits and costs discounted to present value, often lacks explanatory power.[18] To begin with, the action that would maximize a substantive actor's utility may not even be considered, because actors limit their search for and their deliberation on alternatives.[19] Furthermore, actors are unrealistically optimistic as a systematic matter.[20] Moreover, actors systematically utilize heuristics that are irrational or pathological in the sense that they yield systematic errors. For example, actors make decisions on the basis of data that is readily available to their memory, rather than on the basis of all the relevant data; in particular, actors systematically give undue weight to instantiated evidence as compared to general statements, to vivid evidence as compared to pallid evidence, and to concrete evidence as compared to abstract evidence.[21] Similarly, actors are systematically insensitive to sample size, and erroneously take small samples as representative samples. In particular, the sample consisting of present events is often wrongly taken to be representative—and therefore predictive—of future events.[22] Actors also have faulty telescopic faculties; that is, they systematically give too little weight to future benefits and costs as compared to present benefits and costs.[23] Finally, actors underestimate most risks.[24]

These cognitive defects bear with special force on contracts to govern thick, intensive relationships. By virtue of the nature of such a relationship, it will be almost impossible to predict, at the time such a contract is made, the contingencies that may affect the relationship's future course. Furthermore, at the time such a contract is made each party is likely to be unduly optimistic about the likelihood of the relationship's long-term success, and about the willingness of the other party to avoid opportunistic behaviour or unfair manipulation of the relevant contractual rules during the course of the relationship. Finally, the parties to such a contract are likely to give undue weight to the state of their relationship as of the time the contract is made, which is vivid, concrete, and instantiated; erro-

[18] See T Ulen, 'Cognitive Imperfections and the Economic Analysis of Law' (1989) 12 Hamline L Rev 385.

[19] See H Simon, 'Relational Decisionmaking in Business Organizations' (1979) 69 Am Econ Rev 493.

[20] See N. Weinstein, 'Undue Optimism About Future Life Events' (1980) 39 J Personality and Social Psychology 806.

[21] See RDawes, *Rational Choice in an Uncertain World* (1988) 92–4.

[22] See K Arrow, 'Risk Perception in Psychology and Economics' (1982) 20 J Econ Inquiry 1, 5.

[23] See M Feldstein, 'The Optimal Level of Social Security Benefits' (1985) 100 QJ Econ 303.

[24] See TJackson, *The Logic and Limits on Bankruptcy Law* (1986) 232–40. On these cognitive issues, see generally M Eisenberg, 'The Limits of Cognition and the Limits of Contract,' (1995) 47 Stan LR 211.

neously to take the state of their relationship at that point as representative of the relationship's future state; and to give too little thought to, and place too little weight on, the risk that the relationship will go bad. Long duration accentuates all these problems.

The solution to the problems presented by such contracts, which are the most relational of all contracts, is not to attempt to hold the relationship together, as the relational-contract literature suggests. The law can make rules that will prevent a party from getting away with breaking a deal by opportunistically exploiting the other party's minor breach by inducing the other party's breach, or the like, but it cannot make rules that will hold a personal relationship together, and should not do so, because rules that would do so would *invite* opportunistic exploitation. Rather, the solution to the problems presented by such contracts is to allow either party to dissolve the relationship on fair terms, even if the right to dissolve is not written into the contract.

The law already takes a number of half or full steps toward easy dissolution of contracts to govern thick, intensive relationships. For example, contracts to govern the ongoing conduct of a marriage are unenforceable,[25] and under modern no-fault divorce statutes, marriage itself is freely dissoluble. Under US law, employment contracts that do not state a duration are interpreted to be at will rather than for a reasonable time.[26] Under English law, such contracts with manual workers are, in the absence of custom, terminable on reasonable notice—typically one day or one week.[27] A partnership that is not for a stated term or for the completion of specific enterprise is deemed to be at will and can be dissolved at any time by any partner,[28] and even a partnership that is for a term can be dissolved at any time by any partner.[29]

A similar rule has been advocated for close corporations by Hetherington and Dooley, on essentially cognitional grounds:

The emphasis on contractual arrangements reveals a fundamental misunderstanding of the nature of close corporations. Whether the parties adopt special contractual arrangements is much less important than their ability to sustain a close, harmonious relationship over time. The continuance of such a relationship is crucial because it reflects what is perhaps the fundamental assumption made by those who decide to invest in a close corporation: they expect that during the life of the firm the shareholders will be in substantial agreement as to its operation.

Time and human nature may cause a divergence of interests and a breakdown in consensus, however . . .

---

[25] See *Miller* v *Miller* 78 Iowa 177, 35 NW 464, 42 NW 641 (1887); *Balfour* v *Balfour* [1919] 2 KB 571.

[26] See, eg, C Summers, 'Individual Protection Against Unfair Dismissal: Time for a Statute' (1976) 62 Va L Rev 481, 484–5.

[27] See Freedland, *The Contract of Employment* (1976) pp 142–54.

[28] See Uniform Partnership Act, s 31(1).   [29] *Ibid.*, s 31(2).

Our thesis is that the problem of exploitation is uniquely related to liquidity and, for that reason, it is resistant to solution by *ex ante* contractual arrangements or by *ex post* judicial relief for breach of fiduciary duty. Accordingly, we propose that the law should require the majority to repurchase the minority's interest at the request of the latter and subject to appropriate safeguards.[30]

Although corporation law has not yet moved as far as Hetherington and Dooley advocate, the general trend of US law is to make mandatory buy-outs of minority share-holders in close corporations markedly easier, and to dilute a requirement of fault as a condition to granting such relief.[31] English law has exhibited a comparable trend. Section 210 of the Companies Act 1948, which gave remedies to minority shareholders on a showing of 'oppression', has given way to s 459 of the Companies Act 1985, which effectively provides a buyout right to a minority shareholder on a showing that 'the company's affairs have been conducted in a manner which is unfairly prejudicial' to the shareholder's interests.[32] As Prentice has pointed out, the 'focal point of the court's inquiry in determining whether conduct has been unfairly prejudicial is its impact and not its nature',[33] and application of the test should and probably does depend on the shareholder's expectations.[34]

Conclusion

The literature on relational contracts has brought home a fundamental weakness of classical contract law, that is, the flawed nature of its implicit empirical premise that most contracts are discrete. The literature has also been illuminating in its economics and its sociology. Legally, it has excelled in the treatment of specific types of contracts, like franchise agreements; specific types of express or implied terms, like best-efforts provisions; and specific types of relationships, like those in which one party must make a transaction- or relation-specific investment.

What the literature has not done, and cannot do, is to create a special law of relational contracts. To begin with, although different types of economic relationships present different kinds of economic problems to potential contract partners, these problems do not derive from the fact that the contracts are relational, but from the specific attributes of the proposed relationship. An aspect of this point has been aptly made by Cento Veljanovski:

[30] J Hetherington and M Dooley, 'Illiquidity and Exploitation: A Proposed Statutory Solution to the Remaining Close Corporation Problem' (1977) 63 Va L Rev 1, 2–3, 6.
[31] See, eg, *In re Judicial Dissolution of Kemp & Bradley, Inc* (1984) 64 NY 2d 63, 484 NYS 799, 473 NE 2d 1173.
[32] See generally D Prentice, 'The Theory of the Firm: Minority Shareholder Oppression: Sections 459–61 of the Companies Act 1985' (1988) 8 Ox JLS 55.
[33] *Ibid.*, 78.   [34] *Ibid.*, 73–5.

[W]ithin long-term contracts, there are problems of designing control devices to ensure each party acts in the interests of the relationship. But such problems are more prevalent in certain types of contracts, eg franchising and construction contracts, than in others. A focus on such principal-agent problems of ensuring that the agent acts to maximize the profit of both parties would produce a different classification from that offered by the distinction between discrete and relational contracts . . .[35]

Correspondingly, although various types of relational contracts present various kinds of legal problems, these problems derive not from the fact that the contracts are relational, but from more specific attributes. Long-term contracts, contracts involving transaction- or relation-specific investments, contracts to govern thick, intensive relationships, and all other subcategories of relational contracts may each present problems that stem from their distinguishing features. Some of these problems, like the question what constitutes performance in good faith, can be resolved by the application, in each context, of properly formulated general principles of contract law. Other problems, like the desirability of making thick, intensive contractual relationships easy to dissolve on fair terms, may require a special rule that applies to that distinguishing feature. No special legal rules, however, can be formulated for relational contracts as a class. Rather, the general principles of contract law can and should be formulated to be responsive to relational as well as discrete contracts. By and large, that is just the position to which modern contract law has been moving.

---

[35] Veljanovski's remarks are reported in Appendix to Bell, 'The Effect of Changes in Circumstances on Long-Term Contracts' in DR Harris and D Tallon (eds), *Contract Law Today: Anglo-French Comparisons* (1991) pp 195, 219–20.

12

The Regulation of Long-term Contracts* in English Law

Ewan McKendrick

A glance at the leading textbooks on English contract law would suggest that English law makes no special provision for long-term contracts.[1] Such contracts appear to be subject to the same rules as those which pertain to other contracts. But is this initial appearance correct? If it is not, what special provision is made for long-term contracts? If it is, should English law make particular provision for long-term contracts? What is so special about these contracts that could demand the formulation of new rules or the adaptation of existing rules to fit their needs?

In this chapter I shall suggest that it is largely for the parties to such long-term contracts to insert into their contracts clauses which deal with the particular problems encountered by those who enter into long-term contracts. The only demand which this places upon the courts is the traditional one, namely to enforce and give effect to the intention of the parties as expressed in the clauses in which their obligations are contained. In particular, long-term contracts must often be phrased in broad, flexible terms to enable the parties to adjust their bargain to meet changing circumstances. Recognition of this fact on the part of the courts should lead them to adopt a more flexible approach to the interpretation of such clauses, and suggests that they should not be too astute to declare such contracts unenforceable on the ground of uncertainty or vagueness.

What is a long-term contract?

There is no legal definition of a long-term contract: it is a 'sociological, not a legal, category'.[2] Yet in discussing long-term contracts it is important to attempt to provide a definition of the type of contract with which we are

---

* Copyright © 1994, Ewan McKendrick.

[1] An exception is provided by HG Beale, WD Bishop and MP Furmston, *Contract Cases and Materials* (2nd ed 1990) which includes a chapter on the subject of the adjustment of long-term contracts (ch 28).

[2] J Bell, 'The Effect of Changes in Circumstances on long-term Contracts' in D Harris and D Tallon (eds), *Contract Law Today: Anglo-French Comparisons* (1989) p 195.

concerned. There are two problems here. The first relates to the definition of 'a contract' and the second to the definition of 'long-term'.

It is obviously beyond the scope of this chapter to provide a precise definition of a contract. Broadly speaking, a contract may be said to consist of 'an agreement giving rise to obligations which are enforced or recognised by law'.[3] But contracts come in different shapes and sizes and Professor Atiyah has argued that 'we must try to extricate ourselves from the tendency to see contract as a monolithic phenomenon.'[4] Many contracts are now the subject of distinct regulation and, as a result of this fragmentation, we seem to be moving in the direction of the recognition of a law of contracts rather than a law of contract and the so-called 'general principles' of the law of contract 'remain general only by default, only because they are being superseded by detailed ad hoc rules lacking any principle, or by new principles of narrow scope and application.'[5] This point is important to the present discussion because, to take one example, the contract of employment appears to be an example of a long-term, relational contract but it is now the subject of separate legislative regulation which, although built upon common law concepts, has developed its own particular jurisprudence.[6] But contracts of employment are increasingly the preserve of the labour lawyer, not the contract lawyer. Should we therefore include them within the scope of the present discussion? The question is not an insignificant one because the issue is not confined to contracts of employment. Contracts between landlords and tenants and between providers of credit and consumers are also the subject of distinct regulation, reflecting the particular needs of these types of contract. If these contracts are to be excluded from consideration then the problem of long-term contracts becomes 'in many ways a residual area of the law'.[7] Yet it is important to know why these contracts are the subject of distinct regulation. Is it because they are examples of long-term contracts or is it for some other reason, such as the inequality of relationship between the parties to the contract? Although these contracts will not form the central focus of this chapter, they will not be entirely ignored because they may shed some light on the reasons why the law may accord special treatment to certain types of long-term, relational contracts.

The second problem relates to the meaning of 'long-term'. How long is 'long'? Are we simply concerned with the duration of the contract or are

[3] GH Treitel, *The Law of Contract* (8th ed 1991) p 1.

[4] PS Atiyah, 'The Modern Role of Contract Law' in his *Essays on Contract* (1986) p 8.

[5] PS Atiyah, 'Contracts, Promises, and the Law of Obligations' in his *Essays on Contract* (1986) p 19.

[6] In countries where collective agreements are legally enforceable, they too can provide examples of long-term relational contracts.

[7] J Bell, 'The Effect of Changes in Circumstances on Long-Term Contracts' in D Harris and D Tallon (eds), *Contract Law Today: Anglo-French Comparisons* (1989) p 197.

there other issues at stake? The duration of the contract does seem to be a relevant factor: the longer the period of time for which a contract is intended to subsist, the more difficult it is to allocate the risks of future events at the moment of entry into the contract. But acceptance of the proposition that duration of *the contract* is the conclusive factor would result in a series of individual contracts falling outside the definition of 'long-term' contracts.[8] Take the following example. A farmer regularly supplies a major supermarket chain with vegetables. There is no continuing contract between the parties. But there is a tacit understanding that the supermarket will purchase its produce from the farmer while the quality remains of a certain standard. The farmer begins to rely on the supermarket chain as a secure outlet for his goods. In legal form this is simply a series of individual contracts with no ongoing relationship between the parties. Yet the reality is otherwise because, for practical purposes, there may be little difference between a series of individual contracts and a single contract which is stipulated to last for a considerable period of time.

If a series of individual contracts is to be drawn within the category of 'long-term contracts', then it suggests that the duration of *the contract* is not the definitive characteristic of a 'long-term contract'. Rather, it is the nature and duration of *the relationship* between the parties which is the definitive feature. If this is correct then the focus of our inquiry should be on what has been termed 'relational contracts' and not simply contracts which last for a long period of time. While contracts of long duration are more likely to be relational than contracts of short duration, 'temporal extension per se is not the defining characteristic'[9] of a relational contract. But, although the phrase 'relational contract' is regularly used in the literature, its meaning is not at all easy to elucidate.

What is a relational contract?

One of the reasons why it is so difficult to define a relational contract is that many of the writers who employ the term seem to define it negatively, that is to say, they commence their analysis with the classical discrete, commercial, executory contract and then state that the relational

---

[8] A proposition which was accepted by T Daintith, 'The Design and Performance of Long-Term Contracts' in T Daintith and G Teubner (eds), *Contract and Organization: Legal Analysis in the Light of Economic and Social Theory* (1986) 164, 175 where a duration of five years was accepted, on the basis of industry practice, as the minimum period which justified calling the contract 'long-term'.

[9] CJ Goetz and RE Scott, 'Principles of Relational Contracts' (1981) 67 Va LR 1089, 1091.

contract departs from that model in a number of respects.[10] There are a number of respects in which it is argued that the relational contract departs from the classical model.

DISCRETE

The first is that the classical model of contract is 'discrete', whereas the relational contract is not. The exact meaning of 'discrete' is not, however, entirely clear. A dictionary definition is 'individually distinct' or 'separate' but it has been used in the literature in a fuller, more sophisticated sense.[11] Thus, Goldberg has defined a discrete transaction as one 'in which no duties exist between the parties prior to the contract formation and in which the duties of the parties are determined at the formation stage'.[12] This is, however, to overstate the case because it cannot seriously be maintained that 'no duties' exist between the parties prior to the formation of the contract for, as Macneil has pointed out, if this was the case then 'theft by the stronger party is more likely to occur than is exchange'.[13] The claim that contracts are discrete is the more modest one that a contract is a self-contained code which sets out the rights and obligations of the parties thereto.

Macneil has identified a number of ingredients of a discrete transaction which, he argues, are not present in the case of a relational contract. These are:

(1) a clearly defined beginning, duration and termination;
(2) clear and precise definition of the subject-matter of the transaction, its quantity and the price;

---

[10] See, for example, IR Macneil, 'Contracts: Adjustments of Long-Term Economic Relations Under Classical, Neoclassical, and Relational Contract Law' (1978) 72 Northwestern Univ L Rev 854; IR Macneil, 'Economic Analysis of Contractual Relations: Its Shortfalls and the Need for a "Rich Classificatory Apparatus" ' (1981) 75 Northwestern Univ L Rev 1018; CJ Goetz and RE Scott, 'Principles of Relational Contracts' (1981) 67 Vir LR 1089; and D Campbell and D Harris, 'Flexibility in Long-term Contractual Relationships: The Role of Co-operation' (1993) 20 J Law & Soc 166. But contrast the approach adopted by MA Eisenberg, ch 11 above, where the word 'relational' is used in its everyday sense to mean that there is a 'relationship' between the parties which is more than a simple exchange. This approach provides a sharper, more satisfactory definition of the topic and leads us on to a clearer identification of the issues which are at stake.

[11] See, for example, IR Macneil, 'The Many Futures of Contracts' (1974) 47 S Cal L Rev 691, 738–40 and IR Macneil, 'Economic Analysis of Contractual Relations: Its Shortfalls and the Need for a "Rich Classificatory Apparatus" ' (1981) 75 Northwestern Univ L Rev 1018, 1025–39.

[12] V Goldberg, 'Toward an Expanded Economic Theory of Contract' (1976) 10 J Econ Issues 45.

[13] IR Macneil, 'Economic Analysis of Contractual Relations: Its Shortfalls and the Need for a "Rich Classificatory Apparatus" ' (1981) 75 Northwestern Univ L Rev 1018, 1020. For further criticism of this definition, see MA Eisenberg, ch 11, above.

(3) the substance of the exchange is planned at the moment of formation of the contract;

(4) the benefits and burdens of the contract are clearly assigned at the moment of formation;

(5) there is little emphasis upon interdependence, future co-operation and solidarity between the parties;

(6) the personal relationship created by the contract is extremely limited; and

(7) the contract is created by a single exercise of bilateral power.

PRESENTIATION

The second point at which it is alleged that relational contracts depart from the traditional model of contracts is that it is argued that the classical contract is an 'economic allocative mechanism' and that its goal is 'presentiation, the goal of making a present decision about all—including future—aspects of a contractual relationship'.[14] Thus Goetz and Scott have defined a contract as being relational 'to the extent that the parties are incapable of reducing important terms of the arrangement to well-defined obligations'.[15] Thus, the definitive feature of a relational contract appears to be, not only that all the terms are not sharply defined by the parties at the outset, but that *it is not possible* to do so at the moment of entry into the contract.[16]

THE MARGINAL ROLE OF CONTRACT LAW IN THE GOVERNANCE OF CONTRACTUAL RELATIONS

The third point at which it is alleged the relational contract departs from the classical model is that the professed aim of classical contract law, and the remedies which it provides, is to protect the expectation interest which is engendered by a binding promise to perform.[17] In a relational contract, on the other hand, it is suggested that legal remedies play a secondary role in disputes which arise between the parties and that other non-legal factors, such as the need to maintain business relationships, play a critical role in the resolution of disputes between the parties or in

[14] D Campbell and D Harris, 'Flexibility in Long-term Contractual Relationships: The Role of Co-operation' (1993) 20 J Law & Soc 166, 169 and see generally IR Macneil, 'Restatement (Second) of Contracts and Presentiation' (1974) 60 Va L Rev 589.

[15] CJ Goetz and RE Scott, 'Principles of Relational Contracts' (1981) 67 Virg LR 1089, 1091; criticised by MA Eisenberg, p 294, above.

[16] Contrast GG Triantis, 'Contractual Allocations of Unknown Risks: A Critique of the Doctrine of Commercial Impracticability' (1992) 42 UTLJ 450 who takes issue with the proposition that contracting parties are unable to allocate risks that they cannot foresee.

[17] Classically expressed by Parke B in *Robinson v Harman* (1848) 1 Ex 850, at 855; 154 ER 363, at 365.

the means of allocating the risk of some unforeseen event, such as a collapse in the market or currency fluctuations.[18]

CO-OPERATION

The fourth argument which has been put forward is that a long-term contract is 'an anology to a partnership' and must be 'understood as consciously co-operative'.[19] Long-term contracts, it is argued, differ from other contracts in the extent of the commitment which one party must make to the other; they invest so heavily in the relationship that they are effectively locked in to each other. This is in contrast to the traditional 'arm's length bargaining' which takes place in non-relational contracts where the aim of the parties is to maximise their own wealth.

Why treat relational contracts differently?

Given these alleged differences between relational contracts and the classical model of contract, do they demand the creation of a separate body of rules to govern relational contracts? A number of points of distinction may be said to arise.

THE NEED FOR FLEXIBILITY

The first is the need for flexibility, which is suggested by the first two points of distinction. A relational contract may have no clearly defined beginning or duration and the specifications relating to the subject-matter of the contract, its quantity and price may be phrased in rather vague terms. At the moment of entry into the contract, the parties are unlikely to be able to foresee all of the events which may impinge upon performance of the contract. The world is constantly changing and the commercial world must change with it, or ahead of it, in order to anticipate needs. Technology becomes obsolescent at a frightening rate. Prices can fluctuate wildly, as can exchange rates. Natural disasters can occur, as can man-made disasters, such as the intervention of government. In such a turbulent world, the ability to adapt and to adjust is vital. Contracting parties who anticipate that their relationship will endure for a long period of time are therefore likely to have to phrase their contractual obligations in

---

[18] For an example of this process see T Daintith, 'The Design and Performance of Long-Term Contracts' in T Daintith and G Teubner (eds), *Contract and Organization: Legal Analysis in the Light of Economic and Social Theory* (1986) 164, 182–5.

[19] D Campbell and D Harris, 'Flexibility in Long-term Contractual Relationships: The Role of Co-operation' (1993) 20 J Law & Soc 166, 167.

rather vague, aspirational terms to enable them to deal with future, as yet unidentified problems. This suggests that the courts should not be too ready to strike down a long-term contract which is expressed in rather vague terms.

THE NEED TO ADJUST THE TERMS OF THE BARGAIN

The second and, in many ways, related point is that the parties may wish to adjust their relationship as time goes on to take account of unforeseen factors which disrupt the performance of the contract. But it is important to note that this does not necessarily demand that the courts develop a power to adjust contracts to meet new, unforeseen contingencies. If the parties can make provision for such adjustments in the contract itself, or provide a framework within which these adjustments can be made, then it demands no more of the courts than the point which has already been made, namely that the courts should not be too astute to strike out such clauses on the ground of the vagueness of their expression. At first sight, the proposition that the parties can make provision for unforeseen contingencies appears to be open to attack on the ground that, by definition, contracting parties cannot make provision for unforeseen events when drafting their contract.[20] But this is not so. Force majeure and hardship clauses[21] regularly make provision for the consequences of various catastrophic events which may make performance of the contract more onerous. It is true that, very often, the precise event which has disrupted the contract cannot be foreseen, but the risk of disruption can be allocated at a broader level of generality.[22] For example, the precise cause of an abnormal increase in price may not be foreseen (hyperinflation, labour shortages, scarcity of supplies, exchange rate fluctuations, outbreak of war etc) but the risk of any abnormal increase in price may be allocated by the terms of the contract. The task which is then left to the court is an interpretative one, namely to ascertain whether the events which have occurred fall within the definition of an 'abnormal increase in price'. So it is only where, for some reason, the parties are unable to make these adjustments themselves, or have failed to make such provision, that an argument can be made out that it is necessary for the courts to develop a power of adjustment.

---

[20] *Davis Contractors Ltd v Fareham UDC* [1956] AC 696, at 728, per Lord Radcliffe.
[21] Discussed in more detail at pp 323–9 below.
[22] See generally GG Triantis, 'Contractual Allocations of Unknown Risks: A Critique of the Doctrine of Commercial Impracticability' (1992) 42 UTLJ 450.

THE MARGINAL ROLE OF CONTRACT LAW

The third point of distinction, concerning the marginal role of contract law in the governance of contractual relations, is difficult to assess for a number of reasons. The first is that resort to non-legal sanctions or consideration of non-legal factors, such as the need to maintain a business relationship with the other contracting party, may not be confined to long-term contracts, although it may be more prevalent in that context.[23] The second is that it is not at all clear what this conclusion tells us about the role of the law of contract. The fact that the rules are not the decisive factor in the resolution of disputes surely does not require us to abandon or modify our rules of contract law so that the rules mimic the bargaining which takes place in the 'real world'? A contracting party may drive a hard bargain but decide, at the end of the day, not to enforce it for non-legal reasons. That is the choice of that party and it should be respected. But it is an altogether different proposition to say that the law should positively intervene to prevent such a party from enforcing its strict legal rights because many parties in similar situations would reach an acceptable compromise and refrain from enforcing their legal rights. The fact that, in practice, a contracting party chooses not to insist upon her full contractual entitlement, does not mean that the law should actively debar her from insisting upon that entitlement should she so choose.

Important points can, however, be gleaned from a study of contract law in action. A realization of the limited impact which the rules have in practice gives us a fuller picture of the actual operation of the law of contract and underlines the specialist nature of the inquiry which is undertaken by contract lawyers. But it does not render that inquiry valueless: rather it becomes a study of more limited application than lawyers might initially suppose. A further point which emerges from a number of empirical studies and an analysis of the clauses which contracting parties habitually insert into their contracts is that contracting parties may prefer to keep the contract alive, albeit under different terms, rather than witness its termination. In the light of this finding, it can be argued that English law places too much emphasis upon termination as a remedy, at the expense of alternative, more flexible remedies such as the suspension of the contract or the provision of a right to cure defective performance.[24]

One final point which may be made when discussing the marginal role of contract law in the governance of contractual relations is that, for a vari-

---

[23] See generally H Beale and T Dugdale, 'Contracts between Businessmen: Planning and the Use of Contractual Remedies' (1975) 2 Brit J Law & Soc 45; S Macaulay, 'Non-Contractual Relations in Business: A Preliminary Study' (1963) 28 Am Soc Rev 55; S Macaulay, 'An Empirical View of Contract' 1985 Wisc L Rev 465.

[24] However it does not follow that the rules of contract law should mimic the clauses which contracting parties insert into their contracts: see below.

ety of reasons, the parties to the contract may not provide for a number of contingencies when drawing up their contract. The expense of drawing up a detailed contract, the trust developed between the parties over a number of years, or an unduly optimistic outlook on future events may result in the parties drawing up a contract which does not contain the usual battery of price escalation, force majeure and hardship clauses. In such a case, what is to be done when a foreseeable, but unprovided for event occurs which renders contractual performance more onerous for one of the parties?

According to orthodox law, such a party may find it difficult to invoke the doctrine of frustration because, where the event in question was foreseeable, but was not provided for in the contract, the contract will not generally be frustrated.[25] This proposition rests, to a large extent, on the assumption that a failure to provide for the event implies that the promisor intended to assume the risk of that contingency occurring. This assumption has been criticized on the ground that it 'ignores the commercial reality that contracting businessmen normally do not consider or provide for the full range of possible impediments to performance'.[26] There is an element of truth in this argument, but such truth as exists is not confined to long-term contracts: it can apply with equal force to short-term contracts. A court may be called upon to fill in gaps in short-term contracts as well as long-term contracts. The rules as to implied terms, the parol evidence rule and the rules relating to frustration and foreseeability should be the same, regardless of whether the contract is long- or short-term. The argument that difficulties in predicting future events and the lack of formality which sometimes attends long-term contracts should result in the courts being given a special power to adjust long-term contracts[27] must be firmly rejected. Of course, there can be no objection to an express term in the contract making provision for adjustment, or an implied term to that effect, provided that the term passes the stringent tests required for the implication of a term into a contract.[28] But the courts

---

[25] *Paal Wilson & Co A/S v Partenreederei Hannah Blumenthal* [1983] 1 AC 854, at 909. Cf. *WJ Tatem Ltd v Gamboa* [1939] 1 KB 132 and *Ocean Tramp Tankers Corpn v V/O Sovfracht (The Eugenia)* [1964] 2 QB 226, at 239. Much of the debate would appear to hinge upon the degree of foreseeability which is required to exclude the doctrine of frustration: see GH Treitel, *The Law of Contract* (8th ed 1991) pp 800–2 and CG Hall, 'Frustration and the question of foresight' (1984) 4 LS 300.

[26] Comment, 'Contractual Flexibility in a Volatile Economy: Saving UCC Section 2–615 from the Common Law' (1978) 72 Northwestern Univ L Rev 1032, 1040. See more generally EA Farnsworth, 'Disputes over Omission in Contracts' (1968) 68 Colum L Rev 860 and RA Hillman, 'Court Adjustment of Long-Term Contracts: An Analysis Under Modern Contract Law' 1987 Duke LJ 1, 4–6, 12–13.

[27] Such an argument is put forward by RA Hillman, *ibid*.

[28] On which see *Liverpool City Council v Irwin* [1977] AC 239; *Hughes v Greenwich London BC* [1994] 1 AC 170. It can of course be argued that English law should adopt a more liberal approach to the implication of terms into a contract but such an argument cannot be confined in its scope to long-term contracts.

should not have a broad power to imply such a term simply because it would, according to the court, produce a 'fairer' outcome. Nor should the courts embrace 'the fairness principle that the parties should agree to share unallocated losses'.[29] The courts do not have the expertise to engage in contract adjustment on a wide scale. Nor, in the absence of a frustrating event or a recognized ground for setting aside a contract on the ground of unfairness or unconscionability,[30] do they have any justification for re-writing the contract simply because it has turned out to be an onerous one. Finally, contracting parties should be encouraged to plan and to take the obligations which they assume seriously. Contracting parties who wish to reserve to themselves the ability to adjust the contract can insert an express term into the contract to that effect: otherwise they should be bound by the deal which they have struck (in the absence of a consensual adjustment of that bargain). To give to contracting parties the ability to cry 'unfair' and to run off to court in search of an 'equitable adjustment' is objectionable because it places insufficient weight upon the bargain initially struck by the parties, it is productive of uncertainty and it places the party seeking to uphold the bargain in a difficult position because, were the courts to be given such a discretionary power, she could never be sure what the outcome of the case would be.[31] In consequence, such a party would feel pressurized into accepting a compromise and so to give away the rights which she has carefully negotiated. It is not the function of the law of contract to compel parties to give up the rights which they have negotiated. Rather, it should uphold and give effect to these rights and this can best be done by rejecting any attempt to give to the courts a broad power to adjust long-term contracts in the name of 'fairness'.

THE ROLE OF CO-OPERATION

The final point of distinction, relating to the co-operative relationship engendered by a relational contract, can be pushed too far. Co-operation in the face of change should not be considered in isolation from the need

---

[29] RA Hillman, 'Court Adjustment of Long-Term Contracts: An Analysis Under Modern Contract Law' 1987 Duke LJ 1, 3.

[30] English law has traditionally been very reluctant to embrace a general principle entitling the court to set aside a contract on the ground of unfairness or unconscionability: see *National Westminster Bank Plc* v *Morgan* [1985] AC 686. The courts retain various residual powers to set aside a contract on fairness-related grounds but have refused to elevate these individual examples into a general principle (see the judgment of Lord Scarman in *Morgan, ibid.*, 707–9). This restrictive attitude is, of course, a contestable one but the point which must be made here is that any such criticism must be made on general grounds and cannot be confined in its application to long-term contracts.

[31] See generally the excellent article by JP Dawson, 'Judicial Revision of Frustrated Contracts: the United States' (1984) 64 BUL Rev 1. Some of the difficulties which can arise when courts are given a broad power of adjustment are chronicled by Dawson in the companion article 'Judicial Revision of Frustrated Contracts: Germany' (1983) 63 BUL Rev 1039.

to ensure a degree of stability and control at the moment of formation of the contract; risks must be allocated between the parties and the ability to shift that risk must be limited, if not eliminated. While a contracting party may choose, for extra-legal reasons, to co-operate with the other contracting party and to adjust the bargain on the occurrence of some unexpected event, this is not the same thing as saying that that party should be compelled to forego her legal rights in the interest of 'co-operation' and the preservation of a harmonious relationship. But, where the parties choose to express themselves in co-operative language, as where they accept a duty to re-negotiate the contract in good faith on the occurrence of an event which causes exceptional hardship to one of the contracting parties, then it suggests that such a clause serves a useful purpose from the perspective of the parties which should, if possible, be enforced by the courts.

Yet, should the courts go further and recognize the existence of a 'legal duty to bargain in good faith', which duty can override the express terms of the contract? One author has gone so far as to argue that a party to a long-term supply contract, who is advantaged by a change in circumstances which upsets the initial balance struck by the parties, should 'have a legal duty to accept an "equitable" adjustment proposed in good faith by the disadvantaged party'.[32] The justifications proffered for the existence of such a duty are 'the judgment that the advantaged party should share through compromise the unbargained for gains and losses caused by unanticipated change'[33] and the view that 'when unanticipated change imperils the long-term supply contract, the advantaged party should make every reasonable effort to preserve and adjust the relationship and to harmonize conflict'.[34] It is difficult to accept the reliance which is here placed upon notions of 'good faith' to support the existence of such a bargaining duty. The fundamental difficulty which is produced lies in seeing how a party can be in bad faith on the ground that she has refused to give up the rights which she enjoys under the contract. Of course, where the disadvantage which has been produced by the unforeseen event is extreme, then the contract may be held to be frustrated and, in such a case, the court will be called upon to identify the rights of the parties following upon the discharge of the contract. But the situation is altogether different where the contract remains on foot, but one party is alleged to be in bad faith because she has refused to give up her contractual right to demand that the contract be performed according to its original terms. As the court remarked in *Louisiana Power & Light Co* v *Allegheny Ludlum Industries Inc*,[35] the proposition that a contracting party 'was in bad faith for failure to do

---

[32] RE Speidel, 'Court-Imposed Price Adjustments Under Long-Term Supply Contracts' (1981) 76 Northwestern Univ L Rev 369, 404–5.

[33] *Ibid.*, 405. [34] *Ibid.* [35] 517 F Supp 1319 (1981).

what it had no obligation to do cannot withstand scrutiny'.[36] A duty to bargain in good faith, which demands that co-operation take the form of a requirement that the advantaged party accept an equitable adjustment proposed in all good faith by the disadvantaged party, must therefore be rejected.

THE CASE FOR RECOGNITION

The case for the recognition of a formal category of relational contracts does not seem to be particularly strong. It would give rise to considerable problems of demarcation. The definition of a category of relational contracts would be no easy task and, arguably, would cause more problems than it would solve. On the other hand, although no formal category of relational contracts should be recognized, some points of distinction do arise and these should be recognized by the courts. The first is the need for flexibility and the second is the need to adjust the contract to meet changed circumstances. We shall now consider these issues in more detail.

The need for flexibility

We have already noted that long-term contracts may have to be expressed in rather vague terms because of the difficulty in predicting how future events will impact upon contractual performance. There is some evidence that contracting parties today express their contracts in increasingly broad terms, having discovered from experience that long-term contracts in the 1960s and early 1970s were drafted too rigidly.[37]

Many examples can be found of contracts which are drafted in broad terms, leaving room to adjust the scope and the terms of the contract to meet unexpected or uncertain events. For example, unexpected increases in prices can be covered by price escalation clauses, under which the contract price can be raised in line with an index, such as the Retail Prices Index or some other objective benchmark. Price escalation clauses of considerable sophistication can be found in many construction contracts.[38]

---

[36] 517 F Supp 1319, at 1330 (1981).

[37] See T Daintith, 'The Design and Performance of Long-Term Contracts' in T Daintith and G Teubner (eds), *Contract and Organization: Legal Analysis in the Light of Economic and Social Theory* (1986) pp 164, 177–8 and 185.

[38] See, for example, the Contract Price Fluctuations Clause prepared by the Institution of Civil Engineers, the Association of Consulting Engineers and the Federation of Civil Engineering Contractors, in consultation with the Government, in its revised form for use in appropriate cases as a Special Condition of the Conditions of Contract for use in connection with Works of Civil Engineering Construction (6th ed) dated January 1991.

Standards of work can be regulated by professional bodies, or third parties can be relied upon to determine the appropriate standards of performance. Variations to the original contractual specifications can be determined and policed by third parties. A good example in the latter category is provided by clause 51 of the Institute of Civil Engineers Conditions of Contract[39] which provides:

(1) The Engineer
   (a) shall order any variation to any part of the Works that may in his opinion be necessary for the completion of the Works and
   (b) may order any variation that for any other reason shall in his opinion be desirable for the completion and/or improved functioning of the Works.
   Such variations may include additions omissions substitutions alterations changes in quality form character kind position dimension level or line and changes in any specified sequence method or timing of construction required by the Contract and may be ordered during the Defects Correction Period.

A clause permitting variation of the work is an essential ingredient of any construction contract to ensure that the contractor is obliged to carry out such additional work and, in turn, to entitle the contractor to be paid for that work under the terms of the contract. These provisions are invariably complex. Limits, of varying degrees, must be placed upon the ability of the engineer or other third party to order variations. Provision must be made for the procedure to be followed when ordering a variation, for the valuation of any variations so ordered and for the payment for such variations.

The only legal obstacle which lies in the path of the enforcement of such a clause is the requirement that the parties express their contract with a minimum level of certainty because otherwise, in the words of Viscount Maugham, 'consensus ad idem would be a matter of mere conjecture'.[40] The parties can, in fact, preserve a considerable degree of flexibility in their contracting and not fall foul of the uncertainty rule because the courts are generally reluctant to 'incur the reproach of being the destroyer of bargains'.[41]

A good example of the approach which a modern court is likely to adopt is provided by the case of *Queensland Electricity Generating Board* v *New Hope Collieries Pty Ltd*.[42] The parties entered into a contract under which New Hope Collieries agreed to supply the Board with coal for a period of fifteen years. For the first five-year period of the contract, provision was made for a scale of base prices and the contract contained

---

[39] Sixth Edition.   [40] *Scammell and Nephew Ltd* v *Ouston* [1941] AC 251, at 255.
[41] *Hillas & Co Ltd* v *Arcos Ltd* (1932) 147 LT 503, at 512, per Lord Tomlin.
[42] [1989] 1 Lloyd's Rep 205.

elaborate escalation or price variation clauses for adjusting the base prices for changes in New Hope's costs. Although provision was made for the general terms of the contract to continue beyond the initial five-year period, clause 2.5 of the agreement stated that '[t]he base price and provisions for variations in prices for changes in costs for purchases after 31 December 1982 shall be agreed by the parties prior thereto in accordance with clause 8'. The agreement also contained a comprehensive arbitration clause. One of the issues which arose before the Privy Council was whether or not the contract was unenforceable after the first five years because no price had been agreed for the supply of coal. The Privy Council rejected this argument. What is important is not simply the conclusion that the contract was enforceable, but the robust manner in which the conclusion was expressed. Sir Robin Cooke, delivering the judgment of the Privy Council, stated:

in cases where the parties have agreed on an arbitration or valuation clause in wide enough terms, the Courts accord full weight to their manifest intention to create continuing legal relations. Arguments invoking alleged uncertainty, or alleged inadequacy in the machinery available to the Courts for making contractual rights effective, exert minimal attraction ... their Lordships have no doubt that here, by the agreement, the parties undertook implied primary obligations to make reasonable endeavours to agree on the terms of supply beyond the initial five-year period and, failing agreement and upon proper notice, to do everything reasonably necessary to procure the appointment of an arbitrator. Further, it is implicit in a commercial agreement of this kind that the terms of the new price structure are to be fair and reasonable as between the parties. That is the criterion or standard by which the arbitrator is to be guided.[43]

This approach suggests that considerable latitude will be given to contracting parties when drafting their contracts. Further evidence of such latitude can be found in the following passage from the judgment of the New South Wales Supreme Court in *Banque Brussels Lambert SA* v *Australian National Industries Ltd*:

[t]he whole thrust of the law today is to attempt to give proper effect to commercial transactions. It is for this reason that uncertainty, a concept so much loved by lawyers, has fallen into disfavour as a tool for striking down commercial bargains.[44]

But there are limits to the benevolence of the courts, as can be seem by reference to the case of *May & Butcher Ltd* v *The King*.[45] The parties entered

---

[43] [1989] 1 Lloyd's Rep 210.
[44] (1989) 21 NSWLR 502, at 523C. However, it should be noted that *Banque Brussels* involved the construction of a letter of comfort in which the New South Wales Supreme Court refused to follow the approach which had been taken by the English Court of Appeal in *Kleinwort Benson Ltd* v *Malaysia Mining Corpn Berhad* [1989] 1 WLR 379. So it cannot be assumed that this liberal approach would find favour in an English court.
[45] [1934] 2 KB 17.

into a written agreement under which the British government agreed to sell tentage to the plaintiff and the agreement provided that the price and date of payment 'shall be agreed upon from time to time'. It was held that, the parties not having reached agreement on these matters, no contract had been concluded. According to Lord Buckmaster, 'an agreement between two parties to enter into an agreement in which some critical part of the contract matter is left undetermined is no contract at all'.[46] The limits of this case must, however, be made clear. The parties need not agree on all points; but what they must do is provide criteria by which an incomplete matter can be resolved[47] or provide for machinery, such as arbitration,[48] to resolve any dispute between the parties.[49] A failure to do so may result in the contract being held to be unenforceable. But, provided the contract is drafted with sufficient care, the obstacle erected by *May & Butcher* should not be too difficult to overcome.

A rather more significant obstacle was, however, placed in the path of contracting parties by the decision of the House of Lords in the recent case of *Walford* v *Miles*.[50] The defendants were the owners of a company and they entered into negotiations with the plaintiffs for the sale of the company to the plaintiffs. On 17 March 1987 the parties entered into an agreement under which the plaintiffs promised to provide a comfort letter from their bank which confirmed that they had the financial resources to meet the purchase price of the company. In return, the defendants agreed to deal exclusively with the plaintiffs and to terminate any negotiations then current between the defendants and any other prospective purchasers of the company. The plaintiffs complied with their side of the 'bargain', but the defendants subsequently decided not to deal with the plaintiffs and agreed to sell the company to a third party on 30 March 1987. The plaintiffs' claim to recover damages in respect of the defendants' breach of the agreement of 17 March was dismissed on the ground that the agreement was unenforceable.

The agreement of 17 March was both a 'lock-in' agreement (in that it purported to oblige the defendants to negotiate exclusively with the plaintiffs) and a 'lock-out' agreement (in that it sought to prevent the defendants from continuing negotiations with third parties). The plain-

---

[46] *Ibid.*, 20. [47] As in *Hillas & Co Ltd* v *Arcos Ltd* (1932) 147 LT 503.

[48] See, for example, *F & G Sykes (Wessex) Ltd* v *Fine Fare Ltd* [1967] 1 Lloyd's Rep 53; *Vosper Thornycroft Ltd* v *Ministry of Defence* [1976] 1 Lloyd's Rep 58. Although arbitration clauses can be used to resolve uncertainties which the parties have left, it appears that it is not possible to leave it to the court or to the judge to resolve these uncertainties because of the well-worn maxim that the courts will not make the contract for the parties. The distinction thus drawn between an arbitrator and a judge appears to be a questionable one.

[49] As in *Sudbrook Trading Estate Ltd* v *Eggleton* [1983] 1 AC 444.

[50] [1992] 2 AC 128, on which see P Neill, 'A Key to Lock-Out Agreements?' (1992) 108 LQR 405 and N Cohen, ch 2 above. It has, however, been argued that the actual result in the case was correct: see *Chitty on Contracts* (27th ed 1994) s 2–097.

tiffs argued that, in order to give 'business efficacy' to the agreement of 17 March, the defendants were obliged to continue the negotiations in good faith, so that they were only entitled to terminate the negotiations if they had a 'proper reason', subjectively assessed, for doing so.

One difficulty which faced the plaintiffs was that in *Courtney & Fairbairn Ltd v Tolaini Brothers (Hotels) Ltd*[51] it was held that an agreement to negotiate was not an enforceable contract because, in the words of Lord Denning MR, 'it is too uncertain to have any binding force'.[52] The plaintiffs, placing reliance upon a line of United States authority in which it was held that an agreement to use best endeavours was enforceable, argued that *Courtney* was wrongly decided. The House of Lords rejected the argument and chose to affirm that an agreement to negotiate lacked certainty. Lord Ackner doubted whether a court could properly be expected to decide whether a contracting party subjectively had a good reason for terminating negotiations. He stated, perhaps rather more controversially, that a 'concept of a duty to carry on negotiations in good faith is inherently repugnant to the adversarial position of the parties when involved in negotiations . . .' and that '[e]ach party to the negotiations is entitled to pursue his (or her) own interest, so long as he avoids making misrepresentations'.[53] Thus either party was entitled to withdraw from the negotiations at any time and for any reason and the plaintiffs' claim was therefore held to be without foundation.

The decision and the reasoning of the House of Lords is regrettable for three reasons. The first is that their Lordships' refusal to countenance the existence of an undertaking to negotiate in good faith sits rather uneasily with the willingness of the Privy Council in *Queensland Electricity Generating Board v New Hope Collieries Pty Ltd*[54] to imply an obligation to use reasonable endeavours to agree on the terms of supply of coal after 5 years. The difference between an obligation to use reasonable endeavours and to negotiate in good faith is not at all clear.[55]

The second is that one effect of this decision is to make it difficult to draft an enforceable 'lock out' or 'lock in' agreement, despite the commercial purposes which are served by such clauses.[56] Lord Ackner did, however, concede that a lock-out agreement could, in certain circumstances, be enforceable, provided that the agreement was for a specified

---

[51] [1975] 1 WLR 297.　　　　　　　　　　　　　　　　　　　[52] *Ibid.*, 301H.

[53] [1992] 2 AC 128, 138E. Contrast the approach taken by the New South Wales Court of Appeal in *Coal Cliff Collieries Pty Ltd v Sijehama Pty Ltd* (1991) 24 NSWLR 1, at 25–6.

[54] [1989] 1 Lloyd's Rep 205, discussed in more detail at pp 317–18 above.

[55] Although it is suggested in *Chitty on Contracts* (27th ed 1994) s 2–098 that a 'possible distinction between them is that an agreement to use best endeavours could be interpreted as referring to the *machinery* of negotiation, while one to negotiate in good faith is more plausibly interpreted as referring to its *substance*'.

[56] See the forceful criticism levelled against the decision of the Court of Appeal by BJ Davenport, 'Lock-out Agreements' (1991) 107 LQR 366.

period of time and that the parties were not under any obligation to negotiate with each other in good faith for the period in which they were prohibited from conducting negotiations with third parties.[57]

The third point is that the rejection of a role for an obligation to negotiate in good faith may render a number of clauses in long-term contracts
unenforceable in English courts. The following example of a hardship
clause would now seem to be but a pious aspiration after *Walford* v *Miles*:

Both Buyer and Seller recognise a long-term relationship requires mutual collaboration and assistance should either Buyer or Seller suffer hardship or unfairness.
Both Buyer and Seller agree that they will make their best efforts to solve any
problem due to any such circumstances in the spirit of mutual understanding and
collaboration.[58]

It may still be possible to give effect to such a clause by drafting a third
party intervener clause,[59] where a third party is empowered to resolve the
problem should the parties themselves fail to reach an acceptable solution. But a bare clause of the type set out above would appear to be unenforceable.[60] Had the House of Lords in *Walford* been fully aware of the
need to preserve a degree of flexibility and co-operation in long-term contracts, they might have been rather more ready to embrace the concept of
an enforceable obligation to negotiate in good faith.

The adjustment of long-term contracts

A second problem which frequently arises in the case of long-term contracts is the need to adjust the contract in the light of changed circumstances. A contract which was concluded 50 years ago was drawn up in a
world very different from the world of today.[61] Fifty years ago Britain was
fighting World War II, modes of communication were very different than

---

[57] [1992] 2 AC 128, at 139. An example of a lock-out agreement which was held to be
enforceable is provided by *Pitt* v *PHH Asset Management Ltd* [1994] 1 WLR 327.

[58] Quoted by T Daintith, 'The Design and Performance of Long-Term Contracts' in
T Daintith and G Teubner (eds), *Contract and Organization: Legal Analysis in the Light of
Economic and Social Theory* (1986), pp 164, 182.

[59] See p 329 below for a fuller discussion of third-party intervener clauses.

[60] Although it could be argued that *Walford* does not apply where the obligation to negotiate in good faith relates to an issue which is not 'essential' to the agreement: see *Chitty on
Contracts* (27th ed 1994) s 2–098. The difficulty with this view relates to the problems
involved in distinguishing between essential and non-essential issues.

[61] An example of the changes which can occur over a 50-year period and the impact which
such changes can have on a contract is illustrated by *Staffordshire Area Health Authority* v
South Staffordshire Waterworks Co [1978] 1 WLR 1387. The case itself provides an interesting
example of a flexible approach to the implication of terms into a contract, in this case a term
entitling a party to terminate a long-term contract upon the giving of reasonable notice (see
also *Re Spenborough Urban District Council's Agreement* [1968] Ch 139, but contrast *Islwyn
Borough Council* v *Newport Borough Council*, *The Times* 28 June 1993).

they are today, technology has since advanced out of all recognition and the taste of consumers has changed radically. How can a contract be adjusted to meet such changed circumstances?

Before seeking to answer that question, one preliminary point must be made. It should not be assumed that adjustment is necessarily a good thing. There is a value in holding contracting parties to a bargain deliberately made and this is so in long-term as well as short-term contracts. As a general rule, 'specific planning in contractual relations governs in spite of changes in circumstances making such planning undesirable to one of the parties'.[62]

When considering the ways in which a contract can be adjusted to meet unforeseen circumstances, an important question which has to be answered is: who should do the adjusting? There are two possible answers to this question. The first is that it is the courts who could be entrusted with adapting the bargain to meet changed circumstances. The second is that the courts could leave it to the parties themselves to do the adjusting.

It is clear that, as far as English law is concerned, the courts are reluctant to adjust the bargain between the parties. The courts are in general unwilling to imply a term into a contract and a term will not be implied simply because it is reasonable to do so.[63] Nor can frustration lightly be invoked.[64] The narrowness of the doctrine of frustration has been criticized on the ground that it can lead to harsh results.[65] The remedial rigidity of frustration has also been criticized on the ground that its effect is automatically to bring the contract to an end: yet the parties will often want the contract to continue, albeit with the terms adjusted to reflect the new situation in which they find themselves.

But the narrowness of the doctrine of frustration does not act as a barrier to the parties themselves inserting into their contract a range of clauses which will enable them to adapt their contract to meet changing conditions. A wide range of devices is available to contracting parties to enable them to adjust or suspend the contract in the light of unforeseen events. The following examples can be given of clauses commonly encountered in commercial contracts which enable the parties to adjust the contract in the light of unforeseen circumstances.

---

[62] IR Macneil, 'Contracts: Adjustment of Long-Term Economic Relations Under Classical, Neoclassical, and Relational Contract Law' (1978) 72 Northwestern Univ L Rev 854, 873.

[63] *Liverpool City Council v Irwin* [1977] AC 239; *Hughes v Greenwich London BC* [1994] 1 AC 170.

[64] See, for example, *Davis Contractors Ltd v Fareham Urban District Council* [1956] AC 696.

[65] See, for example, McInnis, 'Frustration and Force Majeure in Building Contracts' in E McKendrick (ed), *Force Majeure and Frustration of Contract* (2nd ed 1995).

FORCE MAJEURE CLAUSES

Textbooks on English contract law devote a considerable amount of space to the doctrine of frustration but little, if any, to a discussion of force majeure clauses. This approach fails to reflect the experience of the vast majority of legal practitioners: for them a frustrated contract is a novelty rarely, if ever, encountered. Force majeure clauses are, on the other hand, an everyday occurrence. In defence of the textbooks, it could be argued that it is not their principal function to reflect the life of the average commercial practitioner. But the issue is of more fundamental significance than that. A focus on frustration to the exclusion of force majeure clauses leaves the impression that a contract which is governed by English law cannot be adapted to take account of unexpected events. Such contracts can be adapted and often are. But the source of the power of adjustment is not the common law but the terms of the contract itself.

That this is so can be illustrated by reference to the most important frustration case in recent years: the decision of the Court of Appeal in *J Lauritzen AS* v *Wijsmuller BV (The Super Servant Two)*.[66] The defendants agreed to transport the plaintiffs' oil rig using at their option either Super Servant One or Super Servant Two, both of which were self-propelling, semi-submersible barges especially designed for the transportation of rigs. Prior to the time for performance of the contract, the defendants made an internal decision, which they admitted was not irrevocable, to allocate Super Servant Two to the performance of the contract with the plaintiffs. Super Servant One was allocated to the performance of other concluded contracts. After the conclusion of the contract, but before the time fixed for performance, Super Servant Two sank while transporting another rig in the Zaire river. The plaintiffs' rig could not be transported by Super Servant One because of its allocation to the performance of other concluded contracts. So the parties entered into without prejudice negotiations and it was agreed that the defendants should transport the rig by another, more expensive, method. In these circumstances the plaintiffs sued to recover the losses which they had incurred as a result of this more expensive method of transportation, alleging that the defendants were in breach of contract in failing to transport the rig in the agreed manner. The defendants denied liability on two principal grounds.

The first was that the contract was frustrated by the sinking of Super Servant Two. This argument was rejected by the court on the ground that the cause of the defendants' failure to perform was not the sinking of Super Servant Two but their decision or choice not to use Super Servant One in the performance of the contract with the plaintiffs.[67] It can be

---

[66] [1990] 1 Lloyd's Rep 1.
[67] See also *Maritime National Fish Ltd* v *Ocean Trawlers Ltd* [1935] AC 524.

countered that the defendants had no *real* choice in the matter; had they allocated Super Servant One to the contract with the plaintiffs they would simply have found that they were unable to perform, and hence in breach of, another contract which they had concluded. The choice was a theoretical one only and the conclusion that the contract was not frustrated leaves a seller or supplier of goods in an impossible position, as far as the common law is concerned, where her source of supply partially fails for some unforeseen reason. A failure to perform any contract in full will constitute a breach of contract which cannot be 'excused' by resort to the doctrine of frustration. The case therefore provides a graphic illustration of the narrow confines within which frustration currently operates in English law.

The second ground on which the defendants denied liability was based on clause 17 of the contract, a force majeure clause which stated that:

Wijsmuller has the right to cancel its performance under this Contract whether the loading has been completed or not, in the event of force majeure, Acts of God, perils or danger and accidents of the sea, acts of war, warlike-operations, acts of public enemies, restraint of princes, rulers or people or seizure under legal process, quarantine restrictions, civil commotions, blockade, strikes, lockout, closure of the Suez or Panama Canal, congestion of harbours or any other circumstances whatsoever, causing extraordinary periods of delay and similar events and/or circumstances, abnormal increases in prices and wages, scarcity of fuel and similar events, which reasonably may impede, prevent or delay the performance of this contract.

The Court of Appeal held that clause 17 was effective to exonerate the defendants provided that Super Servant Two did not sink as a result of the negligence of the defendants or their employees. The province of the clause, as a matter of construction, was held to be confined to events which were beyond the control of the defendants and so could not encompass negligently inflicted damage caused by the failure of the defendants or their employees to exercise reasonable care and control.

There is some evidence, albeit slight, that the court was influenced in its decision on the frustration point by the knowledge that it was open to the parties to include in their contract a force majeure clause such as that contained in clause 17. Prior to the decision of the Court of Appeal in *The Super Servant Two* there was some English authority for the proposition that, in the event of a partial failure of supply, a seller who could not satisfy all her contractual obligations in full could seek to share the partial supply among her customers without being in breach of contract to those customers who did not receive the original contracted-for supply.[68] But in

[68] See, for example, *Intertradex SA* v *Lesieur-Tourteaux SARL* [1978] 2 Lloyd's Rep 509; *Bremer Handelsgesellschaft mbH* v *C Mackprang Jr* [1979] 1 Lloyd's Rep 221; *Continental Grain Export Corpn* v *STM Grain Ltd* [1979] 2 Lloyd's Rep 460; *Bremer Handelsgesellschaft mbH* v

The Super Servant Two these cases were held to be cases which turned upon the construction of force majeure clauses and were not illustrative of any common law power to prorate. Hobhouse J, the trial judge in *The Super Servant Two*, was most explicit on this point. He stated that if a promisor wished protection in the event of a partial failure of supplies 'he must bargain for the inclusion of a suitable force majeure clause in the contract'.[69] On this view, it is for the parties to protect themselves from the consequences of an improvident bargain by making appropriate provision in the contract: they cannot rely on the courts to act as their saviour.

It can be argued that this approach unnecessarily increases the transaction costs of the parties because, had the Court of Appeal concluded that the contract was frustrated, there would be no need to draw up these and other elaborate force majeure clauses. There is also some evidence that the scope of force majeure clauses is influenced by the narrow limits of the doctrine of frustration. For example, clause 17 listed closure of the Suez Canal and an abnormal increase in prices as force majeure events, both of which have been held not to constitute frustrating events.[70] Would it not reduce transaction costs to conclude that such events frustrate the contract and thereby save contracting parties the cost of drafting a suitable force majeure clause?

Although initially attractive, the argument is a difficult one to accept for a number of reasons. The first is that to give the doctrine of frustration a greater role would increase uncertainty which, in turn, would increase transaction costs. Until a significant body of case-law emerged, contracting parties could never be sure whether a court would conclude that performance had become sufficiently onerous to permit them to invoke the doctrine of frustration and, in such a situation, many contracting parties might seek to reduce that uncertainty by continuing to use their own force majeure clauses. A related point is that doubts have been expressed about the ability of the judiciary to play a more expansive role: they are not trained as businessmen and it is not at all clear that they have the competence to adapt and adjust complex commercial transactions.[71]

The second point is that it would take more than a widening of the scope of frustration to make it correspond with the apparent wishes of the parties. One limitation of the doctrine of frustration is that it brings the

---

Continental Grain Co [1983] 1 Lloyd's Rep 269 and, more generally, AH Hudson, 'Prorating in the English Law of Frustrated Contracts' (1968) 31 MLR 535.

[69] [1989] 1 Lloyd's Rep 148, at 158.

[70] See *Tsakiroglou & Co Ltd v Noblee Thorl GmbH* [1962] AC 93 (closure of the Suez Canal) and *Davis Contractors Ltd v Fareham UDC* [1956] AC 696 (abnormal increase in prices).

[71] See JP Dawson, 'Judicial Revision of Frustrated Contracts: the United States' (1984) 64 BUL Rev 1, 17–18, 36–7.

contract to an end 'forthwith, without more and automatically'.[72] The court cannot allow the contract to continue and to adjust its terms. Yet a glance at force majeure clauses suggests that immediate termination is not generally what the parties want. It is true that clause 17 in *The Super Servant Two* gave the defendants an option to terminate the contract on the occurrence of a force majeure event but many force majeure clauses make provision for an extension of time or the suspension of the contract for a period before resorting to the more drastic remedy of termination.[73]

The third point is that the diversity and sophistication of the various force majeure clauses which are currently in use underlines the complexity of the issues dealt with by these clauses and they are best resolved by the parties, not the courts. A force majeure clause can be expected to define the events which are to trigger the clause, make provision for the procedure to be followed upon the occurrence of such an event, stipulate the effect which the event is to have on the contract itself and, possibly, make provision for the adjudication of any disputes arising out of the application of the clause.[74] Although force majeure clauses deal with a number of common issues, they resolve these issues in many different ways. For example, the definition of what constitutes a force majeure event will differ between contracts. A buyer may insist that an unanticipated increase in prices be excluded from the list of force majeure events on the ground that it is a risk which must be borne by the seller; in other cases such an event may be included as a force majeure event. Some contracting parties will attempt to draw up a list of force majeure events followed by a general wrap up provision such as 'similar events, which reasonably may impede, prevent or delay the performance of this contract'. Other contracting parties have abandoned the attempt to list the force majeure events and rely simply on a general force majeure clause applying to events which are beyond the (reasonable) control of the parties. A wide variation also exists in relation to the obligation to report the occurrence of a force majeure event: the length of time which is given to report the occurrence of the event varies, usually between 7and 21 days. Sometimes the form of the notice is regulated (for example by 'telegram,

---

[72] *Hirji Mulji* v *Cheong Yue Steamship Co Ltd* [1926] AC 497, at 505; *Maritime National Fish Ltd* v *Ocean Trawlers Ltd* [1935] AC 524, at 527; *Joseph Constantine Steamship Line Ltd* v *Imperial Smelting Corpn Ltd* [1942] AC 154, at 163, 170, 171, 187, 200; *Denny, Mott & Dickson Ltd* v *James B Fraser & Co Ltd* [1944] AC 265, at 274.

[73] See, for example, clause 23 of the Grain and Feed Trade Association's standard form Contract for Bulk Shipment of Feeding Stuffs (GAFTA 97).

[74] See, more generally, M Furmston, 'Drafting of Force Majeure Clauses – Some General Guidelines' and A Berg 'The Detailed Drafting of a Force Majeure Clause' in E McKendrick (ed), *Force Majeure and Frustration of Contact* (2nd ed, 1995) and Yates, 'Drafting Force Majeure and Related Clauses' (1991) 3 JCL 186.

telex or teleprinter or by similar advice'), sometimes not. The form of the report may be mandatory or it may not.[75]

The consequences of the occurrence of a force majeure event also vary. In some cases one party is given an immediate option to terminate, but the more common consequence is that provision is made for the grant of an extension of time (the precise period of time being variable), or for the suspension of the contract for a period of time. In the latter case, consideration must be given to what is to happen if the force majeure event is still operative at the end of the period of suspension. In some cases provision is made for a further period of suspension, in others one party is given an option to terminate, while in others the contract is declared in such a case to be void. The diversity of force majeure clauses suggests that it is impossible to draft a 'boiler-plate' force majeure clause which will be suitable for all occasions and that it would be equally impossible for the courts to provide a simple all-encompassing solution to all these problems via a wider doctrine of frustration. No one solution can be effective for all cases, yet to give the courts a flexible, discretionary power to adapt the contract to meet the new situation would create an unacceptable level of uncertainty. Force majeure clauses provide a better vehicle for the resolution of these issues and, given the wide variety of force majeure clauses currently in existence, it should be possible for the parties to find or draft one which corresponds to their own particular needs.

HARDSHIP CLAUSES

Another clause which can be inserted into a contract to deal with unforeseen events which make performance of the contract more onerous than originally anticipated is a hardship clause.[76] An example of such a clause can be found in *Superior Overseas Development Corpn v British Gas Corpn*[77] in the following terms:

(a) If at any time or from time to time during the contract period there has been any substantial change in the economic circumstances relating to this Agreement and (notwithstanding the effect of the other relieving or adjusting provisions of this Agreement) either party feels that such change is causing it to suffer substantial economic hardship then parties shall (at the request of either of them) meet together to consider what (if any) adjustment[s] in the prices ... are justified in the circumstances in fairness to the parties to offset or alleviate the said hardship caused by such change.

---

[75] Clear words are required if the requirements are to be mandatory, see *Tersons Ltd v Stevenage Development Corpn* [1965] 1 QB 37.
[76] See generally CM Schmitthoff, 'Hardship and Intervener Clauses' [1980] JBL 82.
[77] [1982] 1 Lloyd's Rep 262, at 264–5.

(b) If the parties shall not within ninety (90) days after any such request have reached agreement on the adjustments (if any) in the said prices . . . the matter may forthwith be referred by either party for determination by experts . . .

(c) The experts shall determine what (if any) adjustments in the said prices or in the said price revision mechanism shall be made . . . and any revised prices or any change in the price revision mechanism so determined by such experts shall take effect six (6) months after the date on which the request for the review was first made.

Such a clause should define the circumstances in which 'hardship' exists and should then lay down a procedure to be adopted if any of those circumstances occur. Generally such a clause will create an obligation to use best endeavours to renegotiate the contract in good faith in an attempt to alleviate the hardship which has been caused by the unforeseen event, and it is here that the decision of the House of Lords in *Walford v Miles*[78] may have unfortunate consequences in rendering any obligation to renegotiate in good faith (but not an obligation to use best endeavours to reach agreement) unenforceable. Sanctions should be provided to deal with the possibility that the parties will be unable to or refuse to re-negotiate the contract. A common sanction, employed in the *Superior Overseas Development Corpn* case, is to provide for the intervention of a third party expert or arbitrator should the parties fail to reach agreement themselves.

The advantage of such a clause is that it is designed to enable the relationship between the parties to continue, albeit on different terms. Given that the courts at common law have no power to adjust the terms of a contract to meet changed circumstances,[79] this can be a useful clause to incorporate should the parties wish to make provision for the adjustment of the contract. Professor Schmitthoff has concluded from his brief study of hardship and intervener clauses that it

has revealed a serious defect in English commercial law: the inability of courts and arbitrators to adapt a contract to uncontemplated fundamental changes of economic, political or social nature, if the parties intend to abide by their contract and to implement it.[80]

But this is not necessarily so. The fact that the courts permit the parties to adjust the contract between themselves does not mean that the court should itself have the power to adapt the contract. As has been noted in the context of force majeure clauses,[81] there is nothing necessarily inconsistent in a court refusing to adjust the contract itself but enforcing party

---

[78] [1992] 2 AC 128, discussed in more detail at pp 319–21 above.
[79] *British Movietonews Ltd v London and District Cinemas Ltd* [1952] AC 166.
[80] CM Schmitthoff, 'Hardship and Intervener Clauses' [1980] JBL 82, 91.
[81] See pp 323–7 above.

agreed provisions which stipulate for such adjustment. Contracting parties and their lawyers then know where they stand. If they want to reserve a power of adjustment in the contract, then they must negotiate for it: otherwise they are bound by the terms of their contract in the absence of a frustrating event.

INTERVENER CLAUSES

A third type of clause which may be employed by the parties is a third-party intervener clause. The International Chamber of Commerce has drafted two model intervener clauses in the following terms:

In the event that the parties are unable to agree to apply all or any of the provisions of this article . . . of this contract [or any other appropriate wording chosen by the parties in the particular circumstances of the contract] . . . they shall apply to the Standing Committee for the Regulation of Contractual Relations of the International Chamber of Commerce (ICC) in order that a third person* who shall be appointed in accordance with the Rules on the Regulation of Contractual Relations of the ICC, and who shall carry out his mission in accordance with the said Rules—may issue a recommendation** or may on their behalf make a final decision which shall be binding on the parties and shall be deemed to be incorporated in the contract.** (* Should the parties wish to have the decision or recommendation made by a board of three persons instead of one person, they should make this clear in the clause. ** Only one of these alternatives can be adopted.)

Given the difficulty which parties to long-term contacts experience in terms of predicting the impact which future events will have on the obligations contained in the contract, an intervener clause can enable the parties to draft their obligations in broader terms, leaving it to the intervener clause to provide a means of resolving any disputes which arise in the future. Intervener clauses are regularly employed as a sanction in the event of a failure by the parties to reach agreement under a hardship clause.[82]

THE INFERENCE TO BE DRAWN FROM SUCH CLAUSES

The argument which has been put forward thus far is that there is less need to give the judiciary a broad power to adjust the contract once it is realized that the parties themselves can make provision in the contract itself for its adjustment. However, what is to happen where the parties make provision in the contract but, from the perspective of one of the parties, that provision proves to be inadequate in the light of the events which have actually occurred? The approach which has been suggested here is

---

[82] See pp 327–8 above.

that no special provision should be made for such an eventuality. The parties remain bound by the contract which they have concluded, unless the supervening event is of sufficient gravity to frustrate the contract.

But it is possible to take another view, according to which the presence of clauses, such as price escalation and force majeure clauses, is used to demonstrate that the parties intended to adjust the bargain should an unforeseen event disrupt contractual performance. The court is then justified in intervening, for example, to adjust the price escalation clause when, for some unforeseen reason, it proves to be inadequate. Such was the approach taken by Judge Teitelbaum in the infamous case of *Aluminum Company of America (Alcoa)* v *Essex Group Inc.*[83] Under the terms of their contract, Alcoa agreed to smelt specified quantities of alumina supplied to them by Essex and to re-deliver it to Essex as aluminium. Alcoa prepared their pricing formula with considerable care. Having closely examined the past reliability of certain indices, Alcoa included in their pricing formula three components whose prices were tied to three different indices. But the turmoil produced by the energy crises of the 1970s resulted in these indices failing to perform the task which Alcoa had believed they would do and left Alcoa contemplating a loss of US $60 million over the life-time of the contract. In these circumstances, Alcoa sought relief from the court in the form of, *inter alia*, an equitable adjustment of the contract. One obvious argument against the grant of such relief was that the contract was carefully drawn up by the parties and that this was a risk which Alcoa must bear. The parties had given careful consideration to the choice of indices and the court was not justified in intervening to impose upon the parties a pricing formula other than that agreed upon by them.

But Judge Teitelbaum did not perceive the indices in this light. He stated that, by the formula chosen, 'Alcoa sought a formula which would cover its out of pocket costs over the years and which would yield it a return of around four cents a pound'.[84] This seems an unlikely construction of the role of the indices: the inference which will usually be drawn from reliance upon an index is that the parties intended that that index and no other should govern the relationship between the parties. Otherwise, why go to the trouble of agreeing a particular formula? It is suggested that the construction adopted by Judge Teitelbaum, although a possible one, is, in fact, inherently improbable and is unlikely to be adopted in many other cases. After all, why should Essex intend so to guarantee the profits of Alcoa? Had the loss to Alcoa been of very small proportions, there would have been no question of protecting the return of Alcoa. So why should the size of the loss make any difference to the

---

[83] 499 F Supp 53 (1980).   [84] *Ibid.*, 63.

ability of Alcoa to recover their expected return? The arguments which have been given against a judicial power to adjust long-term contracts[85] must apply with equal force here. Judges are no more entitled to reformulate the price or the terms of a force majeure clause than they are to reformulate any other term of the contract. *Alcoa* also demonstrates the doubts which exist about the competence of the judiciary to engage in such adjustment. Thus, Professor Dawson has noted that a settlement was reached in *Alcoa* which was not based upon Judge Teitelbaum's adjustment and he concludes that judge-made adjustment can only be said to encourage the parties to settle their own disputes in the sense that 'when basic provisions are revised by a judge, who knows only what he can learn from presiding at a trial, the result will probably be so unacceptable to both parties that by their own agreement they will reject the dictated terms and reassert the right that they fortunately still retain, to recover control over their own affairs'.[86] The inference which should generally be assumed from the presence of force majeure, hardship and price escalation clauses is that the parties intended the particular clause and no other to govern their relationship.[87] Their presence does not and should not give the courts a power which they would not otherwise have to adjust the contract.

SUBSEQUENT PARTY ADJUSTMENT

Contracting parties who take legal advice should thus be able to adjust their bargain by the incorporation into the contract of a suitably drafted force majeure clause, hardship clause, third party intervener clause or by some similar device.[88] But what of contracting parties who do not have access to such advice? They are unlikely to be able to invoke frustration except in the most extreme of cases. They can, however, seek to re-negotiate the contract. In the past the doctrine of consideration has placed limits on the enforceability of re-negotiations by insisting that the new agreement be supported by fresh consideration but, since the decision of the Court of Appeal in *Williams* v *Roffey Bros & Nicholls (Contractors) Ltd*,[89] it is likely that the consideration hurdle will be easily overcome by pointing to a practical benefit which has been obtained as a result of the

---

[85] See p 322 *et seq.* above.

[86] JP Dawson, 'Judicial Revision of Frustrated Contracts: the United States' (1984) 64 BUL Rev 1, 28.

[87] For an example of this approach see *Eastern Air Lines Inc* v *Gulf Oil Corpn* 415 F Supp 429, at 439 (1975).

[88] Examples of related devices might include price escalation clauses, clauses which make provision for variation by a third party of the precise specifications of the subject-matter of the contract. See p 317 above.

[89] [1991] 1 QB 1, discussed in greater detail by M Chen-Wishart, ch 5 above.

re-negotiation. Duress has therefore become the major regulator of re-negotiations, so the principal remaining difficulty arises where the re-negotiations fail to bear fruit. In such a case the parties remain bound by the terms of their original contract, in the absence of a frustrating event. It can be argued that this is an unnecessarily harsh result but it is suggested that, to give the courts a general power of adjustment to cover the case where a party is not legally advised or is otherwise unaware of the need to insert protective clauses in the contract, would cause too much uncertainty and that the disadvantages which would accrue as a result of such a reform would outweigh its advantages.

The regulation of certain relational contracts

The argument that English law should not create a formal category of relational contracts appears to be undermined by the fact that certain long-term contracts, such as employment contracts and consumer credit contracts, are the subject of distinct legal regulation. Does this not suggest that there should be a broader category of relational contracts recognized in English law? It is suggested that it does not. Such contracts are the subject of distinct regulation because of the inequality of relationship between the parties and the inability of the weaker party to insert appropriate protective clauses in the contract. Where the parties can protect themselves, by the inclusion of force majeure clauses, hardship clauses etc, in the contract there is no justification for any further, distinct regulation of the contract. Conversely, in cases where the parties cannot bargain on a footing of equality, then Parliament may be justified in intervening to protect the weaker party to the transaction, but the justification for the intervention is the inequality of relationship, not the fact that the parties are party to a relational contract.

Conclusion

English law would not be justified in taking the step of recognizing the existence of a formal category of relational contracts. In the vast majority of cases parties can insert into their contracts provisions which will provide the flexibility necessary to enable them to adapt their contract to changing circumstances. There is, however, a need for the courts to recognize this need to preserve flexibility and to avoid being too astute in refusing to enforce contract terms which are drafted in vague, flexible terms. Against this background, the decision of the House of Lords in

Walford v Miles[90] can be seen as a regrettable decision and the approach of the Privy Council in *Queensland Electricity Generating Board* v *New Hope Collieries Pty Ltd*[91] seems to be the preferable one. This flexible approach should be applied in other contexts, such as requirement contracts, where the need to preserve a degree of flexibility is also of great importance. But, apart from being aware of the reasons why parties to long-term contracts express their obligations in broad, flexible terms and giving effect to these clauses, long-term contracts do not demand distinctive regulation by the courts or by Parliament.[92] The parties can do it themselves. All they ask of the courts is that they give effect to the contracts which they have concluded.

---

[90] [1992] 2 AC 128.   [91] [1989] 1 Lloyd's Rep 205.

[92] Although consideration might usefully be given to the development of a more flexible remedial regime on the occurrence of a breach of contract, such as that contained in Part III of the Vienna Convention on Contracts for the International Sale of Goods. English law arguably places too much emphasis upon termination as a remedy for breach in preference to other more flexible remedies, such as suspension of the contract and the right to cure defective performance. But once again this argument is of general application and cannot be confined to long-term contracts.

(d) Extent of contractual obligation

13

Fault and Breach of Contract*

BARRY NICHOLAS

The title of this paper rings artificially in the ears of a common lawyer. The dictum in *Paradine* v *Jane*[1] is part of the basic furniture of his mind. His conventional starting-point is that contracts are absolute, and that fault plays no part in liability for breach.[2] So it has been said in the House of Lords that:

It is axiomatic that, in relation to a claim for damages for breach of contract, it is, in general, immaterial why the defendant failed to fulfil his obligation, and certainly no defence to plead that he had done his best.[3]

Similarly in the Introductory Note to Chapter 11 of Restatement 2d Contracts it is said that:

Contract liability is strict liability . . . The obligor is therefore liable in damages for breach of contract even if he is without fault . . .

And it is in accordance with this approach that fault makes little or no appearance in books and articles on contract.[4]

On the other hand, the civil lawyer's starting-point is that fault is a requisite of liability for non-performance of a contract.[5] This is explicitly laid down in the German Civil Code[6] and the principle is taken for granted in French law, although the French Civil Code has no express provision.

Superficially, therefore, there is a total contrast between common and

---

* Copyright © 1994, Barry Nicholas
[1] (1647) Aleyn 26; 82 ER 897.
[2] The word occurs in several places in, for example, the Sale of Goods Act 1979 (ss 7, 9(2), 20(2)) but s 61 gives it the meaning simply of 'wrongful act or default'. It can also be found occasionally in judgments, with much the same meaning, eg *Poussard* v *Spiers* (1876) 1 QBD 410.
[3] *Raineri* v *Miles* [1981] AC 1050, at 1086G, per Lord Edmund-Davies.
[4] An important exception is the work of Professor GH Treitel. See his article 'Fault in the Common Law of Contract' in M Bos and I Brownlie (eds), *Liber Amicorum for Lord Wilberforce* (1987) pp 185 *et seq*. This chapter is indebted to his examination of the modern case-law, which it does not attempt to repeat. The main conclusions of his article are embodied in his *The Law of Contract* (8th ed 1991) pp 737 *et seq*, 803 *et seq*. For a comparative treatment see his *Remedies for Breach of Contract: A Comparative Account* (1988) pp 7 *et seq*. I have not been able to take account of his *Frustration and Force Majeure* (1994).
[5] See, eg, GH Treitel, *Remedies for Breach of Contract: A Comparative Account* (1988); K Zweigert and H Kötz, *An Introduction to Comparative Law* (2nd ed 1992) pp 524 *et seq*.
[6] § 276; N Horn, H Kötz, HG Leser, *German Private and Commercial Law: An Introduction* (1982) pp 112 ff.

civil law but, if one looks more closely, one finds that the difference in practical result is small. This paper is not directly concerned with the civil law but, if one is to determine how far fault does play a part in the common law, it may be useful to have, in bare outline, a model of what one fault-based system looks like. For this purpose French law provides a better model than German law, both because structural defects[7] make the German law of breach of contract less easy to penetrate than the French law, and because French law provides closer parallels with the common law.[8]

A French model[9]

In the present context, French law has two important features. As in the common law, a contract is the creation of the parties and they are free, subject to the general law, to make what agreement they please, but this unitary conception of contract is superimposed on a framework, inherited from Roman law, of particular contracts with their own incidents or rules. Many of these 'nominate' contracts are to be found in the Civil Code or in other legislation, but others have evolved, by analogy or otherwise, in the hands of writers and the courts. When faced with an agreement, therefore, a French lawyer will first try to 'qualify' or categorize it under one of the headings thus provided and, subject to any contrary intention of the parties, to apply to it the appropriate incidents or rules. In other words, the presumption in French law is that the incidents of a contract are fixed by law, subject to the parties' power to vary them.

The second feature of French law is more directly relevant to the question of fault. The need to reconcile two apparently conflicting articles of the Civil Code[10] had led to a further categorization, in this case of the obligations which a contract lays on the parties. These are of two kinds. In the case of what is called an *obligation de moyens*, the party in question is obliged to exercise reasonable care, but is exempt from liability if nevertheless he fails to achieve the expected result. The familiar example is that of the doctor, who is (presumptively) bound to take reasonable steps to cure his patient, but is not liable if, in spite of such steps, no cure is

[7] K Zweigert and H Kötz, *An Introduction to Comparative Law* (2nd ed 1992) pp 524 *et seq*; N Horn, H Kötz, HG Leser, *ibid.*, pp 93 ff. But for a discussion of one aspect of the German law see p 353 below.

[8] The difference between the German law, on the one hand, and the French law or the common law, on the other, is in fact much smaller than the formulation in the German Civil Code would suggest: B Nicholas, 'Prerequisites and Extent of Liability for Breach of Contract Under the UN Convention' in P Schlechtriem (ed), *Einheitliches Kaufrecht und nationales Obligationenrecht* (1987) pp 283 *et seq*, 285.

[9] See B Nicholas, *The French Law of Contract* (2nd ed 1992) pp 31, 40, 46 and 49 *et seq*.

[10] Articles 1137 and 1147; see B Nicholas, *The French Law of Contract* (2nd ed 1992) p 52.

achieved. In the case of an *obligation de résultat*, however, the party is obliged not simply to show due diligence, but to achieve the result envisaged. If he fails to do so, he is liable in damages. Thus, in the case of a contract for the carriage of persons or goods, it has long been settled that the transporter is bound not merely to exercise due care, but to carry the persons or goods safely to the destination. The obligation is not, however, absolute. The party obliged will be exempt if he can show that his failure was due to a cause for which he was not responsible, and which he could neither foresee nor surmount (*cause étrangère*, also called *force majeure*, or *cas fortuit*).

The essential difference between these two kinds of obligation lies in the burden of proof. In both cases the burden of showing that the party obliged has not performed his obligation lies, as usual, on the other party and, since in an *obligation de moyens* the failure to take care is an essential element in the breach, he must prove fault. In an *obligation de résultat*, on the other hand, he has only to show that the result has not been achieved, and it is then for the party obliged to prove a *cause étrangère*. (It should be noted that it is not sufficient for him to prove that he has used all reasonable care. The practical difference lies in the case where the cause is unknown.)

Two other points should be briefly noted at this stage:

(1) This is a classification of obligations. One contract may obviously give rise to a number of obligations, some of which may be *de moyens* and others *de résultat*. So a restaurateur is under an *obligation de moyens* in regard to the safety of his premises, but under an *obligation de résultat* to provide food which does not endanger his customer's health.

(2) While the distinction is universally accepted, and the voluminous case-law will usually make it possible to say which obligations are created by any particular contract, and while there has been much doctrinal discussion of the distinction, no entirely satisfactory theoretical basis for it has emerged.[11]

Finally, French law recognizes in some cases a third category of obligation, the *obligation de garantie*, under which the party obliged is absolutely liable, regardless of the absence of fault or the presence of a *cause étrangère*.[12] The simplest examples of such an obligation are found in the seller's guarantees against eviction and against latent defects.

French law therefore provides a model of a system in which liability for breach of contract is seen as being based on fault. The liability can be

---

[11] See p 351 below. The obligations in some situations do not fit precisely into either category, see B Nicholas, *ibid.*, p 54.

[12] Liability is limited, however, to reliance damages unless bad faith is shown: B Nicholas, *ibid.*, pp 56 and 82.

analysed under three heads: liability for fault; strict liability, displaceable by proof of what we may call an exempting circumstance (in French law a *cause étrangère*); and absolute liability. It should be said, however, that references in English to this subject, whether judicial or academic, often use the terms 'strict' and 'absolute' interchangeably. In what follows they are used in the senses given here.

The common law equivalents

STRICT LIABILITY

If we turn to the common law with this analysis and terminology in mind, we can say that, in the conventional view, liability was originally absolute in the sense that any non-performance would ground an action for damages. It is generally accepted,[13] however, that this can never have been entirely true, at least in the cases, for which there is early authority and which were the forerunners of *Taylor* v *Caldwell*,[14] in which performance becomes illegal after the contract is made, or the contract requires performance by the promisor himself (in a contract for services for example) and he dies or is incapacitated. In cases like these, liability is not absolute, but strict, in the sense that the supervening impossibility constitutes an exempting circumstance. We shall return to this analysis.

ABSOLUTE LIABILITY

As far as absolute liability is concerned, there are parallels to the French *obligation de garantie* in such cases as the seller's liability for defective goods.[15] Moreover, the concept of the warranty can be used to create other cases of absolute liability. Since the common law, unlike the civil law, has no principle that a promise to perform the impossible is necessarily void, such a promise may be construed as incorporating a warranty that performance is possible, as in *McRae* v *Commonwealth Disposals* Commission.[16] Apart from such warranty cases, absolute liability may attach to a promise to pay money.[17] In general inability to pay, for whatever reason, does not exempt the debtor from liability.

---

[13] GH Treitel, *The Law of Contract* (8th ed 1991) p 763; *Farnsworth on Contracts* (1990) s 9.5.
[14] (1863) 3 B & S 826, 122 ER 309.
[15] *Frost* v *Aylesbury Dairy Co Ltd* [1905] 1 KB 608.   [16] (1951) 84 CLR 377.
[17] See GH Treitel, 'Fault in the Common Law of Contract' in M Bos and I Brownlie (eds), *Liber Amicorum for Lord Wilberforce* (1987), pp 186 *et seq*; for a discussion of the nature of a seller's liability for failure to deliver generic goods, see *ibid*. 188–93.

FAULT LIABILITY

There are, however, some types of contractual situation which surely cannot at any time have been seen as giving rise either to absolute or to strict liability. A contract for services for a fixed period no doubt does prima facie create a strict obligation to serve for that period (in the sense that failure to do so will, unless excused as above, found an action for damages), but the obligation to perform the services will, unless the terms of the contract or the circumstances in which it is made suggest otherwise, call for no more than the exercise of due care. There is in other words simply fault liability. Thus, if one takes the paradigm instance, given above, of the *obligation de moyens*, namely a doctor's obligation to his patient, it is clear that in the common law also the doctor's duty is presumptively only to exercise reasonable skill and care.[18] More widely, there is authority in the modern cases that this is true of contracts for services generally,[19] and the principle is now enshrined in the English Supply of Goods and Services Act 1982.[20]

The technique of the implied term[21]

One can therefore without difficulty find situations in which the common law in substance recognizes all three of the categories of liability which we derived from French law (though the situations which each system allocates to each category may differ). And yet fault appears to play almost no part in common law thinking about liability for breach of contract. The reason lies, of course, in the conceptual forms in which the substance is cast. Whereas both French law and the civil law generally, proceed from rules appropriate to particular types of contract, the common law looks for implied terms. This is so even where what is plainly in substance a rule is enacted in a statute. Thus the Supply of Goods and Services Act 1982 provides:[22]

In a contract for the supply of a service where the supplier is acting in the course of a business, there is an implied term that the supplier will carry out the service with reasonable care and skill.

---

[18] *Lanphier* v *Phipos* (1838) 8 Car & P 475; 173 ER 581 (see text below, at n 35); *Eyre* v *Measday* [1986] 1 All ER 488; *Thake* v *Maurice* [1986] QB 644.

[19] GH Treitel, *The Law of Contract* (8th ed 1991) pp 740 *et seq*; but see p 349 *et seq* below.

[20] Section 13 (see text immediately below); s 16(3)(a), however, preserves 'any rule of law which imposes on the supplier a duty stricter than that imposed by section 13 . . .'

[21] What follows draws in part on B Nicholas, 'Rules and Terms—Civil Law and Common Law' (1974) 48 Tul LR 946.

[22] Section 13.

We take this approach for granted in all contractual situations. The Sale of Goods Act 1979 offers the most familiar statutory examples. Even the Uniform Commercial Code,[23] otherwise so willing to innovate, adopts the traditional method.

That the common law should have adopted this technique is not surprising. Although we recognize some typical contracts—sale of goods is an obvious example—we do not have a systematic structure of such 'nominate' contracts, and therefore in theory treat each contract as the unique creation of the parties. Where this approach is not sufficient, the courts proceed by implying terms of one kind or another. In spite of many judicial pronouncements and much academic discussion,[24] an examination of which lies beyond the scope of this paper, the nature and classification of these terms remain to some extent fluid, but it is generally accepted[25] that there is a broad distinction to be drawn between, on the one hand, terms implied in fact, in the sense that, as a matter of construction, they represent what the parties must have intended, and, on the other hand, terms implied by law. Of terms implied by law one may distinguish two types: those which apply generally to all contracts of a given type, and those which are imported by the court into a particular contract in order to give it, as is sometimes said, 'business efficacy'. So in *Lister* v *Romford Ice & Cold Storage Co Ltd*[26] Lord Tucker said:

Some contractual terms may be implied by general rules of law. These general rules, some of which are now statutory, for example, Sale of Goods Act, Bills of Exchange Act, etc, derive in the main from the common law by which they have become attached in the course of time to certain classes of contractual relationships, for example, landlord and tenant, innkeeper and guest, contracts of guarantee and contracts of personal service. Contrasted with such cases as these are those in which from their particular circumstances it is necessary to imply a term to give efficacy to the contract and make it a workable agreement in such manner as the parties would clearly have done if they had applied their minds to the contingency which has arisen.

It is with the first of Lord Tucker's categories of terms implied by law that we are concerned. It is tempting to conjecture[27] that such terms originated as terms implied in fact, and that in the course of time the implication became so habitual that it hardened into law. But there seems to be no evidence to substantiate such a conjecture. The nineteenth-century cases in which the use of such terms becomes established plainly recog-

---

[23] §§ 2–314 and 2–315.

[24] See GH Treitel, *The Law of Contract* (8th ed 1991) pp 185 *et seq*, with references.

[25] For a recent judicial example see *Reid* v *Rush & Tompkins Group Plc* [1990] 1 WLR 212, at 227; *The Choko Star* [1990] 1 Lloyd's Rep 516, at 526.

[26] [1957] AC 555, 594.

[27] See *Halsbury's Laws of England* (4th ed 1974), vol 9, s 354, note 27.

nize that the court is in substance laying down a rule. If one looks for the antecedents of, for example, the terms which were eventually incorporated as conditions in the Sale of Goods Act 1893, one sees that the courts made no pretence that they were deriving the terms from the intentions of the parties.[28] Thus in 1815, in a case of a sale of twelve bags of what was described as waste silk, Lord Ellenborough declared that:

under such circumstances, the purchaser has a right to expect a saleable article answering the description in the contract. Without any particular warranty, this is an implied term in every such contract.[29]

And in *Shepherd* v *Pybus*,[30] in reply to an objection that where there was a written contract which contained no such warranty, none could be implied, Tindal CJ declared, citing *Gardiner* v *Gray*,[31] that:

where the warranty is one which the law implies, it is clearly admissible, notwithstanding there be a written contract.

To turn to cases more directly relevant to the subject of this paper, in *Smith* v *Marrable*,[32] a case of a furnished letting of a house found by the tenant to be uninhabitable, Parke B held, citing some rather tenuous authority, that:

a person who lets a house must be taken to let it under the implied condition that it is in a state fit for decent and comfortable habitation . . .[33]

Lord Abinger CB declared more robustly:

I am glad that authorities have been found . . . but . . . no authorities were wanted . . . [C]ommonsense alone enables us to decide. A man who lets a ready-furnished house surely does so under the implied condition or obligation—call it what you will—that the house is in a fit state to be inhabited.[34]

Again, in *Lanphier* v *Phipos*[35] the plaintiff had called in the defendant, a surgeon and apothecary, to treat his wife, who had injured her hand and wrist. At the end of the treatment, however, the hand had become almost useless. Tindal CJ told the jury:

Every person who enters into a learned profession undertakes to bring to the exercise of it a reasonable degree of care and skill. He does not undertake, if he is an attorney, that at all events you shall gain your case, nor does a surgeon undertake that he will perform a cure; nor does he undertake to use the highest possible degree of skill.[36]

---

[28] The cases are surveyed by Brett JA in *Randall* v *Newson* (1877) 2 QBD 102.
[29] *Gardiner* v *Gray* (1815) 4 Camp 144, at 145; 171 ER 46, at 47.
[30] (1842) 3 Man & G 868, at 878; 133 ER 1390, at 1394.
[31] (1815) 4 Camp 144; 171 ER 46. [32] (1843) 11 M & W 5; 152 ER 693.
[33] *Ibid.*, 7; 152 ER 693, at 694. [34] *Ibid.*, 9; 152 ER 693, at 694.
[35] (1838) 8 Car & P 475; 173 ER 581. [36] *Ibid.*, 479; 173 ER 581, at 583.

Similarly in *Harmer* v *Cornelius*,[37] a case in which a painter, employed for a month, had been dismissed for incompetence. Willes J said:

When a skilled labourer, artisan, or artist is employed, there is on his part an implied warranty that he is of skill reasonably competent to the task he undertakes ... Thus, if an apothecary, a watch-maker, or an attorney be employed for reward, they each impliedly undertake to possess and exercise reasonable skill in their several arts.[38]

It is not, as far as my reading goes, until the latter part of the nineteenth century, when greater attention was being paid to the concept of consensus as the basis of contract, that the need is felt to link these implied terms to the intention of the parties. An instance is found in the case of *Readhead* v *Midland Railway Co*,[39] in which the Exchequer Chamber refused to extend to carriers of passengers the strict liability which had long been imposed on carriers of goods. Carriers, it was pointed out, did not have the same control over passengers as they did over goods. Moreover, how could strict liability, if thus extended, be confined to the actual carrying of the passenger, as opposed to his presence on railway premises before and afterwards? And, further, why should it not then be extended to other public places, such as theatres?[40] The court therefore held that the duty of carriers of passengers was limited to the exercise of due care. Montague Smith J, giving the judgment of the court, based the duty on an implied warranty and linked this to the intention of the parties:

Warranties implied by law are for the most part founded on the presumed intention of the parties, and ought certainly to be founded on reason, and with a just regard to the interests of the party who is supposed to give the warranty, as well as of the party to whom it is supposed to be given.[41]

But plainly this nod in the direction of the intention of the parties adds nothing of substance, although it, and others like it, have tended to confuse the distinction between warranties implied in fact and those implied by law.

The use of the instrument of the implied term is not therefore surprising. Moreover, as a matter of history it no doubt had the advantage of concealing the law-making function of the courts. It also has the advantage of making it plain that, since the term is in theory the creation of the parties, it can be excluded by the parties[42]—a matter which in the civil law is again

---

[37] (1858) 5 CB (NS) 236; 141 ER 94.   [38] *Ibid.*, 246; 141 ER 94, at 98.
[39] (1869) LR 4 QB 379.
[40] French law, which went the other way (see p 339 above) on the issue before the Exchequer Chamber has indeed had difficulties with these questions.
[41] *Readhead* v *Midland Railway Co* (1989) LR 4 QB 379, at 392.
[42] It was presumably for this reason that the draftsman of the Sale of Goods Act expressed the seller's obligation in regard to the quality of the goods in the form of an implied term (ss 13, 14, 15), whereas his obligation to deliver, and the buyer's obligation to accept delivery

left to a rule.[43] Nowadays however, this advantage is limited by the presence in a number of statutes of a provision that the term shall be implied notwithstanding any stipulation to the contrary.[44]

It could be said therefore that what in the civil law is expressed overtly in rules governing the incidence of different types of contractual liability, is expressed in the common law under the guise of terms implied by law, and that these implied terms are fictitious expressions of what are in truth rules. The difference, it could be said, is merely a matter of verbal formulation. The implication of such terms is a matter of law, and it is widely accepted that they are, as Professor Treitel puts it, 'in truth, simply duties prima facie arising out of certain types of contracts'.[45] Similarly *Halsbury's Laws of England* says that:

terms implied by law are not happily described as 'implied terms': they are rather duties which (frequently subject to a contrary intention) are imposed by the law on the parties to particular types of contract. In deciding whether to create such duties, the courts tend to look, not to the intention of the parties, but to considerations of public policy.[46]

This view is reflected in the language of the courts. So in *Smith* v *Eric Bush*,[47] in the context of the standard of conduct required of a surveyor or valuer, Lord Templeman said:

The common law imposes on a person who contracts to carry out an operation an obligation to exercise reasonable skill and care. A plumber who mends a burst pipe is liable for his incompetence or negligence whether or not he has been expressly required to be careful. The law implies a term in the contract which requires the plumber to exercise reasonable skill and care in his calling.[48]

Fault is therefore absent from the conventional common law conception of liability for breach of contract only because it is in substance incorporated in the meaning of 'contract'. So in a formulation such as that in Restatement 2d Contracts, § 235(2): 'When performance of a duty under a contract is due any non-performance is a breach', the part played by fault is incorporated in the duty. To put the matter in another way, the implied term approach has the disadvantage that it obscures the part played by fault and discourages systematic discussion of it. As Professor Treitel has

and pay the price, are expressed as duties (s 27). A contract in which either of these latter obligations was excluded would simply not be a contract of sale. The Uniform Commercial Code is drafted in the same way (§§ 2–314, 2–315 and 2–301).

[43] B Nicholas, *The French Law of Contract* (2nd ed 1992) pp 33–6.
[44] eg Unfair Contract Terms Act 1977, s 6; Landlord and Tenant Act 1985, s 8.
[45] *The Law of Contract* (8th ed 1991) p 190.
[46] (4th ed 1974) vol 9, s 354. To similar effect: *Chitty on Contracts* (27th ed 1994), vol I, s 13–003.
[47] [1990] 1 AC 831.
[48] *Ibid.*, 843. Cf. *Independent Broadcasting Authority* v *EMI Electronics* (1980) 14 Build LR 1, 47–8, per Lord Scarman.

said, 'common law courts are not used to thinking of standards of liability in a contractual context'.[49]

We should now look further at the development of what I have called strict liability, in the sense that the promisor is liable for non-performance unless he can show what I have called an exempting circumstance, such as supervening illegality or, in the case of contracts requiring personal performance by the promisor, supervening death or incapacity.

Before *Taylor* v *Caldwell*[50] the exempting circumstance was seen as providing the promisor with a defence to an action by the promisee. The promisor was excused. This is clear in the case of *Hall* v *Wright*,[51] in which the plaintiff contended that the defendant had failed to perform a promise to marry her within a reasonable time. The case turned on the defendant's plea that he was now afflicted by a dangerous disease which made him incapable of marrying without great danger to his life. There was a majority of four to three for the plaintiff in the Exchequer Chamber, but for our purposes the important judgments are those of Pollock CB and Bramwell B, both of whom were in the minority. Bramwell B held that it was an implied term of an ordinary agreement to marry that, in circumstances such as those before the court and in the absence of any stipulation to the contrary, the man should be excused. Pollock CB spoke similarly of an implied exception which relieves from liability in damages.

If one leaves aside the characteristic common law technique of the implied term, the practical result is the same as that of the French *obligation de résultat*. The plea of the defendant in *Hall* v *Wright* was, in French terms, that his illness constituted a *cause étrangère*.

The consequences of *Taylor* v *Caldwell* in English law

The decision in *Taylor* v *Caldwell*,[52] however, led to a diversion of the course of at least the English branch of the common law. In his judgment, Blackburn J retained the language of excuses, but it was no longer only the promisor who was excused by the supervening impossibility, but both parties. Instead of an implied term which limits the extent of the promisor's liability for the non-performance which has occurred, Blackburn J introduced the device of an implied condition which auto-

---

[49] 'Fault in the Common Law of Contract' in M Bos and I Brownlie, *Liber Amicorum for Lord Wilberforce* (1987) p 194. It is significant that the context in which standards of liability are consciously discussed is that of bailment, where the law is based on Lord Holt's borrowings from Roman law in *Coggs* v *Bernard* (1703) 2 Ld Raym 909; 92 ER 107.

[50] (1863) 3 B & S 826; 122 ER 309.

[51] (1858) El Bl & El 746; 120 ER 688. For a fuller discussion of the case see B Nicholas, 'Rules and Terms—Civil Law and Common Law' (1974) 48 Tul LR 946, 962–5.

[52] (1863) 3 B & S 826; 122 ER 309.

matically terminates the whole contract.[53] Not only did this not follow from the examples on which Blackburn J based it, it was not necessary to the decision, which concerned only the liability of the defendant.[54]

This change of course did not take effect immediately, but it was firmly established by Lord Sumner in *Bank Line Ltd* v *Arthur Capel & Co*[55] and *Hirji Mulji* v *Cheong Yue SS Co*.[56] In the latter case, he set out the justification for it as follows:

> . . . [I]t is [the parties] common object that has to be frustrated, not merely the individual advantage which one party or the other might have gained from the contract. If so, what the law provides must be a common relief from this common disappointment and an immediate termination of the obligations as regards future performance.[57]

And yet an echo of what the principle might have been is found 16 years later in Lord Porter's speech in *Joseph Constantine Steamship Line Ltd* v *Imperial Smelting Corpn Ltd*:[58]

> The true principle seems to be, not that all contracts must prima facie be performed . . . but that there are some contracts absolute in their nature where the promisor warrants the possibility of performance. These he is bound to perform in any event or to pay damages, but there are other cases where the promisor is only obliged to perform if he can. In a contract for personal performance where he dies, or in certain other cases where the subject-matter of the contract is destroyed, he cannot implement his promise. In such cases he is excused unless he be in fault . . . Where the promisor makes an absolute promise he takes the risk of his ability to fulfil his contract and must do so or pay damages. No question of frustration does or can arise. Whatever occurs the promisor is bound. The very fact, however, that in certain cases impossibility of performance is an excuse shows that in those cases there is no absolute promise. It is conditional on something, ie, the possibility of performance.

In the American branch of the common law, which still thinks in terms of an excuse, Lord Porter's approach would, I think, be accepted. In Restatement 2d Contracts, § 261, the effect of supervening impracticability is stated in terms of the discharge of the promisor's duty to perform. And the Uniform Commercial Code, § 2–615, provides that a seller's failure to deliver in circumstances amounting to impracticability 'is not a breach of his duty'.

Of course, in most cases the difference between the two approaches is without practical importance, but the automatic termination of the

---

[53] For an examination of the confusions which led to this see B Nicholas, 'Rules and Terms—Civil Law and Common Law' (1974) 48 Tul LR 946, 959–66.

[54] On this and the next paragraph see GH Treitel, *Unmöglichkeit, 'Impracticability' und 'Frustration' im anglo-amerikanischen Recht* (1991) 10.

[55] [1919] AC 435.   [56] [1926] AC 497.   [57] *Ibid.*, 507.

[58] [1942] AC 154, at 203–5.

contract does have the consequence that either party can invoke the frustrating event, and not merely the party whose performance is affected by it.[59] From our point of view, however, the importance of the change of course initiated by *Taylor v Caldwell*[60] is that it stunted the growth of a doctrine of excuses and therefore obscured the law's attitude to the place of fault in liability for non-performance. This is clearly to be seen in two features of the modern law.

PARTIAL IMPOSSIBILITY[61]

Since frustration has the single catastrophic effect of automatically terminating the contract, what is to be said if impossibility (or illegality) affects only one of the obligations undertaken by the promisor—and, let us assume, not one which affects the main purpose of the contract so as to satisfy the requirements of frustration? In French law there is no difficulty. Impossibility or illegality is treated in the same way whether it affects all the obligations created by the contract or a single one. If the impossibility satisfies the requirements of a *cause étrangère*, the promisor is excused. English law, however, having no concept of the frustration of a single obligation, is in difficulty,[62] and what case-law there is provides no clear guidance.

In *Eyre v Johnson*[63] a tenant was held liable in damages for breach of his covenant to repair even though war-time regulations made it illegal for him to do the work. Denning J held that:

... [A]lthough illegality which completely forbids the performance of a contract may give rise to frustration in some cases, illegality as to the performance of one clause which does not amount to frustration in any sense of the word, does not carry with it the necessary consequence that the party is absolved from paying damages.[64]

But this is surely unsatisfactory.[65]

Sainsbury v Street[66] provides an instance of partial impossibility (as opposed to partial illegality), although the ways in which the arguments of the two sides were formulated tended to obscure the issue. The defendant had contracted to sell to the plaintiff 275 tons of barley to be grown

---

[59] GH Treitel, *The Law of Contract* (8th ed 1991) p 808; B Nicholas, 'Rules and Terms—Civil Law and Common Law' (1974) 48 Tul LR 946, 956–7. It should also logically follow that the party whose performance has become impossible is under no duty to inform the other of that fact.

[60] (1863) 3 B & S 826, 122 ER 309.

[61] B Nicholas, '*Force Majeure* and Frustration' (1979) 27 Am J Comp L 231, 235–6.

[62] See for example *Chitty on Contracts* (27th ed 1994), vol I, s 23–051.

[63] [1946] KB 481.

[64] *Ibid.*, 484.

[65] GH Treitel, *The Law of Contract* (8th ed 1991) p 789.

[66] [1972] 1 WLR 834.

on the defendant's farm. In the event, through no fault of the defendant's, no more than 140 tons were produced. The plaintiff conceded that he was not entitled to damages for non-delivery above the figure of 140 tons, but claimed damages up to that amount. In other words, he argued that the partial failure of the crop constituted an excuse, but that the contract remained valid as to the balance. The defendant contended that there was an implied condition precedent that there should be a crop of at least 250 tons and that the failure of that condition meant that he was excused from delivering any at all. This was in substance a claim that the contract had been frustrated. The judge treated the matter as one of construction and, having rejected the defendant's construction as unreasonable, formulated an 'implied condition' which enabled him to give judgment for the plaintiff.

SELF-INDUCED FRUSTRATION

Since frustration automatically terminates the contract, and since fault plays no acknowledged part in liability for breach, English law needs this additional heading. In French law it is simply embodied in the concept of *cause étrangère*. It is noticeable that in American law, which, as we have seen, still thinks in terms of an excuse, there is no independent heading for self-induced impracticability. It is simply a necessary feature of the concept of an excuse that the failure to perform should have occurred without the promisor's fault. So Restatement 2d Contracts, § 261 provides:

Where, after a contract is made, a party's performance is made impracticable without his fault . . . his duty to render that performance is discharged . . .

Border-line difficulties[67]

I have suggested that the device of the implied term has discouraged systematic discussion of the place of fault in contractual liability. A particular difficulty lies on the border-line between absolute or strict liability and fault liability. Liability for defects in goods supplied under a contract of sale is absolute, and the same is probably true where goods are supplied under a contract for the supply of goods other than one of sale, eg one of hire or hire-purchase. On the other hand, contracts for the supply of services presumptively give rise to no more than fault liability.[68] Difficulties arise in situations involving elements of both service and the supply of

---

[67] See generally GH Treitel, 'Fault in the Common Law of Contract' in M Bos and I Brownlie, *Liber Amicorum for Lord Wilberforce* (1987) pp 194–200.
[68] See p 341 above.

some physical object. It is clear that a contractor who does building or repair work is absolutely liable for components which he fits, even when the other party specified the supplier from whom the components were to be obtained.[69] But there is room for doubt where the case involves the design responsibilities of a professional man, such as an architect or an engineer. As far as their supervisory functions are concerned, it is clear that they are normally liable only for fault,[70] but what is the position if the loss complained of arises from defective design or advice?

In *Independent Broadcasting Authority* v *EMI Electronics Ltd*[71] engineering sub-contractors had designed and erected a television mast which collapsed because of a defect of design. The decision against them was on the ground of negligence, but Lord Scarman said:

The extent of [EMI's] obligation is, of course, to be determined as a matter of construction of the contract. But, in the absence of a clear, contractual indication to the contrary, I see no reason why one who in the course of his business contracts to design, supply, and erect a television aerial mast is not under an obligation to ensure that it is reasonably fit for the purpose for which he knows it is intended to be used . . . I do not accept that the design obligation of the supplier of an article is to be equated with the obligation of a professional man in the practice of his profession . . . If a dentist takes out a tooth or a surgeon removes an appendix, he is bound to take reasonable care and to show such skill as may be expected from a qualified practitioner. The case is entirely different where a chattel is ultimately to be delivered.[72]

George Hawkins v *Chrysler (UK) and Burne Associates*[73] presented the problem of the liability of a designer or design-adviser who was not involved in the production or supply of the thing designed. The third party defendant, a sub-contractor of the first defendant, had advised on the design of a shower-room floor which had proved to be unsafe; there was no element of supply on the part of the defendant. The plaintiff, seeking to extend the liability envisaged by Lord Scarman for design-and-supply, argued that, where a professional man designed or advised on design, his design was really a product. It would be anomalous if an architect were treated less stringently than a builder. The court, however, pointing out that Lord Scarman's dictum was confined to the case of the

---

[69] *Young & Marten Ltd* v *McManus Childs Ltd* [1969] 1 AC 454. For reasons of policy for the decision see the speech of Lord Reid; cf. GH Treitel, 'Fault in the Common Law of Contract' in M Bos and I Brownlie, *Liber Amicorum for Lord Wilberforce* (1987) p 196.

[70] See authorities cited by GH Treitel, *The Law of Contract* (8th ed 1991) pp 739 *et seq.*

[71] (1980) 14 Build LR 1.

[72] *Ibid.*, 47–8 (quoting du Parcq LJ in *Samuels* v *Davis* [1943] KB 526). The same view had been expressed by Lord Denning in *Greaves & Co (Contractors) Ltd* v *Baynham Meikle & Partners* [1975] 1 WLR 1095; the other members of the Court of Appeal emphasised the special nature of the facts of the case.

[73] (1986) 38 Build LR 36.

supply of some physical thing, held that it was not open to them to go further in extending the responsibility of a professional man. Neill LJ said:

I recognize that it can be strongly argued that there is no logical basis for drawing a distinction between on the one hand the responsibilities of a contractor who designs and *erects* a building, and on the other hand the responsibilities of an engineer or the consultant who merely designs it.[74]

He recognized also the anomaly that whereas the contractor who incorporates into a building a defective component has recourse against the supplier of the component without proof of fault, he has no similar recourse in matters of defective design.[75]

It may be useful to inquire how French law would approach such a question. The particular matter of the liability of architects or engineers responsible for the design and construction of building works is governed by a statute[76] which imposes an *obligation de résultat*. But this would not cover the case of the sub-contracting designer. There has been much discussion of the appropriate criterion for determining whether an obligation is *de resultat* or *de moyens*, without any universally accepted conclusion.[77] The most widely favoured criterion, however, is that of the aleatory character of the contract, ie the extent to which the achievement of the result envisaged is speculative. This fits well enough the case of the dentist, whose liability is, as in English law,[78] *de moyens* for ordinary treatment, but *de résultat* for the provision of false teeth or, French law would add, for the provision of safe and sterile equipment. It is of course a very imprecise criterion, but it does at least indicate the nature of the question which a French court should ask, namely whether, in the light of current standards of skill and knowledge and of the inherent risks in the area of activity in question, it is reasonable to expect the envisaged result to be achieved. This, it may be thought, provides a more sensitive criterion than simply to ask whether the contract calls for the supply of a physical thing.

Fault in the Vienna Convention on International Sales[79]

In this matter, as in others, the UN Convention on Contracts for the International Sale of Goods (1980) embodies the ideas drawn both from

---

[74] *Ibid.*, 55 (emphasis in original).
[75] Similarly, in *Basildon District Council v JE Lesser (Properties) Ltd* [1985] QB 839, the view was expressed that strict liability was confined to the case where the professional person not merely designed, but made something, as in *Samuels v Davies* [1943] KB 526.
[76] Incorporated in the Civil Code as Art 1792 and 1792–1.
[77] See B Nicholas, *The French Law of Contract* (2nd ed 1992) pp 54 *et seq.*
[78] *Samuels v Davies* [1943] KB 526.
[79] See B Nicholas, 'Prerequisites and Extent of Liability for Breach of Contract Under the UN Convention' in P Schlechtriem (ed), *Einheitliches Kaufrecht und nationales Obligationenrecht*

the common law and from the civil law and may therefore serve to point up some of what has been said above.

The Convention does not directly address the initial question whether, as in the civil law, liability is in principle founded on fault or whether, as in the common law, the party obliged in principle guarantees his performance. The obligations of seller and buyer[80] are expressed, however, in terms which suggest the Common law approach. This is borne out by the one exception. Article 60 provides that:

The buyer's obligation to take delivery consists:
(a) in doing all the acts which could reasonable be expected of him in order to enable the seller to make delivery; and
(b) in taking over the goods.

The obligation in (a) is an *obligation de moyens*. The buyer is in breach of it only if he is (objectively) at fault. Neither the obligation in (b) nor any of the other obligations is expressed in this qualified way. All these obligations may therefore be taken to be strict, in the sense in which that term is used in this paper, ie that non-performance of the obligation entails liability unless there is shown to be what I have called an exempting circumstance. This is provided for in Art 79, to which we must now turn.

The exempting circumstance is defined in terms of an impediment which causes the non-performance:

Article 79(1) A party is liable for a failure to perform any of his obligations if he proves that the failure was due to an impediment beyond his control and he could not reasonably be expected to have taken the impediment into account at the time of the conclusion of the contract or to have avoided or overcome it or its consequences.

This is in substance very close to the French approach.[81] A *cause étrangère* (or *force majeure* or *cas fortuit*) is conventionally defined as an event or obstacle which was unforeseeable, insurmountable and irresistible and which has made performance of the obligation impossible. Article 79(1) requires that the non-performance in question should have been due to an impediment and, in substance, that the impediment should have been:

(1) beyond the control of the person obliged;
(2) unforeseeable at the time of the conclusion of the contract;
(3) irresistible in itself or its consequences.

(1987) pp 283 *et seq*, 285. For a survey of the Convention see B Nicholas, 'The Vienna Convention on International Sales Law' (1989) 105 LQR 201. There are now a number of more or less extended commentaries on the Convention; see especially JO Honnold, *Uniform Law for International Sales* (2nd ed 1991); P Schlechtriem, *Uniform Sales Law* (1986); CM Bianca and MJ Bonell (eds), *Commentary on the International Sales Law* (1987); von Caemmerer/ Schlechtriem, *Kommentar zum Einheitlichen UN-Kaufrecht* (1990); F Enderlein and D Maskow, *International Sales Law* (1992).

[80] Articles 30–60; cf arts 71–3.   [81] See pp 338 *et seq* above.

If Art 79(1) yields results in practice which are different from those reached by French courts, it will be because of the meaning given to 'impediment',[82] not because of the other provisions in the paragraph.

In this connection a difficulty should be noticed which is relevant for our purposes because it arises out of the foundation of German contractual liability in fault.[83] In a sale of specific goods German law makes the seller liable for defects of quality (what the Convention calls 'lack of conformity') on the basis of a guarantee which entails a liability which, like that under the warranties in the Sale of Goods Act 1979, is absolute. But where the sale is of generic goods, matters are otherwise.[84] The presence of a defect may be treated as defective performance of the contract and therefore governed by the principle of fault, although the burden of proof is reversed so as to require the seller to show that he was not at fault. If one approaches the Convention from this point of view, one finds that the main provision on lack of conformity (Art 35) is indeed expressed in terms of an obligation to perform:

(1) The seller must deliver goods which are of the quantity, quality and description required by the contract.
(2) Except where the parties have agreed otherwise, the goods do not conform with the contract unless they:
   (a) are fit for the purpose for which goods of the same description would ordinarily be used . . .

German lawyers, starting from the pre-suppositions of their own system, may therefore expect the seller to be able to escape liability by showing that he was not at fault. And they may find a basis for this in Art 79. The seller, on this view, can escape liability under Art 35 if he can show that his failure to perform his obligation was due to an 'impediment' as defined in Art 79. The difficulty lies, however, in imagining a situation in which such an impediment might make the delivery of conforming goods impossible. The most likely case is that in which, in the state of technical knowledge at the time of the contract, the seller could not have discovered the defect. What here is the impediment? If it is the fact that the seller could not know, then one is simply saying that it is enough for the seller to show absence of fault (ie that the lack of conformity was beyond his

---

[82] For the reasons for this choice of word and, more generally, for the difficulties to which the article gives rise see B Nicholas, 'Impracticability and Impossibility in the UN Convention' in NM Galston and H Smit (eds), *International Sales: The UN Convention on Contracts for the International Sale of Goods* (1984).

[83] On what follows see B Nicholas, *ibid.*, pp 5–10 *et seq* and 'Prerequisites and Extent of Liability for Breach of Contract Under the UN Convention' in P Schlechtriem (ed), *Einheitliches Kaufrecht und nationales Obligationenrecht* (1987) pp 283 *et seq*, with references. See also H Stoll in the same volume, pp 275 *et seq*.

[84] See K Zweigert and H Kötz, *An Introduction to Comparative Law* (2nd ed 1992) pp 528 ff.

control), whereas Art 79 requires both this and the existence of an impediment. One is in fact driven to say that it is the mere fact that the goods do
not conform that constitutes the impediment. The seller is then using the
circular argument that he cannot deliver conforming goods because of an
impediment, namely that the goods are not conforming.[85]

Four other features of article 79 assimilate it to French law and differentiate it from the English common law as it has developed since *Taylor* v
Caldwell.[86]

(1) The impediment relates to the performance of 'any of his obligations'
and not, as in the common law, to the performance of the contract as
a whole.
(2) The consequence of an impediment is to allow the person obliged to
plead exemption from liability in damages, not to produce an automatic termination of the contract.[87] Paragraph (5) of article 79 therefore provides that:
Nothing in this article prevents either party from exercising any right
other than to claim damages under this Convention.[88]
(3) There is no need to provide that the impossibility shall not have been
'self-induced', since this is a necessary part of the definition of the
impediment.[89]
(4) There is no provision for impracticability as opposed to impossibility
and a fortiori none for frustration. This is in accord with French law,
which takes a strict line that nothing short of impossibility suffices.[90]
German law, on the other hand, as is well known, has evolved a very
wide doctrine of the disappearance of the foundation of the transaction. The absence of any treatment of the matter in the Convention
was not, however, the result of any decision of policy to adopt a
'French' position, but of a reluctance to embark on a complex and con-

---

[85] B Nicholas, 'Impracticability and Impossibility in the UN Convention' in NM Galston
and H Smit (eds), *International Sales: The UN Convention on Contracts for the International Sale
of Goods* (1984) n 78, 5–10–5–14; 'Prerequisites and Extent of Liability for Breach of Contract
Under the UN Convention' in P Schlechtriem (ed), *Einheitliches Kaufrecht und nationales
Obligationenrecht* (1987) 283 f; *contra*, H Stoll, in von Caemmerer/Schlechtriem, *Kommentar
zum Einheitlichen UN-Kaufrecht* (1990), 654, who finds the impediment in the circumstances
which made it impossible for the seller to know of the defect. But this again reduces the
requirement in article 79(1) simply to the absence of fault.

[86] (1863) 3 B&S 826; 122 ER 309.   [87] See above pp 346 *et seq.*

[88] The paragraph as drafted is, however, defective in that on its face it leaves open the possibility of a claim for specific performance. On this difficulty, which lies outside the scope of
this paper, see commentaries on the Convention, cited above, especially P Schlechtriem,
Uniform Sales Law (1986) pp 102 *et seq*; cf (on an earlier draft of article 79) B Nicholas, '*Force
majeure* and Frustration' (1979) 27 Am J Comp Law 231, 241–5.

[89] See above, p 349.

[90] This is the position in regard to private law contracts. For public law contracts the
administrative courts have developed the doctrine of *imprévision*. See generally B Nicholas,
The French Law of Contract (2nd ed 1992) pp 208 *et seq.*

troversial problem which was not likely to have much importance in the international sale of goods.

Conclusion

If we return to the two quotations with which this chapter began,[91] we find that they are correct only because the matter of fault is hidden in the term 'contract'. But there is a more substantial difference which helps to account for the common law assumption that contract liability is absolute. The difference is compounded of three elements. The first is that the common law has nothing to correspond to the civil law principle that one cannot be obliged to do the impossible (*impossibilium nulla obligatio*).[92] The second is that the civil law sees the primary remedy for breach of contract as enforced performance, whereas for the common law the primary remedy is damages.[93] The third is embodied in the dictum of that most typical of common lawyers, Mr Justice Holmes, that 'the duty to keep a contract at common law means a prediction that you must pay damages if you do not keep it—and nothing else'.[94] And the payment of damages is never impossible. In principle therefore if one makes what can be construed as an unqualified promise to perform the impossible, one must pay damages for breach of contract, whereas, for the civil lawyer, liability, if any, will not be in contract, but for *culpa in contrahendo*.[95] In other words, one area of what the common lawyer sees as absolute contractual liability is not usually regarded by the civil lawyer as a matter of contract at all, and the liability, if any, in the civil law will not be absolute, but for fault.

[91] See above, p 337.
[92] See above, p 340. Sale of Goods Act 1979, s 6, is a Romanistic intrusion: B Nicholas, 'Rules and Terms—Civil Law and Common Law' (1979) 48 Tul LR 946, 966 ff.
[93] B Nicholas, *The French Law of Contract* (2nd ed 1992) pp 211 and 216 *et seq.*
[94] 'The Path of the Law' (*Collected Legal Papers*, 175; 10 Harv L Rev (1897) 462); cf. Holmes, *The Common Law*, pp 297–300. Of course the dictum is an exaggeration: see eg WW Buckland, 'The Nature of Contractual Obligation' (1944) 8 C LJ 247; WW Buckland, *Some Reflections on Jurisprudence* (1945) pp 97 *et seq.*
[95] F Kessler and E Fine, '*Culpa in contrahendo*, Bargaining in Good Faith and Freedom of Contract: A Comparative Study' (1964) 77 Harv L R 401.

14

Contract Modification as a Result of Change of Circumstances*

Werner Lorenz

Introduction: some comparative aspects

Although this chapter concentrates on German law, some preliminary comparative observations, particularly in regard to English and French law, are necessary in order to show that the present problem is universal. It is the age-old conflict between two principles which a civil lawyer is likely to express in a Latin phrase: *pacta sunt servanda versus clausula rebus sic stantibus*. While it is clear that all developed legal systems must be based upon the principle that contractual obligations validly concluded must be fulfilled, it is not equally clear when a contract ceases to be binding because 'matters did not remain the same as they were at the time of conclusion of the contract'. Obviously, the *clausula* is a potentially dangerous inroad in the sacred principle of *pacta sunt servanda*.

No investigation into the origin and history of the *clausula* will be attempted here. The reader who is interested in the historical development is referred to the excellent account given by Reinhard Zimmermann who has traced it back to Seneca, Cicero and St Augustine.[1] Later on, the *clausula* doctrine was adopted by the *usus modernus* of the seventeenth century, and it fitted also very well in the ideas of the natural lawyers, particularly in the field of international law (Grotius and Pufendorf), but it had no visible influence on English law. On the contrary, the case of *Paradine* v *Jane*,[2] decided in 1647, which confirmed that contractual duties must be regarded as absolute, remained a distinctive feature of English law until the middle of the nineteenth century, when Blackburn J, in his judgment in *Taylor* v *Caldwell*, laid the foundations of the modern doctrine of frustration of contract by taking recourse to civilian doctrine, '[a]lthough,' he added, 'the Civil Law is not of itself authority in an

---

* Copyright © 1994, Werner Lorenz.

[1] R Zimmermann, *The Law of Obligations: Roman Foundations of the Civilian Tradition* (1990) pp 579–82. See also Kegel, 'Empfiehlt es sich, den Einfluss grundlegender Veränderungen des Wirtschaftslebens auf Verträge gesetzlich zu regeln und in welchem Sinn?' *Verhandlungen des 40 Deutschen Juristentages*, vol I (1953) 135, 139–43; K Zweigert and H Kötz, *An Introduction to Comparative Law*, (2nd ed 1992) p 557.

[2] *Paradine* v *Jane* (1647) Aleyn 26; 82 ER 579, at 897.

English Court, it affords great assistance in investigating the principles on which the law is grounded'.[3] This case concerned a contract to use a music hall which was destroyed by fire after the making of the agreement and shortly before the concert was to be given. In German law the solution reached by the English court would follow from § 323 of the Civil Code (BGB) dealing with impossibility of performance for which neither party is responsible. Such cases of factual impossibility for which the debtor cannot be blamed, and where the object of the obligation is a certain thing, do not yet present the difficult questions with which the courts are confronted when it comes to other supervening changes of circumstances affecting the foundation of a contract. Nevertheless, *Taylor* v *Caldwell*[4] is a memorable decision, because it helped to bridge the gulf then existing between civilian doctrine and the common law. The just result was reached by implying in such a contract a condition 'of the continued existence of the thing', a condition which is said to follow from the nature of the contract. If viewed in retrospect, it does not really matter very much whether or not one agrees with this theory of the implied condition, for what matters is that Blackburn J's judgment paved the way to the solution of the famous set of 'coronation cases' which have inspired comparative lawyers all over the world.[5]

Before turning to German law, a brief look at two leading French cases may be helpful: a few years after the decision in the case of *Taylor* v *Caldwell*[6] the *Cour de cassation* had to deal with a contract dating from the sixteenth century in which Sieur de Craponne had agreed for a certain sum to build a canal. Since the water of this canal could also be used for irrigating the orchards of the community of Pélissane, the inhabitants had to pay a modest sum for the maintenance of the canal. When the case came before the courts this contribution, agreed upon three centuries earlier, was totally insufficient to cover the maintenance costs of the canal. The lower courts, having based their decisions only on *équité*, had raised the sum to what was thought to be a reasonable amount. However, the *Cour de cassation* quashed these decisions because: '*dans aucun cas il n'appartient aux tribunaux, quelque équitable que puisse leur paraître leur décision, de prendre en considération le temps et les circonstances pour modifier les conventions des parties et substituer des clauses nouvelles à celles qui ont été librement acceptées.*'[7] This ruling still represents the attitude of the civil courts in France.

---

[3] *Taylor* v *Caldwell* (1863) 3 B & S 826, at 835; 122 ER 309, at 313, per Blackburn J.
[4] *Ibid.*
[5] *Krell* v *Henry* [1903] 2 KB 740 applying the ratio decidendi of *Taylor* v *Caldwell, ibid.*; contrast with *Herne Bay Steam Boat Co* v *Hutton* [1903] 2 KB 683 where the fact that a naval review was due to take place on the occasion of the coronation was not the sole basis of the contract. The court's holding that the venture was at the defendant's risk touches upon the decisive criterion for the correct solution of the present problem.
[6] (1863) 3 B & S 826; 122 ER 309.   [7] Cass civ 6 March 1876, D 1876 I p 193.

However, a different approach has been taken in the area of administrative law: the *Conseil d'Etat* did not hesitate to adapt contracts to altered circumstances which could not have been foreseen by the parties (*'théorie de l'imprévision'*).

The leading case is the 'arrêt Gaz de Bordeaux' decided in 1916 concerning a concession of a utility company for the provision of gas and electricity within the city for a period of 30 years. The contract had been concluded in 1904. After the outbreak of World War I, the price of coal used for the production of gas consumed for public lighting had risen from roughly 28 francs per ton to 117 francs, and the company wanted to have the price of gas adapted to the changed circumstances. Since no amicable settlement could be reached, the administrative courts were called upon to decide the dispute. The company's claim was rejected in the court of first instance, but the *Conseil d'Etat* granted it. The public interest in the continuous supply of gas as well as the fact that *'l'économie du contrat se trouve absolument bouleversée'* militated in favour of a contract modification. In a situation of 'force majeure' reasonable interpretation (*interprétation raisonnable*) must lead to the result that the utility company can claim a contribution (*indemnité*) from the consumer so as to cover part of the loss which would otherwise be caused if the price remained unchanged.[8]

This different treatment of contracts of public law on the one hand, and contracts operating in the private law sphere on the other hand, can hardly be justified by considerations of public interest, which prevail in the reasoning given by the administrative courts. It is not surprising, therefore, that the legislator had to intervene repeatedly: the *loi Failliot* promulgated on 21 January 1918 marks the beginning of a long chain of legislative acts aimed at adapting contractual relations of private law to a totally changed economic situation. It concerned contracts concluded before the outbreak of World War I where the performance would have caused hardship or loss greatly in excess of what the parties could reasonably have foreseen at the time of contracting. In a case like this, the courts were given the power to rescind or suspend such contracts. Moreover, the judge could make an order obliging the parties to renegotiate their contract. After World War II similar legislation was necessary in order to adapt private law relations to radically changed economic conditions.[9] Owing to the restrictive attitude of French civil courts, and the piecemeal intervention of the legislator, businessmen making contracts governed by French law are mindful of this jurisprudence when it comes

[8] *Conseil d'Etat* 30 March 1916, Gaz de Bordeaux, D 1916.3.25. The case is analysed by Denis-M Philippe, *Changement de circonstances et bouleversement de l'économie contractuelle* (1986) 71 *et seq*; see also K Zweigert and H Kötz, *An Introduction to Comparative Law* (2nd ed 1992) p 565.

[9] For details see Denis-M Philippe, *Changement de circonstances et bouleversement de l'économie contractuelle* (1986) pp 105 ff.

to the conclusion of a long-term contract. They usually incorporate clauses guarding against all sorts of risks which would make the performance of contractual obligations excessively onerous.

Legislative inroads in the principle of *pacta sunt servanda*

GENERAL RULES: GERMANY AND ITALY

The brief look at French law has already shown that the legislator may be compelled to intervene in an extreme situation where the underlying basis of the transaction has collapsed due to radical and unforeseen changes of the surrounding economic conditions. But, in spite of this experience, legislators in civil law countries have been hesitant to lay down general rules on the effect of such changes of circumstances on contractual obligations. Leaving aside cases of supervening impossibility of performance, where the subject-matter of the contract is a specific thing which has perished, the influence of other frustrating events was rarely considered. The Prussian General Land Law (ALR) of 1794 is one of the few codifications which tried to cope with the present problem in general terms. It starts out with the principle that: 'apart from the case of factual impossibility, performance of a contract may not, as a rule, be refused on the ground of altered circumstances,'[10] but then goes on to add an important qualification:

If, however, such an unforeseen change makes it impossible to achieve the final aim pursued by the parties as expressed in the contract or inferable from the nature of the transaction, then each of them may withdraw from the unperformed contract.[11]

This general rule is supplemented by a number of detailed provisions concerning indemnification (*Entschädigung*) if the alteration is a risk to be borne by one of the parties alone.[12]

The general rule of the Prussian General Land Law did not recommend itself to the draftsmen of other civil codifications which were attempted in several German states during the nineteenth century. The Civil Code of the Kingdom of Saxony of 1863, for instance, explicitly ruled out any one-sided withdrawal from a contractual obligation because 'the circumstances under which the contract was made have changed, or perfor-

---

[10] § 377 I 5 ALR.   [11] § 378 I 5 ALR.

[12] The Austrian Civil Code of 1811 contains a comparable general rule. However, it applies only to an 'agreement to make a contract', ie a preliminary contract which remains binding only if the circumstances prevailing at the time of the agreement have not so changed in the meanwhile as to frustrate the purpose of the intended contract (Art 936 ABGB). English law does not recognize such 'contracts to make a contract'.

mance and counterperformance have become disproportionate'.[13] It was different only where the parties had either envisaged this situation by an express stipulation, or where a special provision in the Code allowed the refusal of performance.[14]

Although most of the German scholars of nineteenth century legal science rejected the doctrine of *clausula rebus sic stantibus*, because of its vagueness and danger to the certainty of the law, one of the eminent 'Pandectists', Professor Windscheid, came forward with a theory which made it possible to give effect to unforeseen supervening events. In several publications between 1847 and 1892, he established the 'doctrine of (tacit) presupposition' (*Lehre von der Voraussetzung*).[15] His ideas deserve mention at this point because they had considerable influence on the deliberations of the Commission which was responsible for the first draft of the BGB. Space does not permit to give a full account of this complex theory, with its Romanist background. Accepting the risk of oversimplification, the core of this theory may, perhaps, be stated thus: a contracting party usually assumes that the intended legal consequences will occur only under certain circumstances. However, this assumption that a certain state of affairs will prevail has not been elevated to the status of an express 'condition' of the transaction. If this assumption is falsified, it may not always be just and reasonable to insist on the fulfilment of a contractual promise, always provided, however, that the promisee was in a position to realise that the 'presupposition' had a determining influence on the will of the promisor. As a consequence, the promisor should be entitled to demand rescission of the contract. It is therefore fair to say that Windscheid's theory comes very close to a contract concluded under a 'condition' (*Bedingung*) that the assumed state of affairs remain the same throughout the period of the contractual relation. This explains why Windscheid called the (tacit) assumption an 'inchoate condition' (*unentwickelte Bedingung*).

The main objection raised by Windscheid's opponents was that unilateral motives, even though recognizable by the other party, could not be treated like conditions unless they had become terms of the contract. Both legal certainty and the security of commercial dealings would be in great danger if one party were allowed to pass on his contractual risk to the other party.[16] Although Windscheid's theory was not generally accepted

---

[13] § 864.

[14] But these were rare cases only concerning gratuitous promises eg Art 1174 (gratuitous loan for use) and Art 1261 (gratuitous deposit of movables).

[15] The principal work was his monograph on 'Die Lehre des römischen Rechts von der Voraussetzung' (1850). Another English translation of this theory would be 'doctrine of the contractual assumption' (see Tony Weir's translation of K Zweigert and H Kötz, *An Introduction to Comparative Law* (2nd ed 1992) p 557.

[16] O Lenel, 'Nochmals die Lehre von der Voraussetzung' AcP 79 (1892) 49–107 was Windscheid's most influential opponent.

by legal science in his time, we now know from experience that the problem of achieving a fair balance between the binding force of contracts and equity cannot easily be disposed of by a mere reference to the certainty of the law. 'I am firmly convinced', Windscheid remarked at the end of this discussion, 'that the tacit presupposition . . . will time and again claim recognition. Thrown out by the door, it will always re-enter through the window.'[17]

The first draft of the BGB, published in 1887, contained a provision along the lines of Windscheid's basic idea of the 'tacit presupposition'. The *condictio causa data causa non secuta* (= *condictio ob rem*) was drafted in a manner reminiscent of this doctrine.[18] This is not surprising, because Windscheid was a member of the First Commission, and it is well known that he was dominant in the deliberations leading to the first draft. However, the Second Commission, which revised the first draft, reversed this decision. The main reason for rejecting this doctrine was that it would endanger the security of commercial transactions. Moreover, the German Supreme Court (the *Reichsgericht*) had questioned the soundness of this doctrine, although it had paid it lip-service in some earlier decisions.[19] The Commission also pointed out that the 'presupposition', even though this word is often used in everyday life, was not a useful legal concept which could clearly be distinguished from mere unilateral motives of a contracting party. It might be different only where the parties have referred to a presupposition in such a way that it must be regarded as a term of their contract. If such an assumption is falsified, the legal consequence may then be that the effect of the transaction lapses because it was subject to a condition subsequent (*auflösende Bedingung*), or the contract may be construed as if it contained a reservation of a right of rescission (*Vorbehalt eines Rücktrittsrechts*). These legal devices, it was thought, would enable the courts to cope with those cases where it was just and equitable to absolve a party from a contractual obligation.[20]

Although the BGB has refrained from adopting a general provision dealing with the problem of modification of contracts in the event of changing circumstances, there are a few isolated rules which may be associated with the basic idea underlying the *clausula rebus sic stantibus*. Only some of them will briefly be mentioned here.

---

[17] Windscheid, 'Die Voraussetzung' AcP 78 (1892) 197.

[18] § 742 Entwurf I; see Motive zu dem Entwurfe eines Bürgerlichen Gesetzbuches für das Deutsche Reich, Vol II, Recht der Schuldverhältnisse. Amtliche Ausgabe (2nd ed 1896) 842–3.

[19] Reichsgericht 13 May 1889, RGZ 24, 169.

[20] Protokolle der Kommission für die zweite Lesung des Entwurfs des Bürgerlichen Gesetzbuches, Vol II: Recht der Schuldverhältnisse (1898) 690–1.

Section 779

A contract whereby the dispute or the uncertainty of the parties concerning a legal relationship is ended by way of mutual concession (compromise = *Vergleich*) is invalid if the state of affairs regarded as essential according to the terms of the contract do not correspond with the actual facts, and if the dispute or the uncertainty would not have arisen if the state of affairs had been known.

Section 321

If a person is obliged by a mutual contract to perform his part first, he may, if after the conclusion of the contract a significant deterioration in the financial position of the other party occurs whereby the claim for the counter-performance is endangered, refuse to perform his part until the counter-performance is made or security is given for it.

Section 610

A person who promises to make a loan may, in case of doubt, revoke the promise if a serious worsening in the financial circumstances of the other party comes about whereby the claim for repayment is endangered.

Strictly speaking, only §§ 321 and 610 are dealing with fact-situations where the decisive change of circumstances occurred after the conclusion of the contract, whereas s 779 concerns a case in which both parties made a contract in the mistaken belief that their basic assumption was correct, even though it was non-existent from the beginning.

The position of the BGB may be contrasted with Arts 1467–1469 of the Italian Codice Civile of 1942: an entire section is reserved for long-term contracts, the performance of which has become excessively onerous ('*eccessivamente onerosa*') for one of the parties due to extraordinary and unforeseeable events. In such a case this party may demand rescission of the contract, but the other party can avoid this by offering an equitable modification of the terms of the contract ('*offrendo di modificare equamente le condizioni del contratto*'). However, no rescission will be granted if the supervening '*onerosita*' is still within the normal risk of the contract.[21]

---

[21] Article 1467. For further details see Art 1468, applying these principles to contracts where only one of the parties has assumed an obligation, and Art 1469 dealing with contracts which by their very nature are 'aleatoric'. Obviously, the general principle enunciated in Art 1467 cannot apply to the last-mentioned type of contract. As to the Italian case-law turning on these provisions, see G Cian and A Trabucchi, *Commentario breve al Codice Civile* (4th ed 1992) Art 1467 sub II–V. In the opinion of these commentators Italian courts applying Art 1467 have introduced 'nel nostro ordinamento l'istituto della *presupposizione*' (emphasis in original).

SPECIAL RULES FOR BUILDING CONTRACTS: FRENCH AND SWISS LAW

Contracts for work on goods and, in particular, building contracts, give rise to a continuing legal relationship. After the drawing up of plans and specifications which led to the conclusion of the contract, a considerable time may elapse before the work is completed. In such a contract the risk of price increases is obvious, especially during an inflationary period. Contracts concluded on a lump sum basis may then be ruinous for the contractor, because the price thus stipulated will remain valid under all circumstances. This is the solution offered by French law: an architect or contractor who has made a lump sum contract ('*marché à forfait*') may not demand a higher price, neither under the pretext of a rise in costs of labour and materials, nor for changes and extensions of the plan, unless a new price was agreed upon with the employer.[22] This applies also to extraordinary or unforeseeable circumstances which strike at the root of the contract price. This is in keeping with the general rejection of the theory of unforeseen circumstances ('*théorie de l'imprévision*') by French courts in the field of private law. However, the practice necessity to recognize price escalation clauses has so widely been felt in France that, under extraordinary circumstances, the *Cour de cassation* nowadays regards them as valid in lump sum contracts within the meaning of Art 1793 Code Civil. While a general reference to a possible increase in costs of labour and materials would still be incompatible with the nature of a lump sum contract, it will be different if the parties have introduced a special index clause which provides a firm method of computation.[23] Thus, as has aptly been expressed by Borricand 'the unchangeability of the lump sum to be paid has been replaced by the unchangeability of its mode of calculation'.[24] This clause mitigates the conflict of interests inherent in a lump sum contract. In this context it is interesting to note that in some countries belonging to the French legal family Article 1793 Code Civil has not been adopted literally, but has been modified by an open recognition of the '*théorie de l'imprévision*'. The civil codes of Argentina (Art 1633 referring to Art 1198), Chile (Art 2003(2)) and Egypt (Art 658(4)) may serve as examples of this development overcoming the rigidity of the lump sum contract.

The Swiss Code of Obligations starts out with the rule that a person who contracts to produce a work for a fixed price may not demand a higher price, even if it proves more arduous or expensive than was

---

[22] Article 1793 Code Civil.
[23] Cass com 28 May 1963, Gaz Pal 1963.2.402; Cass civ 30 May 1963, Bull civ 1963 I 246 no 289; Cass civ 11 February 1964, Bull civ 1964 I 57 no 79.
[24] Borricand, *Observations sur le marché à forfait* DS 1965 Chr 106(107).

foreseen.[25] If, however, extraordinary circumstances which could not be foreseen or which were beyond the assumptions made by both parties make it impossible to produce the work, or make its production disproportionately difficult, the judge has a discretion to raise the price or rescind the contract.[26] Thus, in a case concerning a lump sum building contract which came before the Swiss Federal Tribunal after World War I, the contractor had expressly agreed to take all risks of 'mistakes, omissions or wrong interpretations of plans and specifications'. Owing to the sudden change of economic conditions during the war, the costs of labour and materials had increased by 60 per cent during the contract period. The court admitted the abstract possibility that the contractor could have waived the benefit flowing from Art 373(2) OR, but was not prepared to construe the clause contained in the contract in such a way.[27]

As has already been indicated in the context of French law, the problem of taking into account unforeseen and abnormal circumstances in the fulfilment of a fixed price contract has lost some of its former significance, due to contractual price escalation clauses widely used in the building industry. This is true also in Swiss law, in spite of the express recognition of the *clausula rebus sic stantibus* in contracts for work and labour. Obviously, the operation of such a rule fitting only exceptional cases of general economic disaster is no longer regarded as sufficient, particularly in the building industry. A review of cases which turn on Art 373(2) OR shows why this is so. The circumstances which may either give rise to an adjustment of the contract sum, or entitle a court to authorize the termination of the contract, must not merely have been quite extraordinary ones, but they also have to be beyond the parties' reasonable contemplation at the time of contracting. However, in times of constantly rising costs of labour and materials this last condition will not easily be satisfied, because the parties could have adapted their contract to this situation.[28]

German case-law and its doctrinal bases[29]

ECONOMIC IMPOSSIBILITY

The decision of the German legislator not to incorporate a general provision on the influence of change of circumstances into the BGB is

---

[25] Article 373 OR. [26] Article 373(2) OR.
[27] Bundesgericht 8 May 1924, BGE 50 II 158. The court added that the burden of proof for such an absolute obligation would be on the employer.
[28] This is pointed out by the Swiss Federal Tribunal; see Bundesgericht 27 March 1922, BGE 48 II 119; for more cases referring to Art 373(2) OR, see Bundesgericht 14 July 1921, BGE 47 II 314; Bundesgericht 8 May 1924, BGE 50 II 158.
[29] See WF Ebke and B Steinhauer, ch 7 above.

compensated, at least in part, by detailed rules concerning supervening impossibility of performance. It is not surprising, therefore, that attempts were made to cope with the present problem by expanding the notion of impossibility, so as to comprise cases in which it would mean 'asking too much of the debtor' (*dem Schuldner unzumutbar*) if the creditor insisted upon performance according to contract. The first crucial cases which reached the German Supreme Court shortly after the BGB had come into force were decided along these lines. A new concept, economic impossibility, was introduced: in a case decided in 1904, the defendant had agreed to sell the plaintiff a large quantity of a special type of flour to be produced by a secret recipe in the seller's own mill. Unfortunately, the mill was destroyed by fire before delivery of the goods. The case turned on the proper construction of § 279: 'If a debt described by class is owed, and so long as delivery of this class of object is possible, the debtor is responsible for his inability to deliver, even though no fault may be imputed to him.' In that case a larger quantity of this type of flour had been shipped to another buyer shortly before the fire broke out. Strictly speaking, therefore, it could not be maintained that such merchandise was no longer available, even though this batch of goods had already been consigned to somebody else. But in the opinion of the court, a debtor, in a case like this, is not obliged to obtain substitute deliveries from remote foreign markets. Where the fortuitous event has rendered the performance of the contractual obligation so difficult that commercial men would regard such extraordinary difficulty as amounting to impossibility, the debtor is relieved from his obligation to perform.[30]

This reasoning derives some support from an important provision of the general part of the law of obligations, which may be regarded as the *sedes materiae* of 'German Equity' (*sit venia verbo*). The provision usually referred to in the cases to be discussed here is § 242 of the BGB: 'The debtor is bound to effect performance according to the requirements of good faith, giving consideration to commercial usage'.[31] Cases of bulk sales of generic goods have given the German Supreme Court the opportunity to refine the rule concerning economic impossibility. Three cases turning on the sale of tin may be taken as examples for the proposition that a mere increase in prices, even though exceeding 100 per cent, will not be sufficient to release the seller from his obligation to deliver the

---

[30] Reichsgericht 23 February 1904, RGZ 57, 116, 119; see also Reichsgericht 6 July 1898, RGZ 42, 114 concerning a comparable fact situation decided under the *Gemeines Recht*, ie Roman law as it was in force at that time in some parts of Germany.

[31] In German: *Der Schuldner ist verpflichtet, die Leistung so zu bewirken, wie Treu und Glauben mit Rücksicht auf die Verkehrssitte es erfordern.* Another provision which is often relied upon by the courts in the present context is Art 157: 'Contracts shall be interpreted according to the requirements of good faith, giving consideration to common usage'.

goods for the stipulated amount.[32] The contracts were concluded a few weeks before the outbreak of World War I. When delivery was due, the world market price for tin had risen considerably, the increase ranging from 100 to 300 per cent, but there was still a market in the goods. The court also took into consideration that, in all of these cases, the sellers were experienced wholesalers who were accustomed to price fluctuations in the import trade. If they were released from their contracts, the effect on retailers who had been more cautious in calculating resale prices would have been disastrous and manifestly unjust, because the percentage of price increases in their resale contracts would be much lower. The result might then be that the retailer could not plead 'economic impossibility'! It was held, therefore, that the wholesaler is not released on the ground of § 242 of the BGB if such merchandise is still available on the wholesale market, even though the price has risen to an extraordinary, hitherto unthinkable, degree. In the words of the court:

On the contrary, for such transactions the principle holds good that the seller will never be released as long as such goods are still being sold and bought on the market and are available in sufficient quantity for the performance of the contract. What the situation would be if only a few parcels of goods could be obtained by a fantastic offer or from a single supplier at an exorbitant price need not now be decided.[33]

The decisions in these tin cases must not lead to the generalization that mere price increases could never be relevant. A closer analysis of the cases decided after the end of World War I shows that a distinction was made between wholesale contracts of generic goods obtainable on a world market, and other types of contract where the debtor had no opportunity to choose between several suppliers. The point may then have been reached at which it will be held that performance of the contractual obligation at the stipulated price would be 'utterly ruinous' ('*geradezu ruinös*').[34] This may be illustrated by two cases decided in 1920. In the first, a lease of business premises had been concluded in 1912 for a period of eight years. Under this contract, the lessor was also obliged to supply steam for the lessee's commercial enterprise. The annual rent had been fixed at 9.363 Marks. Owing to an enormous increase in prices of coal, the lessor had incurred additional costs to the amount of 89.000 Marks during the time between September 1917 and July 1919. His demand for rectification of

[32] Reichsgericht 21 March 1916, RGZ 88, 172; Reichsgericht 15 March 1918, RGZ 92, 322; Reichsgericht 25 February 1919, RGZ 95, 41.
[33] Reichsgericht 21 March 1916, RGZ 88, 172, 177.
[34] Reichsgericht 8 July 1920, RGZ 99, 258, 260 concerning a long-term lease of rooms in a factory building including an obligation to supply steam and electricity. However, on the facts of this case as found by the courts below, it was held that the point of 'ruination' had not yet been reached. For a different outcome of a similar case, see note 35 below.

the lease to the effect that the lessee should be obliged to make an additional payment had been rejected in the lower courts, on the ground that the lessor had to blame himself for his miscalculation. He should have taken into account the consequences of a possible war. While admitting that mere miscalculations of a contracting party cannot, without more, be a sufficient ground for rectification of the price, the Supreme Court took a different view: it was beyond human foresight to anticipate such an economic development at the time of contracting. Hence it could not be laid to the blame of either party not to have incorporated a 'war clause' into their contract.[35] In the second case, in which the 'defence of ruination' (*Einrede der Existenzvernichtung*) was also successful, the sole distributor for Southern Germany of Opel motor-cars had made a contract of sale on the basis of a price list dated February 1919. When performance was due a few months later the manufacturer had increased these prices considerably owing to the inflationary development in the immediate post-war period. After having emphasized that, as a matter of principle, the seller must bear the risk of price increases just as the buyer, correspondingly, must bear the risk of a sudden fall in prices, the court pointed out that the distributor had made about thirty similar contracts. Fulfilment of all these contracts at the price originally agreed upon would cause him a total loss of almost 800.000 Marks within a few months. This would ruin his business and result in immediate bankruptcy.[36]

The reasoning of this decision of the third civil division of the Supreme Court was soon criticized in a judgment of the second division of this court: the 'defence of ruination' leads to a distinction between a wealthy debtor and an impecunious debtor. This was not regarded as a valid distinction, because every debtor must be prepared to face bankruptcy. The decisive criterion in these cases should rather be the disproportion of performance and counter-performance caused by an unexpected supervening change of circumstances. The radical disturbance of this equilibrium may reach the point at which standards of good faith militate against the creditor's claim to performance as originally agreed upon. It will suffice, therefore, that the value of the currency is diminished to such a degree that the debtor would receive a counter-performance which is not in the least an equivalent for his performance.[37] The decision marks the transition to a new general theory designed as a basis for the courts' decision on the problem of altered circumstances.

---

[35] Reichsgericht 21 September 1920, RGZ 100, 129, 133–4.
[36] Reichsgericht 22 October 1920, RGZ 100, 134, 137.
[37] Reichsgericht 29 November 1921, RGZ 103, 171, 173.

COLLAPSE OF THE UNDERLYING BASIS OF THE TRANSACTION

The doctrine to which the German Supreme Court began to adhere after 1921 is usually associated with a monograph published by Paul Oertmann in the same year. The title of this book, translated into English, is *The Basis of the Transaction* (*Die Geschäftsgrundlage*) with the subtitle *A New Legal Concept* (*Ein neuer Rechtsbegriff*). Oertmann took up Windscheid's doctrine of the (tacit) presupposition, and reformulated and improved it considerably. In this effort he was guided by the desire to provide a solid dogmatic basis for the solution of the legal problems caused by the radical changes of the economic conditions in the early 1920s which could not possibly have been contemplated by Windscheid. 'Basis of the transaction', according to this theory, is the assumption shared by the contracting parties that certain circumstances which they regard as important are either existing or will come about, even though this assumption was not expressed in their declarations exchanged when making the contract. This distinguishes Oertmann's theory from Windscheid's doctrine, for it is not sufficient that the assumption belied by the future course of events was privately entertained by the party to whose disadvantage things have turned: it must have been manifested by him at the conclusion of the contract and acquiesced in by the other party.[38]

It must, however, be admitted that Oertmann's theory is also open to serious objections. This is already apparent in the somewhat outmoded hypothetical case still to be found in students' textbooks: the father of the bride buys furniture for the forthcoming marriage of his daughter. The circumstances are such that the seller knows exactly for what purpose this purchase is made. Shortly afterwards the husband-to-be changes his mind, and the wedding is called off. Everybody, including Oertmann, seems to agree that it would be an absurd legal consequence if this contract of sale had lapsed as a result of altered circumstances. But why is this so? The simplest answer would be that this is not within the sphere of a seller's contractual risk.[39] Oertmann's theory also runs into difficulties in all those cases where the subsequent alteration of circumstances was not foreseeable by the parties at the time of contracting. All that can be said in a situation like this is that the parties regarded the continuance of the present circumstances as self-evident. This excludes any assumptions about the future course of events. In the end it boils down to the substance of the

---

[38] P Oertmann, *Die Geschäftsgrundlage: Ein neuer Rechtsbegriff* (1921) pp 37-8.
[39] Oertmann's explanation, *ibid.*, 149, remains in the dark when he refers to 'the special interconnection of interests on the part of the one who acted under this assumption'. For competent criticism see Kegel, 'Empfiehlt es sich, den Einfluss grundlegender Veränderungen des Wirtschaftslebens auf Verträge gesetzlich zu regeln und in welchem Sinn?' *Verhandlungen des 40 Deutschen Juristentages*, vol I (1953) 135, 139–43, 155–7.

classical *clausula*, namely that matters remain the same as they were at the time of conclusion of the contract.

Oertmann's theory has become famous because the Supreme Court adopted it and cited it in numerous leading cases. However, a perusal of these cases leaves the reader with the impression that these citations are mere ornaments. It thus appears that the decisions in cases where performance has unexpectedly been rendered more onerous for one of the parties depend very much on their own particular facts. Moreover, the weight to be attached to such supervening events is not the same in all types of contract. The allocation of risk inherent in each type of contract seems to be the most important element in these crucial cases, turning on the 'collapse of the underlying basis of the transaction'. A brief look at some of these spectacular decisions should confirm this impression.

The first decision paying lip-service to Oertmann's theory concerned a contract concluded on 21 May 1919: the defendant had agreed to sell real property which did not yet belong to him, but which he hoped to obtain from a partnership which was in process of liquidation because he had given notice of its dissolution. The purchase price was in keeping with the market value of the premises at the time of contracting. However, the liquidation of the partnership was delayed and, meanwhile, the price of real property increased rapidly owing to the sudden depreciation of currency. The vendor, therefore, considered himself no longer bound by the contract. The Supreme Court agreed in principle, holding that the court below had not sufficiently taken into consideration the 'defence of the so-called *clausula rebus sic stantibus*'. The fear that recognition of this defence might lead to 'complete lawlessness in the field of contracts' would be unfounded if the necessary caution were observed. Referring to Oertmann's theory, it was held that the depreciation of currency occurring after autumn 1919 had totally upset the equivalence of performance and counter-performance which had been the underlying basis of the transaction. But this did not mean that the defendant vendor could regard the contract as having lapsed; instead, the court below was instructed to re-examine the basis of the transaction and, if possible, to adjust the price in view of the existing devaluation so as to avoid the rescission of the contract. Only if the plaintiff purchaser was not willing to renegotiate the price could the defendant resile from the contract.[40] Professor Kegel, who has made a profound analysis of this German postwar case-law, rightly remarks that the true criterion on which the decision of these cases hinges is the proper distribution of risk on the basis of policy considerations: whether the buyer of the furniture in the above-mentioned hypothetical case will be able to use these goods as contemplated must remain his risk.

---

[40] Reichsgericht 3 February 1922, RGZ 103, 328, 333–4.

The seller neither knows of such risk nor could he control it if he knew about it. But it is different with the risk of currency depreciation as a result of a lost war which cannot be allocated to one party alone and, hence, must be borne by the people at large.[41]

The above decision deserves special attention because it foreshadows the famous line of cases on 'revalorization' (*Aufwertung*). As has already been explained,[42] § 242 of the BGB was the provision usually relied upon by the courts in their attempts to achieve an equitable distribution of the currency risk. In a landmark decision handed down on 28 November 1923, the Supreme Court made the owner of mortgaged property pay the mortgagee a supplementary sum, over and above the nominal amount of the mortgage, so as to make good, at least in part, the devaluation of paper money in Germany.[43] The mortgage, securing a loan of 13.000 marks, had been entered into the Land Register (*Grundbuch*) before World War I. When the loan was due for repayment in 1920 the owner/mortgagor had offered the mortgagee the sum of 18.980 marks (capital plus interest in arrears). It goes without saying that the purchasing power of this sum in paper money was ridiculous if compared with the value of a pre-war loan under the gold standard. The Supreme Court, therefore, sent the case back to the court below with precise instructions as to the factors determining the amount of revalorization: apart from the increased value of immovables in general, the nature of the real property in question—whether agricultural, industrial or residential—had to be taken into account in fixing a reasonable sum. For the present purpose it is not necessary to discuss further details of this case. But it is a remarkable fact that two years later the legislation, which usually lags behind in emergency situations, adopted the ratio decidendi of this case in the Law of Revalorization ('*Aufwertungsgesetz*') passed on 16 July 1925: the owner could only extinguish a mortgage on his property by paying a sum amounting to 25 per cent of the value of the mortgage in gold marks.

The legal situation was particularly complicated in cases where the vendor of real property was obliged to extinguish any mortgages or land charges (*Grundschulden*) with which the object was encumbered.[44] If he had fulfilled this obligation before the transfer of ownership to the purchaser, but the creditor had been paid in worthless paper money he could now demand the reinstatement of the mortgage in the Land Register. As a consequence of this 'resuscitation' of the mortgage under the Law of Revalorization, the vendor could no longer be regarded as having transferred the property 'free of all encumbrances' (*lastenfrei*). He had to pay off

---

[41] Kegel in Kegel, Rupp and Zweigert, *Die Einwirkung des Krieges auf Verträge* (1941), pp 111, 151–2 and *passim*.

[42] See above.

[43] Reichsgericht 28 November 1923, RGZ 107, 78.

[44] See also § 439(2) BGB.

the mortgage a second time, but now in hard currency. Since he had received the purchase price in paper marks this was very hard on him, because the sum he had to pay the creditor exceeded the purchase price by far if converted into gold marks. Thus the Supreme Court had to strike a balance: the vendor was granted a 'contribution claim' (*Ausgleichsanspruch*) against the purchaser, who had to share the expense of paying off the mortgage with the vendor, the amount depending upon a number of circumstances still to be examined by the court below. If the purchaser refused, the vendor was given the option to rescind the contract.[45]

In this context another class of cases is worth mentioning, in which the principle of good faith as embodied in § 242 of the BGB was applied, or at least considered: in view of the shaken belief in the stability of the German mark, merchants in some branches of trade were in the habit of contracting on the basis of foreign currencies, even though the inflationary period had come to an end. Such contracts were governed by German law because the only foreign element was the stipulation as to the currency. The English pound was regarded as a highly reliable currency because it was based on the gold standard. Therefore contracts were concluded on the tacit assumption that England would remain on the gold standard. The Gold Standard Act of 21 September 1931, came as an unpleasant surprise to these sellers who had made contracts on the basis of this assumption. In one of the leading cases, decided in 1933, the Supreme Court held that, as a matter of principle, a devaluation of 20–30 per cent could give the seller of cotton the right to claim an increment (*Ausgleichsanspruch*) towards the loss attributable to the devaluation. However, in remitting the case to the court below the Supreme Court gave detailed instructions as to certain relevant facts still to be found, only two of which will be mentioned here. Could it be that the seller, in his capacity as an importer of cotton, had taken advantage of the devaluation of the English pound? Did the buyer export cotton and, if so, did he suffer any losses due to the diminished value of the pound?[46]

After World War II, some of the problems mentioned above recurred on a much larger scale. Their socio-economic background need not be described here. Suffice it to say, therefore, that millions of refugees and

---

[45] Reichsgericht 10 February 1926, RGZ 112, 329, 333–4; see also Reichsgericht 30 January 1928, RGZ 119, 133 concerning a case where the contract of sale of real property had been made after the currency reform (ie introduction of the so-called *Gleichstellungsmark*). It was held that the vendor had a good claim against the purchaser.

[46] Reichsgericht 21 June 1933, RGZ 141, 212, 219–20. But see also Reichsgericht 28 June 1934, RGZ 145, 41 concerning a loan given on the basis of the English pound, because the creditor had no faith in the stability of the mark. The contract was governed by German law, the only foreign element having been the reference to the English currency. In the opinion of the court the creditor was not entitled to an *Ausgleichsanspruch* as explained in the text, because such loans could not be placed on the same footing as exchange contracts where performance and counter-performance are concurrent conditions.

the destruction of homes and business premises caused unprecedented problems. In this chapter only their influence on contractual relations will be considered. Again, the courts had to find their way through a jungle of legal problems. Only the Law of 26 March 1952, concerning debts incurred before the currency reform of 23 June 1948, provided any help. It conferred upon the courts the power to defer or to reduce payment of a debt if the debtor made a declaration of his assets. Under this so-called *Vertragshilfegesetz* the judge could find that, in view of the altered circumstances, complete performance by the debtor would be too onerous having regard to the economic situations of both parties.[47]

A critical review of the large number of pertinent cases decided by German courts after 1945 permits the generalization that, at least at the beginning, there was some inclination to make a rather liberal use of Oertmann's theory of the *Geschäftsgrundlage*. There are decisions which have met with sharp criticism, because they had neglected the proper distribution of the contractual risk in favour of vague equitable grounds. A case decided by the Federal Supreme Court (Bundesgerichtshof = BGH) on 16 January 1953, usually called the 'pneumatic drill case' (*Bohrhämmerfall*) is a typical example: a contract for the production and delivery of 600 pneumatic drills had been concluded between parties doing business in West Germany. The model was already obsolete, but the defendant intended to send them to East Germany, where pneumatic drills of this type would still be used. This was known to the contractor. More than 200 pieces had already been produced when it became certain that the Berlin Blockade would make delivery of such goods to East Germany impossible. Had this contract for the delivery of work (*Werklieferungsvertrag*),[48] become frustrated thereby? One should have thought that this question admits only a negative answer, the more so because the Bundesgerichtshof rightly started out with the principle that a contracting party must bear the risk of not being able to use the goods as originally planned. However, the court went on to state that the intended resale of these pneumatic drills to East Germany was not merely an irrelevant motive on the part of the defendant, but constituted the 'basis of the transaction' even though the intended use of these pieces of equipment had not become a 'term of the contract'. In the opinion of the court 'both parties shared the assumption that delivery of the pneumatic drills to the East Zone would become possible in the foreseeable future, in spite of the blockade existing at the time of contracting'.[49]

[47] For details see Kegel, 'Empfiehlt es sich, den Einfluss grundlegender Veränderungen des Wirtschaftslebens auf Verträge gesetzlich zu regeln und in welchem Sinn?' *Verhandlungen des 40 Deutschen Juristentages*, vol I (1953) 135, 139–43, 224 *et seq*.
[48] Cf. § 651 BGB.
[49] Bundesgerichtshof 16 January 1953, Lindenmaier-Möhring, Nachschlagwerk des Bundesgerichtshofs, § 242 (Bb) BGB no 12. The defendant was released from his obligation

A more recent case, decided in 1978, shows that the courts are 'back to normal' in this area of the law. It concerned the energy crisis resulting from hostilities in the Middle East in 1973. Under a contract made in 1972, the plaintiff had ordered from the defendant, an oil importer, certain quantities of fuel oil to be delivered by instalments. When the contract was made the average price had been less than 100 DM per ton. During the following year the price increased gradually until it had reached 600 DM per ton, whereupon the defendant informed the plaintiff that no further deliveries at the agreed price would be made unless the price were adjusted to the present value. But the plaintiff refused any renegotiation of the price and warned the defendant of the legal consequences in case of non-fulfilment of the contract. When the defendant stopped all deliveries, the plaintiff obtained the fuel oil from another supplier at the higher price. This additional expenditure was the basis of his claim for damages on the ground of breach of contract.[50] The action succeeded. The Bundesgerichtshof admitted that, as a rule, bilateral contracts where promise stands against promise are concluded on the assumption that performance and counter-performance are equivalent. But this principle does not apply if it may be ascertained from the terms of the contract how the parties intended to delimit their spheres of risk. In that case, the parties had agreed on a fixed price, which evinced an intention on the part of the defendant to assume the risk of price fluctuations. But even if this assumption of risk were limited to 'normal' fluctuations, the defendant should have realized by the middle of 1973 that further drastic price increases were imminent, and avoided at least part of his risk by purchasing larger quantities of oil for storage. In view of the paramount importance of the principle of *pacta sunt servanda* (*Vertragstreue*) 'the defence of collapse of the underlying basis of the transaction may only be invoked if this is indispensable for avoiding an intolerable result irreconcilable with law and justice'.[51]

Numerous other cases were decided along these lines. Only a few will be mentioned before concluding this review of German case-law: a firm of building contractors which had sold family homes had also offered to provide these homes with direct heating produced in a power station of their own. The prices were to be determined by the tariffs charged by the

to accept and pay for all of the pneumatic drills ordered, but the contract was 'adapted to the new situation' in accordance with standards of good faith (§ 242 BGB). As a result of this reasoning, the defendant had to pay one-quarter of the total agreed sum. This was meant to compensate the contractor for the expenditure incurred in beginning to carry out the contract. The decision is criticized by K Larenz, *Geschäftsgrundlage und Vertragserfüllung* (3rd ed 1963) pp 122–4; see also the critical remarks of K Zweigert and H Kötz, *An Introduction to Comparative Law* (2nd ed 1992) p 563.

[50] See § 326 BGB dealing with the legal consequences of default in performing a 'mutual contract' (*gegenseitiger Vertrag*).
[51] Bundesgerichtshof 8 February 1978, BGH, JZ 1978, 235, 236.

public utility of this community. However, soon after the conclusion of this contract it turned out that the building contractors had made a bad bargain, because the public utility did not shift the full burden of the price increase of coal and oil on to its customers. Apparently, this undertaking had been able to make up for these rising costs by other means. Again, the Bundesgerichtshof insisted upon fulfilment of the contractual promise. Although the building contractors' firm had suffered a financial loss, amounting to 58.000 DM per year, this was no reason to plead 'collapse of the underlying basis of the transaction' (*Wegfall der Geschäftsgrundlage*), because the circumstances causing these losses were clearly within their sphere of risk. Moreover, the court was of the opinion that an enterprise of that size should be able to absorb such a loss.[52]

In a later decision concerning the long-term lease of a hotel situated at the sea front, the lessee had found it impossible to run the establishment at a profit. Since considerable investments would have to be made for its modernization, he wanted to renegotiate the lease. When the lessor refused any modification of this contract, the lessee stopped payment of the rent. The lessor's action for payment of the arrears succeeded. The main reason given by the Bundesgerichtshof for rejecting the lessee's plea of *Wegfall der Geschäftsgrundlage* was that the problem of modernization could have been foreseen at the time of contracting.[53]

Conclusion

This chapter has dealt with supervening events striking at the root of a contract, and their effect on contractual obligations. As was explained in the Introduction, cases of factual impossibility of performance where the object of the obligation is a specific thing which has perished were not discussed because the BGB contains a set of clear-cut rules dealing with this situation.[54] However, we have seen in the cases of so-called 'economic impossibility'[55] that these code provisions are too narrow for coping with other fundamental changes of circumstances, which in English law are covered by the doctrine of frustration. In German law the 'doctrine of the underlying basis of the transaction' (*Lehre von der Geschäftsgrundlage*) does

---

[52] Bundesgerichtshof 25 May 1977, BGH, NJW 1977, 2262, 2263.
[53] Bundesgerichtshof 19 April 1978, BGH, NJW 1978, 2390, 2392; see also Bundesgerichtshof 1 June 1979, BGHZ 74, 370 concerning the sale of a piece of land sold as 'land set aside for building' (*Bauerwartungsland*). In the end it turned out that no planning and building permission could be obtained. The parties had contracted under the mistaken belief to have made provision for this case. However, in reality, the contract was silent on this point. This gap was filled by way of *ergänzende Vertragsauslegung* ('suppletive construction') based upon § 157 BGB (see note 31 above). The result was that the vendor had to bear this risk.
[54] See Introduction, above.   [55] See above.

not merely refer to supervening events causing the 'collapse of the under-lying basis of the transaction'[56] (*Wegfall der Geschäftsgrundlage*): it also comprises cases where the contract was concluded on the basis of a wrong assumption. An example of such 'absence of the underlying basis of the transaction' (*Fehlen der Geschäftsgrundlage*) is § 779 of the BGB.

The overlap between this group of cases and the law of mistake is obvi-ous, but the intricate problems concerning the borderline between irrele-vant motives of the parties and relevant common mistakes were outside the scope of this chapter.

I have concentrated on the law in action, and deliberately refrained from discussing the manifold theories surrounding the *Geschäftsgrundlage* in German law. Only those theories which had a noticeable influence on the courts have been considered. From a comparative point of view, the scepticism expressed by Professor Treitel in regard to the 'so-called theo-retical or juristic basis of the doctrine of frustration' deserves special investigation.[57] Similar observations could easily be made in German law. Stripped of their theoretical ornaments, the German decisions show that satisfactory solutions in the crucial cases can only be reached after careful analysis of the distribution of risks inherent in each type of contract.[58]

---

[56] See above.   [57] GH Treitel, *The Law of Contract* (8th ed 1991) p 818 *et seq.*
[58] This is also the substance of the theory propounded by Kegel, 'Empfiehlt es sich, den Einfluss grundlegender Veränderungen des Wirtschaftslebens auf Verträge gesetzlich zu regeln und in welchem Sinn?' *Verhandlungen des 40 Deutschen Juristentages*, vol I (1953) 135, 139–43, pp 199 ff.

15

Alternatives and Frustration*

GH TREITEL**

Alternatives are a tricky concept. The point may perhaps be illustrated by one of the many stories about Groucho Marx who, when asked by an air hostess to 'put out that cigar or you'll annoy the ladies,' is said to have replied 'do you mean I have a choice?' Tradition abandons the story at this interesting point, leaving followers of Groucho to sympathize with him in his perplexity. No less difficult are the problems posed by alternatives in the law of contract. Such problems have arisen in a variety of contexts: e.g., in order to determine whether the requirements of offer and acceptance[1] and those of certainty[2] have been satisfied, and (where the alternatives relate to the time of performance) when performance becomes due.[3] It is, however, the effect of supervening events on alternative obligations which has been the most frequently litigated issue, and which forms the subject of the following discussion.

General rule

A contract is said to impose an alternative obligation if it gives one of the parties the right to chose between two or more specified performances (e.g. delivery of X or Y) or between two or more specified ways in which a single performance is to be rendered (e.g., delivery of X today or tomorrow, delivery of X at one of two or more specified places). If one or more of the specified alternatives become impossible or illegal after the contract is made, the general rule is that the contract is not discharged so long as at least one of those alternatives remains possible and lawful.[4]

The cases provide many illustrations of this general rule. Thus where a contract for the sale of goods provided for shipment from a

* Copyright © 1994, GH Treitel
** This essay consists, in substance, of the text of Chapter 10 of the author's book on *Frustration and Force Majeure*.
[1] *Peter Lind & Co v Mersey Docks & Harbour Board* [1972] 2 Lloyd's Rep 234.
[2] *David T Boyd & Co v Louis Louca* [1973] 1 Lloyd's Rep 209.
[3] *Reed v Kilburn Co-operative Society* (1875) LR 10 QB 264.
[4] *Barkworth v Young* (1856) 4 Drew 1, at 25; *Reardon Smith Line Ltd v Ministry of Agriculture, Fisheries and Food* [1963] AC 691, at 730; *Board of Education v Townsend* 59 NE 223, at 225 (1900); Restatement § 469; Restatement 2d Contracts § 261, and see the authorities cited in notes 5–20 below.

Mediterranean port, it was not discharged when shipment from the port from which the seller had intended to ship was prohibited by the authorities there, for shipment could lawfully be made from other ports within the contractual range.[5] Conversely, where a contract of sale provided for shipment to a range of ports, some of which later became enemy ports, it was held that the seller was bound to ship to a neutral port declared by the buyer, even though the buyer had previously declared a port which, at the time of declaration was an enemy port.[6] Similarly, where an f.o.b. contract required the seller at the buyer's option either to ship the goods from Hamburg or to warehouse them there, the seller was not discharged by an export embargo since this only prohibited the shipment of the goods and in no way prevented him from warehousing them.[7] The same rule applies in the case of a charterparty giving the charterer the right to select one of a number of ports of discharge: if it becomes illegal for the ship to go to the selected port, but remains lawful for her to go to one or more of the others within the contractual range, fresh orders must be given.[8] Again, if a contract of carriage provides that goods are to be carried in one of two named ships, the contract will not be frustrated by loss of only one of those ships: it must be performed by use of the other.[9] The position is similar where a contract gives a party a choice as to the time of shipment: e.g. where a c.i.f contract provides for shipment during 'October and/or November'. If shipment is prohibited on some of those days, but remains possible on others which have not yet gone by at the time of the prohibition, then the seller must ship on one of the latter days.[10] The rule applies, again, where a contract provides for alternative methods of payment: e.g. 'to pay in gold in New York or in sterling in London. If after the contract it becomes illegal to pay in gold in New York, [the party who was to pay] is not thereby relieved altogether from his obligation, he is merely deprived of his option'.[11] Similarly, where an insurer promises to restore damaged premises or to pay the sum insured, he must make the payment if restoration becomes impossible or illegal:

---

[5] *Warinco AG v Fritz Mauthner* [1978] 1 Lloyd's Rep 151.

[6] *Hindley & Co Ltd v General Fibre Co Ltd* [1940] 2 KB 517; and see text accompanying note 82, below.

[7] *Smith Coney & Barrett v Becker Gray & Co* [1916] 2 Ch 87. Contrast *Edward Grey & Co v Tolme & Runge* (1915) 31 TLR 551, where both alternatives had become illegal: the first by prohibition of export from the country of origin and the second by the English prohibition against trading with the enemy: see GH Treitel, *Frustration and Force Majeure* (1994), s 7–026.

[8] *Seabridge Shipping Ltd v Antco Shipping Ltd (The Furness Bridge)* [1977] 2 Lloyd's Rep 377; cf. *Kuwait Supply Co v Oyster Marine Management Inc (The Safeer)* [1994] 1 Lloyd's Rep 637, at 642.

[9] *J Lauritzen AS v Wijsmuller BV (The Super Servant Two)* [1990] 1 Lloyd's Rep 1.

[10] *RT Smyth & Co Ltd (Liverpool) v WN Lindsay Ltd (Leith)* [1953] 1 WLR 1280.

[11] *Ibid.*, at 1283; and see note 39 below.

this is so even if he has elected to restore before the supervening impossi-bility or illegality, or in ignorance of it if it already existed.[12]

The position is the same where the creditor claims to be discharged on the ground of frustration of purpose: such a claim will fail if the contract provides for alternative methods of performance, one of which would, while the other would not, frustrate his purpose in entering into the con-tract. This was the position in one of the coronation cases, in which the contract provided that the viewing facilities were to be made available on the day originally specified for the procession in question or (in the event of its cancellation) on such other day on which that procession passed the premises from which it was to be viewed. Such express provisions were held to exclude the doctrine of discharge by frustration of purpose.[13]

In the cases so far described, the contract expressly provided for alter-native methods of performance, but the general rule equally applies where the alternative is provided by law, or inferred by law from the nature of the contract or other surrounding circumstances. Thus under a c.i.f. contract the seller can perform either by shipping goods or by appro-priating to the contract goods which have already been shipped, whether by himself or by another shipper.[14] The general rule is that the seller is not discharged merely because a supervening event has made shipment impossible or illegal: if goods which had been shipped before the super-vening event are available, he must (in general) buy those goods afloat and tender them to his buyer under the original contract.[15]

The general rule further applies where the party claims to be excused, not under the general doctrine of discharge, but under an express term of the contract. Thus a c.i.f. seller who is prevented by supervening events from shipping goods of the contract description will not be able to rely on an express *force majeure* clause, protecting him in the event of failure to deliver by reason of causes beyond his control, unless he can show that such causes also prevented him from buying afloat.[16] A similar rule was applied where a charterer who had undertaken to load 'a cargo of wheat and/or maize and/or rye' sought to excuse his delay in loading by refer-ence to a term providing that time during which the cargo could not be loaded by reason of certain obstructions beyond his control was not to count for the purpose of calculating demurrage. The obstruction in

---

[12] *Alchorne v Favill* (1825) 4 LJ Ch (OS) 47; cf. *Anderson v Commercial Union Insurance Co* (1865) 55 LJ QB 146, at 150.

[13] *Victoria Seats Agency v Paget* (1902) 19 TLR 16 (first contract).

[14] *Benjamin's Sale of Goods*, 4th ed (1992), ss 19–011, 19–121.

[15] eg, *Ashmore & Son v CS Cox & Co* [1899] 1 QB 436, as explained in *Benjamin's Sale of Goods* 4th ed (1992), s 19–113; for an exception to the general rule see *Tradax Export SA v André & Cie* [1976] 1 Lloyd's Rep 416 discussed in *Benjamin's Sale of Goods*, 4th ed (1992), s 19–121 and GH Treitel, *Frustration and Force Majeure* (1994), s 4–083.

[16] *PJ van der Zijden Wildhandel NV v Tucker & Cross Ltd* [1975] 2 Lloyd's Rep 240.

question affected only wheat, which was the cargo which the charterer had decided to load (but did not affect maize or rye), and it was held that the charterer was not relieved by the clause from his obligation to load one of the other commodities;[17] and even the view that the charterer should be allowed such reasonable time as was required to enable him to decide what alternative course of action to pursue,[18] when it became clear that the supply of wheat would be delayed, has been doubted.[19] In cases of this kind, the contractual provision for alternative methods may, again, be inferred from the surrounding circumstances. Thus a contract to load a cargo at a particular port, and containing an exception for delay in loading due to ice, may not specify the method of loading. This will then be determined by reference to the method usual at that port; and if there is more than one such method the charterer will only be able to rely on the exception if *all* those methods have become physically impossible or at least 'commercially impracticable' as a result of the freezing of the port.[20]

Exceptions

It has been said that 'If one of two things which have been contracted for, subsequently becomes impossible, it becomes a question of construction whether . . . the obligor is bound to perform the alternative or is discharged altogether'.[21] Such a question of construction can arise in two ways. First, even where the contract imposes an alternative obligation, it may on its true construction exclude the general rule stated above. Secondly, it may be a question of construction whether the obligation imposed by a contract is a true alternative one. The presence (or absence) of the disjunctive conjunction 'or' is not decisive: it will be necessary, in the following discussion, to distinguish alternative obligations from a number of analogous concepts.

CONTRARY PROVISION

A contract imposing an alternative obligation may contain an express provision which, on its true construction, excludes the general rule applicable in cases of supervening impossibility affecting some (but not all) of the

---

[17] *Brightman & Co v Bunge y Born Limitada Sociedad* [1924] 2 KB 619, affirmed on another ground [1925] AC 799; and see *post* pp 283–4.
[18] [1924] 2 KB 628, at 631, 637.
[19] *Reardon Smith Line Ltd v Ministry of Agriculture Fisheries and Food* [1963] AC 691, at 717, 733.
[20] *Owners of Steamship Matheos v Louis Dreyfus & Co* [1925] AC 654, at 660.
[21] *Anderson v Commercial Union Insurance Co* (1885) 55 LJ QB 146, at 150, a dictum cited with approval in *AV Pound & Co Ltd v MW Hardy & Co Inc* [1956] AC 588, at 612.

specified alternatives. This was, for example, held to be the position where a c.i.f. contract contained a clause excusing the seller in the event of strikes preventing shipment.[22] The clause was construed so as to apply where the port of shipment which the seller intended to use became strike-bound, even though the seller had not shown that other ports from which he might have shipped were similarly affected.

LIBERTY TO SUBSTITUTE

Where a contract imposes a true alternative obligation, one cannot tell at the time of contracting which alternative the debtor is bound to perform. Such a contract must be distinguished from one which requires a party to render a specified performance but gives him a liberty to substitute a different performance. In a contract of the latter kind, the specified performance alone is originally due and remains due until the substitution is made;[23] when the substitution is made, the substituted performance becomes due (and that originally specified ceases to be due). Three things should follow. First, if the originally specified performance becomes impossible or illegal before the substitution is made, the contract should be discharged, so that the party having the liberty to substitute is not bound to render the substitute performance (nor is the other party bound to accept and pay for it). Secondly, if the substitute performance becomes impossible or illegal after the substitution has been made, the contract is likewise discharged, with corresponding effects: ie, the originally specified performance need no longer be rendered or accepted. Thirdly, the supervening impossibility or illegality of the substitute performance before the substitution is made has no effect on the obligations to render (and to accept and pay for) the originally specified performance: it makes no difference that the party entitled to make the substitution had intended to make it, if he had not actually made it in accordance with any relevant provisions of the contract (e.g., as to giving notice of the substitution). Only in this respect can the present group of cases be said to resemble those of true alternative obligations.

The situation here under discussion is illustrated by cases in which a charterparty relating to a named ship (X) gives the shipowner a 'liberty to substitute'[24] or an 'option to substitute' another similar vessel. In one such

---

[22] *Sociedad Iberica de Molturacion SA v Tradax Export SA* [1978] 2 Lloyd's Rep 545; cf. *Koninglijke Bunge v Cie Continentale d'Importation* [1973] 2 Lloyd's Rep 44, at 50, where, however, the seller failed to prove the facts required by the exception; GH Treitel, *Frustration and Force Majeure* (1994), s 12–022.

[23] *Coastal (Bermuda) Petroleum Ltd v VTT Vulcan Petroleum SA (The Marine Star)* [1993] 1 Lloyd's Rep 329.

[24] *SA Maritime et Commerciale of Geneva v Anglo-Iranian Oil Co* [1953] 1 WLR 1379, at 1382, affirmed without reference to this point [1954] 1 WLR 497.

case it was said at first instance that the object of such a provision was to ensure 'that a mere accident to one particular ship is not necessarily going to bring the charterparty to an end'.[25] This suggests that, in the event of such an accident, the owner is entitled (and possibly that he is bound) to make a substitution. But the only point actually decided[26] was that, after the owner had substituted vessel Y for X, and Y had had to undergo repairs during the currency of the charter, the owner was, on the true construction of the contract, entitled to make a second substitution (reverting to vessel X). There was no destruction of vessel Y, nor even any finding of frustrating delay caused by the need for repairs to her. The suggestion quoted above was said in *The Badagry*[27] not to apply where there had been 'an actual or constructive total loss of the originally named vessel'. That case concerned a demise charter of a named ship which gave the owners an 'option to substitute' a similar vessel. The named ship having become a constructive total loss, it was held that the contract was thereby discharged, so that the owners were not entitled to make the substitution. It would, of course, have been possible to exclude the doctrine of frustration by providing that the substitution could be made even in the event of the loss of the originally named ship; but that was held not to be the meaning of the substitution clause in this case.

'CONTRACT OPTIONS' AND 'PERFORMANCE OPTIONS'

These phrases do not introduce new concepts; they are used (at least generally) to draw the distinctions already explained between true alternative obligations and liberties to substitute. They require further explanation partly because they carry forward the discussion of how those distinctions are to be drawn, and partly because they have, unfortunately, been used in more senses than one.

The distinction between the two kinds of options is derived from the speech of Lord Devlin in *Reardon Smith Line Ltd.* v. *Ministry of Agriculture, Fisheries & Food.*[28] In that case a charterparty was held on its true construction to require the charterer to load a full and complete cargo of wheat in bulk, with the 'option' of loading up to one-third barley in bulk or up one-third flour in bulk, at somewhat higher rates of freight than that specified for wheat. The charterparty contained an exception covering delays caused by strikes, and a strike at the port of loading delayed the loading of wheat, but it was assumed that the strike did not affect the loading of barley or flour. It was held that the charterer was entitled to

---

[25] [1953] 1 WLR at 1382.   [26] See [1954] 1 WLR 497.
[27] *Terkol Rederierne* v *Petroleo Brasileiro SA (The Badagry)* [1985] 1 Lloyd's Rep 395, at 402; cf. *ibid.* at 401.
[28] [1963] AC 691.

rely on the exception, so that he was not liable for delay caused by the strike in the loading of wheat. By contrast, in *Brightman & Co v Bunge y Born Limitada Sociedad*[29] a charterparty required the charterer to load 'a cargo of wheat and/or maize and/or rye', with an exception covering 'obstruction beyond the control of the charterers on the railways'. The charterers were delayed in loading their intended cargo of wheat by industrial action which affected the railway they had intended to use, and in the end they decided instead to load maize. It was held that they were not protected by the exception (save to the minor extent of being allowed a reasonable time to consider their position and to make arrangements for loading the alternative cargo[30]).

No attempt was made in either case to argue the contracts were discharged, presumably because the delays were not sufficiently serious for this purpose[31] and because in each case the cargo was actually loaded: the issue simply was as to the charterers' liability to pay demurrage. But it follows from the reasoning of the two cases that, if the delay in loading wheat had been a 'frustrating' one and if no similar delay had affected the other specified commodities, then the contract would have been frustrated in the *Reardon Smith* case, but not in the *Brightman* case. It is these assumptions and the reasons for them (rather than the actual decisions) which are significant for the purpose of the present discussion.

Two tests for distinguishing between the two situations emerge from the speeches in the *Reardon Smith* case. The first concentrates on the way in which the choice open to the charterer is to be made. In the *Reardon Smith* case, the obligation was one to load wheat unless the charterer exercised his option to substitute barley or flour, and did so in the usual way in which options are exercised, i.e., by notice to the other party.[32] In the *Brightman* case, by contrast, the charterer was entitled simply to load any one of the specified commodities without having to give prior notice to the carrier. It was even said that he retained his freedom of action 'till the last ton was put on board'.[33] Such an extreme view may be open to doubt,[34] but this does not affect the distinction between the two cases: in the *Reardon Smith* case, 'wheat [was] to be the basic cargo, to be displaced only if and as the charterers decide';[35] while in the *Brightman* case, there was no 'basic cargo,' so that it was not possible to tell when the contract was made which of the specified commodities the charterer was obliged to load.

The second test for distinguishing between the two situations concentrates on the purpose for which the choice is given: in Lord Devlin's

---

[29] [1924] 2 KB 619, affirmed on another ground [1925] AC 799.
[30] For later doubts on this point, see note 19 above.
[31] GH Treitel, *Frustration and Force Majeure* (1994), s 5–031 *et seq*.
[32] See [1963] AC 691, at 719, 730, 731.
[33] [1924] 2 KB 619, at 637.
[34] See p 395, below.
[35] [1963] AC 691, at 719.

words, 'the question is whether or not the freedom of choice is intended solely for the benefit of the charterer'[36] or for the benefit of both parties. In the *Reardon Smith* case, Lord Devlin regarded the choice as being for the benefit of the charterer alone, as it was not the intention of the parties to oblige him to ship barley or flour, should wheat be unavailable. In the *Brightman* case the alternative was for the benefit of both parties: it was their intention to confer a right of choice on the charterer, but not to relieve him from his obligation to load merely because the commodity chosen by him was unavailable.

This test may give rise to some difficulty in that what the parties intend is defined by reference the legal consequences of that common intention; but in reply to this objection it can be said that the test of the parties' intention is not infrequently applied to contractual situations in which it gives rise to similar difficulties.[37] A factor which is relevant to the intention of the parties in the present context is whether it matters to the other party which of the alternatives is performed by the party having the right of choice.[38] If it does, the case is likely to fall on the *Reardon Smith* side of the line; if it does not, on the *Brightman* side. This is also true of the type of case, already discussed, where a c.i.f. contract provides for goods to be shipped by the seller 'in October and/or November'. In one such case it was said that the seller had '61 options'.[39] The case would fall on the *Brightman* side of the line in that the seller would not be required to give advance notice to the buyer specifying on which of the 61 days he intended to ship the goods, and in that it would presumably not matter to a buyer who had contracted on such terms on exactly which day within the shipment period the shipment was to be made. It follows that the option as to the date of shipment is for the benefit of both parties in the sense already discussed. That is, it is for the benefit of the seller in that he can ship on any of the 61 days if no obstacle supervenes; but it is for the benefit of the buyer in that, if the seller intended to ship in October but is prevented by supervening events from doing so, and shipment in November remains possible and lawful, then the buyer is entitled to insist on shipment in November.

It thus appears from the preceding discussion that the 'option' in the *Reardon Smith* case was in its legal nature similar to that in *The Badagry*.[40]

[36] [1963] AC 691, at 730.
[37] eg, in distinguishing between 'mere' representations and representations which are intended to have contractual force: see GH Treitel, *The Law of Contract* (8th ed 1991) pp 315, 319.
[38] *SA Maritime et Commerciale of Geneva* v *Anglo-Iranian Oil Co* [1953] 1 WLR 1379, at 1381, and see note 24 above.
[39] *RT Smyth & Co Ltd (Liverpool)* v *WN Lindsay Ltd (Leith)* [1953] 1 WLR 1280, at 1283 per Devlin J, although in *Reardon Smith Line Ltd* v *Ministry of Agriculture, Fisheries and Food* [1963] 1 All ER 545, at 559 Lord Devlin doubted whether this description would be apt 'in ordinary language'.
[40] [1985] 1 Lloyd's Rep 395, see text accompanying note 27 above.

The actual issues discussed in the two cases differed in the sense that in the *Reardon Smith* case the question was whether the party having the right to choose was *bound* to render the substitute performance, while in *The Badagry* the question was whether he was *entitled* to do so (and consequently whether the other party was bound to accept it). Logically, however, it would seem that the same principle should determine the answer to both questions, for in cases of this kind the contract (unless varied at the election of the party having the 'liberty' or 'option') is to render the originally specified performance; and once that performance has become impossible the contract is automatically discharged,[41] so that the option or liberty is no longer capable of being exercised for the benefit of either party.[42] Thus in *The Badagry* the shipowner was no more bound than he was entitled to make the substitution, once the originally named ship had been lost.[43] Conversely, in the *Reardon Smith* case the charterer would no more have been entitled than he was bound to load one of the alternative cargoes if, before exercise of his 'option', an event had occurred which imposed a frustrating delay on the loading of wheat. These propositions may, indeed, require some modification where the supervening impossibility or illegality relates only to the *method* of performance. This point is further discussed below;[44] it arises not because of the nature of the option but because impossibility even in a stipulated method of performance is not necessarily a ground of discharge.[45]

Lord Devlin's speech in the *Reardon Smith* case does not actually make use of the expressions 'contract option' and 'performance option', but it does make use of the two concepts to which these labels have been attacahed in the preceding discussion, calling the former 'business options' and the latter simply (though with some unease) 'options'.[46] The terminological distinction between 'contract' (or 'contractual') and 'performance' options is derived from the more recent case of the *The Didymi*;[47] but there the distinction is used in two quite different senses.

The first is that given to it by Staughton J. when he described a 'contract option' as one 'which alters the nature of the obligation laid down in the contract', and a 'performance option' as one which arises 'where only one obligation is provided by the contract and it remains unchanged; but there are different ways of performing it'.[48] This distinction appears to be

---

[41] GH Treitel, *Frustration and Force Majeure* (1994), s 15–002.

[42] Cf. *Blane Steamships* v *Minister of Transport* [1951] 2 KB 965 (where an option to purchase a chartered ship was held not to have survived her constructive total loss).

[43] For an apparently contrary suggestion in *SA Maritime et Commerciale of Geneva* v *Anglo-Iranian Oil Co* [1953] 1 WLR 1379, at 1382, see notes 24 and 26 above.

[44] See pp 386–7 below.

[45] GH Treitel, *Frustration and Force Majeure* (1994), s 4–064.   [46] [1963] AC 691, at 729.

[47] *Atlantic Lines & Navigation Co Ltd* v *Didymi Corp* (*The Didymi and the Leon*) [1984] 1 Lloyd's Rep 583.

[48] *Ibid.*, at 585.

between what is owed and how (or by what method) it is to be performed. Thus an example of a 'contract option' is said to be 'a contract to load a cargo of wheat with an option to change to barley', while an example of a 'performance option' would be 'a contract to load a cargo in September or October, which in one sense provides a choice of 61 days'.[49] If an option of the former kind is exercised, 'the contract ceases to be one to load wheat and becomes one to load barley', so that if it becomes impossible to load barley the contract is discharged.[50] On the other hand, in the case of a 'performance option' impossibility affecting one method of performance does not discharge the contract, which must be performed in the way (or in one of the ways) remaining possible.

The second explanation of the distinction between 'contractual options' and 'performance options' is that given by Sir John Donaldson M.R. in the *The Didymi*; but it will be seen that the difference between his view and that of Staughton J. is less significant than might at first sight appear. According to Sir John Donaldson, the distinction between the two types of option depends on the steps required to be taken to exercise the choice: 'A "contractual option" enables the beneficiary to define what the contract requires of him. An example would be "vessel to be redelivered at a European port to be nominated by the charterer".'[51] By contrast, a 'performance option' is one which 'itself defines the alternative ways in which the contrast is to be performed and calls for no action on the part of the beneficiary, save the perform the contract in a permissible way. An example would be "vessel to be redelivered at a European port".'[52]

Sir John Donaldson's explanation of the distinction appears to correspond (more closely than Staughton J.'s) with that drawn by Lord Devlin. It also differs from Staughton J.'s explanation in that each of the examples given by Sir John Donaldson concerns an option as to the method of performance, rather than one as to what is owed: what the charterer has to do in each case is to redeliver the ship, and his option merely determines where he has to perform this act. Nor are the consequences of the exercise of a 'contract' or 'contractual' option the same under the two explanations. In Staughton J.'s example, if the charterer exercised his 'contract option' to load barley, and if the loading of barley then became illegal, the contract would be discharged so that there would be no obligation to load wheat. Yet in Sir John Donaldson's example if the charterer exercised a 'contractual option' by nominating a particular port, and if redelivery there subsequently became illegal, it can scarcely be supposed that there would be no obligation to redeliver the ship; the more probable solution would be that the charterer would have to make a fresh nomination of

---

[49] *Atlantic Lines & Navigation Co Ltd* v *Didymi Corp* (*The Didymi and the Leon*) [1984] 1 Lloyd's Rep 583.
[50] *Ibid.*   [51] *Ibid.*, at 587.   [52] *Ibid.*

another port at which the ship could lawfully be redelivered.[53] In this respect, the effect of the exercise of a 'contractual' option which related only to the method of performance may be the same as the effect of the exercise of a 'performance' option.

What the judgments of Staughton J. and Sir John Donaldson M.R. have in common in their description of a 'contract(ual)' option is that the exercise of such an option can alter the original obligation of the beneficiary (of the option), but that it does so only when he notifies the other party of its exercise. By contrast, no such notice need be given of the exercise of a 'performance' option nor does such exercise alter the beneficiary's obligation (which remains to perform in any of the specified ways remaining possible). As Sir John Donaldson says, an option 'without any requirement as to how or when the option is to be exercised has all the characteristics of a performance option'.[54] Such an option may determine what is owed (no less than how it is to be performed) as in the *Brightman*[55] case (where the 'option' to load wheat or maize or rye did not require the charterer to give advance notice of his choice and where, on the unavailability of wheat, he was bound to load maize or rye). Conversely, it is submitted that the selection between one of two or more methods of performance could, in principle, be a contract option if this was clearly the intention of the parties. This might be the case if a contract were made to carry goods in one of two specified ships, the choice to be made by the carrier and notified to the buyer by a specified date. If one of the ships were duly selected in accordance with these provisions, it seems that the contract would be turned into one to carry the goods in that ship, and accordingly it could be frustrated by the loss of that ship before commencement of performance.[56] But although options which relate to the method of performance can in principle be contract options, they are in practice less likely to be construed in this way than are options which relate to the substance of what is to be performed. The reason for this is that the parties can generally be supposed to attach more importance to the definition of what is owed than to provisions which state how it is to be performed; and effect would be given to their intention in this respect by making discharge more likely where impossibility affects the former than where it affects the latter aspect of performance. This would be the effect of a greater readiness to classify options as to what is owed as contract options (where impossibility of performing the selected alternative is a ground of

[53] Cf. *Hindley & Co Ltd* v *General Fibre Co Ltd* [1940] 2 KB 517 (option as to port of destination to be declared by a c.i.f. buyer).
[54] [1984] 1 Lloyd's Rep 583, at 587.
[55] [1924] 2 KB 619, [1925] AC 799, see text accompanying note 29 above.
[56] The example given in the text differs from *J Lauritzen AS* v *Wijsmuller BV* (*The Super Servant Two*) [1990] 1 Lloyd's Rep 1 in that there no selection had been communicated before loss of one of the ships.

discharge) while classifying most options as to the manner of performance as performance options (where impossibility of performing the
selected alternative is not a ground of discharge).

The foregoing discussion is based on the assumption that the party entitled to choose between the two alternatives is (either by the express terms
of the contract, or by operation of law[57]) the debtor, i.e., the person who is
to perform one of the alternatives. It is, of course also possible for that
right to be given to the creditor: e.g. where A agrees to sell to B 'my Rolls
or my Bentley, at buyer's option'. Such an option resembles a performance option in that neither alternative can be described as the primary
obligation. But in two more significant ways it resembles a contract
option: namely in that the option must be exercised by notice to the seller
(since until this is done he cannot perform); and in that, once the option
has been exercised, the contract becomes one to perform the selected alternative and that alternative only. Hence if B selects the Rolls and that car is
stolen or destroyed without fault of either party before the risk has
passed, then the contract will be discharged, so that B can neither demand
nor be compelled to accept the Bentley. It would clearly be unjust to
require A to deliver the Bentley if he had acted in reliance on B's choice of
the Rolls, e.g. by spending money on preparing that car for delivery or by
disposing elsewhere of the Bentley; and while the argument for relieving
B from any obligation to accept the Bentley is less strong, he too may have
acted in reliance on his selection (e.g., by contracting to resell the Rolls);
and his release also follows from the principle that frustration automatically discharges both parties.[58] None of these arguments apply where one
of the cars is destroyed *before* the selection is made, so that in such a case
B would be entitled to select the other, and A bound to deliver it. It is less
clear whether or not B would be bound to select the surviving car: this
would depend on whether the contract on its true construction merely
gave B the right, or imposed on him a duty, to make the selection. The latter concept is by no means implausible: thus an f.o.b. buyer may have a
duty to select a port of shipment where the contract merely specifies a
range of ports.[59] In our example, it might similarly be held that B had a
duty to make the selection. If so, destruction of one of the cars would not
discharge the contract but merely narrow B's range of choice to one.

---

[57] For rules of law determining which party has the option, see (for example) *Reed* v
Kilburn Co-operative Society (1875) LR 10 QB 264; *Benjamin's Sale of Goods* (1992), 4th ed,
s 20–029 (time of shipment in f.o.b. contracts).
[58] GH Treitel, *Frustration and Force Majeure* (1994), s 15–002.
[59] *David T Boyd & Co Ltd* v *Louis Louca* [1973] 1 Lloyd's Rep 209.

ALTERNATIVE METHODS OF DISCHARGE

A contract may impose an obligation on a debtor to perform one thing (X) but give him the liberty to discharge that obligation by doing another thing (Y). Civil lawyers sometimes describe this liberty as a *facultas alternativa;*[60] it differs from an alternative obligation in that it at no stage gives rise to an obligation to do Y. Even if the debtor declares that he will do Y, he does not become bound to do it, but if he in fact does Y his obligation to perform X is discharged. It follows that if X becomes impossible or illegal, the debtor is not bound to do Y, while if Y becomes impossible the debtor must do X and loses his liberty to perform in the alternative way.

Civil lawyers illustrate this type of provision by reference to the purchase of a car for which the customer agrees to give his own car in part exchange.[61] In such a case, the customer will not normally undertake an obligation to deliver his own car: he is merely given a liberty to satisfy part of the price for the car which he is acquiring by delivery of his own car. If his own car is destroyed between the making of the contract and its performance, he must prima facie pay the full price in money; such a rule will not cause him any prejudice where (as will often be the case) he is put into a position to make the extra payment by his receipt of the proceeds of insurance on the destroyed car. It is of course possible for the contract expressly or by implication to provide that payment is to be made *only* on the part-exchange basis: the case would then not be one of *facultas alternativa* but one of failure in an agreed method of performance. Whether the destruction of the buyer's own car would discharge such a contract would depend on whether the partial impossibility defeated the seller's main purpose in entering into the contract;[62] an important factor would be the proportion which the part-exchange value of the buyer's own car bore to the value of the transaction as a whole.

The converse situation to that discussed above is that in which supervening events affect the principal obligation but not the alternative method of discharge: e.g. if the above example of the contract for the sale of a car were varied by supposing that the money element of the price were payable on credit terms or in a foreign currency, and that legislation passed after the sale had made such payment illegal. In such a case the contract would be discharged: the buyer would not be bound to deliver his own car, even if it accounted for as much as 90 per cent. of the agreed 'cash' price. This follows from the concept of *facultas alternativa* as imposing *no* obligation to perform the 'alternative'.

In the examples so far discussed, the alternative method of discharge

---

[60] eg, *Münchener Kommentar zum Bürgerlichen Gesetzbuch* § 262 Comment 2.
[61] *Ibid.* Comment 8; see the German decisions in BGHZ 46, 338, 340, BGH, 18 January 1967.
[62] GH Treitel, *Frustration and Force Majeure* (1994), s 5–002.

relates to part only of the debt, but it can equally relate to the whole. This makes no difference to the position stated above: e.g. where a contract obliges a buyer to pay in cash but provides that the cash price may be satisfied by payment wholly in kind. Supervening impossibility of making the payment in kind does not discharge the debtor's liability to pay cash, any more than in the case of a true alternative obligation; but the case differs from one of alternative obligation in that, if payment in cash became illegal, the debtor would not be bound to pay in kind. This would be so even if he had declared his intention to pay in this way: again this follows from the nature of the *facultas alternativa* as imposing no obligation to perform the alternative.

So far it has been assumed that the choice between the two methods of discharge lies entirely with the debtor. It may equally lie with the creditor: e.g. he may be entitled to demand payment in cash or, if the creditor so elects, by delivery of some specific thing (e.g. a picture). Such a case differs from a *facultas alternativa* in that the exercise of the creditor's choice does alter the nature of the obligation. It follows that if he had elected to seek delivery of the picture and if the picture were then destroyed the debtor would no longer be bound to pay cash, while if, before any such election, payment in cash became illegal the contract would be discharged so that that creditor would lose his right to demand the picture.[63]

ALTERNATIVE AND CONTINGENT OBLIGATIONS

An alternative obligation is often expressed by saying that 'X or Y' must be performed; but (as already noted) the use of the conjunction 'or' between two performances specified in a contract does not necessarily mean that the obligation imposed by the contract is an alternative one. A distinction between alternative and contingent obligations was apparently drawn in *Deverill* v. *Burnell*[64] where the plaintiff had shipped goods to Rosario where they were to be delivered to one Bollaert on his accepting certain drafts. Bills of lading covering the goods were entrusted, together with the drafts, to the defendant for presentation to Bollaert, who accepted the drafts but did not pay on them. The defendant promised the plaintiff that, if the drafts were paid, he would transmit the proceeds to the plaintiff 'and if the drafts should not be paid the defendant should either return the same to the plaintiff or pay him the amount'. The defendant, having neither returned the drafts nor paid the amount, argued that he was liable for no more than nominal damages: his contentions were that the obligation was alternative, that he could have performed it by

[63] The case would then be comparable to *The Badagry* [1985] 1 Lloyd's Rep 395, see text accompanying note 27 above.
[64] (1873) LR 8 CP 475.

returning the drafts (which were worthless), and that damages for breach of an alternative obligation were to be assessed by reference to the alternative least beneficial to the claimant.[65] But the court by a majority rejected this argument and held the defendant liable for the full amount of the drafts. In the words of Grove J. (one of the majority), the defendant's undertaking 'was not in the strictest sense an alternative promise, but a promise that the defendant would return the bills, and if he did not return them he would pay the amount of them'.[66] Grove J. went on to give an example which he evidently regarded as *in pari materia*: 'If I say to a man, I will return your horse tomorrow or pay you a day's hire of him, the only reasonable construction is that, if I do not return the horse, I will pay a day's hire.'[67] The other judgments likewise treat the question whether the contract imposed an alternative obligation as one of construction. Bovill C.J. (who dissented) gave an example similar to that just quoted: a contract by which a man promised 'to deliver up his horse Ajax or pay £1000'[68] would, in his view, impose an alternative obligation. He, too, treated the question whether this was the nature of the obligation as one of construction. What the court has to determine, therefore, is what the parties intended to be the effect of the contract. On the majority view in *Deverill* v. *Burnell*, the defendant had not said 'I will choose between performing X or Y' but 'I will perform X, but if I fail to do so I will perform Y'. The duty to perform Y can be regarded as a contingent rather than as an alternative obligation. This would certainly distinguish the case from 'contract options'[69] and from liberties to substitute[70] of the kind discussed above, in which X, and X alone, is due unless and until the debtor communicates his election instead to perform Y (which then alone becomes due). But a 'performance option' in one of the senses discussed above[71] amounts in substance to much the same thing as the type of obligation discussed in *Deverill* v. *Burnell*: in the case of such an option, it is also true that if the debtor does not perform X he must (without the need for any prior election on his part) perform Y. The distinction between the two types of case appears to be this. In the case of an alternative obligation of the performance option type, it cannot be said that either X or Y is the content of the principal obligation. In the case of the type of obligation under consideration in *Deverill* v. *Burnell*, it seems that X is the primary obligation, Y only becoming due in the event of the non-performance of X. Thus in the example given by Grove J. the primary obligation is 'I will return your horse tomorrow' and the obligation to pay a day's hire is secondary and conditional on non-performance of the primary obligation. The question

---

[65] For this rule, see GH Treitel, *The Law of Contract* (8th ed 1991) p 848.
[66] (1873) LR 8 CP 475.   [67] *Ibid.*   [68] *Ibid.*, at 480.
[69] See pp 382–8 above.
[70] See pp 381–2 above.   [71] See text accompanying note 52 above.

then arises what legal consequences would follow from the supervening impossibility or illegality of either obligation. If the supervening event affected only the secondary obligation (e.g. if making the payment became illegal), then the primary obligation would remain due. If on the other hand the supervening event affected the primary obligation (e.g., if without fault of either party the horse died or was stolen), then it is arguable that the contract would be frustrated so that the secondary obligation could not become due. This in turn is a question of construction: the contract may mean merely that if the debtor *in breach of contract* fails to do X he must do Y, or that if *for any reason* he fails to do X, then he must do Y. If it means the latter, then there is for the purpose of the doctrine of frustration no practical difference between contingent obligation of the kind discussed in *Deveril* v. *Burnell* and alternative obligations of the 'performance option' type. It is however submitted that the former is the more obvious meaning of the contract in Grove J.'s example, and that it was this meaning which he had in mind in distinguishing the case from an alternative obligation. This type of contract is also distinct from one containing a *facultas alternativa*[72] in that under a contract of the present kind Y becomes due on non-performance of X (and only on failure to perform X); and in that failure or perform X gives rise to an *obligation* to perform Y, while under a contract containing a *facultas alternativa* the debtor is never obliged to do Y.

A similar analysis applies where a charterparty provides that a ship is to proceed to a named port (or dock) 'or so near thereto as she may safety get'. In such a contract the named port or dock has been described as 'the primary place of discharge',[73] while the phrase 'or so near thereto as she may safety get' has been referred to as an 'alternative destination'.[74] But a contract of this kind does not impose an alternative obligation in the true sense of that expression, since it is not open to either party to select the 'alternative destination'. That 'alternative' in fact expresses not an alternative but a contingent obligation: the contract means that if (and only if) the ship cannot reach the 'primary place of discharge', then she must (and need only) proceed to the 'alternative destination'. Neither party has any choice in the matter: so long as the ship can get to the primary place of discharge, the shipowner is not entitled to perform, nor is the charterer entitled to demand performance, at the 'alternative destination'. The 'alternative' is not in fact an alternative but a substitute which becomes available only in previously defined circumstances. Indeed, it follows from the meaning of the words 'so near thereto as she may safely get', that there can be no place which answers this description if safe access to the named port (or dock) is possible. If, on the other hand, obstacles arise

---

[72] See pp 389–90 above.
[73] *Robert H Dahl* v *Nelson, Donkin* (1881) 6 App Cas 38, at 62.   [74] *Ibid.*

which prevent the ship from reaching the 'primary destination' named in the contract, this will amount to the occurrence of the condition which brings the obligation to perform at the substitute destination into operation. Taken literally, the phrase 'so near there to as she can safely get' may appear to mean that the substitute destination is one of which it can never be said that it has become impossible to reach. Nevertheless it is submitted that there may be cases in which impossibility in reaching the 'primary' destination could discharge the contract. This might be the position if the place of primary destination were a port which ceased wholly to exist, e.g. because it was totally destroyed by an earthquake. On the true construction of the contract, the 'alternative' could be said not to apply to such a drastic change of circumstances, or perhaps to have become meaningless since once cannot get near to a place which no longer exists. This would be in accordance with the process by which express contractual provisions which might literally cover a supervening event are narrowly construed so as not to apply where that event, or its effects, are so drastic that they cannot have been in the contemplation of the parties at the time of contracting.[75] Such a process of construction would, on the other hand, be less likely to be adopted where the contract required the ship to proceed (within a named port) to a named dock or so near to that dock as she could safely get, and it was only the named dock which was destroyed. The question in each case would be whether the events which had made it impossible to reach the 'primary' destination were such that it would fundamentally alter the nature of the originally agreed performance to require one party to render and the other to accept the performance at the substitute destination; and where it was only a named dock which was destroyed, a negative answer might well be given to this question.

Effect of selection

A contract which imposes an alternative obligation to do X or Y is not discharged merely because the debtor intended to do X and that performance has become impossible or illegal, while Y remains both possible and lawful. But further questions arise where the selection of X has been communicated to the other party and X (but not Y) has then become impossible or illegal. Such communication may alter the nature of the obligation from one to perform X or Y to one to perform X alone; if so, the supervening impossibility of performing X will discharge the contract.

[75] See (in another context) *Metropolitan Water Board* v *Dick, Kerr & Co* [1918] AC 119, and other similar cases discussed in GH Treitel, *Frustration and Force Majeure* (1994), ss 12-006 to 12-007.

Whether the selection has this effect depends on two further points: whether the effect of making the choice is to alter, or redefine, the contractual obligation, and whether the choice has been validly made.

WHETHER SELECTION REDEFINES THE OBLIGATION

In some cases, the selection of one of the permitted alternatives redefines the contractual obligation so that the selected alternative alone becomes due. Whether this is the effect of the selection depends on the factors already discussed. Thus if the contract confers a liberty to substitute and the substitution is made, or if it confers a 'contract option' and the option is duly exercised, the contract becomes one to perform the selected alternative. If, for example, in the *Reardon Smith*[76] case the charterer had exercised his option to load one of the commodities (other than wheat) specified in the contract, he would have become bound to load that commodity to the extent specified in the contract, and if the loading of that commodity had been delayed by strikes he would have been protected by the exception. By contrast, an indication by the debtor that he intends to exercise a 'performance option'[77] or to avail himself of an alternative method of discharge does not alter the nature of the contractual obligation, so that supervening impossibility or illegality of the selected performance is not of itself a ground of discharge. Thus if in the *Brightman*[78] case the charterer had given notice to the shipowner of his intention to load wheat, this would not have altered the nature of his obligation, which would have remained one to load whichever of the specified commodities remained available. This appears from the statement of Atkin L.J. that 'In such a contract as this, there is no such thing as an appropriation of cargo binding shipowner to shipper or shipper to shipowner, nor any question of a final election of an option'.[79] Scrutton L.J. seems to have had a similar point in mind when he said that he could find 'nothing ... to bind the character to load only what';[80] though this view might be based simply on the fact that the charterer's decision to load wheat had not been communicated to the shipowner.

While the mere communication of the selection does not alter the nature of the obligation imposed by a 'performance option', it is arguable that subsequent events may have such an effect. In the *Brightman* case, indeed, Atkin L.J. went so far as to say that 'The shipper retains control of his powers until the final ton is put on board, and as he retains his powers, so he retains his liabilities.'[81] But this statement is, with respect, open to some

---

[76] [1963] AC 691.   [77] See text accompanying note 52 above, *et seq.*
[78] [1924] 2 KB 619, [1925] AC 799; see text accompanying note 29, above.
[79] [1924] 2 KB 619, at 637.   [80] *Ibid.*, at 630.
[81] *Ibid.*, at 637.

doubt. A shipper who has undertaken to ship 'a cargo of wheat' can hardly be entitled to substitute 'a cargo of maize' when almost the whole of a cargo of wheat has been shipped. In such a case the more reasonable view would appear to be that the shipper's obligation has become one to ship a cargo of wheat, not by the mere selection of that commodity, but by subsequent events. If so, he should no more be bound than he is entitled to substitute maize if supervening events made it impossible for him to complete the loading of a cargo of wheat.

WHETHER SELECTION WAS VALIDLY MADE

This point can arise only in the case of a 'contract option', the exercise of which will redefine the contractual obligation. The point is illustrated by *Hindley & Co Ltd* v.*General Fibre Co Ltd*;[82] where a contract for the sale of jute was made c.i.f. a range of European ports (including Bremen and Antwerp) to be declared by the buyers. Shortly after the outbreak of the Second World War, the buyers declared Bremen, but as this declaration was illegal and hence invalid it was held that a subsequent declaration of Antwerp (then a neutral port) was valid. The declaration of Bremen being a 'nullity', the buyers 'were entitled to withdraw it and make the declaration which was made'.[83] It follows from this reasoning that if Bremen had been *validly* selected and if it had subsequently become illegal to carry the goods to that port, then the contract would have been discharged.[84] The principle applies in cases of supervening physical impossibility just as much as in cases of illegality. Thus in the *Hindley* case it was said that the buyers' declaration of Bremen 'had no more effect than if they had declared Timbuctoo';[85] (the point being that that was a place which no ship could ever have reached). But if they had declared a port which was subsequently destroyed by an earthquake, then the contract would, it is submitted, have been discharged. This submission is supported by a case[86] in which a charterparty provided for discharge at one of a number of specified berths and contained an exception for strikes. It was held that the charterer was protected by the exception when, after he had selected one of the berths, a strike broke out there: he was not bound, after that event, to select one of the other berths. The position would be the same if a contract was made to carry goods in one of two named ships to be selected by the shipowner. If before he had made his selection one of those ships was lost, he would prima facie be bound to select the other;[87] and

---

[82] [1940] 2 KB 517.   [83] *Ibid.*, at 553.
[84] Cf. *The Teutonia* (1872) LR 4 PC 171.
[85] [1940] 2 KB 517, at 553.
[86] *Bulman & Dickson* v *Fenwick & Co* [1894] 1 QB 179.
[87] *J Lauritzen As* v *Wijsmuller BV* (*The Super Servant Two*) [1990] 1 Lloyd's Rep 1.

this would be so even though he had selected the first after the loss but in ignorance of that fact. But if after a valid selection (i.e., one complying with any contractual terms as to the time of selection and as to its notification to the shipper) had been made, the selected ship had been lost, then it is submitted that the contract would have been discharged.

Conclusion

Is there any moral to all this? The answer seems to be: at best, only a weak one. The general rule with which this discussion began is satisfactory; and the same may be said of the results of the cases concerned with the exceptions. But objection might reasonably be raised to the complexity of the exceptions, particularly to those which arise from the distinction between 'contract(ual)' and 'performance' options, and from that between alternative and contingent obligations. In the cases from which these distinctions are derived, the courts have done their best with obscurely drafted contracts; and the tools which they have had to use for this purpose can scarcely be said to have much to do with the intention of the parties, which should in principle be the determining factor, but has in practice been almost impossible to discover. Hence the moral (if any) is to avoid drafting obligations in alternative terms, and (ideally) where obligations are alternative by operation of law, to solve the problem of the effect on them of supervening events by express contractual provisions.

Part 4
Remedies

16

Good Faith and Remedies for Breach of Contract*

DANIEL FRIEDMANN**

Introduction

There are two aspects to good faith in the context of remedies for breach of contract. The one relates to the conduct of the party in breach (the defendant), and the question is whether more severe sanctions are to be imposed on him if he acted in bad faith.[1] The second relates to the conduct of the innocent party (the plaintiff) and the issue is whether the remedies available to him are affected by the requirement of good faith.[2] This chapter confines itself to the second issue.[3]

It may be asked whether an attempt to explain rules obtaining in English law by reference to the principle of good faith, which English law has hitherto not adopted, serves a useful purpose. Why 'translate' rules and concepts that appear under titles known to English lawyers and jurists into legal terminology with which they are less acquainted? The answer is that such a project has a number of distinct advantages.[4] Good faith may provide a unifying concept for a number of distinct rules dealt under different headings, and contribute to a greater consistency in the

* Copyright © 1994, Daniel Friedmann
** I am indebted to Melvin Eisenberg, Meir Dan-Cohen and John Dwyer for comments and suggestions.

[1] US courts have in some instances awarded punitive damages for bad faith breach of contract, notably in the field of insurance. See, generally, Keeton & Widiss, *Insurance Law* (1988) p 916 *et seq*; Farnsworth, *Contracts* (2nd ed 1990) 826–9; JD Calamari and JM Perillo, *The Law of Contracts* (3rd ed 1987) s 14–3. It has also been argued that, in general, the wilfulness of the breach should be relevant to remedies: PH Marshall, 'Wilfulness: A Crucial Factor in Choosing Remedies for Breach of Contract' (1982) 24 Arizona L Rev 733.

[2] I am using the term 'requirement' of good faith in a broader sense than 'duty', so as to include in it not only conduct the breach of which gives rise to a claim by the party to whom the duty is owed, but also in the senses of a condition which if it is not met, forms a 'disability' or prevents the creation of a legal right, as in the case of failure to mitigate damages. See Corbin on *Contracts* (1964), vol 5, s 1039, note 4.

[3] The conduct of the defendant may, however, be relevant to the second issue. A reaction by the injured party which may be regarded as excessive in the case of an inadvertent breach, may be perfectly justified if the breach was intentional.

[4] Cf R Powell, 'Good faith in Contracts' [1956] CLP 16; The Hon Mr Justice Steyn, 'The Role of Good Faith and Fair Dealing in Contract Law: A Hair-Shirt Philosophy?' [1991] Denning LJ 131.

law by exerting pressure upon rules which are incompatible with the idea of good faith. It is also of particular importance for the purpose of comparative law. As is well known, different legal systems may reach similar solutions using different routes. The study of the English counterparts of good faith is likely to facilitate mutual understanding with the very many legal systems in which the concept plays a dominant role. A question which is highly relevant to this point relates to unification of the laws. Every significant attempt in this direction will require an examination of the role of good faith. Indeed, voices supporting the adoption of good faith in English contract law have been raised, and there are some indications that they may be heeded.[5]

This chapter is devoted in the main to expound the proposition under which the gap created in English law by the lack of a doctrine of good faith, is filled in part by the law of remedies. In other words, the rules on remedies are used to compensate for the absence of a good faith principle. The effectiveness of the law of remedies in serving this end is greatly enhanced by virtue of the very severe limitations on freedom of contract in this area. A discussion of this point will be preceded by a brief comment on the meaning of good faith.

The meaning of good faith

No attempt will be made to define good faith. The term itself has more than one meaning.[6] Here one specific sense is examined, namely the requirement of certain, usually minimal, restraints upon self-interest in deference to a much heavier interest of another party. Accordingly, a legal right or power is not to be used excessively or in an oppressive way, or for a purpose for which it was not intended. Excessive use means use which

---

[5] The Hon Mr Justice Steyn, 'The Role of Good Faith and Fair Dealing in Contract Law: A Hair-Shirt Philosophy?' [1991] Denning LJ 131, 135, who suggests that '[t]here are international portents of change' in this direction and that the representatives of the UK were among those approving the Vienna Convention on International Sale of Goods. Article 7(1) of the CISG provides that, in the interpretation of the convention, regard is to be had inter alia 'to the need to promote uniformity in its application and the observance of good faith'. On the controversy about the UK's adoption of the Vienna Convention, see J Beatson and D Friedmann, p 5 above.

[6] RG Summers, ' "Good Faith" in General Contract Law and the Sales Provisions of the Uniform Commercial Code' (1968) 54 Va L Rev 195. Broad definitions of 'good faith' are to be found in §§ 1–203 and 2–103 of the UCC. It has also been suggested that good faith is an 'excluder', an idea that is best explained as serving to exclude various types of undesired conduct: RG Summers, 'The General Duty of Good Faith—Its Recognition and Conceptualization' (1982) 67 Cornell L Rev 810. For a different approach, see SJ Burton, 'Breach of Contract and the Common Law Duty to Perform in Good Faith' (1980) 94 Harv L Rev 369. On good faith see also EA Farnsworth, ch 6 above, and WF Ebke and BM Steinhauer, ch 7 above.

greatly exceeds that required for the protection of one's legitimate interest or for its legitimate exploitation, where such conduct leads to a disproportionate loss to another party. This of course is not a precise
definition, since such terms as 'excessive use' and 'legitimate interest' are
inherently vague.

The case of the rescuer who charges an exorbitant amount for his services demonstrates the type of conduct which is contrary to the requirements of good faith in this sense. The rescuer may be under no duty to
rescue yet, if he exploits the other party's predicament in order to demand
a disproportionate payment, the contract is voidable on the ground of economic duress.[7] The basic concept of freedom of contract means that a person is ordinarily free to demand for his services whatever price he deems
fit, but overcharging a party who is in urgent need of rescue services
amounts to an excessive use (or abuse) of freedom of contract.[8]

This does not mean that every exercise of one's rights which inconve-
niences others, is contrary to the requirement of good faith. Thus, the fact
that A declines to sell his property to B or to allow B to use it, although A
has little need for the property and B could use it profitably, does not
mean that A abused his legal right. Much more is required in order to
establish the absence of good faith. Sometimes, as in the rescue example,
it can be a huge disproportion between one party's legitimate interest and
the other party's desperate needs. In other instances, the parties' motives
and conduct can be taken into account. Instances are also conceivable in
which, despite a great disparity between the value of the interests, insistence upon the rights representing the less valuable interest will be justified and vindicated. Much depends on the nature of the parties' conduct
and the circumstances which led to the creation of the situation in which
one party became dependent upon the way in which the other party exercises his rights.

Freedom of contract and remedies for breach

The idea of freedom of contract in Anglo-American law has always been
confined to the formation of contractual rights. In the field of remedies it
has but limited application. The parties are free to determine their rights,

[7] *Post* v *Jones*, 60 US 150 (1856); *The Port Caledonia and the Anna* [1903] P 184; MA Eisenberg,
'The Bargain Principle and Its Limits' (1982) 95 Harv L Rev 741, 754–63; SM Waddams,
'Unconscionability in Contracts' (1976) 39 MLR 369, 385. Cf. also *B & S Contracts and Design
Ltd* v *Victor Green Publications Ltd* [1984] ICR 419; *Atlas Express Ltd* v *Kafco* (*Importers and
Distributors*) *Ltd* [1989] QB 833.

[8] A term often used in this context is 'unconscionability,' see MA Eisenberg, 'The Bargain
Principle and Its Limits' (1982) 95 Harv L Rev 741, 754–63; SM Waddams, 'Unconscionability
in Contracts' (1976) 39 MLR 369, 385.

but they are very limited in their power to agree upon the remedies which will follow should these rights be infringed. This proposition was valid even during the heyday of freedom of contract, when Sir George Jessel MR made his famous statement that:

[I]f there is one thing which more than another public policy requires, it is that men of full age and competent understanding shall have the utmost liberty of contracting, and that their contracts when entered into freely and voluntarily shall be held sacred and shall be enforced by Courts of justice.[9]

This concept of extreme freedom of contract was, however, confined to the creation of contractual rights. It stopped at the gates of remedies, a kingdom almost completely regulated by pre-determined legal rules, which the parties have little power to modify.

It goes without saying that the parties have no power to agree upon sanctions other than those recognized by the law of contract. They may not, for example, decide that the breach will constitute a criminal offence, nor that physical punishment be inflicted upon the party in breach (Shylock's sanction). But even within the area of contract law proper there is only a narrow scope for agreement. The foremost interest of the parties, at the time the contract is concluded, is that it will be honoured. But enforcement, either by way of specific performance or by injunction, is discretionary. The parties may, of course, stipulate in their contract that in case of breach the innocent party will be entitled to specific performance or to an injunction, but such a stipulation is not binding upon the court. Although weight may be attached to the parties' wishes, it is clearly not conclusive.

It is submitted that if the contract was fairly negotiated and if its terms are fair, much greater weight ought to be accorded to the parties' intention, and that this limitation upon the freedom of contract is too severe.[10] Yet, it is symptomatic of the technique of control maintained in Anglo-American law over the exercise of legal rights.[11]

The foremost remedy for breach in Anglo-American law is damages. This remedy is granted as a matter of right. Yet the limitations upon the parties' power to agree upon the consequences of breach are also manifested with regard to this remedy.

---

[9] *Printing & Numerical Co* v *Sampson* (1875) LR 19 Eq 462, at 465.

[10] Cf. A Schwartz, 'The Myth that Promisees Prefer Supracompensatory Remedies: An Analysis of Contracting for Damage Measures' (1990) 100 Yale LJ 369.

[11] The limited availability of specific performance led to the 'right to breach a contract' theory. It is, however, based on oversimplification. See D Friedmann, 'The Efficient Breach Fallacy' (1989) 18 JLS 1. See also, generally, SM Waddams, 'The Choice of Remedy for Breach of Contract', ch 18 below. For the present discussion it suffices to point out that the discretion regarding remedies aimed at protecting a legal right in specie exists also in the context of property rights. See text to note 16 below *et seq*. Nevertheless, specific recovery is more readily available where the claim is based upon property right than in cases of contractual right, though it is discretionary in both instances.

The fundamental rule, which was already well established in the time of Sir George Jessel MR days, is that penalty clauses are void, although the parties may agree upon stipulated damages. Equitable relief is ordinarily available against various kinds of forfeiture, and it was rightly pointed out that '[t]here can, surely, be no doubt that this equitable jurisdiction amounted to a direct interference with freedom of contract'.[12] Yet, as already pointed out, such interference in the field of remedies is the rule rather than the exception.[13]

The purpose of this chapter is neither to examine in detail the ambit of freedom left to the parties in the field of remedies, nor to deal with such issues as whether the parties can agree that the rules of mitigation or remoteness of damages will not apply. For our purposes it suffices to point out that a very substantial part of the law of remedies is beyond the parties' control, and that while the parties may, at least in theory, create 'absolute' contractual rights, their hands are tied so far as the remedies are concerned.

In the examination of this point it will be convenient to distinguish between:

(1) discretionary (equitable) remedies;
(2) non-discretionary (legal) remedies; and
(3) self-help.

DISCRETIONARY REMEDIES

The very nature of the discretion in specific performance and injunctive relief means that the plaintiff is not entitled, as a matter of course, to that which the tribunal may in its discretion withhold. Some of the legal paradoxes are to be found where a legal right is defined as absolute, while the remedy for its protection is discretionary.[14] The point is best

[12] SM Waddams, 'Unconscionability in Contracts' (1976) 39 MLR 369, 370. Cf. also the rule regarding the measure of damages where a party exercises a contractual right to terminate a contract for non-repudiatory breach. The basic approach is that such a party is not entitled to damages for loss of the bargain, on the ground that this loss results from his decision to terminate. The question whether the contract can be drafted in a way which will overcome this rule gave rise to considerable difficulties: *Financing Ltd* v *Baldock* [1963] 2 QB 104; *Lombard North Central plc* v *Butterworth* [1987] QB 527. The issue is discussed in GH Treitel, *The Law of Contract* (8th ed 1991) pp 748–52; RM Goode, 'Penalties in Finance Leases' (1988) 104 LQR 25; H Beale, 'Penalties in Termination Provisions' (1988) 104 LQR 355; JS Ziegel, 'Damages for Breach of Finance Leases in Canada' (1988) 104 LQR 513.

[13] See, however, PS Atiyah, *An Introduction to the Law of Contract* (4th ed 1989) pp 30–1, 453–7 who suggests that, since 1980, English law evidences a resurgence of the freedom of contract ethos and, consequently, courts have recognized the validity of various contractual devices, circumventing the rules against penalties and forfeitures. See also below, text to n 82 *et seq.*

[14] Cf. EL Sherwin, 'An Essay on Private Remedies' (1993) 6 Can J of Law and Jurisprudence 89.

demonstrated in the field of property, in which English law has unequivocally rejected the idea that the use of property rights is subject to a requirement of good faith.[15] In this context the case of *Woollerton & Wilson Ltd v Richard Costain Ltd*[16] is of interest. The facts were as follows: the defendants installed a tower crane on a building site. When the crane was operated, its jib swung at a height of about fifty feet over the plaintiffs' factory. This did not inconvenience the plaintiffs in the slightest, yet the plaintiffs objected to the invasion of their air space and, to quote Stamp J 'something more than £250 which the defendants have offered would have been required to induce them to change their mind'.[17] An injunction was granted, but the court exercised its discretion to postpone its operation for about a year, ie, until the work was expected to be completed.[18]

Detailed discussion of the case is not within the ambit of this chapter. It is, however, relevant to point out the parameters which are characteristic of the Anglo-American approach. It is assumed that the plaintiff has an absolute right in his property. The defendant is in no way entitled to infringe this right, no matter how great is his need to do so,[19] nor how trivial the infringement will be. Nowhere in *Woollerton* is there a reference to the question of good faith. The implicit assumption is that the plaintiffs are perfectly entitled to insist on their property rights, no matter what the consequences for others are, and that such an insistence is not subject to the requirement of good faith.

However, when the issue of the appropriate remedy is addressed, the approach changes. The right may be absolute, but its protection by means of an injunction is discretionary, and in the exercise of this discretion, the court may, as a practical matter, deprive the party of the ability to do that

---

[15] *Bradford Corpn v Pickles* [1895] AC 587. American law has on occasion adopted a different approach. See Powell, *Real Property* vol 5 (1971, revised ed, Rohan) s 696 p 276–9 (with regard to 'spite fences'). See also s 725 at p 420 on 'malicious' appropriation of percolating water, and s 726 p 421 on the development of the US doctrine of reasonable use.

[16] [1970] 1 WLR 411.

[17] *Ibid.*, at 413.

[18] The *Woollerton* decision was doubted in *Charington v Simons & Co Ltd* [1971] 1 WLR 598, at 603. The decision is nevertheless sound.

Whether injunction might be refused where the interference with the plaintiff's rights is permanent, is more problematic. There are statements to the effect that this result might ensue in exceptional situations if a number of conditions exist, one of which is that 'it would be oppressive to the defendant to grant an injunction': *Shelfer v City of London Electric Lighting Co* [1895] 1 Ch 287, at 323, per AL Smith LJ; *Woollerton & Wilson Ltd v Richard Costain Ltd* [1970] 1 WLR 411, at 414. Cf. also *Boomer v Atlantic Cement Co*, 26 NY 2d 219, 257 NE 2d 870 (1970), in which injunctive relief to end a serious nuisance was denied in view of the huge economic loss that it would entail. However, the cases are in conflict, see Clerk & Lindsell on *Torts* (16th ed 1989) pp 328–33.

[19] An exception is, however, recognized where the property of one person is essentially needed to salvage the life of another and possibly also in order to salvage property of much greater value. See text to notes 67–71 below.

which in theory it is entitled to do, namely, to insist upon his 'absolute' right in disregard of the circumstances and interests of others.

The implications for contracts are obvious. If the use of a discretionary remedy to protect the 'strong' property right can be denied because of the plaintiff's lack of good faith or because it is oppressive to the defendant, it could be a fortiori withheld in the contract situation.[20] Indeed, equity has a long tradition of using its discretionary remedies to control or mitigate contractual unfairness. This was mainly done with regard to the process of contract formation ('procedural unconscionability'), namely where the contract was obtained by unfair means, or where the will of the party was impaired.[21] In these cases, specific performance may be denied even if the unfairness does not invalidate the contract.[22] Whether inadequacy of consideration, in itself ('substantive unconscionability'), will lead to the denial of specific performance is not altogether clear.[23] It is, however, well settled that specific performance will not be granted if there has been no consideration at all.[24]

The plaintiff's unfairness may lead to the denial of specific performance not only if it occurred at the formation of the contract, but also when it happened during its performance.[25] *Shell UK Ltd v Lostock Garages Ltd*[26] provides a conspicuous example. In that case the defendant was contractually bound to purchase from the plaintiff (Shell) all the petrol required for its business. The defendant, in breach of the contract, was buying

---

[20] The initial position of Anglo-American law was that the promisee is not entitled to specific performance if damages are adequate, so that enforcement of the contract was the exception rather than the rule. However, modern developments have greatly expanded the availability of specific performance, and it seems that the modern test is not the 'adequacy' of damages but which remedy is the most appropriate: GH Treitel, *The Law of Contract* (8th ed 1991) p 902. Cf. also Farnsworth, *Contracts* (2nd ed 1990) p 858.

[21] It seems that specific performance may be denied in cases of mistake, although there is some conflict on this point. See GH Treitel, *The Law of Contract* (8th ed 1991) pp 280–1; G Jones and W Goodhart, *Specific Performance* (1986) pp 67–70.

[22] GH Treitel, *The Law of Contract* (8th ed 1991) p 908.

[23] *Ibid.*, p 909, indicates that the authorities on this point 'are not easy to reconcile'. English text books, generally, conclude that mere inadequacy of consideration does not preclude specific performance and that an additional element, such as mistake, unfair advantage taken by the other party or even 'surprise', is required. See also G Jones and W Goodhart, *Specific Performance* (1986) p 73. But where the inadequacy of the consideration is gross or 'shocking', the existence of such an additional element will be presumed. Cf. *Underhill v Horwood* (1804) 10 Ves Jun 209, at 219; 32 ER 824, at 828, per Lord Eldon. Under the modern US approach, gross inadequacy of consideration may amount to 'substantive unconscionability' which could lead to the avoidance of the contract.

[24] GH Treitel, *The Law of Contract* (8th ed 1991) p 916.

[25] *Ibid.*, p 909. See also Hanbury and Martin's *Modern Equity* (14th ed 1993) p 762, who base this rule on the maxim that in equity the plaintiff must come with 'clean hands'. In *Shell UK Ltd v Lostock Garage Ltd* [1976] 1 WLR 1187, at 1199 Lord Denning MR referred to the maxim that 'he who comes to equity must do equity'.

[26] [1976] 1 WLR 1187; GH Treitel, *The Law of Contract* (8th ed 1991) pp 188, 909; PS Atiyah, *An Introduction to the Law of Contract* (4th ed 1989) pp 224, 244.

petrol from other suppliers. An injunction was, however, denied on the ground that Shell was selling petrol to competing petrol stations at a much lower price than that demanded from the defendant, making it commercially impractical for the defendant to keep its contract with Shell. In a legal system that recognizes a duty of good faith, it might have been concluded that the plaintiff was in breach of this duty. In English law resort could have been made to implied term. However, the Court of Appeal, by a majority, declined to imply a term prohibiting such a discrimination against the defendant that would force it to trade at a loss. Instead, the Court used its discretion to deny an injunction. The reasoning and the result, based upon the rights-remedies dichotomy, are instructive. They also demonstrate how the law of remedies is used to control contractual behaviour. It is assumed that the plaintiff has a contractual right which is not subject to the requirement of good faith, and which is unaffected by the plaintiff's unfairness. However, once the question of the remedy arises, the attitude changes and the plaintiff is, in effect, deprived of the main advantage which the theoretically valid legal right is supposed to grant him.

The court's power to withhold discretionary remedies is, thus, an important tool of controlling unfair conduct. It is a particularly potent weapon where the alternative non-discretionary remedy, usually damages, is unavailable or of little value, as where the plaintiff suffered no loss or where the loss cannot be proved.[27] The problem becomes more complex where the non-discretionary remedies, which the plaintiff has prima facie at his disposal, can potentially be effective. We now turn to consider whether, and if so how, these remedies are affected by the lack of good faith.

NON-DISCRETIONARY REMEDIES

Introduction

The well-known decision in *White & Carter (Councils) Ltd* v *McGregor*[28] demonstrates the importance of the distinction between discretionary and non-discretionary remedies. In that case the plaintiffs agreed to advertise the defendants' business for three years. The defendants repudiated the contract on the day it was made. Nevertheless, the plaintiffs advertised

---

[27] In the case of *Shell UK Ltd* v *Lostock Garage Ltd* [1976] 1 WLR 1187, at 1202, Ormrod LJ mentioned that it is by no means certain that Shell could prove that they had suffered any loss. PS Atiyah, *An Introduction to the Law of Contract* (4th ed 1989) p 224 also suggests that damages in this case were probably nil.

On the practicability of suing at law after the discretionary equitable remedy has been denied, see JP Frank and J Endicott 'Defenses in Equity and "Legal Rights" ' (1954) 14 La L Rev 380 and comment on this study in A Leff, 'Unconscionability and the Code—The Emperor's New Clause' (1967) 115 U Pa L Rev 485, 541, n 237. See also n 30 below.

[28] [1962] AC 413.

the defendants' business in accordance with the original terms of the contract. The House of Lords held by a majority that the plaintiffs were entitled to recover the whole amount due under the contract. Although the recovery of the contractual price amounts to specific performance, it is classified in English law as an action for debt, which is a non-discretionary common-law remedy.[29] Had the claim been for a discretionary remedy, no doubt recovery would have been denied, but since the remedy was non-discretionary, the majority felt bound to allow it.

In assessing the influence of good faith in contract remedies, the denial of injunctive relief and specific performance, and thus the overall influence of good faith, is of less significance if the promisee can get another, equally potent, remedy as a matter of right. In the present context, much depends on the answer to two questions. First, to what extent are the non-discretionary remedies as effective as the discretionary ones?[30] Secondly, are there rules embodied in the non-discretionary remedies that take lack of good faith into account?

These questions are interrelated, because if one remedy takes into account factors like good faith, while the other remedy disregards them or accords them a different weight, their effectiveness is likely to differ considerably.

It may also be noted that specific performance (the discretionary remedy) and damages (the major non-discretionary remedy) are meant to serve precisely the same purpose.[31] Both are intended to put the innocent party in as good a position he would have been in had the contract not been breached.[32] The difference is that specific enforcement grants the plaintiff the promised performance in specie while damages are intended to provide him with the precise equivalent in monetary terms. But although the two remedies are meant to serve the same purpose, the practical result of awarding one rather than the other may differ

---

[29] *Ibid.*, at 445, per Lord Hodson. The case and the qualification of its principle are discussed below at text to n 111 *et seq.*

[30] Comment, 'Equitable Contract Remedies—Denial of Both Specific Performance and Rescission' (1934) 32 Mich LR 518; SM Waddams, 'Unconscionability in Contracts' (1976) 39 MLR 369, 387–8 and n 27 above and accompanying text. Cf. also EL Sherwin, 'Law and Equity in Contract Enforcement' (1991) 50 Maryland LR 253. In some instances the cost of performance to the defendant is much greater than the benefit of performance to the plaintiff. In these situations, specific performance will enable a plaintiff, who is not genuinely interested in performance to force the defendant to pay for his release an amount exceeding the plaintiff's real interest, see text to notes 43–56 below and S Waddams, ch 18 below.

[31] Restatement (2d) Contracts, § 347, Comment a (with regard to damages); EL Sherwin, 'Law and Equity in Contract Enforcement' (1991) 50 Maryland LR 253, 260.

[32] A different result ensues in the exceptional cases in which punitive damages are awarded in US jurisdictions against the party in breach. See note 1, above. This remedy offers the plaintiff a windfall which is beyond the ordinary reach of the equitable remedies. However, in rare situations, injunction or specific performance may also indirectly offer a windfall to the plaintiff. Such a situation may arise if the defendant is greatly interested in being released and following the court's order decides to 'buy himself out'.

considerably.[33] The extent of the difference depends, inter alia, upon the rules on the appraisal of damages. The discussion below seeks to show that the concept of good faith has a considerable effect on the law of damages, and that the rules on damages, although in theory non-discretionary, in fact allow considerable flexibility.[34] It will be argued that the factors allowing flexibility in awards of damages, if properly taken into account, tend to reduce the practical gap between specific performance and damages. This approach will be examined in the context of the following topics:

(1) penalties;
(2) the requirement of mitigation;
(3) measure of recovery: diminution in value or cost of repair;
(4) measure of recovery: the plaintiff's loss or the defendant's gain.

Penalties

The rule discussed above, under which penalties are void, prevents their use in order to gain an undue advantage, which specific performance does not offer.

Mitigation

It has rightly been pointed out that the rules on mitigation reflect a requirement of good faith.[35] A person is usually likely to do his best to avoid losses which will be imposed upon him. Mitigation requires the victim to avoid losses for which another, albeit a wrongdoer (a tortfeasor or a party in breach of a contract), would otherwise be responsible. It is predicated on the ground that if properly carried out, migration will benefit the wrongdoer without harming the victim. The requirement duly

---

[33] See also note 27 above and accompanying text.

[34] In addition, US law openly grants the courts discretion, in certain circumstances, with regard to some items of damages: Restatement (2d) Contracts, § 351(3); WB Harvey, 'Discretionary Justice Under the Restatement (Second) of Contracts' (1982) 67 Cornell LR 666; MN Kniffin, 'A Newly Identified Contract Unconscionability: Unconscionability of Remedy' (1988) 63 Notre Dame LR 247.

[35] See F Kessler and G Gilmore, *Contracts: Cases and Materials* (2nd ed 1970) ch 12. This chapter is entitled 'The Duty to Act in Good Faith . . .' and it includes the doctrine of anticipatory breach and the duty to mitigate damages. (In the third edition by Kronman, these topics appear, at p 1269, under the title: 'The burdens of innocence'.) Farnsworth, *Contracts* (p 897, note 3) points out that since the rule on mitigation does not reflect a duty, failure to mitigate is not a breach of the general duty of good faith. For this reason I have used the term 'requirement' of good faith (above, note 2). See also MA Eisenberg, 'The Responsive Model of Contract Law' (1984) 36 Stan L Rev 1107, 1153, suggesting that for the purpose of mitigation the substantive decision of a wrongfully dismissed employee whether to take a replacement job is to be tested by a standard of good faith. A similar test is offered in other replacement situations.

to consider the interest of another is thus an application of the concept of good faith in the sense already discussed.[36]

The following examples may be used to test the interrelationship of specific performance, damages and mitigation:

(1) S agrees to sell his house to P for £100,000. S reneges because he fell ill and is unable to move to another city as planned. P can obtain a similar house for about the same price, but seeks specific performance. By the time judgment is to be rendered, the value of the house is £200,000.

(2) The facts are the same as in example (1), except that when P learned about the breach he was unable to acquire another house, because no similar house was available in the area or because at this time prices already went up and P could not afford it.

It should be noted that the rules on mitigation are confined to damages and do not form part of the law of specific performance. Consequently, example (1) presents a situation in which there is a huge economic difference between specific performance and damages. If specific performance is granted, P will get a house which has doubled in value,[37] and the fact that he could have mitigated the damages would become irrelevant. On the other hand, the damages may be nil, since the whole loss could have been avoided. Yet the possibility of mitigation may indirectly effect the outcome. The court, in exercising its discretion, may deny specific performance on the ground that the plaintiff did not act in good faith,[38] because he failed to mitigate the loss.[39] In other words, the fact that mitigation, although not formally part of the law of specific performance, may be taken in account, is likely to reduce the possibility of incongruity between the remedies.[40]

Example (2) assumes that the plaintiff could not have mitigated his loss. In that case the economic results of specific performance and damages should, therefore, be similar. If specific performance is granted, P will get the house which is now worth £200,000.[41] If specific performance is denied on the ground of S's sickness, P would be entitled to damages which ought to be calculated on the basis of the value of the house at the

---

[36] Above, at text after note 6.

[37] Quaere, can the court as part of its discretion in granting specific performance make the order subject to the condition that the price be increased?

[38] Cf. the equitable maxim requiring the one who seeks equity to come with 'clean hands'.

[39] This is but one consideration, albeit an important one, but there may be others that will outweigh it, eg bad faith on the part of the defendant. In this type of situation, specific performance will prove more advantageous to the plaintiff than damages, for the obvious reason that the possibility of mitigation, which would have reduced the award of damages, is disregarded in the award of specific performance.

[40] Another way of reducing the discrepancy between the remedies is by granting specific performance subject to conditions. See note 37, above.

[41] P should, however, pay interest upon the balance of the price, although its payment has been delayed because of the defendant's breach. Indeed, specific performance may be conditional upon such payment.

time judgment is rendered.[42] Damages would, thus, be equal in value to specific performance.

Measure of recovery: diminution in value or cost of repair

A well-known problem of damage assessment arises where the defendant in breach of the contract renders a defective performance or a performance that does not accord with the contract requirements.[43] The problem becomes particularly acute where the cost of curing the defect is highly disproportionate to the loss in value.[44] Will the plaintiff get an undeserved windfall if he recovers the cost of repair and sells the property without having repaired it? Or will the defendant be unjustly enriched if he is allowed to pay the mere difference in value, and thus save himself the cost of due performance?[45] This problem will not be discussed in detail. It suffices to point out that scholars and courts sometimes determine the issue by reference to factors directly relevant to the good faith of both parties. So far as the plaintiff is concerned, an emphasis is sometimes laid on his subjective attitude[46] and it is asked whether he is genuinely interested in curing the defect.[47] With regard to the defendant's good faith, the result is often said to depend on whether he acted wilfully or inadvertently.[48]

---

[42] _Worth_ v _Tyler_ [1974] Ch 30.

[43] GH Treitel, _The Law of Contract_ (8th ed 1991) pp 836–9; Farnsworth, _Contracts_ (2nd ed 1990) 908–12.

[44] _Tito_ v _Waddell_ (No 2) [1977] Ch 106; _Jacob & Youngs_ v _Kent_, 129 NE 889 (1921); _Groves_ v _John Wunder Co_, 286 NW 235 (1939); _Peevyhouse_ v _Garland Coal & Mining Co_, 382 P. 2d 109 (1963); _Rock Island Improvement Co_ v _Helmerich & Payne Inc_, 698 F 2d 1075 (1983); _Ruxley Electronics_ v _Forsyth_ [1994] 1 WLR 650 (CA). See also D Friedmann, 'Restitution of Benefits Obtained Through the Appropriation of Property or the Commission of a Wrong' (1980) 80 Colum LR 504, 522–5.

[45] There may be a considerable difference between the cost of performance originally saved and the cost of curing the defect. Suppose that in building a house the contractor used pipes that were less expensive than those specified in the contract. The difference in price reflects his saving at the time of performance and represents a clear case of unjust enrichment. Cf. _Samson & Samson Ltd_ v _Proctor_ [1975] 1 NZLR 655. The costs of repair, ie replacing the pipes in the already built house may, of course, be much higher and do not represent an enrichment. Cf _Jacob & Youngs_ v Kent, 129 NE 889 (1921).

[46] _Radford_ v _De Froberville_ [1977] 1 WLR 1262; _Dean_ v _Ainley_ [1987] 1 WLR 1729.

[47] MA Eisenberg, 'The Responsive Model of Contract Law' (1984) 36 Stan L Rev 1107, 1160–5. But cf. _Ruxley Electronics_ v _Forsyth_ [1994] 1 WLR 650 (CA) in which the Court of Appeal applied the test of reasonableness. Staughton LJ stated that the plaintiff will not get 'an expensive remedy if there is some cheaper alternative which would make good his loss' (p 659). This is in line with the idea of good faith. However, the concept of reasonableness as interpreted by the majority led to a rather harsh result upon the defendant. The majority also held that the plaintiff is free to use the damages awarded to him as he pleases and is not bound to apply them to remedy the defect for which they were granted.

[48] See the references in Farnsworth, _Contracts_ (2nd ed 1990) pp 911–12. See also PH Marshall, 'Wilfulness: A Crucial Factor in Choosing Remedies for Breach of Contract' (1982) 24 Arizona L Rev 733.

Measure of recovery: the plaintiff's loss or the defendant's gain

In England the Court of Appeal has recently denied the innocent party's right to recover the gains made by the other party from breach of the contract.[49] A different result has been reached in other jurisdictions.[50] The issue has been extensively discussed[51] and it is not proposed to repeat the arguments here. However, an indication will be given of the relevance of good faith to the issue of whether restitution is to be granted as well as to the question how is the defendant's gain to be measured.

Let us return to the case of *Woollerton* discussed above.[52] This, it will be remembered, was a property case, in which a discretionary remedy (injunction) was denied. The plaintiffs could have of course claimed damages to which they were entitled as a matter of right. But what was their loss? The underlying assumption was that they suffered no loss at all, so that only nominal damages could be recovered. But can it be argued that the defendants' wrong deprived the plaintiff of the opportunity to 'sell' the right to use air space?[53] Had such an opportunity been given, the plaintiffs might presumably have charged an amount reflecting much of value to the defendants of the use of their air space. It is, however, obvious that in this type of case it would be inappropriate to award damages equal to the amount that the plaintiffs could have extracted. The reason is this: charging an exorbitant amount for such a case is an excessive exercise of the plaintiffs' property right.[54]

The owner could, presumably, recover either as damages or in restitution a fair amount for the use of his air space.[55] This, however, is clearly

---

[49] *Surrey County Council* v *Bredero Homes Ltd* [1993] 1 WLR 1361.

[50] *Hickey and Co Ltd* v *Roches Stores* (1975) (1993) 2 Restitution LR 196 (Ireland); *Samson & Samson Ltd* v *Proctor* [1975] 1 NZLR 655 (New Zealand); FH 20/82 *Adras Ltd* v *Harlow & Jones GmbH* 42(1) PD 221, noted (1988) 104 LQR 383. There are also a number of US decisions which allowed recovery of gains made through breach of contract. See, eg, *Unita Oil Refining Co* v *Ledford* 244 P 2d 881 (1952).

[51] D Friedmann, 'Restitution of Benefits Obtained Through the Appropriation of Property or the Commission of a Wrong' (1980) 80 Colum LR 504; G Jones, 'The Recovery of Benefits Gained From a Breach of Contract' (1983) 99 LQR 443; EA Farnsworth, 'Your Loss of My Gain? The Dilemma of the Disgorgement Principle in Breach of Contract' (1985) 94 Yale LJ 1339; J Beatson, *The Use and Abuse of Unjust Enrichment* (1991) pp 15–17; SM Waddams, 'Restitution as Part of Contract Law' in A Burrows (ed), *Essays on the Law of Restitution* (1991) 197, 208. R O'Dair, 'Restitutionary Damages for Breach of Contract and the Theory of Efficient Breach: Some Reflections' (1993) 46(2) CLP 113.

[52] Text to note 16, above.

[53] RJ Sharp and SM Waddams, 'Damages for Lost Opportunity to Bargain' (1982) 2 Ox JLS 290. See, however, *Surrey County Council* v *Bredero Homes Ltd* [1993] 1 WLR 1361.

[54] Quaere, had such a contract been made, would it have been voidable on the ground of economic duress?

[55] Cf. *Wrotham Park Estate Co Ltd* v *Parkside Homes Ltd* [1974] 1 WLR 798. Recovery in restitution of the value of the use of another's land was denied in *Phillips* v *Homfray* (1883) 24 Ch D 439. The result is unsatisfactory: R Goff & G Jones, *The Law of Restitution* (4th ed 1993) pp 717–20. Recovery was, however, allowed in torts: *Whitwham* v *Westminster Brymbo Coal and*

not the amount he could extract by virtue of a monopolistic situation.[56] Hence, where the discretionary remedy is denied because it is considered that the plaintiff is trying to exercise his property right in a way which is oppressive to the defendant, the plaintiff may still recover damages to which he is entitled as a matter of right. But the availability of damages will similarly not enable an excessive use of the proprietary right, since the award in monetary terms (either as damages or in restitution) will not take into account the possibility of an unfair exploitation of the plaintiff's right.

To sum up: although the remedy of damages is non-discretionary and English law does not recognize a general principle of good faith, the rules on damages often take the element of good faith into account. This is sometimes reflected in the mode of calculating damages, and in other instances through the principle of mitigation.

SELF-HELP

Introduction

The exercise of self-help enables the aggrieved party to obtain redress without resorting to an action in court.[57] Self-help can, of course, be challenged in court, but it has the advantage of shifting the onus of initiating litigation to the other party.[58] The discussion below will concentrate on the question whether self-help has other advantages reflected in substantive rules, which actually lead to a different result, depending on whether a party can exercise self-help or is bound to apply for a court-controlled legal remedy.

Coke Co [1896] 2 Ch 538. Cf. also *Strand Electric & Engineering Co Ltd* v *Brisford Entertainments Ltd* [1952] 2 QB 246. See also *Ministry of Defence* v *Ashman; Same* v *Thompson* (1993) 66 P & CR195 discussed by E Cooke, 'Trespass, Mesne Profits and Restitution' (1994) 110 LQR 420. Contrast *Stoke-on-Trent City Council* v *W & J Wass Ltd* [1988] 1 WLR 1406 (CA), in which the defendants infringed the plaintiffs' monopoly right to hold a market. It was held that the plaintiffs can recover only nominal damages and that they are not entitled to an amount equal to the reasonable fee they would have charged. The decision is rightly criticized in G Jones, 'The Law of Restitution: The Past and the Future', in A Burrows (ed), *Essays on the Law of Restitution* (1991) pp 1, 7–8.

[56] Contrast *Edwards* v *Lee's Administrators*, 265 Ky 418, 96 SW 2d 1028 (1936), in which the defendant discovered an underground cave. The entrance to the cave was from the defendant's land, but part of the cave was under the land of the plaintiff. The defendant used the whole cave for tourist business which he developed. In a claim for restitution, the defendant was required to disgorge all profits made by the use of the plaintiff's part of the cave (the profits were divided in proportion to the ratio between defendant's part of the cave and that of the plaintiff). This harsh, and in a sense punitive, result was predicated on the ground that the defendant was a conscious wrongdoer.

[57] On self-help remedies in contractual context see PS Atiyah, *An Introduction to the Law of Contract* (4th ed 1989) pp 436–41.

[58] *Ibid.*, pp 438–9.

There are two types of self-help. One, which may be termed physical, takes such forms as recaption of stolen goods or abatement of nuisance. Legal self-help refers to an extra-judicial legal act[59] which affects the rights of the parties. Typical examples are set-off and termination of a contract on the ground of breach or its rescission for fraud.

It is in this area of self-help in which we find some of the sharpest differences between property rights and contractual rights. The typical way in which self-help is exercised in defence of property rights is physical, while that exercised in defense of contractual rights is legal. Instances of physical self-help in a contractual setting can, however, be conceived.[60]

Physical self-help

In *Woollerton*[61] the court decided to postpone an injunction and thus enabled the defendants to trespass the plaintiffs' air space for about a year. Suppose the plaintiffs, instead of applying to the court, would have erected a steel pole on their own land, which would have hindered the movement of the crane's jib over their land and thus prevent the operation of the crane. In this situation the owner does not depend on judicial remedies such as injunction or damages. Consequently, the techniques examined above which, from the owner's point of view, limit their effectiveness, are inapplicable. Indeed, *Woollerton* can be contrasted with the famous decision in *Bradford Corpn v Pickles*[62] in which the defendant made an excavation on his own land, thus preventing the flow of underground water to the plaintiffs' reservoir. The defendant explained that this was done for the purpose of extracting minerals. The plaintiffs claimed, however, that the defendant did not act bona fide and that his real intention was to injure the plaintiffs and so 'to induce them either to purchase his land or to give him some other compensation'.[63] The House of Lords held that, since a landowner had a right to appropriate water percolating in undefined channels within his land, his motives are totally irrelevant. Furthermore, their Lordships saw no reason why the defendant 'should not insist on [the plaintiffs] purchasing his interest'[64] at a price he thinks fit. Indeed, the plaintiffs 'are welcome to the water, and to his land too, if they will pay the price for it'.[65]

It is not proposed to discuss possible distinctions between *Bradford Corpn v Pickles* and *Woollerton*. However, what needs to be pointed out is

---

[59] The term 'legal act' is used in continental law. A notable example is the German BGB.
[60] See below, note 73.
[61] [1970] 1 WLR 411. See above, note 16 and accompanying text.
[62] [1895] AC 587.   [63] *Ibid.*, at 589.   [64] *Ibid.*, at 595, per Lord Halsbury.
[65] *Ibid.*, at 601, per Lord MacNaghten. See, however, n 15 above with regard to American law.

the relevance of the remedy. In *Bradford Corpn* v *Pickles* the landowner did not seek judicial remedy. It was the other party who asked for it. The landowner simply exercised his right. It was, so to speak, akin to self-help, though it was clearly not self-help in the legal sense, since no force was used against another person or another person's property. The landowner merely exploited his property in a manner detrimental to the other party.[66]

This demonstrates that there may be practical differences between imposing a good faith limitation upon the legal right and the indirect technique of restricting the availability of judicial remedies. Had the legal right (ownership) itself been limited by the good faith doctrine and had it applied to the *Woollerton* type of situation, the owner would not have been entitled to use self-help to prevent the encroachment of his air space.

In this context, the incomplete privilege theory developed in US law is of interest.[67] It provides in essence that a person 'may trespass upon the property of another to save himself or his own property or even a third person or his property from harm',[68] although he will be required to pay for the damage done and presumably also for the value of the use of the owner's property.[69] In this type of situation, the restriction upon the owner does not stem from the court's discretion regarding the *remedy* (injunction), but from a limitation imposed upon the owner's *right* of property. For this reason the owner may not resort to self-help.[70] This limitation upon the owner's right seems to be based upon the idea of good faith, which requires that the owner will not insist upon his 'absolute' property right when the life or even property of another person is in imminent danger.[71]

---

[66] An interesting explanation of *Bradford Corpn* v *Pickles* was offered by Glanville Williams saying that 'the plaintiffs' grievance was simply that they would have liked to appropriate something that the defendant succeeded in appropriating or diverting first': GL Williams, 'The Foundation of Tortious Liability' (1939) 7 CLJ 111, 128–9. See also JG Fleming, 'Negligence and Property Rights' (1988) 104 LQR 183. Cf. also *United Steel Works* v *United States Steel Corpn* (1980) 631 F 2d 1264 (owners who decided to close a steel plant preferred to demolish it rather than sell it to the union of the dismissed employees. It was held that the union had no right to purchase the plant from the unwilling owners). The decision is criticized in JW Singer, 'The Reliance Interest in property' (1988) 40 Stan LR 611.

[67] *Vincent* v *Lake Eerie Transportation* 109 Minn 456, 124 NW 221 (1910); FH Bohlen, 'Incomplete Privilege to Inflict Intentional Invasions of Interests of Property and Personality' (1926) 39 Harv L Rev 307; Restatement, Restitution § 122; Restatement (2d) Torts, § 263.

[68] Prosser and Keeton on *The Law of Torts* (5th ed 1984) pp 147–8.

[69] On the nature of this claim see D Friedmann, 'Restitution of Benefits Obtained Through the Appropriation of Property or the Commission of a Wrong' (1980) 80 Colum LR 504, 540–3.

[70] Expelling the endangered trespasser will entail liability in torts and may also constitute criminal offense: Prosser and Keeton on *The Law of Torts* (5th ed 1984).

[71] The distinction between *Woollerton* and the limited privilege situation is that *Woollerton* did not involve a salvage situation. The work performed by the defendants was intended to improve the property, not to protect it from imminent danger. Borderline situations between salvage and improvement can, of course, be envisaged.

The comparison between *Woollerton* and the limited privilege rule highlights the present borderline of good faith. The remedy approach adopted in *Woollerton* is ambivalent. On the one hand, the defendant is treated as a wrongdoer. He had no right to trespass upon the plaintiffs' property. On the other hand, when it comes to the appropriate remedy, the court refrains from enjoining the further commission of this wrong, at least for another year.[72]

The question of physical self-help arises only rarely in the context of contractual rights,[73] and it will not be discussed in this chapter. Legal self-help is, however, quite common in contractual contexts, and it will now be addressed.

Legal self-help: forfeiture, termination and the right to 'earn' the contractual payment

Forfeiture

Typically, forfeiture is a self-help remedy. Where the forfeited interest greatly exceeds the loss suffered by the aggrieved party, the forfeiture is penal. The issue is closely related to termination and is discussed in that context.[74]

Termination

There are many statements in the books, supported by innumerable decisions, to the effect that a breach, no matter how serious, 'does not automatically discharge the contract'.[75]

Contracts cannot be unilaterally terminated. 'An unaccepted repudiation is a thing writ in water'[76] and '[s]ince . . . termination is the converse of . . . creation, principle demands that it should not be recognized unless this is what both parties intend.'[77] The breach merely confers upon the innocent party an option either to terminate (or rescind) the contract, or to treat it as subsisting. If he chooses the latter, the contract remains binding.

[72] For a possible explanation of this type of ambivalence, cf. M Dan-Cohen, 'Decision Rules and Conduct Rules: On Acoustic Separation in Criminal Law' (1984) 97 Harv L Rev 625. The discretionary rules are directed to the judge. The party is advised that he has no legal right, yet there are prospects that the court will not enjoin the wrongful conduct. The result is a 'half-way' deterrence which may be preferable to an open recognition of a right involving conflict of values.

[73] The right to a lien, which sometimes arises in contractual contexts, may be regarded as one of the physical self-help. Other examples include contract provisions which empower a landlord to evict a tenant or allow a hire-purchase company to repossess the goods. See PS Atiyah, *An Introduction to the Law of Contract* (4th ed 1989) p 439.

[74] See below, text to note 82 *et seq.*

[75] GH Treitel, *The Law of Contract* (8th ed 1991) p 743; Anson's *Law of Contract* (26th ed 1984) p 467; Cheshire and Fifoot and Furmston's *Law of Contract* (12th ed 1991) p 541.

[76] *Howard v Pickford Tool Co Ltd* [1951] 1 KB 417, at 421, per Asquith LJ.

[77] Cheshire and Fifoot and Furmston's *Law of Contract* (12th ed 1991) p 541.

This option to terminate the contract or to keep it in force is an option to exercise legal self-help. The innocent party is given a power which he is free to use without resorting to court. The option to rescind is a powerful weapon which, if complete freedom in its application is allowed, would in many instances result in overprotecting the innocent party's interest while unduly penalizing the party in breach.

There are a number of specific rules which limit the possibilities of unfair or unreasonable termination. The doctrine of substantive performance introduced by Lord Mansfield in *Boone* v *Eyre*[78] provides a clear example. Under this doctrine the party in breach who has substantially performed is entitled to recover the contractual price. This means, of course, that the injured party cannot terminate the contract, although he may claim damages for the breach.

However, since the remedy of termination is one of self-help, we find that judicial control over its exercise is only partial. Gaps can be found in which the power of termination can be used in a way which overprotects the legitimate interests of the aggrieved party, and unduly penalizes the party in breach. Let us examine a number of typical situations.

Termination in order to escape from a bad bargain

Suppose A agreed to sell B a piece of property, payment is to be made by instalments and time is of the essence. B is unable to pay the first instalment on time and asks for a one-week extension. A is not prejudiced by the delay, but he decides to terminate the contract because the property has greatly appreciated in value. Here it seems that the mere fact that the innocent party is motivated by the wish to avoid a disadvantageous contract is insufficient to prevent termination. But it has been pointed out that, in this type of situation, the court is more likely to hold that the breach was not sufficiently severe as to warrant termination.[79] Where, however, the seriousness of the breach is beyond doubt, it seems that the innocent party should be allowed to terminate, even though his main purpose is to avoid a bad bargain.[80]

In balancing the interests of the innocent party who wishes to escape from a disadvantageous contract that has been seriously breached, with that of the party in breach, who loses the advantages of the contract but is not otherwise unduly penalized, the scales are not clearly tipped in the latter's favor.[81] This approach can be justified, notably in jurisdictions in

[78] (1779) 1 H Bl 273, n(a); 126 ER 160. See also *Hoenig* v *Isaacs* [1952] 2 All ER 176. Cf. also the rule regarding the measure of damages in the case of non-repudiatory breach (above, note 12).

[79] GH Treitel, *The Law of Contract* (8th ed 1991) pp 628–9.

[80] This factor may, however, be taken into account if there are additional circumstances that make termination disproportionately harsh. Cf. *Stern* v *McArthur* (1988) 165 CLR 489.

[81] Thus, Israeli law recognizes a general principle of good faith. It was, however,

which the consequences of termination are not too harsh upon the party in breach and, in particular, if he does not lose his right to restitution for his part performance.

Termination which leads to forfeiture

There are some situations in which English law enables the injured party to utilize the right of termination in a way that provides him with undue advantages and harshly penalizes the party in breach. Arguably, this overprotection is not in line with the concept of good faith as described above. The typical situation is that in which the aggrieved party is free from the obligation to restore the benefits received under the contract prior to the breach, so that these benefits are in fact forfeited. A possible example is that of a serious breach by a party who undertook to supply services under an entire contract. In such a case, the injured party may terminate the contract, apparently without being required to make restitution for the benefit received.[82]

In similar contexts, the courts did not permit the right of rescission to be exercised in a way that would yield such results. Thus, under English law, a contract cannot be rescinded for misrepresentation or duress if *restitutio in integrum* is impossible.[83] In *Clarke v Dickson*,[84] Crompton J said that, in order to exercise an option to rescind a contract for fraud, the defrauded party 'must be in such a situation as to be able to put the parties into their original state before the contract'.[85]

It has also been stated that '[t]hough the defendant has been fraudulent, he must not be robbed, nor must the plaintiff be unjustly enriched . . .'[86] It is not clear why this reasoning is inapplicable to termination for

consistently held that the mere fact that the aggrieved party exercises his right of termination in order to avoid a disadvantageous contract, does not constitute an infringement of the good faith duty. See eg, CA 158/80 *Shalom v Mota* 36(4) PD 793, 811–12 (Shamgar J); CA 189/86 *Levy v Faygenblat* 42(4) 206 (Beiski and S Levin JJ). Cf. also *Armstrong v Jackson* [1917] 2 KB 822, at 829 (rescission on the ground of fraud).

[82] *Boston Deep Sea Fishing & Ice Co v Ansell* (1888) 39 ChD 339. This rule is, however, subject to the Apportionment Act 1870. See GH Treitel, *The Law of Contract* (8th ed 1991) pp 721–3. On the denial of restitution to the party in breach, see also *Sumpter v Hedges* [1898] 1 QB 673; *Bolton v Mahadeva* [1972] 1 WLR 1009. This rule does not apply to the supply of chattels, in which a party in breach is entitled to recover for part performance: *Oxendale v Whetherell* (1829) 9 B & C 386; 109 ER 143. Payment is to be made at the contract rate: the Sale of Goods Act 1979, s 30(1).

[83] A better solution would have been to allow rescission subject to payment for that which cannot be restored. But at least in the context of fraud and duress, in which the common law found this solution beyond its reach, it chose to disallow rescission and confine the rights of the injured party to damages: JW Salmond and J Williams, *Principles of the Law of Contract* (2nd ed 1945) p 965. The position of equity has been more flexible: *Spence v Crawford* [1939] 3 All ER 271.

[84] (1858) El Bl & El 148; 120 ER 463.

[85] (1858) El Bl & El 148, at 154; 120 ER 463, at 466.

[86] *Spence v Crawford* [1939] 3 All ER 271, at 288–9, per Lord Wright.

breach, and why a defrauder should be in a better position than a party in breach.

Other common law jurisdictions have, generally, avoided the harsh rule which denies restitution to the party in breach of a contract for the supply of labour or services,[87] and are thus more in congruity with the requirement of good faith.

The rule which enables the injured party to terminate a contract on the ground of its breach while keeping the benefits he received under it, does not apply to part payments,[88] nor to goods which have been supplied.[89] Recovery is, however, based on total failure of consideration, so it will presumably be denied if the party in breach received some benefit under the contract which he is unable to restore. It will also be denied in a contact for the supply of labour or services which has been performed, even in part, by the injured party.[90]

In addition, the basic position of English law is that the payment cannot be recovered if it was made as a deposit or security for performance.[91]

Equity has a long tradition of granting relief against forfeiture. It was not, however, applied in favour of a party in breach who rendered part performance under an entire contract for the supply of labour of services.[92] But even in other contexts, the scope and application of the equitable jurisdiction recently became the subject of debate. A distinction has been drawn between forfeiture of proprietary or possessory interest, and forfeiture in a commercial context, notably a deposit or part payment.[93]

Under the restrictive approach, equitable jurisdiction to grant relief is confined to the first category, namely, the forfeiture of proprietary or possessory interests.[94] A more liberal view supports the extension of the jurisdiction to relieve against forfeiture to other situations.[95] It has been

[87] American law generally allows restitution for part performance by the party in breach: Farnsworth, *Contracts* (2nd ed 1990) pp 626 *et seq*. But in cases of wilful breach, restitution is sometimes denied: *ibid*., p 630.

[88] *Dies v British and International Mining and Finance Corpn Ltd* [1939] 1 KB 724.

[89] See note 82, above.

[90] *Hyundai Heavy Industries Co v Papadopoulos* [1980] 1 WLR 1129 (shipbuilding contract).

[91] On the distinction between a deposit and part payment see GH Treitel, *The Law of Contract* (8th ed 1991) pp 890–1. The rule that a deposit is ordinarily not recoverable by the party in breach, has been modified by s 49(2) of the Law of Property Act 1925 with regard to contracts for the sale of land. See GH Treitel, *The Law of Contract* (8th ed 1991) pp 891–2.

[92] See eg *Bolton v Mahadeva* [1972] 1 WLR 1009; *Hyundai Heavy Industries Co v Papadopoulos* [1980] 1 WLR 1129.

[93] Part payment is generally recoverable (above, notes 88 and 91) unless the contract validly provides otherwise: GH Treitel, *The Law of Contract* (8th ed 1991) p 891.

[94] *Sport International Bussum BV v Inter-Footwear Ltd* [1984] 1 WLR 776, at 787, per Oliver LJ; aff'd [1984] 1 WLR 790 (HL). For a detailed discussion see R Goff and G Jones, *The Law of Restitution* (4th ed 1993) pp 433–8. The narrow approach can perhaps be explained by the return to the freedom of contract idea. See PS Atiyah, above n 13.

[95] *Stockloser v Johnson* [1954] 1 QB 476. The case concerned a sale of machinery, the price to be paid by instalments. The purchaser received the machinery and used it, but defaulted

convincingly argued that the validity of forfeiture clauses should depend on the same tests that differentiate penalties from liquidated clauses and that the court should accordingly have power to grant relief where the forfeiture provision is penal in nature.[96]

Where the party in breach is willing and able to perform, equity can sometimes grant relief against forfeiture by extending the time of performance.[97] In this type of situation, the equitable rules on specific performance, coupled with the rules against forfeiture, may prevent the imposition of a disproportionate penalty on the party in breach. Thus, a party in breach may sometimes obtain specific performance subject to compensation for the breach. In *Aspinalls to Powell and Scholefield*[98] the vendor was able to obtain an order for specific performance for the sale of a piece of land the size of which was about twenty per cent smaller than that described in the contract. The price was reduced accordingly. Needless to say, the very award of specific performance indicates that termination is excluded.

The decision of the High Court of Australia in *Stern v McArthur*[99] provides a modern example of the equitable jurisdiction. In that case the purchasers, a man and a woman, entered into a contract in 1969 for the purchase of land for Aus $5,000. A deposit of Aus $250 was made, while in payment of one instalment. In accordance with the terms of the contract the vendor forfeited the instalments already paid. The Court of Appeal held that the forfeiture was not penal. Denning and Somerwell L JJ held obiter that had the forfeiture been penal equity could order repayment if it was unconscionable for the seller to retain the money. Romer LJ held that there was no such equitable jurisdiction, and that relieve from forfeiture could only be granted by extending the time of performance to the party in breach if he was willing and able to perform. Subsequent decisions did not resolve this conflict. See note 94, above. See also R Goff and G Jones, *The Law of Restitution* (4th ed 1993) pp 433–8 who support the position under which there is jurisdiction to relieve from forfeiture in commercial contracts, but consider that 'relief should be granted only in exceptional circumstances' (p 438). A liberal approach was recently adopted by the Privy Council in *Workers Trust & Merchant Bank Ltd v Dojap Investments Ltd* [1993] AC 573. The Privy Council found it unnecessary to decide the specific issue which arose in *Stockloser v Johnson*. Yet it held the rule regarding deposits 'is plainly capable of being abused' (at 579) and that the parties cannot 'attach the incidents of a deposit to the payment of a sum of money unless such sum is reasonable as earnest money (at 579). The Council concluded that the 25 per cent deposit was not a true deposit and 'a provision for its forfeiture in the event of non-performance is a penalty from which the court will give relief by ordering repayment of the sum so paid . . .' (at 582D).

[96] GH Treitel, *The Law of Contract* (8th ed 1991) p 892. Cf. also *Workers Trust & Merchant Bank Ltd v Dojap Investments Ltd* [1993] AC 573.

[97] On the distinction between the case in which the party in breach is unable or unwilling to perform, and the case in which he is willing and able to do so, see GH Treitel, *The Law of Contract* (8th ed 1991) p 892. Cf. also *Stern v McArthur* (1988) 165 CLR 489.

[98] (1889) 60 LT 595; GH Treitel, *The Law of Contract* (8th ed 1991) p 673. The rule as to specific performance with compensation was developed in the context of sale of land. Under English law it does not apply to the sale of goods (GH Treitel, *ibid.*, pp 674–5).

[99] (1988) 165 CLR 489. The case if discussed by SM Waddams, 'Restitution as Part of Contract Law' in A Burrows (ed), *Essays on the Law of Restitution* (1991) pp 197, 204–5. See also G Jones, 'The Law of Restitution: The Past and the Future' in A Burrows (ed), *Essays on the Law of Restitution* (1991) p 10.

the remaining part of the price was to be paid by instalments with interest. The purchasers took possession and built a home on the land. In 1973 they separated. The man left the house, but continued to pay the instalments until March 1977 when he ceased to do so. The woman was unaware that he had ceased the payments, but when she found out she made a payment, which she believed would bring the instalments up to date. Sometime afterwards the vendor, relying on the contractual terms, demanded full payment of the remaining price. When this demand was not complied with, he terminated the contract and sought to recover possession. It was held by majority that relief ought to be granted to the purchasers who also succeeded in obtaining specific performance. It was pointed out that the contract was in force for about ten years. In the meantime, the land has greatly appreciated in value, and the purchasers had built a house on it. In addition, the breach was not a result of a deliberate disregard of the vendor's rights, and the unpaid arrears were small in comparison to the price. Deane and Dawson JJ also referred to 'The . . . notion . . . underlying much of equity's traditional jurisdiction to grant relief against unconscientious conduct, namely, that a person should not be permitted to use or insist upon his legal rights to take advantage of another's special vulnerability or misadventure for the unjust enrichment of himself'.[100]

Translated into the good faith terminology, *Stern v McArthur* can be regarded as applying a good faith limitation upon the aggrieved party's right to terminate the contract.

It is not, however, clear whether the liberal approach reflected in the above quotation from *Stern v McArthur* is indeed of universal application. The High Court of Australia has adopted a broad concept of unconscionability and gives relief on a wider basis than in England.[101] In addition, *Stern v McArthur* was concerned with proprietary interest in land, and we have already noted the reservations expressed in modern English law regarding the extension of the equitable doctrine against forfeiture to ordinary commercial contracts.[102]

For our discussion, it suffices to point out that forfeiture clauses often prove more effective from the aggrieved party's point of view, than penalty provisions. The discrepancy can be explained by the tendency to subject judicial remedies to a more stringent control than that exercised over self help.

---

[100] (1988) 165 CLR 489, at 526–7. It may be pointed out that at a certain stage the vendors offered to pay for the improvements on the land. But Gaudron J, one of the majority justices, considered that as it was not done at the time of termination, and in view of the terms attached to this concession, it does not alleviate the unconscionability of the vendors in asserting and insisting upon their contractual right (*ibid*, 541).

[101] See J Beatson, *The Use and Abuse of Restitution* (1991) pp 92–3. See also J Beatson & D Friedmann, ch 1 above.   [102] Above, notes 91–5 and accompanying text.

Termination causing a disproportionate loss

Termination may sometimes cause a huge loss to the party in breach. Where this loss does not yield a corresponding gain to the aggrieved party, the situation is not strictly within the equitable rules against forfeiture, even in their broad sense. A possible example, discussed by Professor Atiyah,[103] is that of goods imported from overseas which fail to conform in some insignificant way to the contract. Rejection by the buyers may cause the seller an enormous loss. He will be required to deal with goods which are now stored in a foreign country often subject to heavy charges. English law deals with the problem indirectly, by holding that the breach is not sufficiently serious to justify termination.[104] This avenue may, however, be blocked if the breach was serious, or if the contract specifically defines the breach as fundamental. A good faith requirement would enable the issue to be dealt with directly.

Keeping the contract open

The foregoing discussion has dealt with good faith in termination of the contract. We now turn to some of the questions which arise when the injured party decides to keep the contract in force. As already indicated, the basic position of English law is that the party in breach cannot, by his unilateral action, dissolve the contract. This privilege is reserved to the injured party. But just as the power to terminate a contract can be abused, so can the power to keep it in force. A typical case in which the issue arises is where the contract is kept in force so that the injured party can gain the promised performance.

In many instances the injured party may be perfectly justified in insisting on performance. After all, contracts are made to be fulfilled, and the injured party may have a perfectly legitimate interest in its performance. However, intricate problems arise if the performance is likely to harm the party in breach to an extent which seems out of proportion to the benefit which the injured party is likely to gain. In this type of situation a conflict arises between the injured party's right to keep the contract open and the concept of good faith. As already indicated, English law, which does not openly admit that the rights of the injured party are subject to the requirement of good faith, usually solves the dilemma via the law of remedies.

The injured party who insists upon keeping the contract open will

---

[103] PS Atiyah, *An Introduction to the Law of Contract* (4th ed 1989) pp 423–4.
[104] GH Treitel, *The Law of Contract* (8th ed 1991) pp 628–9; PS Atiyah, *An Introduction to the Law of Contract* (4th ed 1989) pp 423–4; *Cehave NV v Bremer Handelsgesellschaft mbH* [1976] QB 44 discussed by PS Atiyah, *op cit*.

normally seek a judicial remedy.[105] He is, however, unlikely to obtain specific performance, because it is a discretionary remedy and, if the plaintiff lacks good faith, it will in all probability be denied. If the injured party claims damages, the rules on mitigation, which actually reflect a requirement of good faith,[106] will apply. Consequently, damages will be reduced when, in order to mitigate the loss, the injured party is expected to terminate the contract and make a substitute arrangement. In other words, the injured party's insistence on keeping the contract open will not shield him from the rules on mitigation which may lead to calculating the damages on the assumption that the contract ought to have been terminated.[107]

Some of the most difficult problems arise where the injured party insists on keeping the contract in force in order to recover in *debt* the amount promised to him under the contract. The source of the difficulty lies in the fact that recovery of an amount due under the contract is tantamount to specific performance. However, this is not a discretionary remedy, but a common law action[108] to which the party is entitled as a matter of right. In this situation a distinction is drawn between two categories:[109] the one in which the co-operation of the party in breach is needed in order to earn the promised amount, and the one in which no such co-operation is needed. The case of the contractor who undertakes to perform work in the homeowner's house belongs to the first category. If the homeowner, in breach of the contract, does not allow the contractor to carry out the work, the contractor will not be able to earn the amount stipulated in the contract. In order to do so he would need a judicial remedy, namely mandatory injunction, which will compel the homeowner to enable him to perform.[110] But this remedy, being discretionary, is unlikely to be granted where the injured party does not act in good faith, or where damages are regarded as the appropriate remedy.

The second category has given rise to great difficulties. Mechanical application of the rules discussed above would lead to the conclusion that in this category the injured party can force performance. The result is

---

[105] If, however, the innocent party was paid in advance there may be no need for him to resort to court. Consequently, his position is likely to become even stronger.

[106] See note 35, above and accompanying text.

[107] Compare the converse situation in which termination increases the loss (note 12, above).

[108] AL Corbin, 'Discharge of Contracts' (1913) 22 Yale LJ 513. Cf. however, the Israeli Contracts (Remedies for Breach) Law under which an order for the payment of the agreed amount is regarded as specific performance and can be denied if it will lead to an unjust result.

[109] GH Treitel, *The Law of Contract* (8th ed 1991) p 898.

[110] On the other hand, if payment was made to him in advance and he has already partly performed, he will, under English law, be entitled to keep the whole amount received. Restitution to the homeowner will be denied on the ground that there has been no total failure of consideration: see note 90, above and accompanying text.

predicated on two propositions. The first is that the option to terminate belongs solely to the injured party. The second is that the action for the agreed amount is at law and, therefore, the court has no discretion to deny it. Furthermore, the rules as to mitigation are confined to actions for damages, and do not apply to an action for the recovery of a mere debt. The well-known decision of the House of Lords in *White & Carter (Councils) Ltd* v *McGregor*[111] represents the high water mark of this reasoning. In that case the plaintiff advertising contractors agreed with the defendant, a garage proprietor, to display his advertisements for three years. The defendant repudiated the contract on the very date it was made, but the plaintiffs chose to disregard the repudiation, displayed the advertisements and claimed the amount due under the contract. The House of Lords, by a majority, upheld the claim.

Despite the seemingly logical foundation of the majority approach, the decision is highly problematical. Lord Reid, one of the majority judges, stated that the result would be otherwise if the injured party has 'no substantial or legitimate interest' in continuing performance.[112] This statement, which is generally taken to form part of the *McGregor* rule,[113] greatly undermines the doctrinal approach. It demonstrates that the right to keep the contract open, coupled with the right to claim the agreed sum, are not absolute but in fact subject to a requirement of good faith.

Moreover, the decision itself seems to represent the exception rather than the rule. Indeed, in analogous situations, English law has reached the opposite result. A conspicuous example is that of an employment contract which is wrongfully repudiated by the employer. It seems that, in principle, the employee earns his salary by being ready and willing to work.[114] But can the employee who has been wrongfully dismissed claim that he declines to accept the repudiation, keep the contract alive and continue to claim his salary? Such a position was maintained in nineteenth century cases which adopted the so-called doctrine of 'constructive service'.[115] Modern decisions have systematically held otherwise. They seem, however, to conflict with the basic doctrinal approach of English law and are not easily explicable. One view is that the wrongful dismissal automatically terminates the contract.[116] This explanation runs counter to the very

[111] [1962] AC 413.
[112] *Ibid.*, 431. See also GH Treitel, *The Law of Contract* (8th ed 1991) p 899 in which examples of such a legitimate interest are given.
[113] GH Treitel, *op cit*. See also *The Alaskan Trader* [1984] 1 All ER 129, discussed by PS Atiyah, *An Introduction to the Law of Contract* (4th ed 1989) p 450.
[114] Obviously, the employer cannot refuse to pay the salary of an employee, who has not been discharged, simply on the ground that during the relevant period there was no work to be done.
[115] *Gandall* v *Pontigny* (1816) 4 Camp 375; 171 ER 119; Farnsworth, *Contracts* (2nd ed 1990) p 900, note 17.
[116] GH Treitel, *The Law of Contract* (8th ed 1991) p 744.

basic assumption of English contract law, namely, that the party in breach cannot unilaterally terminate the contract.

Another explanation, offered by Professor Treitel,[117] is based upon the distinction between rights and remedies. The injured employee has a right to insist upon the continued existence of the contract, but his remedy is confined to damages.[118] However, if recovery of the agreed amount is precluded, then the question arises: for what purpose is the contract regarded as binding? In addition, if in this type of situation the remedy can be confined to damages, why did the plaintiff in *McGregor* recover the agreed price?

It, thus, seems that the *McGregor* decision, which carried the injured party's right to keep the contract open to its ultimate conclusion, is an exception. It also seems that the qualification under which it will not apply if the injured party has no legitimate interest in performing is likely to be expanded, and will perhaps overshadow the rule itself.

The good faith requirement and the 'right' to break a contract

The requirement of good faith imposes a certain limitation upon contractual rights. Its adoption means that even those who believe in the innocent party's right to the contractual performance accept that this right is sometimes to be confined, in order to prevent its abuse. This, however, is a far cry from a general recognition of a 'right to breach a contract'.

On the other hand, those who believe in the 'right to break a contract' are apparently willing to concede that this right is not to be abused, and that such an abuse ought to be deterred.[119]

Hence, the good faith concept somewhat narrows the gap between these two approaches, although it clearly does not bridge it. A substantial number of situations can be envisaged in which the innocent party may in

---

[117] GH Treitel, *The Law of Contract* (8th ed 1991) pp 744–5.

[118] *Ibid.*, pp 896–8. Treitel also points out that the position is similar in the case of a contract for the sale of goods. If the buyer wrongfully repudiates the contract, the seller may elect to keep the contract in force, but this remedy is normally in damages and not in an action for the price. However, the case of the seller is distinguishable on the ground that the seller cannot perform without the buyer's cooperation, ie, without his acceptance of the goods. Indeed, if property in the goods has passed, the seller will be under English law, entitled to the price. This result is contrasted with the position adopted by the UCC, § 2–709: Treitel, *ibid.*, p 900, n 62. On the other hand, in the employment situation the employee can probably earn his salary by being ready to perform (note 114, above) and, under the *McGregor* rule, if the injured party keeps the contract open and if he is able to complete his performance, he will be entitled to the contractual price and will not be confined to the remedy of damages.

[119] EA Farnsworth, 'Your Loss of My Gain? The Dilemma of the Disgorgement Principle in Breach of Contract' (1985) 94 Yale LJ 1339 (regarding 'abuse of the contract'); RA Posner, *Economic Analysis of Law* (4th ed 1992) pp 117–18 (regarding 'opportunistic breach').

good faith insist on performance, while the other party, if a 'right to breach' is recognized may wish to exercise it, without the breach being regarded as opportunistic or as an abuse of the contract. In these situations, those who support the initial approach that contracts are made to be performed, would favour remedies which deter the breach.

Conclusion

In this chapter I have tried to show that the absence of a general principle of good faith in English law is partly compensated by the law of remedies, which greatly limits the possibility of abuse of rights. To this end, it has proven an effective tool, both because remedies are controlled by the courts and because the parties' freedom of contract in this field is limited.

No doubt some of the rules discussed here can be explained on other grounds,[120] but the idea of good faith offers considerable advantages. It is highly relevant to the bridging of the gap between English law and other common law and continental legal systems. It also has a unifying feature and its consistent application is conducive to greater congruity between the remedies. Thus, if the injured party in bad faith fails to mitigate his loss, the failure should be reflected both in damages and specific performance.[121]

The requirement of good faith can most easily be taken into account where the remedy is discretionary. But even where it is not, as in the case of damages there are specific rules, notably those on mitigation, in which the concept of good faith is embedded. There are, however, a number of situations in which English law tolerates an excessive use of legal rights. These include, in particular, cases in which the party asserting a legal right can resort to self-help, and in which it is the other party who seeks a remedy.[122]

---

[120] Thus, the rule on mitigation is clearly supported by the policy of avoiding economic waste.

[121] See text after note 36, above.

[122] See the discussion of forfeiture and termination above, at text to n 82 *et seq.*

17

Expectation Damages and Uncertain Future Losses*

Michael G Bridge**

Introduction

In the law of torts, it is noticeable that factual causation has generated numerous, often intractable, difficulties. A plaintiff must demonstrate not only that the injury was in fact caused by the tortious behaviour of the defendant, but also that the resultant damage comes within the range of what is reasonably foreseeable, so as to satisfy the rule of remoteness of damage (or legal causation). The same obstacles to recovery face the contract plaintiff, except that remoteness of damage is framed in different terms. The plaintiff is equally required to show that the injury was caused by the defendant's breach of contract. Yet any examination of the way the various authors deal with the subject of factual causation in contract law will reveal that explicit coverage is slight,[1] dwarfed by the attention paid to remoteness of damage.

Remoteness of damage is a more difficult obstacle for a contract plaintiff to surmount than it is for a tort plaintiff. The principal difficulty in tort law has been to define the remoteness rule rather than to apply it, whereas both aspects have given difficulty in contract law. This may have something to do with the general confinement of the tort of negligence to the protection of physical interests and the use of the duty concept to handle economic loss issues. The contractual equivalent of the use of duty in this way is the blanket refusal of the law, without turning to the remoteness rule, to permit the recovery of certain items of loss, such as (in most categories of cases) damages for emotional loss. Remoteness of damage in contract is affected by the nature of the bargain struck, express or implied, a consideration not present in tort (though the existence or not of a tort claim may depend upon whether the plaintiff might have protected his interests by contracting with a third party). Nevertheless, a strong argument can be advanced that factual causation should be more of a problem

* Copyright © 1994, Michael G Bridge
** I should like to thank my Nottingham colleague, Stephen Weatherill, and participants at the Merton Colloquium on Contract Law for their helpful comments.
[1] HLA Hart and A Honoré, *Causation in the Law* (2nd ed 1985), p 308.

to contract lawyers than to tort lawyers. The function of tort law is to put the plaintiff back, so far as a money award allows it, in the pre-tort position, which necessitates an historical inquiry into the relation between the defendant's past behaviour and the plaintiff's past injury. It is generally known or knowable what the condition of the plaintiff was before the injury occurred. Contract law, on the other hand, seeks, by promoting the plaintiff's expectation interest, to place him in the position he would have occupied had the contract been duly performed, a position that cannot be known, and one which the defendant's breach of contract makes unknowable. It is inherently, therefore, a more speculative exercise.[2]

A plaintiff, whether suing in contract or in tort, bears the burden of proving that his injuries were in fact caused by the defendant. The argument advanced in this chapter is that, almost by sleight of hand, contract law assists certain plaintiffs, embarrassed by difficulties in proving an expectation lost as a result of the defendant's breach, by various devices that empty the category of factual causation and distribute its contents elsewhere. The law's response to a number of instances of evidentiary incompleteness will be examined, including cases that appear on their face to point away from protecting the plaintiff's expectancy because of such causation or remoteness difficulties. It will be argued that these cases may be seen in another light as strongly supportive of the plaintiff's expectancy. Before the examination of the above instances is conducted, there will be a preliminary inquiry into the expectation interest to provide necessary background. The contractual recovery of an expectancy is less starkly different than might be supposed from some instances of tort recovery; the principal distinction in this area is not so much that between contract and tort, but that between present and future (or vested and contingent) interests. The prospective future earnings of a tort plaintiff, not to mention diminished earning capacity, can be much more difficult to quantify than the lost profits of a contract terminated as a result of the defendant's breach. On the other hand, it will often be easier to say that a tort plaintiff would have had future earnings but for the tort, than that a contract would have yielded profits to the plaintiff. Contract plaintiffs cannot demonstrate from the mere fact of entry into a contract that it would have generated profits, although they sometimes benefit from

---

[2] From time to time there have been suggestions that the rules of causation are applied differently to contract and tort claims: *Heskell* v *Continental Express Ltd* [1950] 1 All ER 1033, at 1047. This became particularly marked when apportionment legislation was introduced in the case of contributory negligence in tort but not in contract: *Quinn* v *Burch Bros* (*Builders*) *Ltd* [1966] 2 QB 370, at 375, 378; *Sole* v *WJ Hallt Ltd* [1973] QB 574, at 582. The contemporary awareness of so much overlap between tort and contract makes it difficult to perpetuate any notion that the rules of causation for the two are different. The recent Court of Appeal decision in *Galoo Ltd* v *Bright Grahame Murray* [1994] BCC 319 gives support to the like treatment of causation in contract and tort.

benevolent assumptions in this area.[3] In addition, any analytical distinction that can still be made between tort and contract recovery is blurred further if consequential damages[4] are awarded. Recovery of this kind in a contract action is not designed to give the plaintiff the benefit of any bargain, but rather to erase the effect of a breach. Consequential damages are available in tort too, and thus help to bridge the gulf that supposedly separates contract and tort damages. They cut across supposed differences between tort and contract in the fundamental approach to damages entitlement.

The nature of the expectation interest

It is the cornerstone of damages in contract law that the plaintiff is entitled, by being put in the position he would have been in if the contact had been performed, to recover his expectation interest, a proposition supported by reference to the words of Baron Parke in *Robinson* v *Harman*[5] and of Lord Atkinson in *Wertheim* v *Chicoutimi Pulp Co.*[6] Rhetoric apart, it must be asked how committed is the law in practice to this principle, for the generosity of the law to the plaintiff whose case is deficient in the stuff of factual causation depends upon the strength of that commitment. It must also be asked just how distinctively contractual expectation damages are, for this inquiry has implications for the comparison of tort and contract claims in areas covered in this chapter.

In the classical analysis of Fuller and Perdue,[7] the expectation interest was one of three different interests that might be served by the award of contract damages, and the only one that sought to project the plaintiff into a world of post-contractual fulfilment defined by means of a substitutive damages award. Reliance damages were designed to put the plaintiff back in the pre-contractual position, while a restitutionary award could be seen as a category of reliance relief, in that the disbursements made by the plaintiff and occasioned by the contract were received by the defendant as opposed to some third party.[8] This tripartite analysis triumphed in the Restatement 2d of Contracts where it is writ large in § 344. A striking feature of that section is that the catalogue of interests is not clearly

[3] The subject of discussion in *The Commonwealth* v *Amann Aviation Pty Ltd* (1991) 174 CLR 64.

[4] See discussion in GH Treitel, *Remedies for Breach of Contract: A Comparative Account* (Oxford, 1988), pp 87–8.

[5] (1848) 1 Ex 850.

[6] [1911] AC 301. See also *The Commonwealth* v *Amann Aviation Pty Ltd* (1991) 174 CLR 64 and authorities therein cited.

[7] 'The Reliance Interest in Contract Damages' (1936) 46 Yale LJ 52.

[8] This schematic statement of the relationship between restitution and reliance does not, of course, detract from the formidable difficulties facing restitution lawyers in calculating benefit to the enriched individual and its relation to the impoverishment of the other.

prescriptive or articulate about the purpose or purposes that contract damages ought to serve. Rather, it appears to be a piece of disembodied legal analysis with no necessary practical significance.[9] An obvious consequence of this, for present purposes, is that the relationship between the reliance and expectation interests is left obscure. Fuller and Perdue advanced the thesis that protecting the expectation interest was a peculiarly effective way of vindicating the reliance interest, in that it was 'the measure of recovery most likely to reimburse the plaintiff for the (often very numerous and very difficult to prove) individual acts and forbearances which make up his total reliance on the contract'.[10] Given the lack of formal recognition accorded in the evolution of contract law to the reliance interest (as Fuller and Perdue concede), nevertheless, the formal standing and primacy of the expectation interest cannot so easily be elided.

It is arguable that common lawyers make too much of the difference between reliance and expectation damages. In practical terms, the liability of a contract-breaker for consequential damages is often of greater significance than the issue of whether there should be liability for loss of bargain. Moreover, we should not complacently assume that, just because the expectation interest cannot be subsumed under the reliance interest advocated by Fuller and Perdue, there exists a clear distinction between the two. In a competitive market, the difference between expectation and reliance is analytical rather than substantive. Consider a contract entered into on 1 July for the delivery of a quantity of widgets on 1 October at a price of £1,000. The seller fails to deliver, and that same quantity of widgets will cost the buyer £1,200 on a rising market on 1 October. The market damages rule in the Sale of Goods Act 1979[11] grants the buyer the difference between the contract price and the later market price, which allows us to quantify the buyer's net expectancy as £200. The buyer needs to be in a position on 1 October to secure the promised quantity of widgets, which means that he needs to have £200 in addition to the £1,000 that he still has if he has not yet paid the seller. That same sum of £200, however, may also be seen as the loss incurred by the buyer in relying upon this particular seller to deliver, instead of upon another seller who actually would have delivered. Strictly speaking, if reliance becomes the measure of damages, the recoverable sum should be (slightly) discounted to reflect the risk that an alternative seller might also have defaulted. The

---

[9] RE Hudec, 'Restating the "Reliance Interest" ' (1982) 67 Cornell LR 704, 707—'a most curious black-letter proposition'.

[10] LL Fuller & WR Purdue, 'The Reliance Interest in Contract Damages' (1936) 46 Yale LJ 52, 60, criticized by SJ Stoljar, 'Promise, Expectation and Agreement' [1988] CLJ 193, 209–12.

[11] Section 51(3).

reason for this is that, if we assume that such alternative seller could also have been sued for £200, we beg the question of the recoverable award.

This merger of reliance and expectation is given recognition in certain tort cases where reliance is an element in the plaintiff's cause of action. In the Canadian Supreme Court decision in *VK Mason Construction Ltd* v *Bank of Nova Scotia*, a bank negligently misrepresented to a builder that it had advanced sufficient funds to a developer to cover the cost of a construction project. In reliance on the misrepresentation, the builder entered into a construction contract with the developer and suffered loss when the developer proved to be undercapitalized. The bank held liable was bound to pay in damages the profit that the builder would have made under the construction contract since 'the lost profit in *this* contract represents the lost opportunity for profit on *any* contract'.[12] In other words, the builder was not as such being awarded its contractual expectancy under a contract to which the bank was a stranger, but rather the value of an opportunity to contract with a different developer lost when, as a result of the bank's misrepresentation, the builder contracted with the actual developer. The court was prepared to assume that the anticipated and alternative profits were one and the same amount. Such a congruence of the tort and contractual measures of recovery is appropriate too where the plaintiff could have lain concurrent actions in tort and contract against the same defendant, since it would be anomalous to have different measures of recovery in such a case.[13]

A similar approach in the matter of tort damages emerges in the Court of Appeal decision in *East* v *Maurer*.[14] The seller of a hairdressing business represented fraudulently that he would not compete with the purchaser within a stated area and then proceeded to do so, with the consequence that the purchaser's business suffered and she later had to sell the lease at a loss. The defendant seller argued that the recovery of damages in the tort of deceit did not admit the award of any sum for lost profits. Yet the Court of Appeal was prepared to award damages under this head as 'directly flowing from the fraudulent inducement'.[15] The sum awarded was calculated according to what the plaintiff could reasonably have expected to make from running a similar hairdressing business bought for the same sum. If this reasoning is expanded to include a justification for an award of lost profits which would have flowed from the pursuit of an alternative contractual opportunity, as it is in the short judgment of Mustill LJ ('the hypothetical profitable business in which the plaintiffs

---

[12] (1985) 16 DLR (4th) 598, at 608 (emphasis in original).

[13] *British Columbia Hydro and Power Authority* v *BG Checo International Ltd* [1993] 1 SCR 12.

[14] [1991] 1 WLR 461. Cf. *Davis* v *Churchward* (6 May 1993 (Unreported)), noted by PA Chandler, 'Fraud: Damages and Opportunity Costs' (1994) 110 LQR 35.

[15] Lord Atkin's words in *Clark* v *Urquhart* [1930] AC 28, at 68.

would have engaged but for buying the [defendant's] business'),[16] the result in *East* v *Maurer* is of a piece with the Canadian decision in *VK Mason Construction Ltd* v *Bank of Nova Scotia*.[17] There is no difference in principle between deceit and negligent misrepresentation in this respect.[18] An award of the money paid for the business, coupled with interest for the period of its detention by the defendant, would not have been enough for a plaintiff who was plainly set upon putting her money into a profit-making venture: it would not truly have returned her to the pre-tort position of one who had a range of opportunities from which to choose.

Beldam LJ was insistent that the plaintiff was not entitled to recover on a contractual warranty basis which he regarded as being framed in terms of an assurance that the defendant's clientele would continue to patronize the plaintiff's establishment. If instead he had considered a rather different warranty, that the plaintiff would not compete, an award of damages under this head should only have yielded a measure in excess of tort if the business sold had been demonstrably more profitable than similar businesses in other places. It is, of course, perfectly easy to devise warranties which yield a measure of damages that does not differ from the tort measure.[19]

This leaves the issue of how the value of the alternative opportunity ought to be measured. The Canadian Supreme Court in *VK Mason Construction Ltd* was rather too prepared to evaluate the opportunity in the same amount as the one accepted by the builder when it contracted with the developer who later failed. This fails to explain why the builder contracted with that particular developer, instead of with some other developer offering an equally profitable opportunity. The court's approach cannot be defended on the ground that the plaintiff has been placed by the defendant in a forensically difficult position, so that the defendant ought to bear the burden of showing that the plaintiff's alternative opportunities were less profitable. Why should the plaintiff be spared the task of bringing in evidence of alternative opportunities? Unless the plaintiff is required to take this extra step, it is difficult to see why the decision should not be used to justify the routine displacement of the normal burden of proof in civil proceedings, a point that should be borne in mind for all aspects of damages recovery considered in this chapter. In any event, the burden of proof is not addressed by the court

[16] *East* v *Mauver* [1991] 1 WLR 461, at 468. Cf. *ibid.*, at 467, per Beldam LJ.
[17] (1985) 16 DLR (4th) 598.
[18] Note that the interpretation, in *Royscot Trust Ltd* v *Rogerson* [1991] 2 QB 297, of the fiction of fraud in s 2(1) of the Misrepresentation Act 1967 would not allow a distinction between recovery under that provision and in the tort of deceit.
[19] See *Esso Petroleum Co Ltd* v *Mardon* [1976] QB 801.

which tackles the problem of the exceptionally lucrative contract by ruling out full recovery on the ground of remoteness. This remoteness argument is misconceived, because it focuses on the actual contract entered into, rather than a typical contract the plaintiff might have entered into instead.

The above cases show that the difference between expectation recovery and reliance recovery is not so great as might be supposed. The confluence of contract and certain areas of the law of tort is also revealed in a number of cases where tort plainly allows a form of expectation recovery. For example, a solicitor can be held liable in negligence for the loss of a legacy where this is forfeited as a result of the solicitor's professional negligence.[20] In such cases, the disappointed legatee acts as a surrogate contract claimant on behalf of a testator who is not alive to sue the solicitor for breach of contract, and of an estate that can only recover nominal damages for the breach. Moreover, the recovery of damages in tort for interference with contractual relations may in appropriate cases be calculated according to the profits which would have arisen from that contract.[21]

A fruitful comparison of tort and contract approaches emerges also in those instances where the tort relationship between plaintiff and defendant is akin to contract. The 'wayleave' and similar cases[22] afford a good example. These involve a trespassory use of the plaintiff's property, usually land, where the defendant is required to pay in damages a sum equivalent to the amount that would have been paid in an arm's length transaction for the use of the land. Although the mechanics of relief could benefit from a more detailed articulation, it is as if a contract between plaintiff and defendant were simulated, and damages then awarded as consideration for the use of the land. It is important to observe, however, that the action is in form one for trespass to land. Hence, in *Phillips* v *Homfray*,[23] it did not survive the death of the tortfeasor, as it would have done if it had taken the form of an action for an account of profits, or an action based on a genuine implied undertaking to pay for the use of the

[20] *Ross* v *Caunters* [1980] Ch 297. The Court of Appeal has signalled recently the survival of this endangered example of economic loss liability in the tort of negligence: *White* v *Jones* [1993] 3 WLR 730 (failure of solicitors to deal expeditiously with testator's expressed desire to alter his will, to detriment of prospective legatees). For the use of specific performance to avoid problems in the award of substantial damages, see *Beswick* v *Beswick* [1968] AC 58, which cannot however assist in resolving the above difficulty.

[21] *Gunter* v *Astor* (1819) 4 Moo PC 12.

[22] See also *Strand Electric and Engineering Co* v *Brisford Entertainments Ltd* [1952] 2 QB 26; *Watson, Laidlaw & Co Ltd* v *Pott, Cassels & Williamson* (1914) 31 RPC 104, per Lord Shaw of Dunfermline. The authorities are helpfully reviewed in *Stoke-on-Trent City Council* v *W & J Wass Ltd* [1988] 1 WLR 1406. See EJ Cooke, 'Trespass, Mesne Profits and Restitution' (1994) 110 LQR 420.

[23] (1883) 24 Ch D 439, dealing with the principle of recovery earlier laid down in the same litigation at (1871) LR 6 Ch App 770. Cf. Lord Mansfield's example of the unauthorized use of the horse in *Hambly* v *Trott* (1776) 1 Cowp 371; 98 ER 1136.

land (which the circumstances negatived), or if the plaintiff had timeously waived the tort and brought an action in quasi-contract instead. The court, moreover, declined to see in the avoidance of expense in paying for the wayleave an addition to the assets of the estate of the deceased tortfeasor sufficient to displace the old rule that personal actions died with the death of the tortfeasor.[24]

When counsel for the successful defendant in *Phillips* v *Homfray* later sat as Rigby LJ in the case of *Whitwham* v *Westminster Brymbo Coal and Coke Co*, a case dealing with the very similar problem of unauthorized use of the plaintiff's land for dumping waste, he emphasized that the defendant was not required to pay on a restitutionary basis for the use of the land: 'We cannot take an account of the profits derived from [the] user; and in fact it is a matter of indifference whether the defendants made a profit or loss out of the transaction.'[25] The plaintiff recovered, not the defendant's gain, but the plaintiff's own loss, which was not to be equated with a diminution in the value of the land. Instead, damages should be calculated as whatever might be 'the customary rate of charge for way-leave in the locality'.[26] Is it really too fanciful to regard damages in a case of this kind as awarded for the loss of a chance to bargain,[27] at least in those cases where the defendant acts by stealth? Where the defendant's action is open and based upon a mistaken view of entitlement, Lord Hatherley[28] obscures the principle of recovery by his refusal to see that the plaintiff has suffered any injury at all (the point was not raised in the court below and was not dealt with by the other members of the House).

The principle of the wayleave cases was extended in *Wrotham Park Estate Co Ltd* v *Parkside Homes Ltd*[29] in circumstances where the tangible property rights of the plaintiff had not been infringed. A developer, in breach of covenant, failed to submit plans for approval to the owners of an estate from which a portion had been carved out in favour of a predecessor in title of the developer. The owners did not seek an interlocutory injunction to prevent development, but sought a mandatory injunction at trial. This was refused because of the advanced state of the development,

---

[24] This accounts for the dissent of Baggallay LJ, *ibid.*, at 466–77.

[25] [1896] 2 Ch 538, at 543.   [26] *Ibid.*

[27] As argued by SM Waddams and RJ Sharpe, 'Damages for Lost Opportunity to Bargain' (1982) 2 Ox JLS 290. This approach was rejected by Steyn LJ in the Court of Appeal in *Surrey County Council* v *Bredero Homes Ltd* [1993] 1 WLR 1361, noted by PBH Birks, 'Profits of Breach of Contract' (1993) 109 LQR 518; AS Burrows [1993] LMCLQ 453. See also AS Burrows, *Remedies for Torts and Breach of Contract* (2nd ed 1994), pp 307–14.

[28] *Livingstone* v *Rawyard's Coal Co* (1880) 5 App Cas 25, at 38.

[29] [1974] 1 WLR 798, distinguished in *Stoke-on-Trent City Council* v *W & J Wass Ltd* [1988] 1 WLR 1406, at 1414, 1420, as 'stand[ing] very much on its own' (Nourse LJ) and as 'far removed from the present case' (Nicholls LJ). See also *Bracewell* v *Appleby* [1975] Ch 408 (right of way); *Carr-Saunders* v *Dick McNeil Associates Ltd* [1986] 1 WLR 922 (access of light easement).

and the ensuing waste that would occur if houses had to be demolished. Instead, Brightman J awarded damages under Lord Cairns's Act,[30] which he calculated according to the terms of a hypothetical bargain which might have been struck between the owners of the estate and the developer in return for a relaxation of the covenant. The bargain thus concocted set the fair price of relaxation at five per cent of the anticipated profits of the developer. It was not a question of disgorging gains from the developer, but rather of recapturing lost ground and trying to imagine the kind of contract that might fairly have been concluded between the parties, given the developer's evident desire to emerge from the venture with a profit. The damages figure seems to have been pitched in such a way as not to disgorge the developer's profit completely and to make the development project still worth pursuing. Going one step further than those courts which find conjectural sums for unprovable future profits,[31] Brightman J was prepared to infer a contract, even though it might never have been concluded given the evident unwillingness of the estate to relax the covenant. But it was due to the fault of the developer that this uncertainty was created and the damages accruing to the owners can be seen as compensating them for the loss of a chance to bargain.[32] Delay in seeking an interlocutory injunction to stop the building works may prejudice the grant of specific relief, but it does not follow that it should have the same impact on the award of damages.

The standing of the *Wrotham Park* decision[33] is in some considerable doubt as a result of the recent Court of Appeal decision in *Surrey County Council v Bredero Homes Ltd*.[34] A district council, the planning authority, had given permission for the number of houses on a site to be increased, but the developers were acting in breach of a covenant owed to the appellants, who had transferred the land to them, in availing themselves of this permission. The appellants were seeking only damages, by way of a 'reasonable premium . . . for contractual permission',[35] for breach of covenant (at common law and not under Lord Cairns's Act), as opposed to an interlocutory injunction restraining the building of the extra houses. There was no question of any property rights of the appellants being injured or affected by the additional building work, and therefore the action could not be laid in trespass; the action had instead to be in contract.

The Court of Appeal declined to extend the wayleave and similar decisions to a case of this nature, asserted the compensatory nature of contract damages and awarded only nominal damages since the appellants had

---

[30] Chancery Amendment Act 1858. [31] See below.

[32] Cf. the criticism of this approach by Steyn LJ in the *Surrey County Council v Bredero Homes Ltd* [1993] 1 WLR 1361.

[33] *A fortiori* of *Penarth Dock Engineering Co Ltd v Pounds* [1963] 1 Lloyd's Rep 359.

[34] [1993] 1 WLR 1361. [35] *Ibid.*, at 1364D, per Dillon LJ.

not suffered a real loss. Curiously, the court was prepared to assume that the covenant had been inserted in the conveyance in order to compel the developers to pay for any future relaxation of the covenant, and so laid itself open to reproach for baffling the legitimate expectation of the appellants. It saw no reason to take account of loss of bargaining power in calculating contract damages.[36] In this respect, the contract approach applied by the court is less generous to the plaintiff than the tort approach in similar cases.

Whether the decision in *Wrotham Park* is still good law vexed counsel for the appellants in *Surrey County Council* v *Bredero Homes Ltd* in his argument for leave to appeal to the House of Lords. It was supported by Steyn LJ, as a restitutionary decision, although how it is to be distinguished from *Surrey County Council* itself is left obscure. This is a point of some considerable importance, because the judgment of the court (and explicitly that of Steyn LJ) rejects the restitutionary approach to the quantification of contract damages.[37] No distinction can be made between the two on the ground that the earlier decision occurred under Lord Cairns's Act, since the House of Lords in *Johnson* v *Agnew*[38] held that the Act was a procedural statute; it did not establish a difference of substance between equitable and common law damages.

A contract decision like that in *Surrey County Council* v *Bredero Homes Ltd* should provoke another hard look at the expectation which is supposedly protected by contract remedies. It can fairly be argued that the common law's bias towards substitutive monetary relief, as opposed to specific relief, has in certain cases a strong effect on the quantum of recovery itself. Suppose that the owner of land sells an adjoining portion to a purchaser who enters into a covenant not to erect certain works upon the land, but later does so in breach of contract. If specific relief is still available, a mandatory injunction for the vendor's contractual expectancy is vividly protected: the undoing of any forbidden work already accomplished restores the land to the condition it was in before the covenant was breached. But suppose it is too late to obtain injunctive relief of this sort and that, in its approach to damages, the court yields to the view that these should be computed according to what the vendor has lost as a result of the breach as measured according to the diminished value of the vendor's retained land. How can it be said that the vendor's contractual

---

[36] See Steyn LJ; also Dillon LJ, *ibid.*, at 1368, who put it in terms of a similarity with the so-called duty to negotiate (sed quaere?).

[37] See also *Tito* v *Waddell* (*No 2*) [1977] Ch 106. The Law Commission in *Aggravated, Exemplary and Restitutionary Damages* (1993) Law Com Consultation Paper No 132 is currently seeking views on whether restitutionary remedies should be made generally available in contract cases (Part VII). The Commission observes (*ibid.*, p 159 and authorities therein cited) that the award of specific performance may serve the goal of restitution.

[38] [1980] AC 367.

expectancy is being protected at all? The motive behind the expectancy may well have been to preserve the vendor's remaining land, but that is not the expectancy itself, which was that the unlawful work should not be suffered to be done. And there may be other motives too, such as aesthetic taste, which are not at all protected by damages measured according to diminished value.

To a significant extent, courts can get away from a reduced value approach in cases where the defendant fails to do something that ought to have been done, as opposed to doing something that ought not to be done, if assured that any damages recovered will actually be dedicated by the successful plaintiff to the performance promised by the defendant.[39] But this does not work where the defendant's breach is an act of commission rather than omission. In such a case, the defendant may not have saved money by the breach, so there is no restitutionary impulse to make up for the evidentiary deficiencies of an expectation damages claim. Furthermore, the very requirement of such an assurance from the plaintiff is discordant with the market-based approach to damages under the Sale of Goods Act 1979, where a successful plaintiff is at perfect liberty to treat the defendant's damages as a speculative gain. A buyer recovering damages for non-delivery is, in principle, compensated according to the market at the delivery date: the fact that the market, having risen from the contract date to the delivery date, then declines is not a matter to be taken into account.[40]

Surrogates for the expectation interest

The argument that will be advanced in this section is that a plaintiff's contractual expectancy may be protected in a surrogate way by means that fall short of its explicit recognition.[41] Such protection stems from the evidential difficulties facing a plaintiff who seeks to prove the make-up of a world that has not come into existence as a result of the defendant's breach of contract. It is the defendant's breach of contract, a wrong, that

---

[39] *Radford* v *De Froberville* [1977] 1 WLR 1262; *Tito* v *Waddell* (*No 2*) [1977] Ch 106.

[40] For a recent affirmation of the abstract market differences approach to damages in sale of goods cases, see *Kaines (UK) Ltd* v *Osterreichische Warrenhandelsgesellschaft*[1993] 2 Lloyd's Rep 1, noted by MG Bridge [1994] JBL 160. The Uniform Commercial Code, starting with concrete cover and resale transactions and when and if these are made, thereby subordinates the market differences approach (§§ 2–706, 2–712). A similar approach is found in the Vienna Convention on Contracts for the International Sale of Goods (1980), Art 75.

Johnson v *Agnew* [1980] AC 367 allows a measure of flexibility as to the *date* of assessment. It would obviously be undesirable to avoid conjecture as to whether, if the seller had duly delivered the goods, the buyer would have unloaded them before the market fell or would have done so at some point during the market's fall.

[41] See generally *McGregor on Damages* (15th ed 1988), ch 8.

causes the plaintiff's evidential embarrassment; this justifies the taking of steps to ease the plaintiff's forensic burden. A breach of contract is actionable without proof of special damage. The civil burden of proof may remain, that the plaintiff's case be proven on the balance of probabilities, but the weight of this burden varies, not just according to the available facts, but also according to the way the plaintiff characterizes his loss and formulates his claim.

DAMAGES FOR THE LOSS OF A CHANCE: THE TORT CASES

The leading contract case is *Chaplin v Hicks*,[42] which involved the deprivation of a contractually agreed opportunity to participate in the later stages of a talent competition. Before that case and its position in contract law is examined, it would be useful to set the scene by considering the insights to be gained from tort law,[43] since there is no difference in principle between the two in the matter of contingent assessments.[44] *Chaplin* has been invoked to further the cause of recoverability of damages for loss of a chance in tort law, where this head of recovery has been subject to a more critical and sustained assessment than it has so far received in contract. This is not surprising, given that the amounts at stake in the contract cases have so far been rather small, and the contract cases have been individualistic and not emblematic of classes of similar claims. In some contract cases, damages for loss of a chance may represent a pragmatic response to the uneconomic pursuit of truth in the definition of the plaintiff's true expectation loss. Breach of contract is also, unlike the tort of negligence, actionable per se, which possibly encourages a more receptive treatment to claims of this nature in contract law.[45] By way of contrast, tort cases have involved large claims that have threatened a succession of similar claims and so have been very strenuously contested.

The case of *Hotson v East Berkshire Area Health Authority*[46] encapsulates the issue of whether damages for loss of a chance may be recovered in tort. It concerned a boy who fell from a tree and was later treated negligently in one of the defendant's hospitals: he was sent away without a proper examination of his hip. He subsequently developed a major physical deformity of the hip joint, due to the failure of the blood supply to the cartilage, which impaired the proper development of the femur. It was the plaintiff's contention that, had his hip injury been competently diagnosed when he first visited the hospital, instead of when he went back five days

---

[42] [1911] 2 KB 786.   [43] See further *McGregor on Damages* (15th ed 1988).
[44] See *Hardware Services Pty Ltd v Primac Association Ltd* [1988] 1 Qd R 393.
[45] *Hotson v East Berkshire AHA* [1987] AC 750.
[46] *Ibid*. See B Coote, 'Chance and the Burden of Proof in Contract and Tort' [1988] ALJ 761, 771.

later, there was a chance that the injury could have been treated and the onset of the deformity arrested. The plaintiff was not able to establish that the deformity would have been arrested by timely and competent treatment, so he would have failed altogether on the balance of probabilities if his claim had been pressed in the conventional way. Instead, he sought damages for the loss of a chance of recovery, relying upon a finding of fact by the trial judge that there was a twenty-five per cent chance that the deformity would not have set in with competent diagnosis and treatment. At first instance, he succeeded, damages being assessed at twenty-five per cent of the full value of the permanent disability. The defendant's appeal was unsuccessful in the Court of Appeal, but was allowed in the House of Lords.

In reaching the conclusion it did, the House of Lords resisted the plaintiff's attempt to show that the loss of a chance of cure was an independent head of loss. It ruled that recovery was precluded by the trial judge's finding that, on the balance of probabilities, the plaintiff's condition had already set in by the time he reached the hospital. And yet it did not confront head on the argument that the gist of the plaintiff's claim[47] could be characterized as the loss of a chance of recovery, as opposed to the injury itself. There is certainly a strong argument to be made that a plaintiff, willing to settle for a lower level of recovery, should yet be prevented from playing fast and loose with the rules of civil proof by invoking the loss of a chance whenever in forensic difficulties. Otherwise, the results for all cases in a particular group would be incoherent, some defendants paying damages in full, although the plaintiff's case was by no means certain, with others being liable for partial damages, provided the plaintiff's case crossed a threshold barrier however defined, but falling significantly short of the balance of probabilities.

The argument has been pressed, however, that while plaintiffs should not freely be allowed to define the gist of their case to maximum advantage, this ought to be permitted if the tortious behaviour of the defendant consists of an undertaking, for example, to exercise due care, and this undertaking is met by a corresponding reliance by the plaintiff on that undertaking.[48] The justification for allowing a plaintiff to change the gist of the action from the injury itself to the chance of avoiding the injury is said to be that the plaintiff's reliance means that he fails to exercise an opportunity to go elsewhere. The decisions of the lower courts in *Hotson* are defended on the ground that, had the plaintiff not relied on the hospital for careful treatment, he might have gone to another hospital to receive treatment which might have spared him his deformity. This approach is

[47] See J Stapleton, 'The Gist of Negligence II' (1988) 104 LQR 389.
[48] See S Perry, 'Protected Interests and Undertakings in the Law of Negligence' (1992) 42 UTLJ 247.

plainly of interest when it comes to justifying contract awards modelled on the loss of a chance, since it is formulated in contractual terms. If anything, it fits rather better those contractual relations that are concluded to produce speculative gains, for risk is the essence of such activities. Bodily wellbeing in contrast, often the subject of both tort and contract relations, is rarely a matter for speculative activity in contract.[49]

In the lower courts in *Hotson*, it was asserted that the result should be the same whether the plaintiff was suing a hospital authority in tort or a private consultant in contract. Furthermore, the undertaking/reliance approach is congruent with the notion, expressed above, that reliance recovery can be justified as the loss of an alternative expectation when the plaintiff contracts with the future contract-breaker, instead of someone else who might well have performed. Yet the approach has to be refined to satisfy those critics who would say that it is artificial, and insensitive to particular facts. What of the plaintiff rushed in for emergency treatment who is unconscious or who is in no condition to go elsewhere for treatment? Is the ambulance team to be regarded as the plaintiff's agent for the purpose of dealings with a hospital?

The *Hotson* case is somewhat disappointing for its failure to analyse fully the meaning of the finding that the plaintiff had a twenty-five per cent chance of avoiding the deformity. In the Court of Appeal, Croom-Johnson LJ, while not dissenting, rejected the notion that the plaintiff should recover if all the finding meant was that twenty-five per cent of the population would have responded well to prompt treatment, and the remaining seventy-five per cent would not. In the House of Lords, Lord Mackay observed that this indeed was the way counsel for the plaintiff sought to justify a twenty-five per cent chance as being an asset personal to the plaintiff. It is hard to resist the conclusion that this 'epistemic probability'[50] had nothing to do with the state of this particular plaintiff on his first arrival in the hospital. Either he had a hundred per cent chance of complete recovery or a hundred per cent chance of deformity: it all depended upon whether he belonged to the twenty-five per cent of the population who in similar circumstances would have made a complete recovery. This could never be known once the opportunity to demonstrate it had been lost.

---

[49] The Unfair Contract Terms Act 1977 disallows attempts to exclude liability for personal injuries and death (s 2(1): tort and contract), so one may not pay less to stay in a hotel in return for chancing the condition of the lift or the scrupulousness of the kitchen staff. One may, however, undertake risky employment that pays danger money. Moreover, one may bargain for better bodily treatment than the law would otherwise accord: *Hawkins v McGee* (1929) 146 A 641. On contracts dealing with the chance of avoiding physical harm, see B Coote, 'Chance and the Burden of Proof in Contract and Tort' (1988) 62 ALJ 761, 771 note 74.

[50] S Perry, 'Protected Interests and Undertakings in the Law of Negligence' (1992) 42 UTLJ 247.

It is nevertheless quite possible to identify a chance that is personal to the plaintiff in circumstances where the plaintiff should be allowed to make his loss the gist of a claim against the defendant. Such was the case in *Davies v Taylor*,[51] where an estranged widow brought a fatal accidents claim for the loss of her dependancy against a tortfeasor whose negligence led to the death of her husband. Such claims, by their nature, are forward-looking and conjectural, in a way that contract claims can sometimes be. The dependant is not in his pre-accident existence offered by the deceased the opportunity of a capital sum in lieu of periodic payments and support. It has long been held that the dependant's statutory claim is for a reasonable expectation of pecuniary benefit lost as a result of the defendant's wrongdoing.[52] The loss of a chance is the very gist of the plaintiff's action in such a case, but a claimant can still lose, as the plaintiff in the *Davies* case did, if unable to cross the threshold and show that there was at least a significant prospect of a matrimonial reconciliation. The *Hotson* preclusion of a chance-based recovery is confined to proving events that have already occurred and does not extend to events that are possible future events.[53] It is commonplace in personal injuries cases to award damages in respect of the chance of a future setback in the plaintiff's condition.[54] The plaintiff, for example, might later experience osteo-arthritis in an injured joint[55] and might, if such occurred, require an operation to replace an injured joint and even a subsequent operation to replace a replacement joint. Such claims are permitted, provided they cross the threshold barrier of not being speculative, whereupon damages are calculated in the light of the percentage chances.[56]

In addition, it is possible to recover where the most the plaintiff can establish is that the defendant's tortious behaviour contributed materially

---

[51] [1974] AC 207. See also *Mallett v McMonagle* [1970] AC 166; *Malec v JC Hutton Pty Ltd* (1990) 169 CLR 638.

[52] *Taff Vale Railway Co v Jenkins* [1913] AC 1.

[53] *Mallett v McMonagle* [1970] AC 166, at 176, per Lord Diplock; *The Commonwealth v Amann Aviation Pty Ltd* (1991) 174 CLR 64.

[54] This is a consequence of the once-and-for-all way in which such tort claims have traditionally been settled or litigated. It is however possible to put on one side possible future risks and seek instead provisional damages, reserving the right to go back to court at a later date if the excluded chance of further injury does eventuate: RSC, Ord 37 r 8. But the provisional damages route has its critics who argue that it prevents settlements with insurance companies, since the provisional damages claim must be the subject of a court order. Moreover, it encourages in the plaintiff an unhealthy continuing preoccupation with the accident and the possible onset of further injury. There is also the chance that at a later date the insurance company will become insolvent.

[55] An illustration used by Lord Simon in *Davies v Taylor* [1974] AC 207, at 220.

[56] Another consequence of the once-and-for-all tort approach is that damages have to be assessed before the plaintiff's present injuries have crystallized for good or ill. Similarly, restitution lawyers may argue that the difficulty of valuing incontrovertible benefit, due to future uncertainties, ought not to lead the court to dismiss a claim: AS Burrows, *The Law of Restitution* (Butterworths 1993), p 10.

to the plaintiff's injury, but it is impossible to isolate that behaviour from a complex environment of causal matter. What is striking in this instance is that the plaintiff recovers in full and does not have his damages discounted to reflect the uncertainty. Such was the case in *Bonnington Castings Ltd* v *Wardlow*,[57] where the plaintiff was able to show that his illness was caused by silica dust, but was unable to show whether the dust that caused it came from the source produced by a breach of statutory duty (guilty dust) or a different source for which the defendant was not responsible (innocent dust). Similarly, a workman recovered damages in *McGhee* v *National Coal Board*[58] when suffering dermatitis plainly caused by brick dust, although he was able only to show that his employer's culpable failure to provide washing facilities after work materially contributed to the risk of injury. Decisions of this type come perilously close to reversing the civil burden of proof, as Lord Wilberforce in the latter case candidly accepted they did. In the assistance they give to the plaintiff, they may be compared to the application of remoteness of damage rules in contract and tort where the defendant is required to foresee or contemplate not the quantity of harm, but merely the type.[59] The drift of these authorities was, however, firmly arrested by the House of Lords in *Wilsher* v *Essex Area Health Authority*,[60] where the blindness of a premature baby could have been caused by an excessive and negligent administration of oxygen, but could quite independently have been caused by any one of a number of altogether different reasons for which the defendant was not liable. In the circumstances, since oxygen could not play the role of silica and brick dust in the earlier cases of being clearly the cause of the plaintiff's condition, the plaintiff's action failed for he could not show that the administration of the oxygen materially contributed to the injury. Confused causes in what might be termed process cases and alternative causes in accident cases were not to be confounded.

DAMAGES FOR THE LOSS OF A CHANCE: THE CONTRACT CASES

An adequate review of contract cases should include under this head not only decisions where a loss has been quantified and then discounted in accordance with the strength of the plaintiff's lost chance, but also those decisions where the loss suffered by the plaintiff is conjectural and the process of computation impressionistic. It is rather rare to find a case that falls squarely within the first of these two categories. Furthermore, the difference between discounted recovery on the basis of a strong chance, and

---

[57] [1956] AC 613.   [58] [1973] 1 WLR 1.
[59] For example, *Victoria Laundry (Windsor) Ltd* v *Newman Industries Ltd* [1949] 2 QB 528 (contract) and *Smith* v *Leech Brain & Co Ltd* [1962] 2 QB 405 (tort).
[60] [1988] AC 1074.

complete recovery for a loss so hard to fathom that any damages awarded will be conjectural, may be so slight as to be merely an analytical one. In a very real sense, it is not a matter of providing the plaintiff with a surrogate for the expectation interest since, in these cases, the plaintiff's expectancy is the chance itself rather than the assurance of gain. Sometimes, the computation of damages in cases of evidentiary difficulty is compounded by the existence of a discretion concerning the defendant's contractual performance. In other cases, the plaintiff facing evidentiary difficulties in estimating the expectation interest will assert instead a reliance claim. It is a very real question whether the plaintiff seeks here a radically different form of recovery, or simply a variant of an unprovable expectation claim. The following categories have in common certain difficulties in tracing a causal link between the defendant's breach and the plaintiff's expectancy.

Mingled causes

Corresponding to decisions such as *McGhee* are numerous contract authorities whose similarity is not immediately obvious. It is likely that the decision in *McGhee* would have attracted less interest if the plaintiff's injuries had been due to both his employer's breach of statutory duty and to his own contributory negligence, with a consequent reduction in his recoverable damages. In contract, except where the defendant's breach of contract is also the breach of a duty of care in tort, there is no apportionment for the plaintiff's contributory negligence.[61] Rather, the question is whether the defendant's breach continues to have causal relevance despite the plaintiff's negligence. Since, if this is the case, the plaintiff recovers in full, no proper distinction is to be taken between the plaintiff's negligence and an external event in those cases where the defendant's breach is mingled with other causal matter.

In *Mowbray v Merryweather*,[62] the hirers of a chain, having settled an action brought against them by an injured employee, were able to recover damages from the defendant suppliers for breach of a common law fitness warranty, despite their own admission at trial that they might with reasonable care have discovered the defect in the chain. The resultant accident to the workman was the natural consequence of the breach of warranty, and was within the contemplation of the parties at the contract date. The same broad approach was adopted by the Court of Appeal in

---

[61] See *Forsikringsaktieselskapet Vesta v Butcher* [1989] AC 852; *Schering Agrochemicals Ltd v Resibel NV SA* (CA 1992), noted by AS Burrows, 'Contributory Negligence in Contract: Ammunition for the Law Commission' (1993) 109 LQR 175; *Barclays Bank plc v Fairclough Building Ltd*, *The Times* 11 May 1994; Law Commission, *Contributory Negligence as a Defence in Contract* (1993 Law Com No 219).

[62] [1895] 2 QB 640.

Lambert v *Lewis*,[63] where a negligent farmer sought to recover from the suppliers of a defective towing hitch damages for breach of the implied terms of reasonable fitness and merchantable quality. He was initially able to recover in full, despite the mingling of his own negligence and the suppliers' strict liability, since his negligence was not so unreasonable as to break the chain of causation linking the injury with the breach of the implied terms, or to fall outside the reasonable contemplation of the parties. The House of Lords,[64] by a different route that spared them the obstacle of unhelpful findings and admissions in the lower courts, reversed this decision and put the loss on the farmer: the implied obligations of the suppliers had a limited post-contract life and there was no separate undertaking that the farmer could continue to use the hitch despite its obviously damaged state.[65]

Neither of the above cases handles complex causal material in a particularly convincing way. The same can be said of *H Parsons (Livestock) Ltd* v *Uttley Ingham & Co Ltd*,[66] where a farmer's misgivings at the state of pig nuts issuing from his hopper were neatly sidelined by the court's preoccupation with the more general question whether the supplier of an unfit hopper might have contemplated that it would lead to illness in the pigs fed from it. How the injury is characterized, and how the breach is defined, can have profound effects upon the relevance of causal material and the outcome of the case. In addition, if the doctrine of mitigation comes into play, the causation debate is transformed. Instead of asking the question whether the defendant's breach continues to have causal relevance, the focus is put upon the behaviour of the plaintiff, and his ability to obviate or alleviate the effect of the defendant's breach.[67] This sidesteps the causation issue.

Contracting for a chance[68]

The contract cases discussed above, far from involving any bargain for a chance, involve a strict assurance by the supplier that goods will be merchantable or reasonably fit for their purpose. Taking a simplified view of causation, they settle upon an all-or-nothing solution: the plaintiff recovers in full or not at all. The principle that damages should be discounted has been accepted where the subject matter of the contract is a chance

---

[63] [1982] AC 225.   [64] [1982] AC 268 *et seq.*

[65] See MG Bridge, 'Defective Products, Contributory Negligence, Apportionment of Loss and the Distribution Chain' (1982) 6 Can Bus LJ 184.

[66] [1978] QB 791.

[67] See MG Bridge, 'Mitigation of Damages in Contract and the Meaning of Avoidable Loss' (1989) 105 LQR 398.

[68] CT McCormick, *Handbook on the Law of Damages* (1935), pp 117–23; GH Treitel, *Remedies for Breach of Contract: A Comparative Account* (1988), pp 193–4.

rather than an assurance of profit. In *Chaplin v Hicks*,[69] the defendant impresario offered terms of employment for three years as actresses to the twelve successful contestants in a national talent competition that involved the selection of fifty finalists (five each from ten different regions) by members of the public. From these finalists, the twelve winners would be personally selected by the defendant. In breach of contract, the defendant failed to give the plaintiff adequate notice of the session at which the twelve winners were selected, and she brought the present action for damages when he declined to offer her an engagement, claiming that she had lost the chance of selection.

She was successful, the amount of damages being fixed by the jury at one hundred pounds, despite the defendant's contention that the damages were not capable of being assessed because of the contingent nature of the contract. As Vaughan Williams LJ put it: 'But the fact that damages cannot be assessed with certainty does not relieve the wrong-doer of the necessity of paying damages for his breach of contract.'[70] He went on to say that, although the right to participate in the contest could not be valued according to the market since it was incapable of transfer, yet a jury was entitled to put a value on it as if it could be transferred.[71] Fletcher Moulton LJ found 'an unchallengeable case of injury'[72] and, plainly unwilling to see such injury compensated in just a nominal damages award, upheld the jury's right to do its best in such a case.

This attitude lies at the heart of the *Chaplin* decision. As much as the plaintiff has to show loss in order to recover damages, and can always recover nominal damages on pointing to a breach, the law tends away from a nominal damages award where a loss of some kind has been experienced but the plaintiff, in consequence of the defendant's breach, cannot put a figure on it. Thus awards have been made against a publisher for the loss of the author's opportunity to enhance his reputation,[73] against a hairdresser whose wrongful dismissal deprived him of the opportunity to earn tips from various customers,[74] against the owner of a hotel for selling it otherwise than through the sole agency of the plaintiffs[75] and against the hirer of a racehorse wrongfully holding over for the owner's lost opportunity to bet on the horses in races and pass on information about it for reward.[76] Damages have also been awarded to an actor, wrongfully dismissed, for the loss of the chance to further his

---

[69] [1911] 2 KB 786; and see also the earlier case of *Richardson v Mellish* (1824) 2 Bing 229; 130 ER 294. Cf. *The Alecos M* [1991] 1 Lloyd's Rep 120.

[70] *Chaplin v Hicks* [1911] 2 KB 786, at 792.   [71] *Ibid.*, at 793.

[72] *Ibid.*, at 795.   [73] *Joseph v National Magazine Co* [1959] Ch 14.

[74] *Manubens v Leon* [1919] 1 KB 208.

[75] *Hampton & Sons Ltd v George* [1939] 3 All ER 627.

[76] *Howe v Teefy* (1927) 27 SR (NSW) 301.

reputation.[77] The methodology of the tort cases, requiring a probability threshold to be crossed before any award of substantial damages may be made, has had an impact.[78]

The jury has in the past been the salvation of English judges in quantifying real injuries that are impossible to calculate: it does not have to justify its award, and an appeal court will intervene only if the award is wholly out of line with what a reasonable jury might have awarded. It is not so easy for the judge sitting alone and delivering a reasoned judgment to conceal his deliberations from external scrutiny. There were initially six thousand contestants in the *Chaplin* case and the plaintiff, chosen by members of the public as the first of the five winners in her region, had very real prospects of success. The gross earnings of the winners over the three-year period were set at £768 (for the first four), £624 (for the next four) and £468 (for the last four). There was no indication of what the plaintiff's actual earnings during that time were or might have been: the engagements promised to the winners had not expired at the time of the present action. The defendant appeared to be subject to no constraints in the choice of the twelve finalists, yet nothing was made of this in the case or of the defendant's refusal to offer a satisfactory engagement to the plaintiff in settlement of the dispute. The award of £100 appears to be as round as it is unfathomable. In other cases, the process can be rendered more scientific. So, sole agents deprived of the opportunity to sell a hotel did not get the £104 that would have been received on the sale, but the lesser figure of £80, which explicitly took into account various factors such as the agents' experience and efficiency, and the fact that they were not specialists in this particular type of property.[79]

The principle of recovery in *Chaplin v Hicks* is applicable to any contract that involves the right to compete. It could quite properly underpin the award of damages in those cases where a pre-contract exists imposing conditions on the submission and treatment of bids in competitive

---

[77] *Clayton* v *Oliver* [1930] AC 209; *White* v *Australian and New Zealand Theatres Ltd* (1943) 67 CLR 266. But note the refusal to award damages to a dismissed manager whose employer in breach failed to make him a director and who had claimed damages for the ensuing loss of prestige and publicity: *Re B Golomb and W Porter & Co* (1931) 144 LT 583.

It has been held that a performing artist not permitted to appear may recover damages for the loss of a chance to enhance his reputation, though not for the damage thereby done to his reputation: *Withers* v *General Theatre Corpn Ltd* [1933] 2 KB 536, disapproving *Marbe* v *George Edwardes (Daly's Theatre) Ltd*[1928] 1 KB 269, at 281 (Bankes LJ), a distinction compelled by *Addis* v *Gramophone Co Ltd* [1909] AC 488, which denies damages for harm done to the plaintiff's reputation by the manner of his dismissal.

[78] *Obagi* v *Stanborough Developments Ltd, The Times* 15 December 1993 (defendant failed to apply for planning permission that, if granted, would have given plaintiff an option to buy half of a plot of land—no recovery because threshold not crossed).

[79] *Hampton & Sons Ltd* v *George* [1939] 2 All ER 627.

tendering conditions.[80] An alternative to the award of damages for loss of a chance might have been damages representing the plaintiff's reliance expenditure in entering the competition, for example the cost of transport, photography sessions, and hairdressers' fees. There is, however, no evidence that this measure was ever considered in the case, and the amount of expenditure incurred might fall too far short of the considerable rewards of successful competition to be palatable to any court setting the damages award. This measure might nevertheless be more useful for awards in commercial tendering conditions. Public procurement regulations, dealing with the breach of a statutory duty to consider bids, authorize the award of the bidder's costs of tendering and participation in the bidding process where the bidder would have had a 'real chance' of being awarded the contract.[81] Recovery at this level may be criticized for giving the plaintiff significantly less than the value of the lost chance. What is the incentive for tendering in normal economic conditions, if the value of the chance of success amounts to nothing more than the sum of costs incurred in preparing and submitting the bid? Yet, it is likely to be a closer approximation to the plaintiff's loss than it would be in a case like *Chaplin*.

Chaplin v *Hicks* is to be distinguished from a decision of Jelf J made shortly before, in *Sapwell* v *Bass*.[82] In that case the defendant disabled himself from performing his contract to have his stallion, Cyllene, serve one of the defendant's brood mares when he sold the stallion to an overseas buyer before the date of performance. Though the agreed stud fee of 300 guineas had not yet been paid, the plaintiff placed his mare with another stallion, Cicero, for the lesser sum of £100 and sought to recover as damages for breach the average profits made from yearlings he had obtained in the past with the help of Cyllene. He was unable to formulate a reliance claim:

No other expenses had been incurred or steps taken by the plaintiff in special preparation for the expected service by Cyllene, for such expenses and steps were all available for the service by Cicero. Neither party could suggest nor could I discover any tertium quid by way of compensation.[83]

Jelf J held that damages could not be computed on the basis that the plaintiff was purchasing a profit-earning chattel[84] because of the contingent character of the contract.[85] He further stated that in general damages were

---

[80] See *Blackpool & Fylde Aeroclub Ltd* v *Blackpool Borough Council* [1990] 1 WLR 1195 where the damages award was not subject to scrutiny in the Court of Appeal. Cf. the difficulty posed by the argument that there is no duty to negotiate: *Walford* v *Miles* [1992] 2 AC 128; *Courtney and Fairbairn Ltd* v *Tolaini Bros (Hotels) Ltd* [1975] 1 WLR 297.

[81] See The Utilities Supply and Works Contracts Regulations 1992, SI 1992 No 3279, reg 30(7).

[82] [1910] 2 KB 486.   [83] *Ibid.*, at 492.

[84] See *Fletcher* v *Tayleur* (1855) 17 CB 21; 139 ER 973.

[85] *Sapwell* v *Bass* [1910] 2 KB 486, at 492–3 (Jelf J lists nine contingencies).

too remote to be recoverable where they depend 'entirely on chances',[86] a proposition that would be hard to reconcile with *Chaplin v Hicks* and with his own later intimation[87] that the loss of a chance could be compensable if 'of sufficiently ascertainable value at the time the contact was made to be within the contemplation of the parties'.[88] Even so, the recoverable amount would have to 'be ascertained with reasonable certainty',[89] not possible in the present case where the plaintiff's mare had been served by Cicero for a very much smaller sum. The loss in the present case was too remote, but the successful defendant was required to pay his own costs.

The result in *Sapwell v Bass* may be justified[90] on the ground, not so much that the plaintiff's right was too contingent to value,[91] but rather that there was no evidence to show that the chance had a greater value than the figure the parties themselves had put upon it when agreeing the stud fee of 300 guineas,[92] an amount which the plaintiff was not in the end called upon to pay. There is much in this, at least if one puts aside the possibility that in some cases there might be wasted reliance expenditure. The defendant was selling a chance to the plaintiff under a straightforward exchange contract, hardly an accurate portrayal of the facts in *Chaplin* where the defendant's reasons for allocating a chance to the plaintiff had nothing to do with any consideration coming from the plaintiff. But if the chance was worth no more than the contractually agreed fee, there would again be no incentive for the plaintiff to enter into the contract, unless he were an inveterate gambler with interests going beyond the turning of a profit on contracts of this kind, and there was no sign of this in the case. The making of a profit from contracts for stud services is hardly so unusual an event as to justify the rather restrictive approach of Jelf J who—and it may not have been entirely coincidental—was sitting without a jury.

A number of professional negligence cases have turned upon the award of damages for the loss of a chance.[93] Except in unusual cases, professionals do not guarantee a result. Sometimes, it is a question of an action being sustainable against a third party but barred for limitation reasons. In *Kitchen v Royal Air Force Association*,[94] a widow recovered from the negli-

---

[86] *Sapwell v Bass* [1910] 2 KB 486, at 493.

[87] When discussing *Watson v Ambergate, Nottingham and Boston Rly Co* (1851) 15 Jur 448.

[88] *Sapwell v Bass* [1910] 2 KB 486, at 494.   [89] *Ibid.*

[90] See Fletcher Moulton LJ in *Chaplin v Hicks* [1911] 2 KB 786, at 797.

[91] As Jelf J appears himself to put it.

[92] See also *McGregor on Damages* (15th ed 1988), para 362 note 67.

[93] See eg *Cook v Swinfen* [1967] 1 WLR 457: solicitor failed to apply for maintenance in negligently conducted divorce proceedings. On the loss of opportunity to bring proceedings, see *Jackson and Powell on Professional Negligence* (3rd ed 1992), ss 4–182 to 4–193.

[94] [1958] 1 WLR 563. Cf. *Malyon v Lawrence, Messer & Co* [1968] 2 Lloyd's Rep 539, where the solicitors' negligence related to the conduct of a running down action in West Germany and the court proceeded to a trial within a trial of the West German action, concluding with a result in the plaintiff's favour which became the measure of the solicitors' damages

gent solicitors approximately two-thirds the amount that she might have recovered, if successful, from an alleged tortfeasor against whom her action had become statute-barred. It was thought not to be a practical matter to try an action against the tortfeasor within the contract action[95] against the defendant solicitors but, in upholding the trial award, the Court of Appeal was not satisfied that her action would fail. The plaintiff was entitled to more than nominal damages and the trial judge's award though generous was allowed to stand since no appeal had been taken on quantum.

Sometimes the plaintiff's action is based on a solicitor's failure to advise, and the question then is how the plaintiff would have acted had proper advice been given. Where the prospects are good that the advice would have been taken, substantial, though discounted, damages have been awarded.[96] A plaintiff unable to demonstrate that he would have responded differently to competent advice will receive only nominal damages.[97] Similarly, a court will not go beyond nominal damages if a solicitor fails to act, and there is nothing to show what the value of that action would have been.[98] The plaintiff has to prove the loss of a *valuable* chance.

THE LOSS OF PROFITS[99]

The reluctance of the law to get involved in the profits of buyers and sellers is revealed by its predeliction for a more-easily administered rule basing damages on the market price prevailing at the breach date. Although this approach has its drawbacks, notably its treatment of the parties as speculators intent on bargaining over market differences instead of dealers with a material interest in the subject-matter of the contract, it has the merit of simplicity and the avoidance of uncertainty in the computation of damages. But it is not always possible to refer to a market to assess damages, especially where the subject matter of the contract is a profit-earning chattel. In such cases, damages have been awarded for lost profits, despite considerable uncertainty in their quantification. The English courts have

liability in negligence. Thus there was no broad assessment of the plaintiff's chances with a suitable discount to reflect the chances of failure.

[95] But note that pleading practice is to recite in the statement of claim against the negligent solicitor the action that might have been maintained, and the prospects of success against the defendant who now cannot be reached as a result of the solicitor's negligence.

[96] *Otter v Church, Adams, Tatham & Co* [1953] Ch 280 (deceased might well have augmented his estate by executing a disentailing assurance); *Hall v Meyrick* [1957] 2 QB 455 (husband might have executed new will if informed that marriage revoked old will).

[97] *Sykes v Midland Bank Executor & Trustee Co* [1971] 1 QB 113.

[98] *Clarke v Kirby-Smith* [1964] Ch 506.

[99] 'Lost Profits as Contract Damages: Problems of Proof and Limitations on Recovery' (1956) 65 Yale LJ 992.

not imposed a control that at one time was prominent in the United States, namely that the profits must have been 'certain' if the plaintiff is to be indemnified for their loss.[100]

The law reports are full of illustrations of awards where there was plainly a loss, but its valuation could only be made impressionistically. In the past, the 'common sense and experience' of the jury[101] have been helpful. In *O'Hanlon v Great Western Railway Co*,[102] an 'intelligent jury' of Glamorganshire businessmen awarded damages against a carrier for lost goods based upon their value at the place where they should have been received, which necessarily supposed an importer's profit, instead of upon their value at the place of shipment together with the cost of freight. Traders do not go to the trouble of having goods shipped in just to sell them at cost. Again, in *Simpson v London and North Western Railway Co*,[103] a carrier's failure to transport timeously trade samples from one agricultural fair to another led to an award of damages for loss of business. In the words of Cockburn CJ, '[damages] must be [a] matter of speculation, but that is no reason for not awarding damages at all.'[104] One US case explicitly justifies a degree of leniency in favour of plaintiffs who have difficulty in establishing their lost profits where this is due to the defendant's repudiatory breach before performance took place.[105] However, a plaintiff engaged in a highly speculative business is unlikely to benefit from such a presumption of profitability. The loss of a general opportunity to trade in a speculative commodities market was too imprecise to have a value put upon it in *E Bailey & Co v Balholm Securities Ltd*.[106] Unlike the plaintiff in *Chaplin v Hicks*, the plaintiff in that case was exposed to the risk of being worse off. The experience and skill of the brokers gave a better than even chance of making money, but not enough to justify the award of damages for loss of a chance.

---

[100] 'The Requirement of Certainty in the Proof of Lost Profits' (1950) 64 Harv LR 317; *Evergreen Amusement Corp v Milstead* 112 A 2d 90 (1955) Md; CT McCormick, *Handbook on the Law of Damages* (1955), pp 97–115.

[101] *O'Hanlan v Great Western Railway Co* (1865) 6 B & S 484.

[102] *Ibid.*   [103] (1876) 1 QBD 274.

[104] *Ibid.*, at 277. Indeed the case law is full of observations that the difficulty of computing damages is no reason for not awarding damages at all: *Ratcliffe v Evans* [1892] 2 QB 524, at 532–3 (Bowen LJ); *Jones v Schiffman* (1971) 124 CLR 303, at 308 (Menzies J); *Fink v Fink* (1946) 74 CLR 127, at 143 (Dixon and McTiernan JJ); *Chaplin v Hicks* [1911] 2 KB 786; *Biggin & Co Ltd v Permanite Ltd* [1951] 1 KB 422, at 438 (Devlin J).

[105] *Vitex Mfg Corp v Caribtex Corp* (1967) 377 P 2d 795. This point is also made by the High Court of Australia in *The Commonwealth v Amann Aviation Pty Ltd* (1991) 174 CLR 64 when, in the face of the plaintiff's claim for the recovery of reliance expenditure, it placed on the defendant the burden of proof that the contract would have been a losing venture. See generally the note by GH Treitel, 'Damages for Breach of Contract in the High Court of Australia' (1992) 108 LQR 226.

[106] [1973] 2 Lloyd's Rep 404.

Where the plaintiff has suffered a genuine loss, an award of surrogate damages may have to be made if the alternative is nominal damages only. In some cases, the actual profit lost by the plaintiff is too remote to be recoverable but an alternative award is made instead. In *Cory v Thomas Ironworks and Shipbuilding Co*,[107] the sellers of a large iron hulk vessel were 6 months late in delivering it, so that the buyers lost certain profits from its use. The buyers intended to employ the vessel as a point of transhipment of coals from colliers to barges, an innovative and lucrative use, but not sufficiently within the contemplation of the sellers to comply with the remoteness rule of recovery. There was however a use that the sellers did reasonably contemplate at the contract date: the hulk could have been used less profitably as a floating warehouse. Despite this not being at all what the buyers had in mind, damages were awarded on this basis. It is worth emphasizing the result. The buyers recovered damages for a loss they did not suffer, but the refusal of any recovery for lost profits in a case where the sellers plainly contemplated that the buyers would earn profits from the hulk would have left them undercompensated, and the seller's breach without a sanction. The same result could not have been reached by applying the remoteness rule so as to permit recovery only of those commercial profits that fell within the contemplation of the sellers. Profits from transhipment and profits from warehousing had to be treated as separate losses, because the remoteness rule requires only that the type of loss and not its extent be contemplated. Too rigorous an application of the remoteness rule, which cuts down rather than expands the plaintiff's expectancy,[108] would undermine fatally the law's commitment to the expectation principle of recovery. It is perhaps no accident that the result in *Cory* gave the buyers less than they would have received if they had disclosed their plans to the sellers and had no doubt paid a higher price for the hulk. If in principle the result is wholly deficient, it has a lot pragmatically to defend it.

A similar point can be made about the celebrated case of *Victoria Laundry (Windsor) Ltd v Newman Industries Ltd*.[109] The plaintiffs failed on the ground of remoteness to recover the profits on particularly lucrative dyeing contracts, but were awarded instead a more modest sum representing profits on the type of dyeing contracts they might within the defendants' contemplation have made though in fact did

---

[107] (1868) LR 3 QB 181.

[108] *The Commonwealth v Amann Aviation Pty Ltd* (1991) 174 CLR 64, at 174 per McHugh J, dissenting on the recovery of damages for factual expectations (discussed below). Cf. Mason CJ and Dawson J in the majority at 89–90 ('the parties clearly contemplated that the contractor would be in an advantageous and preferred position to secure a renewal of the contract . . .').

[109] [1949] 2 KB 528.

not. The court saw no reason why the plaintiffs should not recover 'some general (and perhaps conjectural) sum for loss of business in respect of dyeing contracts to be reasonably expected'.[110] Again, they recovered for a loss they did not suffer, a more acceptable result than not recovering anything at all for the loss of dyeing business.

The damages recovered in *Cory* and in *Victoria Laundry* were no doubt substantial. There are examples, however, of the surrogate award being palliative and declaratory, falling well short of indemnifying the plaintiff in full but yet, like nominal damages, vindicating a right. A good example of this is the award sometimes made against carriers for the investment value of cargo lost or delayed in transit as a result of the carrier's default. The plaintiffs in *British Columbia Saw-Mill Co v Nettleship*[111] were not allowed to recover the profits lost because they were unable to run their mill as a consequence of vital machine parts going missing in transit. The mill was closed down for almost a year while fresh parts were shipped in from London, and the profits claim was expressed, not in conjectural terms relating to the transactions that might have been entered into, but rather in more down-to-earth terms as the rental value for the mill and its machinery during the period of delay. Although not receiving damages for this loss, the plaintiffs yet recovered, in addition to the replacement cost of the parts, interest upon this amount for the period of delay.[112] A similar concession in respect of the lock-up value of a cargo of sugar was made by the defendants in *The Heron II*,[113] but the recovery of profits lost when the ship failed to arrive in Basrah in time to catch a favourable market obviated the need for any such award to be made.

Uncertain future profits can also emerge as a contentious issue in cases where they amount to consequential losses. A buyer, for example, might claim the loss of repeat orders from his customers as a result of the injury done to his trade reputation by the seller's breach of contract. In the past, a number of cases have applied the remoteness rule strictly to prevent recovery,[114] the nearest the courts in this country have got to the US rule requiring certainty if loss of profits are to be recovered. There is, however, no rule debarring recovery in such cases, the matter being simply one of the application of remoteness in the instant case, and the Court of Appeal allowed damages in *GKN Centrax Gears Ltd v Matbro Ltd*[115] where, because of the supply of defective axles, the buyers were able to establish the loss of repeat orders from 'dissatisfied and incensed' customers.

---

[110] *Ibid.*, at 543 per Asquith LJ.   [111] (1868) LR 3 CP 499.
[112] No interest on the locked up intellectual capital of the delayed Calcutta barrister in Willes J's example, *ibid.*, at 510.   [113] [1969] 1 AC 350.
[114] See Scrutton LJ in *Simon v Pawsons and Leafs Ltd* (1932) 38 Com Cas 151.
[115] [1976] 2 Lloyd's Rep 555.

Chance and discretion

The plaintiff's expectation interest has come in for particular scrutiny where the defendant has a measure of discretion in the performance of the contract and, at the time that damages are to be assessed, that discretion has not yet been exercised. Should it be assumed that the defendant would have exercised the discretion in the way least favourable to the plaintiff, or in the way most favourable to himself? Or should a prediction be made as to the way the discretion would actually have been exercised if the defendant had not broken the contract? Further, is the discretion an unbridled one, or is its exercise subject to any limitations arising, for example, out of an implied term?

In the plaintiff's action for wrongful dismissal in *Lavarack* v *Woods of Colchester Ltd*,[116] one of the issues concerned the loss of future bonus payments. These were determined by the directors on a purely discretionary basis, but the plaintiff had in the recent past been awarded sums almost equal to his annual salary. After the plaintiff's dismissal, the bonus system was withdrawn, but most employees of the defendant obtained an increase in salary. There was a finding of fact that the plaintiff's annual salary would have risen by £1,000 had he remained in employment. By a majority, the Court of Appeal refused to take account of this finding. In the words of Diplock LJ: 'The law is concerned with legal obligations only . . . not with the expectations, however reasonable, of one contractor that the other will do something that he has assumed no legal obligation to do.'[117] The case was indistinguishable from an 'absurd' claim for the loss of a chance that a term appointment might have been renewed.[118] The result was therefore entirely in accord with the dictum of Maule J in *Cockburn* v *Alexander*: 'Generally speaking, where there are several ways in which the contract might be performed, that mode is adopted which is the least profitable to the plaintiff, and the least burthensome to the defendant.'[119]

Yet the mode of performance least profitable to the plaintiff and the mode least burdensome to the defendant may not be the same thing. Moreover, that dictum of Maule J speaks to the definition of the defendant's primary obligation, and permits an obligee to choose the less onerous of alternative methods of performance. It has nothing to say about the quantification of contingent performance in secondary (ie, damages) terms. *Cockburn* v *Alexander* was not concerned with the quantification of damages upon a repudiatory breach, but rather with the construction of a charterparty and the computation of freight rates

---

[116] [1967] 1 QB 278.   [117] *Ibid.*, at 294.
[118] Cf. *The Commonwealth* v *Amann Aviation Pty Ltd* (1991) 174 CLR 64.
[119] (1848) 6 CB 791, at 814; 136 ER 1459, at 1468–9. Cf. GH Treitel, ch 15 above.

according to the charter.[120] The decision in *Lavarack* may also be compared with personal injury litigation. Against a third party tortfeasor, account will be taken of likely bonuses and discretionary payments: it will not avail the defendant to say the employer might have chosen not to pay. And if the tortfeasor were the employer himself, the result would in this respect surely be the same, whether the action were laid in tort or in contract.

So what is it about *Lavarack* that justifies a different result? English courts have not accepted the Holmes thesis[121] that the contract-breaker may elect between the alternative primary obligations of performing the contract or paying damages, which would make relevant the dictum of Maule J. There is something distinctly curious about tort law better protecting a contractual expectancy than contract law. In employment relations, the practical answer may be the inference of an implied term that employees will fairly be considered for discretionary payments at least where such payments form a structural part of a remuneration package; this certainly permits the damages issue to be estimated in terms of the loss of a chance. Even without such an implied term, there is much to be said for vindicating a plaintiff's factual expectancy when he sues a defendant who had a future discretion to exercise. If a defendant's breach prevents a discretion from being exercised by a third party, it would be no defence that the third party was not bound to exercise the discretion in the plaintiff's favour. If the defendant, in breaking the contract, denies himself the opportunity to exercise a discretion against the plaintiff, then the plaintiff might be required to prove that he has lost the benefit of a more than speculative chance. Any possibility that the discretion might have gone against the plaintiff could then be used to discount the plaintiff's damages as though it were any other negative contingency, like the chance that the plaintiff might have changed his job or have suffered a fatal accident before the discretion came to be exercised. The assessment of damages is designed to put the plaintiff in the position he would have occupied if the breach had not taken place.[122] The starting point for the rule of remoteness is the contract date, not the date when the defendant committed the breach which forestalled the exercise of the discretion. This defendant forfeits his contractual right to exercise a future discretion against the plaintiff. Why should it be assumed, in

---

[120] See the analysis of it by Mustill J in *Paula Lee Ltd v Robert Zehil & Co Ltd* [1983] 2 All ER 390, at 395–6.

[121] Stated in *Globe Refining Co v Landa Oil Cotton Co* (1903) 190 US 540.

[122] *Livingstone v Rawyards Coal Co* (1880) 5 App Cas 25, at 39 per Lord Blackburn:

[Y]ou should as nearly a possible get at that sum of money which will put the party who has been injured, or who has suffered, in the same position as he would have been in if he had not sustained the wrong for which he is now getting his compensation or reparation.

order to minimize the defendant's liability, that he would have gone on to exercise that discretion against the plaintiff?

In the wrongful dismissal case of *Bold v Brough, Nicholson & Hall Ltd*,[123] the plaintiff recovered compensation for the loss of certain pension rights. The employers were entitled to terminate the pension scheme for their entire workforce, but they had not done so and the court would not assume they had just to minimize their liability. In *Lavarack*, Diplock LJ distinguished *Bold* on the ground that the employers' discretion 'was not a discretion as to the manner of performing their contract of service with the plaintiff but a discretion as to the way in which they would conduct their business as a whole.'[124] Further, 'one must not assume that [the defendant] will cut off his nose to spite his face and so . . . reduce his legal obligations to the plaintiff by incurring greater loss in other respects'.[125] Damages were thus measured by the defendant's minimum disadvantage, and not by the plaintiff's minimum advantage. A defendant in this position will probably make a rational choice. Once probability is admitted into the resolution of a case like *Bold*, it is not easy to see why it should not be given full rein in all cases, so that the actual award in a case like *Lavarack* is made to turn on evidence of probabilities[126] rather than upon any principle of elective choice between alternative primary obligations.[127] It is worth remembering that the plaintiff in *Chaplin v Hicks* received damages for loss of a chance, even though the defendant had a seemingly unfettered discretion in the selection of the twelve winners.

The *Lavarack* view was applied recently in *The World Navigator*.[128] Under an fob contract for the sale of a quantity of maize, the sellers were in breach in failing to supply the buyers with certain documentation. The buyers' ship was therefore severely delayed in taking its position at the loading berth. A loading rate clause also prescribed the rate at which the sellers should load the ship: anything less was a breach and the sellers could not be required to exceed the rate even if

---

[123] [1964] 1 WLR 201.

[124] *Laverack v Woods of Colchester Ltd* [1967] 1 QB 278, at 296.   [125] *Ibid.*, at 295.

[126] See cases like *The Mihalis Angelos* [1971] 1 QB 164 and *Berger & Co Inc v Gill & Duffus SA* [1984] AC 382 for the calculation of damages according to what the defendant in the future might lawfully and most likely would have done had it not been for the termination of the contract by the plaintiff because of the defendant's unlawful repudiation.

[127] Cf. *Re Thornett and Fehr and Yuills Ltd* [1921] 1 KB 219 an action for damages for short delivery of '200 tons 5 per cent more or less' of Australasian beef tallow. Damages were based on the sellers' minimum obligation within the quantitative range defining their primary obligation, the amount of 190 tons. As Scrutton LJ put it in *Abrahams v Herbert Reiach Ltd* [1922] 1 KB 477, at 482: '[A] defendant is not liable in damages for not doing that which he is not bound to do.' See also *Withers v General Theatre Corpn Ltd* [1933] 2 KB 536, at 549 (Scrutton LJ).

[128] [1991] 2 Lloyd's Rep 23.

physically able to do so. The ship was loaded twelve times more quickly than it had to be, and within the time that would have been taken if no breach had occurred and loading had then been completed at the prescribed rate and no faster. Were the buyers entitled to damages for the unlawful detention of the ship prior to loading when the necessary documentation was not made available by the sellers?[129] Could they recover such damages on the ground that the ship would probably have left port even earlier had the documentary breach not occurred?

The Court of Appeal held that the buyers were not entitled to damages for the breach, since it had to be assumed that the sellers, if not in breach of the earlier duty, would have loaded the ship only at the prescribed rate. It was not permissible to look at factual probabilities and estimate the loss of the buyers' chance that the ship might have left port earlier or, it seems, to ask whether the loading rate adhered to in the present case was adopted by the sellers in order to abate the effect of their earlier breach. This was not a case of events 'extraneous' to the contract[130] that could be taken into account in calculating damages, although the sellers' duties in relation to loading and documentation were quite separate. The decision goes beyond *Lavarack*, for it is not a question of what the sellers *might* in future have done. They had in fact loaded at a speedy rate, although it was not known how and why this rate was achieved, or even whether the defendant sellers in the present action were the shippers of the maize.[131] It is difficult to justify excluding evidence surrounding an event that has actually occurred. Staughton LJ put the matter in terms of the defendant sellers being entitled to perform in the way least beneficial to the buyers.[132] If this were to be rephrased in terms of what was least disadvantageous to the sellers,[133] the sellers should have been compelled to explain why they (or the original shippers) loaded at the rate they did.

The approach taken in *Lavarack* is ruled out if the sellers' discretion

---

[129] The buyers were claiming to be indemnified for the demurrage payments they had to make to the ship.

[130] An expression used by Diplock LJ in *Lavarack* to sanction reference to future probabilities.

[131] The litigation concerned two contiguous string sales in which the intermediate party of the three dropped out of the proceedings leaving them to be fought by the first seller and the last buyer. But there is no indication of how long the string was. If the shipper and the defendant seller were different entities, the result in the case seems positively strange. Further, the speed of loading might have been due to a charterer seeking to recover dispatch money.

[132] *The World Navigator* [1991] 2 Lloyd's Rep 23, at 33. See also the judgment of Sir David Croom-Johnson.

[133] The two approaches can yield different result, as observed by Mustill LJ in *Paula Lee Ltd* v *Robert Zehil & Co Ltd* [1983] 2 All ER 390, at 393.

is later crystallized by a contractual variation[134] or is subject to an implied term governing its exercise (as a modern *Lavarack* case might be argued) or is defined in some way by the construction of the language that gives rise to it. An example of constructive limitation is *Abrahams* v *Herbert Reiach Ltd*,[135] where the defendants undertook to publish a book and pay the authors a royalty for each copy of the book sold. They failed to publish a book as agreed and argued that their liability ought to be confined to the smallest number of books that could be said to be a publication. According to the Court of Appeal, this was not a case of alternative performance where a 'standard which is the least onerous to the defendant'[136] applies. Rather, it was a question of what was intended by the word 'publication', which here meant a reasonable number that took account of various circumstances, such as the possibility that the defendants might have underestimated the book's sales prospects by printing too few copies. Publishers do not normally put out books if the expected sales are unlikely to exceed a break-even point for copies sold, and do not define a publication in the way that a libel lawyer might.

An example of an implied term limiting the defendant's discretion is to be found in the rather complex judgment of Mustill J in *Paula Lee Ltd* v *Robert Zehil & Co Ltd*,[137] where the defendants were the sole distributors of the plaintiff manufacturers' dresses in certain Middle Eastern countries. They were bound to buy no fewer than 16,000 garments per season, and were to have control over the marketing and sales policy for their territory. The defendants unlawfully repudiated the contract and argued that their damages liability should be based upon buying in the 16,000 garments at the lowest possible prices, even if it meant buying garments in a limited range of sizes and styles which could not possibly have been marketed successfully in the allotted territory and could only have damaged the plaintiff's reputation if an attempt to do so had been made. Mustill J held that the defendants were impliedly bound to make a reasonable selection, but that damages should be assessed according to the method of reasonable selection that was least unfavourable to them.[138] The process of implying a term looks to performance by the parties to a contract of this type which maximises their joint interests, while the established approach to damages where performance is to occur within discretionary limits

---

[134] See AH Hudson, 'Alternative Methods of Performance in Contract – Assessment of Damages' (1975) 91 LQR 20, discussing *F&G (Wessex) Ltd* v *Fine Fare Ltd* [1967] 1 Lloyd's Rep 53.

[135] [1922] 1 KB 477.   [136] *Ibid.*, at 480.   [137] [1983] 2 All ER 390.

[138] A result consistent with the approach taken in *Abrahams* v *Herbert Reiach Ltd* [1922] 1 KB 177.

assumes contractual breakdown and a self-serving minimization of liability by the defendant.

Apart from the above gloss on the *Lavarack* assertion that the plaintiff is entitled only to his legal expectancy, the English courts have declined to recognize factual expectations where these depend upon a discretion exercised by the defendant himself. But the High Court of Australian in *The Commonwealth* v *Amann Aviation Pty Ltd*[139] has recently broken the factual expectation barrier. The factual expectation in that case was that the respondent would be able to secure, at the end of a three-year border surveillance contract, the renewal of this contract by the appellant for a further period. As a matter of probability, the expectation was a strong one: at the end of the three-year term the respondent would have been the contractor in position, and would already have incurred the substantial capital cost of equipment and aircraft, an impediment to market entry that would have deterred competitors. The unusual feature of this case was that the respondent's factual expectancy claim was framed in terms of reliance damages since it was in no position to quantify its expectancy. The majority of the High Court[140] was prepared to assume, subject to a discount for unfavourable contingencies,[141] that the contract would have been renewed, and that this should be reflected in the respondent's damages. In invoking the remoteness rule to establish that renewal was in the contemplation of the parties, however, they used a restrictive rule[142] in aid of creating an award of damages which, without the rule, had to be justified. Nevertheless, the decision of the majority accords with the criticism made above of the rule of no recovery. It recognizes that the contract-breaking appellant would, at the date of renewal, have acted in accordance with its own best interests. It was not to be assumed that, regardless of these interests, it would have acted in the way most injurious to the respondent.[143] If the respondent was to be put in the position it would have occupied but for the appellant's breach, then the appellant's future behaviour should not be assessed

---

[139] (1991) 174 CLR 64. See also GH Treitel, ch 15 above.

[140] Mason CJ, Brennan, Deane, Dawson, Toohey and Gaudron JJ; McHugh J dissenting.

[141] All the majority judges would have discounted by 20 per cent, with the exception of Toohey J who would have discounted by 50 per cent to take account of the double contingency that (1) the Secretary of State would if called upon to do so have applied the termination machinery at the outset in favour of the appellant; and (2) even if the contract had not been terminated in this way, the appellant for various reasons might not have renewed the contract after the end of the initial three year period.

[142] See note 108 above and accompanying text.

[143] Indeed, the appellant's repudiation of the contract and award of it instead to the previous contractor, who for a limited period only was in a position to resume the service, suggested that the appellant might have had no practical choice but to award the contract once more to the respondent after three years in view of the dearth of competition.

as though it knew it had committed a breach and was seeking to minimize its liability.

Reliance claims

It is an established principle of contract law that the plaintiff may freely seek[144] expectation or reliance damages, although he may not obtain double recovery by claiming both.[145] Since the purpose of contract damages is to project the plaintiff forward into a world of post-contractual fulfilment, and the structure of remedies is predicated upon a contract that is not rescinded ab initio, this position needs to be explained. The view advanced in this chapter is that the recovery of reliance damages amounts to a concession made by the law to the plaintiff who, because of the defendant's breach, is unable to prove his lost expectancy. A plaintiff able to prove the lost expectancy will not want to pursue a reliance claim, apart from the case of a losing contract where, as we shall see, the plaintiff's power of election is curtailed.

We saw earlier that a case could be made for the proposition that there is no qualitative difference between reliance and expectation claims in market conditions, in that a reliance-based recovery ought to put the plaintiff back in the pre-contract position where there existed a range of contractual opportunities similar to the one actually taken with the defendant. Taking up the opportunity afforded by the defendant, at least where the plaintiff's performance capacity is not infinitely elastic, could involve forgoing a contractual opportunity with an alternative partner.

In the well-known case of *Wallington* v *Townsend*, the defendant vendor of a seaside bungalow refused to complete, and was met by the purchaser's claim for the recovery of conveyancing costs thereby lost. Morton J awarded the purchaser these costs as damages, even though she could not prove that the house was worth more than the agreed purchase price, since 'the damages are at large and the Court can give

---

[144] *Sunshine Vacation Villas Ltd* v *The Bay* (1984) 13 DLR (4th) 93 (British Columbia CA); *Wenham* v *Ella* (1972) 127 CLR 454; *Ware* v *Johnson* [1984] 2 NZLR 518, at 546; *Herbison* v *Papakura Video Ltd* (*No 2*) [1987] 2 NZLR 720.

Note the way the High Court of Australia in *The Commonwealth* v *Amann Aviation Pty Ltd* (1991) 174 CLR 64 criticized certain statements in *Anglia Television* v *Reed* [1972] 1 QB 60 and *CCC Films (London) Ltd* v *Impact Quadrant Films Ltd* [1985] QB 16 which it interpreted as suggesting that reliance recovery was a different sort of recovery from expectation recovery instead of a category thereof.

[145] *Cullinane* v *British 'Rema' Mfg Co Ltd* [1954] 1 QB 292. Note the way the Australian courts have been prepared to allow a plaintiff to combine a claim for disbursements and other expenditure with a claim for net profits: *TC Industrial Plant Pty Ltd* v *Robert's Queensland Pty Ltd* (1973) 37 AJLR 289; *The Commonwealth* v *Amann Aviation Pty Ltd* (1991) 174 CLR 64. This approach, which ought to yield the same result as a claim for just gross profits, was surprisingly rejected by the majority in *Cullinane*.

such damages as, according to general principles, it thinks right'.[146]
The loss of an opportunity to contract with a vendor who would have
completed can be given concrete value in a case of this kind, where the
market appears to have been static, when one considers that fresh
conveyancing costs would have had to be incurred by the plaintiff as
and when she purchased a substitute property. The court's response
may also be seen as supportive of a plaintiff whose difficulty in establishing loss is attributable to the defendant's breach. A similar
approach is demonstrated in the case of *Security Stove & Mfg Co* v
American Railway Express Co[147] where, no profits being contemplated
in the carriage of the plaintiffs' stove to a trade exhibition, they were
permitted to recover their expenditure in arranging for the display.
Otherwise, 'unless plaintiff is permitted to recover the expenses that it
went to, which were a total loss to it by reason of its inability to exhibit
the furnace and equipment, it will be deprived of any substantial
compensation for its loss'.

The observation that contracting with one partner may involve forgoing the opportunity to deal with someone else, besides casting general light upon a contract law supposedly dedicated to the pursuit of
contractual expectancies, is of particular relevance to those cases of
precontractual expenditure by the plaintiff that are hard to rationalize
in terms of reliance upon the defendant. The most striking example of
this is *Anglia Television* v *Reed*[148] where certain production costs had
been incurred by the plaintiff television company for a planned programme, most of them before they engaged the defendant actor[149] to
play the leading role. Shortly after the conclusion of the contract, the
defendant repudiated his undertaking since his agent had double-
booked him. The plaintiffs tried to find a substitute within the limited
time remaining in the rather tight production schedule but, this proving impossible, abandoned the production.

Since the plaintiffs were plainly in no position to prove the profits
that would have arisen from a speculative venture of this kind, they
sought instead to recover their expenditure and were allowed to do so.
They did not seek to formulate a damages claim for the loss of an
opportunity to secure the services of another actor, so their claim was
not as expansive as a reliance claim is capable of becoming. The defendant argued that expenditure incurred before the contract could not be
recovered in this way, because it was incurred by the plaintiffs for

---

[146] [1939] Ch 588, at 593.   [147] 51 SW 2d 572 (1932).   [148] [1972] 1 QB 60.
[149] *Pace* Mason CJ and Dawson J in *The Commonwealth* v *Amann Aviation Pty Ltd* (1991) 174
CLR 64, not Oliver Reed but an American actor, deceased in 1993, prominent for his roles in
television serials like *The Defenders* (a lawyer fearlessly righting wrongs) and *The Brady
Bunch*.

their own benefit at a time when it was uncertain whether a contract would be forthcoming to redeem the expenditure. As expressed, the argument does not explicitly deny the plaintiff's reliance on the defendant at the time of expenditure and, indeed, the word 'reliance' is not mentioned in the judgment of the Court of Appeal delivered by Lord Denning. Asserting that it did not lie in the breaching defendant's mouth to say the expenditure was wasted because of his own breach, and concluding that it was within the contemplation of the defendant at the contract date that expenditure would already have been incurred and would be wasted if the contract were breached, the court granted the plaintiffs their precontractual expenses.

The award in *Anglia Television* has been criticized[150] on the ground that most of the expenses were not incurred in reliance on the defendant's undertaking: there was no causal relation between precontractual expenses and the contract.[151] Against that, it can he argued that the statement of the plaintiff's case as based upon the reliance interest, rather than for example upon the expenditure or investment interest,[152] sets discussion off in the wrong direction. A related criticism advanced against the *Anglia Television* decision is that the award of damages did not so much put the plaintiffs back in the precontractual position as in the position they occupied before incurring the first items of expense.[153] If, indeed, the purpose of awards of this kind is to vindicate the reliance interest as a true alternative to expectation recovery, it is hard to answer this criticism, which however is tempered by its author to allow for recovery where expenditure is incurred at a time when the parties have arrived at a '*substantial agreement*'.[154] This meets the case of formal contracts, such as those for the sale of land, where the parties, although not yet legally committed, have reached a point where the bulk of parties in their position go forward to conclude a binding agreement.[155] Recovery here might in certain cases be justified on the ground that expenses were requested by the defendant. In some cases, the defendant may merely have known that they were being incurred and in others only that they might be incurred. So the only difference is between cases where the parties had

---

[150] AI Ogus, 'Damages for Pre-Contract Expenditure' (1972) 35 MLR 423.

[151] See *Security Stove & Mfg Co* v *American Railway Express Co* 51 SW 2d 572 (1932), however, where the court allowed the recovery of precontractual expenses on the ground that the defendant was a common carrier whom the plaintiffs knew could be called upon to carry their equipment.

[152] The Germans call it the negative interest as opposed to the positive (or expectation) interest, terminology used by Steyn LJ in *Surrey County Council* v *Bredero Homes Ltd* [1993] 1 WLR 1361.

[153] AI Ogus, 'Damages for Pre-Contract Expenditure' (1972) 35 MLR 423, 424–5.

[154] *Ibid.*, 425 (emphasis in original).   [155] See *Lloyd* v *Stanbury* [1971] 1 WLR 535.

not yet reached this stage at the time when the expenses were incurred. It is not easy to see why the line has to be drawn here, unless one infers a collateral pre-contract by one party to answer for the expenses of the other in the event of the main contract being concluded and then breached. This would be a nakedly instrumentalist response to the problem, rather than an outcome flowing from a neutral description of the parties' dealings.

The crux of this problem is really which of these two parties should bear the forensic price for an inchoate factual pattern which does not permit either of them to show that there would or would not have been profits made by the plaintiff from the contract. In the famous duck hunting case of *Cook* v *Lewis*,[156] one of the judges in the Canadian Supreme Court justified the imposition on each of the two defendants of the burden of proving it was not he who fired the injurious shot on the ground that it was owing to their fault in firing in the proximity of the plaintiff that he was unable to prove which of them did it.[157] Similarly, it can be argued that the plaintiffs' forensic embarrassment in *Anglia Television* is due to the defendant's repudiation of the contract. Just as the defendant in *Chaplin* v *Hicks* was compelled to pay damages for the loss of a chance, when it could only be said that the chance to participate was an item of commercial value, as the court required it to be, if one begged the question and assumed there would be damages for its loss, so the defendant in *Anglia Television* is compelled to pay the plaintiff's expenses on the ground that they are really a surrogate for the expectation recovery that the plaintiffs were prevented by the defendant from proving.[158]

Two questions follow from the above analysis. First, what happens if the contract would have yielded for the plaintiff a return less than the amount invested by the plaintiff in or for the purpose of the contract? Secondly, who carries the burden of proof of demonstrating, as the case may be, that the performance of the contract would or would not have given the plaintiffs a return that covered their investment?

As regards the first question, the governing principle is that the

---

[156] [1952] 1 DLR 1.   [157] Rand J.

[158] The treatment of reliance damages as a category of expectation recovery rather than as an independent head of damages is especially marked in *The Commonwealth* v *Amann Aviation Pty Ltd* (1991) 174 CLR 64. See, however, M Owen, 'Some Aspects of the Recovery of Reliance Damages in the Law of Contract' (1984) 4 Ox JLS 393, who refers to this rationalisation of reliance damages as a conservative view of the function of reliance; GH Treitel, 'Damages for Breach of Contract in the High Court of Australia', (1992) 108 LQR 226, 229, who regards the treatment of reliance claims as a category of expectation claims as 'a kind of verbal trick'.

Just as this approach supports the recovery of pre-contractual expenditure, so also it supports the award of damages for the initial contractual investment as well as for subsequent running costs, as was permitted in *Hayes* v *James & Charles Dodd* [1990] 2 All ER 815.

expectation interest sets the ceiling of recovery,[159] hence a reliance claim is not allowed to exceed it.[160] This principle is consistent with reliance recovery as a category of expectation damages. The principle was applied by a Canadian court in *Bowlay Logging Ltd v Domtar Ltd*[161] where the defendants failed to provide sufficient trucks to permit the plaintiffs to haul away timber felled in a particular concession granted to the plaintiffs by a third party. The plaintiffs did not claim for lost profits, but rather for expenditure incurred in providing the timber for carriage. When the defendant successfully established that the plaintiffs were losing money on the contract, Berger J refused the plaintiffs their expenses since they were seeking to recover for losses 'flowing from entering into the contract, not losses flowing from the defendant's breach'.[162] The effect of the breach was to save the plaintiffs from incurring further losses. Further, the defendants ought not to be put into the position of insuring the plaintiffs' enterprise, especially where their burden would increase in direct proportion to the inefficiency of the defendants.

The logic of this decision is hard to refute on the facts present in the *Bowlay* case. No reason was given for the defendants' breach. Suppose, however, they stood to lose even more from the performance of the contract than the plaintiffs did, and that their losses had not yet crystallized, while the plaintiffs' losses had. The outcome begins to look less compelling, although it can strongly be argued that any attempt to factor in the defendants' losses is but a negatively expressed variant of an attempt to calculate damages according to gains made by a defendant in breaking the contract. In some cases, a defendant may need to point to the terms of the contract he is repudiating in order to show that the plaintiff has made a losing contract. This encourages the tendentious response that it does not lie in his mouth to prove the plaintiff's imprudent contracting when this is to be found merely in the terms of the bargain struck with the defendant. In the *Bowlay* case itself, the defendants avoided this pitfall by pointing to the inept way that the plaintiffs felled, prepared and stacked the timber, under the

---

[159] See LL Fuller and WR Perdue, 'The Reliance Interest in Contract Damages' (1936) 46 Yale LJ 52, 79.

[160] Suppose the plaintiff elects to pursue a reliance claim where it exceeds so much of the expectation interest as is recoverable under the remoteness rule. Is the ceiling the expectation interest or the expectation interest as taxed by the remoteness rule? It is submitted the former. The fact that certain damages may not be recovered on breach does not at all mean that if the contract had been performed the plaintiff would have lost money on it. See Stone J in *R v Canamerica Auto Lease & Rental Ltd* (1987) 37 DLR (4th) 591, at 608–9. Cf. *Robophone Facilities Ltd v Blank* [1966] 1 WLR 1428 per Diplock LJ (remoteness and penalty clauses).

[161] (1978) 87 DLR (3d) 325 (British Columbia). See also *Sunshine Vacation Villas Ltd v The Bay* (1984) 13 DLR (4th) 93 where the defendant was unable to discharge the burden.

[162] *Bowlay Logging Ltd v Domtar Ltd* (1978) 87 DLR (3d) 325, at 334.

concession granted by the third party, ready for its removal by the defendants. A further difficulty with the *Bowlay* decision lies in knowing whether the principle asserted by the defendant could prevail against a plaintiff asserting a restitutionary claim. It is surely inconceivable, for example, that a defendant obtaining a substantial deposit could pocket it and refuse either to perform the contract or reimburse the deposit, on the ground that the plaintiff was being spared further contractual suffering. But how does this accord with the view that the measure of a plaintiff's damages in contract is the loss made by the plaintiff, rather than the gain made from the breach by the defendant?

The restitutionary point emerged inconclusively in *CCC Films (London) Ltd v Impact Quadrant Films Ltd*,[163] a case mainly significant for its ruling on the burden of proof. It concerned a licensing agreement permitting the plaintiffs to distribute the defendants' films in a number of named territories. The defendants were in breach of contract in failing to forward certain videos to the plaintiffs, who sought to recover the amount they paid (US $12,000) the defendants for the licence. The plaintiffs made no headway with their restitutionary claim: distribution rights had vested in them so as to prevent a failure of consideration. They were then allowed to amend their claim to seek recovery of the same amount as reliance expenditure. Although the plaintiffs' financial prospects under the licensing agreement did not look very promising, and they entered into the agreement in part for taxation rather than commercial reasons, they succeeded because of the defendants' inability to show that they would have lost money under the contract.

The court in *CCC Films* was not invited to distinguish between reliance expenditure paid to the other contracting party and reliance expenditure paid to third parties, so as to confine the *Bowlay* principle to the latter. There is no reason to suppose that such a distinction would have been accepted. Nevertheless, a plaintiff claiming the recovery of money in restitution should not be met by the defence of a losing contract: the *Bowlay* principle applies to breach of contract actions and not to restitutionary claims.[164] To refer to the above example of the pocketed deposit, it should not be extended to sanction what looks like theft. A more difficult case is the plaintiff seeking a restitutionary award for goods supplied or services rendered but, since the focus in restitution is on the defendant's gain rather than the plaintiff's

---

[163] [1985] QB 16.
[164] American Law Institute, Restatement 2d of Contracts, § 373.

loss, the same rejection of the *Bowlay* principle should apply here too[165] if the defendant has obtained an incontrovertible benefit.[166]

A more substantial discussion of the *Bowlay* principle itself is to be found in *C & P Haulage v Middleton*.[167] The appellant was granted by the respondents a 6-month licence, renewable by mutual consent, of certain industrial premises. One of the terms of the agreement was that any fixtures he put into the premises were 'to be left' upon the expiry of the licence. The appellant built a wall, fitted locks and installed electricity. Ten weeks from the end of the second term, he was peremptorily expelled from the premises. He sought to recover the expenditure he had incurred on the premises, but was unsuccessful. The Court of Appeal saw no reason why he should be better off than he would have been had the contract been duly performed by the respondents, for at the end of the second term they would have been under no obligation to renew the licence. Fox LJ referred to the 'very unsatisfactory and dangerous bargain' entered into by the appellant when he agreed to give up the fixtures. The appellant was therefore made to live with the bargain that he had made.

This highlights one of the difficulties of the case. The respondents had clearly repudiated the very bargain which they had insisted should define the appellant's damages entitlement. The provision that the fixtures be left was surely dependent on the performance by the respondents of their side of the bargain in its essential respects, at least if the general law would otherwise have provided for the fixtures to revert to the appellant at the end of the licence. If the general law were to favour the respondents, they would not need to invoke the terms of the very bargain they were repudiating to justify their entitlement to the fixtures. The alterations made by the licensee to the premises would not appear to have produced fixtures of the sort that a tenant could have removed as tenants' fixtures and there is a further area of uncertainty as to whether, even if they had been, a mere licensee would have had the same rights of removal as a tenant. Thus it seems likely that the licensor did not need the contractual term to justify his right to retain the benefit of improvements made by the licensee. Had the position on improvements been otherwise, it is submitted that the respondents should not have been allowed to show the appellant had

---

[165] *Ibid.* But see Comment *d* (reserving some discretion where the standard of good faith and fair dealing points to measuring the benefit by the contract tariff). The question whether a restitutionary award is limited by the plaintiff's expectation loss is 'closely linked to, but not precisely the same as, the question . . . whether restitution is limited by the pro rata contract price': AS Burrows, *The Law of Restitution* (1993), p 268. On the second question, the authorities on balance favour valuation off the contract tariff: *Lodder v Slowey* [1904] AC 442; *Boomer v Muir* 24 P 2d 570 (1933).

[166] AS Burrows, *The Law of Restitution* (1993, pp 268–71).   [167] [1983] 1 WLR 1461.

made an improvident contract by pointing to the terms of the very bargain they were themselves repudiating. The appellant's position in *C & P Haulage* would be no stronger, even if he were to show that there was a benefit accruing to the landlord equal to the amount of his expenditure on the premises. Unlike the case of a contractual deposit, where a payee's right to retain the money has to be justified by the terms of the contract under which it is paid if a restitution claim is to be resisted, the licensor need only invoke his ownership of the premises, and not the terms of any bargain, to justify retaining the benefit.[168]

The second of the above questions related to the burden of proof. Judge Learned Hand once said that 'it is a common expedient, and a just one ... to put the peril of the answer [to the question what the defendant's performance was worth] upon that party who by his wrong has made the issue relevant to the rights of the other'.[169] In many cases, one suspects, the defendant will be just as hard pressed to show that the contract would have made a loss as the plaintiff would be to show that it would have made a profit. Indeed, whilst a plaintiff may sometimes recover a conjectural sum for lost profits, benefiting from an assumption that the contract was entered into for profitable purposes, a defendant seeking to show that a loss would have been incurred may well be driven to support his position with some hard figures, which may have to be painfully extracted from the plaintiff by means of interrogatories or through the discovery process. Even if the plaintiff makes the particular contract without aiming to make a profit, the due performance of the contract may be but part of a larger profit-making drive. A contract to carry equipment for display at an exhibition may not have been designed to generate an immediate profit, but the plaintiffs' willingness to build up its image and trade interest in its equipment could very well have produced dividends at a later date.[170] It would be very short-sighted to describe the contract of carriage as loss-making for the purpose of reliance recovery.

As for the location of the burden, Berger J in *Bowlay* put it on the defendants and at one point spoke of a loss that would have 'inevitably' been suffered on the contract, but from his judgment overall it seems clear that he was applying the normal civil standard to the defence put forward. The High Court of Australia, in the celebrated case of *McRae v Commonwealth Disposals Commission*,[171] had earlier reversed the burden and required the defendant promising the exis-

---

[168] (1795) 6 TR 320.   [169] *L Albert & Son v Armstrong Rubber Co* 178 F 2d 182 (1949).
[170] For the facts of *Security Stove & Mfg Co v American Railway Express Co* 51 SW 2d 572 (1932), see text to note 147 above.
[171] (1951) 84 CLR 377.

tence of a non-existent wreck to prove what amounted to the impossible, namely, that the plaintiff's expenses in preparing a salvage expedition would have been wasted even if there had been in existence a wreck. The reversal of the normal burden of proof was firmly imported in English law in *CCC Films (London) Ltd v Impact Quadrant Films Ltd*[172] despite the quite vigorous argument of the defendants to the contrary.

It was the defendants' argument, advanced to avoid carrying the burden of proof, in *CCC Films* that the recovery of reliance expenditure occurred in only three categories of cases. These included cases connected with the sale of land,[173] cases where it was proved, conceded or assumed[174] that expenditure would have been recovered out of profits, and cases where it was impossible as a result of the defendant's breach to show that the plaintiff would have earned profits from the contract.[175] The third of the defendants' three categories is the most interesting because, if it is expansively interpreted, it permits a plaintiff to assert a reliance claim in precisely those cases where he should want to. But it seems to have been the defendants' assertion that a plaintiff's inability to prove loss of profits as a result of a defendant's breach would occur only where the contract in question remained executory, which it was not in the present litigation. A general difficulty in making proof of loss of profits could not necessarily be laid at the door of the breaching defendant as being caused by his breach. Hutchison J was not prepared to confine reliance claims in the way the defendants wished, and made it clear that, where such claims were maintained by a plaintiff, the defendant would bear the burden of showing that the plaintiff's expenditure would have been wasted in any event:

It seems to me that, at least in those cases where the plaintiff's decision to base his claim on abortive expenditure was dictated by the practical impossibility of proving loss of profit rather than by unfettered choice, any other rule would largely, if not entirely, defeat the object of allowing this alternative method of formulating the claim.[176]

This is consistent with the general position advanced in this chapter that the law eases the burden placed on a plaintiff of proving loss in

---

[172] [1985] QB 16.

[173] *Wallington v Townsend* [1939] Ch 588; *Lloyd v Stanbury* [1971] 1 WLR 535.

[174] The defendants' own contesting of the plaintiffs' claim showed that it was not conceded that the plaintiffs could claim reliance, and the reference to 'assumed' was designed to take account of *Cullinane v British 'Rema' Mfg Co Ltd* [1954] 1 QB 292 where the point had not been taken.

[175] The cited cases were *McRae v Commonwealth Disposals Commission* (1951) 84 CLR 377 and *Anglia TV v Reed* [1972] 1 QB 60.

[176] *CCC Films Ltd v Impact Quadrant Films Ltd* [1985] QB 16, at 40.

various ways where it is the defendant's breach of contract which puts the plaintiff in a difficult forensic position.

CCC Films has not, however, said the last word on the subject of the burden of proof. In *The Commonwealth v Amann Aviation Pty Ltd*,[177] the High Court of Australia was divided between those judges who thought that the (presumably legal) burden of proof lay on the appellant when the respondent was claiming reliance damages[178] and those who more specifically asserted that the appellant's burden was an evidentiary one. If reliance recovery is, as the majority thought, an alternative expression of the expectation principle, which is a conclusion that is difficult to avoid in a legal system where reliance is rarely an independent damages-driven head of liability, there seems no reason to reverse the legal burden of proof in this but not in other cases of damages liability.[179] A plaintiff claiming expectation damages in their direct form may benefit from a benevolent assumption of profitability when awarded a conjectural sum, but this is not the same thing as a reversed burden of proof. A minority of judgments in the case favoured an evidentiary burden on the appellant,[180] supported by the idea that the appellant's breach impeded the plaintiff in the proof of its expectancy.[181] This is commendably flexible, and truer to the genius of the common law in its recognition of the interplay of substantive and procedural law.

One member of the court was prepared to take the transfer of the burden further than the others, who would all have discounted the respondent's reliance damages in recognition of the possibility that the contract might not have been renewed at the end of the three-year period. This judge, in the absence of proof from the appellant that a discounted expectancy award would be worth less than the sum of the respondent's reliance expenditure, would not have discounted the latter at all. There is a remorseless logic at work here but the overall position—a transfer of the burden of proof coupled with reliance damages for the lost factual expectation of a contract renewal—appears to give the respondent too much, and to come perilously close to penalizing the appellant for the breach of contract.

---

[177] (1991) 174 CLR 64.
[178] Mason CJ, Dawson, Brennan (provided the contract is rescinded for breach—sed quaere?), and Deane JJ.
[179] See the judgment of Toohey *ibid.*, at 137–8, and McHugh J, at 166.
[180] Toohey and Gaudron JJ. McHugh J (*ibid.*, at 165) was not even prepared to subscribe to an evidentiary presemption, on the ground that commercial contracts do not invariably yield a profit (sed quaere?).
[181] See particularly McHugh J *ibid.*, at 166.

Conclusion

A variety of topics has been discussed in this chapter, all united by the theme that the law protects future personal interests, arising typically, but not invariably, in contract, which as a result of the defendant's breach of duty never mature into present interests. Compensation is not an exact science, and pragmatic justice will always be preferred by the common law to conceptual purity when the two are in conflict. Where the defendant's breach has caused a loss but the future element in this loss, which the defendant's breach prevents us from defining, means that it cannot be accurately computed, it is better to award a sum of money conjecturally assessed, rather than to allow the plaintiff's loss to go uncompensated. The aim of the law in this area of damages awards is not to promote general deterrence of breaches of duty, although it may in practice achieve this, nor is it to promote a punitive principle. Rather, we see expressed in these awards the law's firm commitment to the expectation principle in its satisfaction with a less than stringent observance of the usual civil rules of proof. This expectation focus is consistent too with its rejection of the award of restitutionary damages in contract. Contract is a legal institution which encourages individuals to commit themselves to change.

As strongly as the expectation interest stands out in these damages cases, the legal system does not allow damages claimants to sit on their rights and demand future support from wrongdoers. Rules of remoteness of damage and mitigation of damages curb the more extravagant expressions of a plaintiff's loss, and promote the values of a society of individuals. An open-ended commitment by the law to compensation without limit would encourage a backward-looking preoccupation with loss, rather than an active determination to move forward positively from the defendant's breach. The rules discussed in this chapter provide a safety net for injured individuals, not a guaranteed future.

18

The Choice of Remedy for Breach of Contract*

SM WADDAMS

Anglo-American law leans towards a preference for money compensation as a remedy for breach of contract. This preference is not quite so strong as is sometimes suggested: in land sale contracts, specific performance is available as a matter of course, and in some other classes of case specific performance is readily granted. There has been a trend in recent years towards a greater readiness to grant specific performance. However, in general, the preference may be conceded: money damages are available as of right, whereas specific performance is not.

This feature of Anglo-American law is often contrasted with the position in civil law systems. Thus, speaking of Scottish law, Lord Watson said:

In England the only legal right arising from a breach of contract is a claim of damages; specific performance is not matter of legal right, but a purely equitable remedy, which the Court can withhold when there are sufficient reasons of conscience or expediency against it. But in Scotland the breach of a contract for the sale of a specific subject such as landed estate, gives the party aggrieved the legal right to sue for implement, and, although he may elect to do so, he cannot be compelled to resort to the alternative of an action of damages unless implement is shewn to be impossible. . . . I do not doubt that the Court of Session has inherent power to refuse the legal remedy upon equitable grounds, although I know of no instance in which it has done so.[1]

Comparative law, however, is a treacherous enterprise, and it would be very rash for a common law reader to assume an adequate understanding of Scottish law on the basis of these words of Lord Watson. The danger of leaping to conclusions is apparent from looking at a brief extract from a modern academic work on Scottish law:

Cases where specific implement not granted. Though a claim for decree of specific implement is a general right there are a number of circumstances where the court will normally not grant such a decree. These are:
(a) where the requirement is only to pay money . . .

---

* Copyright © 1994, SM Waddams
[1] *Stewart v Kennedy* (1890) 15 App Cas 75, at 102–3 (HL (Sc)).

(b) where the contract involves a personal or intimate relationship . . .

(c) where there is no *pretium affectionis* or special quality attaching to the particular subject of contract, as in the case of generic goods, where the disappointed buyer can be adequately compensated with damages . . .

(d) where compliance with the decree would be impossible . . . The same may apply where implement would cause great public inconvenience.

(e) where the decree would be unenforceable . . .

(f) where in the circumstances the grant of decree would cause exceptional hardship, or it would be inconvenient and unjust to grant it.

(g) generally where the court decides in its discretion that damages are quite sufficient and appropriate in the circumstances . . .[2]

It is clear from this list that Scottish courts have power to reach identical results to those reached by English courts; it might even be the case, so far as Professor Walker's list of exceptions indicates, that in practice specific implement is refused in Scotland in circumstances where specific performance would be decreed in England.

Similar caution is needed in drawing conclusions about other legal systems, where, even though a list like Professor Walker's is not available to the casual searcher, there may be a similar, perhaps unwritten, set of understandings which in practice restrict an apparent right to specific performance. In Quebec law, for example, specific performance of an obligation may be demanded 'in cases which admit of it' ('*dans les cas qui le permettent*').[3] It is very difficult to know, without an intimate knowledge of Quebec law and practice, what is meant by that phrase.

Scotland and Quebec have both been influenced by the common law, and it may be that they are not typical of civilian systems. In other civil law systems, however, there also seems to be room at least for doubt. Professor Treitel has written that the difference between German, French and common law approaches 'is probably more marked in theoretical approach than in practical effect'.[4] Of German law, he says that the 'exceptions are far more important than the general rule'.[5] In French law, orders of the court in contract cases are not enforced by imprisonment, but only by money penalties, which the court has a discretion to remit, taking into account 'the debtor's conduct, his resources, and other circumstances'.[6] Professor Ogus comments cautiously (of French and English law) that

---

[2] DM Walker, *The Law of Contracts and related obligations in Scotland* (2nd ed 1985) s 33.21.

[3] Civil Code of Quebec, art 1601. The former Quebec code had a similar provision.

[4] GH Treitel, 'Remedies for Breach of Contract', *Int Enc Comp L VII Contracts in General* (1976), ch 16, s 16–10.

[5] *Ibid.*, s 16–14.

[6] D Tallon, 'Remedies 2: French Report' in D Harris and D Tallon (eds), *Contract Law Today: Anglo-French Comparisons* (1989) pp 263, 269.

[7] A Ogus, 'Remedies 1: English Report' In D Harris and D Tallon (eds), *Contract Law Today: Anglo-French Comparisons* (1989) p 243.

'there is evidence that in practice the systems converge to some extent'.[7] All in all, there seems to be a warning here against accepting without qualification the assertion sometimes heard that specific performance is available as of right in civilian systems. In some systems, doctrines such as good faith or abuse of rights may prevent the use of specific performance in circumstances where it would be oppressive to the defendant.

Some writers have argued in favour of a general right to specific performance in Anglo-American law.[8] This idea is sometimes supported by the proposition that '[t]he purpose of contract remedies is to place a disappointed promisee in as good a position as he would have enjoyed had his promisor performed'.[9] This proposition sounds at first attractive, and even axiomatic, because it seems to echo well-known statements, such as that:

where any injury is to be compensated by damages, in settling the sum of money to be given for reparation of damages you should as nearly as possible get at that sum of money which will put the party who has been injured . . . in the same position as he would have been in if he had not sustained the wrong for which he is now getting his compensation or reparation[10]

or, in reference to breach of contract:

[t]he rule of the common law is, that where a party sustains a loss by reason of a breach of contract, he is, so far as money can do it, to be placed in the same situation, with respect to damages, as if the contract had been performed.[11]

But these two statements are not at all the same as the proposition mentioned earlier. The judicial statements quoted here lay down rules for measuring damages; they say nothing about the choice between damages and specific performance, and the last-quoted statement is of a common law judge before the union of the courts of law and equity, and specifically restricted to the common law. It is one thing to say that, in measuring damages, the appropriate amount of the award is that which puts the plaintiff in the position that would have been occupied if the contract had been performed; it is quite another thing to say that, in selecting the appropriate remedy, that remedy should be chosen that will put the plaintiff in the position which he would have occupied had the contract been performed. The latter proposition cannot be accepted without heavy qualification.

Then it is sometimes said that, since specific performance is available when damages are inadequate, the plaintiff should be allowed to choose,

---

[8] FH Lawson, *Remedies of English Law* (2nd ed, 1980) p 211; A Schwartz, 'The Case for Specific Performance' (1979) 89 Yale LJ 271.

[9] A Schwartz, *ibid.*, 271.

[10] *Livingstone* v *Rawyards Coal Co* (1980) 5 App Cas 25, at 39 (HL (Sc)), per Lord Blackburn.

[11] *Robinson* v *Harman* (1848) 1 Ex 850, at 855; 154 ER 363, at 365, per Parke B.

and the very choice of specific performance would establish that damages were inadequate for this plaintiff.[12] I do not think that this can be accepted, unless 'inadequate' is defined to mean 'such as the plaintiff does not choose'. The plaintiff will choose specific performance when, at the time the choice is made, this seems advantageous to the plaintiff. Of course, if the law gives plaintiffs a new right, they will exercise it when it is advantageous to do so. But this does not establish that it is desirable, or just, to extend the plaintiff's rights in the first place. Often, too, the plaintiff's motive will be to extract money from the defendant in exchange for forgoing the right to specific performance. So where (as in an important class of cases under consideration) the cost to the defendant of performance is substantially greater than the benefit of performance to the plaintiff, the plaintiff will have a strong incentive to demand specific performance, not because the plaintiff wants actual performance, but because the plaintiff wants the defendant to pay money as the price of release from the obligation, that amount approaching the cost to the defendant of performance, not the benefit of it to the plaintiff. It is inadequate to suggest that good-natured plaintiffs will not do such things. If they are entitled by law to such an advantage they will, quite properly, derive what benefit the law allows, and their advisers will, again quite properly, tell them to do so. It is for the law to fashion a remedy in such a way as to do justice to both parties, not, as was said in an analogous context, 'to deliver over the Defendants to the Plaintiff bound hand and foot, in order to be made subject to any extortionate demand that he may by possibility make'.[13]

Some influential writers have taken the view that the fundamental purpose of contract law is the protection of reliance. Professor Fuller, though defending the 'expectation' measure of damages, rested his defence on the basis that the more fundamental purpose of the law was to protect reliance.[14] More recently, Professor Atiyah has doubted the expectation measure of damages itself,[15] and Professor Gilmore has suggested that contract is being reabsorbed into tort law.[16] There is also a strong body of support for the view that, where a gratuitous promise is enforced, the proper measure of enforcement should aim at protection only of the plain-

[12] See A Schwartz, 'The Case for Specific Performance' (1979) 89 Yale LJ 271, 277.
[13] *Isenberg v East India House Estate Co Ltd* (1863) 3 De GJ & S 263, at 273; 46 ER 637, at 641, per Lord Westbury LC.
[14] LL Fuller and WR Perdue, 'The reliance interest in contract damages' (1936) 46 Yale LJ 52.
[15] PS Atiyah, *The Rise and Fall of Freedom of Contract* (1979).
[16] G Gilmore, *The Death of Contract* (1974).
[17] See Restatement of 2d Contracts, vol 1, § 90, and the remarks of Lord Denning MR in *Crabb v Arun District Council* [1976] Ch 179, at 189–90. The right to resume strict rights on reasonable notice after a gratuitous promise to forgo them is another technique of protecting reliance but not expectation. There are admittedly some cases in which specific performance of gratuitous promises has been decreed, but in my opinion these cases give too generous a remedy to the plaintiff.

tiff's reliance, not of the plaintiff's expectation.[17] This is not the occasion for a full discussion of the reliance theory of contracts, but the fact that the theory is widely held, and that it is widely recognized that there are some kinds of contractual obligations that require enforcement only to the extent of protection of reliance, show that there is nothing 'natural' or 'perfect' or fundamentally 'proper' about specific performance. If, in truth, the fundamental purpose of contract law is to protect reliance, that is, to put the plaintiff in the position that the plaintiff would have occupied if the contract had not been made, it must follow that specific performance should be very rarely available, for seldom would it be necessary to enforce a contract in order to protect the plaintiff's reliance.

Another argument in support of a general right to specific performance is based on restitution. It is argued that a defendant should not profit from breach of contract, and that a right of specific performance will prevent such a profit. The restitutionary question has been extensively discussed elsewhere by several contributors to this book, including myself.[18] This is not the occasion for an extended discussion of the point, but I do not think that a general principle of restitution for profits made in breach of contract can be supported. In the case of personal services, few would argue for such a right. If a person contracts to paint the outside of my house, but then in breach of contract does valuable work for a third party instead, there is no principle on which I am entitled to the value of the work, or the amount the defendant receives for it; if I can get my house painted for the contract price or less, I have suffered no loss. The proper money award, in such a case, is nominal, and I would not be entitled either to a decree of specific performance, or to an injunction restraining the defendant from accepting the third party's commission.[19]

Even in the case of a contract that is not for personal services, for example a building contract, I am doubtful if there is a general right to restitution of benefits derived from breach of contract. Suppose that specifications for a building contract call for the use of a certain material, let us say concrete foundations, and the builder, in breach of contract, uses a cheaper but better material, saving money, but delivering a building better in all material respects than that promised. The argument has been

---

[18] D Friedmann, 'Restitution of Benefits Obtained Through the Appropriation of Property or the Commission of a Wrong' (1980) 80 Colum L Rev 504; EA Farnsworth, 'Your Loss or My Gain? The Dilemma of the Disgorgement Principle in Breach of Contract' (1985) 94 Yale LJ 1339; J Beatson, 'What Can Restitution Do for You?' (1989) 2 JCL 65; SM Waddams, 'Restitution as Part of Contract Law' in A Burrows (ed), *Essays on the Law of Restitution* (1991); P Birks, 'Restitutionary Damages for Breach of Contract' [1987] LMCLQ 421; AS Burrows, *Remedies for Torts and Breach of Contract* (2nd ed 1994) p 310.

[19] I assume that *Lumley v Wagner* (1852) 1 De G M & G 604; 42 ER 687 and *Warner Bros v Nelson* [1937] 1 KB 209 would not apply where the services promised to the plaintiff were not unique or irreplaceable. I leave aside the question of an action against the third party for inducing breach of contract.

made, and with some force, that the owner should be entitled to the money saved, but I am not convinced. If the plaintiff had the power to require the defendant to demolish the building and to rebuild it precisely as promised, of course the plaintiff would be able to compel the defendant to pay over the amount saved, and probably much more. But this does not establish that the plaintiff should have such a right, and damages are not usually measured on that basis.[20] As Professor Sharpe has said:

The argument that the defendant should be required to share with the plaintiff the profit made from breach has not been accepted. Even if it were, making specific performance generally available would be an ineffective and inappropriate way to bring about that objective.[21]

There are cases holding that where the plaintiff is entitled to specific performance (the typical case is a purchase of land) and the defendant profits by selling the land to a third party, the plaintiff is entitled to those profits.[22] The reasoning here is that, since the plaintiff has a right to specific performance the plaintiff has an actual right to become the owner of the land and so, in a sense, already has a proprietary interest in the land. The plaintiff can attach the profits because the land is the plaintiff's, and so the profits are the plaintiff's too. Another way of putting the matter is to say that the defendant circumvents the plaintiff's right to bargain, but this is an apt characterization only when the defendant breaks a contract that is specifically enforceable, or engages in conduct that could have been restrained by injunction.[23]

There is, as often, a circularity here. The plaintiff can attach the profits made by breach of contract if there is a proprietary interest; there is a proprietary interest if there is a right to specific performance; there is a right to specific performance if it is appropriate that a proprietary interest should be recognized. But a circularity in legal reasoning does not establish that it is empty of content, nor does the demonstration of such a circularity in this context establish that the plaintiff should always have a right to specific performance and a proprietary interest.

Let us consider again a contract for personal services. If the plaintiff could get specific performance, then the plaintiff could force the defendant to perform, to pay the price demanded by the plaintiff for release, and to attach any profits made by the breach of contract. If this were permitted it might well be said that the plaintiff had something like a proprietary interest in the defendant's services. This conclusion is intolerable, for it would permit a kind of contractual servitude, and that is one reason

---

[20] See *Jacob & Youngs Inc v Kent* 230 NY 239, 129 NE 889 (1921).

[21] RJ Sharpe, *Injunctions and Specific Performance* (2nd ed 1992) s 7.150.

[22] *Lake v Bayliss* [1974] 1 WLR 1073.

[23] See RJ Sharpe and SM Waddams, 'Damages for lost opportunity to bargain' (1982) 2 Ox JLS 290.

why we know that the premise must be false, and why the law almost never gives a right to specific performance against one who promises to render personal services.

There is another aspect of this circularity. We usually assume that a contractual obligation is a single kind of obligation, and that a breach of contract is a single kind of legal wrong. From this starting point it can be made to seem anomalous that there should be two different kinds of remedy. But is it so clear that all contracts give rise to the same kind of obligation? Right and remedy are intertwined. The maxim *ubi ius ibi remedium* can be read in two ways: the right is first established and the remedy follows; or, there is no right at all unless there is a remedy. Some agreements give rise to an obligation that is specifically enforceable. Others give rise to an obligation to pay money in case of breach. These are very different obligations. Why should they both be called by the same name? If, as I suggest is logically quite possible, we had different names for the two kinds of obligation, the case for a general right to specific performance would disappear entirely.

A comparison with tort might be permitted at this point. There too the general objective of the law might be said to be to put the party complaining in the position that that party would have occupied if the wrong had not been done,[24] but no one suggests that tortfeasors should be required to make specific reparation, or even (generally speaking) specific restitution. Even in cases where an injunction restraining tortious conduct is usually available, it is not available as of right.[25] So long as that position obtains in tort, the case for a general right to specific performance of contracts must be weak, for no reason has been advanced for treating a contract-breaker more harshly than a tortfeasor.

The principle of mitigation requires the plaintiff to act reasonably so as to minimize loss caused by breach of contract. Often this means purchasing substitute performance at the lowest price available. A right to specific performance is not consistent with a duty to mitigate by purchasing substitute performance. If the plaintiff has a right to actual performance by the defendant precisely as promised, the plaintiff cannot at the same time have a duty to seek a substitute. A right to specific performance displaces the duty of mitigation and this, I suggest, would be undesirable as a general rule. Mitigation has the effect of reducing the cost of a breach of contract to the two parties jointly. It is the rule that sensible parties would agree on in advance, not knowing which of them was likely to be in breach of contract.

One aspect of mitigation concerns cases of anticipatory repudiation. If

---

[24] See *Livingstone* v *Rawyards Coal Co* (1880) 5 App Cas 25.
[25] See *Isenberg* v *East India House Estate Co Ltd* (1863) 3 De G J & S 263, 46 ER 637; *Miller* v *Jackson* [1977] QB 966; *Redland Bricks Ltd* v *Morris* [1970] AC 652, and the application of Lord Cairns' Act and its equivalent in various jurisdictions.

the defendant contracts for the performance of a service, and then repudiates the contract in advance of performance, it is generally thought that the plaintiff ought to mitigate loss and accept money compensation. It is true that, in one Scottish case, the House of Lords held that in such circumstances the pursuer was entitled to render the unwanted performance and to recover the resulting contractual debt.[26] But the result has been generally criticized, and was denounced by one of the dissenting judges as 'a kind of inverted specific implement',[27] specific implement itself being unavailable in the circumstances under Scottish law, because the defender's obligation was only to pay money. Recognition of a general right to specific performance would enable the plaintiff in such cases not only to continue an unwanted performance, but to obtain a decree of the court entitling the plaintiff to do so and requiring the defendant also to perform in full. Even if such a result were acceptable on the facts of the case just mentioned, which involved a commercial contract to advertise, there are many cases in which all would concede that such an order would be wholly inappropriate. The example of a patient agreeing to surgery and later revoking the decision may be considered extravagant. A less dramatic case, but one where specific performance, I would suggest, is equally inappropriate, is the case of a defendant agreeing to have work done on property (eg cleaning, repair, alteration, or restoration) or commissioning an elaborate report and then revoking the decision before performance.[28]

The absence of a right to specific performance often has the effect of reducing the cost of breach to the two parties jointly. In the case of a dispute over a sale of commercial goods, for example, it is very costly to keep the goods tied up pending the resolution of the dispute. Consider a disputed sale of perishable goods, for example a farmer's crop, where court orders restraining dealing might well cause losses far greater than the amounts in dispute. It makes commercial sense for the goods to be sold while they are saleable, and for the seller to pay money to the buyer if subsequently found to be in breach of contract. The same is true, in a lesser degree, of non-perishable goods, such as a shipload of timber, or a car in a showroom, because storage of goods is always costly. It is not an adequate answer to suggest that plaintiffs, if given the right to restrain dealing by the defendant, would exercise the right reasonably. Plaintiffs will use to their advantage such rights as the law gives them, as is plainly shown by the use of certificates of pending litigation in land sale cases.

[26] *White & Carter (Councils) Ltd* v *McGregor* [1962] AC 413 (HL (Sc)).

[27] *Ibid.*, 433, per Lord Morton.

[28] See *Clark* v *Marsiglia* 43 Am Dec 670 (NYSC, 1843); *Finelli* v *Dee* (1968) 67 DLR (2d) 393; and the hypothetical example discussed by Lord Reid in *White & Carter (Councils) Ltd* v *McGregor* [1962] AC 413, at 431.

It may be said of these cases that the defendant, being a wrongdoer, has only herself to blame if she suffers. But this reflects a punitive attitude, and, more importantly, it neglects the consideration that the typical case is not one of deliberate breach. Often there is a genuine dispute between the parties as to liability (eg contract formation, mistake, frustration, or purported termination for alleged breach). These are potentially complex questions, and there is no basis for saying that the defendant, even if ultimately the losing party, has necessarily acted unreasonably in disputing the case.

It is usually costly to prolong the relationship between hostile parties. A money remedy has the advantage of cutting the parties free from each other's affairs, a result that is generally advantageous in case of a dispute. Compelling the parties to work together when they have lost confidence in each other is costly both to the community[29] and to the two parties jointly. Moreover, a right to specific performance often means that one party has a strong interest in decisions made by the other (eg a buyer's decision to purchase substitute property on a rising market, or an owner's decision to make repairs to deteriorating property). There is merit in 'crystallizing' the parties' rights, leaving each party free to pursue her or his own interests pending the resolution of the dispute, with compensation to be paid by the losing party in money.[30]

In very many cases—probably in the vast majority in which the courts are called upon to enforce contracts—the defendant's obligation is to pay money. There is a useful analogy to be drawn between a decree of specific performance and the enforcement of a debt, but there is an important difference between them: contempt proceedings are not available for the enforcement of debts. Is it desirable that they should be? The answer to this question must surely be in the negative. The reintroduction of imprisonment for debt through contempt proceedings must be out of the question.[31] Even assuming that imprisonment is not available, however, there remain other methods of enforcing court orders such as fines, sequestration, and denial of access to the court, which are not appropriate in the ordinary case of non-payment of a debt. It is doubtful that the ordinary debtor should be stigmatized as contumacious. It would not be acceptable for a creditor to gain an advantage over other creditors, in case of the debtor's insolvency, by resorting to contempt proceedings. In land sale

---

[29] One aspect of this is the court's reluctance to decree a performance which will require supervision.

[30] See *Asamera Oil Corpn Ltd v Sea Oil and General Corpn* [1979] 1 SCR 633; *Dodd Properties (Kent) Ltd v Canterbury City Council* [1980] 1 WLR 433.

[31] In most jurisdictions the statutes restricting imprisonment for debt probably also restrict the power of the court to imprison for contempt. See *Esdaile v Visser* (1880) 13 Ch D 421, but the statutes vary from jurisdiction to jurisdiction, and the question is not free from doubt. See *Corbin on Contracts*, vol 5A, s 1147.

cases, specific performance is regularly decreed in favour of the vendor, although the purchaser's obligation is only to pay money. The effect is to make available the sanctions for contempt of court to enforce what is in substance a debt, and to excuse the vendor from any obligation to mitigate the loss by reselling the land. In some cases, especially where possession has been transferred, the purchaser will be in a better position to resell, but in many other cases this will be more easily done by the vendor. For these reasons, among others, Professor Sharpe has suggested that the vendor of land should no longer have an automatic right to specific performance.[32]

One of the grounds recognized at present for refusing a decree of specific performance, even where otherwise appropriate, is that the defendant would be left without adequate security for the plaintiff's return performance. This would become a serious problem if specific performance were generally available as of right. In the case of a long term contract, a decree of specific performance would have the effect of attaching penal sanctions over an extended period of time to breaches of contract on one side only. If, as is common in long-term contracts, co-operation between the parties had been anticipated to deal with circumstances not precisely foreseen at the time of the contract, the effect of a decree of specific performance would be drastically to alter the nature of the relationship between the parties, making every dispute an occasion of potential penal consequences to one of the parties only, and would deprive that party of the important power to withhold performance in response to an alleged breach by the other party.

There have been a number of recent English cases on the problem of consideration in contract modification, the tendency of the cases being to enforce promises to render an extra performance, even without consideration, in the absence of duress or unconscionability. This is not the occasion for an extended discussion of these cases, but their clear implication is that, in some circumstances at least, it is permissible for a party to a contract to gain an advantage by threatening breach.[33] This conclusion must assume that the contract is not specifically enforceable, for, if it were, the innocent party would rarely have to submit to such a threat. Where, under present law, a breach of contract might be restrained by injunction, for example a threat to reveal confidential information, or a threat by a lessor to deprive a tenant of the tenant's home, there would be a strong case for arguing that a party ought not to profit by threatening such a breach. But the implication of the recent English cases is that not all contracts are to be so treated, and the notion that all contracts are specifically enforceable

---

[32] RJ Sharpe, *Injunctions and Specific Performance* (2nd ed 1992) s 8.220.
[33] See *Williams v Roffey Bros & Nicholls (Contractors) Ltd* [1991] 1 QB 1 (CA), discussed by M Chen-Wishert, ch 5 above.

would, in my opinion, run directly counter to the tendency of these cases.

Some of the arguments considered above relating to reducing the cost of breach of contract might be called economic arguments. More generally, economists have argued in favour of the present law on the basis of what is called 'efficient breach', the notion being that, if specific performance is refused, the parties jointly are better off: the plaintiff is put in as good a position as if the contract had been performed, and the defendant is better off, as is shown by the decision to break the contract. Although I agree with the general conclusion that this leads to, I am inclined to think that the argument itself is inconclusive. The economist's concept of efficiency takes no account of the division of wealth between the parties, and economists also generally assume that the parties can and will bargain for the result they prefer. If this is so, giving the plaintiff a right to specific performance will not be 'inefficient', because the parties will bargain, and the defendant will pay money for release from the obligation. There is then no 'inefficiency'; the 'wasteful' performance does not occur. All that happens is that the plaintiff becomes wealthier at the expense of the defendant, a consequence that economists generally say is not their concern. But, as suggested above, where the cost of performance greatly exceeds the benefit of performance to the plaintiff, the consequence of a right to specific performance will be to enrich the plaintiff at the defendant's expense, and the justice of this result must be of concern to lawyers.

Another economic argument is that the present law represents the usual preference of rational contracting parties, and that it therefore promotes efficiency by reducing the costs of negotiating contracts.[34] I agree with this argument as far as it goes, but like all tests based on hypothetical preferences it is not wholly independent of general considerations of justice, for what will be preferred by hypothetical rational parties is not very different from what, in the writer's opinion, is required by justice.[35]

Breach of contract is not normally punishable either as a crime, or by the award of exemplary damages. This may be said to reflect a general view that breach of contract, while a wrong, is not so serious a threat to the social order as to require punishment. Though, as I have said, I am sceptical about 'efficient breach', I would accept that a certain amount of freedom to break contracts is socially desirable. Few would consider it morally objectionable for a business person to discontinue the business, provided that the discontinuation were coupled with an offer to pay money compensation for any unfulfilled contractual obligations. The

---

[34] AT Kronman, 'Specific Performance' (1978) 45 U Chi L Rev 351.
[35] See Lord Radcliffe in *Davis Contractors Ltd v Fareham Urban District Council* [1956] AC 696, at 728.

attachment of penal consequences to conduct has its own costs. The reluctance to decree specific enforcement of contracts, although it is not a necessary consequence of the refusal to attach penal consequences to breach, springs from the same root.

Some of the arguments in favour of a right to specific performance are based on the inadequate nature of compensatory damages. One answer to this line of argument would be that, if, in any case, compensatory damages are shown to be inadequate, whether because of the operation of the rules of remoteness or because of the reluctance to compensate certain kinds of loss, the solution is to increase the award of damages, and in several areas the scope of recoverable damages has increased.[36] However, there will always be cases where it is difficult to estimate and quantify damages and this difficulty is one of the traditional reasons in favour of granting specific performance. There is good reason why these considerations should be applied to new cases.

There have been a number of recent cases in which the courts have extended specific performance beyond what were formerly thought to be its limits. One example is *Beswick* v *Beswick*[37] where the House of Lords decreed specific performance of a contract to pay money to a third party. Specific performance has also been ordered of a landlord's obligation to provide services to a tenant,[38] and of the obligation of a supplier of motor fuel to continue supply at a time of shortage.[39] In all these cases specific performance was decreed because damages were not considered to be a satisfactory remedy.

Where there is an express agreement between the parties there is a case to be made for a greater willingness than the courts now manifest to enforce the parties' own selection of remedy, whether this takes the form of an agreement to pay liquidated damages or a recognition that a decree of specific enforcement is appropriate. Even here, however, there can be no absolute right to a specific remedy: a burden that seemed light at the time of the agreement may turn out to be unexpectedly onerous to the defendant at the time for performance, or to require an unacceptable degree of supervision on the part of the court. For these reasons the court can never put it out of its own power to determine the justice of such orders at the time they are issued.

---

[36] For example, intangible losses were held to be recoverable in *Jarvis* v *Swans Tours Ltd* [1973] QB 233, followed and extended in many Canadian cases; losses that the plaintiff cannot mitigate because of impecuniosity are recoverable, if not too remote; *General Securities Ltd* v *Don Ingram Ltd* [1940] SCR 670, *Trans Trust SPRL* v *Danubian Trading Co Ltd* [1952] 2 QB 297.

[37] [1968] AC 58. [38] *Posner* v *Scott-Lewis* [1987] Ch 25.

[39] *Sky Petroleum Ltd* v *VIP Petroleum Ltd* [1974] 1 WLR 576. A series of nineteenth-century Canadian cases similarly decreed specific performance of sale contracts where substitutes were not available; see for example *Farwell* v *Wallbridge* (1851) 2 Gr 332.

In many common law jurisdictions, power is given to courts or to arbitrators to order reinstatement of employees wrongfully dismissed, and in a few cases courts have done this in the absence of any specific legislative authority.[40] But the courts have not accepted any principle that such orders are available as of right, and it is almost certain that a specific order would be refused in a case where the plaintiff was employed in a confidential capacity, and mutual confidence had been lost.[41]

The cases referred to above show that the courts retain flexibility, and that they continue to exercise the power to make specific orders in cases that had not previously been foreseen. To some extent also they indicate an enlargement, which may be expected to continue, of the scope for specific remedies. They do not, however, suggest that specific remedies are available as of right. Of injunctions, it has been said that '[t]he standard question . . . "Are damages an adequate remedy?", might perhaps . . . be re-written: "Is it just, in all the circumstances, that a plaintiff should be confined to his remedy in damages?" '[42] This formulation, which might be applied also to decrees of specific performance, indicates a willingness to consider specific remedies where appropriate, but it is very far from being an abandonment of the old principle that equitable remedies are discretionary. The power of the court to refuse an injunction on the ground that it would be oppressive to the defendant has been illustrated in numerous cases. A fairly recent example is a case in the English Court of Appeal, refusing an injunction against an employee to restrain him from working, contrary to his employment agreement, for a competitor of his employer.[43]

Specific remedies are orders of the court, enforced by the court, by machinery under its control, and by the strictest sanctions available to the community against its citizens; experience shows that such orders are liable to operate in ways which were not foreseen at the time of the contract, and that they are potentially oppressive to defendants and to third parties; they may impose on the court a heavy burden of supervision. In these circumstances the court cannot put out of its own ultimate control the power to refuse such orders where they would not be, in the ancient phrase, 'just or convenient'. This is fundamentally what is asserted when it is said that equitable remedies are discretionary, or that, unlike money remedies, they are never available as of right, or that they are not available unless damages are shown to be inadequate or inappropriate. I do not say

---

[40] *Hill v CA Parsons & Co Ltd* [1972] Ch 305. See also *McCaw v United Church of Canada* (1991) 82 DLR (4th) 289, where a minister of religion was ordered to be restored to the roll of ministers.

[41] See *Page One Records Ltd v Britton* [1968] 1 WLR 157 (Stamp J).

[42] *Evans Marshall & Co Ltd v Bertola SA* [1973] 1 WLR 349, 379, per Sachs LJ.

[43] *Provident Financial Group Plc v Hayward* [1989] 3 All ER 298 (CA).

that the variation in these expressions is insignificant, or that there is no difference between a greater and a lesser readiness to decree specific enforcement; but I do suggest that a distinction between money remedies and specific remedies will always be necessary.

Thus the proposition that the plaintiff should have a 'right' to specific enforcement, if it means that the court should have no discretion ever to refuse the injunction or decree, can scarcely be defended. If the proposition means that cases for refusal of the specific order should be precisely defined so as to remove all need for discretion, I think that it underestimates the difficulty of foreseeing the impact that decrees of specific enforcement will have in varied circumstances. The most that could realistically be envisaged is a prima facie right to specific enforcement, with a series of exceptions to be constructed by the courts to deal with cases where a decree or injunction would be inappropriate. But the burden of such an enterprise would be great; the uncertainty during the period of construction would be high; and the utility of the enterprise would be in doubt, because the net practical effect in most cases would be to restore the position that exists under the present law.

19

Suspending Contract Performance for Breach*

JW CARTER**

General

PERSPECTIVE

'Suspension' of performance may refer either to the suspension of one party's duty to perform or to the suspension of the duty of both parties. The reference in the title to this chapter is to the first sense of suspension. In what circumstances is one party (the plaintiff)[1] entitled to suspend its performance obligations on the basis of a breach (actual or prospective) or repudiation by the defendant? In *Channel Tunnel Group Ltd* v *Balfour Beatty Construction Ltd*[2] Staughton LJ said that although it is well established that for a serious breach a plaintiff may treat the contract as discharged, 'there is not yet any established doctrine of English law' allowing the plaintiff merely to suspend its performance.[3] The position is the same under Australian law. This paper advocates the recognition of a right to suspend performance for some forms of breach, and generally for repudiation.[4]

---

* Copyright © 1994, JW Carter

** I am grateful to Mr Justice Handley, Judge of Appeal of the Supreme Court of New South Wales and Professor DJ Harland of the University of Sydney for their comments on an earlier draft of the paper. I must also record my thanks to Anne Duffield and Greg Tolhurst for research assistance.

[1] To avoid confusion between promisor and promisee I refer to the party seeking to suspend performance as the plaintiff.

[2] [1992] 1 QB 656, at 666 (affirmed without reference to the point [1993] AC 334.

[3] In most situations where suspension occurs neither party is in default. Examples are *force majeure* clauses and suspension under statute or by reason of illegality. See, eg *Hirsch* v *The Zinc Corpn Ltd* (1917) 24 CLR 34, 65; *Tennants (Lancashire) Ltd* v *CS Wilson & Co Ltd* [1917] AC 495; *Re Nudgee Bakery Pty Ltd's Agreement* [1971] Qd R 24; *Libyan Arab Foreign Bank* v *Bankers Trust Co* [1989] QB 728. Compare cases where suspension occurs because an event for which neither party has contractual responsibility disrupts performance. See, eg *Robinson* v *Davison* (1871) LR 6 Ex 269; *Bonney* v *Hartmann* [1924] St R Qd 232.

[4] I do not wish to challenge the general rule that, in the absence of express provision, contracts are not suspended by breach or extraneous events. See *Hanley* v *Pease & Partners Ltd* [1915] 1 KB 698; *Browne* v *Commissioner for Railways* (1935) 36 SR (NSW) 21, at 23; *Cricklewood Property and Investment Trust Ltd* v *Leighton's Investment Trust Ltd* [1945] AC 221, at 232. But cf. cases where employment contracts are suspended by an employee's illness; see *Carmichael* v *Colonial Sugar Refining Co Ltd* (1944) 44 SR (NSW) 233, at 235-6.

Although express provisions for suspension are recognized and enforced, it is commonplace that an express termination provision does not impliedly confer a right to suspend performance.[5] There is similarly no implied right to suspend performance for breach of condition, unless the term also operates as a condition precedent. The courts also deny that a repudiation confers a right of suspension, although it is impossible to reconcile this with the decisions on so-called 'unaccepted' repudiations. The law is generally 'hostile' to suspension, on the ground that it could lead to an undesirable degree of uncertainty'.[6] The suspension regime, such as it is, must be cobbled together from conditions precedent to performance, the consequences of repudiation and specific rules protecting property interests.[7] There is a marked contrast with the law in the United States, where a specific regime for suspension has been developed.[8]

EFFECT OF SUSPENSION

The effect of suspension is best understood by reference to its contrast with discharge. Where discharge occurs, following termination for breach or repudiation, *both parties* are permanently discharged, both from the duty to perform and from the duty to be ready and willing to perform.[9] The remedial issues therefore relate, almost exclusively, to compensation and restitution. On the other hand, where performance is merely suspended, only the plaintiff's performance obligation is affected, and there is no question of either party being permanently discharged. Suspension may provide an excuse for non-performance, but suspension does not, of itself, have remedial consequences.[10]

A 'FUNDAMENTAL QUESTION' OF CONTRACT LAW

In *McRae* v *Commonwealth Disposals Commission*,[11] Dixon and Fullagar JJ described as a 'fundamental question' of contract law the issue 'What did the promisor really promise?'. They were inquiring, in the context of an

---

[5] This is expressed as a conclusion on the scope of the express right. See, eg *Steelwood Carriers Inc of Monrovia Liberia* v *Evimeria Compania Naviera SA of Borough of Islington ex p Building Employers' Confederation* [1989] IRLR 382, at 386. Cf. *Terkol Rederierne* v *Patroleo Brasileiro SA (The Badagry)* [1985] 1 Lloyd's Rep 395, at 399 (substitution clause in charter-party contract did not authorize suspension).

[6] GH Treitel, *Remedies for Breach of Contract: A Comparative Account* (1988) p 405.

[7] See below, text at note 24 *et seq.*

[8] See below, text at note 77. See also below, text at note 15 (contrast with respect to right to demand assurance of performance).

[9] See, eg *McDonald* v *Dennys Lascelles Ltd* (1933) 48 CLR 457, at 476–7; *Photo Production Ltd* v *Securicor Transport Ltd* [1980] AC 827, at 850.

[10] The act of suspension may, however, ultimately amount to a step preliminary to discharge or a claim for specific performance. See further below, text at notes 129 *et seq.*

[11] (1951) 84 CLR 277, at 407.

alleged fundamental mistake, whether the promisor had promised to perform at all events, or only subject to the 'mutually contemplated original existence of a particular subject matter'. Precisely the same question has arisen in many other areas of contract. Thus, in *Davis Contractors Ltd* v *Fareham UDC*[12] Lord Radcliffe said the frustration occurs only where the promisor is entitled to say 'It was not this that I promised to do'.[13]

Just as the decision that a contract is void for mistake or discharged by frustration is a conclusion about the scope of the parties' performance obligations, so the decision that a plaintiff is entitled to treat a contract as discharged for breach or repudiation expresses a conclusion about the scope of a plaintiff's promise. Since the question whether a party may suspend performance depends on whether the plaintiff's performance obligation extends to the facts existing at the time when the plaintiff seeks to suspend performance, it also concerns the scope of the plaintiff's promise. Accordingly, the refusal of Australian and English law to recognize a general right of suspension for breach embodies a presumption that, unless the contract has been validly discharged, a plaintiff's performance obligation extends to cases where the defendant has breached the contract, or may do so.

Risk and the functions of suspension

INTRODUCTION

It has been explained that, because there are no (positive) default rules about suspension analogous to those concerning discharge, a right to suspend performance is not a general implication from breach, even a serious breach. Moreover, although suspension is a lesser right than discharge, the mere fact that a right of discharge exists does not mean that there is a right to suspend performance. There is, in other words, the all or nothing approach typical of the common law. Whether or not the policy basis for the rules on breach justify a concept of suspension has never been properly investigated. There are no Australian or English precedents. Without the precedents there is no legal matrix. The result is a general refusal to treat suspension as an available right on the basis of an imputed intention. The right must be found in express or implied terms.

The conventional wisdom is also that neither party has any right to ask the other for an assurance that performance will occur.[14] This does not prevent a plaintiff asking for an assurance, or preclude the defendant

---

[12] [1956] AC 696. [13] *Ibid.*, at 729 (*Non haec in foedera veni*).
[14] See, eg *Chilean Nitrate Sales Corpn* v *Marine Transportation Co Ltd* (*The Hermosa*) [1980] 1 Lloyd's Rep 638, at 651, affirmed [1982] 1 Lloyd's Rep 570 ('ultimatum had no formal legal status').

providing one.[15] However, the absence of a right to require an assurance where the circumstances suggest that the defendant may not be able, or willing, to perform means that no consequences flow from the failure to provide an assurance or the failure to fulfil an assurance which has been given.[16] At best, the conduct of the defendant is evidence of repudiation.[17] This is clearly unsatisfactory.

The normative question of whether a right to suspend performance should be recognised must be answered, in the first instance, by reference to the risks of non-performance and the functions of suspension.

RISK

When two parties enter into an executory bilateral contract, both parties make promises. The fact that the law sanctions the relationship means that each promise creates a duty, namely, to perform the promise. Each promise also generates an expectation, that it will be performed. The law protects the plaintiff's expectation, and also regards the plaintiff's reliance on the promise as important. Under classical contract law, although each party is deemed to have received the promise as the price of its own promise, there is no pretence that the agreed return of each is equivalent in any monetary sense. The fact that one party may stand to make more out of the contract is irrelevant to the scope of the plaintiff's promise. We could express the difference in value as the risk element in the contract. Analysis of 'risk' in contract law is, however, always problematic and necessarily somewhat controversial. In fact, in making a promise each party takes a number of risks, and the contract allocates risks such as changes in market conditions and non-performance.

For our purposes, the most significant risk which a plaintiff runs is the risk of non-performance by the defendant, that is, that the defendant, when the time for performance arrives, will choose not to perform, not be able to perform, or commit a breach of contract. This risk is in all cases a 'material' one, in the sense that its realization has consequences for the plaintiff, financial or otherwise. If the risk that performance will not be received increases, and the event is not the subject of any contractual provision, there is a discrepancy between the actual (contractual) allocation

---

[15] See *Universal Cargo Carriers Corpn* v *Citati* [1957] 2 QB 401, at 450.

[16] It is at this point that the common law applied in England and Australia contrasts sharply with the United Nations Convention on Contracts for the International Sale of Goods (1980) (hereafter the CISG), Article 2 of the United States Uniform Commercial Code (1990 Official Text) (hereafter the UCC) and the law expressed in the Restatement (2d) Contracts (1979). For the relevant provisions see below, text before and after note 76.

[17] See *Chappell* v *Times Newspapers Ltd* [1975] 1 WLR 482, at 499–500; *Laurinda Pty Ltd* v *Capalaba Park Shopping Centre Pty Ltd* (1989) 166 CLR 623, at 649.

of risk, and the allocation which would then be made on a re-negotiation of the contract.

The risk is particularly significant in contracts where the plaintiff is to perform first, or where the performance obligations are concurrent. Where the plaintiff is obliged to perform first, expenditure will have been incurred. Therefore, the propensity of claims for reliance or restitutionary loss increases in direct proportion to the insecurity of the defendant's performance. In addition, and irrespective of whether compensation or restitution is available, there is a corresponding potential for waste of resources. The risk is also present, though usually to a lesser extent, where the performance obligations are concurrent, since expenditure will usually have been incurred in anticipation of the exchange of performances. Moreover, in cases where the relevant event is breach, so that compensation is claimed, the claim is subject to the rules on mitigation of loss. Whatever the order of performance, in all cases, if non-performance occurs and specific performance is not available, the ability to realize profits through favourable market conditions may be lost, any expenditure in reliance is wasted, and benefits conferred in anticipation of performance go unrewarded. The plaintiff is left with a claim for compensation or restitution, resources are reallocated or lost, dispute resolution procedures come into play, economic activity slows, and the financial burden is, ultimately, passed on to society. Although the position is worst where non-performance leads to discharge, the Anglo-Australian formulation of the discharge rules encourages discharge, simply because there is no middle ground. That middle ground is the main locus for a regime on suspension. In considering whether positive default rules are necessary we should accept that, at least in commercial contracts, discharge is an extreme right, and that a right of suspension is, pragmatically, an acceptable trade-off against the modern tendency to restrict rights of discharge.[18]

The risk of non-performance may be less significant where the defendant is to perform first, since there may be no reliance expenditure by the plaintiff, and no conferral of benefit on the defendant. The risk is still material, particularly if another assumption of classical contract law, that the contract was entered into in order to make a monetary profit, is not present. Thus, if the plaintiff's purpose was merely to establish a relation from which commercial benefits might accrue, the materiality of the risk emerges from the conclusion that non-performance may lead to discharge of the relation. Again, if the purpose of the contract was to increase volume rather than to secure profit on an individual transaction, non-performance is a material risk, since a replacement contract must be

---

[18] Cf. GH Treitel, 'Some Problems of Breach of Contract' (1967) 30 MLR 139, 155; FMB Reynolds, 'Discharge by Breach as A Remedy' in PD Finn (ed), *Essays on Contract* (1987) pp 183, 188.

found, duplicating a substantial part of the plaintiff's transaction costs, to society's detriment. If we remove the myopic focus of classical contract law on individual units, and consider a long-term relation with a large number of transaction units, under each of which the defendant was to pay in advance, the plaintiff's motive may have been to ensure a continuous cash flow, with little or no profit from each unit. Non-performance will interrupt the cash flow, lead to lack of confidence, increase uncertainty and, perhaps, place at risk other more profitable contracts financed from the contract with the defendant.

Whether the risk of non-performance is likely to materialize in any given fact situation depends on the interaction of many factors, including those over which the parties have no control such as changes in market conditions and economic activity in general. The common law deals with such factors in an uneven fashion. In extreme circumstances there may be frustration or a right to treat the contract as discharged. These are marginal cases. However, absent such circumstances, a party is expected to continue to perform, with risks consequent on increased expenditure and uncertainty about the other party's willingness or ability to perform. Moreover, where a plaintiff reacts to non-performance by invoking a discharge rule, the actual motivation for exercise of the right of discharge is, at least under English law, largely irrelevant. An ulterior motive, such as that the bargain has become unprofitable, is not a sufficient reason for saying that discharge was not justified. The robust approach of the common law to strategic behaviour is not easy to justify today. It would be even harder to justify under a contract law which included a regime for suspension. The adoption of such a regime is, therefore, consistent with the recent movement in Australian law, and to some extent also in England, towards the adoption of good faith principles.[19]

From the defendant's perspective, the risk of non-performance is a risk that the defendant will, by breaching the contract, come under an obligation to make compensation or restitution. The extent of the defendant's exposure is determined by the loss or damage which the plaintiff will suffer on breach, or the extent to which the defendant will be unjustly enriched on discharge. If the market is moving against the defendant, there is a risk that the plaintiff will demand a higher expectation loss award. If economic conditions remain constant, the likelihood that the risk will materialize depends principally on the difficulty of performance. So far as consequential loss is concerned, and leaving aside the question of remoteness, the more precarious the plaintiff's position, the greater the

---

[19] See, eg *Faccenda Chicken Ltd v Fowler* [1987] Ch 117; *Interfoto Picture Library Ltd v Stiletto Visual Programmes Ltd* [1989] QB 433, at 439; *Coal Cliff Collieries Pty Ltd v Sijehama Pty Ltd* (1991) 24 NSWLR 1; *Renard Constructions (ME) Pty Ltd v Minister for Public Works* (1992) 26 NSWLR 234. But cf. *Walford v Miles* [1992] 2 AC 128.

indemnity which will be demanded on breach. Thus, the significance of the risk of non-performance is a direct function of the difficulty of performance and the loss which the plaintiff will suffer on breach. The more difficult it is for the defendant to discharge the promise—usually a highly subjective matter—the more likely it is that breach will occur, and the more likely it is that the defendant will come under an obligation to make compensation. Similarly, the greater the impact of breach on the plaintiff—also a highly subjective matter—the more the defendant is at risk when attempting to perform a promise. The focus of discharge rules is on the rights of the plaintiff. It is well known that those rules, particularly in the English sale of goods legislation which was copied throughout the British Commonwealth, are heavily plaintiff-biased. The easier it is for the plaintiff to treat the contract as discharged, the greater the risk of non-performance to the defendant. This is one explanation for the current tendency to narrow the scope of the default rules regulating discharge. Thus, there is a restrictive regime for discharge ('avoidance') under the CISG[20] and it is likely that the perfect tender rule of Art 2 of the UCC will go in the current revision.[21] Moreover, generous discharge rules encourage defendants to withhold information pertinent to discharge in order to protect their contracts.[22] Adoption of a suspension regime may encourage, indeed require, defendants to provide non-performance information. We can be more generous with suspension without exacerbating defendant-oriented risk factors.[23]

FUNCTIONS OF SUSPENSION

Against the background of basic risk analysis, the likely impact of events which would cause a reasonable plaintiff to doubt the readiness, willingness or ability of a defendant to perform may be evaluated. The relevant perspective is in terms of five (overlapping) functions of suspension.

[20] Representatives from developing countries were critical of the generous discharge rules applied in developed countries. See M Gilbey Strub, 'The Convention on the International Sale of Goods: Anticipatory Repudiation Provisions and Developing Countries' (1989) 38 ICLQ 475; JO Honnold, *Uniform Law for International Sales Under the 1980 United Nations Convention* (2nd ed 1991) pp 486–8. See also K Sono, 'UNCITRAL and the Vienna Sales Convention' (1984) 18 International Lawyer 7, 8. The CISG applies in a large number of countries, including Australia, Canada and the United States, but not in England.

[21] See RE Speidel, 'Buyer's Remedies of Rejection and Cancellation Under the UCC and the Convention' (1993) 6 JCL 131.

[22] For an analysis of the interaction between default rules, strategic behaviour and the imposition of an obligation to provide information see I Ayres and R Gertner, 'Filling Gaps in Incomplete Contracts: An Economic Theory of Default Rules' (1989) 99 Yale LJ 87. See also AI Rosett, 'Contract Performance: Promises, Conditions and the Obligation to Communicate' (1975) 22 UCLA L Rev 1083.

[23] Cf B Nicholas, 'The Vienna Convention on International Sales Law' (1989) 105 LQR 201, 233.

(1) Since one object of suspending performance is to determine the likelihood that the risk of non-performance will materialize, there is an *information function*. When doubts arise, reliable information on whether (and the extent to which) non-performance will occur may be obtained.

(2) Related to the first function is a *moral function* of requiring a party to restate its performance obligation in the changed circumstances. The moral insistence that promises be kept, and contracts enforced, is reinforced by suspension.

(3) This leads to an *enforcement function*. Suspension is conducive to the preservation and performance of bargains, since the existence of a right to suspend performance may encourage a party not to invoke dispute resolution procedures, and discourage the exercise of a right of discharge.

(4) Given that exercise of the right of suspension enables a party to control expenditure, there is a *mitigation of loss function*. In other words, suspension may save a party from incurring expenditure which will ultimately be wasted or claimed as compensation or restitution.

(5) These functions suggest corresponding economic objects which may be expressed compendiously as an *efficiency function*. In other words, all things considered, from society's perspective suspension is likely to have economic benefits:

    (a) resources are moved more swiftly to a higher value user or more efficient party, since if discharge does occur it is likely to take place at an earlier time than if suspension was not available;

    (b) bargains are preserved;

    (c) dispute resolution procedures are avoided; and

    (d) resources are conserved.

With these functions in mind, we may turn to the rules which currently govern suspension under Australian and English law.

Current rules for suspension under Australian and English law

INTRODUCTION

Although the logical starting point for an analysis of the current law is to say that there is no common law right to suspend performance, and that the only illustrations are to be found in express clauses, I am not concerned with the scope of express provisions. More general assistance is to be gained from an analysis of conditions precedent and the doctrine of repudiation.

CONDITIONS PRECEDENT

Although seldom recognized as such, suspension of one party's obligation to perform is reasonably common under Australian and English law. Whenever a plaintiff is entitled to refuse to perform, that is, to withhold performance from the defendant, there is in effect a right to suspend performance.[24] Where the plaintiff must perform first, and also where the parties' performance obligations are concurrent, the plaintiff may refuse to perform if the plaintiff's performance obligation was subject to an unfulfilled 'condition precedent'. The condition precedent concept employs a usage of 'condition' which is much older than the 'vital promise' sense of the word, and invokes what English lawyers now regard as a secondary meaning,[25] namely, an (uncertain) event which must occur before a party can be required to perform.[26] The fulfilment of a condition precedent may or may not be the subject of a promise.

The rules on conditions precedent developed long before the emergence of the modern concept of discharge for breach. The most frequent question of contract law at this time was whether the plaintiff's pleadings were in order.[27] Decisions were controlled by the order of performance: they illustrate the distinction between dependent and independent promises.[28] A performance duty subject to the prior or contemporaneous fulfilment of a condition precedent was termed a dependent one. Until the event had occurred, a dependent duty could not be enforced: failure of a condition precedent to performance was, simply, a complete bar to action on the contract. If there was no condition precedent (or the contingency had been fulfilled) the performance duty was independent or absolute.

---

[24] See *Banque Keyser Ullmann SA v Skandia (UK) Insurance Co Ltd* [1990] 1 QB 665, affirmed without reference to the point sub nom *Banque Financière de la Cité SA v Westgate Insurance Co Ltd* [1991] 2 AC 249 (non-fulfilment of a non-promissory condition precedent gives no cause of action for breach but simply suspends the obligations of one or both of the parties).

[25] Cf. *Wickman Machine Tool Sales Ltd v L Schuler AG* [1972] 1 WLR 840, at 850 (affirmed sub nom *L Schuler AG v Wickman Machinen Tool Sales Ltd* [1974] AC 235), per Lord Denning MR ('proper' meaning of the word condition is something demanded or required as a prerequisite to the granting or performance of something else).

[26] It is, however, a familiar one to US lawyers. See *Corbin on Contracts*, ss 1613, 700–12. Cf. JH Baker, 'Contract: Construction of "Condition" ' [1973] CLJ 196, 197–8.

[27] See JW Carter, *Breach of Contract* (2nd ed 1991) s 115.

[28] See SJ Stoljar, 'Dependent and Independent Promises' (1957) 2 Syd LR 217. Conditions precedent are therefore, in theory, determined by construction. However, as Professor Beale points out (H Beale, *Remedies for Breach of Contract* (1980) p 27) a finding of dependency is in many contexts imposed on the parties unless they have agreed to the contrary. This was in fact Lord Mansfield's idea in *Kingston v Preston* cited by counsel in *Jones v Barkley* (1773) 2 Doug 689, at 691; 99 ER 437, at 438. In treating dependency as governed by the 'intent' of the transaction he was using the word in a sense ('intendment') now obsolete, namely, the meaning attached by the common law. Cf. PS Atiyah, *The Rise and Fall of Freedom of Contract* (1979) pp 213, 424.

Not surprisingly, we see much formalism in the rules applied to determine whether a duty was dependent or independent.[29]

In modern law, the order of performance is seldom a contentious issue, pleading rules are much less strict, and we tend to regard the cases on dependent and independent promises as of little more than historical interest.[30] However, even today conditions precedent are important.[31] A performance obligation may be unenforceable because the condition (event) is precedent to formation of the contract, or to the duty to perform an existing contract. Most examples are found in express terms, often introduced by the words 'subject to . . .' Thus, the obligation of a party to perform a contract for the sale of goods may be 'subject to' the other party obtaining an export licence, or the obligation of a purchaser under a sale of land contract may be 'subject to finance'. However, conditions precedent are not always associated with 'subject to' clauses, and are most commonly found in aleatory contracts. An illustration is an option contract, where the obligation of the optionor to perform is subject to the condition precedent of valid exercise of the option.[32] In finance and guarantee contracts, an obligation to perform may be subject to the occurrence of specified events, usually described as provisos, which operate as conditions precedent. For example, the performance duty of a surety may be postponed, even after default by the principal debtor, until the creditor has given notice in accordance with the contract.[33] Less frequently, a condition precedent may be found in an implied term.[34] In all cases, however, if the relevant event has not occurred the condition (contingency) remains unfulfilled and there is no obligation to perform.

The concept of 'condition' has often been a source of confusion.[35] This is mainly due to the fact that failure of a condition precedent is not inevitably associated with breach, and use of the word 'condition' (or the expression 'condition precedent') to describe both the event (contingency)

---

[29] See JW Carter, *Breach of Contract* (2nd ed 1991) s 122.

[30] See *Corbin on Contracts* (1951) vol 3A, s 637 (the terms dependent and independent are now rendering no necessary service).

[31] See JW Carter, 'Conditions and Conditions Precedent' (1991) 4 JCL 90.

[32] See, eg *Hare v Nicoll* [1966] 2 QB 130.

[33] For a recent example see *Tricontinental Corpn Ltd v HDFI Ltd* (1990) 21 NSWLR 689 (entitlement to make demand under underpinning agreement regulated by formal requirements in the nature of conditions precedent).

[34] See, eg *United Dominions Trust (Commercial) Ltd v Eagle Aircraft Services Ltd* [1968] 1 WLR 74 where a promise to repurchase aircraft let out on hire-purchase was subject to an implied condition precedent of notice to re-purchase within a reasonable time following termination of the hire-purchase agreements secured by the promise.

[35] See *Bradford v Williams* (1872) LR 7 Ex 259, at 261; *Skips A/S Nordheim v Syrian Petroleum Co Ltd* [1984] QB 599, at 617–18; SJ Stoljar, 'The Contractual Concept of Condition' (1953) 69 LQR 485; GH Treitel, *Remedies for Breach of Contract: A Comparative Account* (1988) pp 255 *et seq*.

and the term stating the event.[36] Take, for example, the case where a sale
contract states that the buyer will obtain an import licence, or provide a
counter trade guarantee.[37] The tendency of Australian and English
lawyers to ask whether the term is a 'condition' fuses at least two, and perhaps three, distinct questions. The existence of the licence or counter trade
guarantee may or may not be a condition precedent to the seller's obligation to ship the goods.[38] There is also the question whether the buyer is in
breach of contract if the licence is not obtained or the guarantee not provided, a question depending on the standard of the buyer's duty and the
steps taken. Finally, the question may arise whether the seller is entitled
to treat the contract as discharged if the licence or guarantee is not
obtained, or not obtained within the time fixed by the contract.[39] Only if
we keep these questions distinct can we meaningfully determine the
rights of the parties, and in particular whether the seller may suspend performance. In fact, a very significant illustration of the contrast between
discharge and suspension is found in the most basic analysis of sale of
goods contracts.[40] If the contract requires payment in exchange for the
goods, the seller's obligation to deliver is subject to a condition precedent,
namely, the buyer's readiness and willingness to accept and pay for the
goods.[41] If the buyer is not ready and willing to pay on the appointed day,
the seller is not bound to deliver the goods, even though the time for payment will not usually be of the essence. The seller is, in effect, entitled to
suspend performance until the buyer is ready and willing to perform, but
not usually entitled to treat the contract as discharged. Similarly, where a
seller makes a non-conforming tender prior to the expiry of the time for
delivery, the buyer is not required to accept delivery, and the seller may

---

[36] This is by no means a modern phenomenon. It goes back at least as far as Lord
Mansfield's statement in the classic decision in *Boone* v *Eyre* (1777) 1 H Bl 273n(a); 126 ER 160
('where mutual covenants go to the whole of the consideration on both sides, they are
mutual conditions, the one precedent to the other'). See also *Behn* v *Burness* (1863) 2 B & S
751, at 754; 122 ER 281, at 283.

[37] Cf *State Trading Corpn of India Ltd* v *M Golodetz Ltd* [1989] 2 Lloyd's Rep 277 (see GH
Treitel, ' "Conditions" and "Conditions Precedent" ' (1990) 106 LQR 185).

[38] Where a particular event is a condition precedent to formation of contract, the existence
of a binding contract—rather than a performance obligation—is suspended. This is rare
today. Compare *Astra Trust Ltd* v *Adams* [1969] 1 Lloyd's Rep 81 where there was held to be
no binding contract for the sale of a vessel subject to a satisfactory survey because no survey
satisfactory to the plaintiffs was obtained. The decision was doubted in *Varverakis* v
Compagnia de Navegacion Artico SA (*The Merak*) [1976] 2 Lloyd's Rep 250, at 254.

[39] Cf *Ankar Pty Ltd* v *National Westminster Finance (Australia) Ltd* (1987) 162 CLR 549 (terms
in a security deposit agreement were both conditions precedent and vital promises).

[40] See JW Carter, *Breach of Contract* (2nd ed 1991) s 125.

[41] See Sale of Goods Act 1979, s 28. There are corresponding provisions in
Commonwealth legislation derived from the Sale of Goods Act 1893. See KCT Sutton, *Sales
and Consumer Law in Australia and New Zealand* (3rd ed 1983) p 365; MG Bridge, *Sale of Goods*
(1988) p 416.

make a fresh tender, whether or not in breach of contract by making the bad tender.[42]

It would today be too narrow an approach to treat the ability to suspend performance as determined by whether there is an unfulfilled condition precedent, since that would make suspension dependent on the order of performance. The best that can be said of the concept is that it provides some protection against the risks involved in rendering performance prior to receipt of the agreed return.[43] Although the concept encourages mitigation of loss, it ignores the functions of suspension listed above. It relies on a literal and formalistic approach, and pays little regard to the broader questions raised under the modern law.

The law on conditions precedent is reinforced in Anglo-Australian law by specific (special) rights responsive to risks which materialise in the course of performance. For example, sureties are protected by a rule that the surety is discharged by a material variation of the contract between the creditor and debtor.[44] Again, an unpaid seller enjoys specific (statutory) protection against loss of its property interest, and the risk of a buyer's insolvency. Thus, the UK Sale of Goods Act 1979[45] may operate to allow an unpaid seller to exercise rights analogous to suspension of performance. Notwithstanding that the property in the goods may have passed to the buyer, an unpaid seller has a lien on the goods for the price while in possession. Where the buyer is insolvent, there is also a right to stop goods in transit if the seller has parted with the possession.[46] Similarly, if property has not passed, an unpaid seller has (in addition to other remedies) a right of withholding delivery. This is similar to, and co-extensive with, rights of lien and stoppage where the property has passed to the buyer. These rules, which were conceived to provide rights against goods rather than personal contractual rights, have a common law ori-

---

[42] See *Borrowman v Free* (1878) 4 QBD 500; *McDougall v Aeromarine of Emsworth Ltd* [1958] 1 WLR 1126, at 1132; *Motor Oil Hellas (Corinth) Refineries SA v Shipping Corpn of India (The Kanchenjunga)* [1990] 1 Lloyd's Rep 391, at 399. Cf. *Hongkong Fir Shipping Co Ltd v Kawasaki Kisen Kaisha Ltd* [1962] 2 QB 26, at 36, 56, 59 (charterer under no obligation to accept or load an unseaworthy vessel).

[43] This was certainly influential in the development of the condition precedent of readiness and willingness in cases of concurrent performance. See *Goodisson v Nunn* (1792) 4 TR 761, at 764; 100 ER 1288, at 1289; *Glazebrook v Woodrow* (1799) 8 TR 366, at 370–1; 101 ER 1436, at 1439

[44] See, eg *Holme v Brunskill* (1877) 3 QBD 495.

[45] See ss 39, 41, 44. For the meaning of unpaid seller see s 38. See generally *Benjamin's Sale of Goods* (4th ed 1992), ss 15–016, 15–028 *et seq*. There are corresponding provisions in Commonwealth legislation derived from the Sale of Goods Act 1893 (UK). See KCT Sutton, *Sales and Consumer Law in Australia and New Zealand* (3rd ed 1983) pp 397 *et seq*; MG Bridge, *Sale of Goods* (1988) pp 682 ff.

[46] The seller may resume possession as long as the goods are in course of transit, and may retain them until payment or tender of the price.

gin.[47] Professor Reynolds has pointed out[48] that as 'special situations' they cannot form a basis for general rules on suspension. Although the rights conferred are clearly responsive to increased risk, particularly insolvency, and are not tied to discharge,[49] the most obvious use of suspension arises in cases where the plaintiff must perform first, where any failure of condition precedent is merely prospective. It is in this context that the law of repudiation is important.

REPUDIATION OF OBLIGATION

The pragmatic development of the common law of repudiation is well documented.[50] The law on repudiation is based on a particular assumption about the scope of a plaintiff's performance duty. The duty to perform is subject to the qualification that the defendant has not renounced its duty to perform the contract. We could therefore say that once a repudiation has occurred the plaintiff is discharged from the obligation to perform. However, the Australian and English authorities, in requiring 'acceptance' of a repudiation, treat the discharge of a plaintiff as based on an act of the plaintiff, rather than the repudiation itself. This approach is unsympathetic to arguments in favour of suspension.

As many commentators have pointed out, English law exhibits a confusion between whether (and when) a plaintiff is discharged by a repudiation, and the entitlement to sue for compensation or restitution. The failure to keep these issues distinct led in cases such as *Hochster* v *De la Tour*[51] to the view that in order to be discharged a plaintiff must also be accorded the right to sue immediately, even before the time fixed for

---

[47] See, eg *Ex parte Chalmers* (1873) 8 Ch App 289; *Morgan* v *Bain* (1874) LR 10 CP 15, at 21, 26. Cf. *James B Berry's Sons Co of Illinois* v *Monark Gasoline & Oil Co*, 32 F 2d 74 (8th Cir 1929). More generally, the existence of a lien over property will entitle the holder to suspend performance until payment. See, eg *Fraser* v *Equitorial Shipping Co Ltd* (*The Ijaola*) [1979] 1 Lloyd's Rep 103 (lien of consulting marine engineer) and generally *Chitty on Contracts* (27th ed 1994) vol ii, s 32–064.

[48] See FMB Reynolds, 'Discharge by Breach as A Remedy' in PD Finn (ed), *Essays on Contract* (1987) pp 183, 187. See also Sir Michael Mustill, 'Anticipatory Breach', *Butterworths Lectures 1989–90* (1990) p 33 (seller's right to refuse to deliver goods to insolvent buyer has 'no general implications for the law of contract').

[49] On the relation between variation of contracts of guarantee and the law of discharge for breach see *National Westminster Bank plc* v *Riley* [1986] FLR 213; *Ankar Pty Ltd* v *National Westminster Finance* (*Australia*) *Ltd* (1987) 162 CLR 549. See JW Carter and JC Phillips, 'Construction of Contracts of Guarantee and the *Hongkong Fir* Case' (1988) 1 JCL 70. Cf. *Bank of Nova Scotia* v *Hellenic Mutual War Risks Association* (*Bermuda*) *Ltd* (*The Good Luck*) [1992] 1 AC 233 (relation between discharge of insurer and discharge of contract of insurance).

[50] For a recent analysis of the history see Sir Michael Mustill, 'Anticipatory Breach', *Butterworth Lectures 1989–90* (1990).

[51] (1853) 2 El & Bl 678, at 689–90; 118 ER 922, at 926. See also *Roehm* v *Horst*, 178 US 1, at 9–11, 19–21; 44 L Ed 953, at 957, 961 (1900).

performance by the defendant.[52] However, there is no reason today to question the decision to allow actions based on anticipatory repudiation. At the same time, modern contract lawyers must surely wince when they look back at cases where it was reasoned that a repudiation of obligation only becomes a wrongful act if the plaintiff elects to treat it as such,[53] and be sceptical of those which suggest that the plaintiff is required to perform unless the contract has been discharged. But it is clearly the law that no claim for damages or restitution may be made unless there has been an election to treat the whole contract as discharged, and also that discharge occurs only when the repudiation has been 'accepted'.[54]

Conventional wisdom therefore has it that a repudiation confers a right to choose between discharging the contract and continuing with its performance. Thus, in the leading English case, *Fercometal SARL v Mediterranean Shipping Co SA*,[55] Lord Ackner said that there is 'no third choice, as a sort of via media, to affirm the contract and yet to be absolved from tendering further performance'.[56] In the leading Australian case, *Foran v Wight*[57] Brennan J expressly disagreed with Lord Ackner's view. Although this is a sufficient indication of controversy, the resolution of which is crucial to the concept of suspension of performance, there is in reality no difference of substance between English and Australian law. However, the position is different in the United States. Section 253(1) of the Restatement 2d Contracts states that the 'repudiation alone gives rise to a claim for damages for total breach', and § 253(2) states that a repudiation 'discharges' the plaintiff. Thus, although use of the concept of acceptance can no doubt be found in the American cases, the Restatement 2d Contracts treats it as otiose for the purpose of discharge.

The idea of discharge by acceptance of a repudiation is clearly a lawyer's concept. No doubt most people in business might understand that there is a right to retire from a contract where the other party has expressly said that performance will not be given. However, good

---

[52] Williston was never convinced of the correctness of *Hochster v De la Tour*, and it would certainly have been sufficient for the court to treat the plaintiff as discharged from the duty to perform, but required to wait until the defendant's failure to perform to claim compensation. See S Williston, 'Repudiation of Contracts' (1901) 14 Harv L Rev 317 and 421. Cf. JD Calamari and JM Perillo, *The Law of Contracts* (3rd ed 1987) pp 521–2.

[53] See, eg *Johnstone v Milling* (1886) 16 QBD 460, at 472–3. See the recent criticism of the reasoning by Sir Michael Mustill, 'Anticipatory Breach', *Butterworths Lectures 1989–90* (1990) p 45.

[54] See generally JW Carter, *Breach of Contract* (2nd ed 1991) ss 745 ff.

[55] [1989] AC 788. See JW Carter, 'The Higher Altitudes of Contract Law' [1989] LMCLQ 81.

[56] [1989] AC 788, at 805E. The other members of the House of Lords agreed. See also *Tankexpress A/S v Compagnie Financière Belge des Petroles SA (The Petrofina)* [1949] AC 76, at 91, per Lord Porter (no 'half-way house' between termination and the obligation to continue performance).

[57] (1989) 168 CLR 385, at 421. Cf. at 410–11.

business practice suggests that cancellation is preceded by an attempt to preserve the bargain. Litigation is likely to be seen as a further problem, not a solution. The law should not ignore the parties' interest in co-operation.[58] The natural business response, therefore, is to ask why the contract has been repudiated, and to attempt to find a mutually satisfactory solution. In any event, cases of express repudiation are rare. The defendant may have claimed breach by the plaintiff or alleged the occurrence of an (extraneous) event for which there is no contractual responsibility. There is almost always a stark contrast between the clear factual picture presented in a trial court's opinion and the murky and uncertain scenario perceived and presented, in the heat of the dispute, to and by the disputants themselves. Lawyers are seldom consulted immediately, and even when lawyers are consulted there is a period in which the parties jockey for positions. While this occurs, the plaintiff may find that its performance obligations fall due. The idea of acceptance, therefore, exposes the plaintiff to the risk of breach by non-performance. However, the courts have, almost by accident, found a way to protect the plaintiff who delays acceptance and fails to perform.

The protection is found in the principle of *Jones* v *Barkley*,[59] a case decided before there was either a doctrine of repudiation or a principle of discharge. Historically, its proper context is the rules on order of performance.[60] The plaintiffs claimed a sum of money required to be paid on the assignment of the equity of redemption of a property to a third party. The defendants indicated that they would not join in the assignment: in modern terminology, they repudiated their obligation to perform. In demurrer proceedings, as a defence to the plaintiffs' claim, the defendants denied that a condition precedent to their liability had been fulfilled. The defence was held not to be a good one.[61] The King's Bench did not deny that the parties' obligations were dependent, or that performance by the plaintiffs was a condition precedent. However, the plaintiffs' performance obligation—to tender an assignment—was dispensed with so far as it was an element of the plaintiffs' claim on the contract. There was no failure by the plaintiffs to perform the contract. The defendants gained no comfort from the condition precedent, since the law would not require the plaintiffs to do what Lord Mansfield described[62] as a 'nugatory' act.

[58] Cf. IR Macneil, 'Efficient Breach of Contract: Circles in the Sky' (1982) 68 Va L Rev 947, 968.

[59] (1781) 2 Doug 684; 99 ER 434.

[60] In the course of argument one counsel produced a copy of Lord Mansfield's judgment in *Kingston* v *Preston* (1773) 2 Doug 689; 99 ER 437, a landmark case in the recognition of the modern presumption of concurrent (and dependent) performance in the context of sale.

[61] The plaintiffs' claim was later heard on its merits, judgment ultimately being given for the defendants on the ground that the agreement was void as one to secure money due from a bankrupt.

[62] (1781) 2 Doug 684, at 694; 99 ER 434, at 440.

The decision in *Jones* v *Barkley* has been relied on in countless cases throughout the common law world. Almost invariably the context has been repudiation of obligation. Even the cases decided while the question of anticipatory repudiation was being debated recognised the viability of the principle,[63] which therefore does not depend on the presence of an ability to treat a contract as discharged prior to the time for performance. There is also no reason to doubt that the idea that a person should not be required to do a nugatory act is some general (loose) common law maxim. However, it seems patently clear that its application for 200 years in contexts which we now see as involving repudiation justifies a more specific rationalization in that context. Under the modern law of repudiation, the effect of *Jones* v *Barclay* is to provide a defence or excuse for failure to perform even though the contract has not been discharged by an election to terminate for repudiation. In nullifying the condition precedent, the effect is to allow a party to suspend performance. As Devlin J explained in *Sionason-Teicher Inter-American Grain Corpn* v *Oilcakes and Oilseeds Trading Co Ltd*,[64] in practice a plaintiff may 'keep the contract alive' by not accepting the repudiation and yet 'still claim that he is relieved from the obligation of making an empty and formal tender' of performance. Nevertheless, the courts have insisted that the principle is a discrete one. Thus, in *Peter Turnbull & Co Pty Ltd* v *Mundus Trading Co (Australasia) Pty Ltd*[65] Dixon CJ described the dispensation achieved by the application of *Jones* v *Barkley* as independent of the law of anticipatory repudiation.

The perception that an independent rationale is required has the object of preserving the concept of acceptance, the supposed rule that the plaintiff is not discharged *until* the repudiation has been accepted. *Peter Turnbull* illustrates that to deny that the plaintiff is entitled to suspend performance is to engage in legal sophistry. The case involved a sale of goods on terms fob Sydney. The contract required the buyers to nominate a vessel, and they tentatively booked shipping space, but made no formal nomination. The sellers said they could not supply oats from Sydney. This was a repudiation. In response the buyers sought to persuade the vessel

---

[63] See, eg *Laird* v *Pim* (1841) 7 M & W 474; 151 ER 852; *M'Clure* v *Ripley* (1850) 5 Ex 140; 155 ER 60. Cf. Sir Michael Mustill, 'Anticipatory Breach', *Butterworth Lectures 1989–90* (1990) p 31 (Lord Mansfield's statement was 'well on the way to a doctrine of renunciation').

[64] [1954] 1 WLR 935, at 944 (affirmed [1954] 1 WLR 1394). See generally F Dawson, 'Waiver of Conditions Precedent on a Repudiation' (1980) 96 LQR 239. There is a technical question of how far cases (eg *Bunge Corpn* v *Vegetable Vitamin Foods (Pte) Ltd* [1985] 1 Lloyd's Rep 613) applying this principle are affected by the re-evaluation of *Braithwaite* v *Foreign Hardwood Co* [1905] 2 KB 543 in *Fercometal SARL* v *Mediterranean Shipping Co SA* [1989] AC 788. The principle does not depend on the contract ultimately being discharged. See *Mahoney* v *Lindsay* (1980) 55 ALJR 118.

[65] (1954) 90 CLR 235, at 246–7. Dixon CJ's view was adopted by Lord Denning MR in *UGS Finance Ltd* v *National Mortgage Bank of Greece and National Bank of Greece SA* [1964] 1 Lloyd's Rep 446, at 452.

to call at Melbourne, where the sellers claimed to have goods available. These attempts were not successful and the buyers ultimately accepted the sellers' repudiation, but not until the time for nomination had expired. Applying *Jones* v *Barkley*, a majority of the High Court of Australia held that the failure to nominate was no defence, even if the term was a condition, that is, stated a vital promise. It would have been more straightforward to say that the buyers had validly suspended their performance obligation, and that this was justified by the sellers' repudiation.

The closest that the Anglo-Australian cases have come to a rationalization of *Jones* v *Barkley* within the scheme of repudiation is via a concept of estoppel. It is now reasonably clear[66] that a plaintiff's reliance on a repudiation, although falling short of an election to treat the contract as discharged, may estop a defendant from relying on a failure to perform, caused by the repudiation, as a breach of contract. Thus, in *Fercometal SARL* v *Mediterranean Shipping Co SA*[67] Lord Ackner said that it may be open to a plaintiff who has not accepted the defendant's repudiation to contend that 'in relation to a particular right or obligation under the contract', the defendant is 'estopped from contending' that the plaintiff is bound by an unperformed obligation or that the defendant is entitled to exercise the right against the plaintiff. Similarly, in *Foran* v *Wight*[68] the High Court treated estoppel as the appropriate rationale for the rule that a defendant cannot treat a failure to perform as a breach when it was induced by the defendant's repudiation. The common choice of an estoppel solution has the virtue of bringing Australian and English law together.

It is not unusual for courts applying common law principles to find complex solutions to simple problems. Nor it is unusual for perceived defects in the common law to be mended with the aid of equity. In *Foran* v *Wight* Brennan J said[69] that the 'basis' on which a plaintiff is, following repudiation, 'dispensed from tendering performance is that an equity is raised' against the defendant which is 'satisfied' by treating the defendant as having prevented the plaintiff from making the tender. However in this context the equitable justification in inapt. The use of estoppel immediately introduces a fiction. If a defendant has said 'I will not perform' or 'I cannot perform', we are forced by estoppel to treat this as a representation to the plaintiff, namely, 'You need not perform'. This is, perhaps, not too

---

[66] See *Nina's Bar Bistro Pty Ltd* v *MBE Corpn (Sydney) Pty Ltd* [1984] 3 NSWLR 613, at 633; *Fercometal SARL* v *Mediterranean Shipping Co SA* [1989] AC 788, at 805–6; *Foran* v *Wight* (1989) 168 CLR 385, at 431–6, 453–4.

[67] [1989] AC 788, at 805.

[68] (1989) 168 CLR 385. See JW Carter, '*Foran* v *Wright*' (1990) 3 JCL 70; A Beech, 'Terminating a Contract: Dispensing with the Requirement of Readiness and Willingness' (1992) 5 JCL 47.

[69] (1989) 168 CLR 385, at 420.

far away from the more realistic injunction: 'Do not perform'. However, estoppel also forces us to treat conduct from which a repudiation may be inferred as equivalent to a representation that the plaintiff need not perform. This may be an unconvincing analysis. It is also unduly legalistic, and must lead to strained analyses of conduct in response to repudiatory conduct. It is not too late to find a simple common law solution, the starting point for which is a more appropriate analysis of commercial conduct.

Some concept is clearly necessary to control the defendant who seeks to gain an unfair advantage from a plaintiff's failure to perform induced by the defendant's repudiation.[70] Although we might call the concept 'estoppel', it is neither necessary nor appropriate to introduce all the technical elements of that concept. Since a defendant cannot claim damages while repudiating a contract,[71] a defendant who sues the plaintiff for damages for not performing is in effect saying that the repudiation has been withdrawn. It is a sufficient basis for denial of the right to invoke the withdrawal facility that the plaintiff has changed its position on the faith of the repudiation. This was perhaps recognized by Lord Ackner in *Fercometal* when he expressed the estoppel qualification in terms of representation and reliance. The object is simply to prevent retraction without prior notice once there has been reliance by the plaintiff. The solution does not require the court to find (invent) and enforce an equity in the plaintiff's favour.[72] Thus, under § 256(1) of the Restatement 2d Contracts, the effect of a repudiation is nullified by retraction only if the notification comes to the plaintiff's attention before the plaintiff 'materially changes his position in reliance on the repudiation or indicates to the other party that he considers the repudiation to be final'. This does not seek to explain why the failure of the plaintiff to perform is not a breach of contract. That appears to be the second purpose of estoppel under Australian and English law.

There can be no better illustration of the attraction inherent in recognition of a right to suspend performance following repudiation than *Foran v Wight*.[73] The fact situation was very simple, but it produced very complex legal analyses. A vendor of land repudiated its obligations prior to

[70] See C Fried, *Contract as Promise* (1981) p 129.

[71] See *Jinright v Russell*, 123 Ga App 766; 182 SE 2d 328, at 330 (171); *Nina's Bar Bistro Pty Ltd v MBE Corpn (Sydney) Pty Ltd* [1984] 3 NSWLR 613, at 632–3. Cf. *Morris v Baron & Co* [1918] AC 1, at 9.

[72] Cf. *Austral Standard Cables Pty Ltd v Walker Nominees Pty Ltd* (1992) 26 NSWLR 524, at 533, 540 where the estoppel concept was applied to conduct following service of a notice to complete a sale of land contract, in reliance on the purchaser's statement that the notice would not be complied with. Neither Clarke JA nor Handley JA referred to the enforcement of an equity. Cf. Sir Michael Mustill, 'Anticipatory Breach', *Butterworth Lectures 1989–90* (1990) p 68 (estoppel recognized in *Fercometal* 'a quite new kind of estoppel').

[73] (1989) 168 CLR 385.

the time fixed for performance. Instead of immediately exercising the right of termination, the purchaser waited until after the time fixed for performance before serving notice of termination. This treated the contract as discharged on the basis of the vendor's failure to perform the contract. Of course, the purchaser had not tendered the purchase money, and because time was of the essence the vendor claimed to have discharged the contract for breach by the purchaser of an essential term of the contract. A majority of the High Court concluded that the purchaser was entitled to succeed and to recover the deposit which the vendor had purported to forfeit. Suspension of performance provides a simple solution. Since the vendor did not give notice that he was able to perform—the repudiation was not validly retracted—the purchaser was not required to take performance steps. The failure to tender the purchase price was not an election either to discharge or affirm the contract, since performance had in effect been suspended. Nor was it a breach. Accordingly, no claim for damages could be made by the defendant.[74]

Following the lead of the Restatement 2d Contracts, we need merely to take a step back in the analysis and say that whenever one party repudiates the contract the other is entitled to suspend performance. Once performance has been suspended—the plaintiff is temporarily discharged—there can be no breach by the plaintiff. If the defendant then decides to perform, notice must be given to the plaintiff. In the absence of notice, the defendant is estopped to the extent that the plaintiff's failure to perform is causally linked to the repudiation. The causal connection is important. Without it the argument that performance has been suspended will not work. In the words of § 255 of the Restatement 2d Contracts, the repudiation must contribute 'materially' to the failure to perform.[75]

---

[74] There was a factual complication, a finding by the trial judge that the purchaser might not have been able to obtain sufficient funds to complete the sale had the vendor tendered conveyance of title. However, any inability of the purchaser to perform went merely to the extent of the vendor's damages liability. Since damages were not claimed by the purchaser this was not in fact an issue. Mason CJ dissented because he could find no causal connection between the vendor's conduct and the purchaser's failure to tender the purchase price. Although this is essentially a factual question on which the majority differed, the ellipsis involved in treating estoppel as the criterion both for retraction and for whether there was breach by the purchaser may well have had a detrimental influence, and explain the complex analysis of the majority. On the other hand, in *Bowes* v *Chaleyer* (1923) 32 CLR 159 a repudiation by a buyer did not lead to suspension by the seller, since there was a tender of delivery. The tender did not conform with the contractual requirements and was therefore made in breach of the seller's performance duty. The buyer was entitled to retract its repudiation because the seller's failure to perform in accordance with the contract was not connected with the buyer's repudiation.

[75] The provision refers to the non-occurrence of a contingency, which is 'excused' by the repudiation. See also § 245 (excuse where breach by non-performance).

SUMMARY

The discussion above may be summarized as follows:

(1) Anglo-Australian law does not recognise a general right to suspend performance for breach. It is, however, open to contracting parties to agree expressly on a regime for suspension.
(2) In cases where the duty of the plaintiff to perform is subject to the prior (or contemporaneous) fulfilment of a condition precedent, a right to suspend performance arises, in the form of an ability to withhold performance until fulfilment.
(3) Although providing a right to treat the whole contract as discharged, a defendant's repudiation does not of itself permanently discharge a plaintiff from the obligation to perform or to be ready and willing to perform. However, there is a regime under which a plaintiff may rely on the repudiation as dispensing with the requirement of performance. I have suggested that an appropriate rationalisation of this qualification is that a repudiation legitimises causally connected commercial conduct amounting to a suspension of performance.

A regime for suspension

INTRODUCTION

Putting to one side the technical approach of the law on conditions precedent, and the equally technical approach of English and Australian courts to the repudiation doctrine, the main reason for the failure of Anglo-Australian law to develop a theory of suspension for breach is the failure to separate discharge and damages. Suspension of performance is, at the highest, a limited form of discharge, limited in both scope and duration. In putting in place a regime for suspension, the distinction between the right of a party to treat its performance obligations as temporarily discharged must be distinguished from the right, which may or may not exist, to claim damages. It is crucial that suspension not to be used simply as a lever for premature discharge and consequential damages recovery where there is no serious breach or repudiation. At the same time, however, we should not discount suspension merely because there is no right of discharge.

More specifically, four questions need to be answered. First, what events activate a suspension regime? Secondly, what response should be available to a plaintiff where an event triggers the regime? Thirdly, where the plaintiff validly invokes the regime, what response is the plaintiff entitled to call for from the defendant? Finally, and most difficult of all, what rights accrue to the plaintiff as a result of the defendant's response?

To provide a better starting point than the current rules of Australian and English law, it is logical to consider the regimes which already exist, under the CISG, the UCC and the Restatement 2d Contracts. These provide a norm against which the proposed regime may be tested, with due regard to the functions of suspension already outlined, the existing default rules on discharge, the distinction between suspension and discharge and that between discharge and damages.

EXISTING REGIMES

Article 71 of the CISG states:

(1) A party may suspend the performance of his obligations if, after the conclusion of the contract, it becomes apparent that the other party will not perform a substantial part of his obligations as a result of:
   (a) a serious deficiency in his ability to perform or in his creditworthiness; or
   (b) his conduct in preparing to perform or in performing the contract.
(2) If the seller has already dispatched the goods before the grounds described in the preceding paragraph become evident, he may prevent the handing over of the goods to the buyer even though the buyer holds a document which entitles him to obtain them. The present paragraph relates only to the rights in the goods as between the buyer and the seller.
(3) A party suspending performance, whether before or after dispatch of the goods, must immediately give notice of the suspension to the other party and must continue with performance if the other party provides adequate assurance of his performance.

This is, to a large extent, a compromise between specific provisions in the sale of goods legislation[76] and the right of suspension conferred by § 2–609 of the UCC. This provides:[77]

(1) A contract for sale imposes an obligation on each party that the other's expectation of receiving due performance will not be impaired. When reasonable grounds for insecurity arise with respect to the performance of either party the other may in writing demand adequate assurance of due performance and until he receives such assurances

---

[76] See above, text at n 45.

[77] See also UCC § 2–610(a), (c) which permit a plaintiff, following a repudiation by the defendant to await performance for a commercially reasonable time, and to suspend performance. Under § 2–611(2) retraction by a defendant must include any assurance justifiably demanded under the provisions of § 2–609. See RJ Robertson, 'The Right to Demand Adequate Assurance of Due Performance: Uniform Commercial Code Section 2–609 and Restatement (Second) of Contracts Section 251' (1988–89) 38 Drake L Rev 305, 324–5.

may if commercially reasonable suspend any performance for which he has not already received the agreed return.

(2) Between merchants the reasonableness of grounds for insecurity and the adequacy of any assurance offered shall be determined according to commercial standards.

(3) Acceptance of any improper delivery or payment does not prejudice the aggrieved party's right to demand adequate assurance of future performance.

(4) After receipt of a justified demand failure to provide within a reasonable time not exceeding thirty days such assurance of due performance as is adequate under the circumstances of the particular case is a repudiation of the contract.

Whereas the CISG and Article 2 of the UCC apply only to sales, the latter has an analogue not only in relation to leases[78] but, as expressed in § 251 of the Restatement 2d Contracts, in general contract law. Under § 251 a plaintiff may require a defendant to provide an adequate assurance of performance if reasonable grounds exist which suggest that the defendant will breach the contract in such a way as to justify a claim for damages for 'total breach'. Failure by the defendant to provide an adequate assurance may be treated as a repudiation. Unlike the UCC provision, this has been the subject of very little judicial interpretation. Whether the provision will ultimately be adopted as a common law principle is unclear.[79] The support in the cases is not wholehearted.[80]

THE EVENTS CRITERION

Aspects

There are three aspects to the criterion for events which trigger suspension:

(1) whether the criterion should be subjective or objective;

(2) the source of the information alleged to trigger the right; and

---

[78] See § 2A–401 of the UCC.

[79] See *Farnsworth on Contracts* (2nd ed 1990) vol 1, s 8.23.

[80] Compare *Mollohan v Black Rock Contracting Inc*, 235 SE 2d 813, at 816, n 1 (W Va, 1977) where the court was not prepared to adopt a tentative draft of s 251 as part of the 'general contract law', with *Lo Re v Tel-Air Communications Inc*, 200 NJ Super 59; 490 A 2d 344, at 350 (1985) where § 251 was said to describe a 'general contractual principle' which originated with the UCC. See also *Ranger Construction Co v Dixie Floor Co Inc*, 433 F Supp 442 (D SC, 1977) where the existence of a right to call for an assurance in the absence of an applicable statutory rule appears to have been doubted. There are also cases in which the UCC provision has been applied by way of analogy. See, eg *UMIC Government Securities Inc v Pioneer Mortgage Co*, 707 F 2d 251 (6th Cir, 1983) which concerned a sale of Government National Mortgage Association certificates; and *Conference Center Ltd v TRC—The Research Corpn of New England*, 189 Conn 212; 455 A 2d 857 (Conn, 1983) which concerned a mortgage security over leasehold premises.

(3) the character of the event which justifies suspension.

Suspension has a role both in long term—relational—situations and short-term contracts consisting of single unit transactions.[81] The information function of suspension is, perhaps, less important where the parties are in a close long-term relation, since they are more likely to be aware of performance difficulties, and changes in economic conditions are likely to have a more gradual effect. Moreover, long-term contracts are often renegotiated. However, generally, in any contract where performance is spread over a substantial period of time, or is comprised of units with substantial time gaps, the information function of suspension will be significant. Unless there is the facility for inquiring whether performance is to occur, a plaintiff may be left in considerable doubt as to the likelihood that performance will be received. The uncertainty may, to a large extent, be cured by the simple device of a written notice asking for an assurance of performance. Thus, *Hongkong Fir Shipping C Ltd v Kawasaki Kisen Kaisha Ltd*[82] involved in long-term relation, namely, a charterparty which was to last for twenty-four calendar months. The event which caused difficulty was an unseaworthy vessel. The reason why the vessel was unseaworthy was that she was undermanned and her engine-room staff incompetent. The reaction of the charterers should have been to call for an assurance of performance. Had they been able to do so they might well have refrained from treating the contract as discharged. An assurance that the crew would be increased or replaced would have been an adequate response.

Objectivity

The events criterion must be objective. Objectivity suggests a criterion of 'reasonable' doubts as to whether the defendant will discharge its performance obligation. Thus, § 2–609 of the UCC and § 251 of the Restatement 2d Contracts,[83] are couched in terms of 'reasonable grounds' for insecurity. It is not sufficient for the plaintiff to rely on a purely subjective (and perhaps irrational) fear.[84] Whether there are reasonable grounds is manifestly a question of fact.[85]

---

[81] See H Beale, *Remedies for Breach of Contract* (1980) pp 78–9.   [82] [1962] 2 QB 26.
[83] The CISG requires it to be 'apparent'. Although no point of reference is stated, this seems an objective criterion.
[84] See, eg *Cole v Melvin*, 441 F Supp 193 (D SD, 1977); *Pittsburgh-Des Moines Steel Co v Brookhaven Manor Water Co*, 532 F 2d 572, at 581 (7th Cir, 1976). Cf. *UMIC Government Securities Inc v Pioneer Mortgage Co*, 707 F 2d 251 (6th Cir, 1983) (no insecurity where party retained funds pending proposed retention arrangement since substantial sums had already been paid and there was no intention to retain the funds if the proposed arrangement was agreed to).
[85] See, eg *AMF Inc v McDonald's Corpn* 536 F 2d 1167, at 1170 (7th Cir, 1976); *American Bronze Corpn v Streamway Products*, 8 Ohio App 3d 323; 456 NE 2d 1295, at 1303 (1982); *Clem Perrin Marine Towing Inc v Panama Canal Co*, 730 F 2d 186, at 191 (5th Cir, 1984).

Although there is a requirement of objectivity, there is no need to insist either that the conduct be directly related to the contract, or that it show non-performance to be a certainty. What matters is that the plaintiff should have grounds in relation to the contract performance, and that these are reasonable. Thus, under the UCC, it is clear that the insecurity may be based on conduct in relation to other contracts[86] or the defendant's general business activity.[87] Indeed, an expression of doubt as to the validity of the contract may be a reasonable ground for insecurity.[88]

Reliable information

More controversial is whether the evidence must come from the defendant. This is not required by the UCC or the Restatement 2d Contracts. Article 71 of the CISG is couched in terms of an 'apparent' lack of readiness or willingness. Although one of two bases for proving the apparent lack of readiness or willingness is the defendant's conduct in preparing to perform or in performing the contract, it would seem that the provision is not limited to the conduct of the defendant. Thus, it would appear that the other basis—a 'deficiency' in the ability to perform or creditworthiness— may be proved by recourse to evidence other than what the defendant has said or done. English and Australian lawyers may well be uncomfortable with a criterion which treats 'market information' as sufficient.[89] However, provided that we exclude unfounded gossip, there is no reason to insist that the evidence of insecurity come from the defendant.[90] In other words, 'reasonable grounds' should be taken to include all *reliable*

[86] See, eg *Toppert* v *Bunge Corpn*, 60 Ill App 3d 607; 377 NE 2d 324 (1978) where delivery was suspended because the buyer had withheld money under another contract in an attempt to provide leverage in relation to that contract. See also UCC, § 2–609, Comment 3 (law on dependence and independence within a single contract does not control the provision).

[87] See *Clem Perrin Marine Towing Inc* v *Panama Canal Co*, 730 F 2d 186 (5th Cir, 1984) where the charterer under a bareboat charter was held to have grounds for insecurity in relation to the owner's promise to transfer merchantable title on exercise of an option to purchase. This was on the basis that the owner had defaulted on a mortgage given to a third party, and had indeed executed a further mortgage. Contrast *Pittsburgh-Des Moines Steel Co* v *Brookhaven manor Water Co*, 532 F 2d 572, at 581 (7th Cir, 1976) where the fact that loan negotiations were incomplete was not regarded as a ground for insecurity as the money was 'not to be needed for some time'. Cummings J, although concurring in the result, thought otherwise. Applying the test of a 'prudent businessman' he considered that reasonable grounds had arisen and treated the majority as applying a criterion requiring a 'fundamental change' in the financial position of the buyer.

[88] See *Copylease Corpn of America* v *Memorex Corpn*, 403 F Supp 625 (SDNY, 1975).

[89] Cf. Devlin J's rejection in *Universal Cargo Carriers Corpn* v *Citati* [1957] 2 QB 401, at 450 of apparent inability, based on informed 'opinion on the market' as a basis for proving anticipatory breach.

[90] Cf. *United States* v *Great Plains Gasification Associates*, 819 F 2d 831 (8th Cir, 1987) where a press release by the defendant's officers was regarded as neither a communication by the defendant nor a statement of policy.

information. Comment 3 to § 2–609 of the UCC thus states that a report from an apparently trustworthy source is sufficient.[91]

Gravity of the event

Analysis of the gravity of the event justifying suspension involves a comparison between the reasonable grounds, the defendant's performance obligation and the obligation which the plaintiff seeks to suspend. Article 71 of the CISG takes a narrow, and perhaps uncertain, approach. In all cases the insecurity of the plaintiff must relate to a 'substantial part' of the defendant's obligations. This is sufficient where the plaintiff relies on conduct in preparing to perform or in performing. However, where inability to perform or creditworthiness is relied upon, there is an additional requirement of a 'serious deficiency'. It is perhaps easy to explain the requirement of a substantial part, since the CISG is concerned with sale contracts where there is, in essence, an exchange of payment for delivery. It is, however, an unfortunately vague criterion. Moreover, both the 'substantial part' requirement and the 'serious deficiency' element are likely to be affected by the CISG's use of the concept of fundamental breach.

There is no statement in the UCC of whether the insecurity must be such that, if translated to breach, it would justify cancellation. The emphasis is on 'reasonable grounds for insecurity' with respect to the other party's performance. On the other hand, the Restatement 2d Contracts provision requires that the reasonable grounds relate to a breach which would give rise to a claim for damages for total breach.[92] Although the UCC approach is perhaps influenced by the perfect tender rule, this does not explain why grounds for insecurity in relation to payment justify suspension. In any event, courts interpreting the UCC provision have rejected the view that the grounds for insecurity must relate directly to the contract at issue. The point of reference of the ground for insecurity put forward by the plaintiff, as well as the gravity of the event, determine the reasonableness of the ground. This aspect of suspension is related to the response which a plaintiff is entitled to make following a failure to provide an adequate assurance.[93]

---

[91] See, eg *Clem Perrin Marine Towing Inc* v *Panama Canal Co*, 730 F 2d 186, at 191 (5th Cir, 1984) where the information came from a broker who had played a major role in negotiating the deal between the plaintiff and the defendant. Cf. the approach of the Restatement 2d Contracts, § 43 to *Dickinson* v *Dodds* (1876) 2 Ch D 463 (reliable information as knowledge of withdrawal of offer).

[92] For a suggestion that there is no difference of substance see JJ White, 'Eight Cases and Section 251' (1982) 67 Cornell L Rev 841, 842.

[93] See below, text at notes 123 *et seq*.

THE RESPONSE TO THE EVENT

Principal issues

Three principal issues arise when we turn to the plaintiff's response to the event which activates the regime: first, the nature and form of the communication to the defendant; secondly, the obligations which may be suspended by the plaintiff; and thirdly, whether it is appropriate to invoke the regime.

Communication

The existing regimes confer on the plaintiff the right to demand an assurance that performance will occur. The demand must relate to the plaintiff's insecurity: there can be no ability to demand a general assurance. A question of form then arises. It is important that the formal requirements reflect common business practices, the general approach of contract law to form as well as the information needs of the defendant. Article 2 of the UCC contains a Statute of Frauds provision.[94] This may explain why it requires that the demand for an assurance be in writing. By contrast, the Restatement 2d Contracts refers simply to a 'demand' for an adequate assurance and, although the CISG requires 'notice' of the suspension, there is no specification of form.

In commercial contracts the modern approach—which should be applied to the suspension regime—is to treat oral communications as sufficient. Moreover, notwithstanding the apparent insistence of the UCC on writing, it has been held that this is not mandatory. In *AMF Inc v McDonald's Corpn*[95] the Court of Appeals for the Seventh Circuit deprecated a 'formalistic approach'. McDonald's failure to make a written demand was held to be excusable because of 'AMF's clear understanding that McDonald's had suspended performance until it should receive adequate assurance of due performance'. This emphasises that it is knowledge which matters.[96]

A sufficient requirement is that the defendant know that suspension

---

[94] See UCC, § 2–201. On the other hand, in England, and most Australian jurisdictions, requirements derived from the Statute of Frauds 1677 (UK) have little impact today outside contracts relating to land.

[95] 536 F 2d 1167, at 1170–1 (7th Cir, 1976). The court relied on its earlier decision in *Pittsburgh-Des Moines Steel Co v Brookhaven Manor Water Co*, 532 F 2d 572, at 581 (7th Cir, 1976).

[96] See also *Conference Center Ltd v TRC—The Research Corpn of New England*, 189 Conn 212; 455 A 2d 857, at 864, n 4 (1983) where the court, applying § 2–609 by analogy, refused to incorporate the formal requirement. For contrary authorities, insisting on a written demand, see RJ Robertson, 'The Right to Demand Adequate Assurance of Due Performance: Uniform Commercial Code Section 2–609 and Restatement (Second) of Contracts Section 251' (1988–89) 38 Drake L Rev 305, 333.

has been invoked, whether by actual communication or the conduct of the plaintiff. *AMF Inc* v *McDonald's Corpn* is illustrative of one of the most significant features of the United States cases. The UCC provision, in particular, has been interpreted by reference to commercial behaviour. The court's injunction against a formalistic approach has played a significant interpretive role. Thus, a demand for payment has been treated as a demand for an assurance of performance.[97] At the same time, if the suspension regime posits that consequences flow from subsequent conduct of the defendant, it is important that the defendant be informed of those consequences.[98] Again, however, it should be sufficient that the consequences are a logical inference from the plaintiff's conduct.

Obligations which may be suspended

The beneficial purpose of giving effect to the mitigation of loss function is served if suspension is limited to cases where the plaintiff can be saved the expense of rendering a performance which has not already been earned. Such performance may not be remunerated otherwise than by way of a compensation or restitution claim. Under both the UCC and the Restatement 2d Contracts the right of the plaintiff is to suspend any performance for which the agreed return has not already been received. The agreed return must be 'in doubt'.[99] If the agreed return has been received, there is no right of suspension.[100] It would be unjust and illogical to permit a plaintiff to suspend the performance of obligations the right to the performance of which has already been earned by the defendant. It would be inconsistent with the common law approach to conditions precedent and repudiation of obligation for a plaintiff to be entitled to withhold this performance. However, there is no reference in the CISG to what the plaintiff has received: it refers merely to suspension of the performance of the plaintiff's obligations. In effect, the plaintiff is able to suspend the performance of any obligation, whether or not this is connected with the obligation of the defendant in respect of which insecurity has arisen.

The conception of suspension as a preliminary to discharge influences the approach of the UCC and the Restatement 2d Contracts. The fact that

---

[97] See *Toppert* v *Bunge Corpn*, 60 Ill App 3d 607; 377 NE 2d 324 (1978); *T & S Brass and Bronze Works Inc* v *Pic-Air Inc*, 790 F 2d 1098 (4th Cir, 1986).

[98] Compare the requirements applied in the cases on notices to perform complete sale transactions *Charles Rickards Ltd* v *Oppenhaim* [1950] 1 KB 616; *Balog* v *Crestani* (1975) 132 CLR 289; *Laurinda Pty Ltd* v *Capalaba Park Shopping Centre Pty Ltd* (1989) 166 CLR 623; *Delta Vale Properties Ltd* v *Mills* [1990] 1 WLR 445.

[99] See also *Gutor International AG* v *Raymond Packer Co Inc*, 493 F 2d 938, at 943 (1st Cir, 1974).

[100] See *Cherwell-Ralli Inc* v *Rytman Grain Co Inc*, 180 Conn 714; 322 A 2d 984 (1980) where a buyer who sought to rely on the suspension regime had in fact received all goods ordered under an instalment contract.

there is no automatic right of discharge under the CISG, following an inadequate assurance, may explain why there is no attempt to connect the plaintiff's action with the insecurity. At best, this is achieved by the 'substantial part' requirement. What these regimes perhaps underestimate is the importance of the link between what the plaintiff has to do and the aspect of the defendant's performance obligations which is uncertain. The assumption of the CISG and the Restatement 2d Contracts is that there should be a right to suspend only where there is substantial insecurity. However, in many contracts the plaintiff is concerned that although the time for performance of a particular obligation is approaching, there is an uncertainty as to the ability of the defendant to respond in the way which the contract requires. For example, if the plaintiff is a builder obliged to deliver materials to a building site, and required to give notice of this so that the defendant may have the site ready to receive the materials, there is no point in getting in the supplies if the site will not be ready. The builder will want to suspend this obligation unless there is an assurance that the site will be ready, irrespective of whether it can be said that having the site ready (or ready in time) is a substantial part of the defendant's obligations.[101] Therefore, a more precise approach, linking what the plaintiff has to do with the aspect of the defendant's performance obligations which is uncertain, would give effect to the enforcement function of suspension.[102] This is because, in many of these cases, the obligation of the defendant will not be one which is amenable to the remedy of specific performance.[103]

This is reducible to a requirement of proportionality. The ability to suspend all performance obligations should be limited to cases where the insecurity relates to all, or substantially all, of the defendant's executory obligations. Accordingly, either a repudiation of obligation or a serious breach will justify total suspension. However, breach of a term (actual or prospective) will, prima facie, only justify the suspension of interconnected obligations. Consider, for example, the breach of a term classified as a condition under Australian and English law on the grounds of commercial convenience. The plaintiff may exercise a right of dis-

---

[101] It is unclear whether the effect of the notice of suspension under the CISG is to extend the time for performance, although common sense suggests that this must be the case. See JO Honnold, *Uniform Law for International Sales Under the 1980 United Nations Convention* (2nd ed 1991) p 493.

[102] But this is not to deny the enforcement function of § 2–609 itself. See RE Speidel, RS Summers and JJ White, *Sales Teaching Materials* (1987) p 233 ('high incidence of consensual adjustment and continued performance').

[103] There is to some extent an analogy with the condition precedent concept, and the *nachfrist* procedure adopted by the CISG. See Articles 47(1), 63(1). Cf. P Linzer, 'On the Amorality of Contract Remedies—Efficiency, Equity and the Second Restatement' (1981) 81 Colum L Rev 111.

charge,[104] but this does not justify suspension of all the plaintiff's obligations. On the other hand, any interdependent obligations would come within my regime for suspension.

APPROPRIATENESS

Objectivity in the events criterion is a way of ensuring that the act of suspension is a genuine one. A response which is designed merely to harm the defendant is not a bona fide one. Similarly, a response motivated by a plaintiff's uncertainty about its own ability to perform lacks candour and would not be an appropriate one.[105] Again, if the plaintiff is not in a position to perform, the suspension regime is not available as a means to delay performance until the plaintiff is able to perform. Again, there is the plaintiff who attempts to trap the defendant into a discharge situation. Finally, if the plaintiff's accounts department regards the terms agreed by the contracts department as providing inadequate protection against default, the suspension regime cannot be used as a way of correcting the position *ex post facto*.[106] These are good faith considerations, and the regime looks to make better sense in the context of a law of contract where there is a general good faith requirement. However, although the suspension concept is reinforced by the insistence of American law of a general good faith requirement,[107] the CISG indicates that this is not essential, since the CISG stops short of imposing a general good faith obligation.[108] In any event, even lawyers in Australia and England are now coming to terms with a good faith requirement, and suspension introduces good faith in a way which reinforces the law on repudiation.[109]

---

[104] At least where the breach is actual. The position where there is merely a prospective breach is uncertain, at least under English law. See *Afovos Shipping Co SA* v *Pagnan* [1983] 1 WLR 195, at 203 (it is to fundamental breach alone that the doctrine of anticipatory breach applies). Contrast *Federal Commerce and Navigation Co Ltd* v *Molena Alpha Inc* [1979] AC 757, at 778, 783, 785; *Foran* v *Wight* (1989) 168 CLR 385, at 395, 416, 441.

[105] See *United States* v *Great Plains Gasification Associates*, 819 F 2d 831, at 834, n 5 (8th Cir, 1987) (party's demand for assurance a 'subterfuge' to escape its contractual obligations). Cf. *Cherwell-Ralli Inc* v *Rytman Grain Co Inc*, 180 Conn 714; 433 A 2d 984, at 987 (1980) where, in effect, a buyer under an instalment contract was relying on its own non-payment as a basis for suspension. Query how far breach by the plaintiff will itself make a demand for an adequate assurance inappropriate. See *United States* v *Great Plains Gasification Associates*, 819 F 2d 831, at 835 (8th Cir, 1987). Cf. *Mayflower Farms* v *Tech-Mark Inc*, 64 Or App 121; 666 P 2d 1384 (1983).

[106] See *Pittsburgh-Des Moines Steel Co* v *Brookhaven Manor Water Co*, 532 F 2d 572, at 579 (7th Cir, 1976).

[107] See UCC, §§ 1–203, 2–104(1).

[108] Cf. Article 7 of the CISG (in the interpretation of the CISG regard is to be had to its international character and to the need to promote uniformity in its application and the observance of good faith in international trade).

[109] Cf. *Hochster* v *De la Tour* (1853) 2 El & Bl 678, at 691; 118 ER 922, at 927 (below, text at note 121).

The UCC includes a requirement that it be 'commercially reasonable' for a plaintiff to suspend any performance. It is inherent in this that there will be situations in which it is unreasonable for a plaintiff to suspend performance. This is also linked with the time within which any assurance of performance must be given. Under the UCC the assurance must be given without a reasonable time not exceeding thirty days.[110] It is not difficult to conceive of situations where the reasonable period of time must inevitably be short, in which an assurance notice must be given within a day or so. Indeed, under English law, one reason for treating time stipulations as essential is the inappropriateness of notice procedures to commercial contracts with a tight performance schedule.[111] However, this is merely a question of degree and we should not be overly influenced by such cases. The general requirement, that the response allow a reasonable period of time, sufficiently accommodates the condition that the performance schedule contemplated by the contract be such that the defendant has time to respond.

RESPONSES TO WHICH THE PLAINTIFF IS ENTITLED

Introduction

One objection which Australian and English contract lawyers may make to a general regime for suspension is that it must have the effect of increasing the defendant's performance obligation. It can, of course, readily be accepted that a notice of suspension cannot be used to bring forward the defendant's performance obligation. In one sense, the essence of the suspension regime is merely that a plaintiff is entitled to call for information, and to act on the information provided. Courts do not have a jurisdiction to rewrite contracts, and a defendant cannot be required to be presently ready and willing to perform obligations which are to mature due in the future. More generally, a demand cannot call for an assurance which would subject the defendant to an obligation substantially different from that to which the parties agreed.[112]

However, this does not imply that the regime be restricted to insecurity arising from a failure to perform. Nor does it imply that the plaintiff is limited to demands satisfied merely by formal responses. The cases on the

---

[110] Section 251(2) of the Restatement 2d Contracts merely requires that the assurance be given 'within a reasonable time'.

[111] See *Bunge Corpn New York* v *Tradax Export SA Panama* [1981] 1 WLR 711, at 716, 720, 727 where reference is made to 'string' contracts and sale contracts where one party's performance is totally dependent on punctual performance by the other.

[112] See, eg *Pittsburgh-Des Moines Steel Co* v *Brookhaven Manor Water Co* , 532 F 2d 572, at 582, 583 (7th Cir, 1976); *United States* v *Great Plains Gasification Associates*, 819 F 2d 831 (8th Cir, 1987).

UCC regime clearly indicate that legitimate demands include not only those which call for responses which amount merely to a change in form, but also those which call for responses which amount to substantive changes.[113] The response falls to be evaluated not just by reference to the agreed terms but also by reference to the considerations which justify the regime, that is, the functions of suspension, including the interest of society in the success of the regime as a component of contract law.

Adequate assurances

Once the plaintiff has validly demanded an assurance, the plaintiff is entitled to a response which is, in the circumstances, 'adequate'. The provisions of the UCC, Restatement 2d Contracts and CISG all use this criterion of an 'adequate' assurance of performance.[114] A plaintiff is entitled to suspend performance until an adequate assurance is given.[115] The concept of an 'adequate' assurance is clearly a relative one. The approach may therefore differ according to the basis or cause for insecurity, the role of the particular performance obligation and the nature of the contract.

Where there is an express repudiation, an adequate assurance may involve no more than a statement of intention to perform. The moral function of requiring a defendant to restate its performance obligation is satisfied. Apart from such cases, only rarely will a statement of intention to perform be sufficient.[116] Generally, it would be unreasonable to treat a fulfilment of the moral function as adequate.[117] Thus, if there is an element of concern over ability to pay, what is appropriate will depend on the circumstances. A statement of financial arrangements already in place, or capable of being put in place, may be adequate; but if existing arrangements have not been met it may be reasonable to require a statement of assets or the provision of some further financial security for performance,

---

[113] See UCC, § 2–609, Comment 4.

[114] The UCC and Restatement 2d Contracts require an 'adequate' assurance of 'due' performance. Although there is debate as to the meaning of 'due performance' (see RJ Robertson, 'The Right to Demand Adequate Assurance of Due Performance: Uniform Commercial Code Section 2–609 and Restatement (Second) of Contracts Section 251' (1988–89) 38 Drake L Rev 305, 331–2) the cases indicate that this cannot be taken literally. Where the assurance is sought after breach, the defendant's performance cannot be exactly that required by the contract. In effect, due performance means performance which is in accordance with the request of the plaintiff.

[115] Following an adequate assurance, the CISG expressly requires the plaintiff to perform.

[116] A statement recognizing the validity of the contract may be sufficient where insecurity is based on the defendant's assertion of invalidity. See RJ Robertson, 'The Right to Demand Adequate Assurance of Due Performance: Uniform Commercial Code Section 2–609 and Restatement (Second) of Contracts Section 251' (1988–89) 38 Drake L Rev 305, 342.

[117] See, eg *Creusot-Loire International Inc* v *Coppus Engineering Corpn*, 585 F Supp 45 (SDNY, 1983) where a seller's statement that its goods would work when installed was clearly inadequate when other buyers had reported serious problems.

such as payment in cash or the issue of a documentary credit.[118] A higher standard might be expected of a buyer's obligation to obtain a performance guarantee than a purchaser's obligation to obtain mortgage finance. Similarly, the more precarious the defendant's position the more that the plaintiff is entitled to claim. Again, if a seller has delivered defective goods, the response, to be an adequate assurance, may involve a commitment to repair or replace any goods which prove to be defective.[119]

The problem of apparent inability

A clear advantage of the suspension regime is to cope with cases of apparent inability to perform. The common law concept of readiness and willingness to perform embraced ability to perform, so that an absence of ability is equivalent to an absence of readiness or willingness.[120] Under the repudiation doctrine, a defendant who is careful to conceal an inability to perform is more generously treated than the forthright defendant who admits the inability. However, the moral justification for anticipatory repudiation, stated by Lord Campbell CJ in *Hochster* v *De la Tour*[121] in terms that a person who 'wrongfully renounces a contract . . . cannot justly complain if he is immediately sued for a compensation in damages by the man whom he has injured' seems equally applicable to parties who conceal inability and those unwilling to admit inability.

It is consistent with commercial standards of morality that a defendant be required to affirm that its performance obligation will be met, or met on time. The notice may bring home to the unduly optimistic defendant just how perilous its position is. In *Universal Cargo Carriers Corpn* v *Citati*[122] Pedro Citati was having difficulty procuring a cargo to load under a voyage charterparty. His supplier had let him down badly. Pedro was unduly optimistic as to his ability to obtain a cargo from another supplier. The shipowners could not demand an assurance of performance before the end of the lay days, and they therefore took a considerable risk

---

[118] See, eg *International Therapeutics Inc* v *McGraw-Edison Co*, 721 F 2d 488 (5th Cir, 1983); *Creusot-Loire International Inc* v *Coppus Engineering Corpn*, 585 F Supp 45, at 50 (SDNY, 1983). Contrast *Pittsburgh-Des Moines Steel Co* v *Brookhaven Manor Water Co*, 532 F 2d 572, at 583 (7th Cir, 1976) where the concurring judge regarded a request for a personal guarantee on behalf of a corporate buyer as going too far.

[119] See, eg *T & S Brass and Bronze Works Inc* v *Pic-Air Inc*, 790 F 2d 1098 (4th Cir, 1986). See also UCC, § 2–609, Comment 4.

[120] See generally *De Medina* v *Norman* (1842) 9 M & W 820; 152 ER 347; *Griffith* v *Selby* (1854) 9 Ex 393; 156 ER 167; *Noonan* v *Victorian Railways Commissioners* (1907) 4 CLR 1668, at 1680, 1685; *British & Beningtons Ltd* v *North Western Cachar Tea Co Ltd*[1923] AC 48, at 63; *Peter Turnbull & Co Pty Ltd* v *Mundus Trading Co (Australasia) Pty Ltd* (1954) 90 CLR 235, at 253. See further below, text at note 136.

[121] (1853) 2 El & Bl 678, at 691; 118 ER 922, at 927. See also *Roehm* v *Horst*, 178 US 1, at 10; 44 L Ed 953, at 961 (1900).

[122] [1957] 2 QB 401.

in sailing the vessel away prior to the commission of a serious breach. Ultimately, they were able to prove that their discharge of the contract was justified because Pedro was wholly and finally disabled from performing the contract, but this proved very costly and was highly inefficient. Had the shipowners been able to demand an assurance Pedro would have been forced to provide evidence of a source of supply. He could not have done this.

RIGHTS WHICH ACCRUE

The issues

In essence the questions here may be formulated as 'What is the impact of a failure to provide assurance?' and 'What standard should be applied to the plaintiff's assessment of the response?' It is useful to return to the problems raised by prospective inability to perform.

In *Universal Cargo Carriers Corpn v Citati*[123] Devlin J said that an anticipatory breach 'must be proved in fact and not in supposition'. Although made in the context of a charterparty, this ruling is reflected in the CISG. There is a contrast between the criterion for suspension, namely that it is 'apparent' that the defendant will not perform:[124] and that for anticipatory breach, namely, that it is 'clear' that the defendant will commit a fundamental breach of contract.[125] A conscious choice was made, and the requirement (for suspension) that it merely be 'apparent' intended to be less onerous than the requirement (for anticipatory breach) that it be 'clear'.[126] It is also assumed by the UCC and Restatement 2d Contracts that a prospective, but merely apparent (material) breach is not of itself a basis for discharge. On the other hand, it is clearly the law, even in England, that a party may legitimately infer a serious breach from the circumstances in which an actual (although minor) breach occurs. Thus, in *Warinco AG v Samor SpA*,[127] buyers refused to accept delivery of the first instalment under a contract for the sale of rapeseed oil. The goods were in accordance with the contract and the sellers were naturally concerned whether the second instalment would be rejected. When the sellers asked whether it would be accepted the buyers refused to say that they would reject (or accept) oil of the type already tendered. The sellers then terminated the contract for repudiation. They convinced the English Court of

---

[123] *Ibid.*, at 450. See also *Chilean Nitrate Sales Corpn v Marine Transportation Co Ltd (The Hermosa)* [1980] 1 Lloyd's Rep 638, at 650 (aff'd [1982] 1 Lloyd's Rep 570); *Sunbird Plaza Pty Ltd v Maloney* (1988) 166 CLR 245 at 280.

[124] See CISG, Art 71(1).   [125] See CISG, Art 72(1).

[126] Cf. B Nicholas, 'The Vienna Convention on International Sales Law' (1989) 105 LQR 201, 233.

[127] [1979] 1 Lloyd's Rep 450.

Appeal that an inference of repudiation had legitimately been drawn from the buyers' conduct. A right to suspend performance would certainly assist in this type of case, by attaching legal status to the demand for an assurance.[128] However, it also highlights the issue whether there should be both a right of discharge and a right to compensation where an inadequate assurance is provided, or merely a right of discharge.

Impact of a failure to provide assurance

The UCC and Restatement 2d Contracts are very clear on the impact of a failure to provide an adequate assurance. They allow a plaintiff to treat the failure as a repudiation. Therefore, if no assurance is given, or that provided is inadequate, the plaintiff may treat the contract as discharged and also claim compensation as on a total breach. In the context of those provisions the notice has an evidential function. In other words, the failure to comply with the procedure is clear evidence of repudiation or serious breach.[129] Although the provisions of the CISG evaporate when we come to the question of the impact of the failure to provide an adequate assurance, it is certainly arguable that an inadequate response amounts to a *clear* indication of anticipatory breach.[130]

In *Warinco AG v Samor SpA*[131] it was more or less fortuitous that the sellers could establish repudiation. Under a regime for suspension, the sellers would have been entitled to suspend performance until an adequate assurance of performance was given, since the circumstances clearly raised a doubt as to the willingness of the buyers to perform. Instead the sellers were faced with a problematic evidentiary issue. Clearly, *Warinco AG v Samor* was a case where the information and moral functions of suspension would have proved both useful and efficient. Application of the Restatement 2d Contracts to a case like *Universal Cargo Carriers Corpn v Citati*[132] would have provided cogent evidence of repudiation. The shipowners would have been saved the burden of proving anticipatory breach by inability to perform. The question is whether these provisions should be regarded as taking the law too far, particularly in a case of prospective inability, by permitting a plaintiff to claim damages for total breach where the evidence may go no further than showing that

---

[128] Cf. *T & S Brass and Bronze Works Inc v Pic-Air Inc*, 790 F 2d 1098 (4th Cir, 1986) where the seller under an instalment contract delivered defective goods and the buyer was held to be entitled to treat the contract as discharged where its demand for an adequate assurance from the seller was not met.

[129] There is, at least for Australian lawyers, an analogy with failure to comply with a notice to complete a sale of land transaction. See *Louinder v Leis* (1982) 149 CLR 509; *Ciavarella v Balmer* (1983) 153 CLR 438.

[130] See JO Honnold, *Uniform Law for International Sales Under the 1980 United Nations Convention* (2nd ed 1991) p 394.

[131] [1979] 1 Lloyd's Rep 450.   [132] [1957] 2 QB 401.

the defendant is, prior to the date specified for performance, not able to provide an adequate assurance that performance will later be rendered.

In the real world, insecurity may arise for a greater number of reasons, including labour difficulties, shortage of goods in the market, difficulty in obtaining raw materials, lack of funds to obtain supplies and so on. Not all of these are synonymous with the likelihood of breach. It may be clear that the defendant will not perform as the contract requires, but far from clear to the parties how serious such disruptions will be. Equally, but more importantly, it may be clear that the defendant will not perform, but far from clear whether there is contractual responsibility. In other words, is repudiation by anticipatory breach a false analogy?[133]

The refusal of courts to treat apparent inability as a repudiation, and their refusal to treat a likelihood of prospective breach as equivalent to the likelihood that serious consequences will flow from a proved breach, imply that the law regards the combined rights of discharge and compensation as unjustified in cases where the plaintiff is able to show only that inability to render the agreed return *may* be present and the inability *may or may not* arise from events within the areas of the defendant's contractual responsibility. On the other hand, the principle of frustration allows reliance on delay which is merely prospective.[134] This strongly suggests that discharge alone is the solution most consistent with Australian and English law.[135] It is therefore arguable that suspension followed by a failure to provide an adequate assurance should always lead to a right of discharge, but only to a right to damages where it is also established that the defendant would have breached the contract in a sufficiently serious way had discharge not occurred. There can, however, be no objection to a claim for restitution, since this relies on the independent principle of unjust enrichment.

Moreover, this reinforces the suggested requirement of proportionality in relation to the events criterion. If it is correct to regard discharge as the primary right flowing from an inadequate assurance, there is no reason to tie the suspension regime to material *breach*. It should be sufficient to justify discharge that the event relates to a substantial part of the defendant's performance obligations, irrespective of whether the event is synonymous with breach. The difficulty in satisfying the criterion for

---

[133] Cf. GH Treitel, *Remedies for Breach of Contract: A Comparative Account* (1988) p 406. See also FMB Reynolds, 'Discharge by Breach as A Remedy', in PD Finn (ed), *Essays on Contract* (1987) 183, 188 who argues that the effect may be to import a duty to 'appear' to be able to perform.

[134] See *Embiricos v Sydney Reid & Co* [1914] 3 KB 45, at 54, per Scrutton J (approved *Watts Watts & Co Ltd v Mitsui & Co Ltd* [1917] AC 227, at 246; *National Carriers Ltd v Panalpina (Northern) Ltd* [1981] AC 675, at 687, 706).

[135] See GH Treitel, *The Law of Contract* (8th ed 1991) p 760. On New Zealand law see F Dawson and DW McLauchlan, *The Contractual Remedies Act 1979* (1981) pp 94–5. Cf. JW Carter, 'The Embiricos Principle and the Law of Anticipatory Breach' (1984) 47 MLR 422.

anticipatory breach by inability[136]—that the defendant was wholly and finally disabled from performing the contract—is so well known as to be notorious.[137] Suspension does not solve this problem, but it is of great assistance where there is uncertainty as to whether the reason for insecurity is synonymous with breach.[138]

Assessment of the response

Once an adequate assurance has been provided, the plaintiff cannot rely on the defendant's conduct as a basis for discharge.[139] The plaintiff must act reasonably in assessing any assurance provided. In other words, just as suspension is not appropriate in all cases, even if the regime is activated, so we must be wary of the plaintiff who seeks to use the suspension regime for an ulterior motive. The UCC therefore requires that the adequacy of any assurance offered be determined 'according to commercial standards'.[140] This incorporates an objective standard appropriate to the conditions in the market, and the commercial standards applied.

Conclusions

Under Australian and English law suspension is treated as distinct from discharge. This is correct. However, the view that suspension of performance situations are limited to cases involving failure of a condition precedent, and cases of repudiation, is outmoded. A regime for suspension is consistent with the condition precedent concept, but less technical and more general in orientation. Similarly, it is too narrow an approach to limit suspension to situations where a right of discharge already exists. Both doctrinally and in practice, the principal advantage of the right to suspend performance lies in bridging the gap between termination for breach of a condition and termination for repudiation or serious breach.

---

[136] See *British & Beningtons Ltd v North Western Cachar Tea Co Ltd* [1923] AC 48 at 72; *Universal Cargo Carriers Corpn v Citati* [1957] 2 QB 401; *Rawson v Hobbs* (1961) 107 CLR 466; *Sunbird Plaza Pty Ltd v Maloney* (1988) 166 CLR 245, at 264. Cf. *Taylor v Johnston*, 123 Cal Rptr 641; 539 P 2d 425 (1975).

[137] This has led to suggestions that the criterion should be more broadly interpreted. See *Foran v Wight* (1989) 168 CLR 385, at 425.

[138] Cf. *FC Shepherd & Co Ltd v Jerrom* [1987] QB 301 (whether sentencing of employee to custodial term for criminal conduct could be relied on by the employer as frustrating the contract).

[139] See, eg *American Bronze Corpn v Streamway Products*, 8 Ohio App 3d 323; 456 NE 2d 1295 (1982).

[140] Section 251(2) of the Restatement 2d Contracts merely requires that the assurance be judged by reference to the 'circumstances of the particular case'.

Equally, there is no obligation to use the suspension regime where a right of discharge exists, for repudiation or serious breach.[141]

It would be more logical, and more consistent with what the courts actually do in cases where a right of discharge arises for breach or repudiation, to say that the right assumes that the plaintiff may refuse to perform. We should therefore accept, as a general rule, that a plaintiff's duty to perform is subject to the qualification that there is no serious breach or repudiation by the defendant. A plaintiff is entitled to a reasonable period of time in which to exercise a right of discharge. To this extent at least there is inherent in most discharge situations a right to suspend performance. United States lawyers would have no difficulty with this proposition. It is because there is no obligation to perform that a plaintiff may suspend performance.

Although there is generally no need for a right to suspend performance in cases within the principle established in *Hongkong Fir Shipping Co Ltd* v *Kawasaki Kisen Kaisha Ltd*,[142] since ex hypothesi the plaintiff has already been deprived of the benefits which the contract was to confer, and the defendant is unlikely to be in a position to remedy the position, it is nevertheless more logical to say that because the defendant cannot call for performance the plaintiff is discharged from the obligation to perform. Instead we say that the plaintiff is discharged on the exercise of a right of termination for breach of a term. There are cases where this distinction is important.[143]

From this perspective, the general recognition of suspension of performance does not per se impact on the bases for discharge under the existing law. But the argument for mitigation by discontinuing performance is made stronger, and the argument that the plaintiff is faced with a simple choice between active performance and discharge is weakened. If discharge ultimately occurs, the right of suspension reinforces the mitigation rules, and may reduce the incidence (or extent) of claims for restitution.

The number of discharge situations is increased only if we take the view that a failure to provide an adequate assurance of performance confers a right to discharge the contract. However, I have argued in favour for a link between what the plaintiff has to do and the aspect of the defendant's performance obligations which is uncertain in a requirement of proportionality. The effect of this is to make the relevance of suspension independent of the ability to treat the contract as discharged. I have also argued in favour of a distinction between responses of the plaintiff limited to discharge and those which also include a right to claim compensation.

---

[141] This is clearly the position under the UCC. See, eg *Cherwell-Ralli Inc* v *Rytman Grain Co Inc*, 180 Conn 714; 433 A 2d 984, at 986–7 (1980).

[142] [1962] 2 QB 26.

[143] In the *Hongkong Fir* case itself, the contract in fact provided that the charterers were not bound to pay hire while the ship was being repaired. There was therefore an express right equivalent to suspension, but there was no mechanism under which an assurance of performance could be sought.

The range of discharge situations is increased, but the ability to claim compensation is unaffected.

It might also be objected that the law is imposing a regime which the parties did not adopt, even though it was open to them to so. There are certainly examples of cases, particularly those involving building contracts, where express provisions may be found requiring a party to show cause if called upon to do so. It is, however, rare for such provisions to be activated by a prospective breach. It is, moreover, too narrow an approach today to say that if the parties have not agreed a procedure in advance that procedure should not be implied. This really gets back to the fundamental question. Just as we have no difficulty in implying a discharge regime we should not cavil at the implication of a suspension regime merely on the basis that it is impossible to imply terms. As a default rule, the regime for suspension may be excluded by agreement.[144]

A suspension regime provides a mechanism by which legal effect may be given to appropriate, that is, rational commercial conduct.[145] The importance of the suspension regime thus lies in recognising and providing an opportunity for 'dialogue to establish whether the parties intend to repudiate or fulfil their contractual obligations'.[146] The evidence of the United States cases is that suspension is more discerning, that is less extreme in effect, than the discharge rules.

It has to be admitted that the regime for suspension proposed here goes beyond the existing law in Australia and England. It will not develop overnight. However, the existence of a suspension regime under the CISG means that suspension is already part of Australian law. It is certainly important to any revision of domestic sales legislation.[147] However, it is also quite possible that the existence of suspension rules in the CISG will promote the recognition of a general common law right. After all, history shows that sales legislation has exerted a powerful influence on general contract law. Sale may no longer be the 'master contract', but it is certainly a representative one.

---

[144] See *Clem Perrin Marine Towing Inc* v *Panama Canal Co*, 730 F 2d 186, at 189–90 (5th Cir, 1984), where, although the construction was described as a 'close one', the contract did not evidence an intention to exclude the UCC provision.

[145] See EJ Murphy and RE Speidel, *Studies in Contract Law* (4th ed 1991) p 1025.

[146] *Conference Center Ltd* v *TRC—The Research Corpn of New England*, 189 Conn 212; 455 A 2d 857, at 863–4 (1983). RJ Robertson, 'The Right to Demand Adequate Assurance of Due Performance: Uniform Commercial Code Section 2–609 and Restatement (Second) of Contracts Section 251' (1988–89) 38 Drake L Rev 305, 353 describes the assurance device as 'one of the most innovative and commercially sensible developments in contract law in this century'. See also JJ White, 'Eight Cases and Section 251' (1982) 67 Cornell L Rev 841, 856–9; HO Hunter, *Modern Law of Contracts: Breach and Remedies* (1986) s 3.02[6].

[147] The CISG is currently being considered by a UCC Drafting Committee, in a re-draft of Article 2. See P Winship, 'Domesticating International Commercial Law: Revising UCC Article 2 in Light of the United Nations Sales Convention' (1991) 37 Loyala LR 43. See also Law Reform Commission of NSW, *Issues Paper on Sale of Goods*, IP 5, 1988.

Index